The Best Northeastern Colleges

The Best Northeastern Colleges

135 Great Schools to Consider

By Robert Franek,
Tom Meltzer, Roy Opochinski,
Tara Bray, Christopher Maier, Carson Brown,
Julie Doherty, K. Nadine Kavanaugh,
Catherine Monaco, and Dinaw Mengestu

Random House, Inc.

New York

www.PrincetonReview.com

Princeton Review Publishing, L. L. C.
2315 Broadway
New York, NY 10024
E-mail: bookeditor@review.com

ISBN 0-375-76334-1

Editorial Director: Robert Franek
Editors: Robert Franek, Erik Olson, and Erica Magrey
Designer: Scott Harris
Production Editor: Julieanna Lambert
Production Coordinator: Scott Harris

Manufactured in the United States of America.

9 8 7 6 5 4 3 2 1

FOREWORD

Every year, about three million high school graduates go to college. To make sure they end up at the *right* school, they spend several billion dollars on the admissions process. This money pays for countless admissions officers and counselors, a bunch of standardized tests (and preparation for them), and many books similar to—but not as good as—this one.

It's so expensive because most admissions professionals have a thing about being in control. As a group, colleges resist almost every attempt to standardize or otherwise simplify the process. Admissions officers want you to believe that every admissions decision that they render occurs within systems of weights, measures, and deliberations that are far too complex for you to comprehend. They shudder at the notion of having to respond to students and their parents in down-to-earth language that might reveal the arbitrary nature of a huge percentage of the admissions and denials that they issue during each cycle. That would be admitting that good luck and circumstance play a major part in many successful applications. So, in flight from public accountability, they make the process a lot more mysterious than it needs to be.

Even the most straightforward colleges hide the information you would want to know about the way they'll evaluate your application: What grades and SATs are they looking for? Do their reported SAT averages include minority students, athletes, and legacies (kids whose parents went to their school)? Exactly how much do extracurricular activities count? What percentage of the aid that they give out is in loans and what percentage is in grants?

We couldn't get answers to these questions from many colleges. In fact, we couldn't get answers to *any* questions from some schools. Others who supplied this information to us for earlier editions of this guide have since decided that they never should have in the first place. After all, knowledge is power.

Colleges seem to have the time and money to create beautiful brochures that generally show that all college classes are held under a tree on a beautiful day. Why not just tell you what sort of students they're looking for, and what factors they'll use to consider your application?

Until the schools demystify the admissions process, this book is your best bet. It's not a phone book containing every fact about every college in the country. And it's not a memoir written by a few graduates describing their favorite dining halls or professors. We've given you the facts you'll need to apply to the few hundred best schools in the country. And enough information about them—which we gathered from hundreds of counselors and admissions officers and more than 100,000 college students—to help you make a smart decision about which school to attend.

One note: We don't talk a lot about majors. This is because most high school students really don't know what they want to major in—and the ones who do almost always change their minds by the beginning of junior year. Choosing a school because of the reputation of a single department is often a terrible idea.

If you're interested in learning about majors and the colleges that offer them, pick up our *Guide to College Majors* or visit our website, www.princetonreview.com, where we explain majors and list the colleges that offer them.

As complicated and difficult as the admissions process is, we think you'll love college itself—especially at the schools listed in this book.

Good luck in your search.

John Katzman

June 2003

ACKNOWLEDGMENTS

I am blessed year after year with a talented group of colleagues working together to produce our guidebooks. This book, part of our "building out" of the concept of our flagship college guide, *The Best 351 Colleges*, yields, like its predecessor, what prospective college students really want: the most honest, accessible, and pertinent information on the colleges they are considering attending for the next four years of their lives. Collectively including profiles of more than 600 colleges and universities, our *Best Regional Colleges* series was an unprecedented undertaking, requiring well-coordinated student-survey, editorial, and production efforts, and my sincere thanks go to the many who contributed to this tremendous project. I am proud to note here that we have again successfully provided an uncompromising look into the true nature of each profiled college or university, based on the opinions of each college's current students. I know our readers will benefit from our cumulative efforts.

A special thank you goes to our authors, Tom Meltzer, Tara Bray, Roy Opochinski, Christopher Maier, Carson Brown, Julie Doherty, Nadine Kavanaugh, Catherine Monaco, and Dinaw Mengestu for their dedication in sifting through thousands of surveys to produce the essence of each school in three paragraphs! Very special thanks go to two stellar producers from our editorial staff: Erik Olson and Erica Magrey. Erik, our Senior Editor, is an essential resource to our department and a clear driver of this series. I can always trust Erik to provide clear direction in both the voice and sensibilities of The Princeton Review; he has proven himself again here. Erica, in her freshman performance, took this trial by fire with grace and moxie. On a daily basis, Erica brought quiet competence to the student survey process, adhering meticulously to our standards and goals for each book's narrative profiles.

Sincere thanks go to Jillian Taylor, our Student Survey Manager. Jillian provided clear messaging on our survey methodology and editorial procedure, remaining even-handed and approachable throughout the process. A special note goes to Amy Kinney, a veteran student surveyor, for her unwavering dedication to relaying our books' mission to the schools included in these pages. She provided sincere representation of the mission of The Princeton Review. Michael Palumbo also deserves praise for his indispensable contributions in the last days of production.

My continued thanks go to our data collection staff—David Soto, Ben Zelavansky, and Yojaira Cordero—for their successful efforts in collecting and accurately representing the statistical data that appear with each college profile. In turn, my gratitude goes to Chris Wujciak for his competence in all of our book pours.

The enormity of this project and its deadline constraints could not have been realized without the calm presence of our production team, Julieanna Lambert and Scott Harris. Their ability to remain focused throughout the production of this project inspires and impresses me. They deserve great thanks for their flexible schedules and uncompromising efficiency.

Special thanks go to Jeanne Krier, our Random House publicist, for the work she has done on this new series and the overall work she has done on our flagship book, *The Best 351 Colleges*, since its first edition. Jeanne continues to be my trusted colleague, media advisor and friend. I would also like to make special mention of Tom Russell, our publisher, for his continuous investment in our new book ideas.

Lastly, I thank John Katzman and Mark Chernis for their steadfast confidence in both this series and our publishing department, and for always being the champions of student opinion. It is pleasure to work with you both.

Again, to all who contributed so much to these publications, thank you for your efforts; they do not go unnoticed.

Robert Franek

Editorial Director

Lead Author—The Best Regional Colleges

CONTENTS

PART 1

INTRODUCTION

A P _ LIC _ T _ O_.

What's *that*?!?!

It's APPLICATION with P-A-I-N removed from the process.

We removed the paper, too.

With PrincetonReview.com's Online College Applications there are no endless piles to shuffle. No leaky pens, no hand cramps, no trying to figure out how many stamps to stick on that envelope.

The process is so painless, online applications practically submit themselves for you. Watch . . .

Type in your main contact information just once in our application profile and every subsequent application you file from our database—picking from hundreds of top schools—is automatically filled in with your information.

Not only are online applications:

- Faster to fill out

- Completely safe and secure

- Instantly trackable (check your application status online!)

- And . . . impossible to lose in the mail (they reach schools instantly)

But also: On PrincetonReview.com, there's no extra fee to submit your application online—our technology is totally FREE for you to use. In fact, some colleges even *waive* the application fee if you apply online.

Still have questions?

- Can I start an application now and finish it later?

- Are there easy-to-use instructions or someone I can call if I have a question? If I get stuck are there application instructions?

- Do schools *really* want to receive applications online?

Yes, yes, and yes!

It's easy to see the advantages of online applications. Almost as easy as actually applying.

Just log on and apply. It's that easy.

PrincetonReview.com—Applications without the pain.

HOW WE PRODUCE THIS BOOK

Welcome to the first edition of *The Best Northeastern Colleges*, one-fifth of our *Best* regional guidebook series. Our decision to produce this series was fueled by a desire to raise awareness of academically excellent but lesser-known regional colleges for those looking to study within a specific geographic area. Many of the schools within these pages are nationally competitive institutions of higher learning; we therefore also include their profiles in the 2004 edition of our best-selling *The Best 351 Colleges*. In fact, for these regional guides, we employ the same methodology for collecting student surveys and distilling them into college profiles as we do for *The Best 351 Colleges*. An important difference between this series and *The Best 351 Colleges*, however, is that we do not include any ranking lists. The profiles in these regional guides also appear in a slightly different format than those in *The Best 351 Colleges*.

But why are some of the outstanding schools in this book *not* included in *Best 351*? For one or both of two possible reasons. First, it may be because—at this time—they have a regional, rather than a national, focus. That is, they draw their students primarily from the state in which they are located, or from bordering states. A second possible reason is that—again, at this time—they have not met the rather rigorous standards for inclusion in *The Best 351 Colleges*. Is that meant as a snub to the schools that didn't make it into *Best 351*? Absolutely not. There are more than 3,000 institutions of higher learning in the United States, and *The Best 351 Colleges* profiles the top 10 percent, academically, of those schools. These regional guides, on the other hand, offer student opinion–driven information on all of those top colleges as well as the colleges just outside of that highest 10 percent.

For each school, we provide both in-depth statistical data (on admissions, financial aid, student body demographics, and academics) and narrative descriptions of academic and social life based on the opinions of the very students who attend them. Although we have expanded the scope of schools profiled from *Best 351*, we have also narrowed our focus to aid students for whom location is a key consideration.

We avoided using any sort of mathematical calculations or formulas to determine which colleges and universities to include in the regional guides. For each region, we aim to provide an inclusive cross-section of colleges: large and small, public and private, all-male and all-female, historically black colleges and universities, science and technology–focused institutions, nontraditional colleges, highly selective and virtually open-door admissions, great buys and the wildly expensive. Like the other schools in these guides, all are institutions well worth considering. Though not every college included will appeal to every student, this guide represents the top 135 colleges in the

Northeastern states. We've surveyed students at 604 colleges across the nation and sorted their profiles into five regional guides. The following books complete the series:

The Best Mid-Atlantic Colleges

The Best Midwestern Colleges

The Best Southeastern Colleges

The Best Western Colleges

Each college we surveyed this year had to meet two criteria: first, they had to meet our standards for academic excellence within their region, and second, we had to be able to survey their students anonymously, either through our online survey (http://survey.review.com) or through our paper survey, which we distribute and collect during an on-campus visit.

Surveying thousands of students on hundreds of campuses is a mammoth undertaking, but the launch of our online student survey, available 24/7, has made it possible for students to complete a survey anytime and anywhere an Internet-enabled computer can be found. We've surveyed anywhere from all twenty-odd men at Deep Springs College in the California desert to thousands of collegians at places like Clemson University and Utah State University.

So how do we do it? All colleges and universities we plan to visit are notified through established campus contacts that we wish to arrange a survey; we depend on these contacts for assistance in identifying common, high-traffic areas on campus in which to distribute our paper survey and to help us make any necessary arrangements as required by campus policies. When possible, and when the college is willing, our contacts will arrange for an e-mail to be sent to the entire student body encouraging them to fill out our online survey. (In recent years, many schools have chosen to send an e-mail to the entire student body, which in some cases yielded astonishing results.) At colleges in the New York metropolitan area (we call it home), we most often send our own team to conduct the typically half-day surveys; at colleges that are further afield, we typically either send Princeton Review people from our field offices or hire current students at the college to conduct the surveys. Some of the colleges also included in *The Best 351 Colleges* series were surveyed this past year, but not *all*; each is surveyed *at least* once every three years. The reality is that, unless there's been some grand upheaval at a campus, we've found that there's little change in student opinion from one year to the next. Colleges that wish to be resurveyed prior to their turn in the regular survey cycle are accommodated with an earlier visit if at all possible.

The survey itself is extensive, divided into four fundamental sections—"About Yourself," "Your School's Academics/Administration," "Students," and "Life at Your School"—that collectively include more than 70 questions. We ask about everything imaginable, from "How many out-of-class hours do you spend studying each day?" to "How widely used is beer?" Most questions are multiple-response in nature, but several offer students the opportunity to expand on their answers with narrative responses. These narrative responses are the source of the student quotes that appear throughout each college profile in *The Best Northeastern Colleges.*

Once the surveys have been completed and the responses stored in our database, each college is given a grade point average (GPA) for its students' answers to each multiple-response question. It is these GPAs that enable us to compare student opinions from college to college, and to gauge which aspects of the complete experience at each college rate highest and lowest according to the institution's own students. (They are also the basis for three of the ratings—Quality of Life, Financial Aid, and Academic—that appear at the top of each college profile.) Once we have this information in hand, we write the individual college profiles. Student quotes within the profiles are not chosen for their extreme nature, humor, or singular perspective—in all cases the intention is that they represent closely the sentiments expressed by the majority of survey respondents from the college or that they illustrate one side or another of a mixed bag of student opinion (in which case the counterpoint will also appear within the text). And of course, if a student's quote accomplishes this *and* is noteworthy for it's wittiness, it'll definitely make it into the guide.

The profiles in general seek to accomplish that which a college admissions viewbook by its very nature can never really hope to achieve—to provide a (relatively) uncensored view of life at a particular college, and acknowledge that even the best colleges have their shortcomings. Though some college administrators find this book hard to accept, most have come to recognize that college officials no longer enjoy the luxury of controlling every word that students hear or read about their institutions and that the age of consumerism in the college search process is here to stay.

Our survey is qualitative and anecdotal. While this approach sometimes means we blow a result—such as when we surveyed at Stephens College during the week the administration was debating the abolition of women's studies as a major at that small women's college and *(surprise!)* the survey results indicated an unhappy student body—most of our results are confirmed by feedback we get from alums, current students, counselors, and prospective students who visit the campuses. In order to help guard against the likelihood that we produce an entry that's way off the mark, we send administrators at each school a copy of the entry we intend to publish prior to its actual publication date, with ample opportunity to respond with corrections, comments, and/or outright objections. In every case in which we receive a reply, we take careful steps to ensure that we review their suggestions and make appropriate changes when warranted.

Far more important than what college administrators think is what *you* think. Take our information on colleges as you should take information from all sources—as input that reflects the values and opinions of others, which may be helpful to you as you *form your own opinions*. This guide is not an end point from which you should cull your list of possible colleges but rather a starting point, a tool that can help you to probe the surface and get a sense of the college experience. You must do your own investigation, refer to other sources, visit the campuses, and develop your own list of best colleges. Only then will this book be the useful tool that it is intended to be.

HOW THIS BOOK IS ORGANIZED

Each of the colleges and universities listed in this book has its own two-page spread. To make it easier to find information about the schools of your choice, we've used the same format for every school. Look at the sample pages below:

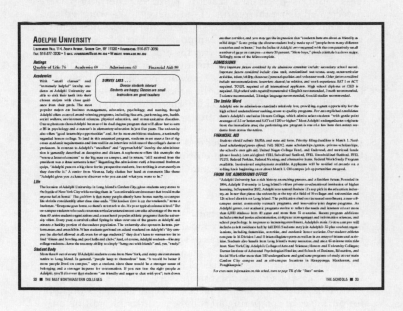

Each spread has several components. First, at the very top of the spread you will see the school's address, telephone and fax numbers for the admissions office, the telephone number for the financial aid office, and the school's website and/or e-mail address. Next, you will find the school's ratings in four categories: Quality of Life, Academics, Admissions, and Financial Aid, which are described further below. Then you will see our "Survey Says . . ." bubble and the first three sections— "Academics," "Life," and "Student Body" —which are drawn primarily from student survey responses for that particular college. Then comes the "Admissions" section with information on how the admissions office weighs the different components of your application; followed by the "Inside Word" on admissions, academics, life, or demographics at that school; "Financial Aid" application pointers; and an institution-authored message under the title "From the Admissions Office." Finally, at the end of the profile is the page number on which the school's statistical data appears. Here's an explanation of each part:

1. Contact Information

Includes school address, admissions phone and fax numbers, financial aid phone number, admissions e-mail address, and school website.

2. Quality of Life Rating

How happy students are with their lives outside the classroom. This rating is given on a scale of 60 to 99. The ratings were determined using the results of our surveys. We weighed several factors, including students' overall happiness; the beauty, safety, and location of the campus; comfort of dorms; food quality; and ease in dealing with the administration. Note that even if a school's rating is in the low 60s, it does not mean that the quality of life is horrible—there are no "failing" schools. A low ranking just means that the school placed low compared with others in our *Best* regional series. This individual rating places each college on a continuum for purposes of comparing all colleges within this edition of the series only. Though similar, these ratings are not intended to be compared directly to those within any subsequent edition, as our ratings computations are refined and change somewhat annually.

3. Academic Rating

On a scale of 60 to 99, how hard students work at the school and how much they get back for their efforts. The ratings are based on results of our surveys of students and administrators. Factors weighed included how many hours students study and the quality of students the school attracts; we also considered students' assessments of their professors' abilities and helpfulness. This individual rating places each college on a continuum for purposes of comparing all colleges within this edition only. Though similar, these ratings are not intended to be compared directly to those within any other edition, as our ratings computations are refined and change somewhat annually.

4. Admissions Rating

How competitive admission is at the school, on a scale of 60 to 99. This rating is determined by several factors, including the class rank of entering freshmen, their test scores, and the percentage of applicants accepted. By incorporating all these factors, our competitiveness rating adjusts for "self-selecting" applicant pools. University of Chicago, for example, has a very high competitiveness rating, even though it admits a surprisingly large proportion of its applicants. Chicago's applicant pool is self-selecting; that is, nearly all the school's applicants are exceptional students. This individual rating places each college on a continuum for purposes of comparing all colleges within this edition only. Though similar, these ratings are not intended to be compared directly to those within any other edition, as our ratings computations are refined and change somewhat annually.

5. Financial Aid Rating

Based on school-reported data on financial aid awards to students and students' satisfaction as collected on our survey with the financial aid they receive. Again, this is on a scale of 60 to 99. This individual rating places each college on a continuum for purposes of comparing all colleges within this edition only. Though similar, these ratings are not intended to be compared directly to those within any other edition, as our ratings computations are refined and change somewhat annually.

6. Survey Says . . .

Our "Survey Says" list, located under the ratings on each school's two-page spread, is based entirely on the results of our student surveys. In other words, the items on this list are based on the opinions of the students we surveyed at those schools (*not* on any numerical analysis of library size, endowment, etc.). Items listed are those that are unusually popular or unpopular on that campus. Some of the terms that appear on the list are not entirely self-explanatory; these terms are defined below.

Diverse students interact: We asked whether students from different class and ethnic backgrounds interacted frequently and easily. When students' collective response is "yes," the heading "Diverse students interact" appears on the list. When student response indicates there are not many interactions between students from different class and ethnic backgrounds, the heading "Students are cliquish" appears on the list.

Cheating: We asked students how prevalent cheating is at their school. If students reported cheating to be rare, "No one cheats" shows up on the list.

Students are happy: This category reflects student responses to the question "Overall, how happy are you with your school?"

TAs teach upper-level classes: At some large universities, you'll continue to be taught by teaching assistants even in your upper-level courses. It is safe to assume that when "Lots of TAs teach upper-level courses" appears on the list, TAs also teach a disproportionate number of intro courses as well.

Students are very religious or **Students aren't religious:** We asked students how religious they are. Their responses are reflected in this category.

Diverse student body: We asked students whether their student body is made up of a variety of ethnic groups. This category reflects their answers, and shows up as "Diversity lacking on campus" or "Ethnic diversity on campus."

Town-gown relations: We asked students whether they got along with local residents; their answers are reflected by this category.

7. Academics, Life, and Student Body

The first three sections summarize the results of the surveys we distributed to students at the school. The "Academics" section reports how hard students work and how satisfied they are with the education they are getting. It also often tells you which academic departments our respondents rated favorably. Student opinion regarding administrative departments often works its way into this section, as well. The "Life" section describes life outside the classroom and addresses questions ranging from "How nice is the campus?" and "How comfortable are the dorms?" to "How popular are fraternities and sororities?" The "Student Body" section tells you about what type of student the school usually attracts and how the students view the level of interaction between various groups, including those of different ethnic origins. All quotes in these three sections are from students' essay responses to our surveys. We choose quotes based on the accuracy with which they reflect our overall survey results for that school.

8. Admissions

This section tells you what aspects of your application are most important to the school's admissions officers. It also lists the high school curricular prerequisites for applicants, which standardized tests (if any) are required, and special information about the school's admissions process (e.g., Do minority students and legacies, for example, receive special consideration? Are there any unusual application requirements for applicants to special programs?).

9. The Inside Word

This section contains our own insights into each school's admissions process, student-body demographics, life on campus, or unique academic attributes.

10. Financial Aid

This section summarizes the financial aid process at the school—what forms you need and what types of aid and loans are available. (More information about need-based aid is listed under "Financial Facts" in the school's statistical profile at the back of the book.) While this section includes specific deadline dates as reported by the colleges, we strongly encourage students seeking financial aid to file all forms—federal, state, and institutional—as soon as they become available. In the world of financial aid, the early birds almost always get the best worms (provided, of course, that they're eligible for a meal!).

11. From the Admissions Office

This section contains text supplied by the colleges in response to our invitation that they use this space to "speak directly to the readers of our guide."

12. For More Information

We refer you to the page number in our school statistics section where you can find detailed statistical information for the particular school you're reading about.

SCHOOL STATISTICS

This section, located in the back of the book, contains various statistics culled from our student surveys and from questionnaires school administrators fill out. Keep in mind that not every category will appear for every school, since in some cases the information is not reported or not applicable. Please note that ratings for Quality of Life, Academics, Admissions, and Financial Aid are explained on pages 10-11.

If a school has completed each and every data field, the headings will appear in the following order:

ADELPHI UNIVERSITY

% graduated top 25% of class	46
% graduated top 50% of class	69

CAMPUS LIFE
Quality of Life Rating	76
Type of school	private
Affiliation	none
Environment	urban

STUDENTS
Total undergrad enrollment	3,391
% male/female	29/71
% from out of state	11
% from public high school	75
% live on campus	26
% in (# of) fraternities	6 (3)
% in (# of) sororities	6 (6)
% African American	12
% Asian	4
% Caucasian	51
% Hispanic	7
% international	4

ACADEMICS
Academic Rating	69
Calendar	semester
Student/faculty ratio	14:1
Profs interesting rating	
Profs accessible rating	
% profs teaching UG courses	100
% classes taught by TAs	0
Avg lab size	10-19 students
Avg reg class size	20-29 students

MOST POPULAR MAJORS
social work
social sciences
business administration/management

SELECTIVITY
Admissions Rating	63
# of applicants	3,705
% of applicants accepted	65
% of acceptees attending	27

FRESHMAN PROFILE
Range SAT Verbal	460-560
Average SAT Verbal	533
Range SAT Math	460-560
Average SAT Math	536
Minimum TOEFL	550
Average HS GPA	3.3
% graduated top 10% of class	17

DEADLINES:
Nonfall registration?	yes

FINANCIAL FACTS
Financial Aid Rating	89
Tuition	$16,100
Room and board	$7,050
Books and supplies	$1,000
Avg frosh grant	$5,653
Avg frosh loan	$3,219

294 ■ THE BEST NORTHEASTERN COLLEGES

Type of school: Whether the school is public or private.

Affiliation: Any religious order with which the school is affiliated.

Environment: Whether the campus is located in an urban, suburban, or rural setting.

Total undergrad enrollment: The total number of undergraduates who attend the school.

% male/female through **# countries represented:** The demographic breakdown of the full-time undergraduate student body, a listing of what percentage of the student body lives on campus, the percentage belonging to Greek organizations, and finally, the number of countries represented by the student body.

Calendar: The school's schedule of academic terms. A "semester" schedule has two long terms, usually starting in September and January. A "trimester" schedule has three terms, one usually beginning before Christmas and two after. A "quarterly" schedule has four terms, which go by very quickly: the entire term, including exams, usually lasts only nine or ten weeks. A "4-1-4" schedule is like a semester schedule, but with a month-long term in between the fall and spring semesters. (Similarly, a "4-4-1" has a short term following two longer semesters.) When a school's academic calendar doesn't match any of these traditional schedules we note that by saying "other." For schools that have "other" as their calendar, it is best to call the admissions office for details.

Student/faculty ratio: The ratio of full-time undergraduate instructional faculty members to all undergraduates.

Profs interesting rating: Based on the answers given iby students to the survey question, "In general, how good are your instructors as teachers?"

Profs accessible rating: Based on the answers given by students to the survey question, "In general, how accessible are your instructors outside the classroom?"

% profs teaching UG courses: Largely self-explanatory; this category shows the percentage of professors who teach undergraduates and doesn't include any faculty whose focus is solely on research.

% classes taught by TAs: Many universities that offer graduate programs use graduate students as teaching assistants (TAs). They teach undergraduate courses, primarily at the introductory level. This category reports on the percentage of classes that are taught by TAs instead of regular faculty.

Avg lab size; Avg reg class size: College-reported figures on class size averages for regular courses and for labs/discussion sections.

Most Popular Majors: The three most popular majors at the school.

% of applicants accepted: The percentage of applicants to which the school offered admission.

% of acceptees attending: The percentage of those who were accepted who eventually enrolled.

 # accepting a place on wait list: The number of students who decided to take a place on the wait list when offered this option.

% admitted from wait list: The percentage of applicants who opted to take a place on the wait list and were subsequently offered admission. These figures will vary tremendously from college to college and should be a consideration when deciding whether to accept a place on a college's wait list.

# of early decision applicants: The number of students who applied under the college's early decision or early action plan.

% accepted early decision: The percentage of early decision or early action applicants who were admitted under this plan. By the nature of these plans, the vast majority who are admitted wind up enrolling. (See the early decision/action description on the next page for more detail.)

Range/Average SAT Verbal, Range/Average SAT Math, Range/Average ACT Composite: The average and the middle 50 percent range of test scores for entering freshmen. Don't be discouraged from applying to the school of your choice even if your combined SAT scores are 80 or even 120 points below the average, because you may still have a chance of getting in. Remember that many schools emphasize other aspects of your application (e.g., your grades, how good a match you make with the school) more heavily than test scores.

Minimum TOEFL: The minimum test score necessary for entering freshmen who are required to take the TOEFL (Test of English as a Foreign Language). Most schools will require all international students or non-native English speakers to take the TOEFL in order to be considered for admission.

Average HS GPA: We report this on a scale of 0.0 to 4.0 (occasionally colleges report averages on a 100 scale, in which case we report those figures). This is one of the key factors in college admissions. Be sure to keep your GPA as high as possible straight through until graduation from high school.

% graduated top 10%, top 25%, top 50% of class: Of those students for whom class rank was reported, the percentage of entering freshmen who ranked in the top tenth, quarter, and half of their high school classes.

Early decision/action deadlines: The deadline for submission of application materials under the early decision or early action plan. Early decision is generally for students for whom the school is a first choice. The applicant commits to attending the school if admitted; in return, the school renders an early decision, usually in December or January. If accepted, the applicant doesn't have to spend the time and money applying to other schools. In most cases, students may apply for early decision to only one school. Early action is similar to early decision, but less binding; applicants need not commit to attending the school and in some cases may apply early action to more than one school. The school, in turn, may not render a decision, choosing to defer the applicant to the regular admissions pool. Each school's guidelines are a little different, and the policies of a few of the most selective colleges in the country have changed quite dramatically recently. Some colleges offer more than one early decision cycle, so it's a good idea to call and get full details if you plan to pursue one of these options.

Early decision, early action, priority, and regular admission deadlines: The dates by which all materials must be postmarked (we'd suggest "received in the office") in order to be considered for admission under each particular admissions option/cycle for admission for the fall term.

Early decision, early action, priority, and regular admission notification: The dates by which you can expect a decision on your application under each admissions option/cycle.

Nonfall registration: Some schools will allow applicants or transfers to matriculate at times other than the fall term—the traditional beginning of the academic calendar year. Other schools will only allow you to register for classes if you can begin in the fall term. A simple "yes" or "no" in this category indicates the school's policy on nonfall registration.

Tuition, In-state tuition: The tuition at the school, or for public colleges, for a resident of the school's state. In-state tuition is usually much lower than out-of-state tuition for state-supported public schools.

Out-of-state tuition: For public colleges, the tuition for a nonresident of the school's state. This entry appears only for public colleges, since tuition at private colleges is generally the same regardless of state of residence.

Room and board: Estimated room and board costs.

Books and supplies: Estimated annual cost of necessary textbooks and/or supplies.

% frosh receiving aid: According to the school's financial aid department, the percentage of all freshmen who received need-based aid.

% undergrads receiving aid: According to the school's financial aid department, the percentage of all undergrads who receive need-based financial aid.

Avg frosh grant: The average grant or scholarship amount awarded to freshmen.

Avg frosh loan: The average amount of loans disbursed to freshmen.

If you have any questions, comments, or suggestions, please contact us at Editorial Department, Admissions Services, 2315 Broadway, New York, NY 10024, or e-mail us at bookeditor@review.com. We appreciate your input and want to make our books as useful to you as they can be.

Glossary

ACT: Like the SAT I but less tricky. Many schools accept either SAT or ACT scores; if you consistently get blown away by the SAT, you might want to consider taking the ACT instead.

College-prep curriculum: 16 to 18 academic credits (each credit equals a full year of a high school course), usually including 4 years of English, 3 to 4 years of social studies, and at least 2 years each of science, mathematics, and foreign language.

Core curriculum: Students at schools with core curricula must take a number of required courses, usually in such subjects as world history and/or western civilization, writing skills, and fundamental math and science.

CSS/Financial Aid PROFILE: The College Scholarship Service PROFILE, an optional financial aid form required by some colleges in addition to the FAFSA.

Distribution requirements: Students at schools with distribution requirements must take a number of courses in various subject areas, such as foreign language, humanities, natural science, and social science. Distribution requirements do not specify which courses you must take, only which types of courses.

FAFSA: The Free Application for Federal Student Aid. Schools are required by law to accept the FAFSA; some require that applicants complete at least one other form (usually a CSS/Financial Aid PROFILE or the college's own form) to be considered for financial aid.

4-1-4: A type of academic schedule. It's like a semester schedule, but with a short semester (usually one month long) between the two semesters. Most schools offer internship programs or nontraditional studies during the short semester. A 4-4-1 schedule is similar to this one, except the short semester comes after the second long semester, usually in the late spring or early summer.

GDI: "Goddamned independent," a term frequently used by students in fraternities and sororities to describe those not in fraternities and sororities.

Greek system, Greeks: Fraternities and sororities and their members.

Humanities: These include such disciplines as art history, drama, English, foreign languages, music, philosophy, and religion.

Merit-based grant: A scholarship (not necessarily full) given to students because of some special talent or attribute. Artists, athletes, community leaders, and geniuses are typical recipients.

Natural sciences: These include such disciplines as astronomy, biology, chemistry, genetics, geology, mathematics, physics, and zoology.

Need-based grant: A scholarship (not necessarily full) given to students because they would otherwise be unable to afford college. Student need is determined on the basis of the FAFSA. Some schools also require the CSS PROFILE and/or institutional applications.

Priority deadline: Some schools will list a deadline for admission and/or financial aid as a "priority deadline," meaning that while they will accept applications after that date, all applications received prior to the deadline are assured of getting the most thorough, and in some instances potentially more generous, appraisal possible.

RA: Residence assistant (or residential advisor). Someone, usually an upperclassman or graduate student, who supervises a floor or section of a dorm, usually in return for free room and board. RAs are responsible for enforcing the drinking and noise rules.

SAT I: A college entrance exam required by many schools.

SAT II: Subject Tests: Subject-specific exams administered by the Educational Testing Service (the SAT people). These tests are required by some, but not all, admissions offices. English Writing and Math Level I or IIC are the tests most frequently required.

Social sciences: These include such disciplines as anthropology, economics, geography, history, international studies, political science, psychology, and sociology.

TA: Teaching assistant. Most often a graduate student, a TA will often teach discussion sections of large lectures. At some schools, TAs and graduate students teach a large number of introductory-level and even some upper-level courses. At smaller schools, professors generally do all the teaching.

Work-study: A government-funded financial aid program that provides assistance to financial aid recipients in return for work in the school's library, labs, etc.

PART 2

THE SCHOOLS

ADELPHI UNIVERSITY

LEVERMORE HALL 114, SOUTH AVENUE, GARDEN CITY, NY 11530 • ADMISSIONS: 516-877-3050
FAX: 516-877-3039 • E-MAIL: ADMISSIONS@ADELPHI.EDU • WEBSITE: WWW.ADELPHI.EDU

Ratings
Quality of Life: 76   **Academic:** 69   **Admissions:** 63   **Financial Aid:** 89

Academics

With "small classes" and "extremely helpful" faculty, students at Adelphi University are able to sink their teeth into their chosen majors with close guidance from their profs. The most popular

> **SURVEY SAYS . . .**
> *Diverse students interact*
> *Students are happy, Classes are small*
> *Instructors are good teachers*

majors are business management, education, psychology, and nursing, though Adelphi offers a cast of award-winning programs, including fine arts, performing arts, health, social welfare, environmental sciences, physical education, and communicative disorders. One sophomore chose Adelphi because of its dual degree program that will allow her to earn a BS in psychology and a master's in elementary education in just five years. The university also offers "good internship opportunities" and, for its more ambitious students, a nationally regarded honors college. To land in this esteemed program, students must meet a list of rigorous academic requirements and fare well in an interview with one of the college's deans or professors. In contrast to Adelphi's "excellent" and "approachable" faculty, the administration is generally described as deceptive and distant. A sophomore offers this example: she "wrote a letter of concern" to the big man on campus, and in return, "all I received from the president was a three sentence letter." Regarding the admissions staff, a frustrated freshman quips, "Adelphi puts on a big show for its prospective students, but nothing is ever exactly as they describe it." A senior from Vicenza, Italy, shakes her head at comments like these: "Adelphi gives you a chance to discover who you are and what you want to be."

Life

The location of Adelphi University, in Long Island's Garden City, gives students easy access to the bustle of New York City while rooting them in "a comfortable environment that would make anyone feel at home." The problem is that many people already have homes nearby, so campus life shrinks considerably after class time ends. "The hardest time is on the weekends," notes a freshman. "Everyone goes home, so there's not much to do. It's your typical suitcase school." But on-campus students who seek out extracurricular entertainment can take advantage of the more than 60 active student organizations and a number of popular athletic programs that the university offers. Every year, a carnival called Spring-In takes over one of the greens at Adelphi and attracts a healthy portion of the student population. The university also sponsors lectures, performances, and art exhibits. When students get bored on a dead weekend on Adelphi's "dry campus (no alcohol allowed at all, even for of-age students)," they don't have to venture too far to find "diners and bowling and pool halls and clubs." And, of course, Adelphi students—like any college students—have the uncanny ability to simply "hang out with friends" and, yes, "study."

Student Body

More than 9 out of every 10 Adelphi students come from New York, and many are commuters native to Long Island. In general, "people keep to themselves" here. "It would be better if more people lived on campus," says a student, since there would be a stronger sense of belonging and a stronger impetus for conversation. If you run into the right people at Adelphi, you'll discover that students "are friendly and eager to chat with you"; turn down another corridor, and you may get the impression that "students here are about as friendly as rabid dogs." Some praise the diverse student body, made up of "people from many different countries and cultures," but the ladies of Adelphi are concerned with the comparatively small number of guys on campus—a mere 30 percent. "More boys," pleads a female business major. Tellingly, none of the fellas complain.

ADMISSIONS

Very important factors considered by the admissions committee include: secondary school record. *Important factors considered include:* class rank, standardized test scores, essay, extracurricular activities, talent/ability, character/personal qualities, and volunteer work. *Other factors considered include:* recommendations, interview, alumni/ae relation, and work experience. SAT I or ACT required. TOEFL required of all international applicants. High school diploma or GED is required. *High school units required/recommended:* 4 English recommended, 3 math recommended, 3 science recommended, 2 foreign language recommended, 4 social studies recommended.

The Inside Word

Adelphi sets its admissions standards relatively low, providing a great opportunity for the high school underachiever seeking access to quality programs. For accomplished candidates there's Adelphi's exclusive Honors College, which admits select students "with grade point averages of 3.5 or better and SAT's of 1200 or higher." Most Adelphi undergraduates originate from the immediate area; the performing arts program is one of a few here that attract students from across the nation.

FINANCIAL AID

Students should submit: FAFSA and state aid form. Priority filing deadline is March 1. *Need-based scholarships/grants offered:* Pell, SEOG, state scholarships/grants, private scholarships, the school's own gift aid, United Negro College Fund, and Endowed, and restricted funds (donor funds). *Loan aid offered:* FFEL Subsidized Stafford, FFEL Unsubsidized Stafford, FFEL PLUS, Federal Perkins, Federal Nursing, and alternative loans. Federal Work-Study Program available. Institutional employment available. Applicants will be notified of awards on a rolling basis beginning on or about March 1. Off-campus job opportunities are good.

FROM THE ADMISSIONS OFFICE

"Adelphi University has a rich history, an exciting present, and a limitless future. Founded in 1896, Adelphi University is Long Island's oldest private co-educational institution of higher learning. In September 2002, Adelphi was named *Business LI*'s top pick in the education industry, an honor that places the university at the top of a field of 19 colleges and universities and 126 school districts on Long Island. The publication cited our increased enrollment, a new off-campus center, community outreach programs, and innovative joint degree programs. As Adelphi grows, our academic programs evolve to reflect the needs and interests of our more than 6,900 students from 40 states and more than 55 countries. Recent program additions include criminal justice administration, computer management and information sciences, and school psychology. In response to increasing enrollment, Adelphi's main 75-acre campus will include a sixth residence hall by fall 2003. Students may join Adelphi's 55-plus student organizations, including fraternities, sororities, and academic honor societies. Our student-athletes compete in 16 Division I and II intercollegiate sports as well as in an array of intramural activities. Students also benefit from Long Island's many resources, and are a 45-minute train ride from New York City. Adelphi's College of Arts and Sciences; Honors and University Colleges; Derner Institute of Advanced Psychological Studies; and Schools of Business, Education, and Social Work offer more than 100 undergraduate and graduate programs of study at our main Garden City campus and at off-campus locations in Hauppauge, Manhattan, and Poughkeepsie."

For even more information on this school, turn to page 294 of the "Stats" section.

ALFRED UNIVERSITY

ALUMNI HALL, ONE SAXON DRIVE, ALFRED, NY 14802-1205 • ADMISSIONS: 607-871-2115
FAX: 607-871-2198 • FINANCIAL AID: 607-871-2159 • E-MAIL: ADMWWW@ALFRED.EDU
WEBSITE: WWW.ALFRED.EDU

Ratings
Quality of Life: 79   **Academic:** 76   **Admissions:** 77   **Financial Aid:** 88

Academics

Alfred University, a school renowned for its ceramics and glassworks programs, provides a "stimulating and rewarding" academic experience. What makes Alfred unique is that it isn't only an art school. Students speak highly of the English and business departments and point out that science courses are quite challeng-

> **SURVEY SAYS . . .**
> *Lots of beer drinking*
> *Students aren't religious*
> *Campus easy to get around*
> *High cost of living, Theater is unpopular*
> *Class discussions encouraged*
> *Lousy off-campus food*
> *Political activism is (almost) nonexistent*

ing. The "brilliant" professors "know you on a first-name basis" and "are often available for help in a class. One-on-one sessions with professors are often available." Class sizes are small and TAs are uncommon. One first-year student writes, "I am a freshman and have already been to two of my professors' homes for dinner." The administration is "friendly" and "quite approachable." They are "willing to discuss any situation that might arise." Some students note that they would like to see more professors in order "to increase the diversity of classes." Several transfer students are extremely fond of AU: "Compared to my previous school, this is heaven." Students note that the computer and library facilities need improvement, as does the food. On-campus parking also needs to be expanded. A junior English major summarizes Alfred University thusly: "Alfred University is a wonderful institution. The buildings are nice-looking, the professors are knowledgeable, and the students are brilliant."

Life

AU's location in a "small, rural town in upstate New York"—two hours away from both Buffalo and Rochester—doesn't inspire its students. "If you expect to have a thrill a minute, then this may not be the best place for you." Still, students say, "there is fun. You just have to find it." The university is aware that students don't have many entertainment options in the surrounding area, and so "they try to plan events for us." Students rent movies or go to AU's on-campus movie theater. Students also go to "the one or two bars in town." Those who partake in winter sports appreciate the campus' proximity to the nearby mountains.

Student Body

Students looking for a diverse population won't find one at AU. "The students are mostly white kids from the East Coast who grew up in upper-middle-class families." Another student adds, "A large number of students have never encountered someone of a different ethnic background." The university's lack of diversity bothers many students. "The white kids mainly hang out with white kids, while black [kids] hang out with black [kids]." AU's small size—about 2,200 undergrads—means that students get to know their peers. "They are a great bunch of people," though "they are sometimes clique-ish." The art students are regarded as the most outgoing. "People mingle freely with ideas, are very friendly, and varied in their dress, interests, and opinions." At the same time, she points out that while "the art school is liberal . . . the school [itself] is rural and in a conservative area."

ADMISSIONS

Very important factors considered by the admissions committee include: character/personal qualities, class rank, extracurricular activities, recommendations, secondary school record. *Important factors considered include:* essays, standardized test scores, volunteer work. *Other factors considered include:* interview, talent/ability, work experience. SAT I or ACT required. TOEFL required of all international applicants. High school diploma or GED is required. *High school units required/recommended:* 16 total required; 4 English required, 2 math required, 4 math recommended, 2 science required, 3 science recommended, 2 science lab required, 3 science lab recommended, 2 social studies required, 3 social studies recommended.

The Inside Word

There's no questioning the high quality of academics at Alfred, especially in their internationally known ceramics program. Still, the university's general lack of name recognition and relatively isolated campus directly affect both the applicant pool and the number of admitted students who enroll, and thus keeps selectivity relatively low for a school of its caliber. (The exception is clearly in ceramic arts, where candidates will face a very rigorous review.) If you're a back-to-nature type looking for a challenging academic environment, AU could be just what the doctor ordered. And if you're a standout academically, you may find that they're generous with financial aid, too—they are serious about competing for good students.

FINANCIAL AID

Students should submit: FAFSA, institution's own financial aid form, state aid form, noncustodial (divorced/separated) parent's statement, business/farm supplement. No deadline for regular filing. The Princeton Review suggests that all financial aid forms be submitted as soon as possible after January 1. *Need-based scholarships/grants offered:* Pell, SEOG, state scholarships/grants, private scholarships, the school's own gift aid. *Loan aid offered:* FFEL Subsidized Stafford, FFEL Unsubsidized Stafford, FFEL PLUS, Federal Perkins, college/university loans from institutional funds, private alternative loans. Federal Work-Study Program available. Institutional employment available. Applicants will be notified of awards on a rolling basis beginning on or about February 1. Off-campus job opportunities are fair.

FROM THE ADMISSIONS OFFICE

"The admissions process at Alfred University is the foundation for the personal attention that a student can expect from this institution. Each applicant is evaluated individually and can expect genuine, personal attention at Alfred University."

For even more information on this school, turn to page 294 of the "Stats" section.

AMHERST COLLEGE

CAMPUS BOX 2231, PO BOX 5000, AMHERST, MA 01002 • ADMISSIONS: 413-542-2328
FAX: 413-542-2040 • FINANCIAL AID: 413-542-2296 • E-MAIL: ADMISSIONS@AMHERST.EDU
WEBSITE: WWW.AMHERST.EDU

Ratings

Quality of Life: 92   **Academic:** 99   **Admissions:** 99   **Financial Aid:** 88

Academics

Small classes, great professors, as much academic freedom as students are willing to grab, and a beautiful campus; no wonder students say, "I could not, in my wildest dreams, imagine an environment better suited for a young adult to grow intellectually than Amherst College." Excellent professors dedicated to undergraduate teaching lie at the heart of the Amherst experience. "Professors make it their business to get to know students and show an interest in them," writes one undergrad. "They are very supportive." Recounts another, "When I wrote my math professor a panic-filled e-mail the night before a test, he called me to help at one in the morning." The administration aggressively encourages close student-teacher relationships, sponsoring "a program [that allows] students to take professors out to dinner and thus extend the educational realm beyond the classroom." Amherst's open curriculum means students "take every course by choice, not because it is required" and can easily "create [their] own interdisciplinary major." Classes are small and selection is limited, so classes close quickly. However, "while on paper it may seem [difficult] to get into classes, Amherst students take the words 'course closed' as a challenge. Here, the administration and many professors encourage us to whine and grovel to get what we want out of our academics. The rules are written so that anyone can be an exception." When students tire of their own college community, it is easy to take a class or audition for a play at one of the other four schools in the Five College Consortium (UMass—Amherst, Smith, Hampshire, and Mount Holyoke). The Five College system, according to students, "gives you all the opportunities of a large university, without any of the drawbacks."

> **SURVEY SAYS . . .**
> *Campus easy to get around*
> *Registration is a breeze, Students are happy*
> *Dorms are like palaces, No one cheats*
> *Very little hard liquor, Very little drug use*
> *Students aren't religious, Lousy food on campus*
> *Student publications are ignored*

Life

According to most students, "Social life at Amherst isn't varied. Mostly it's either parties with lots of alcohol or else just hanging out with your group of friends and talking. But most people seem satisfied with this, and there are a few alternative social events for those who aren't." For fun, students "watch a lot of movies sponsored by campus groups, dance, and go out to dinner with friends." They also attend TAP, a.k.a. The Amherst Party, a regular campuswide blowout held in upper-class dorms. TAP "is huge here, as is drinking. But it's not as if drinking is mandatory for having a good time or fitting in." As an alternative, "some of the substance-free dorms run 'anti-parties' every Saturday in response to TAP." Otherwise, students engage in "lots of preppy activities, e.g. sailing, fencing, and crew"; take advantage of "the Five College system, which brings an endless stream of stuff to do to the Valley"; or just hang out in their amazing dorms. They do not, as a rule, date, since "dating is difficult at a school this small. Most people either randomly hook up on Saturdays or are in long-term relationships." When the campus social scene grows stifling, they head to the close-by fraternities of UMass.

Student Body

Despite a minority population that is uncommonly large among New England private schools, Amherst students still complain that "this is not a very diverse school, and a lot of people don't make efforts to be friends with different kinds of people." Even the more generous undergrads qualify their praise, pointing out that "this school is more diverse than your average bear, but since it's in New England it's still pretty whitewashed." Students "get along very well" and appreciate the fact that their classmates are "very smart, somewhat intimidating, but great company." There are, notes one student, "lots of extremely talented students," and "many fun late-night discussions." Some warn that "too much political correctness is our biggest problem. Lots of complaining about nonexistent problems."

ADMISSIONS

Very important factors considered by the admissions committee include: character/personal qualities, essays, extracurricular activities, recommendations, secondary school record, standardized test scores, talent/ability. *Important factors considered include:* alumni/ae relation, class rank, volunteer work. *Other factors considered include:* geographical residence, state residency, work experience. TOEFL required of all international applicants. *High school units required/recommended:* 4 English recommended, 4 math recommended, 3 science recommended, 1 science lab recommended, 4 foreign language recommended, 2 social studies recommended, 2 history recommended.

The Inside Word

Despite an up-and-down fluctuation in application totals at most highly selective colleges over the past couple of years, Amherst remains a popular choice and very competitive. You've got to be a strong match all-around, and given their formidable applicant pool, it's very important that you make your case as direct as possible. If you're a special-interest candidate such as a legacy or recruited athlete, you may get a bit of a break from the admissions committee, but you'll still need to show sound academic capabilities and potential. Those without such links have a tougher task. On top of taking the toughest courses available to them and performing at the highest of their abilities, they must be strong writers who demonstrate that they are intellectually curious self-starters who will contribute to the community and profit from the experience.

FINANCIAL AID

Students should submit: FAFSA, CSS/Financial Aid PROFILE, noncustodial (divorced/separated) parent's statement, business/farm supplement, income tax returns, W-2 forms (or other wage statements). Regular filing deadline is February 15. The Princeton Review suggests that all financial aid forms be submitted as soon as possible after January 1. *Need-based scholarships/grants offered:* Pell, SEOG, state scholarships/grants, private scholarships, the school's own gift aid. *Loan aid offered:* Direct Subsidized Stafford, Direct Unsubsidized Stafford, Direct PLUS, Federal Perkins, college/university loans from institutional funds. Federal Work-Study Program available. Institutional employment available. Applicants will be notified of awards on or about April 8. Off-campus job opportunities are good.

FROM THE ADMISSIONS OFFICE

"Amherst College looks, above all, for men and women of intellectual promise who have demonstrated qualities of mind and character that will enable them to take full advantage of the college's curriculum. . . . Admission decisions aim to select from among the many qualified applicants those possessing the intellectual talent, mental discipline, and imagination that will allow them most fully to benefit from the curriculum and contribute to the life of the college and of society. Whatever the form of academic experience—lecture course, seminar, conference, studio, laboratory, independent study at various levels—intellectual competence and awareness of problems and methods are the goals of the Amherst program, rather than the direct preparation for a profession."

For even more information on this school, turn to page 295 of the "Stats" section.

ASSUMPTION COLLEGE

500 SALISBURY STREET, WORCESTER, MA 01609-1296 • ADMISSIONS: 888-882-7786 • FAX: 508-799-4412
E-MAIL: ADMISS@ASSUMPTION.EDU • WEBSITE: WWW.ASSUMPTION.EDU

Ratings
Quality of Life: 79   Academic: 76   Admissions: 79   Financial Aid: 79

Academics

Assumption College is a small school with small classes, so professors have a chance to get to know their students. Undergrads feel like "more than a number" to the faculty. Professors are lauded for their ability to "engage the entire class in discussions and encourage thinking that goes beyond textbooks." Undergraduates also praise their instructors' efforts to "get to know you on a personal level," by being "available outside of the classroom all the time." The science departments are particularly heralded. Any student can take honors classes, though this peeves some in the honors program since they have no "special privileges, such as top choice of classes." Class registration is a real concern at Assumption, where "getting classes, even in your major, is next to impossible because of the poor process for registration." Administrators don't enjoy the same high marks the faculty does. While some students claim, "It is so easy to get to know . . . administrators at Assumption," assessments by the majority of survey respondents aren't so sanguine; some simply call the administration "unavailable and inattentive," while others go so far as to comment, "The school is run like a dictatorship."

> **SURVEY SAYS . . .**
> *Students get along with local community*
> *Students are religious, Classes are small*
> *High cost of living, No one cheats*
> *Class discussions encouraged*
> *Student publications are popular*
> *School is well run*

Life

Assumption College has recently gone on a building spree: four new dorms in four years, a "beautiful" new information technology building, and a new science center on the way. Also, "the students did not think there was enough parking, so the school built two parking decks." Located just a half-hour's drive from Boston, students go on day trips to the city and visit the 12 other colleges around hometown Worcester. And the "Worcester area also provides many restaurants, clubs, shops, and events that students take advantage of." Students describe life at Assumption, however, as "pretty boring. There are a lot of parties, but that's about it." The college has tightened its alcohol policy in recent years, but students still say that the "whole weekend revolves" around drinking; "If you are not a drinker then it is not a school for you." Assumption does offer substance-free housing for those in need of "a quiet night's rest." Many students also participate in sports and community volunteer work, as well as campus ministry. (Assumption is Roman Catholic.) Fines abound for infractions such as underage drinking and parking violations, but penalties are inconsistent; "one student can receive extreme censure for an act, while another can get a slap on the wrist for the same thing."

Student Body

Students at Assumption are "polite, easygoing, and fun to hang around with." Most come from "upper-class, white, Catholic families from Massachusetts" The "strong, close-knit student body" is welcoming, but one culturally sensitive student notes, "The student body is not racially diverse at all." Another remarks, "The students here are all the same; how could we not all get along?" Abercrombie & Fitch, the Gap, and J.Crew (in other words, the usual suspects at northeastern colleges) are the brands of choice, meaning that, when out in force, the student body becomes a "walking billboard." One student explains, "I think other campuses are more open and diverse, but the spirituality here somewhat makes up for it." The people in charge of Assumption are aware of its homogenous coloring, though, and are working to "get a greater ethnic diversity with every incoming class."

ADMISSIONS

Very important factors considered by the admissions committee include: class rank, essays, secondary school record, and standardized test scores. *Important factors considered include:* character/personal qualities, extracurricular activities, interview, recommendations, and talent/ability. *Other factors considered include:* alumni/ae relation, geographical residence, minority status, volunteer work, and work experience. SAT I or ACT required. TOEFL required of all international applicants. High school diploma or GED is required. *High school units required/recommended:* 18 total required; 4 English required, 3 math required, 2 science required, 2 foreign language required, 2 history required, 5 elective required.

The Inside Word

Assumption takes the "personal qualities" of its applicants into consideration, looking closely at candidates' co-curricular activities, leadership experiences, and commitment to community service. Essays and letters of recommendation, both required, are also considered important indicators of character. Spend some extra time on the nonacademic part of your application, and choose your recommenders carefully.

FINANCIAL AID

Students should submit: FAFSA. Regular filing deadline is March 1. The Princeton Review suggests that all financial aid forms be submitted as soon as possible after January 1. *Need-based scholarships/grants offered:* Pell, SEOG, state scholarships/grants, private scholarships, and the school's own gift aid. *Loan aid offered:* FFEL Subsidized Stafford, FFEL Unsubsidized Stafford, FFEL PLUS, Federal Perkins, state loans, and college/university loans from institutional funds. Federal Work-Study Program available. Institutional employment available. Applicants will be notified of awards on a rolling basis beginning on or about February 15. Off-campus job opportunities are excellent.

FROM THE ADMISSIONS OFFICE

"The strength of Assumption College can be found in its ongoing commitment to its student-centered mission. This mission provides an intellectual, social, and spiritual environment designed to attract, retain, and graduate students who pursue ethical professional careers and personal lives based on values undergirded by both faith and reason.

"President Tom Plough is fond of saying that 'Assumption features what I call close encounters of the Assumption kind; that is, the relationships between faculty and students and staff here often approach the quality levels of those found in a stable, extended family.' The active engagement of faculty and staff with students in and out of the classroom is a strategic strength of Assumption College. It is relatively easy for graduating seniors to find faculty and staff who know them so well that highly personalized letters of reference to potential employers and graduate schools can be obtained with ease.

"Assumption is explicitly in the business of building compassion, competence, and character through active and aggressive outreach to students. Early attention, availability, interaction, and follow-up with individual new students is a top priority

"As Assumption prepares for its Centennial Celebration in 2004, the College has focused its efforts on providing the resources and facilities its faculty and students need to attain their educational outcomes. It remains primarily residential, believing that the residential learning environment, properly designed, is the superior education model for assisting students to ask the broadest questions at the deepest levels."

For even more information on this school, turn to page 295 of the "Stats" section.

BABSON COLLEGE

MUSTARD HALL, BABSON PARK, MA 02457-0310 • ADMISSIONS: 800-488-3696 • FAX: 781-239-4006
FINANCIAL AID: 781-239-4219 • E-MAIL: UGRADADMISSION@BABSON.EDU • WEBSITE: WWW.BABSON.EDU

Ratings

Quality of Life: 89   **Academic:** 87   **Admissions:** 90   **Financial Aid:** 80

Academics

Entrepreneurship is the name of the game at Babson College. The college has strengths in other areas, surely, but most students arrive here hoping to learn the secret of establishing America's next Jiffy Lube or Continental Polymers (both of whose founders teach here). Babson stresses "hands-on experience" with a curriculum that "really plunges you into the real world, rather than teaching you the-

> **SURVEY SAYS . . .**
> *Diverse students interact*
> *Beautiful campus*
> *Great computer facilities*
> *Students are religious*
> *Campus easy to get around*
> *Campus feels safe*
> *Lousy off-campus food*
> *Theater is hot*
> *Great library*

ories. During first year you actually start a business and then learn how to manage it." (A few naysayers dismiss the freshman project as "small time. . . . The businesses tends to be more of peddle-shops than anything.") Starting a business is only part of a rigorous freshman year that students uniformly refer to as "business boot camp." Warns one undergrad, "Free time is very hard to come by at Babson. You'll always have a business plan to write, a group meeting to go to, or reading to do for a class." Professors are admired for their experience and expertise ("They are typically seasoned businessmen and businesswomen who have a genuine desire to teach students how to be successful in the real world"). While some here complain that "at times Babson can focus too much on 'street smarts' at the expense of 'book smarts'" and others assert that "Babson needs to improve the quality and quantity of the liberal arts curriculum," most here believe the school's assets far outweigh its drawbacks. As one student put it, "From great speakers, like the head of the NYSE, to programs like the Rocket Pitch Event, Business Plan Competition, and entrepreneurship conferences . . . Babson students get what they pay for."

Life

Even though the Babson campus offers "tons of sports events, plays, concerts," and numerous active organizations (including Babson Dance Ensemble, the Babson Players, Student Government, and the Campus Activities Board), most students here agree that "There's lots of stuff offered on campus, but with such a diverse [international] population, it's hard to please everyone. Babson students are so spoiled in so many ways; we get very whiny and complain about things a lot, even though we have it so amazingly good." Some blame the situation on the school's small size; others finger the "super anal" campus police; still others say it's the grueling academic schedule ("Being both happy and successful at Babson requires 36 hours a day"). Fortunately, the school is "not quite in Boston, but close enough to all the action," at least for the majority of students who have cars ("the campus is isolated, so if you don't have a car, you are stuck here," warns one student). "Boston is the choice destination for partying," students tell us, warning that "clubs can set you back $100 in one night with cover charges, drinks, and shared cab fare." Students praise Babson's "small, beautiful campus" and the "extremely safe, lovely neighborhood" surrounding it.

Student Body

The typical Babson undergrad is either "a white suburbanite from an East Coast private school" or "an international who smokes, is always on his/her cell phone, and wears designer threads." Students are "very conservative" and "extremely competitive," leading some to complain that "there are too many unfriendly people here. No one says hello when you walk by them and if you initiate a greeting, it is seldom returned." Reports one undergrad, "Many students are individualistic in nature. They could happily survive on a desert island with a computer, a cell phone, and caffeine." Given the school's focus on entrepreneurship, it is unsurprising that many here are also very materialistic. "If you want to be criticized for not ordering every new gadget in Maxim magazine, or for not having more than one car on campus, this is the place for you," is how one sardonic student here puts it.

ADMISSIONS

Very important factors considered by the admissions committee include: essays, secondary school record, standardized test scores. *Important factors considered include:* class rank, recommendations. *Other factors considered include:* alumni/ae relation, character/personal qualities, extracurricular activities, geographical residence, interview, minority status, state residency, talent/ability, volunteer work, work experience. SAT I or ACT required; SAT II recommended. TOEFL required of all international applicants. High school diploma or GED is required. *High school units required/recommended:* 4 English required, 3 math required, 4 math recommended, 2 science required, 3 science recommended, 4 foreign language recommended, 2 social studies required, 3 social studies recommended.

The Inside Word

Minority representation, including that of women, remains low, which makes for a very advantageous situation for such candidates. In this age of corporate "downsizing" it has become much more commonplace for students to pursue college programs that lead directly to career paths, and Babson has benefited handsomely from this trend. When this trend and the college's fine reputation are combined, the result is a relatively challenging admissions process despite a relatively modest freshman academic profile.

FINANCIAL AID

Students should submit: FAFSA, CSS/Financial Aid PROFILE, noncustodial (divorced/separated) parent's statement, business/farm supplement, federal tax returns, W-2s, verification worksheet. Regular filing deadline is February 15. The Princeton Review suggests that all financial aid forms be submitted as soon as possible after January 1. *Need-based scholarships/grants offered:* Pell, SEOG, state scholarships/grants, the school's own gift aid. *Loan aid offered:* FFEL Subsidized Stafford, FFEL Unsubsidized Stafford, FFEL PLUS, Federal Perkins, state loans. Federal Work-Study Program available. Institutional employment available. Applicants will be notified of awards on or about April 1. Off-campus job opportunities are good.

FROM THE ADMISSIONS OFFICE

"In addition to theoretical knowledge, Babson College is dedicated to providing its students with hands-on business experience. The Foundation Management Experience (FME) and Management Consulting Field Experience (MCFE) are two prime examples of this commitment. During the FME, all freshmen are placed into groups of 30 and actually create their own businesses that they operate until the end of the academic year. The profits of each FME business are then donated to the charity of each group's choice. MCFE offers upperclassmen the unique and exciting opportunity to work as actual consultants for private companies and/or nonprofit organizations in small groups of three to five. Students receive academic credit for their work as well as invaluable experience. FME and MCFE are just two of the ways Babson strives to produce business leaders with both theoretical knowledge and practical experience."

For even more information on this school, turn to page 296 of the "Stats" section.

BARD COLLEGE

OFFICE OF ADMISSIONS, ANNANDALE-ON-HUDSON, NY 12504 • ADMISSIONS: 845-758-7472
FAX: 845-758-5208 • FINANCIAL AID: 845-758-7526 • E-MAIL: ADMISSION@BARD.EDU
WEBSITE: WWW.BARD.EDU

Ratings

Quality of Life: 84   **Academic:** 95   **Admissions:** 95   **Financial Aid:** 87

Academics

Bard College, a Hudson Valley school that puts the "liberal" in "liberal arts," is a bastion of nonconformity and intellectualism. Explains one undergrad, "Bard is like [a] little village in the woods with an eclectic handful of buildings and equally strange and interesting people who are as motivated to delve into some existentialist discussion as they are to get trashed." Professors and academics,

> **SURVEY SAYS . . .**
> *(Almost) everyone smokes*
> *Political activism is hot*
> *Campus is beautiful*
> *Campus feels safe*
> *Lots of beer drinking*
> *Students are happy*
> *No one cheats*
> *Hard liquor is popular*

students tell us, "are both pretty amazing. All the professors seem willing to bend over backward for the students while being respectable members of academia in general." Undergrads may also love the faculty because "the professors are a reflection of the student body: a combination of above-it-all artists, leftist intellectuals, and downright nerds." Students here love the school's "general looseness, which makes it easy to do things—start a club, get a tutorial, make your own major, whatever." Recounts one student, "I wanted to transfer credits so I walked into the registrar's office and was out in five minutes. I wanted a Hebrew tutorial, I found the professor in his office, and he arranged it. . . . Every time I've needed anything, people have graciously given me their time and their advice, minus formality and bureaucracy." According to students, the only exception to the rule is course registration, "which is a nightmare. Professors sit in their offices, and it's first come, first served. Registration opens at noon. People camp out outside the offices up to six hours ahead of time. It's like a Star Wars premiere."

Life

Because Bard is located "an hour from the nearest town that has more than 100 residents," the school "tries to be its own entertainment." The campus scene is enjoyable, if subdued, according to most; explains one undergrad, "For fun we have intellectual conversations, go to the movies, go to campus events, go to see bands, hang out in the library, drive around, go to thrift stores or to Wal- Mart, hang out in the campus center . . . and surf the Internet." There are "always movies at the theatre on weekends, and there are often theatrical productions, art openings, concerts, and lectures" as well. Even so, "It's the party/music scene that runs the place." There "are a lot of herbal activities" here, as "the policies on drugs and alcohol are lenient. For the most part, it should be noted, people respect themselves and one another and do not overuse." Several times a year the school unites for one big party; most popular of these is Drag Race, "where you cannot tell who really is female and who really is male, that is, as long as they have decided to wear clothes for the evening." Many traditional college diversions are absent here; as one student puts it, "These are things people are not into: football, television, dating, and fast food. Things people are into: dance parties, leftist politics, New York City, organic vegetables, and doing their own thang."

Student Body

When conservatives complain about PC campuses and ultraliberal students, they might well be specifically describing Bard. It's the kind of place where students tell you that "we are more concerned with the terrorism for which our government is responsible than the terrorism that targets the United States," and mean it. Most Bard undergrads "didn't really fit in during high school" but feel right at home here among the "leftist white woman who goes to Green Party rallies weekly" and the "friendly white guys with dreadlocks . . . whose joys include learning, music, and getting stoned with close friends." Bard students describe themselves as cerebral, telling us that "a certain level of intellectualism prevails here, and you really feel that the people you are talking to know what they are talking about, and have done research on these topics. Debates get heated, but that's essential to really get to the depth of an issue anyway." Undergrads appreciate the fact that "There is a really high percentage of international students, which gives the Americans a different perspective of the world."

ADMISSIONS

Very important factors considered by the admissions committee include: character/personal qualities, essays, extracurricular activities, recommendations, secondary school record, talent/ability, volunteer work. *Important factors considered include:* work experience. *Other factors considered include:* alumni/ae relation, class rank, geographical residence, interview, minority status, religious affiliation/commitment, standardized test scores, state residency. TOEFL required of all international applicants. High school diploma or GED is required. *High school units required/recommended:* 4 English recommended, 4 math recommended, 4 science recommended, 4 foreign language recommended, 4 social studies recommended, 4 history recommended.

The Inside Word

Bard is highly selective, but it's the match that counts more than the right numerical profile.

FINANCIAL AID

Students should submit: FAFSA, CSS/Financial Aid PROFILE, state aid form, noncustodial (divorced/separated) parent's statement, business/farm supplement. Regular filing deadline is February 15. The Princeton Review suggests that all financial aid forms be submitted as soon as possible after January 1. *Need-based scholarships/grants offered:* Pell, SEOG, state scholarships/grants, private scholarships, the school's own gift aid. *Loan aid offered:* FFEL Subsidized Stafford, FFEL Unsubsidized Stafford, FFEL PLUS, Federal Perkins, college/university loans from institutional funds (for international students only). Federal Work-Study Program available. Institutional employment available. Applicants will be notified of awards on or about April 1. Off-campus job opportunities are fair.

FROM THE ADMISSIONS OFFICE

"An alliance with Rockefeller University, the renowned graduate scientific research institution, gives Bardians access to Rockefeller's professors and laboratories, and to places in Rockefeller's Summer Research Fellows Program. Almost all our math and science graduates pursue graduate or professional studies; 90 percent of our applicants to medical and health professional schools are accepted. The Globalization and International Affairs (BGIA) Program is a residential program in the heart of New York City that offers undergraduates a unique opportunity to undertake specialized study with leading practitioners and scholars in international affairs and to gain internship experience with international-affairs organizations. Topics in the curriculum include human rights, international economics, global environmental issues, international justice, managing international risk, and writing on international affairs, among others. Internships/tutorials are tailored to students' particular fields of study. Student dormitory and classroom facilities are in Bard Hall, 410 West 58th Street, a newly renovated 11-story building near the Lincoln Center District in New York City."

For even more information on this school, turn to page 297 of the "Stats" section.

BARNARD COLLEGE

3009 BROADWAY, NEW YORK, NY 10027 • ADMISSIONS: 212-854-2014 • FAX: 212-854-6220
FINANCIAL AID: 212-854-2154 • E-MAIL: ADMISSIONS@BARNARD.EDU • WEBSITE: WWW.BARNARD.EDU

Ratings
Quality of Life: 91   Academic: 91   Admissions: 97   Financial Aid: 84

Academics

For those looking to be surrounded by "strong-willed, responsible, smart, and independent women" in a school boasting "all the advantages of an Ivy League school, as well as those of a small liberal arts school," look no further. Barnard women agree that their "classes are amazing" and that "the professors are young and excited to be teaching." Also, one

> **SURVEY SAYS . . .**
> *Students love New York, NY*
> *Political activism is hot, Great off-campus food*
> *(Almost) everyone smokes, Campus feels safe*
> *Ethnic diversity on campus*
> *Intercollegiate sports are*
> *unpopular or nonexistent*
> *Very little beer drinking*
> *No one plays intramural sports*

student reflects the overwhelming feeling of the masses in saying that "administrators live to help their students." One of Barnard's big draws is its affiliation with across-the-street Columbia University. "Because of cross-registration with Columbia, the course offerings are endless." And the love flows both ways. One student confides, "Tons of Columbia students come over to Barnard for courses because our professors tend to be better teachers." The college "is very accommodating and open in terms of letting you study what you want." Students get their own "personal major advisor" whom " you don't have to utilize," but who "will ensure you don't get lost." Complaints? "The study abroad program is lacking . . . and [the sciences are] run more like a high school field program than a college science program." Most students agree, however, that "Barnard is one school that loves each student, viewing her as a powerhouse of potential and yearning to help her understand and realize that potential."

Life

"If you can't find something to do in New York City, I really can't help you." That pretty much sums up life at Barnard. Located in the Morningside Heights neighborhood—little more upper than the Upper West Side—Barnard is "separated from the main distractions, but it's close enough to downtown that you can always find things to do." One student raves, "We live on the most exciting island in the world! You can do anything you can possibly imagine here." And while most will agree that "Barnard is all about life in New York City," many are disappointed with their actual campus life. Actually, according to some, "There is no real campus life . . . people come to Barnard because of New York City. As a result, sports . . . clubs in general, suffer from a lack of participation." Parties abound here, but to those intent on Barnard, "Don't come to NYC expecting kegs. Expect vodka." Despite the never-ending off-campus distractions, in-the-know students point out that "there are plenty of student organizations to choose from" (more than 125, actually), which "collectively provide plenty of things to do on campus almost every day and night of the week." Barnard dorms receive low marks. Warns one student, "A lot of the dorms haven't been maintained—rooms are small, there aren't common rooms, stoves/fridges don't work, there's mold everywhere, etc." Getting away from the mold doesn't seem to be too hard, though. Think "New York City: clubs, bars, theatre, opera, music, dance, parks, museums, shops, cruises, tours . . . . You get the idea, right?"

Student Body

Comprising 2,297 individuals, Barnard's students describe themselves as "very diverse—except that we're all women!" These women refer to each other as "dynamic" and "the greatest I have ever known . . . well rounded, cultured, spunky, sophisticated, and fun loving." Here you'll find "liberal feminists, jocks, party girls, gay students, book worms, Orthodox Jews . . . the list goes on and on." One student notes, however, that "although we are friendly toward each other, most groups tend to stay close-knit and don't really diversify." Barnard students are driven; they are "sharks that carry a smile. They are confident, savvy, sophisticated. They embody the city in which they live, constantly evolving and transforming." Prospective students should expect "a very visible gay population," an "active Jewish religious presence," and "a strong feminist sector."

ADMISSIONS

Very important factors considered by the admissions committee include: essays, recommendations, secondary school record, standardized test scores. *Important factors considered include:* character/personal qualities, class rank, extracurricular activities, talent/ability, volunteer work. *Other factors considered include:* alumni/ae relation, geographical residence, interview, minority status, state residency, work experience. TOEFL required of all international applicants. *High school units required/recommended:* 17 total recommended; 4 English recommended, 3 math recommended, 3 science recommended, 2 science lab recommended, 3 foreign language recommended, 2 social studies recommended, 2 history recommended.

The Inside Word

As at many top colleges, early decision applications have increased at Barnard—despite the fact that admissions standards are virtually the same as for their regular admissions cycle. The college's admissions staff is open and accessible, which is not always the case at highly selective colleges with as long and impressive a tradition of excellence. The admissions committee's expectations are high, but their attitude reflects a true interest in who you are and what's on your mind. Students have a much better experience throughout the admissions process when treated with sincerity and respect—perhaps this is why Barnard continues to attract and enroll some of the best students in the country.

FINANCIAL AID

Students should submit: FAFSA, institution's own financial aid form, CSS/Financial Aid PRO-FILE, state aid form, noncustodial (divorced/separated) parent's statement, business/farm supplement, parent's individual and corporate and/or partnership federal income tax returns. Regular filing deadline is February 1. The Princeton Review suggests that all financial aid forms be submitted as soon as possible after January 1. *Need-based scholarships/grants offered:* Pell, SEOG, state scholarships/grants, private scholarships, the school's own gift aid, New York Higher Educational Opportunity Program. *Loan aid offered:* FFEL Subsidized Stafford, FFEL Unsubsidized Stafford, FFEL PLUS, Federal Perkins, state loans, college/university loans from institutional funds. Federal Work-Study Program available. Institutional employment available. Applicants will be notified of awards on or about April 1. Off-campus job opportunities are excellent.

FROM THE ADMISSIONS OFFICE

"Barnard College, a small, distinguished liberal arts college for women that is affiliated with Columbia University, and located in the heart of New York City. The College enrolls women from all over the United States, Puerto Rico, and the Caribbean. More than thirty countries, including France, England, Hong Kong, and Greece, are also represented in the student body. Students pursue their academic studies in over 40 majors, and are able to cross-register at Columbia University."

For even more information on this school, turn to page 298 of the "Stats" section.

BATES COLLEGE

23 CAMPUS AVENUE, LEWISTON, ME 04240-9917 • ADMISSIONS: 207-786-6000 • FAX: 207-786-6025
FINANCIAL AID: 207-786-6096 • E-MAIL: ADMISSIONS@BATES.EDU • WEBSITE: WWW.BATES.EDU

Ratings

Quality of Life: 83   Academic: 98   Admissions: 98   Financial Aid: 82

Academics

The happy students of Bates College agree that "Bates is the small academic atmosphere every liberal arts school brags about." Students' primary source of pride is the faculty, which is "exceptional. I'm taking introductory classes and my profs are all Ph.D.s from Harvard, Yale, and Tufts. I have thought to myself, 'Why are these brilliant people concerning themselves with dorky 18-year-olds?' [In addition], they relate to students very well. I genuinely feel taught, not just a target for information to be thrown at." Students also approve of the 4-4-1 calendar: two conventional semesters in the fall and spring, as well as a "short term" in May that provides students with opportunities to study less traditional topics, or to study or intern off campus. Writes one undergrad, "Short term in May is really fun. Your short term might be in India, or Ecuador, or sea kayaking in Maine. Short terms are great because you only have one class, and there is [a lot of] free time." The administration goes out of its way to involve students: writes one, "Students are involved in almost every single committee in the school, even search committees for professors and staff. I've been on search committees for tenure-track positions in the English and Chinese departments, which meant going for lectures and taking the candidates out to lunch with a couple of other students. My professors made the final decisions, but my opinion had a great deal of weight [with them]."

> **SURVEY SAYS . . .**
> *Dorms are like palaces*
> *Everyone loves the Bobcats*
> *Great food on campus*
> *No one cheats*
> *Campus feels safe*
> *Low cost of living*
> *Students don't get along with local community*
> *Students don't like Lewiston, ME*
> *Student publications are ignored*

Life

Bates' campus is a veritable beehive of extracurricular activity; explains one student, "There is always a diverse array of lectures, seminars, and performances (musical, theatrical, and otherwise) which I attend for fun. On any given day, there are a dozen activities in which students can participate, from club-sponsored movies and dinners to a capella group performances sponsored by the chaplain's office, to seminars targeting young feminists who want to end domestic violence." It's a good thing, too, because hometown Lewiston offers "nothing to do" other than shop at outlets (Patagonia, J.Crew, and especially L.L. Bean in nearby Freeport are campus faves); notes one student, "You can't really escape campus, so you have to be satisfied with on-campus things, like parties, etc., until it gets nice enough to be able to go hiking and so on." Many Bates undergrads are outdoor enthusiasts, and "a lot of people participate in sports, either intercollegiate or intramural as a way of unwinding at the end of the day." On weekends, "There is no doubt that Bates is a drinking school. Beer cans can be seen scattered around dorms on Sunday mornings, and empty beer boxes can be found in almost every trash can." Students appreciate the fact that major cities are not too far off:

"People venture out to Freeport or Portland on the weekends, both of which are within an hour's drive, and the school runs shuttles in case you don't have a car." Boston is approximately 140 miles south.

Student Body

Bates undergrads "range from being excessively rich, private boarding-school educated preppies to mountain crunchies who rush off to climb things between classes. Honest to God, there is a student here who looks like Paul Bunyan with his flannel and scruffy beard, and he will not put on shoes." Diversity also finds itself in a variety of "weird liberal types," as well as an unusual cross-section of "Trustifarian, want-to-be hippies." Students note that "lots of different people can interact together, although there is a sad lack of minority presence other than a very small number of foreign students." According to some, the absence of a Greek system here contributes to the "incredibly friendly" atmosphere; says one student, "There is no hierarchy. You can be friends with people in various groups." Adds another, "I have yet to meet a cruel person at Bates; I think they hide in the basement or something . . . ." Bates draws half of its students from New England. Only about 10 percent of the students are natives of Maine.

ADMISSIONS

Very important factors considered by the admissions committee include: character/personal qualities, class rank, essays, extracurricular activities, interview, recommendations, secondary school record, talent/ability. *Other factors considered include:* alumni/ae relation, geographical residence, minority status, religious affiliation/commitment, standardized test scores, volunteer work. TOEFL required of all international applicants. High school diploma is required and GED is not accepted. *High school units required/recommended:* 15 total required; 19 total recommended; 4 English required, 3 math required, 4 math recommended, 2 science required, 3 science recommended, 1 science lab required, 2 foreign language required, 4 foreign language recommended.

The Inside Word

With or without test scores, the admissions office here will weed out weak students showing little or no intellectual curiosity. Students with high SAT scores should always submit them. If you are curious about Bates, it is important to have solid grades in challenging courses; without them, you are not a viable candidate for admission. Tough competition for students between the College and its New England peers has intensified greatly over the past couple of years; Bates is holding its own. It remains a top choice among its applicants, and as a result selectivity is on the rise.

FINANCIAL AID

Students should submit: FAFSA, CSS/Financial Aid PROFILE, noncustodial (divorced/separated) parent's statement, business/farm supplement. The Princeton Review suggests that all financial aid forms be submitted as soon as possible after January 1. *Need-based scholarships/grants offered:* Pell, SEOG, state scholarships/grants, private scholarships, the school's own gift aid. *Loan aid offered:* FFEL Subsidized Stafford, FFEL Unsubsidized Stafford, FFEL PLUS, Federal Perkins, state loans, college/university loans from institutional funds, private alternative loans. Federal Work-Study Program available. Institutional employment available. Applicants will be notified of awards on or about April 2. Off-campus job opportunities are good.

FROM THE ADMISSIONS OFFICE

"The people on the Bates admissions staff read your applications carefully, several times. We get to know you from that reading. Your high school record and the quality of your writing are particularly important. We strongly encourage a personal interview, either on campus or with an alumni representative."

For even more information on this school, turn to page 298 of the "Stats" section.

BENNINGTON COLLEGE

OFFICE OF ADMISSIONS AND FINANCIAL AID, BENNINGTON, VT 05201 • ADMISSIONS: 800-833-6845
FAX: 802-440-4320 • FINANCIAL AID: 802-440-4325 • E-MAIL: ADMISSIONS@BENNINGTON.EDU
WEBSITE: WWW.BENNINGTON.EDU

Ratings

Quality of Life: 83   Academic: 93   Admissions: 84   Financial Aid: 85

Academics

Bennington College has long been committed to "honoring individuality and the power to create your own education." Students at this unconventional school "don't ever officially declare majors," nor do they take final exams. "We do final projects instead," explained one undergrad. "I got to do a project imitating the style of my favorite poet and a psychological study about student drinking on campus. I feel so involved with my classes!" Instead of grades, students receive written evaluations of their work. Bennington's curriculum "is really dependent on the makeup of the faculty" because "there are not a lot of professors" and also because "the teachers 'teach what keeps them up at night.'" Profs here are "brilliant, amazing people who deeply care about their students"; undergrads also praise the Field Work Term ("a great program of going out for eight weeks to intern or work in your field or a field that you're interested in learning more about"). The visual arts program is one of the school's undisputed strengths. The VAPA (visual and performing arts) building is "open 24/7, and every studio, work space, or lab is open to everyone." Music and language arts instruction also receive praise; the sciences, on the other hand, are considered relatively weak. Many here worry that the student body is growing too rapidly ("We have 200 more students here this year than we had last year") without a proportionate increase in the faculty. "We need more professors," writes a typical student. "If the school is going to continue to accept more students, the college is going to change. Normalization is beginning, and that's sad."

> **SURVEY SAYS . . .**
> Lots of classroom discussion
> Student publications are popular
> Political activism is hot
> Students get along with local community
> Students love Bennington, VT
> Lousy food on campus
> Campus difficult to get around
> (Almost) no one smokes
> Library needs improving

Life

Bennington's "small and secluded" campus is "absolutely beautiful. Imagine the most beautiful haven you have ever been to; that is Bennington in early May. Imagine Norman Rockwell paintings; that is our winter and fall." Students enjoy the luxury of living in actual houses rather than dormitories. "We have both barn houses built in the 1930s and modern houses that were built last year and were featured in architecture magazines," writes one student. All the same, because of the school's remote location, "most people have a really hard time adjusting to life, myself included. If you stick it out, it gets better. . . . There's a positive side to it: if I were in a larger city I would not be devoting as much time to my academics, which is the reason I came here." Bennington is "very isolated from the town, so there are a lot of on-campus events to keep one interested." Students mention "people screening independent films, stand-up comedy shows, and bands playing" as entertainment options. And "students are very supportive about attending others' performances." Undergrads also "tend to have small par-

being on campus can get claustrophobic," "people with cars try to leave for the weekend." Many head to the campus of Williams College, about a half-hour drive to the south.

Student Body

Bennington students range from "vegan, environmentally conscious punks that pretend to be hippies . . . to a significant group of students extremely passionate about their work." The tiny student body "gets oppressive at times, but is very comforting at others. You can say 'I was with Patrick,' and everyone will know who you are talking about." Students tend to subdivide into cliques: "I have a small but very lovable group of friends; that's the tendency here, to form cliques of friends . . . it's just the nature of a small school like this," explains one student. The atmosphere here is politically and socially liberal; "sexuality, religion, social class—none of that matters. I swear, it's like a hippie commune utopia . . . or at least another dimension from The Matrix," is how one student describes it.

ADMISSIONS

Very important factors considered by the admissions committee include: character/personal qualities, essays, interview, secondary school record, talent/ability, volunteer work. *Important factors considered include:* alumni/ae relation, extracurricular activities, recommendations. *Other factors considered include:* class rank, standardized test scores, work experience. SAT I or ACT required. TOEFL required of all international applicants. High school diploma or GED is required. *High school units required/recommended:* 16 total recommended; 4 English recommended, 3 math recommended, 3 science recommended, 3 foreign language recommended, 3 social studies recommended.

The Inside Word

For intellectually curious students Bennington can be a godsend, but for those who lack self-motivation it can represent a sidetracking of progress toward a degree. Admissions standards remain rigorous and enrollment is on an upswing. Candidates will encounter a thorough review process that places great emphasis on matchmaking, which means that strong essays and solid interviews are a must. Intellectual types whose high school grades are inconsistent with their potential will find an opportunity for forgiveness here if they can write well and demonstrate self-awareness and a capacity to thrive in the college's self-driven environment. Minority students are rarities in the applicant pool, and thus enjoy "most-favored candidate" status—provided they fit Bennington's profile.

FINANCIAL AID

Students should submit: FAFSA, institution's own financial aid form, CSS/Financial Aid PROFILE, noncustodial (divorced/separated) parent's statement, parent and student federal tax returns and W-2s. CSS/Financial Aid PROFILE for Early Decision applicants only. The Princeton Review suggests that all financial aid forms be submitted as soon as possible after January 1. *Need-based scholarships/grants offered:* Pell, SEOG, state scholarships/grants, private scholarships, the school's own gift aid. *Loan aid offered:* FFEL Subsidized Stafford, FFEL Unsubsidized Stafford, FFEL PLUS, college/university loans from institutional funds. Federal Work-Study Program available. Institutional employment available. Applicants will be notified of awards on or about April 1. Off-campus job opportunities are fair.

FROM THE ADMISSIONS OFFICE

"Bennington is designed for students with the motivation and maturity to give shape to their own academic lives. It invites you not merely to study the subject you are learning but to put into practice, to act, to compose, to write, to do science: to make the choices through which you become an educated person. Faculty guide the process, but students make it their own at every stage, leaving Bennington prepared to think and create for themselves."

For even more information on this school, turn to page 299 of the "Stats" section.

BENTLEY COLLEGE

175 FOREST STREET, WALTHAM, MA 02452-4705 • ADMISSIONS: 781-891-2244 • FAX: 781-891-3414
FINANCIAL AID: 781-891-3441 • E-MAIL: UGADMISSION@BENTLEY.EDU • WEBSITE: WWW.BENTLEY.EDU

Ratings

Quality of Life: 79   Academic: 77   Admissions: 81   Financial Aid: 80

Academics

A primary focus of the educational process at Bentley College is preparing students for life in the business world. As one student writes, "people, technology, and business—that's what Bentley is about." Many undergraduates affirm that the on-campus trading floor drew them to Bentley. The col-

> **SURVEY SAYS . . .**
> *Musical organizations aren't popular*
> *Classes are small*
> *Great computer facilities*
> *Students aren't religious*
> *Ethnic diversity on campus*
> *Theater is unpopular*

lege's 57-station trading floor is one of only a handful of such real-time trading floor facilities in the U.S. A NASDAQ stock market Premier Partner, Bentley's facility has live data feed from Bloomberg, Reuters, and Dow Jones, among others. Students frequently describe the school's technological and business resources as one of its major strengths. Of course, good technology is not enough to prepare prospective businesspeople. The students save their highest compliments for their professors. "They are all pretty much down to earth," one student writes, and another comments that "the professors are like our best friends. They are there when you need them." When describing professors, a favorite adjective of undergrads is "accessible." Writes one typical student, "All of the professors are extremely helpful and accessible." Classes and seminars are relatively small, which helps to increase student-faculty intimacy. "Because of the small size of our school, it is easy to develop a relationship outside of class between the students and teachers that is comfortable and very helpful." Most students are not as fond of Bentley's administrators, asserting that "it is virtually impossible to get things changed." In general, students believe that the school prepares them well for life after graduation. One muses that Bentley "builds a strong business foundation that will last for a lifetime."

Life

Bentley is located in the small Massachusetts town of Waltham, but because of the school's proximity to Boston (about 20 minutes via a free shuttle), students "can always go there and have a good time." Many especially enjoy Boston's active club scene. Students describe the campus as beautiful and quiet, though many add that there is an obvious lack of school spirit, and according to one morose student, "fun at Bentley consists of sitting in a room and drinking." Still, other students believe that the active Greek life "keeps the campus busy with activities, charities, and parties" that allow them "to meet a lot of people and [enjoy] good times." However you slice it, drinking is a popular activity, and people "party every weekend through Monday." Students agree that the food at Bentley is less than satisfying, but the new residence halls and additional parking lots were the answer to their prayers. Overall, student sentiment about life on campus was perhaps best summarized by the student who told us "Bentley is definitely a fun school with a big party scene," but one which also provides "a very good academic foundation."

Student Body

Though its technologically advanced business curriculum has gained national attention, Bentley remains a college that primarily attracts students from the Northeast. Students lean towards political conservatism, which isn't surprising considering that approximately three-quarters of the students come from New England. Many students list the student body's lack of diversity as one of Bentley's major weaknesses, saying undergrads tend to be very "cliquey, depending on what ethnicity you are." Others write that "everyone is pretty much white, preppy, and rich" and "if you can't afford all A&E and AF, then you won't interact with anyone." Still, most students agree that the campus is very friendly and that students should have "no problem making friends." One student told us, "the people are very nice." International students are not only accepted, but well respected. "The students [at Bentley] are very similar in nature. They all have a really competitive nature," one student wrote, but manage to remain "friendly."

ADMISSIONS

Very important factors considered by the admissions committee include: class rank, essays, recommendations, secondary school record, standardized test scores. *Important factors considered include:* character/personal qualities, extracurricular activities, interview, talent/ability, volunteer work, work experience. *Other factors considered include:* alumni/ae relation, geographical residence, minority status, state residency. SAT I or ACT required. TOEFL required of all international applicants. High school diploma or GED is required. *High school units required/recommended:* 17 total required; 18 total recommended; 4 English required, 4 math required, 3 science required, 2 foreign language required, 3 foreign language recommended, 2 social studies required.

The Inside Word

If you're a solid B student there's little challenge to encounter in the admissions process here. The College's appealing greater Boston location and career-oriented academic strengths account for a sizable applicant pool and the moderate selectivity that it enjoys.

FINANCIAL AID

Students should submit: FAFSA, CSS/Financial Aid PROFILE, noncustodial (divorced/separated) parent's statement, business/farm supplement. Regular filing deadline is February 1. The Princeton Review suggests that all financial aid forms be submitted as soon as possible after January 1. *Need-based scholarships/grants offered:* Pell, SEOG, state scholarships/grants, private scholarships, the school's own gift aid. *Loan aid offered:* Federal Perkins, state loans. Federal Work-Study Program available. Institutional employment available. Applicants will be notified of awards on a rolling basis beginning on or about March 25. Off-campus job opportunities are excellent.

FROM THE ADMISSIONS OFFICE

"Bentley College is a business university focusing on educating students interested in business and related professions, blending the broad curriculum and technological strength of a university with the values and student orientation of a small college. For students interested in business and related professions, Bentley does what the nation's leading technological universities do for students interested in science and engineering. A Bentley education is built on a strong foundation in the liberal arts with an unparalleled array of business courses and hands-on experience with technology. Concepts and theories that students learn in the classroom come alive in several hands-on, high-tech learning laboratories—each among the first of its kind in higher education. The financial Trading Room offers first-hand exposure to financial concepts such as risk management and asset valuation. In the Center for Marketing Technology, undergraduates learn the latest research tools and strategies in marketing and advertising. The Accounting Center introduces students to the cutting-edge tools and technologies that have reshaped the profession of accounting. The Center for Language and International Collaboration is a key resource for language students, international studies majors, and anyone with an interest in international issues. And the Design and Usability Testing Center puts into students' hands the same applications employed by technical communicators. The Mobile Computing Program provides all Bentley freshmen with a fully loaded, network-ready laptop computer."

For even more information on this school, turn to page 300 of the "Stats" section.

BOSTON COLLEGE

140 COMMONWEALTH AVENUE, DEVLIN HALL 208, CHESTNUT HILL, MA 02467-3809 • ADMISSIONS: 617-552-3100
FAX: 617-552-0798 • FINANCIAL AID: 800-294-0294 • E-MAIL: UGADMIS@BC.EDU • WEBSITE: WWW.BC.EDU

Ratings

Quality of Life: 80   **Academic:** 92   **Admissions:** 96   **Financial Aid:** 84

Academics

Boston College has long been known as one of the nation's more elite private undergraduate colleges. Don't let the name fool you, though; this is a research university. But don't let that fool you, either, because BC is as committed to teaching as it is to research. Steeped in strong Jesuit tradition, BC is known for its commitment to providing its students with a rigorous liberal arts curriculum aimed at teaching them not merely what to think, but how to think. Students at BC find some top notch professors, though one student cautions prospects to do their homework: "Research the good professors and take them." The majority of the faculty members at BC are known for taking their "jobs seriously" and being genuinely "interested in helping students learn." While not all the professors are easily accessible, there are definitely more than a handful [who] make the extra effort to reach out to their students. As one student notes, "My professors have been excellent and extremely accessible. I have attended pizza parties and barbecues at professors' homes on a number of occasions." Don't, however, expect to find the same level of openness and warmth with the administration. The students here are often more than just a little disenchanted at the relationship between students and administrators. "I don't know who the administration is really," writes one bewildered student. "They aren't involved much in student life." Many others describe the administration as "aloof" and "overly bureaucratic."

> **SURVEY SAYS . . .**
> *Lots of classroom discussion*
> *Students love Chestnut Hill, MA*
> *Great on campus food*
> *Everyone loves the Eagles*
> *Political activism is hot*
> *Students are cliquish*
> *Student publications are ignored*
> *(Almost) no one listens to college radio*

Life

Despite its rigorous academics, BC is also known for its social scene. For many students here the weekend begins a bit prematurely ("weekends begin on Wednesday") and continue right on up to the last minute. Drinking, whether it's at house parties or Boston bars ("you need a fake ID"), tends to be the social lubricant of choice, especially in Cleveland Circle, where BC parties reign, or on campus in one of the senior student apartments known as "Mods." Now, the fact that BC students may have a readily available supply of alcohol doesn't mean the administration takes it lightly. Underage drinking policies, especially in dorm rooms, are strictly enforced. While much of student life may "revolve around the bottle," that by no means is the end of the story. This is, after all, Boston, "the best college city in the world." As one student notes, "The best thing about BC is that it's just right outside of Boston. Whenever campus gets dull you just hop on the T [Boston's public train system] and you're right in the center of one of the most incredible cultural cities in the country." Whether you're looking for a museum, café, club, or bar, you can bet that you'll be able to find it in Boston. In addition, true to its Jesuit heritage, BC maintains an active social presence through volunteering, with more than "500 students" participating in spring break in Appalachia.

Student Body

The students at BC describe themselves as looking like they have all just stepped out of an "Abercrombie or J.Crew catalogue." As one student notes, "All of the students here look exactly alike. . . . There's pretty much no diversity." Undergrads call their classmates "very nice," while at the same time "rich and cliquish." And while BC certainly is objectively more ethnically and racially diverse than many of its peer institutions, its undergrads by and large don't see it. "This is a pretty cliquey school and groups are formed from freshman year," laments one typical survey respondent. "There's little interaction between different cliques. This is definitely not an ethnically diverse school, and there is often tension between races." For those wishing to break from this standard, student groups often provide a welcoming opportunity to reach across boundaries, regardless of race and background. "The most important thing to do is to get involved with lots of groups, clubs, or sports so that you always have another outlet."

ADMISSIONS

Very important factors considered by the admissions committee include: character/personal qualities, secondary school record, standardized test scores. *Important factors considered include:* alumni/ae relation, class rank, essays, extracurricular activities, minority status, recommendations, religious affiliation/commitment, talent/ability, volunteer work, work experience. SAT I or ACT required. TOEFL required of all international applicants. High school diploma or GED is required. *High school units required/recommended:* 20 total recommended; 4 English recommended, 4 math recommended, 4 science recommended, 4 science lab recommended, 4 foreign language recommended.

The Inside Word

While applications to BC in general have increased over the past couple of years, early action applications have risen more dramatically. Standards remain high, and we more than recommend a strong college-preparatory curriculum in high school—it's a must in order to have a shot. With a large percentage of its students coming from Catholic high schools such applicants are treated well, but there is little room for relaxation in the process. Applicants need to show strong SAT and SAT II scores, but keep the tests in perspective—BC is interested in the whole package.

FINANCIAL AID

Students should submit: FAFSA, CSS/Financial Aid PROFILE, noncustodial (divorced/separated) parent's statement, business/farm supplement, parent and student tax returns and W-2 statements. The Princeton Review suggests that all financial aid forms be submitted as soon as possible after January 1. *Need-based scholarships/grants offered:* Pell, SEOG, state scholarships/grants, private scholarships, the school's own gift aid. *Loan aid offered:* FFEL Subsidized Stafford, FFEL Unsubsidized Stafford, FFEL PLUS, Federal Perkins, Federal Nursing, state loans. Federal Work-Study Program available. Institutional employment available. Applicants will be notified of awards on or about April 15. Off-campus job opportunities are good.

FROM THE ADMISSIONS OFFICE

"Boston College students enjoy the quiet, suburban atmosphere of Chestnut Hill, with easy access to the cultural and historical richness of Boston. Junior Year Abroad and Scholar of the College Program offer students flexibility within the curriculum. Facilities opened in the past 10 years include: the Merkert Chemistry Center, a new dorm and dining hall facility, and a new library. Fifteen Presidential Scholars enroll in each freshman class with a half-tuition scholarship irrespective of need, and funding is available to meet full demonstrated need. These students, selected from the top 1 percent of the Early Action applicant pool, participate in the most rewarding intellectual experience offered at the university."

For even more information on this school, turn to page 300 of the "Stats" section.

BOSTON UNIVERSITY

121 BAY STATE ROAD, BOSTON, MA 02215 • ADMISSIONS: 617-353-2300 • FAX: 617-353-9695
FINANCIAL AID: 617-353-2965 • E-MAIL: ADMISSIONS@BU.EDU • WEBSITE: WWW.BU.EDU

Ratings
Quality of Life: 84   Academic: 91   Admissions: 91   Financial Aid: 87

Academics

Whether they love the school or simply love to hate it, students at BU know how to communicate their beliefs. On the quality of teaching: "Come here and have any life path available to you," writes a first year, "and brilliant, energetic, enthusiastic professors ready to give you the equivalent knowledge of a Ferrari to drive down it." Sound too good to be

> **SURVEY SAYS . . .**
> *Students love Boston, MA*
> *Very little drug use, Lousy food on campus*
> *Great off-campus food*
> *Class discussions are rare*
> *Ethnic diversity on campus*
> *Unattractive campus, Large classes*
> *Very small frat/sorority scene*
> *Athletic facilities need improving*

true? A sophomore puts it into perspective: "I guess the professors here are like those at any university. Some have been wicked funny, awe inspiring, and life changing. Of course there are also a fair share of pompous, misogynistic jerks—but that's why BU has such a great system for dropping classes." Also, "the school's administration resembles a small dictatorship of some Central American country," quips a sophomore. "It is rash, volatile, and hopefully it won't last long." Yet some appreciate the "generally well-run" nature of the school itself. As for the school's large size, one junior remarks, "BU is a large university that may appear overwhelming to a freshman just beginning; however, BU is actually a collection of tiny schools that make up one large institution. Each individual school looks after their individual students, making sure they are not just another number." Not so, counters a sage senior: "If you want individual attention, you need to seek it. Professors (and everyone, really) are receptive if you approach them, but since this is a big school with big classes, they won't seek you out." Most students seem to like the school's deep coffers—financial aid awards are often generous and widespread. Unfortunately, the money doesn't seem to trickle down to the physical plant: a fairly spread-out, urban school, Boston University seems to suffer in the eyes of its students from a lack of a central, well-maintained campus. Writes a senior, "It would be nice to have a campus . . . or at least a patch of shrubs."

Life

While some students view the strictly enforced rules on alcohol, drugs, and guest visitation as providing a safe haven, others, like this sophomore, find the school's strict dorm regulations infantilizing and unnecessarily harsh: "The guest policy creates a type of environment not conducive to socializing or feeling laid-back. We live in a dictatorship!" Still, students at BU seem to get through; as a sophomore describes it, "During the week, students are very focused on class work and courses, but on the weekends, their mindset is completely different. All thoughts lean toward parties, sex, clubs, and alcohol. In short, good old-fashioned college fun." And for those not in the mood for body shots and early morning walks of shame, there's always Boston, "one of the best college towns in the country." Why go to BU? An answer from a particularly expressive senior: "The BU experience goes way beyond the classroom. Just in the last month, I've gone to see the Phantom of the Opera, gone skiing in Vermont, and gone to the Fogg Museum at Harvard. Its location is BU's greatest strength."

Student Body

It might seem incredible that such a large and opinionated student body gets along as well as they do. Writes one junior, "Generally students are unique and independent and encourage healthy competition and collaboration on projects. They are easy to get along with." So it's just like the cast of Friends but on a really big scale? Well . . . not quite, according to a sophomore. "There are, of course, a few cliques on campus composed of students who obviously skipped the day in preschool when they taught 'How to Get Along With Others and Not Be a Eurotrashy Snot.' " Ouch. Fortunately, in a large school there's bound to be someone to click with. How does a typical BUer feel about his or her fellow students? We like this answer: "How should I know?" asks a first year. "Out of 15,000 undergraduates [sic] I have seen about 2,000, spoken to about 500, and hung around with 50." Really good odds, we'd say.

ADMISSIONS

Very important factors considered by the admissions committee include: secondary school record. *Important factors considered include:* class rank, essays, recommendations, standardized test scores. *Other factors considered include:* alumni/ae relation, character/personal qualities, extracurricular activities, volunteer work, work experience. SAT I or ACT required. TOEFL required of all international applicants. High school diploma or GED is required. *High school units required/recommended:* 15 total required; 20 total recommended; 4 English required, 3 math required, 4 math recommended, 3 science required, 4 science recommended, 2 foreign language required, 4 foreign language recommended.

The Inside Word

Boston is one of the nation's most popular college towns, and BU benefits tremendously. The university's last few entering classes have been chock-full of high-caliber students; despite a general decline in applications at colleges in the Northeast it will continue to be competitive to gain admission to BU, as applications keep a steady upward trend and entering class size is kept in check. Those who aren't up to traditional standards are sometimes referred to the less selective College of General Studies, which allows students to continue on to other divisions of the university once they prove themselves academically—but standards here are rising.

FINANCIAL AID

Students should submit: FAFSA, CSS/Financial Aid PROFILE, state aid form, noncustodial (divorced/separated) parent's statement, business/farm supplement. The Princeton Review suggests that all financial aid forms be submitted as soon as possible after January 1. *Need-based scholarships/grants offered:* Pell, SEOG, state scholarships/grants, private scholarships, the school's own gift aid. *Loan aid offered:* Direct Subsidized Stafford, Direct Unsubsidized Stafford, Direct PLUS, Federal Perkins, state loans. Federal Work-Study Program available. Institutional employment available. Applicants will be notified of awards on a rolling basis beginning on or about March 22. Off-campus job opportunities are excellent.

FROM THE ADMISSIONS OFFICE

"Boston University (BU) is a private teaching and research institution with a strong emphasis on undergraduate education. We are committed to providing the highest level of teaching excellence, and fulfillment of this pledge is our highest priority. Boston University has 11 undergraduate schools and colleges offering 250 major and minor areas of concentration. Students may choose from programs of study in areas as diverse as biochemistry, theater arts, physical therapy, elementary education, broadcast journalism, international relations, business, and computer engineering. BU has an international student body, with students from every state and more than 100 countries. In addition, opportunities to study abroad exist through 29 different programs, spanning 16 countries on 6 continents."

For even more information on this school, turn to page 301 of the "Stats" section.

BOWDOIN COLLEGE

5000 COLLEGE STATION, BRUNSWICK, ME 04011-8441 • ADMISSIONS: 207-725-3100 • FAX: 207-725-3101
FINANCIAL AID: 207-725-3273 • E-MAIL: ADMISSIONS@BOWDOIN.EDU • WEBSITE: WWW.BOWDOIN.EDU

Ratings
Quality of Life: 91   **Academic:** 94   **Admissions:** 97   **Financial Aid:** 80

Academics

"Independence," "freedom," and "self-motivation" are words Bowdoin College students frequently associate with their undergraduate experience. Perhaps it has something to do with the size and location of the campus itself—a few

SURVEY SAYS . . .
Great food on campus
Everyone loves the Polar Bears
Very little drug use, Athletic facilities are great
(Almost) no one smokes, Low cost of living

miles from the coast of southern Maine (and its islands, lakes, and wilderness), tiny but highly selective Bowdoin prides itself on its "Walden Pond" atmosphere and challenges its students to, like Thoreau, find their own way. Notes one senior, "You are encouraged to explore all sorts of academic areas, and once you find something you love, you can run with it." Bowdoin's campus is, according to its students, "unbeatable." Remodeled buildings, "pretty good housing—especially for first years," and some of the best college food around all make Joe and Jane College's quest for knowledge a little more, well, comfortable. Professors are, for the most part, accessible (Brunswick is a small town—they can't go far) and full of encouragement. Writes another senior, "Professors are excellent. We've had them over to our house for dinner." Unfortunately, students also note that the "whale of a bureaucracy" at Bowdoin can make retaining such teaching excellence difficult. A savvy junior describes the situation as such: "Great professors, but the school's rush to determine whether to tenure or not leaves their status uncertain and hurries, regrettably, some good ones away."

Life

As one would expect, a major aspect of Bowdoin's social life revolves around—you guessed it—the great outdoors. "There are great opportunities for getting outside," writes a senior. "With the Bowdoin Outing Club you can spend the weekend skiing, camping, hiking, snowshoeing, rock climbing, hanging out at the Outing Club's cabin drinking hot chocolate all weekend." Athletics, too, seem to draw the campus together, whether it's "hockey on the town commons," playing on the rugby team and in other club sports, or watching Bowdoin continue an eons-old rivalry with nearby Colby College during one of their "especially insane" hockey matches. Of course, not everyone is thrilled about all this huffing and puffing in the name of good, clean fun; one junior makes it plain that "athletics and personal fitness activities are a little too popular." In terms of nightlife, there seems to be only a few options at Bowdoin, and most of those involve drinking. Though the administration and the recently transformed "social house" system (sororities and fraternities were banned a few years ago) try to promote non-alcoholic programming such as concerts, dances, and performances, many students stick close to the keg. "I drink for fun," writes a senior, and while one student's soused state might not speak for everyone, at least one first-year agrees: "There's a lot of drinking here."

Student Body

"Everyone here is interesting," says a first year. "We can talk about girls on TV and China's foreign policy as it relates to European trade in the same moment." Another freshman provides a living example of Bowdoin's reputation for turning out aware and independent yet community-minded thinkers and doers: "I am an athlete, don't smoke, and voted Republican. I live next to a kid who smokes, listens to Phish, voted for Nader, and we are now best friends." Too bad much of Bowdoin's diversity is limited to political parties and smoking habits. Another freshman weighs in about what is increasingly seen as a major drawback to an otherwise excellent college experience; "Good thing this campus is traditionally liberal and open minded," she writes. "Otherwise, we would be confused with a white pride meeting." It's a negative the school's administration has not overlooked, and according to students, is working hard to change. "Only recently is Bowdoin attempting to push away from the stale, prep-school boy's attitude that it previously held. Yet the effort is commendable and noticeable." Besides, jokes a sophomore, "It turns out that white, New England prep-school kids are pretty nice. Who knew?"

ADMISSIONS

Very important factors considered by the admissions committee include: character/personal qualities, class rank, essays, diversity of background, recommendations, secondary school record. *Important factors considered include:* alumni/ae relation, extracurricular activities, geographical residence, talent/ability, volunteer work. *Other factors considered include:* interview, standardized test scores, work experience. TOEFL required of all international applicants. *High school units required/recommended:* 20 total recommended; 4 English recommended, 4 math recommended, 4 science recommended, 3 science lab recommended, 4 foreign language recommended, 4 social studies recommended.

The Inside Word

This is one of the 20 or so most selective colleges in the country. Virtually everyone who applies is well qualified academically, which means criteria besides grades and test scores become critically important in candidate review. Who you are, what you think, where you are from, and why you are interested in Bowdoin are the sorts of things that will determine whether you get in, provided you meet their high academic standards.

FINANCIAL AID

Students should submit: FAFSA, institution's own financial aid form, CSS/Financial Aid PROFILE, noncustodial (divorced/separated) parent's statement, business/farm supplement. Regular filing deadline is February 15. The Princeton Review suggests that all financial aid forms be submitted as soon as possible after January 1. *Need-based scholarships/grants offered:* Pell, SEOG, state scholarships/grants, private scholarships, the school's own gift aid. *Loan aid offered:* FFEL Subsidized Stafford, FFEL Unsubsidized Stafford, FFEL PLUS, Federal Perkins, state loans, college/university loans from institutional funds. Federal Work-Study Program available. Institutional employment available. Applicants will be notified of awards on or about April 5. Off-campus job opportunities are fair.

FROM THE ADMISSIONS OFFICE

"Each year Bowdoin sponsors myriad events, including performances by bands, comedians, artists, and dancers as well as lectures and film series, community service events, and the occasional scavenger hunt. Performers who have appeared at the College recently include Savion Glover, Jurassic 5, The Capitol Steps, and Mos Def. Speakers have included Doris Kearns Goodwin, Robert Reich, Spike Lee, Nobel Laureate Thomas Cech, and playwright Tony Kushner. The College has more than 100 active student organizations. About 70 percent of students participate in community service during their time at Bowdoin, and the College's many volunteer programs allow students to interact with the Brunswick community. Club and intramural sports and the Outing Club enable students to get involved in physical fitness without having to be star athletes. Bowdoin is determined to be a place that brings together people from widely diverse ethnic and economic backgrounds, from different parts of the country and the world, and with divergent political beliefs, a full range of religious identities, and broad academic interests."

For even more information on this school, turn to page 302 of the "Stats" section.

BRANDEIS UNIVERSITY

415 SOUTH STREET, MS003, WALTHAM, MA 02454 • ADMISSIONS: 781-736-3500 • FAX: 781-736-3536
FINANCIAL AID: 781-736-3700 • E-MAIL: SENDINFO@BRANDEIS.EDU • WEBSITE: WWW.BRANDEIS.EDU

Ratings
Quality of Life: 80   Academic: 83   Admissions: 91   Financial Aid: 85

Academics

Students who choose Brandeis expect both university-caliber facilities and a small-college experience. For the most part, they feel they get what they came for. "I love the fact that my school feels like a college, yet has so many resources," writes one undergrad. Muses another, "The school is large enough that it isn't stifling, but small enough that it is homey."

> **SURVEY SAYS . . .**
> *Student publications are popular*
> *Political activism is hot, Campus feels safe*
> *Students are happy*
> *Lots of classroom discussion*
> *Students don't like Waltham, MA*
> *No one watches intercollegiate sports*
> *Students are cliquish, Very little drug use*
> *Very small frat/sorority scene*

Only a few complain that "Brandeis tries to be both a small liberal arts school and a research university. I think in trying to be both it succeeds at neither." Typical of a progressive university, "Brandeis has a continued commitment to improving the school. It is constantly reinventing itself." Students warn that "academics are tough and there's not much getting around it. Especially for pre-meds (computer science and biology students also complain of ultraheavy workloads), things can get really stressful at times. However, the professors are very accessible and the advising, both peer and academic, is great." Economics, English, life sciences, theater arts, and Near Eastern and Jewish studies ("One of the best departments in the country!" raves one student) are among the many excellent majors here. Brandeis's core curriculum (math, science, humanities, and foreign language), which takes at least two semesters to complete, "makes sure we get a broad-based education." Students say the "wonderful professors" are "some of the biggest characters I've ever met" and are "genuinely concerned with the academic interests of their students." The administration "keeps the school running quite well, but they seem out of touch with the students."

Life

Brandeis has long been known as a low-key campus, but things are gradually changing. "Social life at Brandeis has slowly been improving since my freshman year," reports one senior. Popular happenings include "the fall weekend, called 'Louie, Louie,' and the spring weekend, 'Bronstein,' " as well as the "The Less You Wear, the Less You Pay" dance, which students deem "very entertaining." Also, "volunteer groups are very popular here and so are student-run theater and a cappella groups," and "the opportunities to join clubs and associations are terrific." Fraternity members say that, though frats are underground, they "try to remain active [even though] the administration does a pretty good job of suppressing our existence and badmouthing us to each year's incoming freshmen." Despite all these options, though, many students still choose to seek entertainment off campus. "Brandeis students tend to fall into two groups: on- and off-campus socializers," points out one undergrad. "Some spend all their time on campus doing various activities and seem to forget about the outside world. Others spend all their time in town (Waltham) or in Boston, stepping foot on campus only for class." An on-campus commuter rail takes students into downtown Boston in a scant half hour. Boston has "so much to offer," but "most things tend to close early."

Student Body

Because Jewish students make up about half the population here, "Brandeis has a reputation for being a solely Jewish school, but in the two months I've been here I've found an amaz-ing[ly diverse] group of friends, and everyone is more than willing to talk about their differ-ences and explain their beliefs. That's one of the main things I love about this place: the lack of intolerance." Efforts to create a more diverse student body appear to be working. Explains one undergrad, "This place may have a 'Jew U' feel, but it's weakening as the student body diversifies . . . it's not the shtetl it used to be." Politically, "Brandeis is for people who are lean-ing to the left." Students "are politically active and working for social justice and awareness. It's an amazing place to be when we rally for recycling, GLBT issues, abortion rights, what-ever." They also "tend to be highly opinionated . . . and passionate about causes." Don't expect the sports teams to win any major championships, though, since "everyone here is someone in your high school PE class that was completely ostracized."

ADMISSIONS

Very important factors considered by the admissions committee include: class rank, secondary school record. *Important factors considered include:* character/personal qualities, essays, extracurricu-lar activities, recommendations, standardized test scores, talent/ability, volunteer work, work experience. *Other factors considered include:* alumni/ae relation, interview, minority status. TOEFL required of all international applicants. High school diploma or GED is required. *High school units required/recommended:* 16 total recommended; 4 English recommended, 3 math rec-ommended, 1 science recommended, 1 science lab recommended, 3 foreign language recom-mended, 1 history recommended, 4 elective recommended.

The Inside Word

While the university has a reputation for quality, the low yield of admits who actually choose to attend Brandeis results in a higher acceptance rate than one might expect. Weak students will still find it difficult to gain admission. The option of submitting ACT scores instead of SAT and SAT II: Subject Test scores should be the hands-down choice of any candidate who doesn't have to take SAT IIs for any other reason.

FINANCIAL AID

Students should submit: FAFSA, CSS/Financial Aid PROFILE, noncustodial (divorced/sepa-rated) parent's statement, business/farm supplement. No deadline for regular filing. The Princeton Review suggests that all financial aid forms be submitted as soon as possible after January 1. *Need-based scholarships/grants offered:* Pell, SEOG, state scholarships/grants, the school's own gift aid. *Loan aid offered:* Direct Subsidized Stafford, Direct Unsubsidized Stafford, Direct PLUS, Federal Perkins, state loans, college/university loans from institution-al funds. Federal Work-Study Program available. Institutional employment available. Applicants will be notified of awards on or about April 1. Off-campus job opportunities are excellent.

FROM THE ADMISSIONS OFFICE

"Brandeis's top-ranked faculty focuses on teaching undergraduates and is accessible to stu-dents during classes, during office hours, and even at home. Students become involved in cut-ting-edge faculty research at the Volen Center for Complex Systems—studying the brain's cognitive process—and throughout the university. Brandeis has an ideal location on the com-muter rail nine miles west of Boston; state-of-the-art sports facilities; and internships that complement interests in law, medicine, government, finance, the media, public service, and the arts. Brandeis offers broad renewable need-based financial aid and scholarships for domestic and international students."

For even more information on this school, turn to page 302 of the "Stats" section.

BROWN UNIVERSITY

BOX 1876, 45 PROSPECT STREET, PROVIDENCE, RI 02912 • ADMISSIONS: 401-863-2378 • FAX: 401-863-9300
FINANCIAL AID: 401-863-2721 • E-MAIL: ADMISSION_UNDERGRADUATE@BROWN.EDU • WEBSITE: WWW.BROWN.EDU

Ratings
Quality of Life: 87   Academic: 96   Admissions: 99   Financial Aid: 79

Academics

Brown's famous "open curriculum," which has no requirements outside of one's major, is "more rewarding for those students who know exactly what they wish to pursue academically." Those lacking the "incredible maturity" it takes "to balance all your courses and choose the right ones" can languish if they're used to rigid structure. Some students warn that good advisement is not always a given. The university, however, prides itself on "helping undergrads achieve their utmost potential." The emphasis is on quality of instruction rather than quantity, with small seminars available from day one of freshman year. Writes one academic junkie, "I go to class because I couldn't deprive myself of listening to what my professors have to say." Students also gush about their "godsend" of a new president, Ruth Simmons, who "simply rocks." Other administrators "understand students and are extremely tolerant of us." They "trust us to do what we want." Complaints primarily involve problems related to Brown's relatively small endowment, citing in particular poor financial aid packages. Students urge those in power to "go need-blind ASAP" in admissions (which the university approved in February 2002). Nonetheless, this "do-it-yourself" experience makes Brown "an Ivy League education without the pretense."

> **SURVEY SAYS . . .**
> *Political activism is hot*
> *Students aren't religious*
> *Great off-campus food*
> *Ethnic diversity on campus*
> *Intercollegiate sports are*
> *unpopular or nonexistent*

Life

"If you understand how this school is both an old, stuffy Ivy League college for boring academics and a laid-back place for chill folk, then you understand Brown," explains one undergraduate. Brown maintains its reputation as a "touchy-feely kind of place" with an "emphasis on individuality and individual choice." Suggests one student, "Think theater, poetry slams, literature." Students beg for some improved facilities for these activities, though, including a concert hall, more meeting space, and easier access to music and sports equipment. In typical departure from the norm, three coed fraternities (two of which are literary in focus) are standard-bearers of the social life at Brown. With "everyone and their dog in an a cappella group," students still find time for politics, being "generally eager to protest anything and everything." Amid this PC climate, students sometimes feel that "debates and conversation are many times stilted by a pathological fear of offending anyone." The campus is "extremely connected to the community" of Providence, where the "weather sucks eight of the nine months you are here." For those with overcoats but without cars, however, inexpensive trolley service runs through the town.

Student Body

Generally, students at Brown refuse to generalize when it comes to their peers, maintaining that "there is no typical Brown student—each individual here is truly unique." Considered a "Birkenstock-wearing, crunchy, granola-eating, nonflushing, tree-hugging crowd" by the outside world, many students contend that in reality "it's much more diverse than that." The population comprises "bright freaks" who are often "book worms with not a lot of social skills" and "rich snobs with little cell phones and fancy clothes." Ideologically, "there is no emphasis to conform to a certain stereotype, and we're quite accepting of all viewpoints." Some students would amend that evaluation by stating that the student body is indeed quite accepting—of liberal viewpoints: "Do not confuse the openness of the curriculum with immediate acceptance of all ideas," writes one undergrad. Though there is "more interracial and inter-class mixing than in the 'real world,' " tho "liberal and agnostic" majority sometimes shows disdain for "the following categories: varsity athletes, Christians, conservatives, frat boys, rich students, midwesterners, or southerners." But in an "activist" place where "everyone wants to change the world," broader acceptance may be the next step toward "unparalleled social consciousness."

ADMISSIONS

Very important factors considered by the admissions committee include: character/personal qualities, secondary school record, talent/ability. *Important factors considered include:* class rank, essays, extracurricular activities, recommendations. *Other factors considered include:* alumni/ae relation, geographical residence, interview, minority status, standardized test scores, state residency, volunteer work, work experience. TOEFL required of all international applicants. High school diploma is required and GED is not accepted. *High school units required/recommended:* 16 total required; 19 total recommended; 4 English required, 3 math required, 4 math recommended, 3 science required, 4 science recommended, 2 science lab required, 3 science lab recommended, 3 foreign language required, 4 foreign language recommended, 2 history required, 1 elective required.

The Inside Word

The cream of just about every crop applies to Brown. Gaining admission requires more than just a superior academic profile from high school. Some candidates, such as the sons and daughters of Brown graduates (who are admitted at virtually double the usual acceptance rate), have a better chance for admission than most others. Minority students benefit from some courtship, particularly once admitted. Ivies like to share the wealth and distribute offers of admission across a wide range of constituencies. Candidates from states that are overrepresented in the applicant pool, such as New York, have to be particularly distinguished in order to have the best chance at admission. So do those who attend high schools with many seniors applying to Brown, as it is rare for more than two or three students from any one school to be offered admission.

FINANCIAL AID

Students should submit: FAFSA, CSS/Financial Aid PROFILE, noncustodial (divorced/separated) parent's statement, business/farm supplement. Regular filing deadline is February 1. The Princeton Review suggests that all financial aid forms be submitted as soon as possible after January 1. *Need-based scholarships/grants offered:* Pell, SEOG, state scholarships/grants, private scholarships, the school's own gift aid. *Loan aid offered:* Direct Subsidized Stafford, Direct Unsubsidized Stafford, Direct PLUS, Federal Perkins, state loans, college/university loans from institutional funds. Federal Work-Study Program available. Institutional employment available. Applicants will be notified of awards on or about April 1. Off-campus job opportunities are excellent.

FROM THE ADMISSIONS OFFICE

"It is our pleasure to introduce you to a unique and wonderful learning place: Brown University. Brown was founded in 1764 and is a private, coeducational, Ivy League university in which the intellectual development of undergraduate students is fostered by a dedicated faculty on a traditional New England campus."

For even more information on this school, turn to page 303 of the "Stats" section.

BRYANT COLLEGE

1150 Douglas Pike, Smithfield, RI 02917 • Admissions: 401-232-6100 • Fax: 401-232-6741
Financial Aid: 401-232-6020 • E-mail: admissions@bryant.edu • Website: www.bryant.edu

Ratings
Quality of Life: 86   Academic: 79   Admissions: 75   Financial Aid: 86

Academics

Bryant College's curriculum allows its undergraduates to have their "whole world . . . incorporated into business." Practical application is emphasized, with classes "always relating back to something you're going to need to know in real life." Professors are also stores of pragmatic knowledge: "Apart from teaching, they bring

> **SURVEY SAYS . . .**
> *Lots of classroom discussion*
> *Great computer facilities, Great library*
> *Lots of beer drinking, Hard liquor is popular*
> *(Almost) no one listens to college radio*
> *Musical organizations aren't popular*
> *Theater is unpopular*
> *Student government is unpopular*

an overwhelming amount of experience on the subject matter we are learning since many of them have other jobs" in the real world. Some students feel the business focus is too tight, though. Writes one, "I realize this is a business school, but they should include some more liberal-arts-oriented courses. As a marketing major, I would like to take an art class or something that promotes creativity." Bryant prides itself on hooking its students up with plum jobs after they graduate. First off, "the career services office is phenomenal" in that they forge "really good connections to local companies that provide internships and possible future jobs." Students also enjoy "excellent networking" and an "extensive alumni network that supports the school and hires its graduates." As far as administrators go, "meeting with them with or without an appointment is never a problem," and "they are always asking students how they can better the school." Overall, Bryant students think "it's too bad that the school does not get the recognition it deserves" because it's "more rigorous academically than the numbers seem to show."

Life

Tucked away on 392 acres outside of Providence, students agree that "you couldn't get a better location." The sense of safety is high, with one student commenting, "I have always liked how we have a one-entrance, guarded campus." In terms of social life, another undergrad explains, "We're out in the woods, so if you aren't clubbing in Providence, you are drinking or hooking up on campus." Reportedly, "the campus is a lot of fun whether you drink or not." The majority of students, however, count themselves among the nonteetotalers. School-sponsored activities are available but considered "childish" and are thus "not readily attended." Student clubs and organizations do exist, and students readily participate in sports, taking advantage of some of the "best athletic facilities in New England." One student writes, "Intramural sports always have a large number of teams, no matter what sport, and the gyms are in constant use, whether for varsity sports or just pick-up games." One of the only complaints is that the school "needs to work on our unity and school pride."

Student Body

If you look at the student body here long enough, according to many, you'll see that "there is definitely a 'Bryant type,'" since "everyone looks the same and does the same thing." One student writes, "I like the people I go to school with because they are a lot like me," meaning that the "majority are from New England" and most share a "sense of professionalism." Students that deviate from this description tend to stick together. "White, minority, and international students predominantly associate with themselves." Further, "Greeks, sports teams, and multicultural students don't always hang out together." Despite this separation, one student reports, "As an openly gay male on a relatively straight campus, I have had no real incidents of discrimination." Another points out, students "feel as though many seem apathetic to greater social causes in the world." The upside of the homogeneity is a sense of "cohesiveness" and "students and alumni that are very loyal."

ADMISSIONS

Very important factors considered by the admissions committee include: class rank, essays, recommendations, secondary school record, standardized test scores. *Important factors considered include:* alumni/ae relation, character/personal qualities, extracurricular activities, interview, talent/ability. *Other factors considered include:* geographical residence, minority status, volunteer work, work experience. SAT I or ACT required. TOEFL required of all international applicants. High school diploma or GED is required. *High school units required/recommended:* 16 total required; 4 English required, 4 years of math required, 3 science recommended, 2 lab sciences required, 2 foreign language required.

The Inside Word

If you're a solid student you should meet little trouble getting into Bryant. The college's admissions effort has brought in qualified applicants from across the country, but the heaviest draw remains from New England. Students attending Bryant will receive a solid business education as well as precious connections in the corporate worlds of Providence and Boston.

FINANCIAL AID

Students should submit: FAFSA, institution's own financial aid form. Regular filing deadline is February 15. The Princeton Review suggests that all financial aid forms be submitted as soon as possible after January 1. *Need-based scholarships/grants offered:* Pell, SEOG, state scholarships/grants, private scholarships, the school's own gift aid. *Loan aid offered:* Direct Subsidized Stafford, Direct Unsubsidized Stafford, FFEL PLUS, Federal Perkins. Federal Work-Study Program available. Institutional employment available. Applicants will be notified of awards on or about March 15. Off-campus job opportunities are good.

FROM THE ADMISSIONS OFFICE

"Bryant College is a student-centered learning community that gives students the tools and resources they need to acquire knowledge, develop character, and achieve success—as they define it. In addition to a first-class faculty, state-of-the-art facilities, and advanced technology, Bryant offers stimulating classroom dynamics; internships at more than 200 companies; 60 student clubs and organizations; varsity, intramural, and club sports for men and women; and opportunities for community service. Bryant is the College of choice for individuals seeking the best combination of a business and liberal arts education. Bryant's rigorous academic standards have been recognized and accredited by AACSB International—The Association to Advance Collegiate Schools of Business. Our academic programs blend the practical with the theoretical; with degrees in business administration, applied psychology, communication, information technology, and liberal studies, Bryant offers academic studies for diverse interests and people. Technology is a fundamental component of the learning process at Bryant. Every entering freshman receives an IBM laptop to use through his or her first two years at Bryant, and is then issued a new laptop in the junior year, which can be purchased upon graduation. Our new Wellness Center employs a full-time wellness coordinator/health educator to help students keep a sense of balance throughout their educational experience. Bryant is situated on 392 acres of beautiful New England countryside and is only 15 minutes from Providence, one hour from Boston, and three hours from New York City and all of the cultural and social amenities of these major metropolitan areas."

For even more information on this school, turn to page 304 of the "Stats" section.

CENTRAL CONNECTICUT STATE UNIVERSITY

1615 STANLEY STREET, NEW BRITAIN, CT 06050 • ADMISSIONS: 800-832-3200 • FAX: 862-832-2295
E-MAIL: ADMISSIONS@CCSU.EDU • WEBSITE: WWW.CCSU.EDU

Ratings
Quality of Life: 77   Academic: 69   Admissions: 67   Financial Aid: 80

Academics

Students at Central Connecticut State University commend the "innovative education" they receive in New Britain, where your enunciation of the town's name determines whether you're a native (it's a Connecticut thing). Indeed, CCSU is the collegiate choice of

> **SURVEY SAYS . . .**
> Very little hard liquor
> Instructors are good teachers
> Great off-campus food
> Classes are small, Profs teach upper levels
> Students don't get along with local community

many Connecticut high school seniors. The university grants students the "ability to tailor and design" their own "programs of study, areas of concentration, and independent study classes." Though CCSU has 10,000 undergrads, students here boast about the "personal" feel of their classes: "We don't have lecture halls, so you usually don't have more than 20 to 30 people in a class." And because "there are great professors at Central that are willing to help out every step of the way," students who take advantage of their profs rarely feel overwhelmed or left at sea. There is also a handful of professors "who have lost touch with reality" and simply can't get through to their audience. Until recently, complaints about registration were ubiquitous at CCSU, but the conversion to "online registration . . . has been a great experience for all." In general, students are pleased with recent steps taken by the administration to improve the campus. "State-of-the-art" computer facilities are available to all students, and "they're rebuilding practically the whole campus"—something that many students say is sorely needed. While some gripe that "the construction has got to end," a thoughtful student interjects, "While we curse and fall over building materials, we can be grateful that future generations will have a lovely campus."

Life

It's true that CCSU "is very much a suitcase school"—a fact that dampens hopes of on-site activity and makes the campus seem "like a ghost town." But campus life is by no means non-existent. The campus is "right across the street from a local park, which is nice to go to when you have to study or just hang out," and when night falls, the few area bars beckon students. "If you're in the in-crowd . . . you go to all the parties" on campus and at nearby off-campus apartments, or you "go to other schools" in the area to carouse. "Drinking is out of control," grouses one undergrad. But there are plenty who scour the area for low-key activities like "movies, dinner, and plays." And with Hartford less than 15 minutes away, there's no excuse for settling for boredom or alcoholism. To travel, though, you'll need a car, and CCSU doesn't make it easy. With about "4,000 parking spots for 11,000 students," commuters and residents alike know the headaches of circling the lots; adds an honors student, "Driving at this university sharpens your cursing ability, as well as your aggressive driving skills."

Student Body

A so-called "commuter school," CCSU hosts only about 20 percent of its students on campus. Whether "commuters or residents," students here "are sometimes friendly," and a layer of superficiality prevents utopian relations. "Everyone dresses like this place is a fashion show," comments one student. "They should be more interested in school work instead of leather jackets and three-inch leg boots, tight shirts, pants, etc." Central has organizations that "give support to every possible group you can of think of—black students, international exchange students, Jewish students, Christian students, gay/lesbian students, etc." Students with a positive attitude and desire for cooperation realize that "everywhere you go, you get to meet new people and get a sense of where other people come from. College is a very cultural experience." And with "tons of diversity at CCSU," this is especially true.

ADMISSIONS

Very important factors considered by the admissions committee include: secondary school record. *Important factors considered include:* class rank and standardized test scores. *Other factors considered include:* essays, extracurricular activities, interview, minority status, recommendations, state residency, and talent/ability. SAT I required; SAT II recommended. TOEFL required of all international applicants. High school diploma or GED is required. *High school units required/recommended:* 13 total required; 4 English required, 3 math required, 2 science required, 1 science lab required, 3 foreign language recommended, 2 social studies required, 1 history required.

The Inside Word

CCSU has fairly generous admissions standards, meaning that the average college-bound high school senior should gain entrance here without much difficulty. Borderline candidates should schedule an interview with the Admissions Office and take the opportunity to present themselves as highly motivated candidates.

FINANCIAL AID

Students should submit: FAFSA. Regular filing deadline is September 24. The Princeton Review suggests that all financial aid forms be submitted as soon as possible after January 1. *Need-based scholarships/grants offered:* Pell, SEOG, state scholarships/grants, and the school's own gift aid. *Loan aid offered:* Direct Subsidized Stafford, Direct Unsubsidized Stafford, Direct PLUS, FFEL PLUS, and Federal Perkins. Federal Work-Study Program available. Applicants will be notified of awards on a rolling basis beginning on or about March 15. Off-campus job opportunities are excellent.

FROM THE ADMISSIONS OFFICE

"Selected as one of the 'Great Colleges for the Real World' and honored as a 'Leadership Institution' by the Association of American Colleges & Universities, CCSU stands as a national example of quality undergraduate education. Offering more than 100 majors in 82 fields of study in its four schools, CCSU also provides a wide array of special curricular opportunities to enrich learning.

"As exemplified in the University's slogan, 'Start with a dream. Finish with a future!' CCSU is committed to preparing students for success in whatever field they choose. The offices of career services and cooperative education provide interesting career-related work experience plus opportunities to make connections with hundreds of participating employers. Nearly 70 percent of participating students are offered permanent, career-starting positions with their co-op employers upon graduation.

"CCSU's campus is attractive, with new and renovated buildings adding to the classic collegiate 'look' of its historical architecture. Academic buildings feature state-of-the-art, fully networked 'smart classrooms.' A newly renovated and expanded student center provides lounges, conference and game rooms, dining and information services, a bookstore, and a range of other support services. With 120 student clubs and organizations covering a broad spectrum of interests, there is a wealth of opportunities to meet new people, broaden horizons, and develop leadership skills. Athletics are a big part of campus life, and students enjoy a state-of-the-art fitness center with training rooms, a swimming pool, a track, and tennis and basketball courts. And CCSU's 18 Division I sports teams provide exciting opportunities to play or watch."

For even more information on this school, turn to page 304 of the "Stats" section.

CITY UNIVERSITY OF NEW YORK—BARUCH COLLEGE

UNDERGRADUATE ADMISSIONS, ONE BERNARD BARUCH WAY BOX H-0720, NEW YORK, NY 10010
ADMISSIONS: 646-312-1400 • FAX: 646-312-1361 • E-MAIL: ADMISSIONS@BARUCH.CUNY.EDU
WEBSITE: WWW.BARUCH.CUNY.EDU

Ratings
Quality of Life: 80   **Academic:** 65   **Admissions:** 63   **Financial Aid:** 82

Academics

Baruch College enjoys a reputation for providing budding business students from New York City with a solid education. In addition to the Zicklin School of Business, Baruch's two other components—the Weissman School of Arts and Sciences and the School of Public Affairs—also receive

> **SURVEY SAYS . . .**
> *Student publications are ignored*
> *Profs teach upper levels*
> *Diverse students interact*
> *Class discussions encouraged*
> *Instructors are good teachers*
> *Very little hard liquor*

high marks from the students. "Baruch's greatest strength is its reputation," reports a student. "As a result, recruiters are very impressed with Baruch applicants." But it's the driven, self-starting "students [who] work full time while attending school full time" that give their alma mater that reputation, especially in the field of accounting. Students do send one warning about Baruch: the professorial pool is a mixed bag. And "the professor makes or breaks the class," adds a student. So what to do? "There is an online rating of professors based on student surveys," an undergrad offers. "By using this information I have had wonderful professors for the most part." And one other warning: "The school's administration is your typical 'Department of Motor Vehicles' bureaucracy. You REALLY need to be patient, persistent, and convincing to get the classes you need, the financial aid you require, and sometimes even accurate information." But when students get frustrated with the administration, they need only walk over to the corner of 3rd Avenue and 24th Street and look up at what the administration has recently built for them: a new 17-story building, called the Vertical Campus, which houses the schools of business and arts and sciences, numerous administrative offices and student organizations, a bookstore, a food court, a full athletic facility, a recital hall, art studios and labs, two auditoriums, 14 research labs, 36 computer labs, 102 classrooms, 375 faculty offices, and plenty more.

Life

Baruch is a commuter school in Manhattan with students coming and going all day long. "When we go out at night, it is generally with friends from other sources, not school," explains a student. But during the day, the school is alive, not only with academics but also with the activities of nearly 130 clubs. From The Ticker—an award-winning student newspaper—to the Hand-to-Hand Combat Club, there's an organization for every interest and every nationality. Because of the campus's central location, Baruch also sees plenty of action from non-campus organizations looking to convert students to their causes. "They post flyers and invite students to attend meetings, think tanks, benefits, and other events," writes an undergrad. But not everyone has time to indulge these crusaders, let alone join a club that suits interests of their own. "A lot of students are busy studying," writes an undergrad, "or having to juggle school and work along with family life." In other words, "they find little time to be involved in anything." When students do have some free time, a popular destination is the new, $38 million Vertical Campus. Below the 17-story building there's a 3-story, underground athletic facility, equipped with recreation and fitness centers, a gymnasium, racquetball courts, a pool, and locker rooms.

Student Body

Because Baruch is a nonresidential campus, the student body is drawn primarily from New York City itself and reflects the city's diverse composition. Baruch's undergraduate population of 12,969 hails from more than 90 shades of identifiable ethnic and cultural background. Students rave that the combination of rich diversity and New York City gusto make the university a dynamic place to learn. A particularly enthusiastic student from New Jersey (which puts her among the mere 4 percent of students who come from out of state) exclaims, "They're the most individualistic and creative people I've ever met! New Yorkers are very assertive and determined to reach their goals." She also says that her Baruch classmates unabashedly confront the big issues of the day, raising "concerns about ethnic diversity, homosexuality, politics, and poverty." Another student adds, "I believe the students all enjoy each other's differences."

ADMISSIONS

Very important factors considered by the admissions committee include: secondary school record and standardized test scores. *Important factors considered include:* essays and recommendations. *Other factors considered include:* alumni/ae relation, class rank, extracurricular activities, interview, talent/ability, and work experience. SAT I required. TOEFL required of all international applicants. High school diploma or GED is required. *High school units required/recommended:* 16 total required; 17 total recommended; 4 English required, 3 math required, 2 science required, 2 science lab required, 2 foreign language required, 4 social studies required, 4 social studies recommended.

The Inside Word

Interest in Baruch has risen greatly in recent years, and so too have admissions standards. Applications are processed through the University Application Processing Center, which handles applications for all CUNY campuses, so don't expect much in the way of individualized attention. Applying early will improve your chances.

FINANCIAL AID

Students should submit: FAFSA and state aid form. Regular filing deadline is April 30. The Princeton Review suggests that all financial aid forms be submitted as soon as possible after January 1. *Need-based scholarships/grants offered:* Pell, SEOG, state scholarships/grants, private scholarships, the school's own gift aid, and City merit scholarships. *Loan aid offered:* Direct Subsidized Stafford, Direct Unsubsidized Stafford, Direct PLUS, and Federal Perkins. Federal Work-Study Program available. Institutional employment available. Applicants will be notified of awards on a rolling basis beginning on or about April 1. Off-campus job opportunities are excellent.

For even more information on this school, turn to page 305 of the "Stats" section.

CITY UNIVERSITY OF NEW YORK—BROOKLYN COLLEGE

2900 BEDFORD AVENUE, BROOKLYN, NY 11210 • ADMISSIONS: 718-951-5001
FINANCIAL AID: 718-951-5051 • E-MAIL: ADMINGRY@BROOKLYN.CUNY.EDU • WEBSITE: WWW.BROOKLYN.CUNY.EDU

Ratings
Quality of Life: 90   Academic: 83   Admissions: 75   Financial Aid: 90

Academics

Students love that "there are a great deal of choices at Brooklyn College," a City University of New York campus located deep within the city's most populous borough. Undergraduates may choose from among 125 different majors; business, computer science, education, accounting, psychology, film and television, and

> **SURVEY SAYS . . .**
> *Ethnic diversity on campus*
> *Beautiful campus, Campus easy to get around*
> *Great computer facilities*
> *Student publications are ignored*
> *Theater is unpopular*
> *Student government is unpopular*
> *Very little beer drinking*

speech pathology are among the most popular here. Students also praise the science departments. Film students note that the school's proximity to a major entertainment capital provides them teachers with broad industry experience. Reports one senior, "My overall academic experience has been great, and though some of my professors have been a little crazy, they are quite knowledgeable." Students' complaints are typical of those lodged by their peers at low-tuition public schools. The primary focus of their discontent is the bureaucracy that rules Brooklyn: "Every little thing requires a form to be filled out," and "the administration is kind of difficult to deal with, so if you wind up at BC, don't expect a ton of help." Instructors, many feel, "are distant. They teach, you learn, there is very little personal interaction." Many students dislike the 10-course core requirement, which obliges students to study a broad range of disciplines. "The requirements are outrageous," grouses one undergrad. "It's supposed to expose you to many different disciplines, which I think is great, but 10 is just too much to me." But, hey BC's students will be renaissance people before they graduate, whether they like it or not! Compounding problems is the fact that "there are not enough classes given in most fields of study for working adults. Most of the important classes that are needed to fulfill degree requirements are given during the day, when most adults are at a full-time job." Even so, most undergrads would agree that "the overall experience is positive" at BC.

Life

With no dormitories and relatively few students living in the area immediately surrounding the campus, Brooklyn College lacks the standard components of an active campus social life, and unsurprisingly, it is relatively quiet when classes end. "Most students are busy, working, raising families, and studying," explains one student. "There is time for student events, but it is hard." Those who get involved tell us that "life at Brooklyn College is a wonderful experience, so long as one takes advantage of all the college has to offer. We have on-campus jazz concerts, dance festivals, plays, lectures from well-known scholars, and a beautiful campus that you can walk through and enjoy." Academic clubs, student organizations, and the Greeks "usually help you meet people quickly, and even though the Greek life on campus isn't really that big, there are often fun fraternity and sorority parties going on at local bars and clubs." Conveniently, "club hours—designated times that all clubs meet and no classes are scheduled—make it easy to join things." Otherwise, campus life is pretty sedate. Located in the Midwood section of Brooklyn, the college "is in a very urban environment," albeit one that has surprisingly few good eateries near campus; warns one student, "The food on campus is absolutely awful . . . . Food off campus is just as bad." Students observe that "what's cool about Brooklyn is it's easy to get places, thanks to the buses and trains, and you can usually find something going on." A subway ride from campus to midtown Manhattan takes approximately 30 minutes.

Student Body

The student body of Brooklyn College "is extremely diverse. Many students have come from foreign countries. You'll meet every nationality you could think of (or maybe didn't) at Brooklyn College. Amazingly, everyone pretty much gets along all right despite the many differences of the diverse student body." Most appreciate the diversity, telling us they "love interacting with people of different cultural groups and learning about foreign cultures." A number of undergrads here are first-generation college students "from a lower economic status. They are working to support their own educations" and, accordingly, are busier and more serious than typical college students.

ADMISSIONS

Very important factors considered by the admissions committee include: secondary school record, standardized test scores. *Other factors considered include:* extracurricular activities, interview, recommendations, talent/ability. SAT I or ACT required; SAT II recommended. TOEFL required of all international applicants. High school diploma or GED is required. *High school units required/recommended:* 4 English recommended, 3 math recommended, 3 science recommended, 3 foreign language recommended, 4 social studies recommended, 4 elective recommended.

The Inside Word

Like other City University of New York (CUNY) schools, Brooklyn College provides easy access to a college education for students who want one. Brooklyn raises the bar, however, with superior offerings in the arts and sciences. You don't have to have a spotless academic record to get into Brooklyn College, but once there you will receive a solid and respected education.

FINANCIAL AID

Students should submit: FAFSA, state aid form. No deadline for regular filing. The Princeton Review suggests that all financial aid forms be submitted as soon as possible after January 1. *Need-based scholarships/grants offered:* Pell, SEOG, state scholarships/grants, private scholarships, the school's own gift aid. *Loan aid offered:* Direct Subsidized Stafford, Direct Unsubsidized Stafford, Direct PLUS, Federal Perkins. Federal Work-Study Program available. Institutional employment available. Applicants will be notified of awards on a rolling basis beginning on or about June 1. Off-campus job opportunities are excellent.

FROM THE ADMISSIONS OFFICE

"Brooklyn College, founded in 1930, ranked first last year in The Princeton Review's The Best 345 Colleges as the most 'Beautiful Campus' in the country. It was also ranked fifth in the country for providing the 'Best Academic Bang for Your Buck' and for its friendly diversity on the 'Students from Different Backgrounds Interact' list. The College, a premiere public liberal arts college, is easily reached by subway or bus, and its accessibility to Manhattan allows students to enrich their educational experience through the city's myriad cultural events and institutions. Brooklyn College's 15,000 undergraduate and graduate students represent the ethnic and cultural diversity of the borough. The College continues on an ambitious drive of expansion and renewal. A dazzling new library opened on campus a year ago. It is the most technologically advanced educational and research library in the CUNY system. Respected nationally for its rigorous academic standards, the College takes pride in such innovative programs as its award-winning Freshman Year College and the core curriculum. The acclaimed Honors Academy houses nine programs for high achievers, including the Mellon Fellowship, which supports minority students, and the BA-MD Program in coordination with SUNY Downstate College of Medicine."

For even more information on this school, turn to page 306 of the "Stats" section.

City University of New York—Hunter College

695 Park Avenue, New York, NY 10021 • Admissions: 212-772-4000 • Fax: 212-650-3336
Financial Aid: 212-772-4820 • E-mail: admissions@hunter.cuny.edu • Website: www.hunter.cuny.edu

Ratings
Quality of Life: 71   Academic: 73   Admissions: 79   Financial Aid: 80

Academics

For many New York residents, Hunter College is the answer to the nagging question, "How in the world can I afford a college education?" With a solid reputation in the natural sciences, health sciences, social work, and English, Hunter offers not only a college degree but also one well regarded in academic circles, all at a price

> **SURVEY SAYS . . .**
> *Ethnic diversity on campus*
> *Political activism is hot*
> *Everyone loves New York, NY*
> *Different students interact*
> *Lots of classroom discussion*
> *Very little beer drinking, Very little hard liquor*
> *Students are not very happy*

that's relatively easy on the bank account. Of course, because the school places a strong emphasis on keeping tuition and fees low, students enjoy few frills along with their learning experience. One student explains that as "with all city schools there are so many students, and sometimes getting exactly what you want is tough, but I think Hunter College does a good job trying to help students in times of need." Administrative issues are the most frustrating here. Another writes, "Classes are at times crowded and hard to get into. Nevertheless, it is possible to speak to professors and get individual attention if you are really interested." While "some profs are really good," others "need more training, and they need to be encouraged to spend time outside the classroom with their students." The honors program here is reportedly "very good."

Life

Hunter is almost exclusively a commuter college. Even the school's few residents live away from campus, in a dormitory two miles south of the school. All others live in apartments scattered across New York's five boroughs, to which they return immediately after classes let out. Accordingly, there is "very little social life at Hunter. Everyone works and studies." Says one student, "Nothing active goes on. I try to get around and hear about social events, but it is usually a drag." Student organizations, intercollegiate and intramural sports, and campus theater help fill the void somewhat, but for most students extracurriculars take place off campus in the city that never sleeps. "New York is the best! The activities don't stop!" explains one enthusiastic student. Hunter's East Side location is close to art galleries, high-end fashion shops, and Central Park ("great for warm weather" and not nearly as dangerous as the movies make it out to be) and also provides easy subway access to Wall Street, Greenwich Village, Yankee Stadium, the Bronx Zoo, and any of a thousand other fabulous destinations. The campus itself, however, a four-building complex between Lexington and Park Avenues, "needs some serious updating."

Student Body

Hunter's student body is among the nation's most racially varied, with African American, Asian, Latino, and Caucasian populations nearly in parity. "It would be impossible to have a more diverse student body," sums up one student. Diversity also manifests itself in students' attitudes. "Hunter is a melting pot of the highly intelligent and the extreme slacker," writes one undergrad. And another notes, "There is a scene here for any type, whether it be religious, studious, political, or stoned." Politically, student opinion ranges from the middle-of-the-road to the left, with very few students admitting to conservatism. Students are also "acutely aware of social, political, and cultural situations in general." With a large nontraditional population and little campus housing, students rarely see each other except in classes or at the library. Explains one, "Hunter students work. They are not, in the usual sense, college students. They live in the real world, not in an isolated, artificial social environment."

ADMISSIONS

Very important factors considered by the admissions committee include: secondary school record, standardized test scores. *Other factors considered include:* essays, recommendations. SAT I or ACT required. TOEFL required of all international applicants. High school diploma or GED is required. *High school units required/recommended:* 14 total required; 16 total recommended; 2 English required, 4 English recommended, 2 math required, 3 math recommended, 1 science required, 2 science recommended, 1 science lab required, 2 science lab recommended, 2 foreign language recommended, 4 social studies recommended, 1 elective recommended.

The Inside Word

Nothing personal here; applications are processed through CUNY's enormous central processing center. Follow the numbers—and be sure to have followed the updated high school curriculum requirements—and gain admission. Looking ahead, expect admissions requirements throughout CUNY to continue to reflect heightened concern with academic preparedness. Hunter will no doubt continue to be among the most demanding CUNY units.

FINANCIAL AID

Students should submit: FAFSA, state aid form. No deadline for regular filing. The Princeton Review suggests that all financial aid forms be submitted as soon as possible after January 1. *Need-based scholarships/grants offered:* Pell, SEOG, state scholarships/grants, private scholarships, the school's own gift aid. *Loan aid offered:* Direct Subsidized Stafford, Direct Unsubsidized Stafford, Direct PLUS, Federal Perkins. Federal Work-Study Program available. Institutional employment available. Applicants will be notified of awards on a rolling basis. Off-campus job opportunities are good.

FROM THE ADMISSIONS OFFICE

"Located in the heart of Manhattan, Hunter offers students the stimulating learning environment and career-building opportunities you might expect from a college that's been a part of the world's most exciting city since 1870. The largest college in the City University of New York, Hunter pulses with energy. Hunter's vitality stems from a large, highly diverse faculty and student body. Its schools—Arts and Sciences, Education, the Health Professions, and Social Work—provide an affordable first-rate education. Undergraduates have extraordinary opportunities to conduct high-level research under renowned faculty, and many opt for credit-bearing internships in such exciting fields as media, the arts, and government. The College's high standards and special programs ensure a challenging education. The Block Program for first-year students keeps classmates together as they pursue courses in the liberal arts, pre–health science, pre-nursing, pre-med, or honors. A range of honors programs is available for students with strong academic records, including the highly competitive tuition-free Hunter CUNY Honors College for entering freshmen and the Thomas Hunter Honors Program, which emphasizes small classes with personalized mentoring by the most outstanding faculty. Qualified students also benefit from Hunter's participation in minority science research and training programs, the prestigious Andrew W. Mellon Minority Undergraduate Program, and many other passports to professional success."

For even more information on this school, turn to page 306 of the "Stats" section.

CITY UNIVERSITY OF NEW YORK—QUEENS COLLEGE

65-30 KISSENA BOULEVARD, FLUSHING, NY 11367 • ADMISSIONS: 718-997-5000 • FAX: 718-997-5617
FINANCIAL AID: 718-997-5101 • E-MAIL: ADMISSIONS@QC.EDU • WEBSITE: WWW.QC.EDU

Ratings
Quality of Life: 67   Academic: 74   Admissions: 75   Financial Aid: 82

Academics

For many New York residents, Queens College offers the best opportunity for an excellent education at cut-rate prices. Explains one student, "The realities of academic life here are top-notch. I have studied and conducted independent research with world-class professors who are eager to devote much time to helping outstanding students achieve their fullest potential. Scholarships and study abroad opportunities abound here." Queens offers honors programs in the humanities, business, and the liberal arts, and the mathematical and natural sciences, which provide enhanced learning opportunities for excellent students." Many expressed frustration over CUNY's financial status, complaining that "continuous budget cuts are destroying the CUNY system." This, however, is the trade-off students make for an affordable education. For most, it is a worthwhile tradeoff because it nets them an education that is "very good overall."

SURVEY SAYS . . .
Ethnic diversity on campus
Political activism is hot
Different students interact
Students love Flushing, NY
Lots of classroom discussion
Campus difficult to get around
Very little drug use
Unattractive campus
Lousy food on campus
Students are cliquish

Life

Because Queens College is a commuter school (QC has no dorms at all), campus life pretty much begins and ends during the day. Writes one student, "This is not a social campus because everyone commutes. You generally become friendly with those in your major, people you constantly have classes with." A few students do take apartments in Flushing; those that do enjoy the nearby Italian, Chinese, and Korean shopping and dining. Extracurricular activities here revolve around "lots of student organizations." Explains one student, "Campus clubs have a lot of activities." Adds another, "The doors to club offices are always open, so people make the rounds of the Student Union, visiting friends as they please. There are always free concerts at the music school during free hour." Students enjoy the fact that "professors like 'doing lunch' with their students; it alleviates a lot of the academic pressure for us." Unlike other CUNY schools such as Hunter and Baruch, Queens has an actual campus, which is "very safe" and "nice and pretty" despite an odd, sometimes clashing variety of architectural styles.

Student Body

The borough of Queens is the residence of choice for many of New York City's immigrant groups. The Queens College student body reflects the international flavor of its home; the school's promotional material boasts that 67 different native languages are spoken on campus. The student body also accurately mirrors New York's demographics, with minority students constituting nearly half the student body. Many students work their way through school here; they are "a hard-working bunch. Most are not well-off financially but are determined to better their lives through education."

ADMISSIONS

Very important factors considered by the admissions committee include: secondary school record. *Important factors considered include:* standardized test scores, talent/ability. *Other factors considered include:* essays, recommendations. SAT I required; SAT II recommended. TOEFL required of all international applicants. High school diploma or GED is required. *High school units required/recommended:* 16 total required; 18 total recommended; 4 English required, 3 math required, 4 math recommended, 2 science required, 3 science recommended, 2 science lab required, 3 foreign language required, 4 social studies required.

The Inside Word

Applicants to Queens follow the usual CUNY application procedures, which have gotten tougher with the implementation of updated high school curriculum requirements. Candidates for the Aaron Copeland School of Music must also successfully pass through a rigorous audition process. CUNY admissions requirements are currently undergoing close scrutiny; beware of the possibility of further changes.

FINANCIAL AID

Students should submit: FAFSA, state aid form. No deadline for regular filing. The Princeton Review suggests that all financial aid forms be submitted as soon as possible after January 1. *Need-based scholarships/grants offered:* Pell, SEOG, state scholarships/grants, private scholarships, the school's own gift aid. *Loan aid offered:* Direct Subsidized Stafford, Direct Unsubsidized Stafford, Direct PLUS, Federal Perkins. Federal Work-Study Program available. Institutional employment available. Applicants will be notified of awards on a rolling basis beginning on or about March 1. Off-campus job opportunities are good.

FROM THE ADMISSIONS OFFICE

"New York State Governor George Pataki calls Queens College 'the jewel of the City University of New York system' for two good reasons: its faculty and its students. Queens College faculty members are renowned for their commitment to scholarship and teaching. Also major contributors to the dynamic learning environment of Queens College are the students, who come from 120 nations. The Queens College curriculum is just as diverse, with nationally recognized programs in many fields, including the Aaron Copland School of Music. In fall 2003, a new Bachelor of Business Administration will offer solid preparation for a business career that is also grounded in the liberal arts and sciences. Aspiring teachers benefit from the Education Division's strength and innovative programs (Queens College educated more teachers than any college in the tri-state area). Located in the most ethnically diverse county in America, the College is a vibrant microcosm of the world, where students interact with peers representing a range of backgrounds and viewpoints. A Queens College education, which is guided by the principal, 'We Learn in Order to Serve,' is the best possible preparation for leadership in today's global village."

For even more information on this school, turn to page 307 of the "Stats" section.

CLARK UNIVERSITY

950 MAIN STREET, WORCESTER, MA 01610 • ADMISSIONS: 508-793-7431 • FAX: 508-793-8821
FINANCIAL AID: 508-793-7478 • E-MAIL: ADMISSIONS@CLARKU.EDU • WEBSITE: WWW.CLARKU.EDU

Ratings

Quality of Life: 71	Academic: 79	Admissions: 82	Financial Aid: 83

Academics

Clark University undergraduates agree that their school's "size is the greatest strength; it allows for personal contact with faculty and administration, as well as fellow students. It feels much like a small community or large family." Explains one student, "Clark is so great because of the student-teacher ratio. I know all of my pro-

SURVEY SAYS . . .
Students don't like Worcester, MA
Students aren't religious
(Almost) everyone smokes
Lousy food on campus
Ethnic diversity on campus
Theater is hot
(Almost) everyone plays intramural sports

fessors and am basically on a first name basis with them. It feels good to know that I can go to them and talk about almost anything. That's the one thing I love most about my school." Professors "are almost always accessible and really care about informing students about their area of expertise." Students agree that Clark's administration is "primarily concerned about academics. In the psychology, geography, international business, and Holocaust studies departments, we have some of the world's best experts, [and] all departments have very intelligent, informative, and open professors in them." Clark is also a "world-class" research university in many ways (rare for such a small, private school). Undergrads here are able to participate to an unusually large degree in "interesting research." Ambitious undergads can take advantage of the "Fifth-Year Free Program," which allows "qualified students" to attend for five years for the price of four and "receive a bachelor's and master's degree," quite a bargain in today's credential-crazed world.

Life

Clark social life is somewhat hampered by the fact that "whereas most schools have one center of campus activities, Clark has two buildings, which really hinders the ability of either to act as a truly central hub. The school needs to become more cohesive in what it offers students socially, because right now the students can't rely on the school for much in that arena." Despite this handicap, "students here are very active. Most belong to at least one group on campus." And "for a population of 2,000," there are "almost 90 different groups" to choose from. Students also enjoy the "frequent concerts held on campus. They are not exactly national bands, but it gives you something to do on the weekend. There are parties, but not many people hold small social events." Hometown Worcester "offers many sources of entertainment but few reliable forms of transportation to get you" to where the action's happening. "Many students, including freshmen, have cars on campus but choose to stay in the general area." That's too bad because "if you are willing to explore and keep an open mind you will find many treasures, like the soul food restaurant not half a mile away, a truly authentic pupuseria, wonderful botanical gardens, decent theatre, and good concerts in the area." Boston is only 40 miles away and is easily accessible by bus and train.

Student Body

"Diversity is a huge strength" at Clark. Observes one student, "It's nice to go from white, suburban America" to a place where you can "learn about so many countries and so many races." The student body "contains all types of people, all of whom live in general harmony with each other: jocks, punks, skaters, indie-rockers, preps, etc." Agrees one undergrad, "Students are the reason Clark has the personality it does. A little offbeat, a little quirky, a little into weird and wonderful things, and all into questioning the status quo, working for positive changes in their world, and asking questions about what is good and right and necessary to make life better. [T]he students here are a great group of people." Students "are very politically active and take part in many different social movements, from animal rights to water quality." A conservative student warns that those "who aren't liberal have a hard time being heard." The international population is large; offers one student, "Sometimes I think the university is better known outside of the U.S." than within it.

ADMISSIONS

Very important factors considered by the admissions committee include: character/personal qualities, recommendations, secondary school record, standardized test scores. *Important factors considered include:* essays, extracurricular activities, talent/ability, volunteer work. *Other factors considered include:* alumni/ae relation, class rank, geographical residence, interview, minority status, work experience. SAT I or ACT required. TOEFL required of all international applicants. High school diploma or GED is required. *High school units required/recommended:* 16 total recommended; 4 English recommended, 3 math recommended, 3 science recommended, 2 science lab recommended, 2 foreign language recommended, 2 social studies recommended, 2 history recommended.

The Inside Word

Clark is surrounded by formidable competitors, and its selectivity suffers because of it. Most B students will encounter little difficulty gaining admission. Given the university's solid academic environment and access to other member colleges in the Worcester Consortium, it can be a terrific choice for students who are not up to the ultra-competitive admission expectations of "top-tier" universities.

FINANCIAL AID

Students should submit: FAFSA, CSS/Financial Aid PROFILE. The Princeton Review suggests that all financial aid forms be submitted as soon as possible after January 1. *Need-based scholarships/grants offered:* Pell, SEOG, state scholarships/grants, the school's own gift aid. *Loan aid offered:* FFEL Subsidized Stafford, FFEL Unsubsidized Stafford, FFEL PLUS, Federal Perkins, state loans, college/university loans from institutional funds. Federal Work-Study Program available. Applicants will be notified of awards on or about March 31. Off-campus job opportunities are good.

FROM THE ADMISSIONS OFFICE

"At Clark University, you are respected for challenging convention, for trying out new ideas and skills, and for inspiring new ways of thinking. You learn how social change is made, and you get to be a part of it. Individual development is nurtured by a dedicated faculty who encourages hands-on learning. Founded in 1887, Clark is home to students from more than 57 countries and 44 states."

For even more information on this school, turn to page 307 of the "Stats" section.

CLARKSON UNIVERSITY

Box 5605, POTSDAM, NY 13699 • ADMISSIONS: 315-268-6479 • FAX: 315-268-7647
FINANCIAL AID: 315-268-7699 • E-MAIL: ADMISSIONS@CLARKSON.EDU • WEBSITE: WWW.CLARKSON.EDU

Ratings

Quality of Life: 73   Academic: 76   Admissions: 82   Financial Aid: 86

Academics

Clarkson University offers students little in the way of bells and whistles (see "Life," below), but it excels in the one area that counts most: academics. Students proudly report that Clarkson "is academically sound. The professors are good and the facilities are even better." Engineering programs are the long-time stalwarts

> **SURVEY SAYS . . .**
> *Library needs improving*
> *Class discussions are rare*
> *Diversity lacking on campus*
> *Student publications are ignored*
> *Large classes*
> *Musical organizations aren't popular*
> *Students aren't religious*

here; business is the rising star. Students appreciate a faculty of educators that "care so much about their students. Your teachers are more like your friends, everyone knows everyone, and teachers are even seen hanging out with students out of class." Writes one student, "My professors show such an enthusiasm for their field of teaching," which makes it hardly surprising that "they are inspirational." It's not all one big engineering love fest, though. Work here is tough ("Everybody who doesn't belong disappears miraculously after their first semester"), but the rewards can be great ("The Career Development Center does an excellent job of getting people work after college") for those who cut the grade.

Life

Like most engineering schools, Clarkson piles the work on its students, providing students with an ideal setting in which to attack it enthusiastically, since "there is not much of anything to do" on or off campus. Writes one typical student, "The common perception around campus is that there is nothing to do but get drunk or high. When people want to do something fun, they go home or visit a high school friend at another university." The Division I powerhouse hockey team is pretty much the only show in town, and students attend the "awesome" games—which are free—enthusiastically. Otherwise they work, gripe about parking ("There is never enough parking, and campus security tickets people who resort to parking on lawns, etc."), campus facilities ("The student union is not a student union. It is a hockey arena with a hockey apparel store that happens to sell candy bars. A true student union would do the campus wonders."), and, of course, the sense that there is nothing to do besides study. Hometown Potsdam, unfortunately, "is the most uneventful town in the U.S." Brutal winters further dampen activity. Is it really all that bad? Not according to at least one dissenter, who writes, "Many students will say . . . well, there's nothing to do here. I tell them they're not looking hard enough. . . . If what you want isn't here, then start it yourself. We have over 100 different clubs and organizations with new clubs being formed every year. The Adirondacks are within a half-hour drive south and Canada is a 45-minute drive north. There are always bands, comedians, and other acts . . . at MidKnights or Club 99. Get away from the computer and you'll find what you're looking for."

Student Body

Clarkson students admit that theirs is not a diverse demographic. But they think you should know that "while diversity here tends to be of the 'What kind of white middle-class male are you?' sort, we really do run the gamut in personality types. Almost everybody finds enough people like them to feel comfortable." Says one engineer, "Though the ratio[s] of females to males and minorities to majorities do not reflect much diversity, the diversity of thought and opinion here is many times greater than at a school whose numbers may reflect extreme diversity." Students here are a "good bunch of people, not cut-throat. Everyone helps each other with work and projects all the time, which is why I like it here. It's a 'we are all here together' attitude instead of 'we are all here, but I want to be the best' attitude." The dearth of women is a problem for most men; wrote one student, "The ratio [of] men to women at my school for my graduating class is 7:1. Sometimes it's hard to get over that, but since I am female, it is quite nice."

ADMISSIONS

Very important factors considered by the admissions committee include: interview, secondary school record. *Important factors considered include:* class rank, extracurricular activities, recommendations, standardized test scores, volunteer work. *Other factors considered include:* alumni/ae relation, character/personal qualities, essays, talent/ability, work experience. SAT I or ACT required. TOEFL required of all international applicants. High school diploma or GED is required. *High school units required/recommended:* 16 total required; 4 English required, 3 math required, 4 math recommended, 2 science required, 3 science recommended.

The Inside Word

Clarkson's acceptance rate is too high for solid applicants to lose much sleep about gaining admission. Serious candidates should interview anyway. If you are particularly solid and really want to come here, it could help you get some scholarship money. Women and minorities will encounter an especially friendly admissions committee.

FINANCIAL AID

Students should submit: FAFSA, institution's own financial aid form, state aid form. The Princeton Review suggests that all financial aid forms be submitted as soon as possible after January 1. *Need-based scholarships/grants offered:* Pell, SEOG, state scholarships/grants, private scholarships, the school's own gift aid, HEOP. *Loan aid offered:* Direct Subsidized Stafford, Direct Unsubsidized Stafford, Direct PLUS, Federal Perkins, college/university loans from institutional funds, GATE Loans. Federal Work-Study Program available. Institutional employment available. Applicants will be notified of awards on or about March 23. Off-campus job opportunities are fair.

FROM THE ADMISSIONS OFFICE

"Clarkson is a blend of vivid contrasts—high-powered academics in a cooperative, friendly community; technically oriented students who enjoy people; a unique location that serves as gateway to all kinds of outdoor recreation and to social and cultural activities of four colleges within a 10-mile radius. Our students are described as smart, hardworking, outgoing, energized, fun-loving, and team players. Our academic programs are rigorous, relevant, flexible, and nationally respected. Our teachers are demanding, approachable, concerned, accomplished, and inspiring. Clarkson alumni, students, and faculty share an exceptionally solid bond and the lifetime benefits that come from an active, global network of personal and professional ties."

For even more information on this school, turn to page 308 of the "Stats" section.

COLBY COLLEGE

4800 MAYFLOWER HILL, WATERVILLE, ME 04901-8848 • ADMISSIONS: 207-872-3168 • FAX: 207-872-3474
FINANCIAL AID: 207-872-3168 • E-MAIL: ADMISSIONS@COLBY.EDU • WEBSITE: WWW.COLBY.EDU

Ratings
Quality of Life: 90   Academic: 94   Admissions: 96   Financial Aid: 79

Academics

An intimate, prestigious, liberal arts college tucked away in a "superb location in the Maine woods not far from civilization," Colby College offers a challenging but manageable undergraduate experience to its small student population. Undergrads report that all the support mechanisms necessary for success in college are

SURVEY SAYS . . .
Great food on campus
Diversity lacking on campus
Athletic facilities are great
Everyone loves the Mules
(Almost) no one smokes
Students don't like Waterville, ME
Class discussions encouraged

in place here. Writes one, "I was intimidated at first by the whole idea of college, but after my first day of classes freshman year, my fears were soon assuaged. My professors were real pros and made otherwise very complex and involved material accessible to the students. At the end of my first semester, I was even asked to be a professor's research assistant." Another explains, "It is a very intimate, personal, inspiring, and wonderful relationship between professors and students. They're always there for you, ready and willing to ease any personal or academic stresses you are under." Not surprisingly, students grow attached to this friendly place. "I consider Colby my home and cannot imagine leaving this community behind," reflects a senior. "Colby has honestly been the most wonderful academic and social experience that I have ever experienced." Unique programs here include "Jan Plan," a short semester that allows students to study nontraditional subjects or intern during the month of January.

Life

Combine a large group of college-age kids and a beautiful, remote, bucolic location and what you get is "summer camp with alcohol. Camp Colby is totally awesome." Students here love the beauty, food, and facilities and are no less than gushy about other kids and professors. Although many students "drink for fun," those who opt for a substance-free social life say "chem-free fun" is readily available as well, especially in the "chem-free" dorms. In addition, "the range of theatre productions, concerts, lectures, and sporting events is incredible." Colby is "a very athletic school" where there are "opportunities for every level of athlete." Outdoor sports are popular year-round, particularly throughout the winter. "Lots of snow. Need I say more?" writes one student. "It's fun, though, [since] the weather provides lots of outdoor activities." As for the school's location, one student let us in on "the best thing about Waterville, Maine—local Karaoke night at the pub in town." Not surprisingly, then, students tend to stay on campus. Fortunately, "life can easily be contained entirely on campus and you will never be bored. There is always something fun going on." Even so, there are those who feel that "we need to integrate students into the surrounding community more, i.e. with more community service projects. We don't have enough contact with locals."

Student Body

Colby undergrads report that the college works hard to increase diversity on campus and should not stop its efforts. "We need to attract kids from a wider range of economic backgrounds," notes one undergrad. However, a sophomore is quick to point out that while "a portion [of the students] are rich, religious, white snobs, the rest are wonderfully adjusting, friendly, and diverse in ideas and beliefs." Students can be "a little too cliquey, but if you catch people on an individual basis, they are usually friendly." Another student agrees, writing, "Everyone here is very approachable. We pride ourselves on it." Students describe their peers as "outgoing and always looking for a good time," though they do admit to being "focused on what is important to them only." As a result, "20 percent of the students here participate in 80 percent of the activities."

ADMISSIONS

Very important factors considered by the admissions committee include: character/personal qualities, secondary school record. *Important factors considered include:* class rank, essays, extracurricular activities, interview, minority status, recommendations, standardized test scores, talent/ability. *Other factors considered include:* alumni/ae relation, geographical residence, state residency, volunteer work, work experience. SAT I or ACT required. TOEFL required of all international applicants. *High school units required/recommended:* 16 total recommended; 4 English recommended, 3 math recommended, 2 science recommended, 2 science lab recommended, 3 foreign language recommended, 2 social studies recommended, 2 elective recommended.

The Inside Word

Colby continues to be both very selective and successful in converting admits to enrollees, which makes for a perpetually challenging admissions process.

FINANCIAL AID

Students should submit: FAFSA and either institutional application or CSS/Financial Aid PRO-FILE with institutional supplement. Regular filing deadline is February 1. The Princeton Review suggests that all financial aid forms be submitted as soon as possible after January 1. *Need-based scholarships/grants offered:* Pell, SEOG, state scholarships/grants, private scholarships, the school's own gift aid. *Loan aid offered:* Direct Subsidized Stafford, Direct Unsubsidized Stafford, Direct PLUS, FFEL Subsidized Stafford, FFEL Unsubsidized Stafford, FFEL PLUS, Federal Perkins, state loans, college/university loans from institutional funds, alternative loans. Federal Work-Study Program available. Institutional employment available. Applicants will be notified of awards on or about April 1. Off-campus job opportunities are fair.

FROM THE ADMISSIONS OFFICE

"Founded in 1813, Colby is one of the nation's oldest and most prestigious independent liberal arts colleges. Colby is known for its diverse and challenging intellectual life, friendly atmosphere, and global reach. On campus, 1,800 students from many different backgrounds and from more than 60 countries live and study together in a vibrant and supportive community. Graduates are well prepared for a broad range of careers or graduate study programs. Colby is recognized as a national leader in undergraduate research and project-based learning, and the quality of the faculty is recognized as the College's greatest asset. The depth of student-faculty interaction and collaboration consistently wins praise from students and alumni. Colby has one of the most ambitious international study programs, with two-thirds of the student body studying abroad at some point in their undergraduate career, and the College maintains an international focus in many of its academic programs. There is a lively interest in political and social activism and volunteer work at Colby, and students get involved in college governance on official boards and committees, including the board of trustees. Colby's 714-acre campus is often cited as one of the nation's most beautiful, and Maine's environment is an ideal setting for the four-year residential college."

For even more information on this school, turn to page 309 of the "Stats" section.

COLGATE UNIVERSITY

13 OAK DRIVE, HAMILTON, NY 13346 • ADMISSIONS: 315-228-7401 • FAX: 315-228-7544
FINANCIAL AID: 315-228-7431 • E-MAIL: ADMISSION@MAIL.COLGATE.EDU • WEBSITE: WWW.COLGATE.EDU

Ratings
Quality of Life: 88   Academic: 92   Admissions: 95   Financial Aid: 82

Academics

Colgate University offers a first-rate undergraduate experience—and with it a well-regarded degree—to its highly intelligent but business-like student body. As one student puts it, "Students here tend to look down on intellectual curiosity." Undergrads here appreciate the value of a good education and realize that they are getting one, praising the "incredible facilities: from classrooms to athletic facilities to the buildings and grounds, this campus is decked out" and professors who "are always more than willing to give extra help, read papers before you turn them in, and offer advice." They also speak highly of the freshman seminar program ("especially great for getting to know your advisor") and the "great abroad program." All Colgate students must complete core courses, "and even these are, for the most part, stimulating." For ambitious students, many opportunities for independent study are available. Sums up one undergrad, "It has the best of two worlds. It has the Greek life [although perhaps not for long; see "Life," below], alumni funding, and academic possibilities of a university, with the charm and community of a small liberal arts school. As scripted as that sounds, it's true."

> **SURVEY SAYS . . .**
> *Frats and sororities dominate social scene*
> *Everyone loves the Red Raiders*
> *Diversity lacking on campus*
> *(Almost) everyone plays intramural sports*
> *Athletic facilities are great*
> *Students don't like Hamilton, NY*
> *Lousy off-campus food*
> *Theater is unpopular*
> *Class discussions encouraged*

Life

Colgate's status as one of the nation's most prestigious party schools ended, perhaps permanently, in the autumn of 2000, when a tragic, alcohol-related automobile accident claimed the lives of four students. Since then, the Colgate administration has aggressively sought to curtail underage drinking and to deter student drunkenness. In an effort to replace the wild parties of the past, "the campus activities staff, the administration, the faculty, etc., are working so hard to try and find alternatives for us. So far this year, we have had speakers come like The Hurricane (Rubin Carter) and Ralph Nader. Tonight we had a comedy group from Chicago. Last weekend, the band Dispatch was here. Although we are in a rural setting, every weekend, there is a concert or other event of some sort taking place." Some warn that "these [events] really aren't attended. These days there is very little for underage students to do on the weekends." Tiny hometown Hamilton offers little ("Well Hamilton, New York, is not quite a bustling town . . . in fact it's not really a town at all") to the chronically bored. Many students occupy their free time with athletics; notes one student, "The fact that students are involved [with] a sport brings everybody together. We all [have to] deal with [balancing] practices and classes."

Student Body

There is most definitely a "Colgate type": explains one of the horde, "Initially, I liked Colgate because I saw so many people who looked a lot like me. However, after three years of attending Colgate, that has come to be one of the aspects about the school that I loathe most. It's a preppy, white-kids-from-New-England kind of place. Khaki pants, white game hats, Jeep Grand Cherokees . . . . Individually, the students at Colgate are great people for the most part. However, all together they are an intimidating crowd." Elaborates another student, "If you are from Long Island, North Jersey, Westchester County [New York], Fairfield County [Connecticut], and like it there, you are in business at Colgate." Students tend to be mostly attractive ("A visiting friend of mine once asked me if Colgate only admits beautiful people. It is true that the vast majority of the students at Colgate are beauty-, health-, and fashion-conscious") and largely monochromatic ("We have black students. Not many though").

ADMISSIONS

Very important factors considered by the admissions committee include: class rank, secondary school record. *Important factors considered include:* character/personal qualities, essays, extracurricular activities, recommendations, standardized test scores, talent/ability, volunteer work, work experience. *Other factors considered include:* alumni/ae relation, geographical residence, minority status. TOEFL required of all international applicants. High school diploma or GED is required. *High school units required/recommended:* 16 total required; 20 total recommended; 4 English required, 3 math required, 4 math recommended, 3 science required, 4 science recommended, 2 science lab required, 3 science lab recommended, 3 foreign language required, 4 foreign language recommended, 2 social studies required, 1 history required, 3 history recommended.

The Inside Word

Like many colleges, Colgate caters to some well-developed special interests. Athletes, minorities, and legacies (the children of alums) are among the most special of interests and benefit from more favorable consideration than applicants without particular distinction. Students without a solid, consistent academic record, beware—the University's wait list leans toward jumbo size.

FINANCIAL AID

Students should submit: FAFSA, CSS/Financial Aid PROFILE, noncustodial (divorced/separated) parent's statement, business/farm supplement. Regular filing deadline is February 1. The Princeton Review suggests that all financial aid forms be submitted as soon as possible after January 1. *Need-based scholarships/grants offered:* Pell, SEOG, state scholarships/grants, private scholarships, the school's own gift aid. *Loan aid offered:* FFEL Subsidized Stafford, FFEL Unsubsidized Stafford, FFEL PLUS, Federal Perkins. Federal Work-Study Program available. Institutional employment available. Applicants will be notified of awards on or about April 1. Off-campus job opportunities are good.

FROM THE ADMISSIONS OFFICE

"Students and faculty alike are drawn to Colgate by the quality of its academic programs. Faculty initiative has given the college a rich mix of learning opportunities that includes a liberal arts core, 50 academic concentrations, and a wealth of Colgate faculty-led, off-campus study programs in the United States and abroad. But there is more to Colgate than academic life, including more than 100 student organizations, athletics and recreation at all levels, and a full complement of living options set within a campus described as one of the most beautiful in the country. A new center for community service builds upon the tradition of Colgate students interacting with the surrounding community in meaningful ways, and an initiative to improve campus culture and social options features a brand-new, state-of-the-art dance club in the heart of downtown Hamilton. For students in search of a busy and varied campus life, Colgate is a place to learn and grow."

For even more information on this school, turn to page 309 of the "Stats" section.

COLLEGE OF MOUNT SAINT VINCENT

6301 RIVERDALE AVENUE, RIVERDALE, NY 10471 • ADMISSIONS: 718-405-3267 • FAX: 718-549-7945
E-MAIL: ADMISSNS@MOUNTSAINTVINCENT.EDU • WEBSITE: WWW.MOUNTSAINTVINCENT.EDU

Ratings
Quality of Life: 77   Academic: 69   Admissions: 63   Financial Aid: 89

Academics

On the banks of the Hudson River in the Riverdale section of the Bronx, the College of Mount Saint Vincent is the temporary home of 1,300 undergrads. "Small size" and "good reputation" are the top reasons that students say they chose CMSV. A liberal arts college, CMSV is run by professors and administrators who "are great at

> **SURVEY SAYS . . .**
> *Very little hard liquor*
> *Students are religious*
> *Diverse students interact*
> *Profs teach upper levels*
> *Theater is unpopular*
> *(Almost) no one listens to college radio*
> *Student publications are ignored*

relating on a personal level." A business major expounds, "Professors are friendly and always willing to help. The administration is readily available and can easily be contacted." The only problem, advises a student, is that "too many professors have a strong accent and are difficult to understand." When it comes time for these undergrads to select a concentration, they choose from 27 majors, 7 pre-professional programs, 5 teacher certificate programs, and 3 certificate programs. Nearly 40 percent of the students leave Mount Saint Vincent with degrees in the health professions or related sciences. And one out of every 20 graduates goes on to pursue a medical degree.

Life

Life "here at the Mount is great," writes a sophomore. Perched in the northernmost borough of America's largest city, Mount Saint Vincent combines a small-school feel with an overwhelming assortment of distractions that are all only a subway ride away. About one-half of the students live on campus, and "the majority of the residents leave on the weekends." One liberal arts major strongly believes that "campus life could be improved." Though campus activities aren't plentiful, they are by no means nonexistent. There are 32 student organizations on campus and 14 Division III athletic clubs. A sophomore offers that she and her friends often "go to different programs held by RAs or clubs." And on those quiet nights, there's nothing wrong with "going out to the local bar or just relaxing."

Student Body

The students at CMSV reflect the multicultural makeup of the city that the college calls home. When a sophomore praises the "good diversity of people" here, he's referring to an undergraduate population that's about 40 percent Caucasian, 26 percent Hispanic, 17 percent African American, and 8 percent Asian. One student notes that people are "a little too grouped by race" in their social circles, but adds that "everyone is friendly" and gets along. A number that some people find a little troubling is the girl-to-guy ratio, which is more than 3:1. (Mostly the female students find this troubling.) Fortunately, they're in a city that provides plenty of fish-in-the-sea to either sex. Many of CMSV's students come from the New York City metropolitan area, and a whopping majority (90 percent) of these students are New York State natives. Whether classmates are from the next neighborhood over, a town in upstate New York, or a different part of the world altogether, it's "an awesome experience meeting them," gushes a communications major. Then he sums up the student body in one word: "Friendly."

ADMISSIONS

Very important factors considered by the admissions committee include: character/personal qualities, recommendations, secondary school record, and standardized test scores. *Important factors considered include:* essays, extracurricular activities, and interview. *Other factors considered include:* alumni/ae relation and class rank. SAT I or ACT required, TOEFL required of all international applicants. High school diploma or GED is required. *High school units required/recommended:* 16 total required; 20 total recommended; 4 English required, 3 math required, 3 math recommended, 2 science required, 1 science lab required, 3 science recommended, 2 foreign language required, 3 foreign language recommended, 3 social studies required, 2 social studies recommended, 3 elective required.

The Inside Word

Mount Saint Vincent does not set terribly high admissions standards, but space is limited at this small school, so candidates are well advised to apply early. Applications are processed on a rolling basis, with decisions rendered within two weeks of submission. The admissions staff at this small school is helpful and attentive.

FINANCIAL AID

Students should submit: FAFSA and state aid form. No deadline for regular filing. The Princeton Review suggests that all financial aid forms be submitted as soon as possible after January 1. *Need-based scholarships/grants offered:* Pell, SEOG, state scholarships/grants, private scholarships, the school's own gift aid, and United Negro College Fund. Merit-based academic scholarship offered. *Loan aid offered:* FFEL Subsidized Stafford, FFEL Unsubsidized Stafford, FFEL PLUS, Federal Perkins, and Federal Nursing. Federal Work-Study Program available. Institutional employment available. Applicants will be notified of awards on a rolling basis beginning on or about March 1. Off-campus job opportunities are good.

FROM THE ADMISSIONS OFFICE

"Overlooking the Hudson River, Mount Saint Vincent's beautiful 70-acre campus is just minutes away from all that New York City offers. With a $40 million building plan underway for the next four years, the College will experience major enhancements in its athletic, residence, and academic facilities and programs.

"The student body is rich in religious, ethnic, and cultural diversity, and a strong sense of community prevails on campus. Small classes, the personal attention the 12:1 student/faculty ratio affords, and an outstanding faculty all provide students with an exceptional learning environment. Leading-edge, quality academic programs include over 60 majors and concentrations to select from, such as business, communications, nursing, and education. Majors in accounting, graphic design, and theatre are planned additions to the curriculum.

"Students take advantage of real-world opportunities and experiences through internships with leading New York businesses like MTV, the NBA, and Merrill Lynch as well as healthcare organizations like Sloan Kettering and New York Hospital. The 32 clubs and organizations, campus radio and TV stations, and several intramural sports offer students many choices for extracurricular activities. In addition, the college has a strong NCAA Division III athletics program, with six men's and nine women's athletic teams, who have averaged two conference championship titles a year over the last decade. A new men's lacrosse team, coached by a three-time All-American, was started in 2002, and new women's lacrosse and men's baseball programs will begin in the spring of 2003."

For even more information on this school, turn to page 310 of the "Stats" section.

THE COLLEGE OF NEW JERSEY

PO Box 7718, Ewing, NJ 08628-0718 • Admissions: 609-771-2131 • Fax: 609-637-5174
Financial Aid: 609-771-2211 • E-mail: admiss@vm.tcnj.edu • Website: www.tcnj.edu

Ratings
Quality of Life: 84   Academic: 84   Admissions: 91   Financial Aid: 80

Academics

For "a price-is-right education with good professors, small class sizes, and extracurricular activities," many are turning to The College of New Jersey, a state liberal arts school "with a lot of potential" that "is just now really starting to expand." While still developing—one manifestation of which is the nonstop construction on campus—the school is already well on its way to "giving the typical college life that one has always

SURVEY SAYS . . .
Lots of beer drinking
Campus easy to get around
Campus is beautiful
(Almost) everyone smokes
Hard liquor is popular
Students are happy
Frats and sororities dominate social scene
Great computer facilities
Students don't like Ewing, NJ
Students don't get along with local community

dreamed about." All the key elements of a great education are here. Classes are "small enough for close attention by professors in class, large enough to constantly meet new people." The school offers "wonderful resources, if you are aware of them. For example, TCNJ has a lot of academic and job placement services that are there, just never utilized by the students." Most important, TCNJ is home to "a lot of smart students" and a faculty who, "on the whole, are available for guidance and help outside of class." Academics are demanding but satisfying here; as one student reported, "I have found that many of my classes have been a lot of work, but that I have come out of them with more knowledge than I would have expected." Students report that "the administration is surprisingly open-minded and constantly exploring new directions for the institution," but warn that day-to-day administrative tasks "often seem very unorganized. . . . You may be sent to a few different departments for the answer to one question."

Life

Most at TCNJ agree that "social life is not as great as you will find in a big college town or a larger school. This is a suitcase college." While "there are parties many weekends at either a fraternity/sorority or sports team house, the scene gets pretty boring pretty quickly," according to many. The biggest party night here, surprisingly, is Tuesday, "because many people don't have any classes on Wednesday until late in the day (12:30–5 is reserved for club meetings, and also sometimes lecturers and things of that nature)." Weekends, in contrast, "can seem kinda desolate." Those who are satisfied with campus life are usually those deeply involved in the Greek scene and student clubs and organizations; as one such student put it, "There are so many great opportunities to take advantage of in terms of organizations and internships!" Sporting events occasionally mobilize the campus, with the annual football game against archrival Rowan the unquestioned highlight of the athletic schedule. "Tailgating for the Rowan game is a must for any fan of football or beer," reports one sports enthusiast. "I know it's not Penn State or anything like that, but it's still a great time." TCNJ's campus is "beautiful, except for the persistent construction." Hometown Ewing, on the other hand, is "lame. It requires some effort to find stuff to do off campus." One suggestion for spicing things up here: "TCNJ should also promote more interaction with other schools such as Rider, which is five miles away, yet I do not know one student from there."

Student Body

The undergrads of TCNJ are "very hardworking and dedicated to academics," but also know how to "maintain a balance between schoolwork and social life." They are an active bunch; explains one undergrad, "Most TCNJ students were involved in high school in something, often a high school sport. So, while the average TCNJ student had a good GPA and SAT score, she was also involved in extracurricular activities." Upon arriving at TCNJ, this student "becomes affiliated with some organization, whether a sorority or fraternity or a student group like government. This student likely wears Abercrombie & Fitch/American Eagle/Gap/Express clothing, [and] is Caucasian and Catholic with a middle- to upper-middle-class background and permanent residence in New Jersey." While the college is "trying to bring kids in from other states and add to the diversity," currently "diversity among the student population is not as great as I think the college would like to brag it is."

ADMISSIONS

Very important factors considered by the admissions committee include: class rank, secondary school record, standardized test scores. *Important factors considered include:* character/personal qualities, essays, talent/ability. *Other factors considered include:* extracurricular activities, minority status, recommendations. SAT I or ACT required; SAT I preferred. TOEFL required of all international applicants. High school diploma or GED is required. *High school units required/recommended:* 18 total required; 4 English required, 3 math required, 3 science required, 4 science recommended, 2 science lab required, 2 foreign language recommended, 2 social studies required, 3 social studies recommended.

The Inside Word

A new name and new-found visibility have given a boost to the applicant pool at The College of New Jersey, but selectivity remains at about the level it has been for the past few years. Since the pool is somewhat better than in prior years, this still translates into a stronger entering class.

FINANCIAL AID

Students should submit: FAFSA. No deadline for regular filing. The Princeton Review suggests that all financial aid forms be submitted as soon as possible after January 1. *Need-based scholarships/grants offered:* Pell, SEOG, state scholarships/grants, private scholarships, the school's own gift aid, Federal Nursing. *Loan aid offered:* Direct Subsidized Stafford, Direct Unsubsidized Stafford, Direct PLUS, Federal Perkins, Federal Nursing, state loans. Federal Work-Study Program available. Institutional employment available. Applicants will be notified of awards on a rolling basis beginning on or about April 1. Off-campus job opportunities are good.

FROM THE ADMISSIONS OFFICE

"Twin lakes form the border of the The College of New Jersey campus, which is set on 289 acres of wooded and landscaped grounds in suburban Ewing Township, New Jersey. TCNJ offers more than 40 baccalaureate degree programs in seven schools: art, media, and music; culture and society; business; education; engineering; nursing; and science. The campus is residential, with nearly two-thirds of the full-time students housed on campus. Classes are small and are all taught by faculty members: there are no graduate teaching assistants. The college is strongly committed to retaining and graduating the students it enrolls. This commitment is reflected in the high return rate of entering students, which has consistently been over 90 percent for the past five years."

For even more information on this school, turn to page 311 of the "Stats" section.

COLLEGE OF THE ATLANTIC

105 EDEN STREET, BAR HARBOR, ME 04609 • ADMISSIONS: 800-528-0025 • FAX: 207-288-4126
FINANCIAL AID: 207-288-5015 • E-MAIL: INQUIRY@ECOLOGY.COA.EDU • WEBSITE: WWW.COA.EDU

Ratings
Quality of Life: 94   Academic: 93   Admissions: 85   Financial Aid: 89

Academics

"It is all about being a better citizen in the world," say the environmentally and politically conscious undergrads of College of the Atlantic, a tiny college whose "strengths include environmental sciences, biology, social sciences, philosophy, and psychology, as well as a tight community [that promotes] intellectual stimulation." COA fosters community spirit and responsibility through its administration, which "is mainly done by committees consisting of students, faculty, and staff, where everyone's opinion counts in decision making." Students love feeling plugged in to the deliberative process and say that the one-for-all approach here also engenders a pervasive feeling of "trust—we don't have locks on our mailboxes, and you can leave your laptop unattended for hours, and it will still be there when you get back." The school allows students "lots of freedom—freedom to take the classes we want, and freedom in those classes to direct our own studies." As one student tells us, "There is so much flexibility here . . . . COA has very few requirements, and they really aren't a big deal." Students praise profs as "energetic and enthusiastic and constantly involved in the students' lives and their learning." Reports one undergrad, "There are posters by each phone on campus, which list the on-campus extension as well as the home phone number of each faculty and staff member. We can call them whenever we need to regarding school, campus committees, and/or personal matters."

> **SURVEY SAYS . . .**
> *Students are cliquish*
> *Very little hard liquor*
> *(Almost) no one smokes*
> *Very little beer drinking*
> *Very little drug use*
> *Students don't get along with local community*
> *Musical organizations aren't popular*

Life

Bar Harbor, COA's hometown, may be the perfect antithesis of a college town; during the summer it's a hopping vacation resort, but during the school year "almost all the stores close up" and students "need to find their own entertainment." Bar Harbor is famous for its bracing winters: "It has been below zero for most of the trimester. It is gray and miserable," notes one undergrad who wishes she were somewhere else. Many here, though, are winter-philes who tout the range of available snow-related activities, which include "skating, cross-country skiing, and snowshoeing." The dearth of in-town options and the small student body combine to create a very subdued campus social scene; "this is not the place for those looking to party, drink, or do lots of drugs (or slack off, for that matter)," explains one student. For fun, "people like cooking together, playing cards, hanging out, going to contra dances, watching movies," and spending as much time outside as they can. Everyone here praises nearby Acadia National Park, "the best backyard a college student could ask for. Finding favorite beautiful hikes, walks, or study spots has become a four-year goal," reports one student. Students party on Tuesdays ("There are no classes on Wednesdays, so Tuesday night is the big social period," explains one student) and on weekends. "Parties are never big, but often fun." Students also want the world to know that "the food is SOOOOO good here! There's no corporate 'food service'—it's just people that work in the kitchen and concoct really tasty (and healthy) food."

Student Body

"Some people think this school is a bunch of granola-eating, flower-child, pot-smoking hippies, but that's not the way it is," reports one COA undergrad. "The typical COA student has a lot of individuality. We're not all cookie-cutter Rastafarians. We're all atypical." Agrees another student, "The COA student tries to be different . . . just like everyone else. There is no 'in' to fit into, just a lot of cliques." Those cliques, students tell us, include "hippies, lobstermen, city kids, trendy people . . . just about every category one could imagine." Students do, on the whole, tend to be "environmentally and socially sensitive" and "liberal in political thought," the type who attend "protests and drive an ancient Volvo or VW with a political bumper sticker and a Darwin fish." "There are quite a few international students, especially from Europe and Asia," at COA, and "they get along well with the rest of the students, but most tend to hang out [primarily] with each other."

ADMISSIONS

Very important factors considered by the admissions committee include: essays, extracurricular activities, interview, recommendations, secondary school record, volunteer work. *Important factors considered include:* character/personal qualities, talent/ability. *Other factors considered include:* alumni/ae relation, class rank, minority status, standardized test scores, work experience. TOEFL required of all international applicants. High school diploma or GED is required. *High school units required/recommended:* 15 total required; 19 total recommended; 4 English required, 4 math required, 2 science required, 3 science recommended, 2 science lab required, 2 foreign language recommended, 2 social studies required, 2 history recommended, 1 elective recommended.

The Inside Word

COA's academic emphasis results in a highly self-selected applicant pool. Fortunately for the college, its focus on human ecology strikes a chord that is timely in its appeal to students. Enrolling here is definitely opting to take an atypical path to higher education. Admissions evaluations emphasize what's on your mind over what's on your transcript, which makes thoughtful essays and an interview musts for serious candidates. It also makes the admissions process a refreshing experience in the relatively uniform world of college admission. The admissions committee includes a few current students who have full voting rights as members.

FINANCIAL AID

Students should submit: FAFSA, institution's own financial aid form, noncustodial (divorced/separated) parent's statement, business/farm supplement. Regular filing deadline is February 15. The Princeton Review suggests that all financial aid forms be submitted as soon as possible after January 1. *Need-based scholarships/grants offered:* Pell, SEOG, private scholarships, the school's own gift aid. *Loan aid offered:* Direct Subsidized Stafford, Direct Unsubsidized Stafford, Direct PLUS, Federal Perkins. Federal Work-Study Program available. Institutional employment available. Applicants will be notified of awards on or about April 1. Off-campus job opportunities are good.

FROM THE ADMISSIONS OFFICE

"College of the Atlantic was created three decades ago at a time when it was becoming evident that conventional education was inadequate for citizenship in our increasingly complex and technical society. The growing interdependence of environmental and social issues and the limitations of academic specialization demanded a wider vision. COA's founders created a pioneering institution dedicated to the interdisciplinary study of human ecology, a college in which students overcome narrow points of view and integrate knowledge across traditional academic lines."

For even more information on this school, turn to page 312 of the "Stats" section.

COLLEGE OF THE HOLY CROSS

ADMISSIONS OFFICE, 1 COLLEGE STREET, WORCESTER, MA 01610-2395 • ADMISSIONS: 508-793-2443
FAX: 508-793-3888 • FINANCIAL AID: 508-793-2265 • E-MAIL: ADMISSIONS@HOLYCROSS.EDU
WEBSITE: WWW.HOLYCROSS.EDU

Ratings

Quality of Life: 83   Academic: 94   Admissions: 92   Financial Aid: 81

Academics

"Academics are very difficult, but very worth the effort" at College of the Holy Cross, a small liberal arts school with "a total sense of community—almost family—just like the admissions propaganda claims." Professors pile on so much work that the school allows students to take only four classes

SURVEY SAYS . . .
Frats and sororities dominate social scene
Beautiful campus
Great library
Diverse students interact
Theater is unpopular
Computer facilities need improving

per semester. Even with this limit, "the work is by all means tough. There's a lot of studying, but it really pays off in the real world." The grading system is equally demanding. Fortunately, HC's stringent standards are well known to the outside world. "A hiring manager from one of the big accounting firms told me the company considers a 3.0 at Holy Cross [equal to] a 3.5 at other schools," explained one student. Students gripe, but they appreciate the results. Wrote one, "I may hate actually being at school, but having Holy Cross on my resume has gotten me a great summer internship, is allowing me to intern in D.C. for the spring semester, and will even indirectly lead into being accepted [by] a reputable law school." They also appreciate the "close personal attention you can receive from professors. I have never had a problem getting extra help from a professor on papers or assignments." This is due in part to the "exclusively undergraduate environment. There are no grad students teaching the classes, and the 'good' professors are also available to everyone, not just upper-level or graduate students." "Active alumni support" further sweetens the deal.

Life

At HC, "everyone works their butt off, but also needs to let off steam. It's a really hard school with very high expectations. The stress can be too much at times." Students "work like mad Sunday through Wednesday" and then start letting off that steam on "Thirsty Thursday," usually at a kegger ("HC is a keg school," students tell us). Alternatives are few. "While the student programming people may put on events that try to bring students together, these events rarely draw many (Spring Weekend and the Opportunity Knocks dance are the exceptions)." Hometown Worcester "does not offer a lot despite the high number of colleges in the area. The city is also not very fond of college students." Nonetheless, a few intrepid souls venture out into the city and report that "dining in Worcester is amazing—many great restaurants. There are usually many choices of things to do here between film series, music performances, theatre, and varsity sports." They warn those who'd follow in their footsteps not to reveal their status as HC students. Undergrads praise their "absolutely gorgeous" campus but warn that its famous picturesque hill "is a real pain in the ass, especially in winter." Intercollegiate athletics, "especially men's and women's basketball teams, are hugely popular," as are intramurals. When escape is essential, students head to Boston or Providence.

Student Body

"There are no surprises" in the Holy Cross student body. "It is a small, private, liberal arts college with a Jesuit identity in New England. Therefore, the population is mostly white, middle class, Irish or Italian Catholics." As one student put it, "A certain type of person, I believe, looks at Holy Cross. This type of person wants a small school in a suburb, with preppy students, small classes, and religion. I am not sure why minorities don't choose Holy Cross; I believe It is because this school just isn't what they want. . . . It is nobody's fault." HC has made some inroads into minority populations through its outreach programs, students here report. The typical HC undergrad is "friendly and outgoing" and conservative. "Religion is big, sports are bigger, and drinking is the biggest." Students like that fact that HC "is a small community, which is nice because you can generally say 'Hi' to anyone and you know them."

ADMISSIONS

Very important factors considered by the admissions committee include: class rank, secondary school record, standardized test scores. *Important factors considered include:* alumni/ae relation, character/personal qualities, essays, extracurricular activities, interview, recommendations. *Other factors considered include:* geographical residence, minority status, talent/ability, volunteer work, work experience. SAT I or ACT required; SAT II also required. TOEFL required of all international applicants. High school diploma or GED is required. *High school units required/recommended:* 20 total recommended; 4 English recommended, 4 math recommended, 4 science recommended, 3 foreign language recommended, 2 social studies recommended, 2 history recommended, 1 elective recommended.

The Inside Word

The applicant pool at Holy Cross is strong; students are well advised to take the most challenging courses available to them in secondary school. Everyone faces fairly close scrutiny here, but as is the case virtually everywhere, the College does have its particular interests. The admissions committee takes good care of candidates from the many Catholic high schools that are the source of dozens of solid applicants each year.

FINANCIAL AID

Students should submit: FAFSA, CSS/Financial Aid PROFILE, noncustodial (divorced/separated) parent's statement, business/farm supplement, parent and student federal tax returns. Regular filing deadline is February 1. The Princeton Review suggests that all financial aid forms be submitted as soon as possible after January 1. *Need-based scholarships/grants offered:* Pell, SEOG, state scholarships/grants, private scholarships, the school's own gift aid. *Loan aid offered:* FFEL Subsidized Stafford, FFEL Unsubsidized Stafford, FFEL PLUS, Federal Perkins, MEFA. Federal Work-Study Program available. Institutional employment available. Applicants will be notified of awards on or about April 3. Off-campus job opportunities are good.

FROM THE ADMISSIONS OFFICE

"When applying to Holy Cross, two areas deserve particular attention. First, the essay should be developed thoughtfully, with correct language and syntax in mind. That essay reflects for the Board of Admissions how you think and how you can express yourself. Second, activity beyond the classroom should be clearly defined. Since Holy Cross is 2,800 students, the chance for involvement/participation is exceptional. The Board reviews many applications for academically qualified students. A key difference in being accepted is the extent to which a candidate participates in-depth beyond the classroom—don't be modest; define who you are."

For even more information on this school, turn to page 312 of the "Stats" section.

COLUMBIA UNIVERSITY

535 WEST 116TH STREET, NEW YORK, NY 10027 • ADMISSIONS: 212-854-2521 • FAX: 212-894-1209
FINANCIAL AID: 212-854-3711 • E-MAIL: UGRAD-ADMISS@COLUMBIA.EDU • WEBSITE: WWW.COLUMBIA.EDU

Ratings
Quality of Life: 84   Academic: 98   Admissions: 99   Financial Aid: 85

Academics

"Academic powerhouse" Columbia University boasts offerings in a staggering array of disciplines, a faculty that includes five Nobel laureates, and one of the nation's few core curricula that students actually love. Even so, "how many schools can boast world-class education and location in the greatest city in the world? One: Columbia." Students here warn that "Columbia truly is hands-off. It's sink or swim, and you are the only person who can help yourself. Advising is minimal and the administration is a celebration of red tape." However, "for the independent-minded student, Columbia is the perfect environment." Central to the CU experience is the Core Curriculum, a sequence that immerses students in western philosophy, literature, and the fine arts. Many here will tell you that the Core "changed my life. It's a great feeling to read something junior year for another class and realize that I know where the ideas originated, and how they progressed." Profs here "are all extremely talented. That doesn't mean they can transmit the material well; in fact, some of them are actually horrible teachers. The exceptions, though, make it all worthwhile." Sums up one undergrad, "You will not have a laid-back, happy-go-lucky type of life at Columbia. Instead of spending your time on sculptured lawns with faculty mapping out the way to go, you will get on a crowded subway, push your way into a door, step over a homeless person, and even if you get tired, you won't be able to rest. Some may think this kind of college experience is terrible. Columbia students are those who think it's the only way to go."

SURVEY SAYS . . .
Students love New York, NY
Campus easy to get around
Great library
Great off-campus food
Ethnic diversity on campus
Campus is beautiful
Campus feels safe
(Almost) everyone smokes
Student newspaper is popular
Political activism is hot

Life

Columbia's campus, a six-block-square plot in the middle of New York's Morningside Heights neighborhood (Harlem is just to the north), includes a surprising amount of open, grassy space for sunbathers and ultimate Frisbee fanatics. Few students linger long on campus when classes and studying are done, however; instead, they set off to explore the overstuffed metropolis that is their home. "One night on the weekends, you might go to a party with friends, a concert on campus, a Columbia-sponsored event; another night, you might go to a Broadway show, a club downtown, a Yankees game." The city provides access to "so many resources and opportunities off-campus. It's wonderful. I found a great internship this summer and since I am only a subway ride away, I can continue to work part-time during the school year." As one student put it, "In my New York City history class, we (150 students) take a bike ride through New York City, leaving campus at 11:00 P.M and returning at 7 in the morning. In my art history class, we go to the Me; in my music class we go to Lincoln Center. Can you easily do this kind of thing at Yale or Harvard? No, you cannot. Yale has New Haven, Harvard has Boston, and Columbia has New York City. Make your choice."

Student Body

Columbia students are "stalwart NYC fans, and support hasn't flagged since 9/11. Students thrive on the city. They don't fear it." Some are from the Big Apple, while many others have merely adopted its mien; they are "very New York: they are not exceedingly polite, but can be; they mind their own business and don't butt into yours; and many are uptight and constantly on the go." These "extremely independent" students can be "hyper-intellectual, high-stress, and snobby"; as one undergrad told us, "Columbia students love being urbane, tortured intellectuals. Superiority complexes run rampant, but most students are like this and thus get along." Diversity is a bragging point for CU. Some here, however, caution that "in terms of a demographic breakdown, Columbia is diverse, but there is far less interaction than one might expect." Conservatives warn that CU "is downright über-liberal . . . . 'Left-wing' is probably an understatement." Agrees one of the pinko masses, "The two Republicans that attend here are burned in effigy fairly frequently."

ADMISSIONS

Very important factors considered by the admissions committee include: character/personal qualities, class rank, essays, recommendations, secondary school record, standardized test scores. *Important factors considered include:* extracurricular activities, talent/ability. *Other factors considered include:* alumni/ae relation, geographical residence, interview, minority status. SAT I or ACT required; SAT II also required. TOEFL required of all international applicants. High school diploma or GED is required. *High school units required/recommended:* 4 math recommended, 4 science recommended, 4 science lab recommended, 4 social studies recommended, 3 elective recommended.

The Inside Word

Columbia's application increases continue to outpace the rest of the Ivy League, and as a result the University keeps moving higher up in the Ivy pecking order. Crime is down in New York City, the football team wins (while still in baby-blue uniforms, no less!), and Columbia has become even more appealing. It's less selective than the absolute cream of the Ivy crop, but offers the advantage of being a bit more open and frank in discussing the admissions process with students, parents, and counselors—refreshing amid the typical shrouds of Ivy mystique.

FINANCIAL AID

Students should submit: FAFSA, institution's own financial aid form, CSS/Financial Aid PROFILE, noncustodial (divorced/separated) parent's statement, business/farm supplement, parent and student income tax returns. Regular filing deadline is February 10. The Princeton Review suggests that all financial aid forms be submitted as soon as possible after January 1. *Need-based scholarships/grants offered:* Pell, SEOG, state scholarships/grants, private scholarships, the school's own gift aid. *Loan aid offered:* FFEL Subsidized Stafford, FFEL Unsubsidized Stafford, FFEL PLUS, Federal Perkins, state loans, college/university loans from institutional funds, alternative loans. Federal Work-Study Program available. Institutional employment available. Applicants will be notified of awards on or about April 1. Off-campus job opportunities are excellent.

FROM THE ADMISSIONS OFFICE

"Located in the world's most international city, Columbia University offers a diverse student body a solid and broad liberal arts curriculum foundation coupled with more advanced study in specific departments."

For even more information on this school, turn to page 313 of the "Stats" section.

CONNECTICUT COLLEGE

270 MOHEGAN AVENUE, NEW LONDON, CT 06320 • ADMISSIONS: 860-439-2200 • FAX: 860-439-4301
FINANCIAL AID: 860-439-2200• E-MAIL: ADMIT@CONNCOLL.EDU • WEBSITE: WWW.CONNCOLL.EDU

Ratings
Quality of Life: 78   Academic: 82   Admissions: 93   Financial Aid: 83

Academics

Students at Connecticut College assert that their professors have "done cool things and they bring those experiences to the classroom." Instructors are approachable and "truly are concerned with our education," and this dedication is complemented by the deans, "who are excellent, understanding people." The small academic setting affords under-

> **SURVEY SAYS . . .**
> *Campus is beautiful*
> *Campus easy to get around*
> *Lots of beer drinking*
> *Hard liquor is popular*
> *Lab facilities are great*
> *(Almost) everyone smokes*
> *Students are happy*
> *Dorms are like palaces*

graduates very personal attention. "In one class, the professor, one of the associate Deans of the college, scheduled a meeting with every student in our 100-plus person class to talk about the take home exam." Another student writes, "Some of my professors are now my personal confidants, and I can go to them for my academic or personal needs." This type of nurturing means that "even though I'm not an exceptional student, [I'm able] to do independent research during my freshman year." Top programs include dance, chemistry, biological sciences, religion, and psychology, and many students also laud the well-organized study abroad programs. In terms of the administration, students comment, "There is supposed to be 'shared governance,' and this is true to a point, but frequently the administration does not consult students on major issues that affect us." The career center receives solid praise, particularly for the variety of "internships that focus on community action, international issues, and the environment."

Life

In general, students at "Conn" feel "pretty pampered" in their "playground for trust-fund babies." The weekend social scene centers largely on alcohol, and several students believe "sometimes it's hard to take part in college activities without being a part of the drinking scene." Those who do indulge "look forward to the huge campus-wide parties, like Festivus or Floralia, which are reason alone to come here—think Woodstock but less hippie." The school organizes Thursday Night Events (TNE's) that draw large numbers of freshmen and sophomores. And an organization called MOBROC (Musicians Organized for Band Rights On Campus), which sets up practice space and a performance venue for campus bands, provides another mainstay of nightlife. ("It's a big deal, but almost underground scene. No other East Coast school has an organization like it.") Alternatives to drinking include "playing out on Harkness Green," attending the "very popular a capella concerts," watching the "amazing student theater productions," "cheering for mediocre sports teams," or venturing in to New London, a town that "takes some time to learn to love."

Student Body

The stereotypical Conn student attended a "fancy boarding school," grew up "just outside Boston," (or somewhere else in New England, New Jersey, or New York) helps to "keep

J.Crew in business," "gets Tiffany's for Christmas," and "drives a Volkswagen with a ski rack on top." Even in this land of self-described WASPs, a few deviants manage to survive, including "our fair share of hippies, punks, straight edge, and D and D magic kids." Reportedly, these atypical students "flock together, just like the rest of the minorities on campus." Many students lament the lack of diversity at Conn, crying, "This is not the real world!" Surveys do point out however, that "a great deal is being done on administrative and student levels to deal with issues of diversity on campus." In the meantime, they content themselves with a "substantial international student population." Some people say the student body is "very supportive of students with differing sexual orientations," while others claim "gays and minorities are segregated." In the end, most students agree, "You basically know everyone on campus, at least by association, [which] makes for a very comfortable, caring environment."

ADMISSIONS

Very important factors considered by the admissions committee include: character/personal qualities, essays, minority status, recommendations, secondary school record. *Important factors considered include:* alumni/ae relation, class rank, standardized test scores, talent/ability. *Other factors considered include:* geographical residence, interview, volunteer work, work experience. SAT II required. TOEFL required of all international applicants. High school diploma or GED is required. *High school units required/recommended:* 4 English recommended, 4 math recommended, 4 science recommended, 2 foreign language recommended, 2 social studies recommended, 3 history recommended, 3 elective recommended.

The Inside Word

Late in 1994, Connecticut became the most recent college to drop the SAT I as a requirement for admission, citing the overemphasis that the test receives from the media and, in turn, students. The college is judicious about keeping their acceptance rate as low as possible. Candidates undergo a rigorous review of their credentials, and should be strong students in order to be competitive. Still, the college's competition for students is formidable.

FINANCIAL AID

Students should submit: FAFSA, CSS/Financial Aid PROFILE, noncustodial (divorced/separated) parent's statement, business/farm supplement, federal tax returns, personal and partnership federal W-2 statements. Regular filing deadline is January 15. The Princeton Review suggests that all financial aid forms be submitted as soon as possible after January 1. *Need-based scholarships/grants offered:* Pell, SEOG, state scholarships/grants, the school's own gift aid. *Loan aid offered:* FFEL Subsidized Stafford, FFEL Unsubsidized Stafford, FFEL PLUS, Federal Perkins. Federal Work-Study Program available. Institutional employment available. Applicants will be notified of awards on or about April 1. Off campus job opportunities are good.

FROM THE ADMISSIONS OFFICE

"Distinguishing characteristics of the diverse student body at this small, highly selective college are honor and tolerance. Student leadership is pronounced in all aspects of the college's administration from exclusive jurisdiction of the honor code and dorm life to active representation on the president's academic and administrative cabinets. Differences of opinion are respected and celebrated as legitimate avenues to new understanding. Students come to Connecticut College seeking opportunities for independence and initiative and find them in abundance."

For even more information on this school, turn to page 313 of the "Stats" section.

COOPER UNION

30 COOPER SQUARE, NEW YORK, NY 10003 • ADMISSIONS: 212-353-4120 • FAX: 212-353-4342
FINANCIAL AID: 212-353-4130 • E-MAIL: ADMISSIONS@COOPER.EDU • WEBSITE: WWW.COOPER.EDU

Ratings
Quality of Life: 80   Academic: 97   Admissions: 99   Financial Aid: 83

Academics

Every student at The Cooper Union for the Advancement of Science and Art gets a full tuition scholarship, undeniably one of the best deals for higher education. Academically, students don't mince words: it's really, really hard. The students of art, architecture, and engineering—Cooper Union offers majors in these three areas only—must survive an "incredibly intense academic atmosphere" in which sleep is rare

> **SURVEY SAYS . . .**
> *Students love New York, NY*
> *Great off-campus food, Dorms are like palaces*
> *Musical organizations aren't popular*
> *Hard liquor is popular*
> *Ethnic diversity on campus, High cost of living*
> *Intercollegiate sports unpopular or nonexistent*
> *Athletic facilities need improving*
> *No one plays intramural sports*
> *Very little beer drinking*

and good grades rarer. Warns one student, "The trick to surviving is knowing what subjects to study and not study for—there simply isn't time to do everything. That and being willing to get a C or even D and accepting that that's just how Cooper is." Notes one engineer, "If you can graduate from this school you can survive anything." Just fulfilling requirements here can be stressful; writes one undergrad, "There is a curriculum for each major, and it's difficult to take electives during the first two years because you have to take the core curriculum first." On the plus side, "the professors at Cooper are excellent and are always ready to give extra help when needed. They are also very fair. The classes are difficult, but everybody struggles together." Students endure, knowing that their programs are "very helpful in terms of finding jobs" and appreciating the fact that "the location in NYC allows many students to hold internships or real jobs during the semester."

Life

Smack dab in the middle of what is arguably America's most exciting and fun city, Cooper Union students struggle to find any time in which to enjoy their surroundings. "Every time a Cooper student plays a game or whatever, he knows he should be studying for a test or doing his calc homework or working on his lab project." Reports another student, "[There are] two kinds of Cooper students: those who go out and those who don't. I would say one out of every four students is interested in a social life. . . . Few actually go out and experience New York City." The tiny campus—actually four buildings in the middle of a busy intersection—"is in the heart of the East Village in New York City. Our campus is our buildings, the streets, traffic lights, crosswalks, and everyone from pointy-haired punks to suit-adorning businesswomen who happen to be walking or sitting or sleeping there." Students feel their extracurricular lives would improve somewhat if Cooper would "offer school housing beyond freshman year since finding an apartment in Manhattan is close to impossible." They also wish the school would "improve its facilities—the buildings are old and dirty"—and add a workout facility.

Student Body

Students report that "The schools of engineering, architecture, and art are VERY separated, each focusing on its own field. Naively speaking, the engineers are dorky, the artists are obtuse, and the architects are recluse. However, there exists a wide range of personalities within each discipline and everyone gets along." Students have a reputation for eccentricity, which some feel is over-hyped; writes one, "There are some really weird people at this school, but overall I think we get a bad wrap. Most of us are normal around here and we mostly get along." Then again, there are also characters like the one this student describes: "One day we discovered that one guy that we all thought was an average Joe was, in fact, a chess prodigy who bet money that he could beat any-one in the school blindfolded and did it with ease. There are lots of people like that at Cooper, peo-ple who work hard on what they're studying but have hidden talents or ideas that are fascinat-ing." Notes one of the relatively few women here, "Due to our extremely large male-female ratio, there is a saying among the girls at Cooper that sums up the student population: The odds are good, but the goods are odd."

ADMISSIONS

Very important factors considered by the admissions committee include: secondary school record, standardized test scores, talent/ability. *Important factors considered include:* essays. *Other factors considered include:* character/personal qualities, extracurricular activities, recommendations, volunteer work, work experience. SAT I or ACT required; SAT I preferred. TOEFL required of all international applicants. High school diploma or GED is required. *High school units required/recommended:* 16 total required; 18 total recommended; 4 English required, 1 math required, 1 science required, 1 social studies required, 1 history required, 8 elective required.

The Inside Word

It is ultra-tough to gain admission to Cooper Union, and will only get tougher. Loads of peo-ple apply here, and national publicity and the addition of dorms have brought even more can-didates to the pool. Not only do students need to have top academic accomplishments but they also need to be a good fit for Cooper's offbeat milieu.

FINANCIAL AID

Students should submit: FAFSA, CSS/Financial Aid PROFILE, state aid form. Regular filing deadline is May 1. The Princeton Review suggests that all financial aid forms be submitted as soon as possible after January 1. *Need-based scholarships/grants offered:* Pell, SEOG, state schol-arships/grants, private scholarships, the school's own gift aid. *Loan aid offered:* FFEL Subsidized Stafford, FFEL Unsubsidized Stafford, FFEL PLUS, Federal Perkins, college/uni-versity loans from institutional funds. Federal Work-Study Program available. Institutional employment available. Applicants will be notified of awards on or about June 1. Off-campus job opportunities are excellent.

FROM THE ADMISSIONS OFFICE

"Each of the three schools, architecture, art, and engineering, adheres strongly to preparation for its profession and is committed to a problem-solving philosophy of education in a unique, scholarship environment. A rigorous curriculum and group projects reinforce this unique atmosphere in higher education and contribute to a strong sense of community and identity in each school. With McSorley's Ale House and the Joseph Papp Public Theater nearby, Cooper Union remains at the heart of the city's tradition of free speech, enlightenment, and entertainment. Cooper's Great Hall has hosted national leaders, from Abraham Lincoln to Booker T. Washington, from Mark Twain to Samuel Gompers, from Susan B. Anthony to Betty Friedan, and more recently, President Bill Clinton."

For even more information on this school, turn to page 314 of the "Stats" section.

CORNELL UNIVERSITY

410 Thurston Avenue, Ithaca, NY 14850 • Admissions: 607-255-5241 • Fax: 607-255-0659
Financial Aid: 607-255-5145 • E-mail: admissions@cornell.edu • Website: www.cornell.edu

Ratings
Quality of Life: 80   Academic: 94   Admissions: 98   Financial Aid: 86

Academics

Ivy League member Cornell boasts a catalog of over 4,000 undergraduate courses, and a top notch faculty to boot. One student boasts "Profs are friendly and approachable." Classes at Cornell are a combination of lectures and sections. Professors teach lectures, and TAs teach sections. And "it's always a pleasant surprise when a TA can speak English." Professor accessibility is also good; as one student notes, "most will give you

> **SURVEY SAYS . . .**
> *Great food on campus*
> *Frats and sororities dominate social scene*
> *Great library*
> *Class discussions are rare*
> *Beautiful campus*
> *Large classes*
> *Campus difficult to get around*
> *Ethnic diversity on campus*
> *Student publications are popular*
> *Musical organizations are hot*

their home number for extra assistance." Most students agree with this sentiment. The hotel school earns high marks from students. And while students have positive feelings about their professors, their opinion of the administration is nearly unanimous. Cornell is "not called 'The Big Red Tape' for nothing." Bear Access, Cornell's computer-based class registration system, "is a nightmare the day classes go open for registration." Switching courses is also a difficult process, and students who attempt to do so find themselves "run[ning] all over campus to accomplish anything." Students complain that the advising system is weak, and "advisors really have no idea what their advisees need to have accomplished for graduation." Supplemental costs are a major sticking point. "Cornell loves to charge fees for whatever it can—Internet, using the gym, buses, parking, cable, many gym classes, printing. You name it, it ain't free." "The general feeling at Cornell is that the undergrads pay for the grad students."

Life

Cornell students work hard all week and "party hard on the weekends." Ithaca is a small but cool town; however, the Greek system corners "the Saturday night entertainment market." The university's mandatory catering rules require all frat parties to be catered by companies "who card people as they come in and give them drinking or nondrinking color-coded wristbands." However, for every "sanctioned" party, there are other unsanctioned parties that "have no qualms about serving alcohol to minors." Some students say that those who don't drink "feel a little bit left out in the cold at times." One student shrugs, "So far, the assumption that students at Ivy League schools drink heavily to ease the pressure of the academic load has proven true." Students enjoy "swimming in the gorges during the summer, traying (on dining hall trays) down the slope during the winter, and going to the mega-grocery store at 2 A.M." Collegetown, which adjoins the campus, "is full of bars, clubs, and cheap eateries with great food." Students also go to the movies in town and take advantage of the many skiing and snowboarding opportunities. Cornell hockey is also extremely popular, and the rink is sold out every year.

Student Body

Cornell's population is "friendly" and "very diverse, not only ethnically, but also in terms of individual personalities, activities, and goals." One student describes his peers as "typical Ivy League students mostly: upper-middle-class suburban kids who have probably never worked in their lives." Different groups of students "tend to interact mostly with members of their own groups." Still, "students for the most part are friendly and open-minded. Pretty much anything goes here." Some complain that their classmates are "cut-throat," especially in the hard sciences, and that engineering students "are hard to get along with."

ADMISSIONS

Very important factors considered by the admissions committee include: essays, extracurricular activities, recommendations, secondary school record, standardized test scores, talent/ability. *Important factors considered include:* class rank. *Other factors considered include:* alumni/ae relation, character/personal qualities, geographical residence, interview, minority status, state residency, volunteer work, work experience. SAT I or ACT required. TOEFL required of all international applicants. *High school units required/recommended:* 16 total required; 4 English required, 3 math required, 3 science recommended, 3 science lab recommended, 3 foreign language recommended, 3 social studies recommended, 3 history recommended.

The Inside Word

Cornell is the largest of the Ivies, and its admissions operation is a reflection of the fairly grand scale of the institution: complex and somewhat intimidating. Candidates should not expect contact with admissions to reveal much in the way of helpful insights on the admissions process, as the university seems to prefer to keep things close to the vest. Only applicants with top accomplishments, academic or otherwise, will be viable candidates. The university is a very positive place for minorities, and the public status presents a value that's hard to beat.

FINANCIAL AID

Students should submit: FAFSA, CSS/Financial Aid PROFILE, noncustodial (divorced/separated) parent's statement, business/farm supplement, prior year's tax forms. Regular filing deadline is February 11. The Princeton Review suggests that all financial aid forms be submitted as soon as possible after January 1. *Need-based scholarships/grants offered:* Pell, SEOG, state scholarships/grants, private scholarships, the school's own gift aid. *Loan aid offered:* Direct Subsidized Stafford, Direct Unsubsidized Stafford, Direct PLUS, FFEL Subsidized Stafford, FFEL Unsubsidized Stafford, FFEL PLUS, Federal Perkins, college/university loans from institutional funds, Key Bank alternative loan. Federal Work-Study Program available. Institutional employment available. Applicants will be notified of awards on or about April 1. Off-campus job opportunities are good.

FROM THE ADMISSIONS OFFICE

"The admissions process at Cornell University reflects the personality of the institution. When students apply to Cornell, they must apply to one of the seven undergraduate colleges. Applications are reviewed within each undergraduate college by individuals who know the college well. Life at Cornell is a blend of college-focused and University activities, and Cornell students participate at both the college and University level. Cornell students can take classes in any of the seven undergraduate colleges and they participate in one of the largest extracurricular/athletics programs in the Ivy League. Prospective students are encouraged to examine the range of opportunities, both academic and extracurricular, at Cornell. Within this great institution, there is a wealth of possibilities."

For even more information on this school, turn to page 315 of the "Stats" section.

DARTMOUTH COLLEGE

6016 McNUTT HALL, HANOVER, NH 03755 • ADMISSIONS: 603-646-2875 • FAX: 603-646-1216
FINANCIAL AID: 603-646-2451 • E-MAIL: ADMISSIONS.OFFICE@DARTMOUTH.EDU • WEBSITE: WWW.DARTMOUTH.EDU

Ratings
Quality of Life: 95   Academic: 98   Admissions: 99   Financial Aid: 87

Academics

There are few schools in North America that can boast the combination of world-class academics and beautiful location that Dartmouth College offers its students. This Ivy-League institution, tucked away in Hanover, New Hampshire, is the home of wonderful, caring professors, who are committed to the academic needs of their students. A sophomore German major speaks for the

> **SURVEY SAYS . . .**
> *Frats and sororities dominate social scene*
> *Great food on campus*
> *Everyone loves the Big Green*
> *Great computer facilities, Campus feels safe*
> *(Almost) no one smokes*
> *Musical organizations are hot*
> *Theater is unpopular*
> *Student publications are popular*
> *(Almost) no one listens to college radio*

majority of students when he writes, "I love Dartmouth because it offers world-class professors who are there because they love to teach." Professors are always accessible, thanks to the Blitz—the campus Internet network—and many students note that they have been invited to their professors' houses for dinner. Students would like too see more study space on campus, though. While the professors are beloved, students don't feel quite the same way about the "draconian" administration. One student writes that the administration "thinks of this school as an advanced placement version of Disney World. You pay, and we hold your hand and kick you out when the park closes." A disheartened senior adds, "Dartmouth's administration has made every effort to destroy a wonderful school. They are attempting to turn Dartmouth into another cookie cutter example of a bland, lifeless university." A more glass-half-full type sophomore provides a little better marketing copy: "Dartmouth's academic experience is unbeatable because it unites a small liberal arts school with all the resources of a top university."

Life

A senior government major reports the concerns of many students: "Students aren't particularly happy with the current administration's attempt to change social life on campus." A history major adds, "The administration likes establishing social guidelines for students even when they [the guidelines] are most often counter to desires or needs." The source of the administration's concerns is the active Greek life, since "frats are the entire social scene." Still, one first-year teetotaler points out, "I was pleasantly surprised to find that [my being such] was not a problem at Dartmouth." Beer pong is one of the most popular intramural sports. A sophomore summarizes campus life: "Dartmouth is the only school that can provide an Ivy League education, the benefits of a small college town, and the cultural and social aspects of a large city without big-city problems." A senior government major asks, "Where else could you attend classes in the morning, spend your afternoons fencing, hiking, or building a snowman, and spend your evenings relaxing with your friends at a coffee house?" While fraternities play a big role in having fun, there are fair amounts of other weekend options. Outdoor activities are a popular recreational alternative in this "beautiful, intimate, and friendly environment." Students hike the Appalachian Trail, play golf, ice skate on local ponds, and ski. One senior engineering major quips, "Sometimes I think Dartmouth has a double role of college and country club."

Student Body

Students genuinely appreciate and respect their peers. Though Dartmouth students work hard, they aren't "cut-throat," as some believe all Ivy Leaguers are. A sophomore beams, "I am continuously surprised at how accomplished, mature, friendly, and fascinating my fellow students are." Despite administration efforts to diversify the student population, it consists of "a standard mix of marginal, pretentious, and extremely intelligent students." A disappointed senior psychology major writes, "There is not very much mixing of racial groups on this campus," and an Asian student adds, "People of different races sit apart from [each] other in [the] food court." Also, a senior computer science major says, "This school is very apathetic in terms of activism and politics. People here come from very privileged backgrounds and so they don't really care about much, except for drinking, academics, and athletics." All in all, students are "cheerful," and "the college is fun, vibrant, and beautiful."

ADMISSIONS

Very important factors considered by the admissions committee include: character/personal qualities, class rank, essays, extracurricular activities, recommendations, secondary school record, standardized test scores. *Important factors considered include:* talent/ability. *Other factors considered include:* alumni/ae relation, geographical residence, interview, minority status, volunteer work, work experience. SAT I or ACT required; SAT II also required. TOEFL required of all international applicants. *High school units required/recommended:* 4 English recommended, 4 math recommended, 4 science recommended, 3 foreign language recommended, 3 social studies recommended.

The Inside Word

Applications for the class of 2006 were up 5 percent from the previous year's totals, making this small-town Ivy more selective in choosing who gets offered a coveted spot in the class. As is the case with those who apply to any of the Ivies or other highly selective colleges, candidates to Dartmouth are up against (or benefit from) many institutional interests that go unmentioned in discussions of appropriate qualifications for admission. This makes an already stressful process even more so for most candidates.

FINANCIAL AID

Students should submit: FAFSA, CSS/Financial Aid PROFILE, noncustodial (divorced/separated) parent's statement, business/farm supplement. The Princeton Review suggests that all financial aid forms be submitted as soon as possible after January 1. *Need-based scholarships/grants offered:* Pell, SEOG, state scholarships/grants, the school's own gift aid. *Loan aid offered:* FFEL Subsidized Stafford, FFEL Unsubsidized Stafford, FFEL PLUS, Federal Perkins, college/university loans from institutional funds. Federal Work-Study Program available. Institutional employment available. Applicants will be notified of awards on or about April 15. Off-campus job opportunities are excellent.

FROM THE ADMISSIONS OFFICE

"Today Dartmouth's mission is to endow its students with the knowledge and wisdom needed to make creative and positive contributions to society. The college brings together a breadth of cultures, traditions, and ideas to create a campus that is alive with ongoing debate and exploration. The educational value of such discourse cannot be underestimated. From student-initiated roundtable discussions that attempt to make sense of world events to the late-night philosophizing in a dormitory lounge, Dartmouth students take advantage of their opportunities to learn from each other. The unique benefits of sharing in this interchange are accompanied by a great sense of responsibility. Each individual's commitment to the Principles of Community ensures the vitality of this learning environment."

For even more information on this school, turn to page 315 of the "Stats" section.

DREW UNIVERSITY

36 MADISON AVENUE, MADISON, NJ 07940-1493 • ADMISSIONS: 973-408-3739 • FAX: 973-408-3068
FINANCIAL AID: 973-408-3112 • E-MAIL: CADM@DREW.EDU • WEBSITE: WWW.DREW.EDU

Ratings
Quality of Life: 87   Academic: 90   Admissions: 89   Financial Aid: 84

Academics

Exciting opportunities abound for undergraduates at Drew University, a small, pretty campus located just 35 miles from midtown Manhattan. Enthuses one student, "The greatest strengths of Drew are the opportunities. We have access to a number of study abroad programs that are both short- and long-term." Another

SURVEY SAYS . . .
Beautiful campus
Students aren't religious
Class discussions encouraged
Athletic facilities are great
Classes are small
Great computer facilities
Diversity lacking on campus

elaborates: "Drew really makes an effort to make sure every student has a study abroad experience, whether it is through a Drew International Seminar that lasts one month, to a semester or year. Drew also has good connections. Because of the close proximity to New York, they are able to offer the 'Wall Street Semester' and the 'Art Semester.' You can also take advantage of the 'U.N. Semester in D.C.' I have never heard a bad review of any of these programs." An "astounding amount of varied internships and job-placement opportunities after graduation" please Drew's largely career-minded student population. Students also appreciate the "phenomenal attention and level of education. The majority of the classes here at Drew are 15 people, so you are constantly interacting with your professor. Basically, you are on a one-on-one basis with people that are experts in the things that they teach. As long as you do your part and exert some effort, it is impossible to do poorly at Drew University." Administrators earn similarly high marks: reports one undergrad, "It is very easy to get an appointment with most of the deans and professors at Drew. The administration is very lenient about things such as academic probation and required leave."

Life

Drew undergrads agree that "Drew doesn't provide enough interesting activities that kids actually want to go to." Explains one undergrad, "Although the student activities board does a great job of planning on-campus events for the week, the weekends can be dead. So many people live close enough that Drew can be called a 'suitcase school'—people are packing up and going home" on the weekends. Hometown Madison doesn't offer much in the way of diversion: the town "isn't right outside your door, and most students don't have cars. There's not much going on in town anyway; it's not really centered on college life." Agrees one student, "The town does not encourage the students to visit their restaurants, stores, and theaters." Fortunately, "New York City is the savior. You cannot complain that there is nothing to do as long as you have ten bucks for train fare." On the upside, students appreciate that "the beauty of the school is incredible. When I first saw campus pictures I was a skeptic, but it is even better than the brochures." Campus speakers, the quality and diversity of whom result from Drew's proximity to a large, international city, are quite popular; notes one student, "Sometimes Drew has speakers on campus that discuss various things, like Buddhism in Japan or African art in Mozambique—stuff like that. Those are popular things to go to and the students enjoy them." Students also like the fact that "there or no frats or sororities, which is wonderful because parties and social gatherings are open to everyone."

Student Body

The "intelligent and hard-working" students of Drew include "a lot of theater students" among the many pre-professionals. Most are Jerseyites "from very rich families, and they act like it." Reports one student, "They all look the same!!! GAP, J.Crew, L.L. Bean. White, white, white. Diversity? Ummm, no! Students are very cliquish." Adds another, "Students here segregate themselves in every way possible. It is amazing how homogeneous the cliques can be . . . . For such a small school, you would think it would force people to interact more." Even so, "there are a lot of nice people here; you just have to really look for them."

ADMISSIONS

Very important factors considered by the admissions committee include: secondary school record. *Important factors considered include:* class rank, standardized test scores. *Other factors considered include:* alumni/ae relation, character/personal qualities, essays, extracurricular activities, interview, minority status, recommendations, talent/ability, volunteer work, work experience. SAT I or ACT required; SAT I preferred. TOEFL required of all international applicants. *High school units required/recommended:* 4 English recommended, 3 math recommended, 2 science recommended, 2 foreign language recommended, 2 social studies recommended, 2 history recommended, 3 elective recommended.

The Inside Word

Drew suffers greatly from the annual mass exodus of New Jersey's college-age residents and a lack of recognition by others. Application totals have increased slightly, but the university must begin to enroll more of its admitted students before any significant change in selectivity will occur. This makes Drew a great choice for solid students, and easier to get into than it should be given its quality.

FINANCIAL AID

Students should submit: FAFSA, CSS/Financial Aid PROFILE. Regular filing deadline is February 15. The Princeton Review suggests that all financial aid forms be submitted as soon as possible after January 1. *Need-based scholarships/grants offered:* Pell, SEOG, state scholarships/grants, private scholarships, the school's own gift aid. *Loan aid offered:* FFEL Subsidized Stafford, FFEL Unsubsidized Stafford, FFEL PLUS, Federal Perkins, state loans. Federal Work-Study Program available. Institutional employment available. Applicants will be notified of awards on or about March 31. Off-campus job opportunities are excellent.

FROM THE ADMISSIONS OFFICE

"At Drew, great teachers are transforming the undergraduate learning experience. With a commitment to teaching, Drew professors have made educating undergraduates their top priority. With a spirit of innovation, they have brought the most advanced technology and distinctive modes of experiential learning into the Drew classroom. The result is a stimulating and challenging education that connects the traditional liberal arts and sciences to the workplace and to the world."

For even more information on this school, turn to page 316 of the "Stats" section.

ELMIRA COLLEGE

ONE PARK PLACE, ELMIRA, NY 14901 • ADMISSIONS: 607-735-1724 • FAX: 607-735-1718
E-MAIL: ADMISSIONS@ELMIRA.EDU • WEBSITE: WWW.ELMIRA.EDU

Ratings
Quality of Life: 78   Academic: 83   Admissions: 78   Financial Aid: 80

Academics

"Most classes are discussion oriented" at this small college in the Finger Lakes region of upstate New York, where professors "make an outstanding effort to get to know each student on a personal level." One undergrad coos, "The faculty are extremely approachable, knowledgeable, excellent teachers." According to some students, however, there are a handful of professors that aren't worth approaching. "Some teachers should get kicked out," suggests a student who's sat across from a few unenthusiastic profs. "If they don't want to teach, they should not." But in the end, the complaints are overridden by the applause. One particularly unique aspect of the curriculum is the mandatory "performing arts program, called Encore, in which [all] students are required to attend 16 performing arts events a year for their first two years. They must also do 60 hours of community service and 240 hours of internship." Elmira also has an innovative calendar that consists of two 12-week terms and a final 6-week block, Term III, during which students study abroad, attend another college, perform fieldwork, conduct lab research, engage in an independent study, or otherwise supplement their education through nontraditional means. Insists one student, "I would not have missed this experience for the world."

> **SURVEY SAYS . . .**
> *Classes are small*
> *Instructors are good teachers*
> *Lousy food on campus*
> *Student publications are popular*
> *School is well run*

Life

While Elmira "is not a party school" and drug use is deterred by "a one strike and you're out" policy, "you can find small parties any night of the week." People "drink a considerable amount" here, reports one student, "although the administration plays it down." When the drinkers aren't mixing cocktails on campus, they'll stroll over to the local bars. These aside, the town of Elmira—described by one student as "a dump," by another as "dull and boring"—doesn't offer much in the way of entertainment. Because the administration keeps "strict" reins on the substance use at Elmira, the college offers an array of alternatives for interested students. For instance, there are "movies on campus every weekend with free admission," as well as "Bingo, talent shows, karaoke," "poetry readings," and "Family Feud, Wheel of Fortune, and other trivia and general knowledge games." The Student Activities Board "also brings in a comedian or other entertainer" every month or so, "and once a year we have a big-name band come to campus, and students get in free." A range of clubs and intramural sports cater to students' individual interests. The mandatory on-campus living draws serious complaints; one student moans, "I think the mightiest injustice this school puts on students is the inability to live off campus, paired with the fact that 90 percent of the housing here is pure crap." Others cite parking as Elmira's major shortcoming; sighs one undergrad, "there is nowhere to park your car at this campus. If you drive, don't bring your car here."

Student Body

"As cheesy as it sounds, as cliché as it may be, I genuinely feel like we are a big family," gushes one student. Many comment on the "friendly atmosphere" that Elmira provides, though there's no question that you'll also find " 'holier than thou' types," "really rich and snobby" students, and "very apathetic" people. In general, students lean toward the "conservative," and "tend to be religious." It also seems that "most everyone is cut from the same Abercrombie mold." This can be a problem for some, like an English major who complains, "I don't fit in with many people here because I'm not a Christian, don't drink, and don't like the Dave Matthews Band." Because many undergrads at Elmira are "middle-upper class" "students . . . from the Northeast," the school could stand some diversity. "A semi-large gay/lesbian population on campus," however, stands as proof that tolerance is not lacking. The we're-all-in-this-together feeling is exactly what Elmira students sense (for better or worse) when they come to campus. The result? "Respect is more common on this campus than in the real world."

ADMISSIONS

Very important factors considered by the admissions committee include: character/personal qualities, class rank, and secondary school record. *Important factors considered include:* alumni/ae relation, essays, extracurricular activities, interview, minority status, recommendations, and standardized test scores. *Other factors considered include:* geographical residence, talent/ability, volunteer work, and work experience. SAT I or ACT required. TOEFL required of all international applicants. High school diploma or GED is required. *High school units required/recommended:* 16 total required; 4 English required, 3 math required, 3 science required, 2 science lab required, 2 foreign language recommended, 3 social studies required, 1 history required, 2 elective required.

The Inside Word

Elmira admissions officers consider the full application package carefully and pay especially close attention to candidates' essays. Notes the admissions office, "The 'fit' between the student and the college is the most important factor." Vegetarians take note: PETA named Elmira one of the nation's 10 most vegetarian-friendly campuses.

FINANCIAL AID

Students should submit: FAFSA and state aid form. No deadline for regular filing. The Princeton Review suggests that all financial aid forms be submitted as soon as possible after January 1. *Need-based scholarships/grants offered:* Pell, SEOG, state scholarships/grants, private scholarships, and the school's own gift aid. *Loan aid offered:* FFEL Subsidized Stafford, FFEL Unsubsidized Stafford, FFEL PLUS, Federal Perkins, and college/university loans from institutional funds. Federal Work-Study Program available. Institutional employment available. Applicants will be notified of awards on a rolling basis beginning on or about February 1. Off-campus job opportunities are good.

For even more information on this school, turn to page 317 of the "Stats" section.

EMERSON COLLEGE

120 BOYLSTON STREET, BOSTON, MA 02116-4624 • ADMISSIONS: 617-824-8600 • FAX: 617-824-8609
FINANCIAL AID: 617-824-8655 • E-MAIL: ADMISSION@EMERSON.EDU • WEBSITE: WWW.EMERSON.EDU

Ratings
Quality of Life: 79   Academic: 75   Admissions: 82   Financial Aid: 84

Academics

"The resources are vast and available" at "funky, offbeat" Emerson College, one of the nation's only four-year colleges devoted exclusively to the study of communications and performing arts. Emersonians tell us they have access to "excellent" computers, "good facilities," and a tremendous internship program, with

> **SURVEY SAYS . . .**
> *Great food on campus, Great library*
> *Lab facilities are great, Theater is hot*
> *Great computer facilities, Beautiful campus*
> *Student government is unpopular*
> *Student publications are ignored*
> *Everyone listens to college radio*
> *Very little beer drinking*

hundreds of positions in Boston, Los Angeles, and other locations in the U.S. and in Europe. Emerson also boasts "great, knowledgeable professors who don't drag on with theory" and who are "always available and willing to go the extra mile" for their passionate students. "Our teachers are, for the most part, struggling artists and writers themselves," notes a writing major. "This makes them especially sympathetic." However, there are also "teachers who don't know how to teach," and "there's too much work." Though Emerson is "not a study school" and "there isn't much book work," the "mostly hands-on" academic life here nevertheless "gets stressful," what with the massive amounts of time consumed by projects and internships. Emerson's administration is "good about allowing for creativity in planning a curriculum" but "red tape is," unfortunately, "everywhere" and "communication among offices is poor for a communications school." Overall, though, "school is fun," according to a satisfied senior. "You come to Emerson to prepare for a career in something you love to do."

Life

In "one word," life at Emerson is "busy." What with "10 billion opportunities," students tell us "the danger here isn't boredom; it's doing too much." Emersonians "may not spend as many hours as a Harvard student hitting the books," but they "get a level of hands-on experience not matched by any other school" and spend a great deal of time "in the video lab editing projects or in rehearsals." "Kids here work 30 to 40 hours per week at real jobs," emphasizes a junior. "Emerson will give you the opportunity to graduate not only with a degree but with a resume." Students are also able to establish "lots of professional contacts" by the time they get their diplomas. Not surprisingly, "social life centers around the arts" and around Boston, America's Great College Town. Emerson is "located in the heart of" Beantown, near Fenway Park, the theater district, and Copley Square. "Living across from Boston Common and the Public Garden is great," and the backdrop provides "a cool, mellow city scene." For the most part, "there's no real campus life. Students go out and do their own thing." Theaters, concerts, clubs, museums, "fabulous restaurants," "pubs," and unparalleled "cultural opportunities" abound. Drug use is more prevalent than drinking here, with marijuana as the opiate of choice, and "everyone—I mean everyone—parties," asserts one student. "That's the reality of college life in Boston." On campus, Emerson has one of the premier college radio stations on the planet.

Student Body

"Picture the strange kid in high school who was really artsy, a little edgy, and had a strange fashion sense. Imagine an entire campus of them and you've got Emerson," says a sophomore. "If you are homosexual, have dyed hair, multiple piercings, and [/or] a creative side, it is the perfect place." Students here range from merely "fairly strange" to "fruity, artsy, atheist, freaky people." You'll find the "brooding, chain-smoking" crowd, "obnoxious theater majors," "zany, artsy types, crazy individualists," and "every color of hair." Though some students here are "sickeningly pretentious," and "everyone wants to be seen in lights," students say theirs is a "very friendly, open environment," "full of creative energy and a solid work ethic." Emersonians are also "very career-oriented" and "enthusiastic about what they are doing." Most "spend every free second rehearsing a monologue, shooting a film, or writing the next Great American Novel." As far as ethnic diversity, "the school prides itself on cultural diversity and a diverse student body but it's 90 percent white," according to a perceptive first-year student.

ADMISSIONS

Very important factors considered by the admissions committee include: secondary school record, standardized test scores. *Important factors considered include:* character/personal qualities, essays, extracurricular activities, recommendations, talent/ability. *Other factors considered include:* alumni/ae relation, class rank, interview, minority status, volunteer work, work experience. SAT I or ACT required. TOEFL required of all international applicants. High school diploma or GED is required. *High school units required/recommended:* 16 total required; 20 total recommended; 4 English required, 3 math required, 3 science required, 3 foreign language required, 3 social studies required, 4 elective recommended.

The Inside Word

Being in Boston does more for Emerson's selectivity than do rigorous admissions standards.

FINANCIAL AID

Students should submit: FAFSA, institution's own financial aid form, CSS/Financial Aid PROFILE, noncustodial (divorced/separated) parent's statement, business/farm supplement, tax returns. The Princeton Review suggests that all financial aid forms be submitted as soon as possible after January 1. *Need-based scholarships/grants offered:* Pell, SEOG, state scholarships/grants, private scholarships, the school's own gift aid. *Loan aid offered:* FFEL Subsidized Stafford, FFEL Unsubsidized Stafford, FFEL PLUS, Federal Perkins, state loans. Federal Work-Study Program available. Institutional employment available. Applicants will be notified of awards on or about April 1. Off-campus job opportunities are excellent.

FROM THE ADMISSIONS OFFICE

"Founded in 1880, Emerson is one of the premier colleges in the United States for the study of communication and the performing arts. Students may choose from over 20 undergraduate majors and 12 graduate programs supported by state-of-the-art facilities and a nationally renowned faculty. The campus is home to WERS 88.9 FM, the oldest noncommercial radio station in New England; the 1,200-seat Emerson Majestic Theatre; and Ploughshares, the award-winning literary journal for new writing. A new 11-story performance and production center houses expanded performance and rehearsal space, a theatre design/technology center, makeup lab, and television studios with editing and control rooms. Located on Boston Common in the heart of the city's Theatre District, the Emerson campus is walking distance from the Massachusetts State House, historic Freedom Trial, Newbury Street shops, financial district, and numerous restaraunts and museums. Emerson's 2,800 undergraduate and 900 graduate students come from over 60 countries and 45 states and territories. There are more than 60 student orginizations and performance groups, 12 NCAA Division III intercollegiate teams, student publications, and honor societies. The college also sponsors programs in Los Angeles, Kasteel Well (The Netherlands), summer film study in Prague, and course cross registration with the six-member Boston ProArts Consortium."

For even more information on this school, turn to page 317 of the "Stats" section.

EMMANUEL COLLEGE

400 THE FENWAY, BOSTON, MA 02115 • ADMISSIONS: 617-735-9715 • FAX: 617-735-9801
E-MAIL: ENROLL@EMMANUEL.EDU • WEBSITE: WWW.EMMANUEL.EDU

Ratings
Quality of Life: 85   Academic: 68   Admissions: 62   Financial Aid: 80

Academics

If you're looking for a small, tight-knit community in the middle of a big, sprawling city, then look no further. With just 700 undergrads, Boston's Emmanuel College provides a liberal arts education in a small-class atmosphere with personal attention from the faculty.

> **SURVEY SAYS . . .**
> *Students are happy*
> *Hard liquor is popular*
> *Students are religious, Classes are small*
> *Students love Boston, Theater is unpopular*
> *Student publications are ignored*

Because professors devote individual attention to each student, "they make you feel important in the classroom." This personalized environment leads students to compare Emmanuel's community to a "small family." Even the administration is close to the student body. "I personally know the dean and president through my involvement on campus, and they are always accessible to me," says a member of student government. On the academic tip, students report that most "courses are challenging," although there simply aren't enough of them. A political science student explains that there are only two full-time professors in her department, which limits the number of courses available: "If I was to enter law school . . . I would be incredibly behind the other students." The programs that garner student praise include biology, business, economics, education, psychology, and writing. If the catalog lacks a course that a student needs, students may take advantage of Emmanuel's membership in the Colleges of the Fenway, a team of schools—also including Massachusetts College of Art, Massachusetts College of Pharmacy and Health Sciences, Simmons College, Wentworth Institute of Technology, and Wheelock College—that cosponsors events and offers students more than 3,000 course options.

Life

When students settle into Emmanuel College, they quickly discover that "Boston is just a gigantic college town," home to Emmanuel and "a zillion other colleges," and rife with every distraction that a college student could dream of. With a campus located in the Fenway—college central of a college city—students have few complaints about social opportunity. "Life in Boston is wonderful," raves a student, pointing to the "museums, bars, and clubs," and "great places to shop"; others list the "great foods," "athletic events, theatre, and the arts" in town. Fenway Park, the Museum of Fine Arts, Symphony Hall, and the well-known Lansdowne Street, Boston's briar patch of dance clubs and concert venues, are all just minutes away. If tranquility is ever in order, students needn't look far; a section of the so-called "Emerald Necklace"—an area of parkland stretching in a six-mile loop—is right across the street from campus. Students also boast that dorms are "comfortable" places where "peace and quiet" can be found. Outside the dorms, students commonly play sports or games "such as Frisbee and baseball." Basketball, in particular, draws school-wide support, especially when the team wins. "We beat NYU!!!" gushes a student about a recent basketball victory. "One of the smallest schools in the country kicked NYU to the curb." Doubtless, a celebration followed, but all debauchery happened far from the court: Emmanuel is a dry campus, so if you're of legal age, you'll have to fill the flask elsewhere.

Student Body

Members of Emmanuel's small community seem to "know each other some way or another" and are always exhibiting their friendliness "with a 'hello' or a smile." One student claims, "I always feel as if I could sit with anyone when I walk into the cafeteria and chat up everyone in the elevator going to class." Aside from being pleasant, students at Emmanuel have traditionally had something else in common: they were all women. All that's changed, though: this fall, the college welcomed men into its fold. Some students are "not thrilled with Emmanuel's decision to go coed," but most seem unfazed. One even admits that "having boys around will give the girls a reason to stay in the dorms. Um . . . ." Moving on to academic aspirations, an undergrad explains, "There is a very defined, motivated group of scholarly students. Everyone wants to go to med or law school after they graduate." But she also concedes that Emmanuel has its stock of "people who do absolutely nothing and get by with 2.0 – 1.0 GPAs, and waste away their college years on Lansdowne Street."

ADMISSIONS

Very important factors considered by the admissions committee include: secondary school record. *Important factors considered include:* essays, interview, recommendations, and standardized test scores. *Other factors considered include:* alumni/ae relation, character/personal qualities, class rank, extracurricular activities, talent/ability, volunteer work, and work experience. SAT I or ACT required. TOEFL required of all international applicants. High school diploma or GED is required. *High school units required/recommended:* 16 total required; 4 English required, 3 math required, 2 science required, 2 science lab required, 2 foreign language required, 2 social studies required.

The Inside Word

Emmanuel admissions officers consider each candidate carefully. The application offers them plenty of information, including two writing samples, extracurricular commitments, and work experience. If you're serious about attending Emmanuel, pay attention to these extras; they could be the difference between admission and rejection.

FINANCIAL AID

Students should submit: FAFSA, institution's own financial aid form, and federal tax returns. The Princeton Review suggests that all financial aid forms be submitted as soon as possible after January 1. *Need-based scholarships/grants offered:* Pell, SEOG, state scholarships/grants, private scholarships, and the school's own gift aid. *Loan aid offered:* Direct Subsidized Stafford, Direct Unsubsidized Stafford, Direct PLUS, Federal Perkins, state loans, MEFA, Nellie Mae Student EXCEL, Signature, CitiAssist, and TERI. Federal Work-Study Program available. Institutional employment available. Applicants will be notified of awards on a rolling basis beginning on or about March 15. Off-campus job opportunities are excellent.

FROM THE ADMISSIONS OFFICE

"Emmanuel College, founded in 1919, prepares men and women with the skills to succeed in tomorrow's world and the social conscience to make a difference in that world. An excellent liberal arts education, shaped by human values and a Catholic heritage, and a strong career development and internship program define the Emmanuel College experience. At Emmanuel, students become engaged learners in small interactive classes and develop leadership skills through participation in campus life. The city of Boston provides an extended classroom, opportunities for community service, and exciting internships with the city's most prestigious, leading-edge employers. And because we recognize the critical importance of information technology, our students have full access to a robust IT network right on campus! A vigorous mind built on an ethical foundation is the hallmark of today's Emmanuel College student."

For even more information on this school, turn to page 318 of the "Stats" section.

EUGENE LANG COLLEGE

65 WEST 11TH STREET, NEW YORK, NY 10011 • ADMISSIONS: 212-229-5665 • FAX: 212-229-5355
FINANCIAL AID: 212-229-8930 • E-MAIL: LANG@NEWSCHOOL.EDU • WEBSITE: WWW.LANG.EDU

Ratings
Quality of Life: 87   Academic: 85   Admissions: 77   Financial Aid: 83

Academics

Like its parent institution, New School University (formerly known as the New School for Social Research), Eugene Lang College has an air of experimentalism about it. Lang was founded in 1978 to extend the New School's tradition as a bastion of free academic inquiry to the undergraduate level. The school demands a large degree of self-sufficiency from its students, imposing only minimal curricular requirements. As one student explains, "Students are treated with respect; there is almost no supervision, so one must take total responsibility for success." Lang's faculty size is necessarily limited by the small student body, but undergraduates can supplement their curricula with courses at other divisions of New School University, including Parsons School of Design, the Adult Division, and the Graduate Faculty for Social and Political Science. They can also cross register at Cooper Union. Sophomores, juniors, and seniors may also take graduate courses at the New School. Students report that "professors are all available for outside help, and small classes are great." Students are less sanguine about the administration, complaining that registration is unduly difficult and that administrators are hard to reach; as one frustrated student put it, "I would think that since we are paying all this money and there are only 500 students in this college that registration and the administration would know what they are doing."

> **SURVEY SAYS . . .**
> *Theater is hot*
> *Students love New York, NY, High cost of living*
> *Student publications are ignored*
> *Great off-campus food*
> *Intercollegiate sports are*
> *unpopular or nonexistent*
> *No one plays intramural sports*
> *Class discussions encouraged*

Life

Lang has no campus to speak of: classrooms are crammed into a single building off the Avenue of the Americas, just above the heart of Greenwich Village in Manhattan. The lack of a true campus, coupled with the seemingly infinite opportunities offered by the city, translate into "no campus life, but that is to be expected because we're in the city." "Our campus is New York City," explains one student, adding that "there is always something to do, museums, galleries, clubs, world-famous restaurants, the greatest shopping, the list is endless." Students enjoy "discounts at almost all museums, opera, and ballet" as well as "incredible access to internships, political organizations, and cultural activities." The downside of all this, of course, is that "it is hard to meet people actually at the school. People go to class and then go home. The school needs to make more programs that make the students interact with classmates." As you might expect, school spirit is practically nonexistent among the student body. Students have no big festivals, no major sporting events to rally around. Even so, most appreciate the situation for what it is; as one student told us, "Hey, we may not have any official sports teams, but we do have the Anarchist Soccer League, which meets once a week in Brooklyn! Now what other college has that?"

Student Body

Lang students "are all very interesting, but that's the biggest problem. Each student represents one of the 'weirdo-individualist' students from their high school. Put a bunch of these students together and you get a lot of social competition to be the 'most' different. Often, it just works out the opposite: the harder they try, the more similar they become." Undergrads share in common "a passion for ideas and the ability to think for ourselves. Students are very articulate and are great people with whom to engage in an impromptu discussion. Lang students are independent and question the status quo (though we might not all agree on what the status quo is and why it should be questioned)." Students are "almost exclusively politically liberal, which gets a little boring after awhile—too much preaching to the choir." Lang students are proud of the diversity of their student body, which ranges over ethnicity, race, gender, and lifestyle.

ADMISSIONS

Very important factors considered by the admissions committee include: essays, recommendations, secondary school record. *Important factors considered include:* character/personal qualities, interview, standardized test scores, talent/ability, volunteer work. *Other factors considered include:* alumni/ae relation, class rank, extracurricular activities, geographical residence, minority status, work experience. SAT I or ACT required. TOEFL required of all international applicants. High school diploma or GED is required. *High school units required/recommended:* 16 total required; 18 total recommended; 4 English required, 3 math recommended, 3 science recommended, 2 foreign language recommended, 3 social studies recommended, 2 history recommended.

The Inside Word

The college draws a very self-selected and intellectually curious pool, and applications are up. Those who demonstrate little self-motivation will find themselves denied.

FINANCIAL AID

Students should submit: FAFSA, state aid form. No deadline for regular filing. The Princeton Review suggests that all financial aid forms be submitted as soon as possible after January 1. *Need-based scholarships/grants offered:* Pell, SEOG, state scholarships/grants, private scholarships, the school's own gift aid. *Loan aid offered:* FFEL Subsidized Stafford, FFEL Unsubsidized Stafford, FFEL PLUS, Federal Perkins, college/university loans from institutional funds. Federal Work-Study Program available. Institutional employment available. Applicants will be notified of awards on a rolling basis beginning on or about March 1. Off-campus job opportunities are good.

FROM THE ADMISSIONS OFFICE

"Eugene Lang College offers students of diverse backgrounds an innovative and creative approach to a liberal arts education, combining stimulating classroom activity of a small, intimate college with rich resources of a dynamic, urban university—New School University. The curriculum at Lang College is challenging and flexible. Class size, limited to fifteen students, promotes energetic and thoughtful discussions and writing is an essential component of all classes. Students design their own program of study within one of five interdisciplinary concentrations in the Social Sciences and Humanities. They also have the opportunity to pursue a five-year BA/BFA, BA/MA, or BA/MST at one of the university's six other divisions. Our Greenwich Village location means that all the cultural treasures of the city—museums, libraries, music, theater—are literally at your doorstep."

For even more information on this school, turn to page 319 of the "Stats" section.

FAIRFIELD UNIVERSITY

1073 NORTH BENSON ROAD, FAIRFIELD, CT 06824 • ADMISSIONS: 203-254-4100 • FAX: 203-254-4199
FINANCIAL AID: 203-254-4125 • E-MAIL: ADMIS@MAIL.FAIRFIELD.EDU • WEBSITE: WWW.FAIRFIELD.EDU

Ratings
Quality of Life: 89   Academic: 79   Admissions: 80   Financial Aid: 84

Academics

With five undergraduate divisions, Fairfield University offers an unusually wide range of academic options to its small student body, and like many Jesuit schools, it manages to do so at a price that nonaffiliated private schools rarely match. Explains one student, "This school has a tremendous amount of academic resources . . . many programs, speakers, and events that are very interesting and intellectual." Another students waxes that "for business students—everything is there," including "great internships." The same student extols the science program, declaring simply that its "professors are awesome." Students report that the workload here is tough but manageable; writes one, "The academic programs are hard enough to be worthwhile, but they don't require a person to study 24/7 to keep a high GPA. It's fair." Professors receive high marks; notes one student, "I never would have imagined a faculty with more diverse thinking and teaching styles." Agrees another, "I have been most impressed with the accessibility and helpfulness of my professors. They are always helpful." The administration "is very accessible, but tends to bounce you around when you have a question—no one knows who has the final say!" Asked to name their school's single strongest suit, most students would agree that "the Jesuit ideals are our strongest points. They are taken seriously, and the quality of education demanded by that tradition is as well."

> **SURVEY SAYS . . .**
> *Lots of beer drinking, Classes are small*
> *Student government is popular*
> *Lousy food on campus, Beautiful campus*
> *Campus easy to get around, Registration is a pain*
> *Diversity lacking on campus*
> *Students don't get along with local community*

Life

Fairfield students "try to balance working hard with playing hard, although the scale is usually tipped a little more" toward the former. Students particularly enjoy recreating at the nearby beach sweeping up from the Long Island Sound, where about 12 percent of students reside in off-campus housing. "We party at the beach! What could be better?" asks one student. Well, town-gown relations, for one. Students agree that "the relationship between the student beach residents and the full-time residents is not good." In response to complaints from the town, the university has stepped up efforts to curtail excessive drinking and unruly behavior. The school "sponsors non-alcoholic events," but these are attended mostly by freshmen. "There is a big emphasis on doing what is 'cool,' and campus events aren't usually considered cool," reports one student. Many students "take the train in to New York City often to see shows or spend time just window shopping." Others "go into New Haven or Norwalk. There's not much to do in the town of Fairfield." Many students are active in community service; writes one, "Fairfield's community service opportunities are unparalleled. If you want to help, Fairfield's the place for you."

Student Body

Students explain that "for years there has been this constant stigma surrounding the typical Fairfield student: the bleach-blonde, Saab-driving, beach-living, Abercrombie-wearing, parent-supported, business major, suburban specimen with his or her nose generally pointed in a skywards direction. While I will not deny that this is a definite type that we have floating about here on this campus, I will say that there are absolutely wonderful students who attend this school. [The] challenge, and this is really not so hard, is to find them." Adds one undergrad, "Some people complain that the student body is rich and spoiled, and much of it is, but that doesn't make us/them bad people." There are "lots of students from New England, especially Massachusetts" and, of course, Fairfield's home state of Connecticut and their border neighbor, New York.

ADMISSIONS

Very important factors considered by the admissions committee include: secondary school record, standardized test scores. *Important factors considered include:* class rank, essays, extracurricular activities, recommendations. *Other factors considered include:* alumni/ae relation, character/personal qualities, geographical residence, interview, minority status, talent/ability, volunteer work, work experience. SAT I or ACT required. TOEFL required of all international applicants. High school diploma is required and GED is not accepted. *High school units required/recommended:* 15 total required; 18 total recommended; 4 English required, 3 math required, 4 math recommended, 3 science required, 4 science recommended, 2 science lab required, 2 foreign language required, 4 foreign language recommended, 3 history required, 4 history recommended, 1 elective required.

The Inside Word

Solid support from Catholic high schools goes a long way toward stocking the applicant pool. Important to note: Steady increases in the number of admission applications has nicely increased selectivity in recent years. Fairfield's campus and central location combined with improvements to the library, campus center, classrooms, athletic facilities, and campus residences make this a campus worth seeing.

FINANCIAL AID

Students should submit: FAFSA, CSS/Financial Aid PROFILE. Regular filing deadline is February 15. The Princeton Review suggests that all financial aid forms be submitted as soon as possible after January 1. *Need-based scholarships/grants offered:* Pell, SEOG, state scholarships/grants, private scholarships, the school's own gift aid. *Loan aid offered:* FFEL Subsidized Stafford, FFEL Unsubsidized Stafford, FFEL PLUS, Federal Perkins, Federal Nursing, state loans, alternative loans. Federal Work-Study Program available. Institutional employment available. Applicants will be notified of awards on or about April 5. Off-campus job opportunities are good.

FROM THE ADMISSIONS OFFICE

"Fairfield University's primary objectives are to develop the creative intellectual potential of its students and to foster in them ethical and religious values and a sense of social responsibility. It also seeks to foster in its students a continuing intellectual curiosity and to develop leaders. As the key to the lifelong process of learning, Fairfield has developed a core curriculum (60 credits) to introduce all students to the broad range of liberal learning. Students choose from 32 majors and 19 interdisciplinary minors. They also have outstanding internship opportunities in Fairfield County and New York City. Fairfield grads wishing to continue their education are highly successful in gaining graduate and professional school admission, while others pursue extensive job opportunities throughout the region. Eighteen Fairfield students have been tapped as Fulbright Scholars in just the past five years."

For even more information on this school, turn to page 319 of the "Stats" section.

FORDHAM UNIVERSITY

441 EAST FORDHAM ROAD, THEBAUD HALL, NEW YORK, NY 10458 • ADMISSIONS: 718-817-4000
FAX: 718-367-9404 • FINANCIAL AID: 718-817-3800 • E-MAIL: ENROLL@FORDHAM.EDU
WEBSITE: WWW.FORDHAM.EDU

Ratings
Quality of Life: 81   Academic: 76   Admissions: 83   Financial Aid: 83

Academics

Fordham University has two campuses: Rose Hill in the Bronx and Lincoln Center in Manhattan. Rose Hill remains a traditional liberal arts and sciences program on a traditional "green lawns and Gothic architecture" campus. Lincoln Center, a "concrete campus," offers a wide range of courses but focuses on media studies, visual arts, and theater. At both campuses, students must complete a "great core curriculum" heavy in the liberal arts before proceeding to their major studies. Students appreciate the benefits of their location, explaining that "Fordham University offers a lot because of its diverse surroundings (the Bronx, New York City). Just by living here you are educated by meeting and seeing new places and things." Professors, who earn high marks, are "strict and difficult but good teachers" and also "humorous and easily accessible. Many are jolly ol' Jesuits who never fail to be passionate about what they teach." The administration is a different story: deans and upper administration receive good grades for being "very involved in the students' lives," but lower-level staff, with whom students more regularly interact, "don't answer student questions or lead you [to] where you can get help. Perhaps they don't know themselves." Still, students feel that the occasional administrative hassle is more than offset by small classes, an excellent library, and overall satisfaction with their academic experience here.

> **SURVEY SAYS . . .**
> *Students love New York, NY*
> *Musical organizations aren't popular*
> *Theater is hot, Classes are small*
> *Dorms are like palaces*
> *Intercollegiate sports are*
> *unpopular or nonexistent*
> *Athletic facilities need improving*
> *Lousy food on campus*

Life

Fordham's two campuses tell a tale of two cities. Rose Hill is located in a working-class Bronx neighborhood. "The boogie-down Bronx is the best," offers one student. "It's a real culture shock for the majority of us who grew up in suburbia." Students are quick to note that both the campus and the immediate area are safe. Among Rose Hill's assets are "a beautiful green campus"; a nearby Little Italy with "great, cheap Italian food"; and easy access to the Botanical Gardens and the Bronx Zoo. Also, the Bronx campus "offers a lot of extracurriculars," writes one student. Reports another, "We have a lot of comedy and music get-togethers. There is always something going on around here." Plus, Rose Hill is only a short subway or bus ride away from Manhattan; many students take advantage of the University Shuttle Service to go between campuses. The other campus is at Lincoln Center, an exclusive area at the heart of Manhattan's West Side. Lincoln Center students have "no real campus." All residential students at Lincoln Center live in a connected campus high-rise and are almost certainly the lowest-income residents of their neighborhood. They report that "New York City provides amazing possibilities. I love to explore Central Park and the Village. Also, the museums are great." The school sits on the south end of the Lincoln Center complex, home to the

New York City Opera and the Metropolitan Opera. Nearby Columbus Avenue provides high-end shopping and many restaurants, some of which, pricewise, are very reasonable.

Student Body

Fordham students "are smart, but they also like to party. Because of the balance most students have, there is a relatively calm atmosphere on campus. Not too much partying, yet not too much stressing over the next exam or paper." Those who choose Fordham "want both a campus community and an independent city life. We all come together for big events, but there can be lulls where nothing seems to be going on." Students are "warm and friendly, but too apathetic" for some, as politics is not a preoccupation of most students here. The student body is "representative of the surrounding population, i.e. Long Island, northern Jersey, and Connecticut." Writes one student, "I feel like the entire population of Long Island goes to school here at times. It's hard to find someone who isn't from New York."

ADMISSIONS

Very important factors considered by the admissions committee include: class rank, secondary school record, standardized test scores. *Important factors considered include:* alumni/ae relation, character/personal qualities, essays, extracurricular activities, interview, recommendations, talent/ability. *Other factors considered include:* geographical residence, minority status, volunteer work, work experience. SAT I or ACT required; SAT II recommended. TOEFL required of all international applicants. High school diploma or GED is required. *High school units required/recommended:* 22 total required; 25 total recommended; 4 English required, 3 math required, 4 math recommended, 3 science required, 4 science recommended, 2 foreign language required, 3 foreign language recommended, 2 social studies required, 3 social studies recommended, 6 elective required.

The Inside Word

Candidates are reviewed by a committee made up of admissions officers, faculty, administrators, and deans. Admission to Fordham is quite competitive and a solid flow of applicants from metropolitan-area Catholic schools keeps their student profile sound.

FINANCIAL AID

Students should submit: FAFSA, CSS/Financial Aid PROFILE, state aid form, noncustodial (divorced/separated) parent's statement, business/farm supplement. The Princeton Review suggests that all financial aid forms be submitted as soon as possible after January 1. *Need-based scholarships/grants offered:* Pell, SEOG, state scholarships/grants. *Loan aid offered:* FFEL Subsidized Stafford, FFEL Unsubsidized Stafford, FFEL PLUS, Federal Perkins. Federal Work-Study Program available. Applicants will be notified of awards on or about April 1. Off-campus job opportunities are excellent.

FROM THE ADMISSIONS OFFICE

"Fordham, an independent institution offering an education in the Jesuit tradition, has three major campuses in the metropolitan New York area. The Rose Hill campus, the largest "green" campus in New York City, is a beautiful 85 acres located next to the New York Botanical Garden and the Bronx Zoo. The Lincoln Center campus is located in the middle of Manhattan across from one of the world's greatest cultural centers, Lincoln Center for the Performing Arts. And in July of 2002, Marymount College in Tarrytown, New York, a women's liberal arts college, will become the 11th school of Fordham. Fordham offers its students a variety of majors, concentrations, and programs that can be combined with an extensive internship program. Fordham works with more than 2,000 organizations in the New York metropolitan area to arrange internships for students in fields such as business, communications, medicine, law and education."

For even more information on this school, turn to page 320 of the "Stats" section.

GODDARD COLLEGE

123 PITKIN ROAD, PLAINFIELD, VT 05667 • ADMISSIONS: 802-454-8311 • FAX: 802-454-1029
FINANCIAL AID: 802-454-8311 • E-MAIL: ADMISSIONS@EARTH.GODDARD.EDU • WEBSITE: WWW.GODDARD.EDU

Ratings
Quality of Life: 94   Academic: 88   Admissions: 73   Financial Aid: 89

Academics

If you loathe the idea of a "traditional school," check out Goddard College, an "artsy, eccentric," "alternative, progressive" school located in rural Vermont where "academic freedom" reigns supreme. At Goddard you can "design" an individual curriculum—"a self-directed, experimental education" if you will—tailored to your own "specific needs." But be warned: "There's no handholding here." The program is "independent, self-directed, and focused." Essentially, "your education is all on you." Classes (called "group studies" in Goddard-speak) are "intriguing and thought-provoking" discussion sessions with "hardly ever more than 10 people." The "open-minded, hip, intellectual" "facilitators"—translation: professors—are "warm and caring and very much a part of the community." There are "no grades or exams, as they interfere with the business of learning." Instead, students receive written evaluations. Also, all students "are a part of the decision making and governance here" and attend "community-based meetings with students/faculty/staff." Suffice it to say, "Goddard is not for everyone" and it has its flaws even for students who thrive in this kind of environment. "The facilities blow," for example, and "the administration is a joke." Nevertheless, students happily declare that Goddard provides a "wonderful, creative, free" atmosphere. "My academic experience has been nothing short of incredible, " boasts a satisfied junior. "I truly love this school."

> **SURVEY SAYS . . .**
> *Political activism is hot*
> *No one cheats*
> *(Almost) everyone smokes*
> *Classes are small*
> *Intercollegiate sports are unpopular or nonexistent*
> *No one plays intramural sports*
> *Very small frat/sorority scene*
> *Class discussions encouraged*
> *Theater is hot*

Life

"Activism, art, punk rock, philosophy, and sex" are all the rage on this tiny campus. Because Goddard is so small, each student has a "tremendous opportunity" to get involved in various activities, including the popular school newspaper, radio station, and Women's Center. Students "go to musical events on campus, hang out in dorms, and spend a lot of time in discussion and debate" as well. Not surprisingly, religious activity is not popular here, although "spiritual" and "pagan clubs" are widely embraced. Community action is vital as well, and each student must work for the college in some constructive way several hours per week. Much campus life is of the "spontaneous" variety. "We held our own Olympics which included streaking, an egg toss, a three-legged race, and other events, followed after dinner by a drag show and lip synch," relates a first-year student. "Parties at Goddard consist of everyone on campus gathering together and getting really drunk." Drug use (especially pot) is profoundly high as well. Skiing trails and plenty of places to hike are nearby, and the quiet and secluded campus feels somewhat disconnected from reality—perhaps too disconnected. Goddard students report that when they "go back to the real world," they have a difficult time assimilating.

Student Body

"The student body consists of all the kids in high school who were alienated because they were weird," making Goddard a leftist paradise which is no doubt "an uncomfortable place for a person with a conservative background." While students at Goddard admit they're "not rocket scientists," they say their campus "is filled with creative, intelligent, and artistic" students "who love life on this planet too much to abandon themselves to the materialism of the modern world." Students call themselves "amazingly unique and creative" and they swear there "is always the potential for enlightening conversations, and connections." The "eclectic" students also say there is "intense diversity of thought" here, as well as "collective ecstasy and depression," but the limited outward diversity ranges "from dirty hippies to even dirtier hippies," as a junior quips.

ADMISSIONS

Very important factors considered by the admissions committee include: character/personal qualities, essays, interview. *Important factors considered include:* talent/ability, volunteer work, work experience. *Other factors considered include:* class rank, extracurricular activities, recommendations, secondary school record, standardized test scores. TOEFL required of all international applicants. High school diploma or GED is required.

The Inside Word

A small applicant pool, the need to have an entering class each year, and a high level of self-selection among candidates makes for Goddard's high acceptance rate. Even though students are not banging down the doors to get into the college, applicants should prepare themselves for a fairly demanding experience. The committee here wants to know a lot about the people who apply, none of which can be supplied in the clean and neat form of transcripts or score reports. This place is not for everyone, and careful self-assessment is the toughest part of the admissions process.

FINANCIAL AID

Students should submit: FAFSA. No deadline for regular filing. The Princeton Review suggests that all financial aid forms be submitted as soon as possible after January 1. *Need-based scholarships/grants offered:* Pell, SEOG, state scholarships/grants, private scholarships, the school's own gift aid. *Loan aid offered:* FFEL Subsidized Stafford, FFEL Unsubsidized Stafford, FFEL PLUS, Federal Perkins, college/university loans from institutional funds. Federal Work-Study Program available. Applicants will be notified of awards on a rolling basis. Off-campus job opportunities are fair.

FROM THE ADMISSIONS OFFICE

"Goddard is a small, coeducational liberal arts college that has an international reputation for appealing to the creative, independent student. Its commitment is to adventurous, capable persons who want to make their own educational decisions and work closely with the faculty. Individually designed programs can be pursued on or off campus."

For even more information on this school, turn to page 321 of the "Stats" section.

GORDON COLLEGE

255 GRAPEVINE ROAD, WENHAM, MA 01984-1899 • ADMISSIONS: 978-927-2300 • FAX: 978-524-3722
E-MAIL: ADMISSIONS@HOPE.GORDON.EDU • WEBSITE: WWW.GORDON.EDU

Ratings
Quality of Life: 79   Academic: 75   Admissions: 71   Financial Aid: 78

Academics

"Gordon attracts students who desire to earn a Christian liberal arts education," sums up one student. But if it's an ethos that attracts them, it's faculty who "are committed to the Lord and have a passion for education" that keep students here; affirms one, "The

> **SURVEY SAYS . . .**
> School is well run
> Very little beer drinking
> Diversity lacking on campus
> Profs teach upper levels
> Classes are small

professors are why I stay at Gordon . . . . They want to see each student succeed and grow not only in academics but as a person as well." Many students appreciate "the integration of faith into" their classes. They also appreciate close and personal interaction with their professors: "When a professor helps you outside the classroom with issues unrelated to class and then tells you they were praying for you, it really means a lot." A freshman conjectures that "after one semester, it seems that the academic rigor will be at a challenging level but not an impossible one." Students' chief concern with the administration stems from a lack of communication between the registrar and the bursar's office, and most believe that many administrative hassles could be avoided if Gordon adopted "online registration and more web-oriented programs." Students would also appreciate more instructional technology in classrooms, and "mandatory chapel attendance" made, well, less mandatory. Otherwise, "Gordon puts an emphasis on Christian life, but trusts its students to make the right decisions by administering helpful guidelines."

Life

Christianity imbues the social lives of Gordon students: "People here are looking for a way to serve God in their everyday lives and do with intelligence as well as heart." Drinking and smoking are forbidden on campus; however, "although it could surprise some people on campus, there are people who drink/take drugs, although most of it is done off campus." Most students, though, find other pastimes: "We love going to the beach that is very close by," and "Gull Pond is the perfect place for walks at any time, especially for late-night stargazing." "Gordon is situated in a wonderful location, close to the North Shore of Massachussets and about half an hour outside Boston," enthuses one student. Gordon may also be single-handedly keeping the local Blockbuster in business; several students report "watching movies with friends" fairly often. Though the T runs into Boston from hometown Wenham, students still cite a need for a car to find any sort of merriment off campus, and many wish for more on-campus activities. A student cautions that "it's very easy to just sit back and wait for the fun to come to you. But it won't." While students request better facilities, "numerous new buildings have been/are being constructed, including a state-of-the-art fine arts center, a music building, and coming soon, a stadium and a brand new science building." A student notes that "there isn't really a casual dating scene—you're either single or attached, no in-betweens," and another complains that "dorm rules are hideous—no boys in the girls' rooms unless the door is open, lights are on, and only during open hall hours."

Student Body

With only about 1,600 students at Gordon, "I easily recognize at least half the faces on campus and have a wide range of friendly acquaintances." Another student feels that "since we are at a Christian school most of us have a lot in common without faith. It brings us together." Women outnumber men at Gordon about two-to-one. Also, "there isn't a lot of diversity—racial or even economic/social—but the administration knows (actually we all know) and we're working on it." But homogeneity has its up side; as one student remarks, "there is very little discrimination in any area because in some ways we are all like-minded."

ADMISSIONS

Very important factors considered by the admissions committee include: character/personal qualities, essays, interview, recommendations, religious affiliation/commitment, secondary school record, and standardized test scores. *Important factors considered include:* class rank. *Other factors considered include:* alumni/ae relation, extracurricular activities, minority status, talent/ability, volunteer work, and work experience. SAT I or ACT required; SAT II recommended. TOEFL required of all international applicants. High school diploma or GED is required. *High school units required/recommended:* 20 total required; 25 total recommended; 4 English required, 2 math required, 3 math recommended, 2 science required, 3 science recommended, 1 science lab required, 3 science lab recommended, 2 foreign language required, 4 foreign language recommended, 2 social studies required, 3 social studies recommended, 5 elective required, 5 elective recommended.

The Inside Word

Interviews are required at Gordon, presumably so admissions officers can gauge candidates' readiness for the rigorous curriculum and high level of religious commitment. Students interested in studying social work must meet a second, more rigorous set of admissions requirements in addition to general requirements.

FINANCIAL AID

Students should submit: FAFSA, CSS/Financial Aid PROFILE, and state aid form. Regular filing deadline is March 1. The Princeton Review suggests that all financial aid forms be submitted as soon as possible after January 1. *Need-based scholarships/grants offered:* Pell, SEOG, state scholarships/grants, private scholarships, and the school's own gift aid. *Loan aid offered:* FFEL Subsidized Stafford, FFEL Unsubsidized Stafford, FFEL PLUS, Federal Perkins, state loans, and college/university loans from institutional funds. Federal Work-Study Program available. Institutional employment available. Applicants will be notified of awards on a rolling basis beginning on or about April 15. Off-campus job opportunities are excellent.

For even more information on this school, turn to page 321 of the "Stats" section.

HAMILTON COLLEGE

198 COLLEGE HILL ROAD, CLINTON, NY 13323 • ADMISSIONS: 800-843-2655 • FAX: 315-859-4457
FINANCIAL AID: 800-859-4413 • E-MAIL: ADMISSION@HAMILTON.EDU • WEBSITE: WWW.HAMILTON.EDU

Ratings
Quality of Life: 89   Academic: 94   Admissions: 92   Financial Aid: 85

Academics

According to a studious junior, Hamilton affords a "grueling but fulfilling education" in a "rigorous yet nurturing" environment. The college "really produces great writers and great thinkers," another student comments, and several respondents highlight the strength of the school's writing program, designed to ensure that graduates

SURVEY SAYS . . .
Registration is a breeze
athletic facilities are great
Classes are small
lots of beer drinking
Students are religious
Political activism is hot
Lots of classroom discussion

can wield the pen as effectively as the institution's namesake, Alexander Hamilton. The college's "very helpful and available" professors conduct classes in a "hands-on" manner and hold students to "very high standards." Luckily, instructors "really communicate the material well" and are always "there for you if you have a problem." The faculty has a reputation for being "eager to meet with students to help prepare for exams or write papers." They also develop camaraderie with their wards: "Only at Hamilton can you go to the pub and have a beer with your professor." Other students concur: "Your teacher is your best friend," and "professors are constantly having entire classes over for dinner." The small classes "concentrate on discussion," which means "you are expected to participate." A music major waxes, "I adore the fact that we call all the professors in our department by their first names." The administration is said to be "exceedingly accessible" as well as "concerned with student opinion and open to suggestions." Hamilton's president holds a weekly "open hour" to meet with students, and most "administrators know student names." In this supportive atmosphere, students aver that "if you have a vision, Hamilton will provide the funding and assistance to [help you] achieve your goals."

Life

For students sometimes it seems that life at Hamilton consists of "nothing but work and alcohol." Students attribute the drinking culture on campus to the fact that "it is always ass-cold winter" in central New York. Although "beer is readily available" and many students say they "drink for fun," a sophomore wants you to know that "drinking isn't compulsory, just common" in Clinton. While some students wish for "more things for people who don't drink to do," others point out "alternatives like movies, dance, theater, comedy, and other low-key activities." Fraternities and sororities are considered "integral" to Hamilton social life, and many students agree that things "would be better if the Greeks still had houses." Others feel that "Greek life is too important," but rest assured, "you can find a party whether you're Greek or not." Students also venture off campus in search of a colder beer. "Three words: The Village Tavern," a senior writes, referring to one of the two bars in town and the scene of many a Hamilton student's fond college memories. Students report that their adopted hometown of Clinton "is the textbook definition of boring," but nonetheless wish for improved town-gown relations. One student notes, "Being isolated on 'the Hill' can sometimes warp students' perception of the real world."

Student Body

Many respondents share the sentiment that "a small percentage of the students account for the Hamilton image of rich, white, and preppy." While the Greek population may be the most visible and "sometimes it seems like everyone is from old-money Greenwich," students emphasize that other types do coexist in Clinton. "The majority of people are friendly, open-minded, and intelligent," and "most people smile, even if they don't know you," contributing to a "nice sense of community." Students note the "homogeneous population" when it comes to race and ethnicity. One junior tells us, "I'm not sure that minorities feel welcome." But others observe, "Hamilton's diversity is increasing. It has come a long way in a few years." According to a senior, "Even though Hamilton is sort of über-whitey land, it's clear that admissions and the administration are trying very hard to diversify the campus."

ADMISSIONS

Very important factors considered by the admissions committee include: class rank, recommendations, secondary school record. *Important factors considered include:* alumni/ae relation, character/personal qualities, essays, extracurricular activities, interview, minority status, standardized test scores. *Other factors considered include:* talent/ability. TOEFL required of all international applicants. *High school units required/recommended:* 16 total recommended; 4 English recommended, 3 math recommended, 3 science recommended, 3 foreign language recommended, 3 social studies recommended.

The Inside Word

Gaining admission to Hamilton is difficult, and would be more so if the college didn't lose many of its shared applicants to competitor schools. The college's position as a popular safety for the top tier of northeastern colleges has always benefited the quality of its applicant pool, but it translates into a tough fight when it comes to getting admits to enroll. Although selectivity has risen significantly of late, Hamilton remains in the position of losing many of its best candidates to other, more prestigious schools. Students who view Hamilton as their first-choice college should definitely make it plain to the admissions committee—such news can often be influential, especially under circumstances like those mentioned here.

FINANCIAL AID

Students should submit: FAFSA, institution's own financial aid form, CSS/Financial Aid PRO-FILE, state aid form, noncustodial (divorced/separated) parent's statement, business/farm supplement, parent and student federal tax returns. Regular filing deadline is February 1. The Princeton Review suggests that all financial aid forms be submitted as soon as possible after January 1. *Need-based scholarships/grants offered:* Pell, SEOG, state scholarships/grants, private scholarships, the school's own gift aid. *Loan aid offered:* FFEL Subsidized Stafford, FFEL Unsubsidized Stafford, FFEL PLUS, Federal Perkins, college/university loans from institutional funds. Federal Work-Study Program available. Institutional employment available. Applicants will be notified of awards on or about April 1. Off-campus job opportunities are fair.

FROM THE ADMISSIONS OFFICE

"One of Hamilton's most important characteristics is the exceptional interaction that takes place between students and faculty members. Whether in class or out, they work together, challenging one another to excel. Academic life at Hamilton is rigorous, and emerging from that rigor is a community spirit based on common commitment. It binds together student and teacher, and stimulates self-motivation, thus making the learning process not only more productive but also more enjoyable and satisfying. Hamilton's Bristol Scholars program is merit-based, offering ten half-tuition scholarships. Both the Bristol and the need-based Schambach Scholars program also offer special research opportunities with faculty on campus. National merit finalists also receive $2,000 a year."

For even more information on this school, turn to page 322 of the "Stats" section.

HAMPSHIRE COLLEGE

ADMISSIONS OFFICE, 893 WEST STREET, AMHERST, MA 01002 • ADMISSIONS: 413-559-5471
FAX: 413-559-5631 • FINANCIAL AID: 413-559-5484 • E-MAIL: ADMISSIONS@HAMPSHIRE.EDU
WEBSITE: WWW.HAMPSHIRE.EDU

Ratings

Quality of Life: 85   **Academic:** 87   **Admissions:** 83   **Financial Aid:** 85

Academics

Independent study and self-designed majors are the norm at Hampshire College, a small Pioneer Valley liberal arts school that "takes you up on your wager that all you need is academic freedom." Hampshire freshmen must complete the recently added First Year Program. ("Actual academic requirements for this year's freshman class have turned Hampshire

> **SURVEY SAYS . . .**
> *Political activism is hot*
> *(Almost) everyone smokes*
> *No one cheats*
> *Campus easy to get around*
> *Great off-campus food*
> *Campus feels safe*
> *Students love Amherst, MA*
> *Lots of beer drinking*

mainstream," gripes one old-timer.) After that, students are pretty much on their own, although they must complete a concentration and an advanced study project. Most students meet the last two requirements through curricula of their own choosing. "Academically, Hampshire is a place where you can do whatever you want, as long as you are able to find a few professors who are willing to work with you on your self-constructed major," explains one student. Although the school is small, students' options are broadened considerably by Hampshire's participation in the Five-College Consortium, which allows students to cross-register at Amherst, Smith, University of Massachusetts, and Mount Holyoke. Some here warn that "Hampshire's academic structure is not for everyone. It's very well suited for people who have a strong idea of what they would like to study, but don't want to squeeze their interests into the confines of traditional majors. It's also good for people who want to explore several interests. . . . However, if you're easily distracted and need someone to point you in a clear, well-defined direction, then Hampshire is probably not the place for you."

Life

"There's not much centralized activity" at Hampshire College, students here agree. As one student put it, "Everything is pretty laid-back and easygoing. People are really into the work they are doing, and they spend a lot of time thinking about that and talking to others about it." While campus is usually quiet, the other four area colleges and the towns of Amherst and Northampton offer all the action most students want. "If you're bored, it's your own fault," writes one undergrad. "The Pioneer Valley is a happening little place. Amherst and Northampton are both funky little college towns with lots to do in nice weather. There's excellent shopping at numerous vintage stores. The Pearl Street nightclub has cheap concerts every week. Ani DiFranco, Carrot Top, BB King, and Sonic Youth have been to Northampton at least once, to name a few." Furthermore, "if you want to escape, you can do that too. There are miles and miles of hiking trails within walking distance of campus, as well as biking trails. I knew that I wasn't going to have a car, so the free bus system was a humongous plus." Activity reaches its lowest ebb "during the long, hard winters." "That's when we start smoking marijuana," explains one student. Campus movies—"Indie, hip-hop, action, anime, classic low camp; we tend to like movies we can laugh with (or at least at)"—are also very popular.

Student Body

The "talented, artistic, quixotic, eccentric, and highly motivated" undergrads of Hampshire include a large group of "those kids in elementary school who were caught trying to dissect the pencil sharpener during math class. We're horrible at following rules." While students like to regard themselves as entirely unique, there is "definitely a stereotype of the pot-smoking, Phish-loving, hippie activist kid at Hampshire, and for the most part, I would say it's true." Critics might accuse these students of being self-absorbed; "I think that's true," agrees one undergrad. "We all spend a ridiculous amount of time thinking about ourselves and what we do, which makes us an incredibly self-aware (if sometimes egocentric) group of people." Politically, "Hampshire students are ultra-liberal. While many would claim that we are an open-minded community because all kinds of lifestyles and ethnic groups are accepted, just try bringing in a conservative speaker to campus and students will be there quicker than the lifespan of a Hollywood marriage to protest, disrupt, and cause mayhem." Students are proud to report that Hampshire is extremely GLBT-friendly.

ADMISSIONS

Very important factors considered by the admissions committee include: essays, recommendations, secondary school record. *Important factors considered include:* character/personal qualities, extracurricular activities, talent/ability. *Other factors considered include:* alumni/ae relation, class rank, interview, minority status, standardized test scores, volunteer work, work experience. TOEFL required of all international applicants. *High school units required/recommended:* 19 total recommended; 4 English recommended, 4 math recommended, 4 science recommended, 2 science lab recommended, 3 foreign language recommended, 2 social studies recommended, 2 history recommended.

The Inside Word

Don Quixote would be a fairly solid candidate for admission to Hampshire. The admissions committee (and it really is one, unlike at many colleges) looks to identify thinkers, dreamers, and the generally intellectually curious. It is important to have a solid record from high school, but high grades only go so far toward impressing the committee. Those who are denied usually lack self-awareness and are fairly poor communicators. Candidates should expect their essays to come under close scrutiny.

FINANCIAL AID

Students should submit: FAFSA, institution's own financial aid form, CSS/Financial Aid PROFILE, noncustodial (divorced/separated) parent's statement. Regular filing deadline is February 1. The Princeton Review suggests that all financial aid forms be submitted as soon as possible after January 1. *Need-based scholarships/grants offered:* Pell, SEOG, state scholarships/grants, private scholarships, the school's own gift aid. *Loan aid offered:* Direct Subsidized Stafford, Direct Unsubsidized Stafford, FFEL PLUS, Federal Perkins. Federal Work-Study Program available. Institutional employment available. Applicants will be notified of awards on a rolling basis beginning on or about April 1. Off-campus job opportunities are fair.

FROM THE ADMISSIONS OFFICE

"Students tell us they like our application. It is less derivative and more open-ended than most. Rather than assigning an essay topic, we ask to learn more about you as an individual and invite your ideas. Instead of just asking for lists of activities, we ask you how those activities (and academic or other endeavors) have shown some of the traits that lead to success at Hampshire (initiative, independence, persistence, for example). This approach parallels the work you will do at Hampshire, defining the questions you will ask and the courses and experiences that will help you to answer them, and integrating your interests."

For even more information on this school, turn to page 323 of the "Stats" section.

HARTWICK COLLEGE

PO Box 4020, ONEONTA, NY 13820-4020 • ADMISSIONS: 888-427-8925 • FAX: 607-431-4138
E-MAIL: ADMISSIONS@HARTWICK.EDU • WEBSITE: WWW.HARTWICK.EDU

Ratings
Quality of Life: 75   Academic: 70   Admissions: 65   Financial Aid: 81

Academics

At Hartwick College, students never have to worry about waiting in line at a computer lab. Why not? Because the price of laptops is "included in the tuition," so when new students arrive on campus, each is presented with his or her own portable computer. "The integration of the laptops in the classes

SURVEY SAYS . . .
Classes are small
Great food on campus
Instructors are good teachers
School is well run
Very little hard liquor

is a strength of school," because it helps students to become comfortable and skilled with up-to-date technology. The professors at Hartwick "range from great to 'Why did they hire that guy'"—though the majority of student opinions land on the "great" side of the fence. "We have a lot of talented professors that care about students learning," says a senior. Profs exhibit their concern for students by holding "BBQs or study sessions at their houses and encouraging home phone calls with any questions." Profs and administrators also encourage students to take advantage of the "many different choices for going abroad." Science students, for instance, can attend specialized programs in the Bahamas, Costa Rica, the Galapagos Islands, Switzerland, the Grand Canyon, and Hawaii. Just eight miles from the main campus, there's also the Pine Lake Environmental Campus, a 920-acre area that provides living laboratories in the forms of deciduous forests, lakes, swamps, and streams. In total, more than 30 majors are available at Hartwick, as well as a handful of special programs, such as the Latin American and Caribbean Studies minor and the museum studies program, and pre-professional programs in engineering, health professions, and law. Despite Hartwick's pros, some students are dubious about the college's claim that it's "a top liberal arts school." As one student comments, "I find that it is not as selective or difficult as the school claims to be in the brochures."

Life

The "small city of Oneonta," in central New York state, is the homeland of Hartwick College. And while Oneonta might not have much to offer in comparison to, say, New York City (which is four hours to the southeast), it does manage to give these students what they crave most: bars. "Pretty much everyone goes out to the bars (underage included) and drinks alcohol," one student tells us. "This is definitely a party school—loads of liquor and a downtown full of bars," says another. Okay, we get the point. But what else is there to do in Oneonta? "The town has all the typical activities like bowling and movies and a little bit of shopping." When the nice weather hits, students like to "play sports outside, sunbathe, and go for walks in the downtown area." The college has many clubs and intercollegiate athletic teams as well as some recreational options, including "comedians and bands and trivia games, etc., etc." And of course, there are the frat parties. While only about 20 percent of the students are members of Greek organizations, they shoulder a large burden for providing on-campus nightlife. And when they throw parties, many students are happy to join in the revelry. If campus life and Oneonta's scene grow old, there's always Albany—just an hour away.

Student Body

Among this student population of about 1,500, "the 'rich kid syndrome' prevails." One student admits, "It can be a difficult transition to make [coming] from a family of lower-middle- to lower-class social status." Difficult, but not impossible—and all in all, "everyone socializes" and "gets along" on the Hartwick campus. In fact, numerous students have described Hartwick as "a very close-knit community." While it's true that "not everyone here is intellectual or way into academics," it's not hard to find "bright students" who are glad to sink their teeth into the challenges of a Hartwick education. And with 30 states and 35 countries represented on the student roster, the undergrads here have the chance to makes friends from all over the globe.

ADMISSIONS

Very important factors considered by the admissions committee include: class rank and secondary school record. *Important factors considered include:* essays, extracurricular activities, and recommendations. *Other factors considered include:* alumni/ae relation, character/personal qualities, geographical residence, interview, minority status, standardized test scores, state residency, talent/ability, volunteer work, and work experience. TOEFL required of all international applicants. High school diploma or GED is required. *High school units required/recommended:* 19 total recommended; 4 English recommended, 3 math recommended, 3 science recommended, 2 science lab recommended, 3 foreign language recommended, 2 social studies recommended, 2 history recommended.

The Inside Word

With stiff area competition from both state universities and more prestigious private colleges, Hartwick cannot afford to be as selective as it would like. The school thus offers a great opportunity to underachievers looking to start over at a challenging liberal arts college.

FINANCIAL AID

Students should submit: FAFSA, institution's own financial aid form, and state aid form. Regular filing deadline is February 1. The Princeton Review suggests that all financial aid forms be submitted as soon as possible after January 1. *Need-based scholarships/grants offered:* Pell, SEOG, state scholarships/grants, private scholarships, and the school's own gift aid. *Loan aid offered:* FFEL Subsidized Stafford, FFEL Unsubsidized Stafford, FFEL PLUS, Federal Perkins, Federal Nursing, and alternative loans. Federal Work-Study Program available. Institutional employment available. Applicants will be notified of awards on or about March 15. Off-campus job opportunities are good.

FROM THE ADMISSIONS OFFICE

"The foundation of a Hartwick education is learning by doing. Students are actively involved in learning, whether it's managing a 'virtual' business, engaging in transcultural nursing in Jamaica, or designing and building environmentally friendly houses on the college's Pine Lake campus. Many Hartwick students conduct research with their professors, sometimes resulting in students co-authoring articles for journals in their disciplines. This hands-on learning helps 96 percent of graduating seniors find jobs or enter graduate or professional school within six months of graduation. Another program unique to Hartwick that leads to the high placement rate in MetroLink. This award-winning annual program takes students to New York, Boston, and Washington D.C. for a weeklong experience in 'shadowing' professionals in those cities. Established Metrolink sites include the Boston Red Sox, Saatchi & Saatchi advertising, the Bronx Zoo, the FBI, and the Smithsonian Institution. Recent full-semester internships have included the National Baseball Hall of Fame, the New York Mets, John Hancock Insurance, the U.S. Congress, and many others."

For even more information on this school, turn to page 324 of the "Stats" section.

HARVARD COLLEGE

BYERLY HALL, 8 GARDEN STREET, CAMBRIDGE, MA 02318 • ADMISSIONS: 617-495-1551 • FAX: 617-495-8821
FINANCIAL AID: 617-495-1581 • E-MAIL: COLLEGE@FAS.HARVARD.EDU • WEBSITE: WWW.FAS.HARVARD.EDU

Ratings
Quality of Life: 94   Academic: 97   Admissions: 99   Financial Aid: 88

Academics

Reputations like Harvard's aren't given to them; they are earned with "unparalleled resources" ("the libraries are great, and my friends who are in the sciences usually have their own desks or offices in the science buildings," writes one student), "excellent professors who definitely do very important things outside of teaching," and a "talented, motivated, unique, brilliant" student body. Students tell us that "the academic experience is amazing. Sitting in an economics class taught by Marty Feldstein . . . is not something that students get to do everywhere." They also warn that "it's humbling to rub shoulders with Nobel laureates and presidential advisors." But don't think anyone caters to your needs alone: "There's no hand-holding. You'd better be an independent, self-motivated type, or else maybe one of those liberal arts schools out in the woods is a better choice." The quality of instruction varies widely; speculates one undergrad, "Profs are an argument for free market economics: in the classes that nobody takes unless they want to they are wonderful. In required classes they go from OK to pathetic." Some advise that while "Harvard is known for the lawyers, doctors, and politicians that come out of it, I have found that if you desire small, personal classes and access to faculty, Harvard is really better for smaller concentrations (majors) since the instruction is equally phenomenal." The administration "is distant and inattentive to students' needs. They can replace you, and don't think they don't know that."

> **SURVEY SAYS . . .**
> *Great library, High cost of living*
> *Registration is a breeze*
> *Students love Cambridge*
> *Great computer facilities*
> *Student government is unpopular*
> *Ethnic diversity on campus*

Life

"Contrary to popular belief," students want you to know, "Harvard is actually a lot of fun." While many people—and nearly all pre-meds—do "nothing but study," others "actually take breaks from studying long enough to down a few beers and hook up." The campus is a cultural hotbed, as "there's always so much going on: plays, concerts, seminars." Parties "are less plentiful," "only occur Thursday through Saturday," and if held in the dorms "end at 1 a.m. (Harvard has a strict policy on that)." However, "it is easy to travel to one of numerous close colleges for parties," or hit the "clubs, bars, and nightlife of Cambridge or Boston." You might also join one of the social clubs (membership by invitation only) "similar to a combination of fraternities and Princeton's eating clubs" that provide some social life, though they are not affiliated with the college. Harvard's "teams are competitive, so if you're an athlete, well, you usually hang out with other athletes." Many students speak highly of campus living quarters; reports one upperclassman, "Freshman year everybody lives in the same general location, The Yard, which is really conducive to meeting people and hanging out and class. Living in the upper class 'houses' is really nice," too.

Student Body

"Everyone here is brilliant," Harvard undergrads report, "and some are very academically competitive. Only come here if you are willing to put up with a fair share of dorks." Because many got here by burying their heads in books, "social graces are very lacking at Harvard. Most people here spent most of high school working hard, so little skills like small talk are not very well developed However, the population is so diverse that you'll no doubt find people that you like to hang out with, and once you get your core group of friends, those are pretty much the only people you'll hang out with for four years." Many note that "there are two types of Harvard people: those who stress too much and those who know the importance of balancing work and play. It's all about that second group." Mixed in among the student body are "a handful of the blue-blooded, prep-school types," but, "on the whole, you will not find a more vibrant, diverse, exciting, and fascinating group of students anywhere in the world."

ADMISSIONS

Very important factors considered by the admissions committee include: character/personal qualities, extracurricular activities, recommendations, secondary school record, talent/ability. *Important factors considered include:* class rank, essays, interview, standardized test scores. *Other factors considered include:* alumni/ae relation, geographical residence, minority status, volunteer work, work experience. SAT I or ACT required; SAT II also required. *High school units required/recommended:* 19 total recommended; 4 English recommended, 4 math recommended, 4 science recommended, 4 foreign language recommended.

The Inside Word

It just doesn't get any tougher than this. Candidates to Harvard face dual obstacles—an awe-inspiring applicant pool and, as a result, admissions standards that defy explanation in quantifiable terms. Harvard denies admission to the vast majority, and virtually all of them are top students. It all boils down to splitting hairs, which is quite hard to explain and even harder for candidates to understand. Rather than being as detailed and direct as possible about the selection process and criteria, Harvard keeps things close to the vest—before, during, and after. They even refuse to admit that being from South Dakota is an advantage. Thus the admissions process does more to intimidate candidates than to empower them. Moving to a common application seemed to be a small step in the right direction, but with the current explosion of early decision applicants and a super-high yield of enrollees, things are not likely to change dramatically.

FINANCIAL AID

Students should submit: FAFSA, CSS/Financial Aid PROFILE, noncustodial (divorced/separated) parent's statement, business/farm supplement, tax returns. No deadline for regular filing. The Princeton Review suggests that all financial aid forms be submitted as soon as possible after January 1. *Need-based scholarships/grants offered:* Pell, SEOG, state scholarships/grants, private scholarships, the school's own gift aid. *Loan aid offered:* Direct Subsidized Stafford, Direct Unsubsidized Stafford, Direct PLUS, Federal Perkins, state loans, college/university loans from institutional funds. Federal Work-Study Program available. Institutional employment available. Applicants will be notified of awards on or about April 1. Off-campus job opportunities are excellent.

FROM THE ADMISSIONS OFFICE

"The admissions committee looks for energy, ambition, and the capacity to make the most of opportunities. Academic ability and preparation are important, and so is intellectual curiosity—but many of the strongest applicants have significant nonacademic interests and accomplishments as well. There is no formula for admission and applicants are considered carefully, with attention to future promise."

For even more information on this school, turn to page 324 of the "Stats" section.

HOBART AND WILLIAM SMITH COLLEGES

639 SOUTH MAIN STREET, GENEVA, NY 14456 • ADMISSIONS: 315-781-3472 • FAX: 315-781-3471
FINANCIAL AID: 315-781-3315 • E-MAIL: HOADM@HWS.EDU • WEBSITE: WWW.HWS.EDU

Ratings
Quality of Life: 82   Academic: 87   Admissions: 86   Financial Aid: 84

Academics

Hobart and William Smith Colleges are separate, single-sex institutions sharing the same campus and classes. In an effort to combine the best aspects of single-sex and coeducational instruction, the schools share classes and even a common faculty, yet maintain separate traditions and coordinate priorities. The effect of this "coordinate education" is particularly prominent at William Smith, the women's school. Acknowledging that women often take a "back seat" at "traditionally male-dominated coeducational colleges," William Smith co-opts the most successful attributes of all-women's colleges, such as self-government and an emphasis on gender studies. According to students at both schools, HWS' chief assets include "small classes and discussion groups" and professors who "are always around to help the students out, giving out e-mail addresses and even home phone numbers and encouraging us to call. They seem to care about the students and want them to do well." Writes one student, "The interaction I've had with the faculty has been extremely helpful and constructive. There is a high expectation in the courses, but the profs are very willing to meet with you [to] help you meet those expectations." Administrators are regarded more ambivalently. While one freshman gushes that "we have administrators who make sure you are adjusting to school easily. They are willing to help if you have any problems," many upperclassmen complain about the administration. Most students, however, feel it's worth enduring some rough spots to be "recognized as an individual, which to me is extremely important. At a large university, I would be recognized as merely a number."

> **SURVEY SAYS . . .**
> Great food on campus
> Everyone loves the Statesmen
> Beautiful campus
> Athletic facilities are great
> Students don't like Geneva, NY
> Theater is unpopular
> Class discussions encouraged

Life

The social scene at HWS runs the whole spectrum from "hanging down town with all the sweet townies to getting drunk or stoned." According to one respondent, "There are two bars that let everyone in. So everyone goes, which means you have to wait 20 minutes before you can get a drink. Either the school should think of better things for us to do or they should build more bars." Plenty of students offered another solution to the situation: "For myself and everyone on campus," writes a typical undergrad, "we have one word for you: fraternities!!!" To its credit, "the school has increased the number of on-campus activities." A typical weekend could include a cold one at the campus pub, taking in a movie at the Friday Flix Series with your main squeeze, or shakin' your booty at the on-campus answer to the Copa Cabana. HWS boasts a "beautiful campus, which is enjoyed by students. People really like the outdoors and will do the craziest things just to have an excuse to be outdoors, like sled downhill on trays from the dining hall." Besides traying, lots of students are involved in athletics, especially lacrosse.

Student Body

Don't come to HWS looking for a melting pot. As one student points out, "I really like a lot of people who go here, but they are all carbon copies of one another." Writes one, "Going to class is like going to a J Crew fashion show and the parking lot is a SAAB dealership." There is "noticeable segregation of the races, particularly in the dining hall. It's a little disturbing." Students also subdivide into "cliques structured along socioeconomic lines, but this does not mean that these groups don't interact with each other." It is clear that cliques, though friendly, are king.

ADMISSIONS

Very important factors considered by the admissions committee include: essays, secondary school record. *Important factors considered include:* character/personal qualities, class rank, extracurricular activities, recommendations, standardized test scores, volunteer work, work experience. *Other factors considered include:* alumni/ae relation, geographical residence, interview, minority status, talent/ability. SAT I or ACT required; SAT I preferred. TOEFL required of all international applicants. High school diploma or GED is required. *High school units required/recommended:* 19 total required; 4 English required, 3 math required, 3 science required, 2 science lab required, 3 foreign language required, 2 social studies required, 2 history required, 4 elective recommended.

The Inside Word

Hobart and William Smith lose a lot of students to their competitors, who are many and strong. This helps open up the gates a bit for more candidates. However, the schools' location, right on Seneca Lake, offers students a great place to study.

FINANCIAL AID

Students should submit: FAFSA, CSS/Financial Aid PROFILE, state aid form, noncustodial (divorced/separated) parent's statement, business/farm supplement, parent's and student's tax return. Regular filing deadline is February 15. The Princeton Review suggests that all financial aid forms be submitted as soon as possible after January 1. *Need-based scholarships/grants offered:* Pell, SEOG, state scholarships/grants, private scholarships, the school's own gift aid. *Loan aid offered:* FFEL Subsidized Stafford, FFEL Unsubsidized Stafford, FFEL PLUS, Federal Perkins. Federal Work-Study Program available. Institutional employment available. Applicants will be notified of awards on or about April 1. Off-campus job opportunities are fair.

FROM THE ADMISSIONS OFFICE

"Hobart and William Smith Colleges seek students with a sense of adventure and a commitment to the life of the mind. Inside the classroom, students find the academic climate to be rigorous, with a faculty that is deeply involved in teaching and working with them. Outside, they discover a supportive community that helps to cultivate a balance and hopes to foster an integration among academics, extracurricular activities, and social life. Hobart and William Smith, as coordinate colleges, have an awareness of gender differences and equality and are committed to respect and a celebration of diversity."

For even more information on this school, turn to page 325 of the "Stats" section.

HOFSTRA UNIVERSITY

ADMISSIONS CENTER, BERNON HALL, HEMPSTEAD, NY 11549 • ADMISSIONS: 516-463-6700
FAX: 516-463-5100 • FINANCIAL AID: 516-463-6680 • E-MAIL: HOFSTRA@HOFSTRA.EDU
WEBSITE: WWW.HOFSTRA.EDU

Ratings
Quality of Life: 70   Academic: 73   Admissions: 76   Financial Aid: 82

Academics

What draws students to Hofstra University, an up-and-coming school located just a half-hour outside New York City, is its "growing academic reputation. It seems everywhere you turn, somebody tells you what a great school Hofstra is." With "good education, law and business majors," "a fine English depart-

> **SURVEY SAYS . . .**
> *Frats and sororities dominate social scene*
> *High cost of living*
> *(Almost) everyone smokes*
> *Students don't get along with local community*
> *Students don't like Hempstead, NY*
> *Students not very happy*
> *Ethnic diversity on campus*

ment," "strong music, drama, film, philosophy, chemistry, and biology departments," and "a really good astronomy observatory," Hofstra boasts a diversity of strengths that larger universities might justifiably envy. And the improvements keep coming: "There's constantly research going on and it's constantly getting better with more students attending. The sports teams are getting better and are getting more recognition, too." Students appreciate the degree of academic freedom accorded them here; as one explains, "Hofstra offers an overwhelming amount of core courses and electives so that students with very specific or very eclectic interests can find something satisfactory." Added bonuses: "It is close to NYC, where there is a great job market," and "alumni heavily support their alma mater." Student complaints center on "long lines" and the perception that some core courses "are mind-numbingly easy."

Life

Hofstra's "beautiful" campus is "an arboretum and a museum, with beautiful flowers, trees, sculptures, and statues lining the sidewalks," offering a pastoral antidote to the bustle outside the school's gates. Campus life offers numerous clubs and organizations such as Hofstra Concerts and Entertainment Unlimited. Athletic facilities are fine and the teams are competitive, if not especially well supported: "It would be great to see more students at games. . . . even for Homecoming, only half the stadium gets filled," complains one student. The Greeks are popular even though they don't have houses; most Greek parties take place in Hofstra USA, the on-campus pub, or in one of the three bars located "just across the street from campus." Those bars are about the only popular sites in hometown Hempstead, which students describe as "a little drab." Fortunately, "the school is only 25 miles away from NYC, so a lot of people like to go there."

Student Body

While the numbers bear out one student's assertion that "there are so many different kinds of people at [Hofstra]; it's very diverse," there is still a widely held perception that "at Hofstra, you see a lot of the typical 'Long Island Kids': Gucci, Armani, stilettos in the middle of December, Beemers . . . the whole deal." Many report that the dividing line runs between the school's resident and commuter populations; as one residential student puts it, "Campus students and commuting students are like fire and ice. The campus students are fun-loving and rowdy . . . . There is always laughing and random acts of craziness going on." Undergrads on both sides of the divide agree that "if you don't have a clique, it is 10 times harder to make friends." Writes one undergrad, "Students tend to stay in their own groups, especially the Greeks. When push comes to shove, though, the students do come together."

ADMISSIONS

Very important factors considered by the admissions committee include: class rank, recommendations, secondary school record, standardized test scores. *Important factors considered include:* character/personal qualities, essays, extracurricular activities, interview, talent/ability. *Other factors considered include:* volunteer work, work experience. TOEFL required of all international applicants. High school diploma or GED is required. *High school units required/recommended:* 16 total required; 4 English required, 2 math required, 3 math recommended, 1 science required, 3 science recommended, 1 science lab required, 2 foreign language required, 3 social studies required, 4 social studies recommended, 4 elective required. Prospective engineering majors need at least 4 years of mathematics, 1 year of chemistry, and 1 year of physics.

The Inside Word

Hofstra wants to be national, and has positioned itself very well with impressive facilities, appealing program offerings, solid athletic teams, and an effective national ad campaign. As a result, Hofstra's current student profile has increased dramatically. Presently, Hofstra is a solidly competitive regional university; it is a school to watch in the future.

FINANCIAL AID

Students should submit: FAFSA, state aid form. The Princeton Review suggests that all financial aid forms be submitted as soon as possible after January 1. *Need-based scholarships/grants offered:* Pell, SEOG, state scholarships/grants, private scholarships, the school's own gift aid. *Loan aid offered:* FFEL Subsidized Stafford, FFEL Unsubsidized Stafford, FFEL PLUS, Federal Perkins, college/university loans from institutional funds. Federal Work-Study Program available. Institutional employment available. Applicants will be notified of awards on a rolling basis beginning on or about March 1. Off-campus job opportunities are excellent.

FROM THE ADMISSIONS OFFICE

"Hofstra's first priority is excellence in teaching. Faculty are experts in their fields, accessible to students, and committed to providing a stimulating education. Classes are small, yet students have extensive choices, including more than 110 majors. Eligible students may enroll in Honors College, which provides additional opportunities for the most academically qualified students. Great emphasis is placed on the role of students in the life of the University. Hofstra's educational offerings are verified by prestigious national accreditations in business, law, education, journalism, and engineering among others, as well as the only chapter of Phi Beta Kappa at a private university on Long Island. The Hofstra libraries are computerized and contain 1.6 million volumes or equivalents. The libraries, and most of the campus, are wired to a computer network allowing immediate access to information, including the Hofstra Online Information System, which provides students quick access to their academic records. The campus has theaters, art galleries, an accredited museum, an FCC-licensed FM radio station, an on-campus television station, a variety of restaurants, an Olympic-size indoor pool, and extensive recreational facilities. Several housing options are provided in on-campus residence halls and off-campus apartments. Students have access to a beauty salon, post office, nightclub, and entertainment center on campus. Hofstra's beautiful campus, just 25 miles from Manhattan, is located on 250 acres designated as an arboretum. A new state-of-the-art facility for the School of Education and Allied Human Services will open this fall. Call 1-800-HOFSTRA to schedule an Admission Information session, which are available Monday through Saturday."

For even more information on this school, turn to page 326 of the "Stats" section.

HOUGHTON COLLEGE

PO Box 128, HOUGHTON, NY 14744 • ADMISSIONS: 800-777-2556 • FAX: 716-567-9522
E-MAIL: ADMISSIONS@HOUGHTON.EDU • WEBSITE: WWW.HOUGHTON.EDU

Ratings

Quality of Life: 75   Academic: 78   Admissions: 71   Financial Aid: 76

Academics

To a large degree, the Houghton identity is forged by its interest in "Christ, his teachings, and how to integrate them into your life." In the classrooms, professors combine "faith and learning," and in so doing, they show students how to integrate these two things into

> **SURVEY SAYS . . .**
> *Very little hard liquor*
> *No one watches intercollegiate sports*
> *Very little beer drinking*
> *Students are religious*
> *Classes are small*

their own everyday lives. At this upstate New York college, 1,200 students benefit from professors who "are available whenever we have a question that pertains to class [or] to life" in general. Professors also promote a sense of teamwork that some of their pupils pick up on: "Students are always willing to help each other in their academic difficulties and beyond," boasts one undergrad. Others think that cooperation isn't anything to count on: "There is a lot of competition scholastically," and when the group projects end it may seem that "students here are only concerned with themselves." With 35 majors to choose from, Houghton's students can focus on traditional subjects like history and chemistry, or delve into faith-oriented majors such as Bible studies, church ministries, or education ministries. While Houghton's most popular majors are education, biology, and psychology, some believe that music is where Houghton really shines. The fact that recent Houghton grads have gone on to the Eastman School of Music in Rochester—one of the nation's premier music institutions—is a testament to the program.

Life

Welcome to the western reaches of upstate New York. You'll notice that as well as being 75 minutes from both Buffalo and Rochester, Houghton's not far from a lake, a river, a few state parks, and a ski area. So it's no surprise that students at Houghton find much of their fun in the great outdoors. "We go to see the amazing falls and beauty of Letchworth State Park and to swim in the great trout waters of Wiscoy Creek," writes one student, while another mentions the phat "snowboarding or sledding" in the winter. A robust outdoor recreation department leads student trips out into the wilderness, too. Life on campus has its ups and downs. "The campus activity board tries to bring things here because there is nothing to do in town. They bring in movies that are playing in the theatres, and they have concerts here all the time." In fact, because "a lot of people are musically inclined," listening to and playing music are common pastimes. Houghton's equestrian program is another draw for students. The 386-acre equestrian center is a horse-rider's dream, with pens, stalls, pastures, an indoor arena, an outdoor arena, and a stadium. On the downside, campus regulations leave students crying, "They need to make the rules less strict!" Drugs and alcohol are prohibited, and using either raises the specter of the "possibility of expulsion."

Student Body

Houghton College draws much of its small student body from New York State, and almost 90 percent of its enrolled students are white. Unsurprisingly, there's a certain uniformity in

Houghton's student body that engenders a "very high-school-like" vibe. "Students can be extremely fake" and "very judgmental," writes an undergrad. But another counters that despite the "tendency to be fake," the majority of Houghton's students are "very nice, caring people." Many argue that "the greatest strength of Houghton is the Christian atmosphere." Others, however, suggest that putting more emphasis on diversity could improve things dramatically.

ADMISSIONS

Very important factors considered by the admissions committee include: character/personal qualities, class rank, religious affiliation/commitment, and secondary school record. *Important factors considered include:* essays, recommendations, and standardized test scores. *Other factors considered include:* alumni/ae relation, extracurricular activities, interview, minority status, talent/ability, volunteer work, and work experience. SAT I or ACT required. TOEFL required of all international applicants. High school diploma is required and GED is accepted. *High school units required/recommended:* 16 total are recommended; 4 English recommended, 3 math recommended, 2 science recommended, 2 science lab recommended, 2 foreign language recommended, 1 social studies recommended, 2 history recommended.

The Inside Word

Houghton is a deeply Christian evangelical school. Students not committed to proselytizing will not be happy here. Admissions counselors know that and will block the applications of those who, in their view, are "bad fits" with the college.

FINANCIAL AID

Students should submit: FAFSA and institution's own financial aid form. No deadline for regular filing. The Princeton Review suggests that all financial aid forms be submitted as soon as possible after January 1. *Need-based scholarships/grants offered:* Pell, SEOG, state scholarships/grants, private scholarships, and the school's own gift aid. *Loan aid offered:* FFEL Subsidized Stafford, FFEL Unsubsidized Stafford, FFEL PLUS, Federal Perkins, college/university loans from institutional funds, and private alternative loans. Federal Work-Study Program available. Institutional employment available. Applicants will be notified of awards on a rolling basis beginning on or about March 15. Off-campus job opportunities are fair.

FROM THE ADMISSIONS OFFICE

"Since 1883, Houghton College has provided a residential educational experience that integrates high-quality academic instruction with the Christian faith. Houghton is selective in admission, attracting a very capable student body from 25 countries and 40 states. The college receives widespread national recognition for the quality of its student profile, faculty, and facilities. Enrolling 1,200 full-time students, Houghton is located on a beautiful 1,300-acre campus in western New York. The college's campus includes a 386-acre equestrian center as well as cross-country and downhill ski trails. Houghton's campus combines classic-style architecture with state-of-the-art technology and facilities, including a campuswide computer network and Internet access. All first-year students and transfers receive laptop computers and printers. Houghton's traditional liberal arts curriculum offers more than 40 majors and programs. Numerous study abroad programs are available, including Houghton's own offerings in Tanzania, Australia, and London. The First-Year Honors Program offers highly qualified students the opportunity to study in England during the second semester of their first year with 25 of their peers and two Houghton faculty members. There is a strong pre-professional orientation, with 30 to 35 percent of graduates moving on to graduate or professional school upon graduation. Houghton alumni can be found teaching at 175 colleges and universities around the United States and abroad."

For even more information on this school, turn to page 326 of the "Stats" section.

ITHACA COLLEGE

100 Job Hall, Ithaca, NY 14850-7020 • Admissions: 607-274-3124 • Fax: 607-274-1900
Financial Aid: 607-274-3131 • E-mail: admission@ithaca.edu • Website: www.ithaca.edu

Ratings
Quality of Life: 74   Academic: 76   Admissions: 83   Financial Aid: 80

Academics

Students identify several standout programs at Ithaca College, the "other school" in the tiny upstate New York town. (It also happens to be home to Cornell University.) Music, theater, physical therapy, and communication (the latter of which "offers four years of hands-on experience, whereas most colleges only offer two years") are considered the finest the school has to offer. On these programs, students heap lavish praise. Writes one, "I absolutely love it here at IC. I mentioned that I was interested in becoming a drama therapist, and the school was more than helpful with arranging a double major. They even went above and beyond and helped me set up a drama therapy program, which I run at a local retirement home." Offers another, "As a music major, I am very pleased with my professors. Their knowledge in their field is impressive; they are very approachable and teach well. As for my liberal arts classes, I'm not as impressed. I've had a few excellent professors, but most seem about average." Students agree that "the professors are the best part of school. They are really here to help us learn, and the school puts value on hiring teachers that are good at teaching." They also report that "the school administration is a good one. However, there is a lot of bureaucracy to get anything done."

> **SURVEY SAYS . . .**
> *Students love Ithaca, NY*
> *Student government is popular*
> *Lots of beer drinking, Great off-campus food*
> *Student publications are popular*
> *Great computer facilities*
> *Very small frat/sorority scene*
> *Musical organizations are hot*
> *Diversity lacking on campus*
> *Lab facilities need improving*

Life

In a nutshell, "life at Ithaca is a college student's dream." Students proclaim that "there are plenty of things to do. Since the town houses two colleges, fun and unique bars and coffeehouses are around every hilly corner. The wine trails are always fun, and swimming and hiking around the 'gorge'ous waterfalls is practically a tradition. Lake Cayuga is fun to boat on, and certain festivals held in the Commons, like the popular Apple Harvest Festival, are sure to bring everyone (both locals and students) downtown together." Adds another undergrad, "The Ithaca Commons are an awesome place to go shopping or to find a huge array of good food, from all-American to more exotic cuisine. And the city has tons of culture (think plays, concerts, art galleries, and seminars in cooking, dancing, etc.)." Students report "a large amount of drinking that goes on here, but there are other things to do besides [that]." Students love athletics ("People are very interested in participating in sports, both intercollegiate and intramural") and outdoor activity ("The campus is located in some of the most beautiful nature to be found east of the Mississippi"). Despite IC's proximity to Cornell, "there isn't as much mingling between the two colleges as one might expect. Relations between the two are okay, but they could be better. They think of IC as the party school on the other hill; we think of them as a bunch of nerds that have no lives." Students can escape when necessary to more exotic locales, as they "are only hours away from Niagara Falls, Boston, Philadelphia, and New York City."

Student Body

Ithaca draws its students from a relatively small demographic, according to student respondents. "If you are not from Massachusetts, Long Island, or New Jersey, you will not fit in," warns one. "Many so-called 'snobs' [attend], but an okay amount of friendly people too." Students recognize that there is religious diversity here—"about one-third Jewish, one-third Catholic, and one-third Protestant"—and report that "as far as discrimination, it is not seen at Ithaca College. There is an especially large homosexual community that is very accepted by all, including a month of Gaypril to celebrate diversity." Students in the school's premier departments are considered serious and studious; others "have a social life as their primary focus instead of academics."

ADMISSIONS

Very important factors considered by the admissions committee include: secondary school record, standardized test scores. *Important factors considered include:* character/personal qualities, class rank, essays, extracurricular activities, interview, recommendations, talent/ability. *Other factors considered include:* alumni/ae relation, volunteer work, work experience. SAT I or ACT required. TOEFL required of all international applicants. High school diploma or GED is required. *High school units required/recommended:* 16 total required; 4 English required, 3 math required, 3 science required, 2 foreign language required, 3 social studies required, 1 elective required.

The Inside Word

Ithaca has enjoyed a renaissance of interest from prospective students of late, and its moderately competitive admissions profile has been bolstered as a result. In addition to a thorough review of academic accomplishments, candidates are always given close consideration of their personal background, talents, and achievements. Programs requiring an audition or portfolio review are among the college's most demanding for admission; the arts have always been particularly strong here.

FINANCIAL AID

Students should submit: FAFSA. CSS/Financial Aid PROFILE is required of early decision applicants and must be submitted by November 1. The Princeton Review suggests that all regular financial aid forms be submitted as soon as possible after January 1. *Need-based scholarships/grants offered:* Pell, SEOG, state scholarships/grants, private scholarships, the school's own gift aid. *Loan aid offered:* FFEL Subsidized Stafford, FFEL Unsubsidized Stafford, FFEL PLUS, Federal Perkins, college/university loans from institutional funds. Federal Work-Study Program available. Institutional employment available. Applicants will be notified of awards on a rolling basis beginning on or about March 15. Off-campus job opportunities are good.

FROM THE ADMISSIONS OFFICE

"Ithaca College was founded in 1892 as a music conservatory and today continues that commitment to performance and excellence. Its modern, residential, 750-acre campus, equipped with state-of-the-art facilities, is home to the Schools of Business, Communications, Health Sciences and Human Performance, Humanities and Sciences, and Music. With more than 100 majors –from biochemistry to business administration, journalism to jazz, philosophy to physical therapy, and with upper-division programs in Rochester, Los Angeles, and London—students get the curricular opportunities of a large university in a personalized smaller college environment. Ithaca's students benefit from an education that emphasizes hands-on learning, collaborative student-faculty research, and development of the whole student. Located in central New York's spectacular Finger Lakes region in what many consider the classic college town, Ithaca College offers 25 highly competitive varsity teams, more than 140 campus clubs, and two radio stations and a television station, as well as hundreds of concerts, recitals, and theater performances annually."

For even more information on this school, turn to page 327 of the "Stats" section.

KEENE STATE COLLEGE

229 MAIN STREET, KEENE, NH 03435 • ADMISSIONS: 603-358-2276 • FAX: 603-358-2767
E-MAIL: ADMISSIONS@KEENE.EDU • WEBSITE: WWW.KEENE.EDU

Ratings
Quality of Life: 78   Academic: 71   Admissions: 67   Financial Aid: 77

Academics

According to one student who attends Keene State College, a public liberal arts institution in the heart of New England, its top feature is "the support it offers to every student who needs it, especially academically." A unique

> **SURVEY SAYS . . .**
> *Diversity lacking on campus*
> *Classes are small*
> *Students don't get along with local community*
> *Very little hard liquor*

example of KSC's supportive approach is Aspire, a program for first-generation college students. Aspire offers services such as individualized tutoring, study-skills workshops, and academic advising. An Aspire participant tells us that the program is among the "things that have made my college life easier." The "small classes" at Keene State make the learning environment more inviting as well. "The professors are always available for outside help or assistance," and the students who take advantage of this availability rave about the personal feel of the school. (But beware, says a student. A number of professors "are dull . . . and seemingly rather unintelligent.") Of the 40 or so undergrad majors offered at Keene State, education and psychology rank near the top in terms of popularity and reputation. But not everyone is primed to take advantage of the academic opportunities here. "Students don't take their educations seriously," grumbles a disappointed student. And because "standards are fairly low" in some corners of campus, slackers are able to slide by without exercising many brain cells.

Life

Keene State's campus shines with "its beauty and its facilities," as "the city and the campus are both well cared for and tasteful." One chemistry major paints this picture for us: "The main road through campus is pedestrian only; there's a beautiful arch at the beginning; trees everywhere, the grassy quad, the hills in the distance, the history of some of the buildings." Social life on this picturesque campus is not dead by any means. "On weekends I have to say I go out and drink," says a student, "but who doesn't?" Another explains, "There is always a party to go to . . . whether a fraternity party or an off-campus party." Greek life is alive here in southern New Hampshire, with about 10 participating organizations. "Think Animal House," someone suggests. Unfortunately for the less keg-oriented among us, some students claim, "school life is horrendous unless you party and drink," while others would consider "horrendous" an unnecessarily strong word. The town of Keene, home to 23,000 residents, has a dance club, a movie theatre, "lots of restaurants," a handful of bars, and a variety of arts venues, and "college students get good discounts all around Keene." When they want to escape from campus, "many students enjoy skiing or snowboarding at one of the many mountains within an hour or two of the campus. Taking a hike up Mount Monadnock is very common and gives a beautiful view of the Monadnock region of New Hampshire." KSC's "location is advantageous," a student adds, "not far from Boston and New York City, and minutes from Massachusetts and Vermont."

Student Body

Though more than 40 percent of Keene State's students come from outside New Hampshire, the local students who migrate from high school to Keene State in flocks lend an air of provincialism to the college. Despite the "cliquish" atmosphere that is sometimes felt in these parts, you'll find students who "are nice, caring, and considerate." Homogeny is the reigning adjective for KSC's student body—nearly 95 percent of students are white, and "most people here come from the same socioeconomic background." "Most students [at KSC] are the typical college students," remarks one survey respondent. "They wear jeans and t-shirts to class." Another undergrad's perception of his classmates is that "they all look alike, talk alike, and act alike." He adds, "The biggest social issue on campus is, 'What frat is throwing a party tonight?'" Still, there are advantages to the common bond between students; one freshman shares that "the feeling of belonging" was the "thing that brought me to Keene State."

ADMISSIONS

Very important factors considered by the admissions committee include: secondary school record. *Important factors considered include:* class rank, essays, interview, recommendations, and standardized test scores. *Other factors considered include:* alumni/ae relation, extracurricular activities, talent/ability, volunteer work, and work experience. SAT I or ACT required, SAT I preferred. TOEFL required of all international applicants. High school diploma or GED is required. *High school units required/recommended:* 14 total required; 4 English required, 3 math required, 3 science required, 1 science lab required, 2 foreign language recommended, 4 social studies required, 2 history required.

The Inside Word

Keene State takes the time to look at your admissions application, primarily in an effort to justify admitting otherwise substandard candidates. The gatekeepers here want to invite you in; all you have to do is give them a good reason.

FINANCIAL AID

Students should submit: FAFSA and income tax forms. Regular filing deadline is March 1. The Princeton Review suggests that all financial aid forms be submitted as soon as possible after January 1. *Need-based scholarships/grants offered:* Pell, SEOG, state scholarships/grants, private scholarships, and the school's own gift aid. *Loan aid offered:* FFEL Subsidized Stafford, FFEL Unsubsidized Stafford, FFEL PLUS, Federal Perkins, and college/university loans from institutional funds. Federal Work-Study Program available. Institutional employment available. Applicants will be notified of awards on a rolling basis. Off-campus job opportunities are fair.

For even more information on this school, turn to page 328 of the "Stats" section.

LESLEY UNIVERSITY

LESLEY COLLEGE: 29 EVERETT STREET, CAMBRIDGE, MA 02138 • ADMISSIONS: 617-349-8800
FAX: 617-349-8810 • E-MAIL: UGADM@MAIL.LESLEY.EDU • WEBSITE: WWW.LESLEY.EDU
ART INSTITUTE OF BOSTON: 700 BEACON ST., BOSTON, MA 02215 • ADMISSIONS: 617-585-6700
FAX: 617-437-1226 • E-MAIL: ADMISSIONS@AIBOSTON.EDU • WEBSITE: WWW.AIBOSTON.EDU

Ratings
Quality of Life: 70   Academic: 71   Admissions: 71   Financial Aid: 68

Academics

Boston's Lesley University is the proud parent of twins: Lesley College and the Art Institute of Boston. But while both institutions operate under the same umbrella, they are, in fact, quite

> **SURVEY SAYS . . .**
> *Students love Cambridge, Campus feels safe*
> *Great off-campus food, Classes are small*
> *Students are happy*

different. Lesley College—right next to Harvard in Cambridge—is an all-women's college with a proclaimed emphasis on giving back to the community and contributing to society as a whole. The most popular fields of study at Lesley College are human services and education, and students dive into internships during freshman year. Lesley offers "intimate class sizes, small student/teacher ratios . . . open class discussions, [and] professors [who] often assess through writing assignments rather than structured exams." And students with an interest in the arts are able to "cross register with the Art Institute of Boston." Located in Boston's Kenmore Square, AIB is a small, co-ed institution, offering a corps of faculty that "are always 'on call' and truly look out for the welfare of the students, academically and socially." AIB students boast that their professors are not only "very knowledgeable and helpful aids in the learning process," but also "smart, unique, and respectable artists" who can shed valuable light on the prospects of earning a living in the visual arts. Any complaints? Some AIB students wish for a tighter connection with Lesley U. and the additional funds that would accompany it, while many at Lesley College gripe about typical administration issues.

Life

"It's Boston, baby!" Whether you're studying at the Art Institute of Boston or at Lesley College, you're sure to find a plethora of activities and events to fit your fancy. AIB is near Boston's clubs, while Lesley College is a stone's throw from Harvard and MIT parties, but most students report similar social habits: "work, go to school, sleep, eat, go back to work, do homework—but not all in that order." Obviously, AIB undergrads are regulars at Boston's art museums and galleries. In fact, AIB's campus consists of only two buildings, so the division between campus life and city life is often blurred. Lesley College, on the other hand, "is its own world [and] sucks you in," says an undergrad. Since Lesley's is a dry campus without males, women seeking alcohol and women seeking men often "leave campus over the weekend." But an upperclassmen reports, "In the past two years, Lesley has made a major attempt at creating a more involved social life for students who are here on the weekend." Some favorite events are Friday-night coffeehouses, the annual Quadfest, and Spa Night.

Student Body

"Everyone here is very open to different lifestyles and cultures," says a Lesley College undergrad, which is true, by many accounts, of the Art Institute of Boston as well. Another common trait of students at these sister institutions is that a liberal mindset predominates. An AIB junior says, "The typical student is left-wing, liberal, vegan . . . . The conservatives are forever under scrutiny." But at an art school like AIB, "atypical is typical." The glue that holds these students together is that they're all "dedicated to their art." At Lesley, you'll find a good "many girlie students" as well as lesbian students. So how to best describe this conglomerate student population? "Like fresh ingredients to a good cook," of course.

ADMISSIONS

Very important factors considered by the admissions committee include: secondary school record. *Important factors considered include:* class rank, interview, recommendations, standardized test scores, character/personal qualities, and volunteer work. *Other factors considered include.* alumni/ae relation, essays, extracurricular activities, geographical residence, minority status, talent/ability, and work experience. SAT I or ACT required. TOEFL required of all international applicants. High school diploma or GED is required. *High school units required/recommended:* 18 total required; 20 total recommended; 4 English required, 3 math required, 3 science required, 1 science lab required, 2 science lab recommended, 2 foreign language recommended, 1 social studies required, 2 social studies recommended, 1 history required, 2 history recommended, 4 elective recommended.

The Inside Word

With few entering students, Lesley can afford to scrutinize each application carefully. Serious candidates are strongly advised to visit campus and interview. Applicants to AIB should carefully assemble their portfolios and prepare to talk passionately about their future art careers.

FINANCIAL AID

Students should submit: FAFSA and institution's own financial aid form. The Princeton Review suggests that all financial aid forms be submitted as soon as possible after January 1. *Need-based scholarships/grants offered:* Pell, SEOG, state scholarships/grants, private scholarships, and the school's own gift aid. *Loan aid offered:* FFEL Subsidized Stafford, FFEL Unsubsidized Stafford, FFEL PLUS, Federal Perkins, state loans, MEFA, TEIR, Fleet 1st, Premier, and Signature loans. Alternative payment plans. Federal Work-Study Program available. Institutional employment available. Applicants will be notified of awards on or about March 15. Off-campus job opportunities are excellent.

FROM THE ADMISSIONS OFFICE

"Located in America's premiere college town, Lesley University prepares students for professional careers in the areas of education, the arts, human services, and management. The university's educational philosophy is rooted in a commitment to the liberal arts, scholarly inquiry, professional practice, and lifelong learning. Both of Lesley University's undergraduate residential colleges—Lesley College and The Art Institute of Boston—offer small-school, intimate attention combined with the resources and diversity of a larger university. Those benefits include access to accelerated bachelor's/master's programs, intercollegiate athletics, and cross-registration with other schools of the university. Teaching undergraduates is the faculty's number one priority, with an emphasis on collaborative learning and small classes.

"Central to Lesley's mission is a commitment to excellence, creative instruction, the integration of academic and field-based learning, and responsiveness to the needs of society and the student. A distinctive and fundamental aspect of education at Lesley University is the conviction that people matter, and that professionals who respond to their needs—such as classroom teachers, human services workers, and professional artists—provide a unique and crucial contribution to society. Faculty and students believe in the power of individuals working collaboratively to bring about constructive change. The vast majority of Lesley graduates work in professions where this philosophy is applied daily. The goal of a Lesley University education is to empower students with the knowledge, skills and practical experience they need to succeed as catalysts and leaders in their professions, their own lives, and the world in which they live."

For even more information on this school, turn to page 328 of the "Stats" section.

MANHATTAN COLLEGE

MANHATTAN COLLEGE PARKWAY, RIVERDALE, NY 10471 • ADMISSIONS: 718-862-7200 • FAX: 718-862-8019
E-MAIL: ADMIT@MANHATTAN.EDU • WEBSITE: WWW.MANHATTAN.EDU

Ratings
Quality of Life: 75   Academic: 76   Admissions: 75   Financial Aid: 70

Academics

Students at Manhattan College, a small Catholic liberal arts school tucked into a lovely residential Bronx neighborhood, report that "our school is best for sciences and engineering." Students in these top programs tell us that their work load is heavy, while the

> **SURVEY SAYS . . .**
> No one watches intercollegiate sports
> Very little beer drinking
> Students are religious
> No one plays intramural sports
> Very little hard liquor, Diverse students interact

programs outside of engineering and science are less academically challenging. Notes one student, "All of the professors I've had have been pretty good, but the liberal arts area seems too easy for college level." Students here praise their profs both for their teaching abilities and accessibility; writes one undergrad, "My professors are all reputable teachers who put their best effort into teaching us the material. So far, all of my professors have been great at doing what they're supposed to: teach. They are all available after class and most show genuine interest in helping out the students." Agrees another, "The professors show interest in helping students on a one-on-one basis. They are always available to give you good, realistic advice, and to listen to your concerns and share a cup of coffee or lunch at the cafeteria. My experience has been very valuable, and it will be treasured." Students also appreciate their "small classes, so you get a more personalized education." Undergrads here wanted us to know that "our location outside of the city makes it hard for Manhattan to compete with schools such as NYU and Columbia, but with a little publicity from publications such as yours, I could see enrollment from higher-tier students increasing." Consider it done!

Life

Manhattan College is not located in Manhattan, as the name would suggest, but it's not far from the bustling nexus of New York City's five boroughs. From their campus in Bronx's Riverdale section along the Hudson River, Manhattan College students can reach the northern tip of Manhattan with a 10-minute subway ride; the trip to midtown and points south takes considerably longer and affords a good opportunity to catch up on your reading. Most students "go down to Manhattan as much as I can. It is pretty expensive, though, so I don't go all that much. I usually just hang out around the dorms with friends or attend school functions." Students appreciate their school's unique situation, whereby "we are located right near Manhattan while we still have a small-campus atmosphere." "Just like any other school, drinking is real popular" at Manhattan, but a recent binge-drinking death at the school has heightened students' awareness of the dangers of alcohol abuse. The school is home to an active Greek community and more than 70 student organizations, as well as the Jaspers, Manhattan's men's and women's intercollegiate athletic teams that compete against small area schools such as Iona, Rider, Marist, and Fairfield. The campus is currently undergoing a major overhaul, which has students optimistic about the school's future: "They are working on fixing up the campus apartments, which really need to be renovated. . . . The library is under construction right now. It should be beautiful [when complete] about a year from now."

Student Body

"The diversity and close-knit environment of my school is one of its greatest qualities," writes one Manhattan undergrad, reflecting the fact that minority students make up one-third of the school's population. Agrees another student, "Students are diverse from one another even though most come from all parts of New York." Students here are "very helpful and considerate. . . . We work together well." Many enjoy how "everyone likes to have fun and party together, but they are respectful when its time to slow down the partying a little bit and do some schoolwork." Some see a dichotomy within the population, telling us that "most students outside of the engineering and sciences areas don't earn their high averages and that most of them look for the easy way out." Others simply wish the student body gelled more, noting that "the only thing that needs to be worked on in my opinion is the amount of school spirit. It needs to be increased a bit."

ADMISSIONS

Very important factors considered by the admissions committee include: secondary school record and standardized test scores. *Important factors considered include:* class rank, essays, extracurricular activities, interview, and recommendations. *Other factors considered include:* alumni/ae relation, character/personal qualities, talent/ability, volunteer work, and work experience. SAT I or ACT required, SAT I preferred. TOEFL required of all international applicants. High school diploma is required and GED is accepted. *High school units required/recommended:* 16 total required; 17 total recommended; 4 English required, 4 English recommended, 3 math required, 4 math recommended, 2 science required, 3 science recommended, 2 foreign language required, 3 foreign language recommended, 3 social studies required, 3 social studies recommended, 2 elective required.

The Inside Word

Manhattan's engineering program may be one of the undiscovered gems of the region. Because of heavy competition from other area engineering schools, however, the college cannot afford to be as selective as it might wish, thus presenting a golden opportunity to prospective engineers who slacked off a bit in high school.

FINANCIAL AID

Students should submit: FAFSA. No deadline for regular filing. The Princeton Review suggests that all financial aid forms be submitted as soon as possible after January 1. *Need-based scholarships/grants offered:* Pell, SEOG, and the school's own gift aid. *Loan aid offered:* Direct subsidized Stafford, Direct Unsubsidized Stafford, and Direct PLUS. Federal Work-Study Program available. Institutional employment available. Applicants will be notified of awards on a rolling basis beginning on or about February 15. Off-campus job opportunities are excellent.

FROM THE ADMISSIONS OFFICE

"This year marks the 150th Anniversary of the founding of Manhattan College. Our Sesquicentennial celebration began on August 19, 2002 with a special stamp cancellation on the Quadrangle. Numerous events are planned during the academic year for students, faculty, staff, alumni, and friends of Manhattan as well as the general public. Among other events, the celebration includes speaking engagements on campus by noted alumni, including novelist James Patterson '69 and the former mayor of New York City, Rudy Guliani '65. The Sesquicentennial will officially close during Alumni Reunion Weekend with Mass celebrated in St. Patrick's Cathedral on Saturday, June 7, 2003, followed by a grand reception for all in Rockefeller Center Plaza."

For even more information on this school, turn to page 329 of the "Stats" section.

MANHATTANVILLE COLLEGE

2900 PURCHASE STREET, ADMISSIONS OFFICE, PURCHASE, NY 10577 • ADMISSIONS: 914-323-5124
FAX: 914-694-1732 • E-MAIL: ADMISSIONS@MVILLE.EDU • WEBSITE: WWW.MVILLE.EDU

Ratings
Quality of Life: 77   Academic: 75   Admissions: 74   Financial Aid: 83

Academics

Ask students to describe the Manhattanville experience, and they'll likely use the word "family" time and again. "Manhattanville is a family. Professors' and administrators' doors are always open," writes a typical student. Giving rise to this homey atmosphere are "small and personal classrooms that contribute to a very engaging learning experience between your-

> **SURVEY SAYS . . .**
> *Political activism is hot*
> *Frats and sororities dominate social scene*
> *Student publications are popular*
> *Lab facilities are great*
> *Lots of classroom discussion*
> *Student government is popular*
> *School is well run*
> *Campus difficult to get around*

self, your professor, and your classmates, all giving and taking equally and efficiently." The success of such an approach, of course, hinges on the quality of the faculty. Fortunately, "The professors are incredible, very down-to-earth . . . . They greet you when they see you, and they give their home phone numbers so you can contact them at any time." Crowed one student, "My profs make me feel important so that I want to work harder for them." Upper-level administration is equally accessible. In fact, many students singled out President Berman as one of Manhattanville's greatest assets. "The president holds monthly dinners at his house, and many of us stay for hours to discuss various issues, both personal and school-related. He also attends most student events. How many other college students can say that they see and interact with the school's president at least once a week?" Students report that "The education department has made quite a name for itself and is helpful getting jobs for grad students," but add that the school is strong in many areas. Wrote one student, "Manhattanville offers a great liberal arts education, with strength in a variety of departments, from drama to computer science." A few warned that the small departments are very small; chemistry majors, for example, cross-register at SUNY Purchase for a few of their classes.

Life

There's "not much to do on campus" at Manhattanville, students here agree, attributing the subdued social scene to a several factors. Many report that "Security is ridiculously tight," and "there are no Greeks on campus, so there isn't even a place to have huge parties." The most compelling reason, perhaps, is that "most people go to NYC for fun. It is only 45 minutes by train" or on the free valiant bus service provided by the school. Being "the most amazing cultural activity center in the world" students find no lack of things to do in the city. Campus fun consists of quiet activities; explains one undergrad, "There's pretty much always someone's room to go hang out in. Watching movies, playing video games, watching TV, playing guitar, drinking, playing Frisbee or lacrosse, and just talking are what people do—among a few other things—to have fun." Undergrads also tell us that "major sporting events and theater productions are lots of fun and are well attended." As one student summarizes, "Situated in a rich Westchester suburb, the campus is beautifully serene. Yet within 10 minutes of the campus is the center of Westchester County, offering plenty of great food, shopping, and night life."

Student Body

The "smart, sociable," "athletic, easygoing" undergrads of Manhattanville generally hail from New York and Connecticut, although there is also a sizeable international student population. Wrote one local, "The greatest strengths [of] my school are the extreme levels of diversity. There are students from Europe, the Orient, the Middle East, and the Caribbean. I have never known so many international people before!" A few complain, however, that "while there is diversity, students are segregated into their own groups." Others gripe that their classmates are "highly concerned with materialistic issues." One student wryly described his peers here as "Attack of the Rich Clones: a look at the parking lot and students' attire speaks volumes."

ADMISSIONS

Very important factors considered by the admissions committee include: secondary school record and standardized test scores. *Important factors considered include:* essays, extracurricular activities, interview, and recommendations. *Other factors considered include:* alumni/ae relation, character/personal qualities, geographical residence, talent/ability, volunteer work, and work experience. SAT I or ACT required. TOEFL required of all international applicants. High school diploma or GED required. *High school units required/recommended:* 16 total required; 4 English required, 3 math required, 2 science required, 2 social studies required, 5 elective required.

The Inside Word

More than 30 years after going coed, this former women's college is still predominantly female and is still looking to boost its male population. The fact that the school accepts only half its male applicants speaks more to the quality of the applicant pool than to selectiveness; if male and female candidates of equal qualifications are vying for the last seat in the freshman class, it will go to the male.

FINANCIAL AID

Students should submit: FAFSA and state aid form. No deadline for regular filing. The Princeton Review suggests that all financial aid forms be submitted as soon as possible after January 1. *Need-based scholarships/grants offered:* Pell, SEOG, state scholarships/grants, private scholarships, and the school's own gift aid. *Loan aid offered:* FFEL Subsidized Stafford, FFEL Unsubsidized Stafford, FFEL PLUS, and Federal Perkins. Federal Work-Study Program available. Institutional employment available. Applicants will be notified of awards on a rolling basis. Off-campus job opportunities are excellent.

FROM THE ADMISSIONS OFFICE

"Manhattanville's mission—to educate ethically and socially responsible leaders for the global community—is evident throughout the College, from academics to athletics to social and extracurricular activities. With 1,500 undergraduates from 53 nations and 37 states, our diversity spans geographic, cultural, ethnic, religious, and socioeconomic backgrounds as well as academic interests. All students are free to express and share their views in this tight-knit community, where we value the personal as well as the global. Any six students with a similar interest can start a club, and most participate in community service projects, club activities, or other campuswide programs. Study abroad opportunities include not only the most desirable international locations, but also a semester-long immersion for living, studying, and working in New York City. In the true liberal arts tradition, Manhattanville students are encouraged to think for themselves and develop new skills—in music, in the studio arts, on stage, in the sciences, or on the playing field. We offer more than 50 areas of study as well as a popular self-designed major, so there is no limit to our academic scope. Our Westchester County location, just 35 miles north of New York City, gives students an edge for jobs and internships. Over the past few years, Manhattanville has been rated among the '100 Most Wired,' the '100 Most Undeservedly Under-Appreciated,' the '320 Hottest,' and *U.S. News & World Report*'s first tier."

For even more information on this school, turn to page 329 of the "Stats" section.

MARIST COLLEGE

3399 NORTH ROAD, POUGHKEEPSIE, NY 12601-1387 • ADMISSIONS: 845-575-3226 • FAX: 845-575-3215
E-MAIL: ADMISSIONS@MARIST.EDU • WEBSITE: WWW.MARIST.EDU

Ratings
Quality of Life: 76   Academic: 86   Admissions: 83   Financial Aid: 79

Academics

Marist College's "simply spectacular" library, called "one of the nicest and most modern with a very high student-to-Internet connection ratio," stands as a testament to the college's commitment to academics. The professors count among "the most devoted I have ever met" and are "active participants in their field outside of class." One of the school's "greatest strengths is the interaction between professor and student." As one student points out, "Getting together to watch college hoops with your professor is not something you can do at every school." Most students save their criticism for the "mediocre assistant professors." "I rarely get into the classes I need for my major," is a common complaint, but most agree: "I go to classes because I enjoy them." The most popular and renowned programs include communications, business, education, fashion, IT, and the Public Praxis Program, "an exceptional blend of philosophy courses and community service." The Marist administration is composed of "consummate professionals" who are "very strict. They try to act like our parents." Students share their residence halls with "mentors who help us with any problems we have, even if it's not related to academics." Marist enjoys a "good reputation with surrounding businesses" and "many connections with large companies, especially IBM." The "great internship program" ensures that Marist undergrads are "well prepared for jobs after graduation."

> **SURVEY SAYS . . .**
> *School is well run*
> *Classes are small*
> *Profs teach upper levels*
> *Instructors are good teachers*
> *Hard liquor is popular*
> *Popular college radio*
> *Student publications are popular*

Life

Many students characterize Marist as a "big bar school," as opposed to your run-of-the-mill "party school," and thus, an ID (of any degree of authenticity) is "crucial." Though the school hosts no on-campus sororities or fraternities, everybody apparently "knows how to have a good time while getting their work done." According to many, the surrounding town of Poughkeepsie is "very ghetto" and "economically challenged and in need of student involvement." Undergrads consider the school's strict guest policy "old-fashioned," making dorms "like a prison, especially for freshmen." Opines one, "We are college students, and having curfew for visiting other students is just inexplicable." A system based on "Priority Points," awarded for all types of campus involvement, dictates the on-campus housing lottery, and some students "think that this is a great thing." Others bitterly note, "This college needs to actually reward the students who spend a majority of their time going to class and studying." In terms of activities, many respondents praise the school-sponsored "bus trips to Broadway shows for only $25. You can't beat that!" The city looms only 90 minutes away, and closer to home, the "Hudson Valley has a large amount of history to explore."

Student Body

Among the population of 4,000, "there isn't a lot of diversity, culturally or socially." Many students are "white middle-class Catholics," often from Long Island; one student notes,

"Sometimes I look around campus and feel like I'm looking at a mirror." Students call for "more minority-oriented events" but still believe "the minority community mixes in very well with everyone, even though there are very few of us." "I know it's cheesy when you see kids of all different types playing Frisbee and laughing on the green outside in brochures," comments a student, "but it really does happen here." Perfect harmony is confronted by obstacles like "segregation between 'normal' students and athletes" and the perception that "commuters are generally not as valued as live-in students." Generally, though, friendliness abounds at Marist, where "everyone says 'hi' to everyone," which "makes you feel like a rock star."

ADMISSIONS

Very important factors considered by the admissions committee include: secondary school record, recommendations, and standardized test scores. *Important factors considered include:* character/personal qualities, essays, extracurricular activities, minority status, volunteer work, and work experience. *Other factors considered include:* alumni/ae relation and talent/ability. SAT I or ACT required. TOEFL required of all international applicants. High school diploma or GED is required. *High school units required/recommended:* 16 total required; 19 total recommended; 4 English required, 3 math required, 4 math recommended, 3 science required, 4 science recommended, 2 science lab required, 3 science lab recommended, 3 foreign language recommended, 2 social studies required, 2 social studies recommended, 1 history required, 2 history recommended, 1 elective required.

The Inside Word

As the school's housing policy indicates, Marist places a strong emphasis on civic responsibility. Candidates who show a strong record of community service and leadership activities will have a definite leg up in the admissions process here.

FINANCIAL AID

Students should submit: FAFSA and institution's own financial aid form. Regular filing deadline is March 1. The Princeton Review suggests that all financial aid forms be submitted as soon as possible after January 1. *Need-based scholarships/grants offered:* Pell, SEOG, state scholarships/grants, private scholarships, and the school's own gift aid. *Loan aid offered:* FFEL Subsidized Stafford, FFEL Unsubsidized Stafford, FFEL PLUS, and Federal Perkins. Federal Work-Study Program available. Institutional employment available. Applicants will be notified of awards on a rolling basis beginning on or about March 15. Off-campus job opportunities are excellent.

FROM THE ADMISSIONS OFFICE

"Marist is a 'hot school' among prospective students. We are seeing a record number of applications each year. But the number of seats available for the freshman class remains the same, about 950. Therefore, becoming an accepted applicant is an increasingly competitive process. Our recommendations: Keep your grades up, score well on the SAT, participate in community service both in and out of school, and exercise leadership in the classroom, athletics, extracurricular activities, and your place of worship. We encourage a campus visit. When prospective students see Marist—our beautiful location on a scenic stretch of the Hudson River, the quality of our facilities, the interaction between students and faculty, and the fact that everyone really enjoys their time here—they want to become a part of the Marist College community. We'll help you in the transition from high school to college through an innovative first-year program that provides mentors for every student. You'll also learn how to use technology in whatever field you choose. We emphasize three aspects of a true Marist experience: excellence in education, service to others, and the pursuit of higher human values. At Marist, you will get a premium education, develop your skills, have fun and make lifelong friends, be given the opportunity to gain valuable experience through our internship and study abroad programs, and be ahead of the competition for graduate school or work."

For even more information on this school, turn to page 330 of the "Stats" section.

MARLBORO COLLEGE

PO Box A, South Road, Marlboro, VT 05344 • Admissions: 802-258-9236 • Fax: 802-257-4154
Financial Aid: 802-257-4333 • E-mail: admissions@marlboro.edu • Website: www.marlboro.edu

Ratings
Quality of Life: 94   Academic: 95   Admissions: 82   Financial Aid: 91

Academics

Like everything else at Marlboro, academics are centered around the individual student. Because students are given "freedom to design" their "own academic programs," "you can study whatever you want." In other words, students tend to believe that "the possibilities are endless." Through the

> **SURVEY SAYS . . .**
> *Lots of beer drinking*
> *Frats and sororities dominate social scene*
> *Popular college radio, Great food on campus*
> *Library needs improving, Low cost of living*
> *Lousy off-campus food*
> *Political activism is (almost) nonexistent*

system of "self-governance," students are intimately involved in the administration of their educations. One student notes that he and fellow classmates even participate in "hiring professors." A senior, however, complains that "the self-governance we advertise is a myth—student government consists only of the 'good kids.'" Other students will tell you that it's the grown-up administration that's "counterproductive to the ideals this school was founded on." (It should be mentioned, though, that the administration is so accessible that even "the president of the college plays basketball with students during lunch hour.") You won't hear any complaints about the faculty. "They're hardworking, quirky, rugged types," describes a freshman. A senior adds, "Professors . . . are here because they sincerely want to teach." While students focus on a range of topics, the school seems particularly proud of its creative endeavors, like theatre and creative writing. Regardless of what you study here, "there's no such thing as sitting in the back and twiddling your thumbs." Of course, the very fact that there's enough schoolwork to "kill an average individual" means that "a true Marlboro student thinks about dropping daily."

Life

While Marlboro neighbors the 12,000-person town of Brattleboro, which has a "spa" and occasional "performances," students manage to find their excitement on campus. Like all college students, Marlboro students "often drink on the weekends." But more than drinking, they like talking. For fun, people regularly "engage in conversation that is usually somewhat intellectual." A freshman says, "We talk about everything from the Muppets to political and religious theories to whether vampires are ticklish." We should mention that these chat sessions often take place in the rustic dorms—one of them a converted ski chalet—where three-quarters of the student body lives. Students also take advantage of school activities, like the Outdoor Program, which loans everything from cross-country skis to kayaks and climbing gear to students at no cost. In fact, Marlboro students have a thing for skis, and outdoor activities in general. When the "cabin fever" sets in, students here start "affixing skis to the bottom of objects and riding them down hills." Thus, things like the "ski-chair" and "ski-bike" are born. But more than anything, schoolwork dominates a student's life at Marlboro. One senior writes, "Students spend a remarkable amount of time studying" at Marlboro. But they enjoy it. "It's like summer camp plus stress." And snow.

Student Body

Marlboro was started by a bunch of young World War II vets who returned from the front and wanted a rigorous education rooted in an ideal of student independence. Their legacy sustains. Marlboro students pride themselves on their independence. Sometimes this backfires. "We tend to stick to our established friends and groups," admits one junior. "Students can get pretty self-absorbed, and it becomes irritating," writes a freshman, adding, "until, of course, you yourself become self-absorbed!" All in all, most members on "Planet Marlboro" "get along" and remain "very open to a diversity of lifestyles." This is a good thing because of "the smallness and isolation of the campus—any enemy you make you will see at every meal for four years." Naturally, though, "there are always assholes, and with only 300 people they can really make themselves known." The biggest gripe that students have with their own flock is the "lack of racial diversity." And, while we're hearing grievances, they also want to break down a stereotype that has long draped over these individualistic, outdoorsy students: "We're NOT a bunch of hippies. We're a bunch of dorks and nerds." And "far more mature than most college students," opines a junior.

ADMISSIONS

Very important factors considered by the admissions committee include: secondary school record. *Important factors considered include:* interview, character/personal qualities, class rank, essays, extracurricular activities, recommendations, standardized test scores, talent/ability, volunteer work. *Other factors considered include:* alumni/ae relation, geographical residence, work experience. SAT I or ACT required; SAT II recommended. TOEFL required of all non-native speakers of English. High school diploma or GED is required. *High school units required/recommended:* 4 English required, 3 math recommended, 3 science recommended, 3 foreign language recommended, 3 social studies recommended, 3 history recommended.

The Inside Word

Don't be misled by Marlboro's high acceptance rate; the College's applicant pool consists mainly of candidates who are sincerely interested in a nontraditional path to their BA. They also possess sincere intellectual curiosity, and students who don't should not bother applying. The admissions process here is driven by matchmaking and a search for those who truly want to learn. For the right kind of person, Marlboro can be a terrific college choice.

FINANCIAL AID

Students should submit: FAFSA, CSS/Financial Aid PROFILE, noncustodial (divorced/separated) parent's statement. Regular filing deadline is March 1. The Princeton Review suggests that all financial aid forms be submitted as soon as possible after January 1. *Need-based scholarships/grants offered:* Pell, SEOG, state scholarships/grants, private scholarships, the school's own gift aid. *Loan aid offered:* FFEL Subsidized Stafford, FFEL Unsubsidized Stafford, FFEL PLUS, college/university loans from institutional funds. Federal Work-Study Program available. Institutional employment available. Applicants will be notified of awards on a rolling basis beginning on or about April 1. Off-campus job opportunities are fair.

FROM THE ADMISSIONS OFFICE

"Marlboro College is distinguished by its curriculum, praised in higher education circles as unique; it is known for its self-governing philosophy, in which each student, faculty, and staff has an equal vote on many issues affecting the community; and it is recognized for its 50-year history of offering a rigorous, exciting, self-designed course of study taught in very small classes and individual tutorials. Marlboro's size also distinguishes it from most other schools. With 300 students and a student/faculty ratio of 8 to 1, it is one of the nation's smallest liberal arts colleges. Few other schools offer a program where students have such close interaction with faculty, and where community life is inseparable from academic life. The result, the self-designed, self-directed Plan of Concentration, allows students to develop their own unique academic work by defining a problem, setting clear limits on an area of inquiry, and analyzing, evaluating, and reporting on the outcome of a significant project. A Marlboro education teaches you to think for yourself, articulate your thoughts, express your ideas, believe in yourself, and do it all with the clarity, confidence and self-reliance necessary for later success, no matter what postgraduate path you take."

For even more information on this school, turn to page 331 of the "Stats" section.

MASSACHUSETTS INSTITUTE OF TECHNOLOGY

77 MASSACHUSETTS AVENUE, CAMBRIDGE, MA 02139 • ADMISSIONS: 617-253-4791
FAX: 617-253-1986 • FINANCIAL AID: 617-253-4971 • E-MAIL: ADMISSIONS@MIT.EDU • WEBSITE: WWW.MIT.EDU

Ratings
Quality of Life: 83   Academic: 99   Admissions: 99   Financial Aid: 88

Academics

How intense is an MIT education? "Say you like Pez candy," posits one MIT undergrad. "MIT, then, is like being forced to eat 10×10^9 Pez candies." Indeed, "the workload is heavy" here, but the crunch is mitigated by an atmosphere of teamwork and a sense that students are getting the very best education money can buy. They study directly under "Nobel Prize–winning faculty, even as freshmen" and enjoy access to "superior labs and outstanding opportunities for undergraduate research." Time management is critical. "Tech is hell if you want to attend every lecture, read everything twice, do the homework perfectly, and ace every test," explains one student. "If you understand what does and does not help you learn, life here becomes much more manageable." Material "is taught extremely fast. It takes a few weeks to get used to, but it makes everything so much more interesting and motivating." Most classes consist of "lectures taught by a full professor and recitations taught by TAs." According to several students, "Usually, recitations by undergraduate and graduate TAs, not the classes taught by distinguished faculty, are the most helpful [in learning] the material." MIT's "world-renowned" profs are, for the most part, "excellent teachers as well as researchers. Some are not good at teaching. Many are famous and offer cutting-edge information." Students appreciate the fact that "freshman year is pass/no record, and that was awesome in helping me adjust," and also that "the administration has gone through a lot of work sorting us out and choosing whom to select. They really hate to see students flunk out or transfer."

> **SURVEY SAYS . . .**
> *Frats and sororities dominate social scene*
> *Great computer facilities*
> *Students love Cambridge, MA*
> *(Almost) everyone plays intramural sports*
> *Lab facilities need improving*
> *Unattractive campus, Large classes*
> *Intercollegiate sports are*
> *unpopular or nonexistent*
> *(Almost) no one smokes*

Life

Students at MIT warn that their studies leave little time for socializing, but because they are located in Cambridge with so many undergraduate institutions nearby, they are well-situated to make the most of their few free hours. Explains one undergrad, "There are always concerts and events on campus, but when we want to get off campus, Boston is a beautiful, cultural city. Walking down Newbury Street, rollerblading along the Charles River, or eating in the North End Italian district are just a few favorites." The Greek scene "is huge, especially on the weekends," and "guest lectures and movies are always available." And there's always time for "hacking," the time-honored school tradition one student defines as "the act of pulling off elaborate, skillful practical jokes." Among the school's most celebrated hacks are placing a replica of a campus police cruiser atop the Great Dome; the creation of a water fountain–fire plug hybrid (because learning at MIT is "like drinking water from a fire hose"); and the distribution of "Buzzword Bingo" cards during Al Gore's 1996 commencement address. On the downside, the campus "is different shades of ugly." Reports one student, "It seems like all the green patches are being taken away because of new building projects."

Student Body

The "very diverse" MIT student body lacks variety in one area only: brains. "People here range from the really smart to the insanely smart," writes one student, although some note that their peers have "plenty of book sense but hardly any common sense." Because "students don't compete with each other as much as with themselves, everyone is willing to help everyone else out." MIT undergrads regard each other as "awesome people, although a bit nerdy." Some are overly introverted ("Too many people are happy to lock themselves in their rooms and study all day. If you come to MIT do not become one of these people"), but mostly this is a happy, sociable group Notes one student, "When you come to MIT, the real you comes out. Everyone here is unique and not afraid to show it. That's because we're all tolerant of each other's differences."

ADMISSIONS

Very important factors considered by the admissions committee include: secondary school record. *Important factors considered include:* character/personal qualities, class rank, extracurricular activities, recommendations, standardized test scores, talent/ability. *Other factors considered include:* student's context, essays, interview, minority status, volunteer work, work experience. SAT I or ACT required; SAT II also required. TOEFL required of all international applicants. High school units recommended: 4 English recommended, 4 math recommended, 4 science recommended, 2 foreign language recommended, 1 social studies recommended, 1 history recommended.

The Inside Word

High academic achievement, lofty test scores, and the most rigorous high school courseload possible are prerequisites for a successful candidacy. Among the most selective institutions in the country, MIT's admissions operation is easily one of the most down-to-earth and accessible. Over the years they have shown both a sense of humor in admissions literature and an awareness that applying to such a prestigious place creates a high level of anxiety.

FINANCIAL AID

Students should submit: FAFSA, CSS/Financial Aid PROFILE, noncustodial (divorced/separated) parent's statement, business/farm supplement, parent's complete federal income tax returns from prior year including all schedules and W-2s. Regular filing deadline is February 1. The Princeton Review suggests that all financial aid forms be submitted as soon as possible after January 1. *Need-based scholarships/grants offered:* Pell, SEOG, state scholarships/grants, private scholarships, the school's own gift aid. *Loan aid offered:* Direct Subsidized Stafford, Direct Unsubsidized Stafford, Direct PLUS, Federal Perkins, college/university loans from institutional funds. Federal Work-Study Program available. Institutional employment available. Applicants will be notified of awards on or about March 15. Off-campus job opportunities are excellent.

FROM THE ADMISSIONS OFFICE

"The students who come to the Massachusetts Institute of Technology are some of America's—and the world's—best and most creative. As graduates, they leave here to make real contributions—in science, technology, business, education, politics, architecture, and the arts From any class, many will go on to do work that is historically significant. These young men and women are leaders, achievers, producers. Helping such students make the most of their talents and dreams would challenge any educational institution. MIT gives them its best advantages: a world-class faculty, unparalleled facilities, remarkable opportunities. In turn, these students help to make the Institute the vital place it is. They bring fresh viewpoints to faculty research: More than three-quarters participate in the Undergraduate Research Opportunities Program. They play on MIT's 41 intercollegiate teams as well as in its 15 musical ensembles. To their classes and to their out-of-class activities, they bring enthusiasm, energy, and individual style."

For even more information on this school, turn to page 331 of the "Stats" section.

MERRIMACK COLLEGE

OFFICE OF ADMISSION, AUSTIN HALL, NORTH ANDOVER, MA 01845 • ADMISSIONS: 978-837-5100
FAX: 978-837-5133 • E-MAIL: ADMISSION@MERRIMACK.EDU • WEBSITE: WWW.MERRIMACK.EDU

Ratings
Quality of Life: 74   Academic: 80   Admissions: 75   Financial Aid: 75

Academics

Though set in the quiet town of North Andover, students say professors bring "real-world experience into the classroom" to Roman Catholic-affiliated Merrimack College. Undergrads describe their instructors as "highly educated and professionally developed individuals" who "have real-world principles to contribute to classes regarding real-world issues." When it comes to teaching, though, students give mixed reviews. Explains one, "I have experienced a full range, from professors I would never recommend to another student to professors whom I would do anything to take a class with." One student reassures us that the administration is "quick to replace [poor professors] and actively seeks out teachers who are better suited to their job and who have better teaching abilities." In addition, "there are tutors for almost every subject with almost unlimited availability," and seniors benefit from "job fairs every other day" as well as "seminars on different jobs one can get with a BA." Many students complain, however, that registration would be easier if there were "more choices [of] classes" available to undergraduates. Most also feel that the "communication problems" between "registrar's office, the financial aid office, and the bursars office" cause a lot of headaches.

> **SURVEY SAYS . . .**
> *Students get along with local community*
> *School is well run, Classes are small*
> *Students are religious*
> *Class discussions encouraged*
> *(Almost) everyone plays intramural sports*

Life

"Life at Merrimack is fun in its own, rural, way," which for many students means "partying, partying, partying." But though you do find "a large population of the campus partying every weekend," Merrimack students advise that that's not all there is to do. One student gushes, "There are so many activities to get involved in. It's impossible to not find something that interests you." In particular, "outdoor games," "watching our sports programs," and "going to the movies," are popular; as is the school's burgeoning Greek system, which students describe as "currently small but growing in a good way." "Most students participate in retreats or excursions offered by Campus Ministry," whether religious or not. One student tells us, "Being a non-Catholic, I can say that I in no way feel uncomfortable attending a Catholic school or its functions, including those offered by Campus Ministry." Merrimack is "just a quick train ride or a half-hour drive," from Boston, "so you can always have the fun and excitement there"; students also like to "go an hour north to ski in New Hampshire."

Student Body

Despite its cosmopolitan professors, students say Merrimack "is not a good reflection of the real world," as "there isn't much diversity" within the student body. Students tell us that the "homogenous student population," comprises "mainly upper-middle-class white people." Some admit that because "most of the students come from the same type of background, they are not very open-minded to new experiences," and one student cautions that "there is a good amount of hidden homophobia present" on campus. Other students counter, however, that, "race, gender, and sexual preference do not seem to be an issue on this campus at all." In fact, students generally describe their classmates as "friendly, sociable, polite, and community-minded." Sums up one undergrad: "Friendliness, compassion, and helping each other is what makes students at Merrimack unique."

ADMISSIONS

Very important factors considered by the admissions committee include: secondary school record and standardized test scores. *Important factors considered include:* character/personal qualities, class rank, essays, extracurricular activities, interview, and recommendations. *Other factors considered include:* alumni/ae relation, talent/ability, volunteer work, and work experience. SAT I or ACT required, SAT I preferred. TOEFL required of all international applicants. High school diploma is required and GED is not accepted. *High school units required/recommended:* 16 total required; 21 total recommended; 4 English required, 3 math required, 4 math recommended, 2 science required, 3 science recommended, 2 science lab required, 3 science lab recommended, 2 foreign language recommended, 2 social studies required, 2 social studies recommended, 1 history required, 2 elective required.

The Inside Word

Applicants should seriously consider applying to Merrimack through the Early Action program. It guarantees priority registration and financial aid for those accepted, provides a variety of school-related discounts, and best of all, is nonbinding.

FINANCIAL AID

Students should submit: FAFSA, CSS/Financial Aid PROFILE, noncustodial (divorced/separated) parent's statement, and business/farm supplement. Regular filing deadline is February 15. The Princeton Review suggests that all financial aid forms be submitted as soon as possible after January 1. *Need-based scholarships/grants offered:* Pell, SEOG, state scholarships/grants, private scholarships, and the school's own gift aid. *Loan aid offered:* Direct Subsidized Stafford, Direct Unsubsidized Stafford, Direct PLUS, Federal Perkins, state loans, and college/university loans from institutional funds. Federal Work-Study Program available. Institutional employment available. Applicants will be notified of awards on a rolling basis beginning on or about March 1. Off-campus job opportunities are excellent.

FROM THE ADMISSIONS OFFICE

"Merrimack has become an increasingly competitive and demanding college with greater expectations of our talented students. For the second year in a row, *U.S. News & World Report* named Merrimack a Top 10 regional school. It also ranked Merrimack as a Top 10 'Best Value' regional college, an indication of a quality education at a competitive cost.

"Student request for admission has increased by more than 70 percent in only four years and freshman residency has grown to 85 percent. To meet the growing demand, many new facilities have been added within the past four years, including an award-winning campus and recreation center, a state-of-the-art center for the arts, and two new residence halls for freshmen and sophomores. A new hockey rink and extensive landscaping designs are putting the finishing touches on an already beautiful campus.

"Co-operative Education is a popular work/study option for all of our students and many are taking advantage of study opportunities around the world, including the most popular placements in Australia, Italy, and Great Britain.

"Merrimack continues to improve its 34 major course offerings in all three of our divisions: Liberal Arts, Science/Engineering, and the Girard School of Business and International Commerce. This makes our college, with its 2,150 students, a most desirable choice for academic preparation. Our student/faculty ratio of 14:1 not only allows close contact with faculty, but also great dialogue with fellow students—a hallmark of the Merrimack curriculum."

For even more information on this school, turn to page 332 of the "Stats" section.

MIDDLEBURY COLLEGE

THE EMMA WILLARD HOUSE, MIDDLEBURY, VT 05753 • ADMISSIONS: 802-443-3000 • FAX: 802-443-2056
FINANCIAL AID: 802-443-5158 • E-MAIL: ADMISSIONS@MIDDLEBURY.EDU • WEBSITE: WWW.MIDDLEBURY.EDU

Ratings
Quality of Life: 81   **Academic:** 92   **Admissions:** 98   **Financial Aid:** 74

Academics

Academically one of the most rigorous programs in the country, "top-rate" Middlebury College, tucked away in rural Vermont (about three and a half hours' drive to Boston, 45 minutes to Burlington, and two hours to Montreal) manages to offer the resources, facilities, and faculty excellence of a much larger school—while keeping enrollment for undergrads at around 2,300. Nationally recognized language, writing, and theater programs share

> **SURVEY SAYS . . .**
> *Everyone loves the Panthers*
> *Athletic facilities are great*
> *No one cheats*
> *Diversity lacking on campus*
> *Great food on campus*
> *(Almost) no one smokes*
> *(Almost) no one listens to college radio*
> *Theater is hot*
> *Musical organizations are hot*
> *Political activism is (almost) nonexistent*

the spotlight with a top-notch science curriculum—which has benefited in recent years from the construction of a new science center. One student is thrilled that "professors here actually teach. They manage classes, advising, and research demands seamlessly." Despite "tons of homework" and tough classes, students say there's little of the "cutthroat competition" that might characterize other schools of Middlebury's caliber. It might have something to do with the pristine location of "Club Midd," their "laid-back" atmosphere, and an excellent alumni network that makes finding a job after graduation a whole lot easier. Or it might be the result of a bit of grade inflation (some kids complain that "if you're smart, you can get A's and B's hardly doing any work"). But most likely, it's just Middlebury's special blend of a quality program, personal attention, and something a little more nebulous one student calls "attitude." In any case, Middlebury's got it. Sums up a senior, "Academically, I've been challenged, but also have had time to breathe and have fun."

Life

You'd think that at a place that gets "so cold your nostrils freeze together" folks would be spending most of their time inside. Not so at Club Midd! "We own our own ski mountain," notes a junior, one of the reasons why, come winter, most students head outside for fun. With skiing, hiking, rock climbing, mountain biking, kayaking, and fishing right in the college's backyard, you can see why "year round people are involved in outdoor activities." "Almost everyone is athletic one way or another," adds another senior. The school's facilities say as much—students can choose between a hockey rink, fitness center, pool, golf course, and "snow bowl" for fun. It's no surprise, then, that "sports are a major preoccupation here." The "work hard, play hard" ethos extends into socializing, too. A senior explains: "As opportunities for nightlife are virtually nonexistent, we drink. While fun, this does take its toll on one's health." And though there doesn't seem to be a shortage of school-sponsored activities and clubs (social houses and a "commons"-style freshman dorm system provide social opportunities for underclassmen), some students complain that the Middlebury experience "varies between having amazing times to wanting to get the hell out of here." What's more, besides the professed lack of academic competition, "life can be very stressful," notes a junior; "everyone around is an overachiever, star athlete, talented musician, and very attractive."

Student Body

"Students here come from every corner of the world . . . and every New England prep school," jokes a first-year on the subject of Middlebury's fairly homogenous student body (80 percent of its undergrads self-identify as "Caucasian"). A junior gives his take on the situation: "They're cool but the same. This is what I heard before I got here, and this is definitely true. . . . [M]ost are rich and white" and from somewhere "just outside of Boston." Still, it's the people that most students say make the Middlebury experience what it is. Take it from this sophomore: "The main reason I fell in love with Midd was the students. At no other school did I see so many happy, outgoing students." Concludes a classmate, "The majority of the students are really smart and really cool, which makes a small school not feel that way."

ADMISSIONS

Very important factors considered by the admissions committee include: character/personal qualities, secondary school record. *Important factors considered include:* class rank, essays, extracurricular activities, recommendations, standardized test scores, talent/ability. *Other factors considered include:* alumni/ae relation, geographical residence, interview, minority status, volunteer work, work experience. *High school units required/recommended:* 4 English recommended, 4 math recommended, 4 science recommended, 4 science lab recommended, 4 foreign language recommended, 3 social studies recommended.

The Inside Word

While Middlebury benefits tremendously from its age-old position as an Ivy League safety, it is nonetheless a very strong and demanding place in its own right. Middlebury has a broad national applicant pool and sees more ACT scores than most eastern colleges, so submitting ACT scores to Middlebury is a more comfortable option than at most eastern schools.

FINANCIAL AID

Students should submit: FAFSA, CSS/Financial Aid PROFILE, federal income tax return (or statement of nonfiling). Regular filing deadline is January 1. The Princeton Review suggests that all financial aid forms be submitted as soon as possible after January 1. *Need-based scholarships/grants offered:* Pell, SEOG, state scholarships/grants, private scholarships, the school's own gift aid. *Loan aid offered:* Direct Subsidized Stafford, Direct Unsubsidized Stafford, Direct PLUS, Federal Perkins, college/university loans from institutional funds. Federal Work-Study Program available. Institutional employment available. Applicants will be notified of awards on or about April 1. Off-campus job opportunities are good.

FROM THE ADMISSIONS OFFICE

"The successful Middlebury candidate excels in a variety of areas including academics, athletics, the arts, leadership, and service to others. These strengths and interests permit students to grow beyond their traditional 'comfort zones' and conventional limits. Our classrooms are as varied as the Green Mountains, the Metropolitan Museum of Art, or the great cities Russia and Japan. Outside the classroom, students informally interact with professors in activities such as intramural basketball games and community service. At Middlebury, students develop critical thinking skills, enduring bonds of friendship, and the ability to challenge themselves."

For even more information on this school, turn to page 333 of the "Stats" section.

MONMOUTH UNIVERSITY

ADMISSION, MONMOUTH UNIVERSITY, 400 CEDAR AVENUE, WEST LONG BRANCH, NJ 07764-1898
ADMISSIONS: 732-571-3456 • FAX: 732-263-5166 • E-MAIL: ADMISSION@MONMOUTH.EDU
WEBSITE: WWW.MONMOUTH.EDU

Ratings

Quality of Life: 79   Academic: 70   Admissions: 60   Financial Aid: 77

Academics

At Monmouth University, professors are the frequent recipients of unrestrained accolades. "Professors are outstanding, highly accessible, and eager to nurture students along into becoming leaders," writes one pleased under-

> **SURVEY SAYS . . .**
> *Lots of beer drinking, Classes are small*
> *No one cheats, Students are happy*
> *School is well run*

grad. Monmouth undergrads can delve into any of 26 majors offered through five colleges. While students are generally satisfied with their courses, getting in is another story. One senior relates the tale of his latest registration escapade, when he went to the registration hall "very early in the morning to ensure admittance into the necessary courses . . . because when registering for fourth-year courses, we must keep in mind that blockage from just one course may postpone graduation for up to seven months." Despite being near the front of the line, he didn't get two needed courses and spent days haggling with administrators to remedy the situation. Without getting into so much detail, let's just say that the housing situation at Monmouth draws similar criticisms: too many people want in to too few rooms. So, yes, "the school can at times be aggravating," readily admits a student. "But if you step back and look at the big picture, usually you'll see that the students are the priority here."

Life

Monmouth's "beautiful campus," a few minutes from the waters of the Atlantic in West Long Branch, New Jersey, is a picturesque amalgam of green gardens and gray sculptures, of historic landmarks and contemporary architecture. Inside the walls of campus, students can sign up for any of about 65 campus organizations, as well as try out for a handful of NCAA Division I athletic clubs, compete in intramural sports, or pledge at one of 13 Greek societies. "There is so much do at the school," remarks one student. "But everyone is too cool to do it. The students here go home pretty much every weekend." As many universities with large constituencies of commuters experience, extracurricular life at Monmouth sometimes has only a faint pulse. But "Greek life is prominent at Monmouth," assures one student, while another adds that an average Monmouth student's life looks something like this: "Go to frat parties, follow our basketball team, go to clubs, follow teams!" Off campus, students hit the beach, drive an hour and a half to New York City or Philadelphia, or an hour to Atlantic City. Students warn incomers, though, to think twice before bringing a car to campus. Residential students get parking decals on a first-come, first-served basis, and parking spots are often hard to come by. Good news: the train station is just minutes from campus.

Student Body

Most Monmouth students hail from New Jersey and the surrounding states, and more than half are commuters. Another, sometimes discouraging, characteristic of the students at this mid-sized, private university is their well-to-do attitudes. "Very snobby, self-centered, and spoiled," remarks one student of her classmates. Another student quips, "I wish my daddy could buy me a Jaguar." But the students with their noses in the air are offset by the students with their feet firmly planted on the ground—the "very warm-hearted and hardworking" contingency, as one student puts it. What would really add to the dynamics at Monmouth is diversity, students tell us. "Student population is mostly Caucasian with small percentages of minority and foreign students," and it often happens that "members of different ethnicities tend not to mix, and actually form 'cliques.'" As one student suggests, if you can't beat the cliques, join one: "It is a matter of finding the people you fit in with and sticking with them. Once you find that, you have found a family."

ADMISSIONS

Very important factors considered by the admissions committee include: secondary school record and standardized test scores. *Important factors considered include:* extracurricular activities and interview. *Other factors considered include:* alumni/ae relation, character/personal qualities, class rank, essays, recommendations, volunteer work, and work experience. SAT I or ACT required. TOEFL required of all international applicants. High school diploma or GED is required. *High school units required/recommended:* 16 total required; 4 English required, 3 math required, 2 science required, 1 science lab required, 2 foreign language recommended, 2 social studies recommended, 2 history required, 5 elective required.

The Inside Word

B students with average standardized test scores should have little trouble getting into Monmouth University. Stiff competition from the area's many quality schools forces MU to accept more students, and less-qualified students, than it otherwise would.

FINANCIAL AID

Students should submit: FAFSA. No deadline for regular filing. The Princeton Review suggests that all financial aid forms be submitted as soon as possible after January 1. *Need-based scholarships/grants offered:* Pell, SEOG, state scholarships/grants, private scholarships, and the school's own gift aid. *Loan aid offered:* Direct Subsidized Stafford, Direct Unsubsidized Stafford, Direct PLUS, Federal Perkins, and state loans. Federal Work-Study Program available. Institutional employment available. Applicants will be notified of awards on a rolling basis beginning on or about February 1. Off-campus job opportunities are good.

FROM THE ADMISSIONS OFFICE

"Monmouth University is a leading independent institution of higher learning, emphasizing teaching and scholarship at undergraduate and graduate levels. The University is committed to helping men and women pursue and achieve a wide variety of bachelor's and master's programs. Monmouth is dedicated to serving its students and actively manages its resources to keep up with its growth. Because of this, the University still offers small classes that are taught by professors who focus on the student's learning and career preparation. Seven schools within the University provide a variety of academic programs. There are bachelor's degree programs in arts and sciences and in professional areas of business, computer science, criminal justice, education, nursing, social work, and software engineering. Master's-level programs include business administration, computer science, corporate and public communication, criminal justice, education, electronic engineering, history, liberal arts, nursing, psychological counseling, social work, and software engineering. Monmouth faculty members are respected scholars, artists, scientists, and professionals, all of whom are committed to helping students achieve their fullest potential. The University's beautiful and historic 153-acre campus is located in attractive, residential West Long Branch, New Jersey, near the ocean and close to New York City and Philadelphia. Monmouth University also enjoys proximity to high-technology firms and financial institutions and a thriving business-industrial sector. Monmouth offers a high-tech learning environment, professors who meet the highest standards for teaching and academic excellence, and the vibrant life of a large university combined with the individual attention typical of small liberal arts colleges."

For even more information on this school, turn to page 333 of the "Stats" section.

MOUNT HOLYOKE COLLEGE

50 COLLEGE STREET, SOUTH HADLEY, MA 01075 • ADMISSIONS: 413-538-2023 • FAX: 413-538-2409
FINANCIAL AID: 413-538-2291 • E-MAIL: ADMISSIONS@MTHOLYOKE.EDU • WEBSITE: WWW.MTHOLYOKE.EDU

Ratings
Quality of Life: 90   Academic: 93   Admissions: 87   Financial Aid: 93

Academics

Rigorous academics in a nurturing environment distinguish the Mount Holyoke undergraduate experience. As one student simply puts it, "Mount Holyoke is an extremely tough school. Students enrolled need to learn to separate their 'fun' time from their study time. If they do not, they will sink like rocks." Mount Holyoke

> **SURVEY SAYS . . .**
> Student publications are ignored
> Students don't get along with local community
> Students don't like Socorro, NM
> Intercollegiate sports unpopular or nonexistent
> Campus easy to get around
> Lousy food on campus
> Popular college radio

demands a lot from its students, but the school also strives to ensure that undergrads have every chance to succeed. Explains one, "At times you feel like you are drowning in work. But there are plenty of lifeguards to help you. By the end of your first semester, not only are you learning to swim, but you're beginning to feel more confident in the water." "The courses are rigorous but not impossible," notes another. Easing the academic burden is a faculty that students universally praise. Writes one typical student, "The professors are unbelievable. I find out every day something new that they have done. They are the top of the line, the most accomplished and most understanding teachers I have ever had. They genuinely care about you and how you are doing, and will make sure that you are performing up to your potential." The administration, "although not as good as the professors, are helpful and cordial." Membership in the Five College Consortium, which also includes UMass—Amherst, Smith, Amherst, and Hampshire, provides access to top profs at other area schools. The MHC Honor Code, which every student signs during their first year and "which the campus takes very seriously," is another plus; it allows ample academic freedom, including "self-scheduled exams." About the only thing the students here really pine for is more "name recognition." As a biology major points out, "No one knows how cool we are."

Life

Hard work means less play for the women of Mount Holyoke. "This is not the school for a stereotypical college social life," explains one undergrad. "However, if you enjoy Friday night study sessions, come on down." Adds another, "Unfortunately, although there are four other colleges in the area, it is very hard to find anything on the weekend besides the general frat parties of UMass and TAP (the Amherst party) at Amherst College." The administration, to its credit, works hard to provide activities such as "improv comedy, free dances, movie showings, and music performances." Students also point out that "if you can't find something to do on campus, hop on the free bus to the neighboring towns with diverse restaurants, fun shopping, and great bars/clubs. The school provides weekly transportation to the mall and the grocery store (one mile down the road)." But don't hang out in South Hadley. Cautions one undergrad, "Mount Holyoke College is located in a very small town called South Hadley, Massachusetts, which we refer to it as 'How Sadly.' The town hates us." Students conclude that "If you want a social life, you can get it. It's just a little more [of an] effort to find."

Student Body

The typical Mount Holyoke woman, students report, "seems to be one that believes that she can single-handedly change the world. Most of the students are exceptionally friendly—many, however, are overly p.c." A large and vocal lesbian community makes Mount Holyoke home, prompting one student to write, "If you're gay, you've entered your heaven." Others add, "We have a few major subcultures, like the athletes, the party girls, the queer community, some religious groups, but most people have diverse groups of friends from all over campus. It is easy to make new friends in classes, in clubs, or over a meal in one of our cafeterias (there is one in every dorm). The friends you make here will last a good long time." Be fore-warned, though. "There are a lot of opinionated women, which means that there tend to be arguments and debates in classes, in the dorms, in online forums, in the newspaper, etc."

ADMISSIONS

Very important factors considered by the admissions committee include: class rank, essays, recommendations, secondary school record. *Important factors considered include:* character/personal qualities, extracurricular activities, interview, talent/ability, volunteer work, work experience. *Other factors considered include:* alumni/ae relation, geographical residence, minority status, standardized test scores. TOEFL required of all international applicants. High school diploma or GED is required. *High school units required/recommended:* 4 English recommended, 3 math recommended, 3 science recommended, 3 science lab recommended, 3 foreign language recommended, 3 history recommended, 1 elective recommended.

The Inside Word

Mount Holyoke has benefited well from the renaissance of interest in women's colleges; selectivity and academic quality are on the rise. Considering that the college was already fairly selective, candidates are well advised to take the admissions process seriously. Matchmaking is a significant factor here; strong academic performance, well-written essays, and an understanding of and appreciation for "the Mount Holyoke experience" will usually carry the day.

FINANCIAL AID

Students should submit: FAFSA, CSS/Financial Aid PROFILE, noncustodial (divorced/separated) parent's statement, business/farm supplement, federal income tax returns and W-2 forms of parents and student. Regular filing deadline is February 1. The Princeton Review suggests that all financial aid forms be submitted as soon as possible after January 1. *Need-based scholarships/grants offered:* Pell, SEOG, state scholarships/grants, private scholarships, the school's own gift aid. *Loan aid offered:* Direct Subsidized Stafford, Direct Unsubsidized Stafford, Direct PLUS, Federal Perkins, state loans, college/university loans from institutional funds. Federal Work-Study Program available. Institutional employment available. Applicants will be notified of awards on or about March 25. Off-campus job opportunities are excellent.

FROM THE ADMISSIONS OFFICE

"Did you know that the majority of students who choose Mount Holyoke do so simply because it is an outstanding liberal arts college? After a semester or two, they start to appreciate the fact that Mount Holyoke is a women's college, even though most Mount Holyoke students never thought they'd go to a women's college when they started their college search. Students talk of having 'space' to really figure out who they are. They speak about feeling empowered to excel in traditionally male subjects such as science and technology. They talk about the remarkable array of opportunities—for academic achievement, career exploration, and leadership—and the impressive, creative accomplishments of their peers. If you're looking for a college that will challenge you to be your best, most powerful self and to fulfill potential, Mount Holyoke should be at the top of your list."

For even more information on this school, turn to page 334 of the "Stats" section.

NAZARETH COLLEGE OF ROCHESTER

4245 EAST AVENUE, ROCHESTER, NY 14618-3790 • ADMISSIONS: 585-389-2860 • FAX: 585-389-2826
E-MAIL: ADMISSIONS@NAZ.EDU • WEBSITE: WWW.NAZ.EDU

Ratings
Quality of Life: 75   **Academic:** 80   **Admissions:** 72   **Financial Aid:** 82

Academics

Many students choose Nazareth College of Rochester for the strong reputations of its education and physical therapy programs, as well as for the variety of unique programs it offers, such as art and music therapy. Students report that Nazareth's growing campus and facilities are great and that "the aca-

> **SURVEY SAYS . . .**
> *Popular college radio*
> *Instructors are good teachers*
> *Lousy food on campus, Classes are small*
> *Diversity lacking on campus*
> *School is well run, Theater is hot*
> *Student publications are popular*

demics are top notch." Writes a senior, "My professors have given me my motivation to learn. My intellectual abilities have [risen] many levels because of [their] help and dedication." The intimate environment really pleases Nazareth students, who claim instructors "will go out of their way to help students and make themselves available." According to one student, "Everyone here is very helpful and available for outside help for any reason, including nonschool related problems." Overall, the academic environment is very supportive. A student explains, "Nazareth has an atmosphere that is competitive without being cutthroat. The teachers challenge you to do your best, but in the classroom there is a general sense of camaraderie." Those looking for the stimulation of a large university, however, might not be at home at Nazareth. Grumbles one dissatisfied student, "It is not even a real college; it is high school for 18 to 21 year olds." Many Nazareth students "haven't had a lot of experience with the administration" and so rightly feel that they "can't really comment on" its performance. Those students who did have something to say about the people running the school, however, give appraisals that range from "inconsiderate" and "out of touch" to "excellent and open to student suggestions."

Life

"Campus life is busy but fun" at Nazareth. From "campus ministry and volunteer organizations" to "pick-up sports," students say "there are always a lot of activities going on." Many Nazareth students report that they enjoy residential living and spend their free time chatting with their classmates in the dining hall or hanging out with their friends on the weekends. "Dorm life is great," as one student simply put it. Claims another, "I have never been happier in my life than I have been at Nazareth College." In addition to on-campus activities, students say they "shop, watch movies, go out to eat, hang out with friends, [or] go to church for fun." Those who prefer the excitement of the urban environment, however, complain that there is "not much to do" at Nazareth. One freshman says, "During the week campus life is extremely boring." A senior reflects, "The T.V. shows about college never happened for me." These students venture into downtown Rochester to participate in "a lot of community service and outreach programs" or to hang out at Java's, a favorite coffee shop for area students in search of a caffeine fix and quasi-intellectual conversation.

Student Body

Nazareth's 3,000 students, the large majority of whom hail from upstate New York, comprise a close-knit campus community. A sophomore recalls that "as a freshman one of the first things I noticed was how friendly everyone was." The spirit of solidarity prevails through one's years of study, as one senior declares, "Everyone seems to go out of their way to be friendly and helpful." The size of the campus and its residential life facilitates relationships between students, and many undergrads believe that their "fellow students will be lifelong friends." Some are, however, discouraged by the tiny size of the school and claim it feels "like high school." And like high school, several students report that Nazareth has "too many cliques." In addition, students claim that, "there is not a lot of communication among races" in what is a generally homogenous student body. As one senior put it, "Talking about diversity and doing something about it are two different things."

ADMISSIONS

Very important factors considered by the admissions committee include: class rank, secondary school record, and standardized test scores. *Important factors considered include:* essays, interview, minority status, recommendations, volunteer work, and work experience. *Other factors considered include:* alumni/ae relation, character/personal qualities, extracurricular activities, geographical residence, state residency, and talent/ability. SAT I or ACT required. TOEFL required of all international applicants. High school diploma or GED is required. *High school units required/recommended:* 4 English required, 3 math required, 4 math recommended, 3 science required, 4 science recommended, 2 science lab required, 3 foreign language required, 4 foreign language recommended, 3 social studies required, 4 social studies recommended.

The Inside Word

Admissions officers at Nazareth College are looking for candidates who will enhance the college community as a whole. This means that a special talent in athletics, music, the arts, or leadership areas counts; it can be especially helpful to candidates whose academic records are less than exemplary.

FINANCIAL AID

Students should submit: FAFSA. Regular filing deadline is May 1. The Princeton Review suggests that all financial aid forms be submitted as soon as possible after January 1. *Need-based scholarships/grants offered:* Pell, SEOG, state scholarships/grants, private scholarships, and the school's own gift aid. *Loan aid offered:* FFEL Subsidized Stafford, FFEL Unsubsidized Stafford, FFEL PLUS, and Federal Perkins. Federal Work-Study Program available. Institutional employment available. Applicants will be notified of awards on a rolling basis beginning on or about March 8. Off-campus job opportunities are excellent.

FROM THE ADMISSIONS OFFICE

"Campus expansion is creating more opportunities for Nazareth students in what they study, where they reside, and how they play. Information Technology, new in 2001, prepares students for careers in demand by all organizations. New campus apartments plus a growing number of single rooms provide more living choices for our growing student body. Soccer, lacrosse, and track athletes will compete in the new 2,200 seat stadium. Recreational athletes will love running on the 400-meter, all-weather oval.

"More students from more places are choosing Nazareth College. The 2002 freshman came from throughout the United States and abroad. In turn, more of our students seek opportunities for international study and internships. The new Center for International Education creates 'two-way traffic' for study; participants are students wishing to come to the United States as well as U.S. students seeking an international experience. The new Center for Teaching Excellence assists Nazareth and other college faculty in honing their classroom skills. Recent campus speakers have included space shuttle astronaut Pamela Melroy, olympic gold medallist Billy Mills, anthropologist Meave Leakey, Marriott CEO Bill Marriott Jr., and former surgeon general of the United States Dr. David Satcher."

For even more information on this school, turn to page 335 of the "Stats" section.

NEW JERSEY INSTITUTE OF TECHNOLOGY

University Heights, Newark, NJ 07102 • Admissions: 973-596-3300 • Fax: 973-596-3461
Financial Aid: 973-596-3480 • E-mail: admissions@njit.edu • Website: www.njit.edu

Ratings

Quality of Life: 66   **Academic:** 79   **Admissions:** 80   **Financial Aid:** 85

Academics

Those looking for "great 'bang for the buck'" in the world of engineering would do well to consider the New Jersey Institute of Technology. While the school also maintains divisions of architecture, management, and arts and sciences, the low-cost, high-return College of Engineering is the undisputed star of the show. According to NJIT, graduates make

> **SURVEY SAYS . . .**
> *Musical organizations aren't popular*
> *Popular college radio*
> *High cost of living*
> *Very little drug use*
> *Unattractive campus*
> *Very little beer drinking*
> *Very little hard liquor*

up one-fourth of all engineers currently working in the Garden State. Important to note, the university is opening the College of Computing Sciences in fall 2001. Students warn "this school is easy to get into, but when it comes to sticking through it and getting a degree from here, life is 'hell.' The professors love to challenge you, and I can say that when I graduate I know I am going to be very well off." NJIT's curriculum is "extremely vigorous and challenging" and "helps provide you with the proper learning skills that are needed in order for you to make it in the world." Professors receive mixed reviews; some "go above and beyond for 'positive and eager-to-learn' students," while others "tend to read from slides instead of using them as aids" and "are rarely available beyond class hours." The administration "is slow to enact changes desired by students" and could use more "financial advisors and otherwise more help for registration, particularly for freshmen!" Students also gripe about the condition of lecture halls, dorms, and other facilities. Even so, most agree that the NJIT experience is an enriching one. Writes one, "It feels like you're in the United Nations school, as there are so many international students and professors. Great cultural experience if nothing else; sometimes, though, it makes it hard to understand what's going on."

Life

Hmm . . . a tech school in Newark, New Jersey. Not exactly the formula for a swinging campus, you have to admit. NJIT has other hurdles to overcome as well. As one student explains, "Because we are so diverse and a large percentage of our students are commuters, it is really hard to form any kind of school unity, whether it be in clubs, student government, or athletics." All the same, "While our school is extremely technology-oriented, we do know how to have fun, regardless of how busy we are." As for NJIT's reputation as a dead campus, several students note that "contrary to popular belief, there is plenty to do on campus. More often than not, it is the lack of student participation that creates the perception of a nonexistent social life on campus." Many students report participating in such sports as bowling, swimming, volleyball, lifting weights, and track and field, while some insist that "pool is the biggest 'sport' on campus. Everyone owns a pool cue." Downtown Newark is enjoying a renaissance with the recent addition of a new performing arts center that draws major international artists in music, dance, and theater. And of course, New York City is only a PATH train ride away.

Student Body

NJIT boasts "good ethnic diversity and individual acceptance," and although "students tend to self-segregate into ethnic/gender/major-related groups," most agree that the atmosphere here is congenial. Writes one student, "I actually often brag about how friendly our campus is. Maybe that's just reflecting the desperation of the male population in [light of] the male-female ratio of 10:1." Students wish there "was more interaction between residents and commuters." Commuters "often come to class and just leave. It's hard to meet nondormers."

ADMISSIONS

Very important factors considered by the admissions committee include: class rank, secondary school record, standardized test scores. *Other factors considered include:* character/personal qualities, essays, extracurricular activities, interview, recommendations, talent/ability, volunteer work, work experience. SAT I or ACT required; SAT I preferred. TOEFL required of all international applicants. High school diploma or GED is required. *High school units required/recommended:* 16 total required; 4 English required, 4 math required, 2 science required, 2 science lab required, 2 foreign language recommended, 1 social studies recommended, 1 history recommended, 2 elective recommended.

The Inside Word

NJIT is a great choice for students who aspire to technical careers but don't meet the requirements for better known and more selective universities. To top it off, it's a pretty good buy.

FINANCIAL AID

Students should submit: FAFSA. The Princeton Review suggests that all financial aid forms be submitted as soon as possible after January 1. *Need-based scholarships/grants offered:* Pell, SEOG, state scholarships/grants, private scholarships, the school's own gift aid. *Loan aid offered:* Direct Subsidized Stafford, Direct Unsubsidized Stafford, Direct PLUS, FFEL Subsidized Stafford, FFEL Unsubsidized Stafford, FFEL PLUS, Federal Perkins, state loans, college/university loans from institutional funds. Federal Work-Study Program available. Institutional employment available. Off-campus job opportunities are good.

FROM THE ADMISSIONS OFFICE

"Talented high school graduates from across the nation come to NJIT to prepare for leadership roles in architecture, business, engineering, medical, legal, science, and technological fields. Students experience a public research university conducting more than $50 million in research that maintains a small-college atmosphere at a modest cost. Our attractive 45-acre campus is just minutes from New York City and less than an hour from the Jersey shore. Students find an outstanding faculty and a safe, diverse, caring learning and residential community. All dormitory rooms have sprinklers. NJIT's academic environment challenges and prepares students for rewarding careers and full-time advanced study after graduation. The campus is computing-intensive. For five consecutive years, Yahoo! Internet Life has ranked NJIT among America's Most Wired Universities."

For even more information on this school, turn to page 335 of the "Stats" section.

NEW YORK UNIVERSITY

22 WASHINGTON SQUARE NORTH, NEW YORK, NY 10011 • ADMISSIONS: 212-998-4500 • FAX: 212-995-4902
FINANCIAL AID: 212-998-4444 • E-MAIL: ADMISSIONS@NYU.EDU • WEBSITE: WWW.NYU.EDU

Ratings
Quality of Life: 88   Academic: 89   Admissions: 90   Financial Aid: 83

Academics

Most colleges would be honored to have a single world-renowned academic department. Then again, most aren't New York University. The programs at NYU's Stern School of Business and the Tisch School of the Arts are among the best undergraduate programs in the country. NYU professors are "very intelligent, informed, and

> **SURVEY SAYS . . .**
> *Students love New York, NY*
> *Great off-campus food, (Almost) everyone smokes*
> *Ethnic diversity on campus*
> *Great library, Campus feels safe*
> *No one plays intramural sports*
> *Very small frat/sorority scene*
> *No one watches intercollegiate sports*

open-minded." They are both "witty" and "well-prepared" and, considering that many of them live in the city, "tend to be very accessible," though some students complain that, because of the university's size, profs occasionally get "lost in the crowd." Explains one student, "They are helpful in guiding students . . . to careers, internships, grad school programs, good restaurants, movies, hairdressers, and all the best deals that New York City has to offer." Undergrads also appreciate the fact that professors are often the authors of the textbooks used in class. A senior broadcast journalism major writes that though he harbors "a lifelong hatred towards school and education, I've enjoyed learning here." Students not interested in an academic culture need not apply since, according to one junior, "as a freshman, I began doing work people don't touch until grad school." Students get practice as the vociferous liberals they are when dealing with the administration, as they must be "persistent and demanding" in order to get things done. Students rave about online registration, though some complain that upper-level classes close too quickly, "often with the speed of Japan's bullet train."

Life

"What do we do for fun?" a senior theater major asks. "We do New York." While studies are undeniably important, NYU is located in the heart of downtown Manhattan's Greenwich Village, within shouting distance of hundreds of restaurants, theaters, clubs, and other cultural opportunities. "Life here is never dull or routine," a junior politics major writes, and "no student can say that she is bored." Students who wish to commune with nature spend time bike riding or inline skating in Central Park. Sports fans not only attend college basketball games on campus (NYU's Division III women's basketball team is among the best in the nation), but can also choose from any of the city's professional baseball, basketball, football, and hockey teams. Numerous museums and theaters provide more cultural stimulation than a student can possibly absorb in four years. The city's extensive concert scene assures that local and national acts can be found somewhere every night of the year. Though there are plenty of on-campus activities, students downplay their importance because of the numerous off-campus opportunities. The lack of a defined campus allows the school to become a part of the city, which, in turn, allows students to smoothly coexist with fellow city dwellers. While on-campus housing is expensive, the "apartment-style dorms" are often looked upon wistfully by those who end up in almost-as-costly off-campus housing.

Student Body

New York is one of the most diverse cities in the world and that doesn't exclude the student body of NYU. "Everyone here is very unique—some you love, some you hate." Students are individualistic and passionate, "but somehow this manages to bond us all," and students create close friendships, writes one senior musical theater major. "People are cool and unique," adds a sophomore. Students are "tolerant and open-minded" and develop neighborly relationships. Students see their peers as adventurous and focused, which "makes for some really interesting people." A junior English major advises, "If you're looking for an accepting community, this is it." If students have any complaints, it is that their peers are sometimes apathetic about campus life, and "as a result, school spirit is negligible." Still, it's unlikely that anyone looking for a diverse educational experience will easily find one that surpasses the one found at NYU.

ADMISSIONS

Very important factors considered by the admissions committee include: essays, secondary school record, standardized test scores. *Important factors considered include:* character/personal qualities, class rank, extracurricular activities, recommendations, talent/ability. *Other factors considered include:* alumni/ae relation, minority status, volunteer work, work experience. SAT I or ACT required. TOEFL required of all international applicants. High school diploma or GED is required. *High school units required/recommended:* 18 total required; 4 English required, 3 math required, 4 math recommended, 3 science required, 2 science lab required, 2 foreign language required, 3 foreign language recommended, 4 history required.

The Inside Word

NYU is more selective than most large private universities but, except for a few particularly choosy programs, no more personal in its evaluation of candidates. A solid GPA and test scores go further toward getting in than anything else. Still, the university is very serious about projecting a highly selective image and it's dangerous to take your application too lightly. Over the past decade, NYU has turned its attention to increasing the national profile of its student body. Applications have increased by more than half over the past four years.

FINANCIAL AID

Students should submit: FAFSA, state aid form. Early decision applicants may submit an institutional form for an estimated award. Regular filing deadline is February 15. The Princeton Review suggests that all financial aid forms be submitted as soon as possible after January 1. *Need-based scholarships/grants offered:* Pell, SEOG, state scholarships/grants, private scholarships, the school's own gift aid. *Loan aid offered:* FFEL Subsidized Stafford, FFEL Unsubsidized Stafford, FFEL PLUS, Federal Perkins, Federal Nursing. Federal Work-Study Program available. Institutional employment available. Applicants will be notified of awards on a rolling basis beginning on or about April 1. Off-campus job opportunities are excellent.

FROM THE ADMISSIONS OFFICE

"NYU is distinctive both in the quality of education we provide and in the exhilarating atmosphere in which our students study and learn. As an undergraduate in one of our seven small- to medium-size colleges, you will enjoy a small faculty/student ratio and a dynamic, challenging learning environment that encourages lively interaction between students and professors. At the same time, you will have available to you all the resources of a distinguished university dedicated to research and scholarship at the highest levels, including a curriculum that offers over 2,500 courses and 160 programs of study and a faculty that includes some of the most highly regarded scholars, scientists, and artists in the country. New York University is a vital, vibrant community. There is an aura of energy and excitement here, a sense that possibilities and opportunities are limited only by the number of hours in a day. The educational experience at NYU is intense, but varied and richly satisfying."

For even more information on this school, turn to page 336 of the "Stats" section.

Northeastern University

360 Huntington Avenue, 150 Richards Hall, Boston, MA 02115 • Admissions: 617-373-2200
Fax: 617-373-8780 • Financial Aid: 617-373-3190 • E-mail: admissions@neu.edu • Website: www.neu.edu

Ratings

Quality of Life: 76   Academic: 76   Admissions: 77   Financial Aid: 88

Academics

The academic calendar at Northeastern comes in an unusual shape. Northeastern runs on four "short quarter terms" each year, rather than the two-semester model used by most universities. Yes, this means four healthy breaks a year, but at the expense of one large summer break. (If this is a concern, take note that the

> **SURVEY SAYS . . .**
> *Students love Boston, MA*
> *Athletic facilities are great*
> *High cost of living*
> *Ethnic diversity on campus*
> *Popular college radio*
> *Campus feels safe*
> *Great off-campus food*

administration plans to convert to the semester model in the fall of 2003.) With an undergraduate population the size of a small city, "students must be self-starters and self-helpers to succeed here." On this note, some students wish the university administrators and professors would offer "more guidance." While students offer unified complaints about the accessibility of professors, they garnish their thoughts with universal praise for the campus's unique "co-op" program. This program is geared toward preparing students for the global marketplace by getting them into real-world internships and linking them up with a variety of resources, including alumni contacts. This experiential program is supplemented by "a good selection of classes" in the scholastic curriculum. Add all of this up and what you get on any given weekday is what one student calls "a revolving door—in and out all the time—between classes and co-op; students are always moving around."

Life

It's probably not surprising that student life at Northeastern revolves around Boston at least as much as it does around the university itself. "There isn't much to do on campus," admits a junior. Despite having nearly 140 student organizations and a living (if not always lively) Greek system, Northeastern constantly spews its students into Boston's "clubs," "museums," "coffee shops," "movies," "concerts," sports "games," and . . . well . . . it's Boston—"you're bound to find something you like." In fact, one student says that it's "everything around campus" that "provides you with culture and social interactions." Of course, before you dive headfirst into the rich social life of Boston, you have to "make sure you can finance yourself." Boston, remember, is not a cheap city. Whether they stay on campus or venture into the city, NU students tend to "party fairly hard on weekends." They also "work relatively hard" on the weekdays. So when all's told, most students here are able to strike "a balance between social life and academics."

Student Body

Situated in the heart of a city that has dozens of universities and professional schools, Northeastern students are not always distinguishable from the other young faces in the Boston crowd. Like Boston itself, Northeastern is composed of "a very diverse" student body. Because the students come from a variety of backgrounds, says one student, "everyone I meet has something new to offer." Although every tax bracket is certainly represented in the NU population, a noticeable core of students comes from a background of deep pockets. "Everyone here has money," a sophomore says, "and they're not afraid to show it." Among the nearly 14,000 undergraduate students, the most interaction occurs in dorms ("The best dorms in Boston," raves one student), classrooms, or, when applicable, campus groups. Overall, though, "everyone seems to only care about their own little clique." Cliques aside, Northeastern students are "very friendly and helpful, especially to freshman." And they plan to make a dent in the world when they leave the campus halls. Declares one undergrad, "Students here are very goal-oriented and know where they want to go."

ADMISSIONS

Very important factors considered by the admissions committee include: secondary school record. *Important factors considered include:* character/personal qualities, class rank, essays, extracurricular activities, recommendations, standardized test scores, talent/ability. *Other factors considered include:* alumni/ae relation, geographical residence, minority status, volunteer work, work experience. SAT I or ACT required; SAT I preferred. TOEFL required of all international applicants. High school diploma or GED is required. *High school units required/recommended:* 17 total recommended; 4 English recommended, 3 math recommended, 3 science recommended, 2 science lab recommended, 2 foreign language recommended, 3 social studies recommended, 2 history recommended.

The Inside Word

Northeastern is one of the moderately selective of Boston's mélange of colleges and universities, which makes it a popular safety for students who must go to school in Beantown. This translates into a large applicant pool and a lower acceptance rate than might otherwise be the case. The source of any true selectivity in NU's admissions process is a heavy reliance on the numbers: GPA, rank, and tests.

FINANCIAL AID

Students should submit: FAFSA, CSS/Financial Aid PROFILE. No deadline for regular filing. The Princeton Review suggests that all financial aid forms be submitted as soon as possible after January 1. *Need-based scholarships/grants offered:* Pell, SEOG, state scholarships/grants, private scholarships, the school's own gift aid, Federal Nursing. *Loan aid offered:* FFEL Subsidized Stafford, FFEL Unsubsidized Stafford, FFEL PLUS, Federal Perkins, Federal Nursing, state loans, MEFA, TERI, Signature, Massachusetts No Interest Loan (NIL), CitiAssist. Federal Work-Study Program available. Institutional employment available. Applicants will be notified of awards on a rolling basis beginning on or about February 15. Off-campus job opportunities are excellent.

FROM THE ADMISSIONS OFFICE

"Northeastern University's energy comes from its bright, ambitious students and their sense of purpose. In the classroom, in campus activities, and in the city of Boston, they make things happen. Backed by the three components of a Northeastern education—a solid liberal arts foundation, professional knowledge and skills, and on-the-job experience—they're ready to take on any challenge, anywhere. Through Northeastern's cooperative education (co-op) program, students alternate classroom learning with periods of full-time paid work related to their majors or interests. Northeastern students try out different jobs, build their résumés, earn money, and understand the connection between work and classes all before they graduate. And they do it in the heart of an exciting city, where culture, commerce, civic pride, and college students from around the globe are all a part of the mix."

For even more information on this school, turn to page 337 of the "Stats" section.

PLYMOUTH STATE COLLEGE

17 HIGH STREET, PLYMOUTH, NH 03264 • ADMISSIONS: 603-535-2237 • FAX: 603-535-2714
E-MAIL: PSCADMIT@MAIL.PLYMOUTH.EDU • WEBSITE: WWW.PLYMOUTH.EDU

Ratings
Quality of Life: 75   Academic: 68   Admissions: 60   Financial Aid: 80

Academics

The professors at Plymouth State College have a reputation for being "well educated in their field and [able to] teach it well to others." A few exceptions "don't have a clue about helping students get interested," and others are characterized as "really quirky

SURVEY SAYS . . .
Very little beer drinking
Very little hard liquor
Diversity lacking on campus
Classes are small
(Almost) no one listens to college radio

and strange, in a good way." The faculty and staff are generally sociable, in part because "some teachers and advisors that live close to campus invite their students or advisees to dinner or a cookout." Another respondent points out, "Because it's a small school, the professors and administration know you by your first name, which makes it a comfortable and successful academic experience." Though several students comment that the school needs to improve the "depth of some programs," most agree that the theatre and education departments are strong. Summing the situation up, one woman writes, "The academics are challenging enough to make it worth going to class but not so hard that I'm forced to drop out." The administration is called "friendly" and "terrific"; others go as far as to say, "They have never failed to meet my needs and usually listen to the opinions of students, and very seriously." A common complaint centers on "how much they charge for fines, parking tickets, dorm charges, parking passes, and late fees." Still, Plymouth State offers an affordable education and "doesn't accept everybody like I once thought."

Life

Located in a town where "there really isn't much to do besides throw back the booze," Plymouth has earned a reputation for its students' interest in the alcohol arts. Specifically, one student writes, "Last time I heard, we were the fifth largest party school in the nation." Reportedly, "studying is done between the drunken stupors and the haze of partying." Another student qualifies this sweeping assessment, stating, "Plymouth used to be known as a huge party school. People still drink, but it has been toned down quite a bit." Still, on the weekends the majority of people "work their way to Russell Street where the fraternities are," causing some students to frown upon "the amount that drinking is accepted, both of-age and underage." Aside from the parties, the school is "mainly sports-oriented." Relishing in "the surrounding beauty" of New Hampshire, students tell us that "in the winter, skiing is the big thing." One undergraduate waxes pastoral: "Sometimes I just take walks because the mountains are so beautiful here." Though some respondents offer mixed reviews ("When you can find something to do, it is great, but when you can't, it's boring"), most agree that "life at Plymouth is spectacular."

Student Body

One community-minded Plymouth student characterizes the school's population as a "tight family" where "everyone is looking out for each other." Plymouth kids also report that when they "make eye contact with a stranger, it's an automatic hello." Plymouth is home to "quite a variety of people," and some claim that "it doesn't matter what kind of clique you're in. It is pretty versatile, and everyone seems to give everyone a chance." Another student agrees by saying, "Everyone is very different but very friendly and usually not biased about anything." However, some respondents note a degree of homophobia, which they find out of place considering the "big theatre department full of gay guys and a female rugby team full of lesbians." Despite pleas for "more political activism," most attendees appear to be "relatively happy with their lives as students."

ADMISSIONS

Very important factors considered by the admissions committee include: secondary school record. *Important factors considered include:* character/personal qualities, class rank, essays, recommendations, standardized test scores, and talent/ability. *Other factors considered include:* alumni/ae relation, extracurricular activities, minority status, volunteer work, and work experience. SAT I or ACT required, SAT I preferred. TOEFL required of all international applicants. High school diploma or GED is required. *High school units required/recommended:* 13 total required; 16 total recommended; 4 English required, 3 math required, 2 science required, 1 science lab required, 2 foreign language recommended, 2 social studies required, 2 social studies recommended, 1 history required, 2 history recommended.

The Inside Word

Plymouth State has upped its admissions standards in recent years, but the school is still a relatively easy admit. With only half its students ranking in the top half of their graduating high school class, the PSC student body closely mirrors the student body of a typical New Hampshire high school.

FINANCIAL AID

Students should submit: FAFSA. The Princeton Review suggests that all financial aid forms be submitted as soon as possible after January 1. *Need-based scholarships/grants offered:* Pell, SEOG, state scholarships/grants, private scholarships, and the school's own gift aid. *Loan aid offered:* FFEL Subsidized Stafford, FFEL Unsubsidized Stafford, FFEL PLUS, and Federal Perkins. Federal Work-Study Program available. Institutional employment available. Applicants will be notified of awards on a rolling basis beginning on or about March 1. Off-campus job opportunities are good.

For even more information on this school, turn to page 337 of the "Stats" section.

POLYTECHNIC UNIVERSITY

6 METROTECH CENTER, BROOKLYN, NY 11201-2999 • ADMISSIONS: 718-260-3100 • FAX: 718-260-3446
E-MAIL: ADMITME@POLY.EDU • WEBSITE: WWW.POLY.EDU

Ratings

Quality of Life: 75   Academic: 82   Admissions: 80   Financial Aid: 80

Academics

Students in search of hardcore engineering, mathematics, and computer science may well find a home at the Polytechnic Institute of Brooklyn. Students tell us that Poly "is an academically sound school, and only people who really know what they are doing get degrees from this place, at least in the technical programs. Also, the school is really trying its best to keep up with the marketplace, adding some classes and majors to help reflect trends in the industry." Students warn that "if you don't really know your stuff, you don't have much of a chance of passing many classes, so you gotta have a grip on the source material," pointing out that only half of the students in most freshman classes graduate from Poly. Notes one student, "If your idea of a fun Friday night is finishing up a computer programming assignment followed by reading three chapters of quantum physics, Polytechnic is perfect for you." Students have a few bones to pick with the faculty and administration; they caution that many professors don't speak English as a first language ("75 percent is a safe estimate"), making lectures difficult, and that the administration is poor (one student refers to the staff in the bursar's office, student accounts, and financial aid as "just plain lazy"). One final warning: "It is impossible to transfer out of Poly without losing a large amount of credits (because the classes are so specialized), so you feel as if you're 'trapped' in Poly without a way out." Despite its drawbacks, "Polytechnic University is a well-established, competitive university with extremely rigorous coursework. My academic experience at this school had given me the incentive that you can always try harder, and the harder you try, the more you can achieve."

> **SURVEY SAYS . . .**
> *Classes are small*
> *Diverse students interact*
> *No one cheats*
> *Registration is a breeze*
> *Great computer facilities*
> *Lousy food on campus*

Life

Be forewarned: "Poly doesn't allow for much of a social life. The workload will keep most of the students in an effective lockdown all but a few times during the semester." Social life here is further stymied by the fact that "95 percent of us do not live on campus, because the only dorms until this upcoming summer have been part of NYU's campus in Manhattan. Most people come for classes and then go home right after." Adds another student, "The standard organizations (a/k/a frats) are not really active. Only one of them actively holds parties, which usually blow, by the way." Commuters find little reason to hang around after class, because "the campus isn't very nice looking, and the main academic building is a converted safety razor factory." On a positive note, "the school is involved in construction projects, including the creation of a new academic building and dorm." Undergrads tell us that "for fun, we have to be proactive and gather some friends together to go do stuff," and that in New York City, "there are more than enough places to go have some fun." The school's location, in Brooklyn's downtown Metrotech complex, is within walking distance of Brooklyn Heights, home to many fine shops, restaurants, and a waterfront promenade. The Brooklyn Bridge is less than a mile from campus, meaning a mere 15-minute stroll leads students to great neighborhoods like Little Italy and Chinatown in lower Manhattan.

Student Body

Poly students are "extremely diverse in race, culture, and nationality and everyone is very accepting of other cultures and ethnicities." As one student put it, "I mean, we're in Brooklyn, NYC. Of course it's a pretty diverse group, and everyone tends to respect one another. It's the Poly philosophy: we're better than the rest of the population, and therefore we stick together. It's all the techno-brainwashing you go through your first year. You tend to bond easily with other techies." Students also bring diverse attitudes to the classroom. Writes one undergrad, "Some of the students are extremely high strung, and others are extremely loose. Some are extremely obsessed about their school work, and some are rather flippant about it. For the most part, they are friendly, helpful, and hardworking, but not obsessive."

ADMISSIONS

Very important factors considered by the admissions committee include: secondary school record and standardized test scores. *Important factors considered include:* class rank. *Other factors considered include:* essays, interview, and recommendations. SAT I or ACT required, SAT I preferred. TOEFL required of all international applicants. High school diploma is required and GED is not accepted.High school diploma is required and GED is accepted. *High school units required/recommended:* 4 English required, 4 math required, 4 science required, 2 foreign language recommended, 3 social studies required, 2 elective required.

The Inside Word

Your chops as a techie must be sharp to meet the effort required by Polytechnic's academics. You'll need to be self-motivated, too; La Isla Manhattan, with its zillions of distractions, is only stone's throw away. But if you can handle big-city life, it's worth the effort to gain admittance and take advantage of this campus's accessibility to interests both professional and personal.

FINANCIAL AID

Students should submit: FAFSA. No deadline for regular filing. The Princeton Review suggests that all financial aid forms be submitted as soon as possible after January 1. *Need-based scholarships/grants offered:* Pell, SEOG, state scholarships/grants, private scholarships, and the school's own gift aid. *Loan aid offered:* FFEL Subsidized Stafford, FFEL Unsubsidized Stafford, FFEL PLUS, Federal Perkins, and college/university loans from institutional funds. Federal Work-Study Program available. Institutional employment available. Applicants will be notified of awards on a rolling basis beginning on or about February 1. Off-campus job opportunities are good.

For even more information on this school, turn to page 338 of the "Stats" section.

PRINCETON UNIVERSITY

PO Box 430, Admission Office, Princeton, NJ 08544-0430 • Admissions: 609-258-3060
Fax: 609-258-6743 • Financial Aid: 609-258-3330 • Website: WWW.PRINCETON.EDU

Ratings

Quality of Life: 86   Academic: 99   Admissions: 99   Financial Aid: 83

Academics

Princeton University is arguably the most undergraduate-friendly member of the Ivy League. "The lack of a large graduate school at Princeton allows professors to focus more on the undergraduate population, which is a significant contrast to other top schools in the nation." Students rate professors from "stars of academia" to

SURVEY SAYS . . .
Lots of classroom discussion
Registration is a breeze, Lousy food on campus
Diverse students interact, No one cheats
(Almost) everyone smokes
Computer lab facilities need improving
Intercollegiate sports are unpopular or nonexistent
No one plays intramural sports

"unknowns who are there because they are great at teaching." With more than 4,500 undergrads, Princeton is no stranger to lecture courses. But "all the bigger lectures are broken down into precepts"—small, once-a-week discussion groups where students are given a greater degree of personal attention. While many of the precepts are run by TAs "who don't always have wonderful teaching skills," others are led by faculty members. One exuberant student says, "I walked into my first precept of the semester and saw that my preceptor was none other than James McPherson, the greatest living Civil War historian." History, politics, English, and economics are the most popular majors. But, argues a student, "there are basically no weak departments at Princeton. Whatever subject you choose to major in, you will have the world's foremost experts in the field instructing you." All students must complete "independent work" in their junior year and "a thesis" as seniors. The university calls these requirements "the hallmark of a Princeton education," and students rave that it "is fantastic because of the close relationships it fosters between students and their professor-advisors who supervise all independent work."

Life

"Two words: THE STREET." "The Street," as students call it, is Prospect Avenue, where one finds Princeton's famous eating clubs. "It's impossible to explain Princeton's social life without describing the Eating Clubs." These are "Princeton's version of coed fraternities," and at the end of sophomore year the majority of students join one—either through lottery or a selection process called "bicker." Members get "free" food and "free" beer, not to mention access to an array of social events. Students' descriptions of the clubs range from "quite good" to "pompous and ridiculous." New students quickly realize that the town of Princeton "offers little diversion for a college student." That's why "most of an undergraduate's social life occurs" on campus. The university provides "various performances, dances, fashion shows, cultural shows, plays, and theatre," not to mention a plentitude of extracurricular clubs and athletics. The new student center "has movies, TVs, a chic coffee shop with live jazz, a smoothie and milkshake bar, plenty of room to chill, computers, and, of course, great food." And, yes, Princeton students study. A lot. "I think most Princeton students find time to keep up with their work, do extracurriculars, and party," surmises a student. "The only thing that gets sacrificed is sleep."

Student Body

"At first, most (students) seem like your typical college kids. It's only after you live with them that you begin to see how incredible they are." While Princeton's administration is still working hard to outrun the university's "preppy white image," it's having no problem drawing in brilliant students. "I learn more talking to my friends at 3 A.M. than I'll ever learn from a Nobel Prize winner," writes one satisfied student. The undergrads here range from championship athletes to award-winning musicians—and everyone in between. And they come from a range of backgrounds. As one student puts it, "Princeton is one of the few schools in the country where the son or daughter of a wealthy senator can befriend a math Olympiad winner whose parents didn't finish high school." Others do complain about the lack of racial diversity on campus: "Princeton is numerically diverse (i.e., they have a healthy percentage of minority students), but it seems somewhat homogenous." This aside, one student assures, "As a minority, I don't feel any discrimination." Sure, students here "can be somewhat pretentious." But hey, every once in a while "it can be difficult being bunched together with a group of overachievers."

ADMISSIONS

Very important factors considered by the admissions committee include: character/personal qualities, essays, extracurricular activities, recommendations, secondary school record, standardized test scores, talent/ability, volunteer work, work experience. *Important factors considered include:* alumni/ae relation, minority status. *Other factors considered include:* class rank, interview. SAT I or ACT required; SAT I preferred; SAT II also required. TOEFL required of all international applicants. High school diploma is required and GED is not accepted. *High school units required/recommended:* 18 total recommended; 4 English recommended, 4 math recommended, 2 science recommended, 2 science lab recommended, 4 foreign language recommended, 2 history recommended.

The Inside Word

Princeton is much more open about the admissions process than the rest of their Ivy compatriots. The admissions staff evaluates candidates' credentials using a 1–5 rating scale, common among highly selective colleges. In the initial screening of applicants, admissions staff members assigned to particular regions of the country eliminate weaker students before the admissions committee makes its evaluation. Princeton's recommendation to interview should be considered a requirement, given the ultra-competitive nature of the applicant pool. In addition, three SAT IIs are required; no joke, indeed.

FINANCIAL AID

Students should submit: Princeton accepts, but does not require, the CSS/PROFILE application. The primary application is the Princeton Financial Aid Application, on the Web at www.princeton.edu. This online form has no fee. The FAFSA is also required. Regular filing deadline is February 1. *Need-based scholarships/grants offered:* Pell, SEOG, state scholarships/grants, private scholarships, the school's own gift aid. Princeton eliminated student loans in 2001–2002 and replaced them with additional grants. Since then, no student has been required to borrow as part of their aid award. Federal Work-Study Program available. Institutional employment available. Applicants will be notified of awards on or about April 1. Off-campus job opportunities are good.

FROM THE ADMISSIONS OFFICE

"Methods of instruction [at Princeton] vary widely, but common to all areas . . . is a strong emphasis on individual responsibility and the free interchange of ideas. This is displayed most notably in the wide use of preceptorials and seminars, in the provision of independent study for all upperclass students and qualified underclass students, and in the availability of a series of special programs to meet a range of individual interests. The undergraduate college encourages the student to be an independent seeker of information . . . and to assume responsibility for gaining both knowledge and judgment that will strengthen later contributions to society."

For even more information on this school, turn to page 339 of the "Stats" section.

PROVIDENCE COLLEGE

River Avenue and Eaton Street, Providence, RI 02918 • Admissions: 401-865-2535 • Fax: 401-865-2826
Financial Aid: 401-865-2286 • E-mail: pcadmiss@providence.edu • Website: www.providence.edu

Ratings
Quality of Life: 79   Academic: 78   Admissions: 83   Financial Aid: 81

Academics

Providence College: Welcome to an enjoyable but "demanding" academic experience. Students attend Providence because it is a small Catholic school with a reputation for its strong liberal arts program. The required two-year humanities course, "The Development of Western Civilization," is highly regarded and "comes in handy when watching Jeopardy." Some students complain that it also "lacks perspective outside" of that

> **SURVEY SAYS . . .**
> *Diversity lacking on campus*
> *Everyone loves the Friars*
> *Hard liquor is popular*
> *Students are cliquish*
> *(Almost) everyone plays intramural sports*
> *Very small frat/sorority scene*
> *Students are very religious*
> *Registration is a pain*
> *Library needs improving*
> *Lousy food on campus*

which is provided by the "white Catholic male" professors. Students appreciate that there are no TAs and that professors are, as one senior political science major puts it, "friendly and easily accessible." Professors "go out of their way to help students—even those not in their classes," a junior communications major brags. Though introductory classes tend to be easy, upper-level classes are "interesting and challenging." The Honors Program is "excellent," and the education program also garners high praise. The administration is "very rigid, keeping in close accordance with traditional Catholic policy," one junior reports, though students admit that the administration is also "very easy to communicate with." Class registration is "frustrating" because some students complain that athletes are provided preferential treatment.

Life

"Life at Providence College involves working hard during the week and partying on the weekends." Speaking of other entertainment options, one senior management major notes, "there are also many theaters, shows, and intellectually stimulating events in and around the Providence College campus." Downtown Providence is a popular destination. The city's numerous quality restaurants are standard haunts. Students also spend a good deal of time working for various community service organizations. The college's basketball team plays in the powerful Big East conference and often fights its way into the NCAA Tournament. The hockey team is also a popular draw. A political science major speculates that "Friar hockey games [have] become the biggest social event on campus." Students are unhappy with the on-campus food, which one sophomore calls "just plain bad," and the dorms. They also complain that the exercise facilities are insufficient and that the school needs an indoor track. Students say that the nearby Indian casinos are a great place to blow off some steam.

Student Body

A great sense of community pervades Providence College, thanks largely to the fact that students are "very involved on campus, especially through volunteer work." Some students sadly note that their peers "are very likely to conform to the latest styles and social norms." One sophomore admits that her fellow students are "mostly white, Irish-Catholic

Republicans, and if you don't fit that mold, you're looked upon as different." Some students tend to be "cliquey" and "overly materialistic" as well as "shallow" and "snobbish," and diversity is sorely lacking. "We need more people from different backgrounds, and not just minorities, to open people up to seeing things another way." One biology major affirms, "The lack of diversity is frustrating." Nevertheless, students overwhelmingly admit that their peers are extremely friendly. "There is a familial atmosphere" at Providence College.

ADMISSIONS

Very important factors considered by the admissions committee include: secondary school record. *Important factors considered include:* character/personal qualities, class rank, essays, extracurricular activities, recommendations, standardized test scores, talent/ability, volunteer work. *Other factors considered include:* alumni/ae relation, geographical residence, minority status, state residency, work experience. SAT I or ACT required; SAT II recommended. TOEFL required of all international applicants. High school diploma is required and GED is not accepted. *High school units required/recommended:* 16 total required; 18 total recommended; 4 English required, 3 math required, 4 math recommended, 3 science required, 4 science recommended, 2 science lab required, 3 science lab recommended, 3 foreign language required, 1 social studies required, 2 history required.

The Inside Word

Providence's reputation for quality is solidly in place among above-average graduates of northeastern Catholic high schools, who account for almost a quarter of the applicant pool. The strength of these candidates is one of the primary factors that allow the college to be choosy about who gets in. Successful candidates usually project a well-rounded, conservative image.

FINANCIAL AID

Students should submit: FAFSA, CSS/Financial Aid PROFILE. Regular filing deadline is February 1. The Princeton Review suggests that all financial aid forms be submitted as soon as possible after January 1. *Need-based scholarships/grants offered:* Pell, SEOG, state scholarships/grants, private scholarships, the school's own gift aid. *Loan aid offered:* Direct Subsidized Stafford, Direct Unsubsidized Stafford, Direct PLUS, FFEL Subsidized Stafford, FFEL Unsubsidized Stafford, FFEL PLUS, Federal Perkins. Federal Work-Study Program available. Institutional employment available. Applicants will be notified of awards on or about April 1. Off-campus job opportunities are excellent.

FROM THE ADMISSIONS OFFICE

"Infused with the history, tradition, and learning of a 700-year-old Catholic teaching order, the Dominican Friars, Providence College offers a value-affirming environment where students are enriched through spiritual, social, physical, and cultural growth as well as through intellectual development. Providence College offers over 35 programs of study leading to baccalaureate degrees in business, education, the sciences, arts, and humanities. Our faculty is noted for a strong commitment to teaching. A close student/faculty relationship allows for in-depth classwork, independent research projects, and detailed career exploration. While noted for the physical facilities and academic opportunities associated with larger universities, Providence also fosters personal growth through a small, spirited, family-like atmosphere that encourages involvement in student activities and athletics."

For even more information on this school, turn to page 339 of the "Stats" section.

QUINNIPIAC UNIVERSITY

MOUNT CARMEL AVENUE, 275 MOUNT CARMEL AVENUE, HAMDEN, CT 06518 • ADMISSIONS: 203-582-8600
FAX: 203-582-8906 • E-MAIL: ADMISSIONS@QUINNIPIAC.EDU • WEBSITE: WWW.QUINNIPIAC.EDU

Ratings
Quality of Life: 74   Academic: 79   Admissions: 75   Financial Aid: 78

Academics

Students looking for a medium-sized university with career-focused programs and a liberal arts foundation should consider Quinnipiac University. Though

> **SURVEY SAYS . . .**
> *Diversity lacking on campus*
> *Classes are small, Lots of beer drinking*
> *Instructors are good teachers*

the school's undergraduate population is a substantial 5,000, Quinnipiac offers the academic support and personal attention typical of small colleges. Students report that "class sizes are usually under 20" and that "the professors make an effort to learn not only your name, but who you really are." Undergrads say that QU professors "are there to teach you, help you, and get to know you, not to fail you or know you by a number." In fact, it is through many channels that the school displays its dedication to helping students succeed, and many note that the school's Learning Center "has tutors, who have been an essential component to hard science classes" and can be a "big help" if you are struggling with academics. Some students, however, feel that the classes at Quinnipiac could stand to be more competitive. In the words of one: "I have been satisfied but not challenged at Quinnipiac." Additionally, many debate the school's use of numerous adjunct professors. While some students claim "the part-time teachers are not devoted to your studies," others insist "the adjuncts here are incredible. They bring their real-world experience to the classroom." Regarding majors, "physical therapy, communications, and pre-med here are all very strong and hard to get into." Though administrators are "friendly and personable" when you get them one-on-one, the overall structure is plagued by a "lack of communication between the different departments in the school."

Life

Students say that "one of QU's greatest strengths is its location: 10 minutes away from Connecticut's cultural center and geographically right between New York and Boston." In addition, there is a "state park directly across from the campus," "the beautiful Sleeping Giant Mountain, which provides a beautiful backdrop for campus every season." Students say they like to take advantage of "concerts, plays, coffeehouses, lectures, restaurants, shopping" in nearby New Haven, as well as the town's "Thirsty Thursdays," which "are almost always happening." For recreation, students say, "it's really relaxing to climb Sleeping Giant or to sit out on the quad and drink a milkshake." In addition, "there are so many different organizations to be involved in, and that creates more opportunity to meet new people and form great friendships." Though students advise that "there is very little academic or intellectual conversation outside the classroom," they also note that "studying is pretty important to most people here." One undergrad summarizes life: "During the week the library is usually full. However, come the start of the weekend (usually Thursday nights) many students choose to drink." On that note, students tell us that, "beer pong, partying, and cigarette smoking are favorite pastimes."

Student Body

"Many of the students at Quinnipiac are alike: well-dressed, upper-middle-class people," according to one undergrad. "Everyone's personality is very similar," adds another.

Considering these observations, it's no surprise that students also report that "there is very little diversity" at QU. Not everyone's complaining, however. Opines one undergrad: "I like my classmates because so many of them are just like me . . . . Sometimes I wish it were more diverse, but then at the same time I think the reason everyone gets along so well is because we're all so much alike." Characterization of the student body runs from "shallow and materialistic" to "warm" and "friendly," but many agree, "Like everywhere else there are certain groups but . . . they are always interacting with each other and it's easy to make friends with them all."

ADMISSIONS

Very important factors considered by the admissions committee include: secondary school record. *Important factors considered include:* class rank, essays, recommendations, and standardized test scores. *Other factors considered include:* alumni/ae relation, extracurricular activities, interview, minority status, volunteer work, and work experience. SAT I or ACT required. TOEFL required of all international applicants. High school diploma or GED is required. *High school units required/recommended:* 16 total required; 4 English required, 3 math required, 3 science required, 2 science lab required, 2 foreign language recommended, 2 social studies required, 3 elective required. Physical and occupational therapy require 4 science and 4 math.

The Inside Word

Quinnipiac boasts a wide range of opportunities for study and social pursuits in a geographic locale equidistant from multiple cultural centers, not to mention a very responsive faculty.

FINANCIAL AID

Students should submit: FAFSA. The Princeton Review suggests that all financial aid forms be submitted as soon as possible after January 1. *Need-based scholarships/grants offered:* Pell, SEOG, state scholarships/grants, private scholarships, the school's own gift aid, and Federal Nursing. *Loan aid offered:* FFEL Subsidized Stafford, FFEL Unsubsidized Stafford, FFEL PLUS, Federal Perkins, Federal Nursing, and state loans. Federal Work-Study Program available. Institutional employment available. Applicants will be notified of awards on a rolling basis beginning on or about March 1. Off-campus job opportunities are excellent.

FROM THE ADMISSIONS OFFICE

"The appeal of Quinnipiac University continues to grow each year, and our students come from a variety of states and backgrounds. Seventy-five percent of the freshman class is from out of state. Students come from 25 states and 18 countries.

"As admission becomes more competitive, the university continues to focus on its mission of providing outstanding academic programs in a student-oriented environment on a campus with a strong sense of community. The development of an honors program, a highly regarded Emerging Leaders student life program, and a 'writing across the curriculum' initiative in Academic Affairs form the foundation for excellence in our Schools of Business, Communications, Health Sciences, Education, Liberal Arts, and Law. To reflect twenty-first-century thinking, innovative programs such as interactive digital design, entrepreneurship, athletic training/sports medicine, and e-media have been developed in recent years. Nearly thirty percent of current undergraduates plan to stay at Quinnipiac to complete their graduate degree.

"More than 65 student organizations, 21 Division I teams (newly named the 'Bobcats'), recreation and intramurals in a newly expanded recreation/fitness center, community service, student publications, and a strong student government offer a variety of outside-of-class experiences to the student body. Multicultural awareness is supported through the Black Student Union, Asian/Pacific Islander Association, Latino Cultural Society, International Student Club, and GLASS. An active alumni association reflects the strong connection Quinnipiac has with its graduates—and they give the faculty high marks for career preparation. An outstanding location and campus atmosphere make Quinnipiac a great choice."

For even more information on this school, turn to page 340 of the "Stats" section.

RAMAPO COLLEGE OF NEW JERSEY

505 RAMAPO VALLEY ROAD, MAHWAH, NJ 07430 • ADMISSIONS: 201-684-7300 • FAX: 201-684-7964
E-MAIL: ADMISSIONS@RAMAPO.EDU • WEBSITE: WWW.RAMAPO.EDU

Ratings
Quality of Life: 80   Academic: 84   Admissions: 79   Financial Aid: 76

Academics

A small public school with strong programs in business, communications, the sciences, and liberal arts, Ramapo College offers undergraduates a small-college experience at a reasonable price. Students agree

> **SURVEY SAYS . . .**
> School is well run, Class discussions encouraged
> Student publications are popular
> Classes are small, Lots of beer drinking

that the size and the school's location near New York City are Ramapo's two chief assets. Writes one student, "It's small enough so everyone can be a part of it. You really feel like you can go to someone if you need help." Class sizes "are capped at 35, so interaction with professors is amazing. In fact, all of my professors know me by name (except for my Shakespeare prof, who keeps calling me Scott)," explains one student, whose name is not Scott. Ramapo's location is prime for the many "work-related opportunities provided by the school (i.e.: co-ops, internships, on-campus jobs, job fairs, resume-writing workshops), [which] are a real strength." Most students here agree that "teachers are top-notch," although some complain that "too many are adjuncts who are here for a semester or two, and then are gone forever." Administrators "stay busy but try and have an open door policy so if you need anything, you just have to ask." The bureaucracy here, however, is more typical of a large state school than of a small college, resulting in "everything from unclear and misleading letters sent to students to the clumsy processes of registration and housing." Students also warn that Ramapo, in its youth, has "no school spirit and no sense of tradition"; on the upside, "the school is still in its growing stages, so that is really exciting. It's only 31 years old, so we are seeing so many improvements."

Life

With barely more than half its students living on campus—and many returning home on weekends—the Ramapo campus is understandably quiet from Friday night to Monday morning, but few seem to mind the situation. Many head to New York City to go clubbing; others stay closer to home, visiting "one of three major malls in the area that are popular hangouts." During the day, many head for "the reservation down the road for a great hike that takes you up the mountains. There are several trails that you can take, which bring you around two lakes and a waterfall. When you get to the top of the mountain there is a great view of New York City as well as an aerial view of the Ramapo College campus." On campus, students complain that "it's tough to have parties because of security or someone complaining about the noise (but a few of us have mastered certain techniques to ensure an undisturbed party)." Unaffordable off-campus housing translates to "only a few frat houses to go party at"; as a result, "Greek life is extremely important here—it basically defines you and who you can hang out with." For weeknight fun, a host of events, speakers, and organizational meetings keeps students busy. One student takes issue with the substantial increase in enrollment: "We could use some more housing, or less students, because this relatively new housing crunch is killing the fact that dorms and apartments used to be spacious. And parking is a bitch!"

Student Body

Undergrads tell us that Ramapo hosts "a highly diversified body of students. We have a lot of international students, a lot of Hispanic students, a lot of African Americans, and a lot of white students." As at many East Coast private schools, "the campus is very liberal, and thus, very open-minded," according to the liberal majority; the conservative opposition counters that "it is very evident in the few classroom discussions that my peers have little knowledge of worldly events, and in fact at times even little common sense." With a preponderance of middle- and upper-middle-class kids here, Ramapo students "seem kind of sheltered, but once they get to know people, they open up to those around them." Some students complain that the school is too cliquish, a problem they feel is exacerbated by the importance of Greek organizations in campus life.

ADMISSIONS

Very important factors considered by the admissions committee include: secondary school record, class rank, and standardized test scores. *Important factors considered include:* character/personal qualities, essays, extracurricular activities, recommendations, and talent/ability. *Other factors considered include:* alumni/ae relation. SAT I required. TOEFL required of all international applicants. High school diploma or GED is required. *High school units required/recommended:* 16 total required; 4 English required, 3 math required, 3 science recommended, 2 science lab required, 2 foreign language required, 2 history required, 3 elective required.

The Inside Word

A young institution, Ramapo desires applicants who can define its future heritage, people from all over the world who will capitalize on both its quiet campus and convenient location near New York City.

FINANCIAL AID

Students should submit: FAFSA. No deadline for regular filing. The Princeton Review suggests that all financial aid forms be submitted as soon as possible after January 1. *Need-based scholarships/grants offered:* Pell, SEOG, state scholarships/grants, private scholarships, and the school's own gift aid. *Loan aid offered:* Direct Subsidized Stafford, Direct Unsubsidized Stafford, Direct PLUS, Federal Perkins, and state loans. Federal Work-Study Program available. Applicants will be notified of awards on a rolling basis beginning on or about April 1. Off-campus job opportunities are excellent.

FROM THE ADMISSIONS OFFICE

"Students admitted to Ramapo College for fall 2002 had an average SAT score of 1140 and ranked in the top 25 percent of their graduating class. Applications to the freshman class were the highest in the history of the college; admission was offered to fewer than half (43 percent) of the freshman applicants. Ramapo students come from all 21 counties in New Jersey as well as 23 states and more than 60 countries. Eight-seven percent of freshmen and 56 percent of all full-time students live on campus, for a total of 2,117 residential students.

"Ranked number two among public comprehensive colleges in the north, Ramapo College of New Jersey is sometimes mistaken for a private college. This is, in part, due to its unique interdisciplinary academic structure, its size of around 5,500 students, and its pastoral setting. Ramapo offers bachelors' degrees in the arts, business, humanities, social sciences, and the sciences as well as in professional studies, which include teacher certification at the elementary and secondary levels, pre-law, pre-med, and social work.

"Undergraduate students choose to concentrate their studies in one of five schools: Administration and Business; American and International Studies; Contemporary Arts; Theoretical and Applied Science; and Social Science and Human Services. Of the 600 course offerings and 40 academic programs, the most popular are business administration, communications, psychology, nursing, information systems, and computer science."

For even more information on this school, turn to page 340 of the "Stats" section.

RENSSELAER POLYTECHNIC INSTITUTE

110 EIGHTH STREET, TROY, NY 12180-3590 • ADMISSIONS: 518-276-6216 • FAX: 518-276-4072
FINANCIAL AID: 518-276-6813 • E-MAIL: ADMISSIONS@RPI.EDU • WEBSITE: WWW.RPI.EDU

Ratings
Quality of Life: 82   Academic: 87   Admissions: 83   Financial Aid: 85

Academics

Prestigious profs and a boot camp–style curriculum distinguish Rensselaer Polytechnic Institute, an engineering and management powerhouse in upstate New York. "One of my professors is the CIO here, and another worked at Amazon.com and chiefly developed the one-click shopping; yet another is a security expert for the network," brags one

> **SURVEY SAYS . . .**
> Great computer facilities
> Lots of beer drinking
> Frats and sororities dominate social scene
> Registration is a breeze
> Lab facilities are great
> Hard liquor is popular
> Ethnic diversity on campus
> Athletic facilities are great

of many students who tout their instructors' credentials. Their teaching ability, of course, is another matter: "While some professors engage students and take an active role, many others mumble and seem to just regurgitate a lecture that they have given hundreds of times before." Undergraduates also want you to know that "some of the professors do not speak English well enough to fully convey their teachings and opinions on certain subjects." Most departments here, however, offer more chances for hands-on research than you'll find at comparable institutions: "The school has a great undergraduate research program for students to get involved in actual research programs that you might have to wait until grad school for otherwise," reports one engineer. Outside the school's areas of specialty, the quality of courses drops off. "Humanities and social sciences are hell," warns one student. "Any hope that reading the course catalog inspires within you will be crushed when you realize that if [a course is] offered (almost never happens), it's filled entirely by seniors." Students also complain of "a continual struggle between students and administration. The administration has an extreme tendency to skip student input before implementing decisions that directly affect the student body."

Life

"Everyone at RPI is pretty focused on academics," students here say, "and if you aren't, you don't last particularly long. I've lost two roommates so far." A heavy academic load isn't the only check on RPI social life. There's also hometown Troy, which one student describes as "every run-down town you've ever seen in a movie." Nearby Albany isn't much better; cautioned one undergrad, "The tour guides hype to prospectives the opportunities to visit Albany for entertainment, but having lived most of my life in Albany, I can honestly say that there isn't much more to do there than there is in Troy." Thus, the job of providing entertainment at RPI falls largely to the Greek system. "The social life at RPI is mostly made up of Greeks," explains one student. "Even non-Greeks go to frat parties because there isn't much else to do." Those uninterested in the Greeks have few options; as one put it, "A large majority of non-Greek students evacuate the campus on every available weekend to go to Montreal, NYC, Boston, and points west." Or they plant themselves in front of their computers, working problem sets and playing video games. Some venture outdoors: "The school has great proximity to the Adirondack Mountains and to southern Vermont for day hikes and skiing all winter." During hockey season—"our only Division I sport"—they follow the Red Hawks.

Student Body

The student body at RPI is divided between "geeky engineer types who never actually interact with the social scene" and "manager types who are more socially adept [and] who shun what they call 'the engineers' to the point of being excessively rude about them behind their backs." The geeks are pretty much all male, which "works out well because the ratio of females to males is quite low, so this alarming trend actually benefits the regular student who likes to socialize and basically have a good time." Not that the women here can't be a bit geeky, too; as one student recounts, "True story: My first week here, I saw a fight in the dining hall between two girls over which was the best Final Fantasy game. . . . So yeah, there are some strange people here." The large international population includes "lots of Chinese and Indians. You learn a lot about different cultures from the people here."

ADMISSIONS

Very important factors considered by the admissions committee include: secondary school record. *Important factors considered include:* standardized test scores. *Other factors considered include:* alumni/ae relation, character/personal qualities, class rank, essays, extracurricular activities, geographical residence, minority status, recommendations, talent/ability, volunteer work, work experience. SAT I or ACT required. TOEFL required of all international applicants. High school diploma or GED is required. *High school units required/recommended:* 15 total required; 4 English required, 4 math required, 4 science required, 3 social studies required.

The Inside Word

Although scores and numbers may not be the only consideration of the admissions committee at RPI, it is important to remember that you have to have high ones in order to stay in the running for admission. Here in Troy and at many other highly selective colleges and universities, the first review weeds out those who are academically weak and without any special considerations. Underrepresented minorities and women are high on the list of desirables in the applicant pool here, and go through the admissions process without any hitches if reasonably well qualified.

FINANCIAL AID

Students should submit: FAFSA. No deadline for regular filing. The Princeton Review suggests that all financial aid forms be submitted as soon as possible after January 1. *Need-based scholarships/grants offered:* Pell, SEOG, state scholarships/grants, private scholarships, the school's own gift aid. *Loan aid offered:* Direct Subsidized Stafford, Direct Unsubsidized Stafford, Direct PLUS, FFEL Subsidized Stafford, FFEL Unsubsidized Stafford, FFEL PLUS, Federal Perkins, college/university loans from institutional funds. Federal Work-Study Program available. Institutional employment available. Applicants will be notified of awards on or about March 20. Off-campus job opportunities are good.

FROM THE ADMISSIONS OFFICE

"Rensselaer emphasizes the study of technology and science, preparing students for today's high-tech world. The university is devoted to the discovery and dissemination of knowledge and its application to the service of humanity. Rensselaer has been in the forefront of scientific and professional education since its founding in 1824, and today its reputation for educational excellence draws students from every state and more than 81 countries. Recently constructed Barton Hall is state-of-the-art housing with Web and Ethernet access in all rooms and conference rooms, plus a fully wired lounge. Rensselaer has recently completed construction of a $6 million fitness center and a $9.5 million renovation to the student union. The Institute will break ground on two major facilities: a center for biotechnology and interdisciplinary studies that will advance the work of expanding research portfolio, and an experimental media and performing arts center that will significantly enrich the campus experience and build programs in the electronic arts."

For even more information on this school, turn to page 341 of the "Stats" section.

RICHARD STOCKTON COLLEGE OF NEW JERSEY

JIM LEEDS ROAD, PO BOX 195, POMONA, NJ 08240 • ADMISSIONS: 609-652-4261 • FAX: 609-748-5541
E-MAIL: ADMISSIONS@STOCKTON.EDU • WEBSITE: WWW.STOCKTON.EDU

Ratings

Quality of Life: 75   Academic: 82   Admissions: 84   Financial Aid: 74

Academics

The Stockton academic experience is, according to students, "the best bang for your buck. Most professors are easy to approach and will bend over backwards to help students." Agrees another, "It is a superior learning environment, very laid back yet at the same time academically challenging." Students at Stockton, for the most

SURVEY SAYS . . .
Popular college radio
Classes are small
Profs teach upper levels
Great food on campus
School is well run
Student publications are popular
Intercollegiate are sports popular

part, just love being there, and adore the "excellent" faculty, who are "so helpful and friendly that they end up becoming friends." Undergrads find the level of academics "challenging" but manageable "if you spend a lot of time on them." The college has done a good job of accommodating nontraditional students, too; according to one working mom, "The selection of distance-learning classes is good also and continues to grow each semester." Students' descriptions of adjunct professors aren't flattering; some undergrads go so far as to call them "incompetent" and "never accessible." While some students think the school bureaucracy is "decent but can be inept," another suggests that "the administration and faculty are like a peanut butter and jelly sandwich. Together" they're great. The dean of students is "very accessible and wonderful to talk to" about whatever issues you may have. Watch out for the housing office, though: while freshmen are guaranteed housing for the first semester, the waiting list for upperclassmen and transfer students can be long.

Life

One student declares, "People here like to party. That is the thing to do. It unites everyone." Another counters "occasionally we throw a good party, but most of the time we are studying unfortunately. Sporting events, concerts, and theatre productions are huge too." Thursday nights are especially lively. From Friday through Sunday, though, Stockton is a "suitcase college," meaning many students pack up and go home, and on campus "nothing is offered on the weekends." Philadelphia and Atlantic City are within driving distance for overnight or even day trips. The campus itself is aesthetically pleasing; one student declares that "Stockton's beauty is breathtaking. From the moment you drive onto College Drive, you feel as if you're in another part of the world. With nature all around from Lake Fred to the Pinelands, outside is very quiet and peaceful. The smells in the spring and fall; it is a beauty unexplained until you experience it for yourself." With all of this natural beauty, it's hardly surprising that "everyone hangs out a lot, especially outside when the weather is nice, which is fun as hell." At Stockton, "it seems like people from diverse backgrounds are generally open to hanging out with people from other ethnicities and religions, and whenever possible, a lot of the student organizations plan 'interfaith' or 'interracial,' etc., types of events to demonstrate some sense of solidarity on campus."

Student Body

"Friendly" is the word students use over and over again to describe Stockton's student body, where "even complete strangers will take time to say 'hello' or 'good morning' when passing by." One student claims that "the students at Stockton are one of the reasons I chose this school. I have never met more open and accepting people in my life." A transfer student adds that one gets "the feeling there are many kids [here who] are the first in their family to attend college." The result is that these students "work very hard."

ADMISSIONS

Very important factors considered by the admissions committee include: class rank, secondary school record, and standardized test scores. *Important factors considered include:* essays and extracurricular activities. *Other factors considered include:* alumni/ae relation, character/personal qualities, recommendations, talent/ability, volunteer work, and work experience. SAT I or ACT required, SAT I preferred. TOEFL required of all international applicants. High school diploma or GED is required. *High school units required/recommended:* 16 total required; 4 English required, 3 math required, 2 science required, 2 science lab required, 2 social studies required, 3 elective required.

The Inside Word

Stockton, named after New Jersey's representative at The Continental Congress and a POW of the British Army in 1776, is equally attractive for the on-campus or commuting student. Its strong academic reputation demands that applicants demonstrate their ability to match the school's standards of academic hunger and social diversity.

FINANCIAL AID

Students should submit: FAFSA. The Princeton Review suggests that all financial aid forms be submitted as soon as possible after January 1. *Need-based scholarships/grants offered:* Pell, SEOG, state scholarships/grants, and the school's own gift aid. *Loan aid offered:* Direct Subsidized Stafford, Direct Unsubsidized Stafford, Direct PLUS, FFEL Subsidized Stafford, FFEL Unsubsidized Stafford, FFEL PLUS, Federal Perkins, and state loans. Federal Work-Study Program available. Institutional employment available. Applicants will be notified of awards on a rolling basis beginning on or about April 1. Off-campus job opportunities are excellent.

FROM THE ADMISSIONS OFFICE

"Stockton College of New Jersey offers the atmosphere and rigorous academics of the very finest private institutions, at a surprisingly affordale cost. Stockton's outstanding faculty includes a Pulitzer Prize winner, two Fulbright Scholars, and the recipient of an Academy Award, several Emmy Awards, and a Grammy Award. Awards don't tell the whole story, though. Stockton's faculty is dedicated to teaching excellence and student success.

"Student life at Stockton is second to none. Our sports teams are nationally ranked, including the 2001 National Division III men's soccer champions. We recently opened a state-of-the-art, $17 million sports center that includes a fully equipped fitness center, and there are new arts and science, health science, and student housing buildings. Stockton's beautiful campus was voted one of the state's Top Ten Architectural Treasures by *New Jersey Monthly Magazine*. Our pristine 1,600 acres are located within the Pinelands national preserves, including four lakes as well as trails for hiking and biking—all within a 10-minute drive to the popular southern New Jersey beach resorts. The numerous attractions of Philadelphia and New York City are easily accessible as well.

"Stockton features small class sizes, professors who are friendly and accessible, and student organizations to serve every interest. For the student seeking a total college experience at the most reasonable cost possible, Stockton College of New Jersey offers the best of both worlds. Stockton truly lives up to its slogan: 'An Environment for Excellence.'"

For even more information on this school, turn to page 342 of the "Stats" section.

RIDER UNIVERSITY

2083 LAWRENCEVILLE ROAD, LAWRENCEVILLE, NJ 08648-3099 • FAX: 609-896-5042
E-MAIL: ADMISSIONS@RIDER.EDU • WEBSITE: WWW.RIDER.EDU

Ratings

Quality of Life: 78   **Academic:** 77   **Admissions:** 75   **Financial Aid:** 84

Academics

Business-related studies and elementary education are the biggest drawing cards at Rider University, an institution that combines the intimacy and mentorship of a teaching college with the broad academic offerings of a university. Students brag that "you can tell an overwhelming majority of the professors really care about their stu-

> **SURVEY SAYS . . .**
> *Hard liquor is popular*
> *Lab facilities need improving*
> *Registration is a breeze*
> *Student publications are ignored*
> *Students aren't very religious*
> *Students don't like*
> *Lawrenceville, NJ*

dents and enjoy their job. They are very easy to find and always willing to help." The College of Business Administration (CBA) receives near-universal accolades; writes one enthusiastic undergraduate, "The CBA offers excellent courses that help you not only learn the materials but also understand them." Students are especially bullish about the accounting program and DAARSTOC, an experiential "executive skill-building program" meant to develop in students "interview skills, stand-up speaking abilities, conflict resolution skills, [and] group dynamics." Smaller but equally prestigious is Rider's Westminster Choir College, a choral school with its campus in beautiful Princeton. Students report that "the performance opportunities, the talent of the teachers (in performance and pedagogy), and the music education program" are top-notch, but complain that "classrooms consist of mostly temporary cottage-like rooms, which is a bad thing. And our budget is tight, as it is with a lot of art schools. . . . [But] if someone wanted to make a few million dollars worth of donations, we'd be set."

Life

Rider undergrads report that "life at Rider is quite laid-back. Most of the week is spent going to class, with work in the evening, but weekends are when the fun starts. Being close to a huge movie theater and having free movies at our student center always gives students something to watch." Rider is also home to an active Greek scene, and students tell us that "during Rush there is always plenty to do because the fraternities are the best hangout spots." Otherwise, life here is subdued but satisfying; according to undergrads, "The campus usually goes to local bars during the week." Such a pace leaves some yearning for more, provoking glass-half-full types to point out that "some students complain that there is nothing to do, when in reality they are lazy. Almost every day a different event is happening, and campus entertainment is also a big part of life here. Famous bands, comedians, lectures, and magicians always are coming to campus." Students at the Choir College tell us that "Westminster is a very quiet campus. . . . It is definitely a conservatory atmosphere. For fun, we walk around Princeton or go see a movie, go out to dinner. Nothing extremely unique." Students on both campuses happily point out that Philadelphia, Trenton, and New York are all easily accessible by train.

Student Body

Rider students want you to know that they are typical college students, no more and no less; writes one, "Some think, some drink, some even stink, but we will all learn our own ways of doing things and what we want from life during our time here at school." African-Americans make up the largest minority group at this predominantly Caucasian campus where "people of different races interact but most stick to their own." Students are quick to point out that "there are many diverse student groups on campus. Each person belongs [to] at least one organization, which caters to his/her interest. These student groups/organizations foster unity, commitment, and social interaction with other students, faculty members, and staff." Some students at the Lawrenceville campus complain of cliquishness, especially among the Greek community. Music students report that Westminster, on the contrary, "is one of the least cliquish environments I have ever experienced. The majority of the students are voice majors, and along with that comes drama queens but also an intense passion for life and music. Since everyone in the school is in a choir, you meet with your whole class for an hour, four days of the week. This creates a bond that I don't think anything else could create."

ADMISSIONS

Very important factors considered by the admissions committee include: essays, secondary school record, standardized test scores. *Important factors considered include:* class rank. *Other factors considered include:* recommendations, character/personal qualities, extracurricular activities, talent/ability. SAT I or ACT required. TOEFL required of all international applicants. High school diploma or GED is required. *High school units required/recommended:* 16 total required; 4 English required, 3 math required, 3 science recommended, 2 foreign language recommended, 2 social studies recommended, 2 history recommended.

The Inside Word

In the admissions world there are two all-important mandates: recruit the college's home state, and recruit JERSEY! As a school in the Garden State, Rider deserves some special attention for the diverse group of students it brings in each year. Students who wish to attend need to have a solid academic record and good test scores. A few bumps in your academic past, however, shouldn't pose too much of a threat.

FINANCIAL AID

Students should submit: FAFSA. Priority filing deadline is March 1. The Princeton Review suggests that all financial aid forms be submitted as soon as possible after January 1. *Need-based scholarships/grants offered:* Pell, SEOG, state scholarships/grants, private scholarships, the school's own gift aid. *Loan aid offered:* FFEL Subsidized Stafford, FFEL Unsubsidized Stafford, FFEL PLUS, Federal Perkins, state loans, college/university loans from institutional funds, alternative loans. Federal Work-Study Program available. Institutional employment available. Applicants will be notified of awards on a rolling basis beginning on or about April 1. Off-campus job opportunities are excellent.

For even more information on this school, turn to page 343 of the "Stats" section.

ROCHESTER INSTITUTE OF TECHNOLOGY

60 LOMB MEMORIAL DRIVE, ROCHESTER, NY 14623 • ADMISSIONS: 716-475-6631 • FAX: 716-475-7424
FINANCIAL AID: 716-475-2186 • E-MAIL: ADMISSIONS@RIT.EDU • WEBSITE: WWW.RIT.EDU

Ratings
Quality of Life: 74   **Academic:** 80   **Admissions:** 85   **Financial Aid:** 81

Academics

The "very prestigious" Rochester Institute of Technology is a demanding arts and technology school with a humanist approach to academics: the school requires every student, regardless of major, to complete a core curriculum of liberal arts courses. Students love or endure the requirements in order to benefit from RIT's modern classrooms, "exceptional" laboratories, and "state-of-the-art" equipment. Classes, students report, are "difficult and require a lot of work," a situation made more intense by a quarterly academic schedule that causes courses to fly by. "It's impossible to get ahead of your work," writes one student. "The trick is to not fall too far behind." Most professors are "accessible" and are "genuinely concerned with their students' success." Students enjoy "classes [that] are small so you can get more individual attention along with the fast pace." All told, students concede that an RIT education is a stressful one, but feel "the stress is worth it" because "graduates are in demand." One reason why grads are able to land prime jobs is RIT's co-op program, which allows students to gain hands-on experience in paid internships. Participating companies include biggies like Xerox, Kodak, and Bausch & Lomb. Each year, over 2,600 RIT co-op students work in more than 1,300 firms around the country.

> **SURVEY SAYS . . .**
> Very little drug use
> Musical organizations aren't popular
> Great computer facilities
> Student publications are ignored
> Popular college radio, Unattractive campus
> Campus difficult to get around
> Student government is unpopular
> Intercollegiate sports are
> unpopular or nonexistent
> Political activism is (almost) nonexistent

Life

"Since RIT is such an intense learning environment, there isn't a lot of time left for extracurricular activities," says one student. When students do find some time to put their books and laptops away, they "go to movies, work out at the gym, or hang out in somebody's room" playing video games. For more lively entertainment, students often "travel to other schools for parties." Greek life provides a social outlet for some students, though at least as many despise fraternities and sororities. The result is a deeply divided campus, with Greeks complaining of an "anti-frat sentiment" and independents griping that fraternities and sororities act like they own the campus. Others complain that "the general setup of the school makes it difficult to meet and interact with those outside your major." However, most agree it is "extremely easy to make friends at RIT."

Student Body

The "hard-working" and "goal-orientated" students of RIT hail from all 50 states and 90 countries. And they say that their peers "are very friendly and mix well together no matter what race." The glue that binds them, according to many, is stress. "Camaraderie is often essential to survive the hellish upper-level courses. Having friends in your major really helps to relieve stress and work better." With heavy workloads burdening them, RIT undergrads have little time for and less interest in the outside world. "If I only had one word with which to describe RIT students," notes one student, "it would be 'focused.' "

ADMISSIONS

Very important factors considered by the admissions committee include: secondary school record. *Important factors considered include:* class rank, minority status, standardized test scores. *Other factors considered include:* alumni/ae relation, character/personal qualities, essays, extracurricular activities, geographical residence, interview, recommendations, talent/ability, volunteer work, work experience. SAT I or ACT required. TOEFL required of all international applicants. High school diploma or GED is required. *High school units required/recommended:* 22 total required; 4 English required, 2 math required, 3 math recommended, 2 science required, 3 science recommended, 1 science lab required, 2 science lab recommended, 3 foreign language recommended, 4 social studies required, 4 social studies recommended, 10 elective required.

The Inside Word

RIT is not as competitive as the top tier of technical schools, but its location and contacts with major research corporations make it a top choice for many students. The acceptance rate is deceptively high when considered in conjunction with the student academic profile and the high yield of admitted students who enroll. There is a strong element of self-selection at work in the applicant pool; the successful candidate is one who is solid academically and ready to hit the ground running.

FINANCIAL AID

Students should submit: FAFSA, state aid form. The Princeton Review suggests that all financial aid forms be submitted as soon as possible after January 1. *Need-based scholarships/grants offered:* Pell, SEOG, state scholarships/grants, private scholarships, the school's own gift aid. *Loan aid offered:* Direct Subsidized Stafford, Direct Unsubsidized Stafford, Direct PLUS, Federal Perkins, private bank loans. Federal Work-Study Program available. Institutional employment available. Applicants will be notified of awards on a rolling basis beginning on or about March 15. Off-campus job opportunities are excellent.

FROM THE ADMISSIONS OFFICE

"A nationally respected leader in professional and career-oriented education, RIT has been described as one of America's most imitated institutions and has been recognized as one of the nation's leading universities. RIT has also been rated the number one comprehensive university in the East for its scientific and technology programs. RIT's strength lies in its dedication to providing superior career preparation for today's students. This has attracted excellent faculty to RIT and has led to the development of academic programs that combine small classes and an emphasis on undergraduate teaching, modern classroom facilities, and work experience gained through the university's cooperative education program. Few universities provide RIT's variety of career-oriented programs. Our eight colleges offer outstanding programs in business, engineering, art and design, science and mathematics, liberal arts, photography, hotel management, computer science, and other areas. RIT's National Technical Institute for the Deaf (NTID) is the world's largest mainstreamed college program for the deaf and hearing impaired."

For even more information on this school, turn to page 343 of the "Stats" section.

ROGER WILLIAMS UNIVERSITY

ONE OLD FERRY ROAD, BRISTOL, RI 02809-0000 • ADMISSIONS: 401-254-3500 • FAX: 401-254-3557
E-MAIL: ADMIT@RWU.EDU • WEBSITE: WWW.RWU.EDU

Ratings

Quality of Life: 75   Academic: 71   Admissions: 64   Financial Aid: 78

Academics

Roger Williams University's biggest draw is its faculty, professors who are "all experts in their own respected fields." Small class sizes, "a good mixture of lecture and discussion," and the fact that professors make sure students know about "every possible way to access them outside of the class-

SURVEY SAYS . . .
School is well run, Students are happy
High cost of living, Classes are small
Instructors are good teachers
Intercollegiate sports are popular
Hard liquor is popular
Student publications are popular

room" are all features heralded by satisfied students. Some students warn that this cozy community is growing too large, too fast, though: "The school tries to market itself as a small school, but in reality . . . class sizes have increased largely over the two years I've been here." Still, students love their "friendly and easygoing professors" and appreciate how well "they know the material and are willing to help students out in any way." Some describe the coursework as "rather hard" while others complain, "Many of the classes, especially the cores, feel like high school because they are taught on such a simple [level]." With its' competitive architecture and biology departments and the new Center for Economic and Environmental Development, RWU enables students to "learn by doing."

Life

Students at RWU appreciate their school's beautiful setting. They should: "The school sits right on the Mount Hope/Narragansett Bay and allows for the continuous view of the bay—even from the dorms," marvels one undergrad. Besides its natural beauty, the school is also able to satisfy the needs and desires of both homebodies and adventurous types. For the former, the Campus Entertainment Network "sponsors on-campus events like comedians, musicians, and movies." For the latter, Bristol is a "quaint little town," but the real action is in Providence and Newport, each about a 20-minute drive from Bristol. Those looking for "real" metropolis distractions head to Boston. Getting there is easy: "RIPTA (the public bus transportation) has a stop right outside the campus, which can bring students to Providence [or Newport] for the night," reports one student. Heading to the beach when it's warm or watching one of the school's Division III teams sweat are also possibilities, and yet many students agree that "life on this campus, as far as weekends go, consists mainly of drinking at parties." With over 30 clubs and organizations, there seems to be something for everyone at Roger Williams. (Attention budding rock stars: "There are a lot of musicians on campus! If you play guitar or drums, you won't have a problem finding someone to jam with!")

Student Body

Most students at Roger Williams love the way the small campus community creates a homey environment. "Everyone is very open and everyone says 'hi' and has a smile when they go to class." It seems that "you can't walk out of your room without getting at least a few 'hellos' thrown your way." There are some who "would like to see a more diverse campus" (one wry student quips that RWU stand for "Rich White Undergrads"), and even though people are extremely nice, most seem as though they've stepped out of one clothing line's notoriously risqué catalogue. Conspicuous consumption here doesn't stop with clothes; one student warns, "Be aware—most of the students here drive better cars than the faculty do"—a fact that grates on the nerves of some students who aren't from such privileged backgrounds. Economic differences don't seem to affect students' warm feelings about one another, though, since "it is very easy to make friends with a lot of people." In fact, "students are not cliquey. Many students hang out with one group of kids one night, and the next night, they hang out with a different group."

ADMISSIONS

Very important factors considered by the admissions committee include: essays, secondary school record, standardized test scores, and talent/ability. *Important factors considered include:* character/personal qualities, class rank, and extracurricular activities. *Other factors considered include:* alumni/ae relation, interview, recommendations, volunteer work, and work experience. SAT I or ACT required, SAT I preferred. High school diploma or GED is required. *High school units required/recommended:* 16 total required; 4 English required, 3 math required, 4 math recommended, 3 science required, 2 science lab required, 2 foreign language recommended, 3 social studies required, 1 social studies recommended, 2 history required.

The Inside Word

Admission to the school's well-regarded architecture program is competitive; all other programs are much less so. Architecture candidates must apply by February 1 and would be well advised to spend considerable effort on their portfolios.

FINANCIAL AID

Students should submit: FAFSA and CSS/Financial Aid PROFILE. The Princeton Review suggests that all financial aid forms be submitted as soon as possible after January 1. *Need-based scholarships/grants offered:* Pell, SEOG, state scholarships/grants, private scholarships, and the school's own gift aid. *Loan aid offered:* FFEL Subsidized Stafford, FFEL Unsubsidized Stafford, FFEL PLUS, Federal Perkins, and state loans. Federal Work-Study Program available. Institutional employment available. Applicants will be notified of awards on a rolling basis beginning on or about April 1. Off-campus job opportunities are good.

FROM THE ADMISSIONS OFFICE

"Located on a beautiful, waterfront campus in historic Bristol, Rhode Island, Roger Williams University is a leading liberal arts university in New England. Our modern, safe, 140-acre campus places you among many nearby resources and attractions. You'll enjoy the region's engaging lifestyles and vibrant cultures. Also, our campus is easily accessible from urban centers such as Providence, Boston, and New York by car or other transportation.

"We offer 35 challenging academic majors through a liberal arts college, five professional schools, graduate programs, and the state's only law school. Accredited by the New England Association of Schools and Colleges, Roger Williams University has 3,300 full-time undergraduates. We're just the right size to offer you the friendliness and attention of a small liberal arts college, but with the professional tracks and research opportunities of a larger university. It's the best of both worlds. You'll also benefit from an array of support services to ease your arrival and make your years here comfortable and enjoyable. We give you what you're looking for—a high-quality education within an ideal academic setting that encompasses excellent facilities, recreation, athletics, and social life. Modern academic and support facilities are within walking distance of residence halls. Students have access to first-rate resources including libraries, state-of-the-art computer centers, and other advantages such as design and art studios. A Roger Williams University education gives you the chance to become a complete person who is successfully able to bridge transitions to a rewarding career and gratifying life."

For even more information on this school, turn to page 344 of the "Stats" section.

ROWAN UNIVERSITY

201 MULLICA HILL ROAD, GLASSBORO, NJ 08028 • ADMISSIONS: 856-256-4200 • FAX: 856-256-4430
E-MAIL: ADMISSIONS@ROWAN.EDU • WEBSITE: WWW.ROWAN.EDU

Ratings
Quality of Life: 77   Academic: 74   Admissions: 66   Financial Aid: 77

Academics

Rowan University, a reportedly "underestimated" New Jersey state school "growing in recognition," draws students with several top-notch programs. Those studying education note, "We have connections to most nearby

> **SURVEY SAYS . . .**
> No one cheats, Classes are small
> Frats and sororities dominate social scene
> School is well run, Lots of beer drinking
> Students get along with local community

school districts, and field experiences are strong in preparing students." The engineering department also offers "cream of the crop" professors and specifically "encourages women to excel." Public relations majors repeatedly praise their active student society, which offers networking, internship, and social opportunities. Professors are called "cooperative and willing to help," and since the school is "more teaching based than research based," students always "get lots of individual attention." Unfortunately, state budget cuts have put a damper on Rowan's "ambitious growth plan," and tuition creeps up to compensate. Due to the scarcity of some crucial classes, many students inadvertently find themselves on the "five-year program," wishing aloud, "I would like to graduate someday." Gripes abound that the administration "only administers stress and headaches," and demonstrates "poor prioritization of funds and altered sense of reality." Nonetheless, students agree that their university is on the up-and-up: "I do believe Rowan will be an amazing school in four or five years." Already, "it is becoming a very popular school and is therefore increasing its admission standards."

Life

Rowan life can be summarized by one student's comment: "We are the kind of school that admires hard work and good grades, yet we admire the ability to do a funnel as well." Drinking attracts a dedicated group of students who "revolve their weekends around frats and sororities" and frequent the "numerous taverns and sports bars." Referring to the recent ban on kegs at frat parties, a student writes, "Administration is foolishly trying to attack the party scene and turn it into a more academic school." Since only one-third of students live on-campus, the school "pretty much shuts down when everyone leaves on the weekends." Though more than 150 chartered organizations function on campus, "turn-out is often low" at group-sponsored activities. Students begin their Rowan career with a "great freshmen orientation program that helps incoming students feel like they want to be a part of the Rowan community." Nonetheless, "not much school spirit" takes hold. Though some feel that it's "actually not a good/safe idea to roam around the campus after dark," others have "NEVER felt unsafe walking around in the night or day" on Rowan's campus, a mere 20 minutes from Philadelphia and 45 minutes from the coast and Atlantic City.

Student Body

Rowan students are mainly "products of New York and New Jersey suburbs." Although the student population is relatively diverse, one student characterizes the situation by saying, "The different ethnic groups don't usually mingle. There is a growing interest, however, in different cultures, and Rowan tries to expose this and bring awareness. The cultural clubs also try to bring in other people." Another student chimes in, "I was one of few African American males in my field of study (business), which means I really think this school needs to do some minority recruiting." Amid the largely "apolitical" population, some students perceive "little tolerance for intellectuals" and "little intellectual diversity." Approximately 40 percent of the population commutes, and "there's very little interaction, if any, among commuters." Since the majority are traditional students, Rowan's nontraditional students can also have a difficult time integrating. Apparently, however, "each year, more and more people stay" on campus, improving the sense of community.

ADMISSIONS

Very important factors considered by the admissions committee include: class rank, secondary school record, and standardized test scores. *Important factors considered include:* character/personal qualities, extracurricular activities, interview, recommendations, and talent/ability. *Other factors considered include:* essays, minority status, state residency, volunteer work, and work experience. SAT I required. TOEFL required of all international applicants. High school diploma or GED is required. *High school units required/recommended:* 16 total required; 4 English required, 3 math required, 2 science required, 2 science lab required, 2 social studies required, 5 elective required.

The Inside Word

Not heretofore known as having a tight admissions process, Rowan is starting to look beyond New York and New Jersey for candidates who want to contribute to its forward scholastic momentum.

FINANCIAL AID

Students should submit: FAFSA. Regular filing deadline is March 15. The Princeton Review suggests that all financial aid forms be submitted as soon as possible after January 1. *Need-based scholarships/grants offered:* Pell, SEOG, state scholarships/grants, private scholarships, and the school's own gift aid. *Loan aid offered:* Direct Subsidized Stafford, Direct Unsubsidized Stafford, and Direct PLUS. Federal Work-Study Program available. Institutional employment available. Applicants will be notified of awards on a rolling basis beginning on or about May 1. Off-campus job opportunities are excellent.

FROM THE ADMISSIONS OFFICE

"Rowan University is a selective, progressive public university with the funds and public support to transform itself into a top regional university. It is using these resources to improve the academic quality of the university while keeping tuition affordable. Because of its large endowment, the University is able to compete with private colleges and produce direct benefits for students. The university has begun a $530 million 10-year plan to expand the campus, improve facilities, and hire more faculty. By implementing a comprehensive plan for enrollment management, Rowan University will maintain its reputation as a high-quality, moderate-price university. New residence halls will be built to allow the university to become a traditional residential campus.

"These efforts have caught the attention of organizations that evaluate colleges and universities nationwide. *U.S. News & World Report* ranks Rowan University in the 'Top Tier' of Northern Regional Universities. The 2000 edition of the Newsweek/Kaplan 'How to Get into College' guide named it a 'Hidden Treasure.' Kaplan included the university in 'The Unofficial, Biased Insider's Guide to the 320 Most Interesting Colleges' and *Kiplinger's* named Rowan University one of the '100 Best Buys in Public Colleges and Universities.'

"At Rowan, students have access to the resources of a large university without sacrificing the personal attention and small class size of a private college. All classes are taught by professors, not teaching assistants. The university enrolls more than 9,600 students among six colleges (Business, Communication, Education, Engineering, Fine & Performing Arts, and Liberal Arts & Sciences). Students can choose from 37 undergraduate majors and 30 graduate programs leading to master's and doctoral degrees."

For even more information on this school, turn to page 345 of the "Stats" section.

RUTGERS UNIVERSITY—NEW BRUNSWICK

65 DAVIDSON ROAD, PISCATAWAY, NJ 08854-8097 • ADMISSIONS: 732-932-4636 • FAX: 732-445-0237
FINANCIAL AID: 732-932-7057 • E-MAIL: ADMISSIONS@ASB-UGADM.RUTGERS.EDU • WEBSITE: WWW.RUTGERS.EDU

Ratings
Quality of Life: 72   Academic: 82   Admissions: 88   Financial Aid: 82

Academics

For most undergrads, the choice to come to Rutgers is primarily an economic one; even for out-of-state students, this public university provides a name-brand education at a discount rate. Once they arrive, though, most students are surprised to discover not just a cheap school but also a top-notch university, one that can offer the 28,000 undergraduates on its New Brunswick campus

SURVEY SAYS . . .
Great library
Athletic facilities are great
Political activism is hot
Students don't get along with local community
Large classes
Campus difficult to get around
Ethnic diversity on campus
Unattractive campus
Lots of long lines and red tape

academic opportunities in practically every field under the sun. Students report finding RU's size daunting at first ("It is very easy to get lost in the crowd here," warns one sophomore), but eventually they learn to work the system and get the most of their myriad opportunities. Writes one, "As I grew up at this school I learned to like it more, especially as I got into research. Based on my experiences I would rate Rutgers as great for doing research—that is, if you know how to use the school." Agrees another, "Rutgers University promotes education that helps individuals to explore learning in an independent manner. Students are challenged by professors to solve problems and expand their critical thinking skills. When entering the working world, I felt totally prepared. Learning is continuous at this school." Professors are "great but the higher up the ladder you go, the bigger the egos," explains a junior. Teaching assistants, unfortunately, are often "unqualified, unprepared, or just unable to effectively teach classes." Consequently, "Rutgers is basically a do-it-yourself school where you have to occasionally look for help." Don't look to the administration, though, unless you're prepared for the "RU Screw," or, as one student put it—less colorfully and more diplomatically—"some bureaucratic difficulty."

Life

At Rutgers "there is no lack of activities for the interested, motivated student," says a sophomore. "It's just a matter of keeping your eyes and ears open to take advantage of everything" Rutgers has to offer. Writes another student, "Rutgers has provided a multitude of opportunities for me to grow through community service," as well as clubs and other organizations. Activities "range from the Rutgers Ambulance Service to Model United Nations to one of the best college newspapers in the country." Intercollegiate sports are popular, and students report a decent variety of movies and plays presented on campus. The Greek system is thriving but not overwhelming, and parties of all kinds are "going on practically every night." Even so, some feel that life in New Brunswick leaves something to be desired. "Thank God we are near New York City," writes one. "Otherwise, I hope you like drinking beer in a basement because that is what everyone does until they turn 21." Philadelphia is also an easy train ride away.

Student Body

As a public university that draws lots of nontraditional students (i.e., part-timers, continuing education students), "RU students are very representative of people in the real world. It takes all kinds." Attests one student, "Few campuses offer the same diversity of lifestyles" or "so many diverse social groups." Students are "friendly, active, and involved. I have made many friendships here that will last an entire lifetime." And while they may not have the time to hang out and grab a beer (since many have families, jobs, and the like), "most are easy to get along with and quite friendly. I do a lot of group work with them and they're just great. . . . Everyone is willing to offer their advice or knowledge."

ADMISSIONS

Very important factors considered by the admissions committee include: class rank, secondary school record, standardized test scores. *Other factors considered include:* extracurricular activities, geographical residence, minority status, state residency, talent/ability, volunteer work, work experience. SAT I or ACT required. TOEFL required of all international applicants. High school diploma or GED is required. *High school units required/recommended:* 16 total required; 4 English required, 3 math required, 4 math recommended, 2 science required, 2 foreign language required, 5 elective required.

The Inside Word

New Jersey residents are finally acknowledging that the flagship of their state university system is among the finest public universities in the nation. As a result, getting in keeps getting tougher every year as more and more New Jersey residents elect to stay home for college.

FINANCIAL AID

Students should submit: FAFSA. No deadline for regular filing. The Princeton Review suggests that all financial aid forms be submitted as soon as possible after January 1. *Need-based scholarships/grants offered:* Pell, SEOG, state scholarships/grants, the school's own gift aid. *Loan aid offered:* Direct Subsidized Stafford, Direct Unsubsidized Stafford, Direct PLUS, Federal Perkins, state loans, college/university loans from institutional funds, other educational loans. Federal Work-Study Program available. Institutional employment available. Applicants will be notified of awards on a rolling basis beginning on or about February 15. Off-campus job opportunities are good.

FROM THE ADMISSIONS OFFICE

"Rutgers, The State Universtiy of New Jersey, one of only 61 members of the Association of American Universities, is a research university, which attracts students from across the nation and around the world. What does it take to be accepted for admission to Rutgers University? There's no single answer to that question. Our primary emphasis is on your past academic performance as indicated by your high school grades (particularly in required academic subjects), your class rank, the strength of your academic program, your standardized test scores on the SAT or ACT, any special talents you may have, and your participation in school and community activities. We seek students with a broad diversity of talents, interests, and backgrounds. Above all else, we're looking for students who will get the most out of a Rutgers education—students with the intellect, initiative, and motivation to make full use of the opportunities we have to offer."

For even more information on this school, turn to page 345 of the "Stats" section.

St. Anselm College

100 Saint Anselm Drive, Manchester, NH 03102-1310 • Admissions: 888-4ANSELM
Fax: 603-641-7550 • Financial Aid: financial_aid@anselm.edu • Website: www.anselm.edu

Ratings

Quality of Life: 80   Academic: 79   Admissions: 86   Financial Aid: 82

Academics

Just about every St. Anselm student will agree that the greatest strength of this school is the faculty. "My professors are all awesome," crows one undergrad. "They're also very accessible and urge us to come to them." With

SURVEY SAYS . . .
Great on-campus food, Students are religious
Lab facilities are great, No one cheats
Registration is a breeze
Student government is popular

just under 2,000 students, St. Anselm adheres to an "anti-inflation grading policy," which one student claims "makes it impossible to get over a C!" Hence, the nickname of the school, "St. A," is sometimes changed to "St. C." The stringent grading policy, however, is "very challenging and encourages the students to work harder." One common complaint is that there should be "a larger selection of majors to choose from," and many students specifically cite a need for more attention to fine arts, eastern theologies, and music. And while some students claims it's "difficult to create change on campus because St. Anselm is deeply rooted in tradition," the majority agree that "the administrators are always open to student input," and, as one students states, "I have been pushed to excel by professors who quickly assessed my abilities and truly wanted me to achieve what I was capable of."

Life

Formed in 1889 in southern New Hampshire by Benedictine Monks, Saint Anselm sometimes has earned a reputation as "a large bunch of Catholic do-gooders, but at the same time . . . a large bunch of fallen Catholic partiers!" Located near Manchester, the students "usually only party on Thursdays, Fridays, and Saturdays. . . . the weekends always revolve around drinking since there's not much else to do." Campus "can be boring because there are not a lot of places to go and have a fun time, but we do have a few clubs near by." No official Greek system adds to the rush off campus when class ends. One student is a big fan of "taking road trips to Boston or Portsmouth" and another is a huge proponent of the many campus events "like outdoor movies on the quad, laser tag, concerts, and our own game shows." For outdoorsmen, one student suggests taking "advantage of the excellent rock climbing, snowshoeing, hiking, camping, and skiing that the area has to offer." For the indoors type, on the other hand, there are a few complaints. While "new, beautiful townhouses were built for upper classmen," one student feels that "dorm availability for freshmen" is a problem.

Student Body

Budgeting one's time is important to a St. Anselm student. "It takes me so long to get to class because every five steps there is someone new to stop and say 'Hi' to and to talk to. Everyone is so friendly." With only 2,000 students, "everyone knows what is going on in everyone's life." And while some think this breeds "high-school-like cliques," another student likes how "the college tries to foster a 'Community of Respect,' and I do believe they succeed in that attempt." Many students hail from New England and are predominantly Catholic and Caucasian. Others, more inclined to fashion metaphors, label their peers "stereotypical Abercrombie-Finch cookie cutter," "snobby J.Crew," and "Gap poster children." In fact, a majority of students feel that "the lack of diversity of races, lifestyles, and backgrounds is St.

Anselm's biggest weakness." But most agree "the school has a lot to offer people. There are sports, groups, SGA, etc. . . . There is plenty for a student to be involved in." Warning to first-time visitors: the school is run primarily by Benedictine monks and although most students feel "the life of the monks who run the school is inspiring to anyone who meets them," another warns that it takes some time to "get used to men walking around in long, black robes."

ADMISSIONS

Very important factors considered by the admissions committee include: character/personal qualities, secondary school record. *Important factors considered include:* class rank, essays, recommendations, standardized test scores, talent/ability. *Other factors considered include:* alumni/ae relation, extracurricular activities, geographical residence, interview, minority status, volunteer work, work experience. SAT I or ACT required. TOEFL required of all international applicants. High school diploma or GED is required. *High school units required/recommended:* 18 total required; 20 total recommended; 4 English required, 3 math required, 4 math recommended, 3 science required, 4 science recommended, 3 science lab required, 2 foreign language required, 4 foreign language recommended, 2 social studies required, 1 history required, 2 history recommended, 3 elective required.

The Inside Word

St. Anselm gets a predominately regional applicant pool, and Massachusetts is one of its biggest suppliers of students. An above average-academic record should be more than adequate to gain admission.

FINANCIAL AID

Students should submit: FAFSA, CSS/Financial Aid PROFILE, federal tax returns for parent(s) and student. The Princeton Review suggests that all financial aid forms be submitted as soon as possible after January 1. *Need-based scholarships/grants offered:* Pell, SEOG, state scholarships/grants, private scholarships, the school's own gift aid. *Loan aid offered:* FFEL Subsidized Stafford, FFEL Unsubsidized Stafford, FFEL PLUS, Federal Perkins, GATE Loans. Federal Work-Study Program available. Institutional employment available. Applicants will be notified of awards on a rolling basis beginning on or about March 10. Off-campus job opportunities are excellent.

FROM THE ADMISSIONS OFFICE

"Why St. Anselm? The answer lies with our graduates. Not only do our alumni go on to successful careers in medicine, law, human services, and other areas, but they also make connections on campus that last a lifetime. With small classes, professors are accessible and approachable. The Benedictine monks serve not only as founders of the college, but as teachers, mentors, and spiritual leaders.

"St. Anselm is rich in history, but certainly not stuck in a bygone era. In fact, the college has launched a $50 million fundraising campaign, which will significantly increase funding for financial aid, academic programs, and technology. New initiatives include the New Hampshire Institute of Politics, where the guest list includes every major candidate from the 2000 presidential race, as well as other political movers and shakers. Not a political junkie? No problem. The NHIOP is a diverse undertaking that also involves elements of psychology, history, theology, ethics, and statistics.

"St. Anselm encourages students to challenge themselves academically and to lead lives that are both creative and generous. On that note, more than 40 percent of our students participate in community service locally and globally. Each year, about 150 students take part in Spring Break Alternative to help those less fortunate across the United States and Latin America. High expectations and lofty goals are hallmarks of a St. Anselm College education, and each student is encouraged to achieve his/her full potential here. Why St. Anselm? Accept the challenge and soon you will discover your own answers."

For even more information on this school, turn to page 346 of the "Stats" section.

SAINT BONAVENTURE UNIVERSITY

PO Box D, Saint Bonaventure, NY 14778 • Admissions: 716-375-2400 • Fax: 716-375-4005
Financial Aid: 716-375-2528 • E-mail: admissions@sbu.edu • Website: www.sbu.edu

Ratings

Quality of Life: 85   Academic: 77   Admissions: 77   Financial Aid: 88

Academics

In the mid-1990s, the faculty at St. Bonaventure created a division of the university called Clare College. The college now serves as the headquarters for all core-curriculum courses. To graduate, each student has to complete 12 of the Clare College courses, in addition to taking care of a major. In essence, it's not much different from most universities. But from the student perspective (and this is one of the nicer students), the "Clare College program needs work." Clare College aside, students at Bona's (as they affectionately call it) appreciate their academic experience—especially the professors. Not only are profs "funny," but they're also always endearing themselves to their students by doing things like giving out "their home phone numbers in case you need help" after close of business. "One of my professors lives in his office, I think," surmises a journalism major. "Profs are very nice," chirps a sophomore business major, adding, "Even if I get bad grades, I still can't hate them." Small class sizes ensure that students are able to work closely with their professors. "This school has provided me with more than $80,000 worth of knowledge," writes a senior.

> **SURVEY SAYS . . .**
> *Great library*
> *Lousy food on campus*
> *Great computer facilities*
> *Beautiful campus*
> *Campus easy to get around*
> *Athletic facilities are great*
> *Low cost of living*
> *Lots of beer drinking*

Life

St. Bonaventure was a thirteenth-century bishop. Translated, his name means, "Oh, good fortune!" If you ask students at St. Bonaventure University, they'll tell you that, when it comes to socializing, it's an apt name indeed. On the whole, people who come to Bona's feel fortunate that they did. Students here basically "live it up," according to one junior. Well, "Bonaventure is a party school," and while the university is not without its list of organizations and activities, most students prefer to find their own fun at the bars or parties. An "estimated 80 percent of students drink four times a week," guesses a junior, adding that those numbers are "not bad if you can moderate it with studies." Of course, not all students find their entertainment in a bottle. And "if a student complains all there is to do is drink, it's their fault!" A sophomore elementary education major says she easily has "fun with . . . friends doing nonalcoholic activities." While the "very small town" of St. Bonaventure doesn't have much to offer the students culture-wise—except for bars—campus activities like intercollegiate sports (participating and spectating), the campus radio station, and "CAB [Campus Activities Board] activities" add to the after-class options. What students don't do for fun is eat. In the apropos words of a freshman, "The food is icky."

Student Body

A profile of the average St. Bonaventure student would look something like this: "Middle-upper class," a strong penchant for drink, a love of sports, and "very friendly." This is just a profile, of course. Some students are "a little stuck up," or "cliquey," though on the whole "no matter where you go on campus, you always say 'hi' and smile to everyone." Actually, the general friendliness of the campus is so pervasive that students feel like "Bona" (as they call it) is just "one big family." While "the strong Catholic tradition leaves" students "very friendly," they're also "very close-minded to alternative lifestyles and ways of viewing" the world. Although many of the students are eager to get out and support the Bona's sports teams, they'll also tell you that "Division I athletes think they are God's gift to the school." But you shouldn't let a few inflated heads stop you from finding your place at St. Bonaventure. As one senior declares, "I make a new friend everyday, seriously."

ADMISSIONS

Very important factors considered by the admissions committee include: character/personal qualities, interview, recommendations, secondary school record. *Important factors considered include:* essays, extracurricular activities, standardized test scores, talent/ability, volunteer work. *Other factors considered include:* alumni/ae relation, class rank, work experience. SAT I or ACT required; SAT I recommended. TOEFL required of all international applicants. High school diploma or GED is required. *High school units required/recommended:* 19 total recommended; 4 English required, 3 math required, 3 science required, 3 science lab recommended, 2 foreign language required, 4 social studies required.

The Inside Word

Saint Bonaventure is a safety for many students applying to more selective Catholic universities, but it does a good job of enrolling a sizable percentage of its admits. Most solid students needn't worry about admission; even so, candidates who rank St. Bonnie as a top choice should still submit essays and interview.

FINANCIAL AID

Students should submit: FAFSA, institution's own financial aid form, state aid form. The Princeton Review suggests that all financial aid forms be submitted as soon as possible after January 1. *Need-based scholarships/grants offered:* Pell, SEOG, state scholarships/grants, private scholarships, the school's own gift aid. *Loan aid offered:* FFEL Subsidized Stafford, FFEL Unsubsidized Stafford, FFEL PLUS, Federal Perkins, college/university loans from institutional funds. Federal Work-Study Program available. Institutional employment available. Applicants will be notified of awards on a rolling basis beginning on or about April 1. Off-campus job opportunities are excellent.

FROM THE ADMISSIONS OFFICE

"The Saint Bonaventure University family has been imparting the Franciscan tradition to men and women of a rich diversity of backgrounds for more than 130 years. This tradition encourages all who become a part of it to face the world confidently, respect the earthly environment, and work for productive change in the world. The charm of our campus and the inspirational beauty of the surrounding hills provide a special place where growth in learning and living is abundantly realized. The Richter Student Fitness Center, scheduled to be completed in 2004, will provide all students with state-of-the-art facilities for athletics and wellness. Academics at Saint Bonaventure are challenging. Small classes and personalized attention encourage individual growth and development for students, Saint Bonaventure's nationally known Schools of Arts and Sciences, Business Administration, Journalism/Mass Communication, and Education offer majors in 31 disciplines. The School of Graduate Studies also offers several programs leading to the master's degree."

For even more information on this school, turn to page 347 of the "Stats" section.

St. John's University—Queens

8000 Utopia Parkway, Jamaica, NY 11439 • Admissions: 718-990-2000 • Fax: 718-990-5728
E-mail: admissions@stjohns.edu • Website: www.stjohns.edu

Ratings
Quality of Life: 80   Academic: 73   Admissions: 66   Financial Aid: 79

Academics

St. John's attracts high-caliber students thanks in part to the "strong alumni base and emphasis on ethics in the Catholic tradition." Once on campus, students find professors who are "very knowledgeable and, above all, very personable." With a student-faculty ratio of 18:1, small class sizes

> **SURVEY SAYS . . .**
> *Theater is hot*
> *Students get along with local community*
> *School is well run*
> *Diverse students interact*
> *Classes are small*
> *Great computer facilities*

ensure "a lot of attention from my professor"; this personal approach extends to student advisors, as "there's plenty of academic advisement for anyone who needs it." The computer science, government and politics, and pharmacy departments receive high marks from undergraduates. This academic rigor doesn't lead to "the fierce, cutthroat competition between students you see at other schools." Students laud the generous financial aid offered by the school and also praise the "attentive" and "helpful" administration. Throw in "superior computer facilities" and a well-run freshman center, and students start gushing, "My academic experience has been a triumphant one thus far."

Life

"I'm involved in a lot of volunteer groups at school, and most of the people I know are too," writes an altruistic student. "St. John's really encourages giving back to the community." Other students spend their time at "comedy shows, talent shows, fashion shows," or other free activities sponsored by the student life committee. Sports are another common obsession: "If you want to play basketball, well then, you've found your haven." Proximity to New York City is also commonly cited as a huge plus: "What isn't there to do in NYC?" Sometimes students lament the strong commuter component of campus life, and even among the 2,000 residents, many go home every weekend: "It's still a commuter school no matter how many dorms there are." Most agree, however, that "overall the campus vibe is good here." Those who do live at St. John's tell us that Jamaica Estates offers "off-campus restaurants, pizza joints, delis, cafes, bars, shops, diners. . . . There is a lot of nightlife in Queens and even more in Manhattan."

Student Body

Many students share the sentiment, "I love how diverse this school is!" Apparently, St. John's admits "students from almost every single background" who still manage to "get along really well." Maybe this is because "Queens is the most ethnically diverse county in the country," reflecting the student body from "many different nations." On the other hand, certain students paint a less harmonious picture with comments like, "My sexual orientation has left me ostracized" and "I just wish that people were more open-minded about certain topics here."

ADMISSIONS

Very important factors considered by the admissions committee include: secondary school record. *Important factors considered include:* class rank, essays, recommendations, and standardized test scores. *Other factors considered include:* character/personal qualities, extracurricular activities, interview, talent/ability, volunteer work, and work experience. SAT I or ACT required. TOEFL required of all international applicants. High school diploma is required and GED is accepted. *High school units required/recommended:* 16 total are required; 4 English required.

The Inside Word

St. John's should receive strong consideration from anyone looking for a large institution with good facilities and resources, as well as a good connection to the community, even amidst the sometimes maddening spread of New York City. Socioeconomic and ethnic diversity ensure a place for you within the student body.

FINANCIAL AID

Students should submit: FAFSA and state aid form (FAFSA preferably online). The Princeton Review suggests that all financial aid forms be submitted as soon as possible after January 1. *Need-based scholarships/grants offered:* Pell, SEOG, state scholarships/grants, private scholarships, and the school's own gift aid. *Loan aid offered:* FFEL Subsidized Stafford, FFEL Unsubsidized Stafford, FFEL PLUS, and Federal Perkins. Federal Work-Study Program available. Institutional employment available. Applicants will be notified of awards on a rolling basis beginning on or about April 1. Off-campus job opportunities are fair.

For even more information on this school, turn to page 347 of the "Stats" section.

SAINT JOSEPH COLLEGE

1678 ASYLUM AVENUE, WEST HARTFORD, CT 06117 • ADMISSIONS: 860-231-5216 • FAX: 860-233-5695
E-MAIL: ADMISSIONS@MERCY.SJC.EDU • WEBSITE: WWW.SJC.EDU

Ratings
Quality of Life: 79   Academic: 73   Admissions: 64   Financial Aid: 80

Academics

Saint Joseph College, a small, four-year women's college in north central Connecticut, is a "small and quiet school, great for the serious student" with "excellent programs in education and

> **SURVEY SAYS . . .**
> *Diverse students interact*
> *Students are religious*
> *Classes are small*

nursing." The good professors, students agree, are what make a Saint Joseph education worthwhile. Gushes one, "I have always found my professors to be willing and eager to assist me in all arenas of study. In several cases, they have referred me to their colleagues who have more experience in a particular area. Note that this occurred when the question I had was completely unrelated to any actual research project—this was occurring when I was merely curious, not desperate for guidance. I respect the commitment and expertise that such openness between faculty and students requires." Students are less happy with administrators, complaining that "the administration is very hard to get in touch with if there is a problem; pretty much we are left to our own devices." Others caution that "we advertise our connection to consortium colleges but lack adequate transportation to them."

Life

Just about any small, single-sex school is going to have a difficult time supporting an extracurricular scene. Throw in a strictly enforced religious moral code, and you have life at Saint Joseph College. "Campus life for the most part is nonexistent outside of studying," sums up one student. "The majority of on campus students go home for the weekends but for those that do stay buses are available for trips to the mall or downtown" West Hartford. Many here deeply resent the "very strict policies regarding overnight male guests in dorms. They aren't allowed after 1 A.M. in your room. This policy is very unpopular with students," reports a typical student. The social scene that does exist is "quiet for the most part. Large parties generally include no more than 12 people and take place on Friday or Saturday. There are no parties during the week." Many here feel that "SJC could improve by incorporating the surrounding schools in more of their functions. With SJC being an all-girls school it would be nice to have more activities that could include guys." Even the glummest here admit that "the college is beautiful in terms of landscape."

Student Body

Saint Joseph's undergrads appreciate "the wide variety of ethnic backgrounds among the students." As one student told us, "I honestly enjoy talking to the different types of students on campus. Students come from different backgrounds, and I can honestly say that talking to students from different backgrounds has had an amazing effect on the person I have become over my four years at Saint Joseph College." Students also report that Saint Joe's is home to "a small residential community, with a lot of people going home on the weekends. However, since it's an all women's college, I think the bonds we form with each other are stronger and you really get to know one another more. The people that stick around the most are the people with the closest friendships, those that will probably be friends forever."

ADMISSIONS

Very important factors considered by the admissions committee include: secondary school record. *Important factors considered include:* class rank, essays, and letters of recommendation. *Other factors considered include:* extracurricular activities. SAT I or ACT required. High school diploma or GED is required. *High school units required/recommended:* 16 total required; 4 English recommended, 4 math recommended, 3 lab science recommended, 2 foreign language recommended, 3 social studies recommended.

The Inside Word

Good thing the campus lies within walking distance of the Hartford scene, as on-campus students still need off-campus mobility to pursue all the school's academic and extracurricular avenues. Saint Joseph is a visually beautiful school unless you find a dearth of boys aesthetically displeasing.

FINANCIAL AID

Students should submit: FAFSA and institution's own financial aid form. Regular filing ASAP after January 1. *Need-based scholarships/grants offered:* Pell, SEOG, state scholarships/grants, private scholarships, and the school's own gift aid. *Loan aid offered:* FFEL Subsidized Stafford, FFEL Unsubsidized Stafford, FFEL PLUS, Federal Perkins, state loans, and Connecticut Family Education Loan Program. Federal Work-Study Program available. Institutional employment available. Applicants will be notified of awards on a rolling basis beginning on or about February 1. Off-campus job opportunities are good.

FROM THE ADMISSIONS OFFICE

"Saint Joseph College was founded in 1932 by the Sisters of Mercy to provide higher education opportunities for women. Over the years, the college has remained true to this vision, offering students solid professional training grounded in a tradition rich in the liberal arts. Consistently cited on the national level for the quality of its academic programs, Saint Joseph College is committed to responding to the needs of an ever-changing society. Today, the college serves the needs of a diverse, intergenerational student body while remaining true to its original mission.

"The beautiful 84-acre West Hartford campus houses The Women's College, the coeducational Prime Time Program and Graduate School, and The Gengras Center. Located one block from campus is the renowned School for Young Children, one of the earliest childhood centers in the state. The School for Young Children also serves as an on-site laboratory for preschool teacher training. The college's newest facility, The Carol Autorino Center for the Arts and Humanities, houses a 350-seat auditorium, five art galleries to showcase the college's extensive fine arts collections, classrooms, faculty offices, and more. The campus is easily accessible and offers ample parking, residence halls, dining facilities, the Pope Pius XII Library with more than 133,700 volumes and online resources, The O'Connell Athletic Center, and a state-of-the-art Information Technology Network Center."

For even more information on this school, turn to page 348 of the "Stats" section.

St. Lawrence University

Payson Hall, Canton, NY 13617 • Admissions: 315-229-5261 • Fax: 315-229-5818
Financial Aid: 315-229-5265 • E-mail: admissions@stlaw.edu • Website: www.stlawu.edu

Ratings
Quality of Life: 83   Academic: 91   Admissions: 86   Financial Aid: 83

Academics

St. Lawrence students love the "really comfortable, home-like atmosphere" engendered by "the size of the student body and the relative isolation of our campus from any real cities." Small class sizes are the norm at this small liberal arts college in the "north country" of New York State, meaning that "classes are discussion seminars rather than lectures.

SURVEY SAYS . . .
Beautiful campus
Students are religious
Everyone loves the saints
Students get along with local community
Frats and sororities dominate social scene
Political activism is hot
Campus difficult to get around
Students are happy

This allows students to make a more personal connection—not only with their fellow students, but also with their fellow professors." Professors "are all passionate about their subjects, easy to talk to, have good senses of humor, and available outside of class. If you can't make it to their office hours, they are willing to schedule a meeting time." Add "great research, independent projects, internships, and study abroad opportunities in 14 countries" as well as "a great diversity of classes offered here that makes it is almost impossible to not become enriched," and you'll understand why students here feel so favorably about SLU academics. But wait; there's more! Students also tell us that "the alumni connections are amazing and a great thing to have later on after college, especially for internships or actual jobs."

Life

"At St. Lawrence, there isn't much to do for fun except make your own fun." Some students here immerse themselves in campus life; writes one, "It's most important to be extremely active and try to enjoy what the campus has to offer to the fullest. From intramurals to the student government, there is always something to interest everyone." Students enthusiastically support their Division I hockey teams, which "add interest on an otherwise dull campus in the dead of winter," and enjoy special events like Peak Weekend ("It's for those who hike, I mean really hike, and those who just like to own hiking stuff. The Outing Club, the nation's oldest collegiate outdoors club, attempts to get college students on all 36 high peaks in the Adirondacks") and Snowbowl ("lots of sledding and beer"). Most students eventually find their way to SLU's lively party scene. "We do drink a lot," confesses one student. "The school tries to hide it, but St. Lawrence students can handle their booze almost any night of the week and still keep pace with the demanding academic program." For many, "the social scene at St. Lawrence gets a little monotonous. The area doesn't have much to offer, and the main weekend activities revolve around drinking with friends." Many warn that winters are long and exceedingly cold. Road trips to Canada, especially to Ottawa or Montreal, are popular diversions.

Student Body

St. Lawrence has long had a reputation as a preppy haven. Students here tell us that about half the student body fits that stereotype; writes one, the typical "Larry" likes "wearing his polo shirt with the collar turned up, [wearing] a North Face fleece, and carrying a Nalgene bottle. A Muffy, the female Larry, can be spotted with her Vera Bradley bags, Tiffany's heart bracelet, and an inordinate number of shoes." Admits one majority student, "St. Lawrence plays into the hands of the classic prep, so many of us seem to come from New England boarding schools, while the remainder are from upscale areas. We look and act like we stepped right out of the pages of The Official Preppy Handbook, and most of us seem proud of it." However, "there are also environmentalists, hippies, the outdoors people, and everyone else" at SLU, although "there aren't many punks and skaters, and people of these types tend to find themselves the token 'oddball' of the dorm." Everyone seems to agree that "we are quite a 'white' school and are lacking a bit in diversity." Many here are "involved in everything. I can't think of anyone who doesn't have extracurriculars. There is an organization for anything you can imagine." Many are active in community service.

ADMISSIONS

Very important factors considered by the admissions committee include: character/personal qualities, recommendations, secondary school record. *Important factors considered include:* class rank, essays, extracurricular activities, interview, minority status, standardized test scores. *Other factors considered include:* alumni/ae relation, geographical residence, talent/ability, volunteer work, work experience. SAT I or ACT required. TOEFL required of all international applicants. High school diploma or GED is required. *High school units required/recommended:* 20 total recommended; 4 English recommended, 4 math recommended, 4 science recommended, 4 foreign language recommended, 2 social studies recommended, 2 history recommended.

The Inside Word

St. Lawrence has a rough time convincing students to commit to spending four years in relative isolation. Serious competition from many fine northeastern colleges also causes admissions standards to be less selective than the university would like. This makes St. Lawrence an especially good choice for academically sound but average students who are seeking an excellent small college experience and/or an outdoorsy setting.

FINANCIAL AID

Students should submit: FAFSA, institution's own financial aid form, noncustodial (divorced/separated) parent's statement, income tax returns/W-2s. Regular filing deadline is February 15. The Princeton Review suggests that all financial aid forms be submitted as soon as possible after January 1. *Need-based scholarships/grants offered:* Pell, SEOG, state scholarships/grants, the school's own gift aid. *Loan aid offered:* Direct Subsidized Stafford, Direct Unsubsidized Stafford, FFEL Subsidized Stafford, FFEL Unsubsidized Stafford, FFEL PLUS, Federal Perkins, college/university loans from institutional funds, GATE Loans. Federal Work-Study Program available. Institutional employment available. Applicants will be notified of awards on or about March 30. Off-campus job opportunities are poor.

FROM THE ADMISSIONS OFFICE

"St. Lawrence is an independent, nondenominational, liberal arts and sciences university located in northern New York. The student body of 2,000 men and women choose from among more than 30 majors and minors; classes are small, with an emphasis on experiential learning, interdisciplinary study, and independent research. St. Lawrence is a residential college where living and learning are combined through the First-Year Program, theme cottages, and international study. St. Lawrence students are well rounded and involved, with many drawn to the 1,000-acre campus for the opportunity it provides for outdoor recreation. The campus, located in the town of Canton, is halfway between the Adirondack Park and the city of Ottawa. Students are active in various organizations centered on the arts, politics, community service, and athletics, with 32 intercollegiate teams offered. St. Lawrence alumni are loyal and active, providing internships for undergraduates and demonstrating their commitment through giving generously of their time and resources."

For even more information on this school, turn to page 348 of the "Stats" section.

SAINT MICHAEL'S COLLEGE

ONE WINOOSKI PARK, COLCHESTER, VT 05439 • ADMISSIONS: 802-654-3000 • FAX: 802-654-2591
E-MAIL: ADMISSION@SMCVT.EDU • WEBSITE: WWW.SMCVT.EDU

Ratings
Quality of Life: 75   Academic: 80   Admissions: 87   Financial Aid: 77

Academics

St. Michael's, according to its undergraduate students, is "pretty liberal for a Catholic college." The professors "care about their students" and "know your name." One professor even "invites students to stop by for some coffee and a talk," inspiring one of his stu-

> **SURVEY SAYS . . .**
> *Student publications are popular*
> *Students are religious, Classes are small*
> *Diversity lacking on campus*
> *Instructors are good teachers, School is well run*
> *Students get along with local community*

dents to rhapsodize: "This is exactly why I came to a small liberal arts school—I have the opportunity to sip coffee and talk philosophy with a brilliant professor, just because." The English department is "outstanding," enticing many students to major in the subject. Undergrads also single out journalism for plaudits; some would "venture to say it is one of the best journalism schools in the country." And students feel confident that their education will prepare them well to succeed in the "real world." Unfortunately, "there is not a wide variety of classes offered," and students often have trouble getting into classes that they need or want, "which sucks." Some students are even forced to remain in school an extra semester in order to fulfill graduation requirements. Students feel as if the administration is overly concerned with fundraising. "There is a recent trend in the world of college administrators to think of college as a business," complains one student. Tuition goes up every year, and students worry that financial aid isn't keeping pace.

Life

St. Michael's is situated just outside Burlington, about five miles from the shores of Lake Champlain in northern Vermont. Favorite activities include skiing, snowboarding, drinking, and smoking pot. Stowe is no more than an hour's drive away, and students hit the slopes there whenever possible. Montreal, about an hour and a half away by car, is a popular weekend destination. Burlington, Vermont, is only a short drive, too, and the college runs a little service called "MORF, which is a van that is two bucks a person into Burlington." "Church Street in downtown Burlington is a very popular place for the college crowd," where students can take in a movie, shop, or go to a bar. Undergrads are candid about drug use at St. Mike's: "There is a lot of alcohol and weed on campus," admits one student. However, "if that's not what you're into, there are also plenty of people just like you." Students also engage in volunteer work, and many are involved in intramural sports. Practicing homebody is also a popular pastime: "My closest friend and I really enjoy just sitting in the room, reading poetry, and sipping on some fine Vermont beer." Students wish the administration would provide more on-campus activities, especially in the winter months, when Vermont gets mighty cold and bleak.

Student Body

Students at St. Mike's get along with one another just fine. Most are "upper-middle-class white Catholics" with a "friendly vibe." Stylewise, the "dirty hippie" look is mod, and there are a fair amount of "left-wing political activists" who encourage their fellow students to hope that "perhaps the world we inherit is not doomed after all." And while "for a Catholic school there is a rather large gay population," students raise questions about the low level of economic and racial diversity. "More and more over the past few years there have been more students from more well-to-do families coming here," says another, making students from lower-income backgrounds feel as if they "don't fit in very well."

ADMISSIONS

Very important factors considered by the admissions committee include: class rank, secondary school record, and standardized test scores. *Important factors considered include:* character/personal qualities, essays, and recommendations. *Other factors considered include:* alumni/ae relation, extracurricular activities, geographical residence, interview, minority status, state residency, talent/ability, volunteer work, and work experience. SAT I or ACT required. TOEFL required of all international applicants. High school diploma or GED is required. *High school units required/recommended:* 16 total required; 20 total recommended; 4 English required, 3 math required, 4 math recommended, 3 science required, 4 science recommended, 2 science lab required, 3 science lab recommended, 3 foreign language required, 4 foreign language recommended, 3 history required, 4 history recommended.

The Inside Word

The school is as selective as it is because it trusts students to live up to its Catholic and academic standards without a lot of handholding after admittance. The noninterventionist attitude on campus spills over into nearby Burlington, but keep in mind that Vermont as a whole is strict about underage drinking.

FINANCIAL AID

Students should submit: FAFSA, institution's own financial aid form, federal tax forms, and W-2s. Regular filing deadline is March 15. The Princeton Review suggests that all financial aid forms be submitted as soon as possible after January 1. *Need-based scholarships/grants offered:* Pell, SEOG, state scholarships/grants, private scholarships, and the school's own gift aid. *Loan aid offered:* FFEL Subsidized Stafford, FFEL Unsubsidized Stafford, FFEL PLUS, and Federal Perkins. Federal Work-Study Program available. Institutional employment available. Applicants will be notified of awards on or about April 1. Off-campus job opportunities are good.

FROM THE ADMISSIONS OFFICE

"With nearly 95 percent of undergraduates living on campus, Saint Michael's College is committed to creating a life-changing educational experience for a diverse student population from throughout the United States and the world. Striking the perfect balance between a busy college town and a spectacular outdoor wilderness, our 440-acre campus is located between Lake Champlain and the majestic Green Mountains, just outside Burlington, Vermont's largest city and home to four colleges, including the University of Vermont. When not excelling in one of the fine academic programs that places Saint Michael's in the top tier of *U.S. News & World Report* rankings, three out of four students spend their time in our wide-reaching Wilderness Programs, in our extensive service program, or in recreational and Northeast-10 sports. Wilderness Programs bring students into the great Vermont outdoors for river rafting, sea kayaking, rock- and ice-climbing, hiking, skiing, snowboarding, and other adventure sports as well as survival training from beginner to advanced certification levels. MOVE, our student-led volunteer corps run in concert with our Edmundite Campus Ministry, earned Saint Michael's a place in history as the 32nd Point of Light for engendering lifelong community service. Some 625 students rack up 42,000 hours of service a year building houses through Habitat for Humanity; working as tutors, youth mentors, and companions for the elderly; and fighting hunger and homelessness. One in four students takes part in 21 NCAA Division II intercollegiate sports (all but six in the Northeast-10 Conference). Meeting the needs of a diverse student population also means providing healthy living options, including GREAT Housing, through which 20 percent of students choose to create and live in a drug- and alcohol-free environment."

For even more information on this school, turn to page 349 of the "Stats" section.

SALVE REGINA UNIVERSITY

100 Ochre Point Avenue, Newport, RI 02840-4192 • Admissions: 401-341-2908 • Fax: 401-848-2823
E-mail: sruadmis@salve.edu • Website: www.salve.edu

Ratings
Quality of Life: 77   Academic: 71   Admissions: 63   Financial Aid: 75

Academics

Salve Regina University's most commonly cited strength has got to be the small class size, which enables "more personal teaching" and "a lot of attention from professors." Not only is it "easy to get extra help," but instructors also "make themselves very accessible

> **SURVEY SAYS . . .**
> *School is well run*
> *Intercollegiate sports are popular*
> *Great off-campus food*
> *Classes are small*
> *Students get along with local community*

to all the students, and they are very understanding." One student reports, "Professors are great and always willing to help and chat whether it be about class or outside things." Additionally, they exhibit a "genuine desire to see students succeed." Surprisingly, certain people may find themselves "having to teach myself in some highly difficult areas," but the education and nursing programs are singled out as exemplary. On the administrative side, offices are notorious for letting "paperwork end up in no-man's land," but students also characterize administrators as "more than helpful" and "willing to let us get our points across." Though some wish the school would raise the bar and "make it harder to get in," most agree with the statement, "I feel that I am getting a well-rounded education at Salve."

Life

One student sums up prevailing opinion with his comment, "If you don't like the atmosphere around Salve Regina University, then something is wrong with you." Attribute this sentiment to the fact that "the dorms are mansions" and the nearby ocean induces a pleasant "calming effect." The town of Newport is considered "quite a wonderful sight to see" and "a beautiful fun place to spend four years." One student reports, "When the weather is right the parties down on the beach are great." The biggest complaint about the Salve Regina experience centers on the predominance of strict rules. First of all, the campus is dry, "which doesn't mean there isn't a lot of drinking," one respondent is quick to point out. Second, members of the opposite sex are not allowed in dorms past the stroke of midnight, a policy many students find, like, "so outdated." An undergraduate astutely writes, "They want us all to act like priests and nuns, which does not prepare us at all for the real world," unless they are joining the clergy, of course. Others agree with the outlook, "They advocate that we are adults now, and I feel that we should be trusted to be making adult decisions." To escape the stricture, many students head to Providence, a mere half-hour and inexpensive bus ride away.

Student Body

Many Salve students comment on the "unity" at their school, the feeling that the student body is "like a large family. Everyone is friendly and charitable." The majority of undergraduates are "very open to making friends" and "tend to live good Christian lives," which includes being "loving and caring and people you can trust." Several students call for "more diversity in race and background," but considering the current environment, "there are few people who are ever excluded or discriminated against." The small population makes for a situation where "you basically know everyone here" and "there is no real sense of who is a senior and who is a freshman." Thus, "most of the students are always looking to say 'hi' to one another, which really makes for a friendly campus."

ADMISSIONS

Very important factors considered by the admissions committee include: class rank, secondary school record, and standardized test scores. *Important factors considered include:* character/personal qualities, essays, extracurricular activities, recommendations, talent/ability, volunteer work, and work experience. *Other factors considered include:* alumni/ae relation and minority status. SAT I or ACT required. TOEFL required of all international applicants. High school diploma or GED is required. *High school units required/recommended:* 16 total required; 4 English required, 3 math required, 2 lab sciences required, 2 foreign language recommended, 1 social studies required, 4 elective recommended.

The Inside Word

Don't be fooled by the easy admissions because Salve Regina students are challenged to reach higher once admitted to achieve their undergraduate and professional goals. This picturesque campus affords you the perfect opportunity to kick back and . . . study. Partying takes place outside Salve's walls, in Newport and Providence.

FINANCIAL AID

Students should submit: FAFSA, institution's own financial aid form, CSS/Financial Aid PRO-FILE, noncustodial (divorced/separated) parent's statement, and business/farm supplement. Deadline for regular filing is March 1. The Princeton Review suggests that all financial aid forms be submitted as soon as possible after January 1. *Need-based scholarships/grants offered:* Pell, SEOG, state scholarships/grants, private scholarships, and the school's own gift aid. *Loan aid offered:* FFEL Subsidized Stafford, FFEL Unsubsidized Stafford, FFEL PLUS, Federal Perkins, Federal Nursing, state loans, college/university loans from institutional funds, and private loans. Federal Work-Study Program available. Institutional employment available. Applicants will be notified of awards beginning on February 1. Off-campus job opportunities are excellent.

FROM THE ADMISSIONS OFFICE

"Salve Regina University is a small university with big opportunity. Located on one of the most beautiful campuses in the country, Salve Regina's historic oceanfront campus is a place where students feel at home. Students study and live in historic mansions, yet receive an education that prepares them for modern careers and a lifetime of serving their communities. Salve offers excellent pre-professional and liberal arts programs (most popular are business, education, administration of justice, and biology). The classes are small and are all taught by professors (no grad assistants). Salve's small size also makes it easy for students to get involved on campus with clubs, activities, athletics, or intramurals. At Salve, it is easy to become a leader—even in your first year.

"Newport offers the perfect location for students who love history, sailing, and the outdoors. Students can surf, ocean kayak from First Beach, or bike ride on the famous Ocean Drive. Newport also hosts several festivals throughout the year. All students get a free statewide trolley/bus pass that takes them throughout Newport or to Providence, only 30 minutes away.

"Admission to Salve Regina is competitive. The Admissions Office looks at several factors in reviewing applications. Most important are applicants' day-to-day academic work and the level of the courses they have taken. Recommendation letters and test scores are also reviewed, as are leadership positions and community involvement."

For even more information on this school, turn to page 350 of the "Stats" section.

SARAH LAWRENCE COLLEGE

ONE MEAD WAY, BRONXVILLE, NY 10708-5999 • ADMISSIONS: 914-395-2510 • FAX: 914-395-2676
FINANCIAL AID: 914-395-2570 • E-MAIL: SLCADMIT@MAIL.SLC.EDU • WEBSITE: WWW.SLC.EDU

Ratings

Quality of Life: 76   Academic: 93   Admissions: 90   Financial Aid: 80

Academics

At Sarah Lawrence, there's no such thing as a test, core requirement, or major. The SLC equivalent of a test, explains one sophomore, involves "sitting in a room with 10 classmates and a brilliant teacher and working hard enough to participate in a discussion without looking like an idiot."

> **SURVEY SAYS . . .**
> *No one cheats, (Almost) everyone smokes*
> *Class discussions encouraged*
> *Classes are small, Political activism is hot*
> *Intercollegiate sports are unpopular or nonexistent*
> *No one plays intramural sports*
> *Campus easy to get around*
> *Students don't get along with local community*

However, don't be fooled, for what SLC doesn't give in tests, it does make up for in papers; many, many papers! The downside of this unrestrictive approach is that students who aren't organized, disciplined, and self-motivated can find themselves fumbling through an "unfocused education." If students find that they're losing their way—or just need to chat about classes, or personal life, or the future—they can always talk to their "don." The system of donning at Sarah Lawrence links each student with a personal advisor (professor) who helps guide the student's education. As you might expect, "good professors are extremely enthusiastic and intelligent," while "bad profs are average and boring." Sometimes it's tough to get into classes—especially popular ones like "photography, writing, and some lit classes." "Work flows steadily" from every academic front on this campus. Students don't mind the rigor, though. In fact, one freshman only wishes "we could take more classes."

Life

Imagine that all the "brilliant weirdos," "introverted poetic types," "artistic geniuses," and "social martyrs" from high school came together in one place—that place is Sarah Lawrence. SLC's extracurricular activities are what you make them. One freshman puts it nicely: "There are tons of activities going on all the time. I don't think a day goes by when there isn't some sort of guest performer or speaker or student performance going on." Other students flee campus every chance they get for everyone's favorite enchanted isle—Manhattan, 15 miles away. On the whole, Sarah Lawrence's hometown gets bad ratings, as "Bronxville is a sleepy little hamlet with an average income of around $350,000, so the neighbors aren't exactly into all-night raging parties." This can be a sore spot if you're a student who likes to "play hard and work hard," but party life does exist, in all its incantations. A sophomore says it's the drugs that serve as the social grease on the rusty hinges of the student body, but another says, "There are people who only want to party and get wasted, but there are also quite a few people who would much rather go to a movie or watch one in their room with some friends." Whatever your bag, Sarah Lawrence can please on many levels. Larger events on campus tend to be big crowd pleasers, like the Cross Dress Cabaret (Drag Queen and King crowned, of course), the Dive-in-Movie (only 65 at this one . . . the pool can't fit anymore!) and more than a handful of poetry slams. And if this all gets to be too much, students can wander over to the library and into The Pillow Room—a space cluttered with big cushions where students can read a book, take a nap, or try to figure out how they're going to come up with the train fare into the city next weekend.

Student Body

On any given day at Sarah Lawrence, you're likely to see a mix of "hipsters, artists, intellectuals, and slackers." And most of these people are intent on fostering and exhibiting their individualism. This translates to a healthy population of creative minds, though, "It's hard to create a community from a lot of individuals," says one student. Another calls Sarah Lawrence the "un-community," and says that the college "focuses so much on individualism" that "no one remembers to stop and say 'hello.'" With about three-quarters of the student population being white as well as "extremely liberal," it sometimes seems that "the student body is much more homogenous than they like to believe." "Students at times can be cold, pretentious, and alienating," concedes one sophomore. "But at other times [they] can be warm, generous, and accepting. It's a bit of a bipolar campus."

ADMISSIONS

Very important factors considered by the admissions committee include: character/personal qualities, essays, recommendations, secondary school record. *Important factors considered include:* extracurricular activities, talent/ability, volunteer work, work experience. *Other factors considered include:* alumni/ae relation, class rank, geographical residence, interview, minority status, standardized test scores. SAT I or ACT required. TOEFL required of all international applicants. *High school units required/recommended:* 4 English required, 2 math required, 4 math recommended, 2 science required, 4 science recommended, 2 foreign language required, 4 foreign language recommended, 4 social studies recommended, 2 history required, 4 history recommended.

The Inside Word

The public generally views Sarah Lawrence as an artsy "alternative" college. The college itself avoids this image, preferring instead to evoke an impression that aligns them with more traditional and prestigious northeastern colleges such as the Ivies, Little Ivies, and former Seven Sisters. Both the total number of applicants and the selectivity of the admissions process have increased over the past few years.

FINANCIAL AID

Students should submit: FAFSA, CSS/Financial Aid PROFILE, noncustodial (divorced/separated) parent's statement. Regular filing deadline is February 1. The Princeton Review suggests that all financial aid forms be submitted as soon as possible after January 1. *Need-based scholarships/grants offered:* Pell, SEOG, state scholarships/grants, private scholarships, the school's own gift aid. *Loan aid offered:* FFEL Subsidized Stafford, FFEL Unsubsidized Stafford, FFEL PLUS, Federal Perkins. Federal Work-Study Program available. Institutional employment available. Applicants will be notified of awards on or about April 1. Off-campus job opportunities are good.

FROM THE ADMISSIONS OFFICE

"Students who come to Sarah Lawrence are curious about the world, and they have an ardent desire to satisfy that curiosity. Sarah Lawrence offers such students two innovative academic structures: the seminar/conference system and the arts components. Courses in the humanities, social sciences, natural sciences, and mathematics are taught in the seminar/conference style. The seminars enroll an average of 11 students and consist of lecture, discussion, readings, and assigned papers. For each seminar, students also have private tutorials, called conferences, where they conceive of individualized projects and shape them under the direction of professors. Arts components let students combine history and theory with practice. Painters, printmakers, photographers, sculptors and filmmakers, composers, musicians, choreographers, dancers, actors, and directors work in readily available studios, editing facilities, and darkrooms, guided by accomplished professionals. The secure, wooded campus is 30 minutes from New York City, and the diversity of people and ideas at Sarah Lawrence make it an extraordinary educational environment."

For even more information on this school, turn to page 350 of the "Stats" section.

SETON HALL UNIVERSITY

400 SOUTH ORANGE AVENUE, SOUTH ORANGE, NJ 07079-2697 • ADMISSIONS: 973-761-9332
FAX: 973-275-2040 • FINANCIAL AID: 973-761-9332 • E-MAIL: THEHALL@SHU.EDU
WEBSITE: WWW.ADMISSIONS.SHU.EDU

Ratings

Quality of Life: 80   **Academic:** 83   **Admissions:** 77   **Financial Aid:** 81

Academics

Students at Seton Hall praise their school's pre-professional and career-specific programs. The education department, for example, "has a wonderful staff who are readily available and very resourceful," writes one future teacher. A nursing student reported having "an overall good experience with my professors." And a business student bragged that everyone in the b-school is "helpful, nice, and accessible." Students generally praise the deans as "very personable," and report that priests "are very nice too." There's general approbation of the full-time professors, who "work hard to help the students" and who, "because of our wireless campus and email system, are very accessible day or night!" Despite all these assets, Seton Hall also receives some very loud complaints from its undergraduates. "Registration and the money aspect are horrible," most here agree. They also warn that "advisors are the worst part of the entire process. They either don't know what they're doing or they just don't care." Others grouse that "the instructors for the core classes haven't been the best quality" and that "a lot of adjunct professors arrive here after a long day's work at their other job and don't teach us anything." Summing up both the good and bad here, one student writes, "At Seton Hall you can find small class sizes, professors who care, students who are willing to help each other and a feeling like you belong to a really big family. Seton Hall . . . has its problems with parking for commuters, living spaces for residents, long lines at the financial aid office, and even longer lines at the bookstore to buy high-priced books."

> **SURVEY SAYS . . .**
> *(Almost) everyone smokes*
> *Lots of beer drinking*
> *Great computer facilities*
> *Everyone loves the Pirates*
> *Frats and sororities dominate social scene*
> *Hard liquor is popular*
> *Popular college radio*
> *Campus easy to get around*
> *Ethnic diversity on campus*
> *Students don't get along with local community*

Life

"A lot of parties go on at Seton Hall" even though the university "has worked really hard to prevent students from doing the typical party scene." Notes one student, "At the beginning of last year, Seton Hall started putting pressure on the South Orange Police. The parties are at Greek houses, which are off campus, and now most parties get broken up by the cops." The university crackdown is the result of frequent complaints from the school's neighbors. As a result, students either hit the frat parties or "travel away from campus, and usually away from South Orange if they plan to do most things." The net result is that many students feel that "Seton Hall University has absolutely no social life for a student who cares naught for alcohol." A good portion of the student body goes home after classes: "On the weekends the place is so deserted." Many who stick around "just take the train to New York City. . . . It's only a 20-minute ride, so it's what most of us do for fun here. We head for a bar or club in the city." About the only time the campus truly comes together is to watch the Pirates shoot hoops.

Student Body

Seton Hall is "a very ethnically and culturally diverse school," but by nearly all accounts, students separate themselves into ethnic and racial enclaves. Students typically "are from New York or New Jersey. They are Catholic and either white or Hispanic. Some complained that their classmates "wear way too much makeup and try to be J.Lo or Ja Rule. It's sick." Adds another critic, "Black pants, tight shirts, and the 'Jersey' look, which is trendy, set the tone. There's Coach, Fendi, Gucci, and Tiffany's everywhere." Undergrads tend to be "uninterested in politics at the local, state, and national levels." Most are "involved in at least one extracurricular activity, have a part-time job, and know when to have fun and when to buckle down to do their work."

ADMISSIONS

Very important factors considered by the admissions committee include: essays, recommendations, secondary school record, standardized test scores. *Important factors considered include:* extracurricular activities, volunteer work, work experience. *Other factors considered include:* character/personal qualities, class rank, interview, talent/ability. SAT I or ACT required. TOEFL required of all international applicants. High school diploma or GED is required. *High school units required/recommended:* 16 total required; 4 English required, 3 math required, 1 science required, 1 science lab required, 2 foreign language required, 2 social studies required, 4 elective required.

The Inside Word

Getting into Seton Hall shouldn't be too stressful for most average students who have taken a full college-prep curriculum in high school. In the New York metropolitan area there are a lot of schools with similar characteristics, and collectively they take away the large proportion of Seton Hall's admits. Above average students who are serious about the university should be able to parlay their interest into some scholarship dollars.

FINANCIAL AID

Students should submit: FAFSA. No deadline for regular filing. The Princeton Review suggests that all financial aid forms be submitted as soon as possible after January 1. *Need-based scholarships/grants offered:* Pell, SEOG, state scholarships/grants, private scholarships, the school's own gift aid. *Loan aid offered:* Direct Subsidized Stafford, Direct Unsubsidized Stafford, Direct PLUS, Federal Perkins, state loans, college/university loans from institutional funds. Federal Work-Study Program available. Institutional employment available. Applicants will be notified of awards on a rolling basis beginning on or about March 15. Off-campus job opportunities are excellent.

FROM THE ADMISSIONS OFFICE

"As the oldest and largest diocesan university in the United States, Seton Hall University is committed to providing its students with a diverse environment focusing on academic excellence and ethical development. Outstanding faculty, a technologically advanced campus, and a values-centered curriculum challenge Seton Hall students. Through these things and the personal attention students receive, they are prepared to be leaders in their professional and community lives in a global society. Seton Hall's campus offers students up-to-date facilities, including an award-winning library facility opened in 1994 and the state-of-the art Kozlowski Hall, which opened in 1997. The university has invested more than $25 million in the past five years to provide its students and faculty with leading edge information technology. The Mobile Computing Program is widely recognized as one of the nation's best. In 1999 and 2000, Seton Hall was ranked as one of the nation's Most Wired universities by Yahoo! Internet Life magazine. Recent additions to Seton Hall's academic offerings include the School of Diplomacy and International Relations and a number of dual-degree health sciences programs, including physical therapy, physician assistant, and occupational therapy."

For even more information on this school, turn to page 351 of the "Stats" section.

SIENA COLLEGE

515 LOUDON ROAD, LOUDONVILLE, NY 12211 • ADMISSIONS: 518-783-2423 • FAX: 518-783-2436
FINANCIAL AID: 518-783-2427 • E-MAIL: ADMIT@SIENA.EDU • WEBSITE: WWW.SIENA.EDU

Ratings
Quality of Life: 75   Academic: 74   Admissions: 74   Financial Aid: 80

Academics

Students at Siena College have very mixed feelings about their education. They praise their favorite professors because they are "always available and willing to help with anything." And they're "creative and open-minded" to boot. The history program gets especially high marks. Professors "not only know what they are talking about, [but] they [also] know how to relay the infor-

> **SURVEY SAYS . . .**
> *Musical organizations aren't popular*
> *Diversity lacking on campus*
> *Students love Loudonville, NY*
> *Classes are small*
> *(Almost) everyone plays intramural sports*
> *Very small frat/sorority scene*
> *Theater is unpopular*
> *Computer facilities need improving*
> *Registration is a pain*

mation to students in a user-friendly way," writes a senior psychology major. Despite the small classes, "some professors tend to lecture too much and don't get the students involved." Students also complain that they have a difficult time registering for the most desired classes, which therefore makes "the good teachers impossible to get." The administration also gets mixed reviews. While a sophomore English major believes, "Those who don't look at the administration as the enemy from day one get listened to with relative seriousness," most students say that the lack of communication between the administration and themselves is a major problem. One senior history major describes the administration as "a bunch of bureaucrats on valium who are underpaid and consequently don't care." She adds that the various administrative offices "treat students like juvenile delinquents."

Life

Although Loudonville is not far from the bars of Albany, the lack of transportation is a problem—one that encourages many students to stay in town, where entertainment options are seriously limited. Some students "get all dolled up in their party best and pile 12 to a taxi"; however, because taxis are expensive, which makes it difficult to get off campus, many students go to the upperclassmen's townhouses to pour a few down the hatch. However, there are other things to do on campus: students attend movies, and a number enjoy their association with a medieval history club—the Society for Creative Anachronism. The gym is well used, the dorms are overcrowded, and students go out to dinner as often as they can because the on-campus food leaves much to be desired.

Student Body

Siena's students are primarily Catholic and conservative. Some believe that the "upper-middle-class Catholic students are unacquainted with reality." An English major describes his fellows as "good people who do very stupid things." Students complain about the evident lack of diversity on campus; this is not surprising considering that over 90 percent of the students are Caucasian. "There is some diversity," a chemistry major says, "but it's primarily Abercrombie-wearing Dave Matthews fans." A senior history major decries the "closed-mindedness" that she observes among her schoolmates. Students describe their peers as "friendly" but "cliquey." Overall, "students here . . . are nice and usually show respect for you," a business major writes. "They are able to get along together pretty well."

ADMISSIONS

Very important factors considered by the admissions committee include: secondary school record. *Important factors considered include:* essays, recommendations, standardized test scores. *Other factors considered include:* alumni/ae relation, character/personal qualities, class rank, extracurricular activities, talent/ability, volunteer work, work experience. SAT I or ACT required. TOEFL required of all international applicants. High school diploma or GED is required. *High school units required/recommended:* 14 total required; 19 total recommended; 4 English required, 3 math required, 4 math recommended, 3 science required, 4 science recommended, 3 science lab required, 4 science lab recommended, 3 foreign language recommended, 1 social studies required, 3 history required.

The Inside Word

Students who have consistently solid grades should have no trouble getting admitted. There is hot competition for students between colleges in New York State; Siena has to admit the large majority of its applicants in order to meet freshman class enrollment targets.

FINANCIAL AID

Students should submit: FAFSA, state aid form. The Princeton Review suggests that all financial aid forms be submitted as soon as possible after January 1. *Need-based scholarships/grants offered:* Pell, SEOG, state scholarships/grants, private scholarships, the school's own gift aid, Siena Grants, Franciscan Community Grants. *Loan aid offered:* FFEL Subsidized Stafford, FFEL Unsubsidized Stafford, FFEL PLUS, Federal Perkins. Federal Work-Study Program available. Institutional employment available. Applicants will be notified of awards on or about April 1. Off-campus job opportunities are good.

FROM THE ADMISSIONS OFFICE

"Siena is a coeducational, independent liberal arts college with a Franciscan tradition. It is a community where the intellectual, personal, and social growth of all students is paramount. Siena's faculty calls forth the best Siena students have to give—and the students do the same for them. Students are competitive, but not at each other's expense. Siena's curriculum includes 23 majors in three schools—liberal arts, science, and business. In addition, there are over a dozen pre-professional and special academic programs. With a student-faculty ratio of 14:1, class size ranges between 15 and 35 students. Siena's 152-acre campus is located in Loudonville, a suburban community within two miles of the New York State seat of government in Albany. With 15 colleges in the area, there is a wide variety of activities on weekends. Regional theater, performances by major concert artists, and professional sports events compete with the activities on the campus. Within 50 miles are the Adirondacks, the Berkshires, and the Catskills, providing outdoor recreation throughout the year. Because the capital region's easy, friendly lifestyle is so appealing, many Siena graduates try to find their first jobs in upstate New York."

For even more information on this school, turn to page 352 of the "Stats" section.

SIMMONS COLLEGE

300 THE FENWAY, BOSTON, MA 02115 • ADMISSIONS: 617-521-2051 • FAX: 617-521-3190
FINANCIAL AID: 617-521-2001 • E-MAIL: UGADM@SIMMONS.EDU • WEBSITE: WWW.SIMMONS.EDU

Ratings
Quality of Life: 86   **Academic:** 88   **Admissions:** 77   **Financial Aid:** 80

Academics

Have you ever heard of "Dan— The Man—Cheever"? Most Simmons students have. "The president is down to earth. He let's the students call him 'Dan—The Man,'" after all. In fact, most students find the administration and the faculty to be "very accessible."

> **SURVEY SAYS . . .**
> *Students love Boston, MA*
> *Profs teach upper levels, Students are cliquish*
> *Great off-campus food, Popular college radio*
> *Students are happy, High cost of living*

Overall, students believe Simmons provides an "academic experience" that is "excellent" and "truly interactive." "Professors here go the extra mile"—though it should be said that "some of them are windbags and like hearing themselves talk." No matter what they think of their professors, students can definitely lodge a complaint or two against the curriculum. For instance, a "performing arts department is needed," and there's "only one music prof—icky." They also could do without Culture Matters, an "extremely disappointing, ineffective, and not challenging" course that all first-year students have to take. But if your cards fall right, you'll find that "every class ends up being your favorite class." Because the "work load is heavy" across the board, Simmons students get the sense that they're "all in this together." A sophomore adds, "Especially when we all have to cross Brookline Avenue, the four-lane road with no crosswalk."

Life

There are more than 50 clubs and organizations at Simmons, though you wouldn't know it by talking to the students. "Campus life is nonexistent," remarks a freshman. "Clubs and sports are often ignored." So what exactly do Simmons students do for fun? For those who choose to stick around campus, not much. "Girls have knitting parties, eat a lot of take out, and do laundry on Saturday nights." Others "just hang out, drink, smoke, and make out." But for those who are looking for a little more excitement, they've got Boston—and 15 nearby colleges—at their fingertips. The city of Boston can provide not only "a great opportunity to go to see movies, plays, musicals, [and] go to museums and shopping," but also the chance to meet other college-agers at "bars and clubs." And when they feel up for a good old-fashioned keg party, the Simmons women "go to frats at the larger schools" that are nearby, especially Boston University and MIT. And for sports fans, "Red Sox and Bruins games" are good ways to spend an evening. But at the end of any good evening, Simmons students return to "quiet" dorms on campus, dorms that according to some, "are like dungeons." So you're not likely to find boys or a party or an Ethernet hookup in your dorm room. But you just have to keep in mind that "Simmons is a great learning environment while Boston is a great social environment."

Student Body

Take 1,200 female undergraduates, drop them in the heart of Boston, and what do you get? Simmons College, of course. "It's all women, white, majority middle class," which makes one Latina student exclaim, "More diversity, PLEASE, GOD!" According to one junior, Simmons "students come in two types: conservative, rich, and closed-minded, and then liberal, middle or lower class, and working for progress and diversity at Simmons." While "there are a lot of activists at Simmons," there is also an apathetic contingent in the student body. One student complains that her classmates are "snobby and stick within their own cliques." "A lot of people say Simmons women are snobby, but I find the complete opposite," dissents a freshman. One thing's for sure: when they're not listening to Britney or waging a political crusade, they're lost in their coursework. The fact that they're "very dedicated" to their studies is the common bond among Simmons students.

ADMISSIONS

Very important factors considered by the admissions committee include: secondary school record. *Important factors considered include:* character/personal qualities, class rank, essays, recommendations, standardized test scores. *Other factors considered include:* alumni/ae relation, extracurricular activities, interview, talent/ability, volunteer work, work experience. SAT I or ACT required. TOEFL required of all international applicants. High school diploma or GED is required. *High school units required/recommended:* 15 total required; 4 English required, 3 math required, 4 math recommended, 3 science required, 3 foreign language required, 4 foreign language recommended, 3 social studies required, 4 social studies recommended.

The Inside Word

Most of the best women's colleges in the country are in the Northeast, including those Seven Sister schools (roughly the female equivalent of the formerly all-male Ivies) that remain women's colleges. The competition for students is intense, and although Simmons is a strong attraction for many women, there are at least a half-dozen competitors who draw the better students away. For the majority of applicants there is little need for anxiety while awaiting a decision. Its solid academics, Boston location, and bountiful scholarship program make Simmons well worth considering for any student opting for a women's college.

FINANCIAL AID

Students should submit: FAFSA. The Princeton Review suggests that all financial aid forms be submitted as soon as possible after January 1. *Need-based scholarships/grants offered:* Pell, SEOG, state scholarships/grants, private scholarships, the school's own gift aid. *Loan aid offered:* FFEL Subsidized Stafford, FFEL Unsubsidized Stafford, FFEL PLUS, Federal Perkins, state loans, college/university loans from institutional funds. Federal Work-Study Program available. Institutional employment available. Applicants will be notified of awards on a rolling basis. Off-campus job opportunities are good.

FROM THE ADMISSIONS OFFICE

"Simmons believes passionately in an 'educational contract' that places students first and helps them build successful careers, lead meaningful lives, and realize a powerful return on their investment.

"Simmons is truly a 100-year-old university in Boston, with a tradition of providing women with a collaborative environment that stimulates dialogue, enhances listening, catalyzes action, and spurs personal and professional growth.

"Simmons honors this contract by delivering a quality education and measurable success through our singular approach to professional preparation, intellectual exploration, and community orientation."

For even more information on this school, turn to page 352 of the "Stats" section.

SIMON'S ROCK COLLEGE OF BARD

84 ALFORD ROAD, GREAT BARRINGTON, MA 01230 • ADMISSIONS: 413-528-7312 • FAX: 413-528-7334
FINANCIAL AID: 413-528-7297 • E-MAIL: ADMIT@SIMONS-ROCK.EDU • WEBSITE: WWW.SIMONS-ROCK.EDU

Ratings
Quality of Life: 84   Academic: 93   Admissions: 91   Financial Aid: 88

Academics

Tiny Simon's Rock College of Bard, which admits exceptional high school sophomores and juniors to its college-level program, "is a fantastic opportunity for students who were either bored in high school (the overachievers) or the really smart kids who never did a damn thing, but want to now. Hating high school isn't enough,

SURVEY SAYS . . .
Ethnic diversity on campus
Lots of classroom discussion
Political activism is hot
Theater is hot
Very small frat/sorority scene
Athletic facilities need improving
Intercollegiate sports unpopular or nonexistent

though; you really have to work hard here." With barely 400 enrollees, "there are usually only about 8 people in a class. You can take the class wherever you want it to go. And if you can't, you can stay after and talk it over with the teacher one-on-one." The school offers students the freedom "to do independent study or take a 300-level course as a freshman or do practically anything else. All you have to do is ask." Notes one student, "This school is really one giant test of one's own motivation and determination." Although "there isn't a huge variety of majors and classes available," students tell us that "every semester when the course catalog comes out, it's never a question of finding interesting courses to take; it's always a matter of working them into a workable schedule." They also explain that "because of the interdisciplinary nature of academics here, the limited number of majors isn't a huge problem." Furthermore, "if something you want to study isn't being covered, it's remarkably easy to set up a tutorial dedicated to that subject because professors are extraordinarily available and receptive."

Life

"Life at Simon's Rock can be very boring since it's located in a small town," undergrads at this tiny college concede, "but you can find happiness with your friends and student life staff." Diversion comes primarily in the form of "a peculiar form of 'hanging out'—Simon's Rock should really be a verb rather than a noun. This sort of hanging out involves either being outside smoking or inside watching the Fight Club DVD a lot, and having conversations that range from the emotionally charged to goofy to intellectual." Go-getters note that "the schools is always really helpful to students. Since many of the students are younger, some too young to drive, they offer town trips every day, and on weekends they often take groups to go ice-skating, bowling, roller skating, miniature golfing, or just to the movies. They also have mall trips, and student groups often go to other colleges to meet other students and to get ideas as to how to incorporate Simon's Rock into the larger college community." Many, however, don't take advantage of these opportunities, instead resorting to immersion in computer games, pot-smoking, or pure tedium. Location and the size of the school are major roadblocks to a more active social scene. "It would be nice if there were stronger campus organizations, but it's difficult for that to happen given the small size of the school and the demanding nature of the classes," explains one student. Notes another, "The location of the school doesn't help one bit." It's so secluded that "there's no television reception, and cell phones are useless, too."

Student Body

Traditionally regarded as a lefty-weirdo haven, Simon's Rock "seems to be getting more conservative and preppy with each entering class." The transition is a slow one, however. According to one student "the average Simon's Rock student probably smokes both cigarettes and marijuana, is interested in arts and humanities, considers him- or herself to be politically active, and is probably vegetarian or vegan." And oddballs still predominate; as one student put it, "We all come from something abnormal, due to the fact that we are entering college a year or two early. And these abnormalities, although strikingly different, form a common bond." Adds another, "The townies call us 'the freaks on the hill.' My mom calls us 'the patients.'" Because it's a school of 400 students, "everyone knows everybody."

ADMISSIONS

Very important factors considered by the admissions committee include: character/personal qualities, essays, interview, recommendations, talent/ability. *Important factors considered include:* extracurricular activities, secondary school record, standardized test scores, volunteer work. *Other factors considered include:* alumni/ae relation, minority status, work experience. SAT I or ACT required. TOEFL required of all international applicants. *High school units required/recommended:* 15 total recommended; 2 English recommended, 2 math recommended, 2 science recommended, 1 science lab recommended, 2 foreign language recommended, 2 social studies recommended, 2 history recommended, 2 elective recommended.

The Inside Word

There is no other college like Simon's Rock in the country, and no other similar admissions process. Applying to college doesn't get any more personal, and thus any more demanding, than it does here. If you're not ready to tap your potential as a thinker in college beginning with completion of the application, avoid Simon's Rock. Simply hating high school isn't going to get you in. Self-awareness, intellectual curiosity, and a desire for more formidable academic challenges than those typically found in high school will.

FINANCIAL AID

Students should submit: FAFSA, CSS/Financial Aid PROFILE, noncustodial (divorced/separated) parent's statement. Regular filing deadline is June 15. The Princeton Review suggests that all financial aid forms be submitted as soon as possible after January 1. *Need-based scholarships/grants offered:* Pell, SEOG, state scholarships/grants, private scholarships, the school's own gift aid. *Loan aid offered:* Direct Subsidized Stafford, Direct Unsubsidized Stafford, Direct PLUS, FFEL Subsidized Stafford, FFEL Unsubsidized Stafford, FFEL PLUS, Federal Perkins, state loans. Federal Work-Study Program available. Institutional employment available. Applicants will be notified of awards on a rolling basis beginning on or about April 15. Off-campus job opportunities are good.

FROM THE ADMISSIONS OFFICE

"Simon's Rock is dedicated to one thing: to allow bright highly motivated students the opportunity to pursue college work leading to the AA and BA degrees at an age earlier than our national norm."

For even more information on this school, turn to page 353 of the "Stats" section.

SKIDMORE COLLEGE

815 NORTH BROADWAY, SARATOGA SPRINGS, NY 12866-1632 • ADMISSIONS: 518-580-5570
FAX: 518-580-5584 • FINANCIAL AID: 518-580-5750 • E-MAIL: ADMISSIONS@SKIDMORE.EDU
WEBSITE: WWW.SKIDMORE.EDU

Ratings

Quality of Life: 94   **Academic:** 84   **Admissions:** 83   **Financial Aid:** 81

Academics

Skidmore College, a small liberal arts school in upstate New York, boasts strengths in the "liberal arts, fine arts, and performing arts." In addition, Skidmore offers excellent pre-professional programs and programs in education and social work. A core curriculum—the

> **SURVEY SAYS . . .**
> *Great library, No one plays intramural sports*
> *Students love Saratoga Springs, NY*
> *Great computer facilities, Dorms are like palaces*
> *Diversity lacking on campus*
> *Class discussions encouraged*

Liberal Studies sequence—exposes students to the "greatest hits" of western arts and sciences and provides "a valuable supplement to a solid liberal arts education." Says one student of the curriculum, "Skidmore embraces versatility. It's the training ground for modern Leonardo da Vincis, Aristotles, and tap-dancing brain surgeons." Students at Skidmore enjoy a relaxed but rigorous academic atmosphere in which "academics are challenging yet manageable" and the workload is "just right. I think I was well prepared for the academic atmosphere here. Just when things seem too easy, something challenging comes along, and vice versa." Professors are "fun and interesting. They seem to love what they do." Writes an undergrad, "Professors are always available to talk to. They are so helpful and friendly. Not only can you talk to them about academics but you can get advice on life in general." About the only beef students have with the faculty is that "we need more professors in order to expand the number of courses offered." Undergrads are more circumspect about the administration, complaining that "students have very little input in what happens on this campus. Decisions are made behind closed doors." For a select group of "highly motivated and talented students," Skidmore offers the Honors Forum, "an enriched combination of academic and co-curricular opportunities."

Life

For those who enjoy crisp autumns, beautiful campuses, and lovely small cities, Skidmore offers an excellent quality of life. "The campus is beautiful, dorms are awesome, and Saratoga Springs is great!" gushes one student. "It's a 30,000-person town with the facilities and entertainment of a town three times its size. Wonderful coffee shops [and a] great night life" are among the most popular amenities. Students are quick to point out that "for the outdoorsy types, the Adirondacks are an hour drive away" and that "Lake George is beautiful and less than 30 minutes away." One student remarks that there's "lots of stuff to do here with nature. Mad nice parks. We usually do outdoor activities for fun (hiking, biking, Frisbee, etc.) until the sun goes down, then we usually consume a lot of alcohol and do a variety of drugs." Students also note that "big cities [New York, Boston] are four hours away . . . a little too far, but there are buses and trains." Albany is close by for students needing an instant fix of urban style. On campus, "students are highly involved in clubs and other extracurriculars," but "sports and school spirit are lacking." Offers one undergrad, "There is always something going on: lectures, bands, plays, free movies on weekends, bowling, laser tag. . . . I think this may account for the low support of sports." Skidmore has no Greek scene, which many here see as "a plus. Off-campus parties are fun, relaxed environments."

Student Body

"Skidmore students," explains one undergrad, "are generally considered wealthy, spoiled, privileged people. To a certain extent, it's true. But at the same time, you can surround yourself with people who do not fit the stereotype. There are many hard-working, down-to-earth people here." Comments another, "Skidmore is, unfortunately, a pretty homogeneous place. The administration works hard to give financial aid. Without it, the cost of tuition would make this place completely exclusive. All issues of diversity directly relate to money." Some report that "all the different types of people—jocks, thespians, artists, hippies, and preps—all interact well together. It isn't uncommon to have friends in all circles." Others complain that students are very cliquey. One woman warns prospective female applicants that "the students at Skidmore are mostly women. The ratio of men to women is about 2:3, which is really good if you're a straight guy because a lot of the men here are gay."

ADMISSIONS

Very important factors considered by the admissions committee include: recommendations, secondary school record. *Important factors considered include:* character/personal qualities, class rank, essays, extracurricular activities, standardized test scores, talent/ability, volunteer work, work experience. *Other factors considered include:* alumni/ae relation, geographical residence, interview, minority status. SAT I or ACT required. TOEFL required of all international applicants. High school diploma or GED is required. *High school units required/recommended:* 4 English recommended, 4 math recommended, 4 science recommended, 3 science lab recommended, 4 foreign language recommended, 4 social studies recommended.

The Inside Word

Although Skidmore overlaps applicants with some of the best colleges and universities in the Northeast, it's mainly viewed as a safety. Still, this makes for a strong applicant pool, and those students who do enroll give the college a better-than-average freshman academic profile. The entire admissions operation at Skidmore is impressive and efficient, proof that number two does indeed try harder.

FINANCIAL AID

Students should submit: FAFSA, CSS/Financial Aid PROFILE, state aid form. Regular filing deadline is January 15. The Princeton Review suggests that all financial aid forms be submitted as soon as possible after January 1. *Need-based scholarships/grants offered:* Pell, SEOG, state scholarships/grants, the school's own gift aid. *Loan aid offered:* FFEL Subsidized Stafford, FFEL Unsubsidized Stafford, FFEL PLUS, Federal Perkins. Federal Work-Study Program available. Institutional employment available. Applicants will be notified of awards on or about April 1. Off-campus job opportunities are good.

FROM THE ADMISSIONS OFFICE

"Skidmore's Liberal Studies Curriculum is a highly interdisciplinary core curriculum that enriches a student's first two years of study. Students take one course in each of four liberal studies areas, beginning that Liberal Studies I: The Human Experience. This is a cornerstone course that is team-taught to all freshmen by 28 professors from virtually every department in the college. It involves lectures, performances, films, and regular small group discussions. Students then take one more liberal studies course in one of the three succeeding semesters. The purpose of these two courses is to show the important academic interrelationships across disciplines, across cultures, and across time. The result is that our students learn to look for connections among the disciplines rather than see them in isolation. With this interdisciplinary foundation under their belts by the end of the sophomore year, students are better prepared to then select a major (or combination of majors) that matches their interests."

For even more information on this school, turn to page 354 of the "Stats" section.

SMITH COLLEGE

7 COLLEGE LANE, NORTHAMPTON, MA 01063 • ADMISSIONS: 413-585-2500 • FAX: 413-585-2527
FINANCIAL AID: 413-585-2530 • E-MAIL: ADMISSIONS@SMITH.EDU • WEBSITE: WWW.SMITH.EDU

Ratings
Quality of Life: 92   Academic: 94   Admissions: 97   Financial Aid: 79

Academics

Ask any student why she decided to come to Smith, and you're bound to hear about its "academic reputation." While students tend to think the classes at Smith are "interesting but not thrilling," they also believe that the school does live up to its reputation. With "small classes" and "no distribution requirements," students are

SURVEY SAYS . . .
Lots of liberals, Profs teach upper levels
Lab facilities are great
No one watches intercollegiate sports
Political activism is hot
Student publications are popular
Class discussions encouraged

given the academic freedom and attention that they need to succeed. "The support systems" provided by professors and other students are crucial aids as "Smithies," as Smith students refer to themselves, dive headlong into the hard work that they find in almost every class. "There's great tutoring and writing help available," reports one junior. "And professors and other students always want to help everyone." In fact, professors are looked upon as "minor deities" in these parts, not only because they "are always accessible and open to questions," but also because they are "extremely intelligent" and dedicated to their fields of study. Students, in turn, become dedicated to their own fields of study. As a result, academics can be very consuming at Smith. "I study my ass off—everyone does," writes one sophomore. "If you don't, you will not last here."

Life

Smithies are known far and wide for their acceptance of alternative lifestyles and a liberal-minded academic and extracurricular dedication to social issues. Notwithstanding these activist principles, Smithies are the kind of students that "study for fun." Because of the campus "house system," which provides "country-club comfort" of living for students, many Smithies reveal that they form their closest friendships with other women in their respective houses. Soon after arriving at Smith, students realize that "this is not a party school," which means it's a "good deal quieter than coed institutions." But that's not to suggest that it's boring. Activities run the gamut from "playing Scrabble on a Friday night" to "organizing a rally" to singing with the campus a cappella group, The Smithereens, to attending "lectures, theatre, dance shows, improv comedy," to just hanging out with friends and talking "a lot about emotions, equality, justice, the government, and larger religious and existential questions." Smith is also part of the Five College Consortium (along with Amherst, Mount Holyoke, and Hampshire Colleges, and the University of Massachusetts—Amherst). When Smithies go looking for parties, they appreciate the "easy access to the other four colleges in the area." And "the good thing is the bus (to these colleges) is free and runs til 3 A.M. on the weekends!" Smithies also take advantage of their location in the heart of Northhampton, which many students believe to be "the greatest town ever!" "Northhampton is a wonderful place—funky and diverse, with tons of activities—movies, shopping, parks, bars and pubs," and "fun stores and restaurants." In other words, if you just look a little, you'll "never have a problem finding something to do here."

Student Body

Smithies are a "rather homogenous" bunch of about 2,600 students almost universally "intent on their studies." A large majority of them are "of a lefty bent" as far as politics go, and they're vocal about their opinions. "If you're not open-minded, you'll be miserable at Smith," one freshman warns. This outspoken liberalism isn't appreciated by all of the students, though. "I feel like I'm going to be lynched if I'm not PC enough," a student says. Some students—who hadn't anticipated the strong presence of liberal and lesbian cultures at Smith—complain that "the college does not present an accurate description of students" in its admissions literature. This means that "Smith can be a hard place to adjust to" when you actually join its ranks as a freshman. For the most part, once students realize that they're a part of a "smart, assertive, wacky" student body, they tend to settle quite cozily into the "beautiful campus" and the challenging college life at Smith.

ADMISSIONS

Very important factors considered by the admissions committee include: character/personal qualities, recommendations, secondary school record. *Important factors considered include:* class rank, essays, extracurricular activities, interview, standardized test scores, talent/ability. *Other factors considered include:* alumni/ae relation, minority status, volunteer work, work experience. SAT I or ACT required; SAT II recommended. TOEFL required of all international applicants. *High school units required/recommended:* 15 total recommended; 4 English recommended, 3 math recommended, 3 science recommended, 3 science lab recommended, 3 foreign language recommended, 2 history recommended.

The Inside Word

Don't be fooled by the relatively high acceptance rate at Smith (or at other top women's colleges). The applicant pool here is small and highly self-selected, and it's fairly tough to get admitted. Only women who have taken the most challenging course loads in high school and achieved at a superior level will be competitive.

FINANCIAL AID

Students should submit: FAFSA, institution's own financial aid form, CSS/Financial Aid PROFILE, noncustodial (divorced/separated) parent's statement, business/farm supplement. Regular filing deadline is February 1. The Princeton Review suggests that all financial aid forms be submitted as soon as possible after January 1. *Need-based scholarships/grants offered:* Pell, SEOG, state scholarships/grants, the school's own gift aid. *Loan aid offered:* Direct Subsidized Stafford, Direct Unsubsidized Stafford, FFEL PLUS, Federal Perkins, state loans, college/university loans from institutional funds. Federal Work-Study Program available. Institutional employment available. Applicants will be notified of awards on or about April 1. Off-campus job opportunities are excellent.

FROM THE ADMISSIONS OFFICE

"Smith students choose from 1,000 courses in more than 50 areas of study. There are no specific course requirements outside the major; students meet individually with faculty advisers to plan a balanced curriculum. Smith programs offer unique opportunities, including the chance to study abroad, or at another college in the United States, and to learn firsthand about the federal government. The Ada Comstock Scholars Program encourages women beyond the traditional age to return to college and complete their undergraduate studies. Smith is located in the scenic Connecticut River valley of western Massachusetts near a number of other outstanding educational institutions. Through the Five College Consortium, Smith, Amherst, Hampshire, and Mount Holyoke colleges and the University of Massachusetts enrich their academic, social, and cultural offerings by means of joint faculty appointments, joint courses, student and faculty exchanges, shared facilities, and other cooperative arrangements."

For even more information on this school, turn to page 354 of the "Stats" section.

STEVENS INSTITUTE OF TECHNOLOGY

CASTLE POINT ON HUDSON, HOBOKEN, NJ 07030 • ADMISSIONS: 800-458-5323 • FAX: 201-216-8348
FINANCIAL AID: 201-216-5194 • E-MAIL: ADMISSIONS@STEVENS-TECH.EDU • WEBSITE: WWW.STEVENS-TECH.EDU

Ratings
Quality of Life: 74   **Academic:** 82   **Admissions:** 85   **Financial Aid:** 89

Academics

Students looking for a highly regarded engineering school near a major city need look no further than Stevens Institute of Technology in Hoboken, New Jersey. Of course, some students point out that Stevens is one of those techie schools that "tries to be broad-based, but isn't." Students don't come to Stevens for the humanities. Professors are "brilliant" but also "often too smart for their own good." They

> **SURVEY SAYS . . .**
> *Students love Hoboken, NJ*
> *Musical organizations aren't popular*
> *Class discussions are rare*
> *Popular college radio*
> *Library needs improving*
> *Lousy food on campus*
> *Lab facilities are great*
> *Political activism is (almost) nonexistent*
> *Computer facilities need improving*

sometimes forget that students are not yet experts in their field and accordingly, "their expectations are quite high." They "need to stop reading the text to us." Many believe that their professors "are basically just here to do research and write books." Also, many of the TAs for labs and recitations are not native speakers of English. "Half the time, you have to guess what the professor is saying," a junior electrical engineering major says. First- and second-year students find the school's mandatory course load a relief—one less thing for them to worry about. Of course, the workload is significant, and many students worry as much about the grading curve as they do about passing classes that they consider superfluous. Nevertheless, the "engineering department and comp-sci programs are great." Students also tell us that the co-op programs are very strong, and the school's career services center is very helpful. The school also reportedly does an excellent job supporting students with any extra tutoring they might need.

Life

Stevens students love the campus because it is located in Hoboken, a town with numerous bars and restaurants across the Hudson from New York City. "It is the best view of New York you could ever get," one student writes. New York offers numerous opportunities for diversion, and students often go to the movies in Greenwich Village. The campus itself is small and "park-like," which makes it "easy to get to classes from the dorms." Students, especially those who are underage, go to parties at the fraternities and sororities. While Stevens is not a commuter school, a large number of students go home on the weekend. However, athletics is a big draw, with over 70 percent of undergraduates participating. Studying is a must on week nights if one is to keep up with the workload. Students also report a dislike for on-campus fare, and all agree that parking is difficult in Hoboken. Also, students wish clubs and student organizations had better support from the school's administration.

Student Body

It's not surprising on a campus whose male population is greater than 75 percent that the primary complaint is that there aren't enough female students. While most students are friendly and noncompetitive, there is a good percentage of "anti-social types who just sit at their computers all day." Those not involved with the Greek community tend to form cliques based on their ethnicity. Students feel like they know everyone because the campus and the student body are so small. While there are many students "who'd rather stay in on a Saturday night and play network games rather than go out and enjoy Manhattan or Hoboken," there are very bright people at Stevens, "so you're bound to come across some interesting characters." In general, Stevens's students get along because they are united by a common goal: "To get a great education that will put us out in the world with a very good salary."

ADMISSIONS

Very important factors considered by the admissions committee include: interview, secondary school record, standardized test scores. *Important factors considered include:* character/personal qualities, class rank, extracurricular activities, talent/ability. *Other factors considered include:* alumni/ae relation, essays, recommendations, volunteer work, work experience. SAT I or ACT required; SAT I preferred. TOEFL required of all international applicants. High school diploma is required and GED is not accepted. *High school units required/recommended:* 4 English required, 4 math required, 3 science required, 4 science recommended, 3 science lab required, 4 science lab recommended, 2 foreign language recommended, 2 social studies recommended, 2 history recommended, 4 elective recommended.

The Inside Word

Stevens is indeed impressive and legitimately near the top of the "second tier" of technical schools. Above-average students who would run into difficulty trying to gain admission to the MITs and Caltechs of the world will find a much more receptive admissions process here. Given its solid reputation and metropolitan New York location, it's an excellent choice for techies who want to establish their careers in the area.

FINANCIAL AID

Students should submit: FAFSA. No deadline for regular filing. The Princeton Review suggests that all financial aid forms be submitted as soon as possible after January 1. *Need-based scholarships/grants offered:* Pell, SEOG, state scholarships/grants, private scholarships, the school's own gift aid. *Loan aid offered:* Direct Subsidized Stafford, Direct Unsubsidized Stafford, Direct PLUS, Federal Perkins, state loans, Signature Loans, TERI Loans. Federal Work-Study Program available. Institutional employment available. Applicants will be notified of awards on a rolling basis beginning on or about March 30. Off-campus job opportunities are excellent.

FROM THE ADMISSIONS OFFICE

"The quality and achievements of our graduates are the greatest hallmarks of the Stevens education. Approximately 100 percent have had technical, pre-professional experience outside the classroom during their undergraduate years. Among other benefits, this enables them to be the finest candidates for prestigious graduate schools or positions of employment in industry. Striking indications of this are that all students seeking a full-time position receive a job offer prior to graduation from the institute, and Stevens ranks 11th among the Top 550 institutions that produce presidents, vice presidents, and directors of U.S. companies. However, outstanding academic excellence needs to be balanced with an outstanding campus life, and at Stevens students will find 70 student organizations and NCAA Division III athletics. Plus, the Hoboken location overlooking the Hudson River and New York City skyline offers a campus environment like no other."

For even more information on this school, turn to page 355 of the "Stats" section.

STONEHILL COLLEGE

320 WASHINGTON STREET, EASTON, MA 02357-5610 • ADMISSIONS: 508-565-1373 • FAX: 508-565-1545
E-MAIL: ADMISSIONS@STONEHILL.EDU • WEBSITE: WWW.STONEHILL.EDU

Ratings
Quality of Life: 74   Academic: 78   Admissions: 76   Financial Aid: 73

Academics

A small Catholic institution, Stonehill College provides an undergraduate experience where students "are not only academically challenged but also guided and encouraged." One student reports that all classes "involve

> **SURVEY SAYS . . .**
> *Instructors are good teachers*
> *Students are religious, Classes are small*
> *High cost of living, Popular college radio*
> *Intercollegiate sports popular*

critical thinking and applications to other areas of the liberal arts education." Although "more female faculty would be nice," professors are typically "highly interested in the welfare of the students." Another content undergrad writes, "As a senior, I have a class with the president. He is great, and there are only four other students in the class." Students are pleased that overall, there's "no problem getting the classes I want." The administration is described as "an enthusiastic group of professionals who put first the goals of the school and the wishes of the students." Those who interact with the staff say, "I am surprised how friendly they are and how much they genuinely want to help me." Students are also appreciative of being afforded "a seat at most decision-making tables." One complaint, however, is the school "accepts too many people and then overcrowds our . . . dorms." In addition to having an impressive "international internship program," Stonehill "is well known and highly praised in the Boston area, where you can find many jobs after graduation."

Life

In a bold statement, one Stonehill student claims his school has "the most beautiful campus in New England." One student perceives Stonehill's social life quite favorably: "Stonehill is a very 'on-campus' school, which is actually really nice. The weekends usually consist of an event on campus and mostly parties at the upper-class townhouses." The school also recently opened "The Hill," a student center with "a bar, restaurant, snack bar, and entertainment area with TV, pool tables, and arcades." Students complain about the high degree of control the administration sometimes exerts on their social lives. As one reports, "We had a 'fun parade' one week and they broke up the little fun we were having and said we were causing a riot." However, "Campus ministry and community service are strong—retreats, alternative spring breaks, and service projects are really popular." And speaking of retreats, Boston and Providence are frequented when campus entertainment runs dry.

Student Body

Earning its nickname "Clonehill," the homogenous population at Stonehill is characterized, as one student puts it, as "Irish Catholic, from the Northeast, and not passionate about much except their drinks." Despite the administration's commitment to diversity, students feel "there are only a handful of minority students on campus, which is something to be ashamed of." "All of the minority students hang out together," begins one student, who then adds, "I don't think it is because Stonehill students are racist—I think it's because they are afraid and do not know how to interact effectively with their peers of color." Another student notes, "Students get along well probably because everyone comes from similar backgrounds and has similar values." In terms of personalities and interests, "you get the whole spectrum" at Stonehill. It's a cordial atmosphere where "people are always holding doors and smiling." Overall, "it's like having another huge extended family to see you through all the good times and the bad."

ADMISSIONS

Very important factors considered by the admissions committee include: class rank, secondary school record, and standardized test scores. *Important factors considered include:* character/personal qualities, essays, extracurricular activities, recommendations, and talent/ability. *Other factors considered include:* alumni/ae relation, geographical residence, minority status, volunteer work, and work experience. SAT I or ACT required. TOEFL required of all international applicants. High school diploma or GED is required. *High school units required/recommended:* 16 total required; 21 total recommended; 4 English required, 3 math required, 4 math recommended, 1 science required, 3 science recommended, 1 science lab required, 2 science lab recommended, 2 foreign language required, 3 foreign language recommended, 3 history required, 4 history recommended, 3 elective required.

The Inside Word

This Beantown stronghold exercises strict policies, but students can easily find social outlets off campus. The pursuit of any of the 30 majors in this family atmosphere is contagious, though you might not feel as much a part of the family if you're not white, Catholic, and Irish.

FINANCIAL AID

Students should submit: FAFSA, CSS/Financial Aid PROFILE, noncustodial (divorced/separated) parent's statement, and business/farm supplement. The Princeton Review suggests that all financial aid forms be submitted as soon as possible after January 1. *Need-based scholarships/grants offered:* Pell, SEOG, state scholarships/grants, private scholarships, and the school's own gift aid. *Loan aid offered:* Direct Subsidized Stafford, Direct Unsubsidized Stafford, Direct PLUS, Federal Perkins, and state loans. Federal Work-Study Program available. Institutional employment available. Applicants will be notified of awards on or about April 1. Off-campus job opportunities are good.

FROM THE ADMISSIONS OFFICE

"Founded in 1948 by the Congregation of Holy Cross, Stonehill's mission is to provide education of the highest caliber, grounded in the liberal arts, comprehensive in nature, and nurtured by Catholic intellectual and moral ideas. Stonehill College is a selective, private, coeducational Catholic college enrolling 2,100 full-time students. Located 20 miles south of Boston on a 375-acre campus with easy access to Boston, we offer 30 challenging majors in the liberal arts, business, and science degree programs. Stonehill also offers students 35 minor programs as well as the opportunity to double major. The college's programs, through an involved and engaging faculty and a commitment to hands-on learning, aim to foster effective communication, critical-thinking, and problem-solving skills in all our students. An Honors Program, undergraduate research opportunities, and area internships enrich the educational experience of many students.

"To gain experience internationally, our students may study abroad, spending four to nine months living and studying in another part of the world. Full-time internships in Dublin, London, Brussels, Paris, Montreal, and Zaragoza, Spain, allow highly motivated students to gain valuable work experience while earning academic credit. On campus, more than 85 percent of our students live in first-rate residence halls that feature large rooms and well-designed layouts. Stonehill's 20 Division II varsity sports, over 60 clubs and organizations, as well as intramural and recreational sports programs provide students with many ways to become involved. Stonehill provides its students with a powerful environment for learning where students are safe, known, and valued."

For even more information on this school, turn to page 356 of the "Stats" section.

SUFFOLK UNIVERSITY

8 ASHBURTON PLACE, BOSTON, MA 02108 • ADMISSIONS: 617-573-8460 • FAX: 617-742-4291
EMAIL: ADMISSION@ADMIN.SUFFLOLK.EDU • WEBSITE: WWW.SUFFOLK.EDU

Ratings

Quality of Life: 73   Academic: 70   Admissions: 69   Financial Aid: 75

Academics

"Suffolk University is about diversity and a solid education in an ideal location," agree students at this comprehensive university in downtown Boston. A large international population—enhanced by Suffolk's permanent campuses in Madrid, Spain, and Dakar, Senegal—accounts for much of the diversity. Nontraditional students also add to the mix ("This school is all about second chances," explains one undergrad who returned to school after a long layoff). All here appreciate how "the school is very dedicated to its students," offering small classes and going the extra mile to line up co-op and internship opportunities. Students in management- and government-related areas especially benefit from the school's downtown location and its strong ties to city businesses and government. Suffolk undergrads save their highest praise for the faculty, however, whom they describe as "a fantastic resource, always willing to help anyone who asks for it. They also do their best to challenge students in classes without setting them up for failure." Brags one student, "Many [adjunct faculty] teach at schools such as Harvard or Boston College. I definitely feel like I'm getting the same education as I would at . . . Ivy League schools but in much smaller classes." Not to mention that they're getting it at a much lower price. Students also appreciate how "the administration is easily accessible and open to student feedback."

> **SURVEY SAYS . . .**
> *Students love Boston, Great computer facilities*
> *Great off-campus food*
> *Ethnic diversity on campus*
> *Students are happy*
> *Intercollegiate sports unpopular or nonexistent*
> *Athletic facilities need improving*
> *No one plays intramural sports*
> *Students aren't religious*

Life

Suffolk does not have a traditional, enclosed campus; rather, the school consists of a collection of buildings scattered across Boston's Beacon Hill neighborhood, not far from the Government Center and the famous Boston Commons. This situation, coupled with the lack of a large resident population, means that school-related extracurriculars are minimal, limited primarily to student clubs and organizations. Few here mind, however, because the city of Boston itself offers undergraduates a rich bounty of experiences. Students tell us that "there is so much to do here, from theater to dining to Red Sox games to movies. Boston is such a cultural city!" Beantown is also home to numerous other colleges and universities (Boston University, Boston College, Harvard, MIT, and Emerson, to name just a few), making it "a giant college campus with endless possibilities!" Suffolk undergrads report that the school "is working hard to improve on-campus housing . . . . A new dorm will be ready for the fall of 2003" that will double the school's residential capacity. Students hope that the increase in residents will result in a more cohesive, active student body, the lack of which many identified as Suffolk's greatest weakness.

Student Body

"Suffolk's greatest strength is the diversity" of its student body. "Everyday I seem to meet someone from another country. Just the other day I met someone from Bolivia," writes one student. Internationals "are a very high percentage" of the population here and "seem to fit in quite well." Suffolk is also home to "a fairly large constituency of adult professionals who have returned to school (often attending night classes intermixed with 'traditional' students)," as well as "a large gay population." "Most [students] come from the New England/New York area" and are of the down-to-earth variety; "there's not a lot of blue-blood here," explains one student. "But that's a good thing, I think. Understand that blue-bloods aren't discouraged or ostracized, just not the norm." Students are generally practical and goal-oriented, the type of people who "get the job done and still make time to spend with friends."

ADMISSIONS

Very important factors considered by the admissions committee include: secondary school record. *Important factors considered include:* class rank, essays, recommendations, and standardized test scores. *Other factors considered include:* alumni/ae relation, character/personal qualities, extracurricular activities, and interview. SAT I or ACT required. TOEFL required of all international applicants. High school diploma or GED is required. *High school units required/recommended:* 4 English required, 3 math required, 2 science required, 1 science lab required, 2 foreign language required, 1 history required, 4 elective required.

The Inside Word

Suffolk University was one of approximately two dozen schools to attend a May 2002 recruitment event geared specifically to gay and lesbian students. The school's commitment to diversity is unquestionable; candidates here benefit from many distinguishing characteristic reflected in their applications.

FINANCIAL AID

Students should submit: FAFSA and institution's own financial aid form. Regular filing deadline is March 1. The Princeton Review suggests that all financial aid forms be submitted as soon as possible after January 1. *Need-based scholarships/grants offered:* Pell, SEOG, state scholarships/grants, private scholarships, and the school's own gift aid. *Loan aid offered:* Direct Subsidized Stafford, Direct Unsubsidized Stafford, Direct PLUS, Federal Perkins, state loans, and college/university loans from institutional funds. Federal Work-Study Program available. Institutional employment available. Applicants will be notified of awards on a rolling basis beginning on or about March 1. Off-campus job opportunities are excellent.

FROM THE ADMISSIONS OFFICE

"Founded in 1906, Suffolk University is a four-year private university with 14 buildings located in the historic Beacon Hill area. This location allows students to enjoy the best of city life while experiencing the benefits of a dynamic, caring, and collegial academic community. Small class sizes as well as faculty-student interaction are hallmarks of a Suffolk education. A practical 'real-world' education, supportive faculty, and a diverse student body make Suffolk and ideal university. The campus is just steps away from the State House and the Boston Public Garden and is within easy walking distance of Quincy Market, Faneuil Hall, Downtown Crossing (the shopping district), the Financial District, Newbury Street, and Copley Plaza. One of our residence halls overlooks Boston Common. A new dormitory will open in September 2003. Suffolk also has campuses in Madrid, Spain, and Dakar, Senegal, and enrolls nearly 1,000 students from more than 100 countries. Suffolk also enrolls 750 out-of-state students from 36 states. The Center for International Education is dedicated to providing advice and assistance not only to international students but to all students who whish to study and travel abroad. Incoming students are told that the University is not just interested in enrolling them, but also in seeing them through to graduation. A University-wide Retention Committee and faculty advising program monitors the academic progress of all students. Free tutoring is available for any students needing assistance. The spring retention rate for freshmen who entered Suffolk in fall 2002 was 93 percent."

For even more information on this school, turn to page 357 of the "Stats" section.

SUNY AT ALBANY

1400 WASHINGTON AVENUE, ALBANY, NY 12222 • ADMISSIONS: 518-442-5435 • FAX: 518-442-5383
FINANCIAL AID: 518-442-5757 • E-MAIL: UGADMISSIONS@ALBANY.EDU • WEBSITE: WWW.ALBANY.EDU

Ratings
Quality of Life: 68   Academic: 70   Admissions: 79   Financial Aid: 74

Academics

SUNY—Albany lures students with an affordable, quality education—an uncommon combination these days. The psychology, business, and English programs are popular. Unfortunately, these departments are often very large, which causes a number of prob-

> **SURVEY SAYS . . .**
> *Class discussions are rare*
> *Students don't get along with local community*
> *Students are cliquish*
> *Ethnic diversity on campus, Large classes*
> *Unattractive campus*

lems. A senior business administration major voices, "Many of the professors are disinterested and lack substance. It just seems as though a substantial portion of the faculty doesn't care about the student body." SUNY—Albany is a research university. Accordingly, professors "don't want to teach and quite a few don't even know how to teach." Students also complain that classes are impersonal. "My name is my social security number," one junior writes, and in popular majors, class sizes do not decrease in upper-level courses. One senior theater major points out that "the [classes] tend to be different from department to department. Some are huge, cold, and impersonal, while others are small and extremely good about giving attention to the individual." Science students love the new research library, and many students rave about the design of the campus. "Everything is in a rectangular area so it's easy to get from class to class," writes one. The administration takes some serious lumps. "Class registration is preposterous. There are too many students and not enough classes or room in classes," one junior psychology major writes. Advisors do not fare well either. A disappointed psychology major comments, "It is nearly impossible to get an appointment with my advisor. He's always too busy." Another adds, "I don't know my advisor's name. I have never met [him] because I've always seen grad students or associates." Despite those disillusioned by little student-faculty interaction, for many students Albany "is a good school if you like big schools."

Life

Students at SUNY—Albany know that studying is only one ingredient in the smorgasbord that is a rewarding college experience. "We're not a party school. We just have lots of parties, drinking, and drugs. Okay, I guess we are a party school," one senior psychology major admits. "Students care more about partying than studying. If they have to choose between studying or going out and getting drunk, the latter usually prevails." Another senior adds that students only make an effort "when it comes to getting drunk. They spend all night trying to accomplish that." On the upside, downtown Albany, though "always cold and gray," provides "many entertainment opportunities." The area contains numerous inexpensive bars and clubs, and "anyone with a library card could get into [them]." Thursday, Friday, and Saturday are popular party nights, though students agree, "there are parties almost every night." Students complain about the cafeteria food and the lack of parking. "If you have a class after 9 a.m., it's difficult to find a spot." The school also needs to improve a few facilities. One senior math major writes, "Many of the classrooms are disgusting. Walls are dirty, desks are small, and the blackboards don't erase."

Student Body

SUNY—Albany is a diverse campus where students "all get along like pigs in a blanket." The university is popular among students who reside in the Northeast because of its central location. A junior criminal justice major writes that "SUNY—Albany is one of the few schools where you can walk around campus and feel like you're in Beverly Hills, then in a minute feel like you're in Flatbush." GDIs do not hold the Greek system in high regard. While students are generally friendly, many of them form cliques "like in high school," leading to some campus tension. Nevertheless, one junior psychology major writes, "Everyone has a generally friendly attitude."

ADMISSIONS

Very important factors considered by the admissions committee include: character/personal qualities, class rank, secondary school record, standardized test scores. *Important factors considered include:* essays, recommendations. *Other factors considered include:* extracurricular activities, geographical residence, minority status, talent/ability, volunteer work. SAT I or ACT required; SAT I preferred. TOEFL required of all international applicants. High school diploma or GED is required. *High school units required/recommended:* 18 total required; 4 English required, 2 math required, 4 math recommended, 2 science required, 3 science recommended, 2 science lab required, 3 science lab recommended, 3 foreign language recommended, 3 social studies required, 2 history required, 5 elective required.

The Inside Word

While the SUNY system's budgetary woes have abated to a degree, funding uncertainties continue to be a problem. Applications and standards are on the rise. Albany is the third most selective SUNY campus. Perhaps the university's status as the training camp site for the New York Giants will bring both revenue and facilities to aid a turnaround. Without increased private funding, Albany is likely to remain a relatively easy path into a SUNY university center.

FINANCIAL AID

Students should submit: FAFSA. New York State residents will receive an Express TAP Application one month after filing FAFSA. The Princeton Review suggests that all financial aid forms be submitted as soon as possible after January 1. *Need-based scholarships/grants offered:* Pell, SEOG, state scholarships/grants, private scholarships, the school's own gift aid. *Loan aid offered:* FFEL Subsidized Stafford, FFEL Unsubsidized Stafford, FFEL PLUS, Federal Perkins, college/university loans from institutional funds. Federal Work-Study Program available. Institutional employment available. Applicants will be notified of awards on a rolling basis beginning on or about April 1. Off-campus job opportunities are good.

FROM THE ADMISSIONS OFFICE

"Albany continues to see a growth in the quality of its applicants and has become increasingly selective, with an admission rate of just above 50 percent. Out-of-state and international enrollments are also increasing as metro Albany receives greater national visibility for its educational opportunities. (It's ranked third in the Places Rated Almanac.) UAlbany will be the new home of the research and development center of International Sematech North, a consortium of the world leaders in computer chip manufacturing. The Presidential Scholars Program continues to attract top-achieving students, and Project Renaissance, the unique freshman-year experience, also remains a very popular option for students interested in UAlbany's high-quality, affordable college experience."

For even more information on this school, turn to page 357 of the "Stats" section.

SUNY AT BINGHAMTON

PO Box 6000, Binghamton, NY 13902-6001 • Admissions: 607-777-2171 • Fax: 607-777-4445
Financial Aid: 607-777-2428 • E-mail: admit@binghamton.edu • Website: www.binghamton.edu

Ratings
Quality of Life: 75   **Academic:** 84   **Admissions:** 92   **Financial Aid:** 75

Academics

A highly regarded state school, SUNY—Binghamton is said to be "perfect for those looking to get in and out with a good and inexpensive education." Reportedly, students "can experiment with ideas, think freely, and get the tools to expand their view of the world."

> **SURVEY SAYS . . .**
> *Class discussions are rare*
> *Students don't get along with local community*
> *Students are cliquish*
> *Ethnic diversity on campus*
> *Large classes*
> *Unattractive campus*

Professors are respected for their intelligence and prominence in their fields, but in terms of teaching skills, students dream, "Maybe I'll eventually get into a class where I don't have to teach myself." According to some, just enrolling in "the courses you want or need can be nearly impossible." While some characterize the administration as "efficient and friendly," most remain decidedly "dissatisfied" with the top brass. One student tells us, "Getting the answers to questions about your major or any other thing is very difficult."

Life

The Binghamton experience includes a "politically active campus" amid a "lack of school spirit." One student notes, "There are really no traditions on campus," though the popular pastime of "smoking in nonsmoking buildings" may soon count as one. Free time is filled with "a huge variety of stuff to do, ranging from cultural, religious, and political events, to lots of artsy stuff, to lots of good old-fashioned getting drunk." Since Binghamton is "by no means a party school," social activities centered on something other than alcohol are common. Reports one student, "They have recently begun showing movies in the Union on weekends, along with late-night billiards and bowling." The surrounding city of "Binghamton is not the best of cities. It is, however, cheap and accessible" with "movie theaters, bowling alleys, skating rinks, restaurants, and shopping galore." Though "the 'townies' don't like us very much," the two-dollar cab fare into town keeps student influx high. The campus is "not too country and only a few hours from N.Y.C.," but upperclassmen can hunker down in their widely praised on-campus apartment housing. In summary, a student explains, "Even though it wasn't anyone's first choice, everyone likes it."

Student Body

SUNY—Binghamton is reportedly home to "a million closet geniuses." A conspicuous segment of the population—who want to achieve good grades and are always pleased with the low price they pay for tuition—is said to be "preoccupied with the latest Gucci and Versace product lines." Regarding students' personal transport, "The cars in the parking lot are worth more than my house." Attracting many students from New York City and Long Island, a rift between down- and up-staters is sometimes apparent, though the majority shares a "typical white middle-class" background. Students believe there is "not much mingling" between racial and ethnic groups; some even report "large racial and ethnic cleavages." One comments, "The many forms of diversity on campus come at the expense of true campus cohesiveness." One gay undergraduate male writes, "I have found the school to be relatively tolerant of my orientation." Tolerance comes with the territory in another's opinion: "New York is a melting pot; therefore, many, if not all, of the students are well aware of the diverse cultures of the world, and this awareness makes them respectful."

ADMISSIONS

Very important factors considered by the admissions committee include: secondary school record, standardized test scores. *Important factors considered include:* class rank, essays, extracurricular activities, minority status, talent/ability. *Other factors considered include:* alumni/ae relation, character/personal qualities, geographical residence, recommendations, state residency, volunteer work, work experience. SAT I or ACT required. TOEFL required of all international applicants. High school diploma or GED is required. *High school units required/recommended:* 16 total required; 4 English required, 3 math required, 4 math recommended, 2 science required, 3 science recommended, 3 foreign language required, 2 social studies required, 3 history recommended.

The Inside Word

Binghamton's admissions process is highly selective, but fairly simple. Candidates go through a process that first considers academic qualifications, primarily through numbers, and then takes a relatively brief look at other components of the application. Out-of-state enrollment is miniscule for a public university of Binghamton's reputation, but the University's enrollment management strategy includes enhancing efforts to recruit students from further afield.

FINANCIAL AID

Students should submit: FAFSA. The Princeton Review suggests that all financial aid forms be submitted as soon as possible after January 1. *Need-based scholarships/grants offered:* Pell, SEOG, state scholarships/grants, private scholarships, the school's own gift aid. *Loan aid offered:* Direct Subsidized Stafford, Direct Unsubsidized Stafford, Direct PLUS, Federal Perkins, Federal Nursing, college/university loans from institutional funds. Federal Work-Study Program available. Institutional employment available. Applicants will be notified of awards on a rolling basis beginning on or about March 15. Off-campus job opportunities are excellent.

FROM THE ADMISSIONS OFFICE

"Binghamton University prides itself on excellent teaching and solid research from a faculty remarkably accessible to students. Students have the opportunity to engage in research with faculty and, together, they have designed projects and coauthored papers. Teaching and mentoring by faculty builds students' confidence and competence, encouraging them to become independent learners. Binghamton University welcomes serious students interested in working toward a productive future in our dynamic academic community."

For even more information on this school, turn to page 358 of the "Stats" section.

SUNY AT BUFFALO

15 CAPEN HALL, BUFFALO, NY 14260 • ADMISSIONS: 888-UB-ADMIT • FAX: 716-645-6411
FINANCIAL AID: 866-838-7257 • E-MAIL: UB-ADMISSIONS@BUFFALO.EDU • WEBSITE: WWW.BUFFALO.EDU

Ratings
Quality of Life: 69   **Academic:** 76   **Admissions:** 82   **Financial Aid:** 80

Academics

A "wonderful variety of majors" and an "inexpensive" education await those willing to brave the frosty winters of New York State's northwestern academic outpost, SUNY—Buffalo. Engineering, business, and pre-med are the major draws here, but other disciplines (especially communications and the liberal arts and sciences) also offer competitive programs. Students report that "classes are big, which kind of sucks." Instruction in large lectures, many feel, is "not very easy. They expect you to understand right away what they understand. Also, they need to get more experienced instructors instead of using TAs to teach courses." Classes improve, though, at the upper levels, where "professors relate well to students, are accessible, and overall, keep learning interesting." Buffalo's administration "communicates very poorly with students," not a very unusual situation at a large state university. Even so, students cheerfully acknowledge Buffalo's many assets, which include "great computer facilities," as well as "wonderful" research opportunities, a great library, and "an [excellent] Honors Program."

> **SURVEY SAYS . . .**
> *Ethnic diversity on campus*
> *(almost) everyone smokes*
> *Lots of beer drinking*
> *Great computer facilities*
> *Great library*
> *Student newspaper is popular*
> *Athletic facilities are great*
> *Hard liquor is popular*

Life

SUNY—Buffalo is situated on two distinct campuses, a "south urban" campus within the city limits of the city and a "north rural (or suburban)" campus just outside of town. South Campus is home to the medical sciences, while most other departments are headquartered to the north. Other departments and the School of Architecture and Planning are split between the two campuses. Students feel that the university is relatively easy to get around. From South Campus "it's very easy to go out and do stuff. We're close to the theater district." Downtown is also home to "the bars of Main Street or Chippewa Street," music venues, and a bevy of great pizzerias. At the northern campus, however, "either you go to frats and dance clubs and get wasted or you don't. If you don't, there's really nothing else for you to do here. If you want a life, you need a car." Adds one student, "Greeks make up only 2 percent of the population but are so evident around North Campus. They don't have a good reputation at all! " For those desirous of more constructive pursuits, "there's something for everyone"; the student newspaper, minority student organizations, student government, and sports are all popular. A sophomore tells us that "getting involved is easy, and it makes a big school like UB feel smaller." Students give parking and campus food an adamant thumbs down and warn all upstate neophytes that "UB lives up to the isolated tundra stereotype of Buffalo."

Student Body

The student body at UB "is broad and diverse, enabling students to gain valuable cultural insight." And therefore, "we treat each other with respect," notes one white student, a sentiment apparently confirmed by an African American student who feels "Buffalo has a great deal to offer minority students." Leaning to the left-of-center politically, most UB students we surveyed don't consider themselves particularly politically active. As a whole, they're a "generally friendly" lot who rate themselves as pretty happy, if lacking a little "school spirit" and a strong sense of community. Writes one, "It's hard to make a lot of friends with such a large commuter population."

ADMISSIONS

Very important factors considered by the admissions committee include: class rank, secondary school record, standardized test scores. *Other factors considered include:* essays, extracurricular activities, minority status, recommendations, talent/ability, volunteer work. SAT I or ACT required. TOEFL required of all international applicants. High school diploma or GED is required. *High school units required/recommended:* 17 total recommended; 4 English recommended, 3 math recommended, 3 science recommended, 3 foreign language recommended, 4 social studies recommended.

The Inside Word

Buffalo was formerly a private university and was absorbed into the SUNY system. Its admissions process reflects this private heritage to the extent possible (applications are centrally processed for the entire system in Albany). It's one of the few SUNY schools with a freshman academic profile higher than its published admissions standards. Although Binghamton is academically the most selective of the SUNY University Centers, Buffalo is in many ways closer to what other states refer to as the flagship of the state system.

FINANCIAL AID

Students should submit: FAFSA. The Princeton Review suggests that all financial aid forms be submitted as soon as possible after January 1. *Need-based scholarships/grants offered:* Pell, SEOG, state scholarships/grants, private scholarships, the school's own gift aid, Federal Nursing. *Loan aid offered:* Direct Subsidized Stafford, Direct Unsubsidized Stafford, Direct PLUS, Federal Perkins, Federal Nursing, college/university loans from institutional funds. Federal Work-Study Program available. Applicants will be notified of awards on a rolling basis beginning on or about February 1. Off-campus job opportunities are good.

FROM THE ADMISSIONS OFFICE

"The University at Buffalo (UB) is among the nation's finest public research universities—a learning community where you'll work side by side with world-renowned faculty, including Nobel, Pulitzer, National Medal of Science, and other award winners. As the largest, most comprehensive university center in the State University of New York (SUNY) system, UB offers more undergraduate majors than any public university in New York or New England. With opportunities for joint degrees and combined five-year bachelor's and master's degrees, you'll be free to chart an academic course that meets your individual goals—you can even design your own major. Our unique University Honors and University at Buffalo Scholars scholarship programs offer an enhanced academic experience, including advanced research opportunities, faculty mentors, and special seminars. The university is committed to providing the latest information technology—UB was ranked as the nation's 10th most-wired university by Yahoo! Internet Life magazine. UB also places a high priority on offering an exciting campus environment. With nonstop festivals, Division I sporting events, concerts, and visiting lecturers, you'll have plenty to do outside of the classroom. We encourage you and your family to visit campus to see UB up close and in person. Our Visit UB campus tours and presentations are offered year-round."

For even more information on this school, turn to page 359 of the "Stats" section.

SUNY AT NEW PALTZ

75 S MANHEIM BOULEVARD, SUITE 1, NEW PALTZ, NY 12561-2499 • ADMISSIONS: 845-257-3200
FAX: 845-257-3209 • E-MAIL: ADMISSIONS@NEWPALTZ.EDU • WEBSITE: WWW.NEWPALTZ.EDU

Ratings
Quality of Life: 75   Academic: 83   Admissions: 82   Financial Aid: 70

Academics

"New Paltz is the perfect place to be," bubbles a contented undergrad; indeed, State University of New York in New Paltz pleases many of its pupils. One student tells us that professors "do not treat us like numbers like I expected from a state university," and a junior calls profs "for the most part, very accessible and helpful. This is even true when I am in classes with 100 or more students in them." Another student beams, "I have never had better professors who go out of their way to make the college experience as rewarding as possible." On the other hand, there are some who find many of the professors to have "a 'my way or the highway' motto." The women's studies, theatre, and art departments are said to be among the school's greatest strengths, and as a result, the whole campus apparently demonstrates a "devotion to creativity and beauty." Getting into classes may be "like pulling teeth" though—"not all classes are offered each semester, so you really have to be on top of what classes you need to take for your major." While one student believes that dealing with "the administration is a nightmare," another writes that the "administration does a wonderful job of keeping in touch with its students. For instance, the college president even has open office hours for students. Recently, he even dressed in tights to help celebrate Shakespeare's birthday."

> **SURVEY SAYS . . .**
> *Classes are small*
> *School is well run*
> *Lots of beer drinking*

Life

Nestled in the Hudson River Valley, in the beautiful Shawangunk Mountains, New Paltz is "the ultimate college town," a "great area for the arts, theatre, and nature lovers." One student elaborates: "Whenever a person with a car offers, we go up to the top of the mountains and hang out for hours." Other points of interest include 130 clubs and organizations, "great apple and pumpkin picking," "hiking, art shows, musicals, movies," and "three art galleries," not to mention that doing "laundry is FREE." The two biggest complaints about living on campus are the food ("the variety of food is lacking, especially for vegans and vegetarians") and the dorms ("small, old, and gross"). The campus is just "an hour from NYC, so it's easy to hop a train and spend a day in the city," and a 10-minute walk into New Paltz will find you surrounded by "the best restaurants (nachos at McGillicuddys!)," "a lot of fun coffeehouses and bars," and "a lot of clubs." Main Street "looks like a classic hippie town, filled with great spiritual shops, palm readings, and enough pizza places to feed the hungriest campus." While some students claim that there is "nothing but frat parties" here, one student assures, "Many people take their academics quite seriously. When it's party time, it's definitely party time, but when finals come around, there's no one at the bar."

Student Body

Misanthropes beware: many students compare the New Paltz college community to "a small town where you know all your neighbors." One transfer student explains that "everyone is down to earth and friendly. People smile and say 'hello' just walking by each other even if they don't know you." Another student claims that "if it is raining, chances are a stranger that passes in a car will slow down and ask if you need a ride." Relations between "the black student union members and the women's lacrosse team and the campus paper reporters and the nerds and the frat guys and the hippies" are reportedly healthy—"we all talk to each other and truly value each other's opinions." Some, however, feel that despite the "great diversity" on campus, "it is not a particularly inviting community. Everyone seems trapped in their individual groups." But most agree that because New Paltz itself "is a very calm, hippy-ish town," "it gives the school the same kind of feel."

ADMISSIONS

Very important factors considered by the admissions committee include: class rank, secondary school record, and standardized test scores. *Other factors considered include:* character/personal qualities, essays, extracurricular activities, and talent/ability. SAT I or ACT required. TOEFL required of all international applicants. High school diploma or GED is required. *High school units required/recommended:* 17 total required; 21 total recommended; 4 English required, 3 math required, 4 math recommended, 3 science required, 4 science recommended, 3 science lab required, 3 foreign language required, 4 foreign language recommended, 3 social studies required, 3 social studies recommended, 1 history required.

The Inside Word

It's a friendly setting in New Paltz, where the distinct closeness and superior academics can fool you into forgetting its state-school structure. The administrative red tape, however, appears quickly enough to remind you it's a SUNY. Be ready as an applicant.

FINANCIAL AID

Students should submit: FAFSA and state aid form. Regular filing deadline is March 15. The Princeton Review suggests that all financial aid forms be submitted as soon as possible after January 1. *Need-based scholarships/grants offered:* Pell, SEOG, state scholarships/grants, private scholarships, the school's own gift aid, and Federal Nursing. *Loan aid offered:* Direct Subsidized Stafford, Direct Unsubsidized Stafford, and Direct PLUS. Federal Work-Study Program available. Institutional employment available. Applicants will be notified of awards on a rolling basis beginning on or about April 1. Off-campus job opportunities are good.

FROM THE ADMISSIONS OFFICE

"SUNY New Paltz prides itself on being a comprehensive, diverse, and selective regional university of roughly 8,000 full- and part-time undergraduate and graduate students.

"This year's freshman class of 900 students has an average SAT score of 1130 and a high school average of 89. These students were selected from a pool of more than 13,500 applications—a 12.5 percent increase over last year's record-breaking pool of 12,000 applicants. For the 11th consecutive year, SUNY New Paltz received more applications than any of SUNY's other university colleges. With an acceptance rate of 41 percent, New Paltz remains one of the most selective universities in the Northeast and among the 5 percent of campuses across the country that accept less than half of their applicants.

"Several recent significant projects have enhanced the quality of academic and student life on campus. A new state-of-the-art Language Learning Center opened for students in fall 2002. The Center allows New Paltz to expand language-learning possibilities using modern technology and establishes New Paltz as the leading venue for foreign language learning within SUNY. Additionally, construction of Lenape Hall, our 13th residence hall, began this fall. The 238-bed residence hall will also include a computer lab and fully equipped exercise room. New Paltz received an endowment from the Dorsky family and a grant from the Rockefeller Foundation to benefit the Samuel Dorsky Museum of Art. The endowment is the lead gift in the campus's campaign to raise $2.5 million in endowment funds for the Museum."

For even more information on this school, turn to page 359 of the "Stats" section.

SUNY AT STONY BROOK

OFFICE OF ADMISSIONS, STONY BROOK, NY 11794-1901 • ADMISSIONS: 631-632-9898 • FAX: 631-632-9898
FINANCIAL AID: 631-632-6840 • E-MAIL: UGADMISSIONS@NOTES.CC.SUNYSB.EDU
WEBSITE: WWW.STONYBROOK.EDU

Ratings

Quality of Life: 68   Academic: 75   Admissions: 80   Financial Aid: 73

Academics

The State University of New York at Stony Brook "is what you make it. You can take a rigorous, challenging curriculum or you can take Basketweaving 101." Most choose the former route, attending Stony Brook in hopes of earning a valuable degree in the sciences and engineering at public-school prices. A nationally renowned graduate research center ("Our research facilities are awesome!!"), Stony Brook comes complete with all of the advantages and drawbacks one would expect to find in a large university. Students "are very much on their own here." Professors "are usually too into lecturing as opposed to making sure students understand what they are being taught. There are few excellent professors, a large sum of nonchalant professors, and a few no-care professors." Notes one student, "Studying electrical engineering at Stony Brook is one of the most brutal and crushing experiences a person can have. The required work is voluminous and extremely challenging and there is almost no support whatsoever: TAs don't speak English and the professors are, for the most part, unhelpful. On the plus side, the professors are extremely knowledgeable." Upperclassmen have access to better teachers and smaller classes and are accordingly more positive about the school. Writes one, "My upper-division professors are fabulous. They do all their own research and have developed their own views on their subjects. The lack of real professors during freshman and sophomore year was awful, but these past two years have made up for it." Students in the Honors College also laud the "priority registration, close-knit group of students," and the fact that the program "encourages students to question everything and to think freely." As for the administration, a typical student asks, "Administration? It's a state school, the people who bring you the DMV. Sadly, the civil-service taint is felt here at the school big time."

> **SURVEY SAYS . . .**
> *Musical organizations aren't popular*
> *High cost of living, Popular college radio*
> *(Almost) everyone smokes*
> *Students don't get along with local community*
> *Large classes, Unattractive campus*
> *Campus difficult to get around*
> *Students are not very happy*

Life

Several factors conspire to make Stony Brook's campus one of the nation's least active socially. First, many students are deeply immersed in science and engineering and thus have little time for socializing. "Most people here," explains one student, "think about chemistry. Once they're done with that, they think about chemistry some more. Then they go home for the weekend." Second, many undergrads commute to Stony Brook for classes only. The parking situation, it should be noted, does little to encourage commuters to stick around: it is "a major crisis for most commuter students" because so few spaces are available. Of those who reside on campus , many go home nearly every weekend. Third, "Port Jefferson and Stony Brook aren't great college towns, although they're getting better" as they add "shopping, entertainment, and many local bars and clubs with a young crowd." As a result, many feel that "there is nothing to do for fun. On weekends this place is dead, a ghost campus until Monday morning." A small but vocal minority protest that "some people feel that there is nothing to do on this campus because our campus is portrayed as a suitcase college . . . but by being part of a group or team, your life on campus is a lot more fun, with parties, mixers, etc." With "Campus Recreation making small improvements every year," perhaps Stony Brook is growing closer to a more typical undergraduate social environment.

Student Body

The diversity of SUNY SB's student body "is a great asset to the campus because it allows students to get to know other cultures, races, etc., and to become more tolerant and understanding of human beings as a whole." Students "generally keep to their own ethnic groups but also get along with other students." While "some students seem exceptionally smart, interesting, etc., others fall into the basic Long Island 'big hair and muscle car' category. And many, of course, are science geeks." Because the many commuters here usually come only for classes and study sessions, "it's hard to meet people."

ADMISSIONS

Very important factors considered by the admissions committee include: secondary school record, standardized test scores. *Important factors considered include:* class rank, essays, extracurricular activities, interview, talent/ability. *Other factors considered include:* alumni/ae relation, recommendations. SAT I or ACT required; SAT II recommended. TOEFL required of all international applicants. High school diploma or GED is required. *High school units required/recommended:* 14 total required; 19 total recommended; 4 English required, 3 math required, 4 math recommended, 3 science required, 4 science recommended, 2 foreign language required, 3 foreign language recommended, 4 social studies required.

The Inside Word

Graduate programs continue to receive national accolades, and the New York State legislature has been somewhat kinder to SUNY of late. Stony Brook's athletic programs have moved to NCAA Division I, America East Conference, in hopes of generating greater visibility and increases in applications. For the near future, admission will remain relatively easy for solid students.

FINANCIAL AID

Students should submit: FAFSA. The Princeton Review suggests that all financial aid forms be submitted as soon as possible after January 1. *Need-based scholarships/grants offered:* Pell, SEOG, state scholarships/grants. *Loan aid offered:* FFEL Subsidized Stafford, FFEL Unsubsidized Stafford, FFEL PLUS, Federal Perkins. Federal Work-Study Program available. Institutional employment available. Applicants will be notified of awards on a rolling basis beginning on or about March 1. On- and off-campus job opportunities are excellent.

FROM THE ADMISSIONS OFFICE

"Stony Brook University has a philosophy of encouraging excellence. This commitment to excellence shows in the many different merit scholarship programs we offer high-achieving students, including special scholarships offered to Intel Science Talent Research and National Merit Scholarship Competition finalists and semifinalists as well as valedictorians and salutatorians.

"At Stony Brook we offer our undergraduates one of the finest educations available. Stony Brook's faculty rank among the best in the country and pride themselves on creating a discovery-rich environment on campus. Just this past year, the American Association of Colleges & Universities recognized Stony Brook as one of only 16 'Leadership Institutions' for innovation and commitment to undergraduates. We invite students who possess both intellectual curiosity and academic ability to explore countless exciting opportunities available at Stony Brook to learn, discover, and create."

For even more information on this school, turn to page 360 of the "Stats" section.

SUNY COLLEGE AT BROCKPORT

350 NEW CAMPUS DRIVE, BROCKPORT, NY 14420 • ADMISSIONS: 585-395-2751 • FAX: 585-395-5452
E-MAIL: ADMIT@BROCKPORT.EDU • WEBSITE: WWW.BROCKPORT.EDU

Ratings
Quality of Life: 80   Academic: 72   Admissions: 67   Financial Aid: 72

Academics

With a "good reputation for teaching," State University of New York College at Brockport excels in the physical education department, where "we have a great

> **SURVEY SAYS . . .**
> *School is well run, Profs teach upper levels*
> *Classes are small, Lots of beer drinking*

bunch of teachers who really care about the students and their effectiveness as future PE teachers." Environmental and computational science programs also excel, as does the dance program, which is reportedly "outstanding and equipped with amazing facilities and a fantastic staff." Additionally, "research opportunities in the science departments are superb." Professors across the board are "very invested in assuring a deep understanding of the material being covered," and they serve as "active participants in my educational goals." Though some students claim that the administration "treats us all like babies," most are fans of the "very visible" President Yu, who is often "spotted eating with students in the dining halls." Many do, however, note a need for "more minority and female role models" amid the faculty and staff. Students here call for more variety among the "challenging but not overly difficult" courses offered. Class size can also be an issue: "The majority of my classes in my psychology major were huge—forget having a professor know that you even exist." Students participating in the Delta program, an interdisciplinary, accelerated course of study, gush that it's "the highest quality academic program offered." Brockport's most noted selling point, however, is the "quality education for an affordable price" it offers.

Life

Participants in Greek life call themselves "a dying breed" at Brockport, claiming they are wrongly "blamed for the so-called 'drinking problem'" on campus. Greek sympathizers warn that if the administration "continues to cut fraternity and sorority life, the application rate will decrease." For now, the beer-centered culture persists, with students proclaiming, "For fun, we drink." Because the "dry campus forces people to be more sneaky," most of the parties take place "off campus in private residences." When students aren't partying, the town of Brockport, "your typical college town," boasts proximity to "a large town like Rochester," the beauty and casinos of Niagara Falls, and Hamlin Beach on Lake Ontario. Students here are "very sports-oriented," constantly attending games and playing in intramurals when the weather allows; otherwise, students occupy themselves with everything "from broom ball to ballroom dancing." The school also hosts "a big concert every spring," with past acts including Method Man, Live, and Outkast. In an unusual event, "last semester we had a travelling reptile show come in, and everyone got to hold a Burmese python and a tarantula."

Student Body

The Brockport crew includes a "slim minority population," and several students note the campus is "not as diverse as it claims to be." Apparently, "many people could be more sensitive to minority groups"; however, one student writes, "As a Hispanic and a female, I feel I am treated with respect." Undergraduates observe some segregation, calling it "unfortunate" and stating that "separation between different types of people certainly stifles an exchange of ideas and beliefs." Race aside, "intellectuals hang out with intellectuals, athletes with athletes, partiers with other partiers." The student body is called "very mainstream," seeing as "there aren't a lot of punks, hippies, nerds, or any other sort of social subsets." Though close to one-third of students are nontraditional, many perceive the student body as "sheltered" from real-world concerns.

ADMISSIONS

Very important factors considered by the admissions committee include: class rank, secondary school record, and standardized test scores. *Important factors considered include:* essays, extracurricular activities, recommendations, and talent/ability. *Other factors considered include:* character/personal qualities, interview, volunteer work, and work experience. SAT I or ACT required. TOEFL required of all international applicants. High school diploma or GED is required. *High school units required/recommended:* 18 total required; 4 English required, 3 math required, 3 science required, 1 science lab required, 3 foreign language recommended, 4 social studies required, 4 elective required.

The Inside Word

If you make the hike from beyond the greater Buffalo region to see what Brockport has to offer and why it is described as an idyllic college-town experience, you'll find vibrant, if not especially demanding, academic and social lifestyles, owing themselves to a somewhat complacent student body—that is, until you arrive.

FINANCIAL AID

Students should submit: FAFSA, state aid form, and alternative bank loans. No deadline for regular filing. The Princeton Review suggests that all financial aid forms be submitted as soon as possible after January 1. *Need-based scholarships/grants offered:* Pell, SEOG, state scholarships/grants, private scholarships, and the school's own gift aid. *Loan aid offered:* Direct Subsidized Stafford, Direct Unsubsidized Stafford, Direct PLUS, Federal Perkins, Federal Nursing, and alternative loans. Federal Work-Study Program available. Institutional employment available. Applicants will be notified of awards on or about February 15. Off-campus job opportunities are good.

FROM THE ADMISSIONS OFFICE

"The SUNY Brockport mission statement puts it in writing: 'SUNY Brockport has the success of its students as its highest priority.' College programs, faculty, staff, and the campus itself all operate with that goal in mind.

"New programs in environmental science, biology, and computational science and the AACSB accreditation for the business programs serve as a complement to the Honors Program and the unique Delta College, the largest study abroad program in SUNY and one of the top ten in the nation. The full range of SUNY Brockport's academic programs offer students a variety of challenging learning options leading to strong post-graduate success. Nearly 25 percent of SUNY Brockport undergraduates go on to graduate school and 93 percent find jobs or are in graduate school within six months of graduation.

"Substantial investments in campus facilities in recent years have included top-to-bottom renovations of the Lennon Hall science center, Hartwell Hall, and Seymour College Union. These, along with other facilities upgrades, make for as vibrant campus life. A spacious suburban campus with easy access to Rochester, Buffalo, and Lake Ontario offers an exciting choice of cultural and outdoor activities.

"Consider SUNY Brockport if you want to study with world-class faculty; be actively involved in cultural, social, and athletic programs; and apply what you've learned to challenges in the real world. We encourage you to visit our campus of more than 300 acres and meet with faculty, staff, and students. It's the best way to discover if our strengths complement your talents and aspirations."

For even more information on this school, turn to page 361 of the "Stats" section.

SUNY College at Cortland

PO Box 2000, Cortland, NY 13045 • Admissions: 607-753-4712 • Fax: 607-753-5998
E-mail: admissions@cortland.edu • Website: www.cortland.edu

Ratings

Quality of Life: 75   Academic: 73   Admissions: 72   Financial Aid: 68

Academics

Students agree that education, physical education, and outdoor education are the major drawing cards at the State University of New York at Cortland, a midsize campus located halfway between Syracuse and Binghamton. Students happily report that "teachers on campus truly care. They are

> **SURVEY SAYS . . .**
> *No one plays intramural sports*
> *Classes are small*
> *Diversity lacking on campus*
> *Very little hard liquor*
> *Instructors are good teachers*
> *Intercollegiate sports unpopular or non-existent*

available at all times of the day, and many even give their home phone numbers to their classes. One thing that is not unusual at Cortland but it is at many colleges is the frequency of which many students go to their professors' houses." They also tell us that "the administration offices are sometimes difficult, but in the end they come through with the right information. The president of the college is involved in day-to-day student activity and is a great asset to the school's culture." However, many undergrads would also agree that quality at Cortland is not uniform: writes one student, "The problem with SUNY Cortland is that in almost every aspect there seems to be a wide range of extremes, meaning that although there are many professors who are outstanding there are just as many that don't even care. The same is true in the aspects of campus facilities, office staff, and dining facilities. While you will find the occasional shining star in any of these areas, such as a really nice facility or dorm, there are way too many horrendous facilities that make the overall appearance and campus atmosphere somewhat discouraging at times." Cortland's outdoor education program is augmented by access to the Adirondack Forest Preserve and the Brauer Memorial Geologic Field Station, the only major geologic research facility in the SUNY system.

Life

Many undergraduates feel that Cortland is "definitely a party school" with "nonstop action on Friday and Saturday." "I think the school is considered a big party school since it's in the middle of nowhere," explains one undergraduate. Agrees another, "There is nothing to do around here but drink. I'm not saying that's a bad thing, but the town of Cortland is horrible. There are lots of bars, which are always packed, no matter what night of the week it is." The Greek community, host to many parties, is of moderate size; fraternities and sororities "are great although very disrespected by the college," some complain. Not everyone here is a party animal, though; writes one undergrad, "Life at Cortland is very diverse. There are many sports-involved students (for lack of better words). However there are very studious people, and then there are those that party a lot." For those who enjoy an active lifestyle, "recreation areas are abundant in the upstate area, so bicycling, camping, and long rides in the countryside are popular amount the students of Cortland State." Students report that "the area around the school could be a lot nicer. It looks kind of run down on some streets." They also gripe that "campus parking needs to be improved big-time. There is not enough parking to accommodate even half of the students with cars." Because roughly half the students here live off campus, this is a major issue for many.

Student Body

"Most of the students here are either from Long Island, Rockland County, or the Buffalo area," reports one Cortland undergraduate. Adds another, "The students at Cortland are great people. Most of the students are from downstate, but they adjust in the environment of rural communities of upstate New York." The influx of downstate students means that "there is a mix of different genders . . . and sexual orientation here." Minority populations are small; all but a tiny fraction of the student body is made up of native New Yorkers.

ADMISSIONS

Very important factors considered by the admissions committee include: secondary school record and standardized test scores. *Important factors considered include:* essays, extracurricular activities, recommendations, and talent/ability. *Other factors considered include:* alumni/ae relation, class rank, geographical residence, interview, minority status, state residency, volunteer work, and work experience. SAT I or ACT required. TOEFL required of all international applicants. High school diploma or GED is required. *High school units required/recommended:* 20 total required; 23 total recommended; 4 English required, 3 math required, 4 math recommended, 3 science required, 4 science recommended, 3 science lab required, 3 foreign language required, 4 foreign language recommended, 4 social studies required.

The Inside Word

Students who plans to keep their eyes open and ears to the ground will be positioned for the best experience possible at Cortland. The depth of your love of the outdoors and education will determine whether you consider the school's location to be a case of easy access or alienation from your interests.

FINANCIAL AID

Students should submit: FAFSA. Regular filing deadline is April 1. The Princeton Review suggests that all financial aid forms be submitted as soon as possible after January 1. *Loan aid offered:* Direct Subsidized Stafford, Direct Unsubsidized Stafford, and Direct PLUS. Federal Work-Study Program available. Institutional employment available. Applicants will be notified of awards on a rolling basis beginning on or about March 1. Off-campus job opportunities are good.

For even more information on this school, turn to page 361 of the "Stats" section.

SUNY College at Fredonia

178 Central Avenue, Fredonia, NY 14063 • Admissions: 716-673-3251 • Fax: 716-673-3249
E-mail: ADMISSIONS.OFFICE@FREDONIA.EDU • Website: WWW.FREDONIA.EDU

Ratings

Quality of Life: 77   Academic: 79   Admissions: 74   Financial Aid: 75

Academics

The "exceptional" music major is what beckons many students to the College of Fredonia. The music department offers bachelor's degrees in eight areas of music, ranging from performance to business. And with 30 related

SURVEY SAYS . . .
Classes are small
Profs teach upper levels
Diversity lacking on campus
Student publications are ignored

extracurricular groups on campus—as well as the 200-plus programs brought into the Michael C. Rockefeller Arts Center each year—music students have innumerable opportunities to supplement their education outside of the classroom. Cousin programs in the arts and theatre are also popular among Fredonia's students. However, not every program at the college inspires enthusiasm in its students. "The academics are a joke at this school," growls a student. Another says, "The professors are terrible." But these criticisms are not the consensus. Just as some students complain, others do nothing but chirp. "I love Fredonia and my professors," exclaims one student. A fellow enthusiast says, "The professors are all very approachable. Overall, I have had a very good academic experience here." So how do incomers align themselves with the contented students? Do some homework before signing up for a class. Ask upperclassmen what they know about Professor X or Professor Y. Before you know it, you'll be singing the praises of Fredonia.

Life

"Fredonia is a college town," which means that when things are quiet on campus, there's always something to do a few steps away. The downtown area, "just a five-minute walking distance from campus," has "a popular nightlife." One of the most frequented spots is a "local dance club" called Sunny's, which the students not-so-reverently refer to as "Scummy's." Just outside of the campus walls, frat houses and sports houses provide the primary sites for college parties, fully equipped "with kegs and pot." Also, the "huge majority of upperclassmen live off campus" and often throw private parties. More sober events include the frequent "sports, comedy, and musical" activities hosted by the campus and sponsored by student groups. Musical performances are particularly common on this campus, ranging from classical to classic rock. "FredFest, the spring musical festival," brings in major music acts. The Michael C. Rockefeller Arts Center on campus also does its part to bring entertainment to Fredonia; every year, almost 60,000 people come to the campus's arts center to enjoy its more than 200 shows, which range from exhibits in the art gallery to concerts in the King Concert Hall to plays in Bartlett Theatre. All this activity aside, some students complain that the campus quiets too much on weekends, when many undergrads pack their bags for a two-day trip to their homes. So if the quiet becomes disquieting, students can fill their gas tanks and take daytrips to places like Buffalo and Niagara Falls, both less than an hour away.

Student Body

Fredonia, the westernmost member of the State of New York university system, attracts much of its populace from the surrounding, rural areas of western New York and northwestern Pennsylvania. But don't jump to any conclusions. While there are certainly a large number of small-town, Caucasian students here, there's also a healthy number of "minority students, as well as those of various sexual orientations." And when you visit the campus, you'll certainly smell the scent of patchouli in the air. That's right—"So many hippies!" Oh, and "lots of good-looking girls," adds a decidedly heterosexual male. With the Buffalo metro area less than an hour away, there's a refreshing waft of city mentality blowing through here. And with the coast of Lake Erie just minutes from campus, there's an appreciation for nature as well. Then there are the many music lovers drawn to the college by its strong music program. All in all, this mixture of students combines to form "a very friendly college."

ADMISSIONS

Very important factors considered by the admissions committee include: secondary school record. *Important factors considered include:* class rank, extracurricular activities, recommendations, and standardized test scores. *Other factors considered include:* alumni/ae relation, character/personal qualities, essays, minority status, talent/ability, volunteer work, and work experience. SAT I or ACT required. TOEFL required of all international applicants. High school diploma or GED is required. *High school units required/recommended:* 17 total required; 19 total recommended; 4 English required, 3 math required, 4 math recommended, 3 science required, 4 science recommended, 3 foreign language recommended, 4 social studies required, 4 social studies recommended.

The Inside Word

Fredonia's strength in music can be converted into great social and extracurricular activity for applicants inclined to demonstrate their talents to the admissions office. A little more than a mile away from Lake Erie, this SUNY is a good target school for any New Yorker of the Great Lakes area.

FINANCIAL AID

Students should submit: FAFSA and state aid form. The Princeton Review suggests that all financial aid forms be submitted as soon as possible after January 1. *Need-based scholarships/grants offered:* Pell, SEOG, private scholarships, and the school's own gift aid. *Loan aid offered:* FFEL Subsidized Stafford, FFEL Unsubsidized Stafford, FFEL PLUS, and Federal Perkins. Federal Work-Study Program available. Institutional employment available. Applicants will be notified of awards on a rolling basis beginning on or about March 15. Off-campus job opportunities are good.

For even more information on this school, turn to page 362 of the "Stats" section.

SUNY College at Geneseo

1 College Circle, Geneseo, NY 14454-1401 • Admissions: 716-245-5571 • Fax: 716-245-5550
Financial Aid: 716-245-5731 • E-mail: admissions@geneseo.edu • Website: www.geneseo.edu

Ratings
Quality of Life: 71   Academic: 77   Admissions: 92   Financial Aid: 79

Academics

Future undergrads seeking a small-school experience at state-school prices would do well to consider SUNY—Geneseo, the competitive liberal arts campus located in one of the system's northern outposts. Gushes one student, "Geneseo's greatest strength is in academics. I

SURVEY SAYS . . .
Lots of beer drinking
Lots of classroom discussion
Athletic facilities need improving
Registration is a pain, Low cost of living
Ethnic diversity lacking on campus

was warned that it would be hard to access professors at a state school, but at Geneseo, nothing could be further from the truth. My class sizes are small, my professors all know me personally, and they are always available to discuss anything with their students. The academic work is incredibly challenging—it requires a lot of time and effort to succeed here. I'm proud of the rigorous academic standards at Geneseo." Other students warn, however, that "professors vary by department, and it's very clear that there is a bias toward specific departments that the school is known for." The school's most prominent programs include "excellent" dance and theatre programs, a "great" school of business, and popular psychology and biology departments. The best professors here "take time to get to know you on a personal level and are extremely accessible inside and outside of the classroom. Because our university is geared more toward the undergraduate as opposed to the graduate, the professors will bend over backwards to help you." The administration, "particularly when it comes to financial aid and bills, is somewhat lacking, but I guess compared to other schools is average."

Life

The studious undergrads of Geneseo report that their campus "is a quiet place, for the most part. [But] if you are looking for parties, you will be able to find them. At the same time, we have so many organizations that put on performances (several choirs, an orchestra, several bands, two drama clubs, etc.) that no one can ever be bored." A sizeable Greek contingent hosts the majority of weekend bashes; explains one frat member, "Many complain about the Greek population, but it offers a great number of opportunities and experiences, and especially friendships. There is a large number of Greeks in Geneseo, and it does create a boundary with some individuals, but for every one of those there are two others who do not feel that way." Outside the Greek scene, students note that "there are also always plays or musical events on campus to attend. Movies are played for reduced prices as well. Most people are content with the activities." Students also praise their "beautiful campus," although they wish there weren't so many hills to climb, especially during the snowy winter months. They also gripe that "because we are a state school, there is not a lot of money, and construction projects seem to take forever, and there always seems to be something that is falling apart." The town of Geneseo gets poor grades; writes one student, "Geneseo can be a bit boring . . . . Sometimes the most fun we can have is riding the bus to and from Wal-Mart." Students roadtrip to Rochester, which is only 30 minutes away by car or school-sponsored bus.

Student Body

Students on the "mostly female" (about two-thirds, to be exact) Geneseo campus agree that "Geneseo is a great place, but it isn't exactly an accurate representation of the real world. The student body is very homogenous, mostly white middle- to upper-middle class. More diversity would be nice." Others do note some diversity, pointing out that "the campus is rather divided socioeconomically. You can go to the overcrowded parking lots to see that. A lot of parents pay for their kids to come here because it is so reasonably priced and will buy them expensive cars and give them spending money and everything. Then there are the students who are holding down several part-time jobs, have loans, and are paying for college themselves." Undergrads here "are extremely friendly." Writes one student, "I would have no problem going to a dining hall alone, and if I saw another student alone, joining them and having a conversation."

ADMISSIONS

Very important factors considered by the admissions committee include: class rank, secondary school record, standardized test scores. *Important factors considered include:* essays, extracurricular activities, minority status, recommendations, talent/ability. *Other factors considered include:* character/personal qualities, volunteer work. SAT I or ACT required. TOEFL required of all international applicants. High school diploma or GED is required. *High school units required/recommended:* 20 total recommended; 4 English recommended, 4 math recommended, 4 science recommended, 4 foreign language recommended, 4 social studies recommended.

The Inside Word

Geneseo is the most selective of SUNY's 13 undergraduate colleges and more selective than three of SUNY's university centers. No formula approach is used here. Expect a thorough review of both your academic accomplishments (virtually everyone here graduated in the top half of their high school classes) and your extracurricular/personal side. Admissions standards are tempered only by a somewhat low yield of admits who enroll; this keeps the admit rate higher than it might otherwise be.

FINANCIAL AID

Students should submit: FAFSA, state aid form. The Princeton Review suggests that all financial aid forms be submitted as soon as possible after January 1. *Need-based scholarships/grants offered:* Pell, SEOG, state scholarships/grants, private scholarships, the school's own gift aid. *Loan aid offered:* FFEL Subsidized Stafford, FFEL Unsubsidized Stafford, FFEL PLUS, Federal Perkins, state loans, alternative loans. Federal Work-Study Program available. Institutional employment available. Applicants will be notified of awards on a rolling basis beginning on or about March 15. Off-campus job opportunities are fair.

FROM THE ADMISSIONS OFFICE

"Geneseo has carved a distinctive niche among the nation's premier public liberal arts colleges. Founded in 1871, the college occupies a 220-acre hillside campus in the historic Village of Geneseo, overlooking the scenic Genesee Valley. As a residential campus—with nearly two-thirds of the students living in college residence halls—it provides a rich and varied program of social, cultural, recreational, and scholarly activities. Geneseo is noted for its distinctive core curriculum and the extraordinary opportunities it offers undergraduates to pursue independent study and research with faculty who value close working relationships with talented students. Equally impressive is the remarkable success of its graduates, nearly one-third of whom study at leading graduate and professional schools immediately following graduation."

For even more information on this school, turn to page 363 of the "Stats" section.

SUNY College at Oneonta

Alumni Hall 116, State University College, Oneonta, NY 13820 • Admissions: 607-436-2524
Fax: 607-436-3074 • E-mail: ADMISSIONS@ONEONTA.EDU • Website: WWW.ONEONTA.EDU

Ratings
Quality of Life: 80   **Academic:** 69   **Admissions:** 64   **Financial Aid:** 74

Academics

State University of New York College at Oneonta may not offer the dizzying variety of academic options available at its larger sister campuses, but it does provide something that's in short supply at

> **SURVEY SAYS . . .**
> *Very little beer drinking*
> *Very little hard liquor, Classes are small*
> *Instructors are good teachers*

those other schools: a cozy, small-school experience. As one undergrad here told us, "The greatest strength of Oneonta is its size. Since it's not a really big school, students can get a lot of individualized attention, and it is very easy to get ahead. Landing a teaching assistant position is very easy, and getting involved with independent research is easy too." Students praise the education department here, reporting that "for the teaching degree programs, the courses are rigorous and the workload is heavy, but the school has an excellent reputation." The school's "interesting and accessible" professors "encourage extra help and are readily available. The school has its share of bad professors too, but I have also had my share of outstanding ones: classes where you walk in and you walk out a different person. Those are the ones that have made my education outstanding." In contrast, "a lot of students here are extremely frustrated by the disorganization of the administration. It's almost as if they have very few set policies. I'll speak to one administrator about an issue, and then to another administrator and get completely different responses from the two. The administration needs to get on track."

Life

According to one undergrad, "most students believe that Oneonta is boring. However, one must remember that the majority of our students are from NYC." Many feel that partying results from a lack of other options; as one student told us, "There's not much to do in Oneonta. It's a very small town. Weekends are all about the bars. If you don't feel like going to the bars and you don't have a car, you're pretty much screwed. If you have a car, you can get to our 24-hour Wal-Mart. Or the bowling alley." Others, however, point out that "there's also a lot to do on campus if you are not a partier. The campus activities committee (CUAC) hosts movies in the campus ballroom on weekends and many other activities as well." Intercollegiate sports are popular, with several successful women's programs: the women's soccer team won the SUNYAC championship and advanced to the NCAA tournament in 2001, while the women's basketball, lacrosse, and softball teams all posted winning seasons during the 2001–2002 academic year. Students complain that town-gown relations are poor; gripes one, "Another thing that really disturbs me is the way the community treats us like children. They give us no respect. And if we want to get anything done, we have to use our parents as a threat."

Student Body

The Oneonta campus is home to "your typical mix of people and personalities. You can pretty much tell who is serious and who may need to pay more attention to academics." Students report a cliqueishness on campus that grows more pronounced as the school year proceeds; explains one student, "The students here in the beginning of the year are incredibly friendly. As you walk through campus you can feel the good attitude that flows around. As the year progresses though, there are cliques, but nothing that is really exclusive and purposely shuts others out." Agrees another undergrad, "There's not an abundance of overly friendly people, but they aren't rude either." One 38-year old "nontraditional student" assures, "My interactions and relationships with the other students here have been excellent." The great majority of undergrads hail from the upstate region immediately surrounding Oneonta; approximately half live off campus.

ADMISSIONS

Very important factors considered by the admissions committee include: secondary school record. *Important factors considered include:* character/personal qualities, extracurricular activities, interview, recommendations, standardized test scores, talent/ability, and volunteer work. *Other factors considered include:* alumni/ae relation, class rank, essays, minority status, and work experience. SAT I or ACT required. TOEFL required of all international applicants. High school diploma or GED is required. *High school units required/recommended:* 16 total required; 4 English required, 2 math required, 3 math recommended, 2 science required, 3 science recommended, 2 science lab required, 2 foreign language required, 3 foreign language recommended, 3 social studies required.

The Inside Word

Oneonta works well for students from central New York State, as they all benefit from a quality of life that's surprisingly high given the relatively low admission standards. The academics and campus activities offer just the right amount of adventure for most applicants, so one will be hard pressed to find many hardcore slackers or curve-burners.

FINANCIAL AID

Students should submit: FAFSA. No deadline for regular filing. The Princeton Review suggests that all financial aid forms be submitted as soon as possible after January 1. *Need-based scholarships/grants offered:* Pell, SEOG, state scholarships/grants, private scholarships, and the school's own gift aid. *Loan aid offered:* Direct Subsidized Stafford, Direct Unsubsidized Stafford, Direct PLUS, FFEL Subsidized Stafford, FFEL Unsubsidized Stafford, FFEL PLUS, Federal Perkins, state loans, and college/university loans from institutional funds. Federal Work-Study Program available. Institutional employment available. Applicants will be notified of awards on a rolling basis beginning on or about March 1. Off-campus job opportunities are good.

FROM THE ADMISSIONS OFFICE

"A liberal arts college with a pre-professional focus, the SUNY College at Oneonta enrolls more than 5,400 undergraduates in 69 majors. The College is noted for outstanding and accessible faculty, students committed to academic achievement and community service, excellent facilities and technology, a beautiful and welcoming campus with a new field house and lighted all-weather field, and a modern library with exceptional print and electronic resources. Popular majors include the NCATE-accredited education programs, business economics, music industry, and psychology. The college's newer majors in computer art, environmental science, and mass communications attract many students, as do traditional arts and sciences programs.

"In the past four years, Oneonta has hired more than 130 new faculty and staff and renovated all dining and residence halls. National accreditations for several major academic programs and a substantial commitment to a merit scholarship program have helped attract increasingly talented freshman classes. The profile of the entering class of 2002 shows a mean combined SAT score of 1100 and mean high school average of 86.5. The class of 1,100 students was drawn from more than 10,300 applicants at an acceptance rate of 47 percent.

"In recent years, the College has been recognized nationally by the Templeton Foundation, which twice named Oneonta to the Honor Roll for Character Building Colleges; *U.S. News & World Report*, which ranked Oneonta fifth among northern universities for graduates who have the least debt; and *Yahoo! Internet Life*, which named Oneonta as one of the nation's 200 Most Wired Colleges."

For even more information on this school, turn to page 363 of the "Stats" section.

SUNY COLLEGE AT OSWEGO

211 CULKIN HALL, OSWEGO, NY 13126 • ADMISSIONS: 315-341-2250 • FAX: 315-341-3260
E-MAIL: ADMISS@OSWEGO.EDU • WEBSITE: WWW.OSWEGO.EDU

Ratings

Quality of Life: 81   Academic: 68   Admissions: 65   Financial Aid: 78

Academics

Students at the State University of New York College at Oswego understand that attending a state school sometimes means accepting the bad with the good.

SURVEY SAYS . . .
Very little hard liquor
Classes are small, Lots of beer drinking

Oswego's assets are compelling: an "outstanding" school of education ("In my major alone, there is a 96 percent job placement right out of graduation, virtually guaranteeing me a job," writes one probable future teacher), "good internship and foreign exchange programs and opportunities," and, of course, a relatively affordable tuition. Because Oswego is one of the smaller SUNY campuses, some students here also enjoy "close relationships" with faculty. Accessibility, however, can be a problem; complains one undergrad, "Well, personally I find it difficult to get a hold of my teachers because a lot of them have other projects going on in their lives other than teaching, and trying to actually get in touch with a dean . . . forget about it." Course conflicts and limited course selection can become major obstacles: "It's hard to graduate in four years if you're going for teaching, but that extra year isn't always bad, it just means that you can meet people and have one more year in the sun before you get out." Sums up one student, "There are kinks in every school and this definitely applies for Oswego. Overall, though, my time here has been quite productive."

Life

For most students, extracurricular life centers on the town of Oswego's watering holes. "The bar scene is pretty happening," explains one student. "There are over 30 bars within three miles of campus. You can basically find a bar that suits your taste and practically call it your own. You always meet your friends there and know everybody in the bar that you go to, making the college as a whole a fairly tight community." Students note that "it is easy to get into a bar and drink, no matter how young you are or how bad your ID is." Dorm, fraternity, and sorority parties offer "a cheaper option, usually three to five bucks for all you can drink." Some here complain that "other than the option of drinking, there actually isn't much to do here. There are only so many times a person can enjoy the sunset before it gets old." Students here also enjoy intramurals and "going to rugby, hockey, and lacrosse games, as well as wrestling matches." Lake Ontario "is absolutely beautiful," but with that beauty comes a weather advisory: "We're on the shore of Lake Ontario, and the lake-effect snow is horrible. The wind whips through the campus and, if you're not careful, can blow you over. To make matters worse, snow removal on campus is terrible." Despite the drawbacks, many here view their years in Oswego as "a good, enjoyable time. It's a great place to be yourself, and to be laid back. Most importantly, it makes you realize that college is the best time of your life."

Student Body

The "nice, goal-oriented" students of SUNY Oswego tell us that they enjoy a convivial campus atmosphere; "It seems like almost everyone gets along," explains one student. "There are little conflicts or people who don't talk to one another, but it's not severe." Adds another, "This is probably one of the only schools were you can hang out with people you don't know and they treat you like you have known them for years. You can go out to a party, introduce yourself, and hang out." Undergrads appreciate the fact that "there is a wide array of students up here from all different backgrounds and upbringings," although some complain that "there are too many Long Island brats for this small, quaint college. They whine constantly, and try to make this college hell on earth for the casual, easygoing people of the world. Hint to them: high school is over!!"

ADMISSIONS

Very important factors considered by the admissions committee include: secondary school record and standardized test scores. *Important factors considered include:* class rank and recommendations. *Other factors considered include:* alumni/ae relation, character/personal qualities, essays, extracurricular activities, interview, minority status, talent/ability, volunteer work, and work experience. SAT I or ACT required; SAT I recommended. TOEFL required of all international applicants. High school diploma or GED is required. *High school units required/recommended:* 18 total required; 4 English required, 3 math required, 4 math recommended, 3 science required, 4 science recommended, 2 science lab required, 3 science lab recommended, 2 foreign language required, 4 foreign language recommended, 4 social studies required, 2 history recommended.

The Inside Word

Two camps of students exist at Oswego: those who maximize their opportunities despite obstacles, and those who maximize their complaints about them. You'll be best off here with a flexible and understanding approach and a knack for planning appropriately for those times when you're socked in by a snowstorm.

FINANCIAL AID

Students should submit: FAFSA. Deadline for priority filing is April 1. The Princeton Review suggests that all financial aid forms be submitted as soon as possible after January 1. *Need-based scholarships/grants offered:* Pell, SEOG, and state scholarships/grants. *Loan aid offered:* FFEL Subsidized Stafford, FFEL Unsubsidized Stafford, FFEL PLUS, and Federal Perkins. Applicants will be notified of need-based awards on a rolling basis beginning on or about April 1. Federal Work-Study Program available. Institutional employment available. *Academic merit scholarships offered:* Merit scholarships will be announced on a rolling basis beginning on or about February 15. Off-campus job opportunities are fair.

FROM THE ADMISSIONS OFFICE

"Oswego offers a great higher education value on a beautiful 690-acre lakeside campus in upstate New York, 35 miles northwest of Syracuse. Oswego is small enough to provide a friendly, welcoming environment and big enough to provide wide-ranging academic and social opportunities. The diverse selection of degree programs ranges from accounting to zoology and includes interdisciplinary options like cognitive science and international trade. The schools of education and business have each won the stamp of excellence from the premier accrediting organizations in their field. The weather makes the college popular with future meteorologists—one of Oswego's best-known alumni is the *Today* show's Al Roker. Oswego is noted for its Honors Program, internships, and international study. Ninety percent of the faculty is full time, one of the highest percentages among public colleges, and all courses are taught by faculty, not graduate assistants. Eighty million dollars in campus construction is under way, which will provide new living accommodations, high-tech classrooms, and recreational facilities. Students participate in 130 clubs and organizations and 23 intercollegiate sports. Half of all students and 90 percent of freshmen live on campus, which has been named one of the safest in the country. Over $2 million in academic merit scholarships are awarded to nearly 30 percent of the entering class in renewable awards worth ranging from $500 to $3,400 per year. The Oswego Guarantee promises both that room and board costs will not increase during a student's four years on campus and that a student can complete a degree in that time."

For even more information on this school, turn to page 364 of the "Stats" section.

SUNY College at Potsdam

44 Pierrepont Avenue, Potsdam, NY 13676 • Admissions: 315-267-2180 • Fax: 315-267-2163
E-mail: admissions@potsdam.edu • Website: www.potsdam.edu

Ratings
Quality of Life: 76   Academic: 70   Admissions: 66   Financial Aid: 76

Academics

The bottom line of the academics at State University of New York College at Potsdam can be summed up by the comment, "If you want to be a music teacher in New York State, you go here." The Crane School of Music has an excellent reputation, and "we just

> **SURVEY SAYS . . .**
> *Very little hard liquor*
> *Students are happy*
> *Classes are small*
> *Great food on campus*
> *Intercollegiate sports unpopular or non-existent*

got a new dean at the music school who is taking a lot of steps to make Crane even better." Overall, professors are characterized as "very friendly," and they "encourage you to come and see them in their offices if you need extra help." Several students proudly note that "we have small classes and a high teacher-to-student ratio"; others point out the "really strong" education and math programs. Some attendees wish the school "could offer more courses," but many respondents claim that the root of many problems is the fact that "as a whole, we just don't have enough money." Certain common state-school complaints can be heard, such as, "There is typically an overpowering plethora of bureaucratic bullsh*t." Others address the problem sans expletives: "It's hard to get any answers or help from people in the administration in both Crane and SUNY Potsdam as a whole." Though "the school presents a pretty picture," a small number of students call the quality of classes "quite average."

Life

Reportedly, "Potsdam is a really small town and at times can seem boring, but there are actually a lot of things to do around the area." According to respondents, these options include "concerts and events at the music school" as well as "camping, fishing, swimming, and all kinds of outdoor things." Many students tout the fact that "there is skiing nearby and a lot of hiking because we are right in the mountains." On the other hand, it's "very, very cold here in the winter! So many people find themselves hanging out indoors with friends, which breeds a good amount of alcohol consumption." Local highlights include a movie theatre in town [which "gives students a discount on Tuesday nights"] and a mall about 20 miles away." The alluring Canadian cities of Montreal, Ottawa, and Toronto are all within striking distance as well. Ultimately, the campus and town are "very safe" though remote.

Student Body

Upon setting foot on the Potsdam campus, younger students notice that upperclassmen "are very welcoming when you first arrive." Considering the small population of 4,000 students, people agree that "this is a diverse bunch for up north in the middle of nowhere!" Another student tells us, "In a music school you find an intensely different group of people. You find people of many different races, abilities, and sexual orientations not to mention different musical ability levels, styles, and goals." One student credits the artsy community with "a lot of acceptance and welcoming of the gay and lesbian community within my campus." Even outside of Crane, most Potsdam students "interact well and are able to conduct their studies without feeling discriminated against by other students."

ADMISSIONS

Very important factors considered by the admissions committee include: secondary school record and standardized test scores. *Important factors considered include:* class rank and talent/ability. *Other factors considered include:* alumni/ae relation, character/personal qualities, essays, extracurricular activities, interview, recommendations, volunteer work, and work experience. SAT I or ACT required. TOEFL required of all international applicants. High school diploma or GED is required. *High school units required/recommended:* 17 total required; 20 total recommended; 4 English required, 3 math required, 4 math recommended, 2 science required, 3 science recommended, 1 science lab required, 2 science lab recommended, 3 foreign language required, 4 foreign language recommended, 4 social studies required, 4 social studies recommended.

The Inside Word

Its strengths in music benefit the whole campus as the Crane School's diverse energy rubs off on the rest of Potsdam. But pity those in other departments who hope to see the school respond to their needs as efficiently as Crane does to its students.

FINANCIAL AID

Students should submit: FAFSA and state aid form. No deadline for regular filing. The Princeton Review suggests that all financial aid forms be submitted as soon as possible after January 1. *Need-based scholarships/grants offered:* Pell, SEOG, state scholarships/grants, private scholarships, and the school's own gift aid. *Loan aid offered:* Direct Subsidized Stafford, Direct Unsubsidized Stafford, Direct PLUS, Federal Perkins, and alternative loans. Federal Work-Study Program available. Institutional employment available. Applicants will be notified of awards on a rolling basis beginning on or about February 15. Off-campus job opportunities are good.

For even more information on this school, turn to page 365 of the "Stats" section.

SYRACUSE UNIVERSITY

201 TOLLEY, ADMINISTRATION BUILDING, SYRACUSE, NY 13244 • ADMISSIONS: 315-443-3611
FINANCIAL AID: 315-443-1513 • E-MAIL: ORANGE@SYR.EDU • WEBSITE: WWW.SYRACUSE.EDU

Ratings
Quality of Life: 84   Academic: 87   Admissions: 88   Financial Aid: 83

Academics

Students choose Syracuse for the tremendous scope of its offerings, its excellent resources (including "a fantastic library!") and of course, its national reputation. Among its nine academic divisions, SU boasts notable programs in business, engineering, visual and performing arts, and natural sciences. It is probably best known, however, for the "amazing"

> **SURVEY SAYS . . .**
> *Student publications are popular*
> *Diverse students interact*
> *Everyone loves the Orangemen*
> *Frats and sororities dominate social scene*
> *Students are cliquish, Athletic facilities are great*
> *Lousy off-campus food*
> *Lab facilities need improving*
> *Students aren't religious*

Newhouse School of Communications, which is universally thought to be "one of the best in the country" and includes one of the nation's top broadcast journalism programs. Like most universities, "this school is very research oriented." Warns one student, "Syracuse University is supposedly a student-centered research campus; however, if the students don't know and act upon that, they'll get lost in the crowd." Instruction varies markedly from one division to the next, with journalism profs earning the highest marks. Notes one sophomore, "Some professors are captivating and others are awful." Complains one math education major, "There is no doubt in my mind that the professors know their stuff, but a large portion of them don't know how to present the material in a beneficial manner." The administration generally receives favorable reviews; writes one student, "The school's administration is very accessible . . . many of them go to great lengths to accommodate your needs as a student. This helps reduce the stress of the whole academic experience." Many students, however, complain that the administration nickels-and-dimes them with "lots of extra charges on top of the very expensive tuition."

Life

Students are split in their assessment of the social scene at Syracuse. Detractors badmouth the town ("dull and depressing . . . the local establishments—stores, shops, etc.—could use some restoration"), the weather ("This is the third most overcast city in the U.S.—lots of rain"), and the variety of available entertainment ("A car is needed to go anywhere that has culture," writes one student. Others disagree, pointing out that "there's more to do in Syracuse than people give it credit for. Many people go to the campus bars for entertainment. By far they are the most popular, but there are other things to do, like bowling, dancing, coffee houses, etc." They also point to a moderately active Greek system that "provides more stuff to do, especially since there isn't much to do in local areas. Bars are big here, as are casual drugs like marijuana. This could be a very depressing place or the best time ever." All students agree that drinking is a popular pastime, explaining that "SU is a drinking school, not a party school." They also agree that intercollegiate sports, especially football, basketball, and lacrosse, are huge. Sums up one student, "If you like sports, snow, and beer, this is a great school for you."

Student Body

"People think that the only type of people that come here are rich spoiled kids from Long Island," writes one SU student. "In reality, those are the ones that stick out the most, but there are many different types of people here." Indeed, undergrads at SU represent "a diverse student population with diverse interests." However, according to most students, different populations rarely intermingle. "I would love to believe that we all get along," writes one African American junior, "but we segregate from each other based on Greek life, race, religion, class, etc. It's rather sad: some just live in a bubble and think SU is A-OK. We have some work to do."

ADMISSIONS

Very important factors considered by the admissions committee include: character/personal qualities, class rank, essays, interview, recommendations, secondary school record, standardized test scores. *Important factors considered include:* talent/ability. *Other factors considered include:* alumni/ae relation, extracurricular activities, minority status, volunteer work, work experience. SAT I or ACT required; SAT I preferred. TOEFL required of all international applicants. High school diploma or GED is required. *High school units required/recommended:* 20 total required; 21 total recommended; 4 English required, 3 math required, 3 science required, 3 science lab required, 2 foreign language required, 3 foreign language recommended, 3 social studies required, 5 elective required.

The Inside Word

Thanks to nationally competitive athletic teams and the Newhouse School of Communications, Syracuse draws a large applicant pool. It has also reduced the size of the freshman class, so the university has gotten more selective over the past few years. Most above-average students should still be strong candidates; though weaker students may also benefit from Syracuse's individualized admissions process, they must show true promise in order to have a shot. Candidates for the Newhouse School will encounter even greater competition.

FINANCIAL AID

Students should submit: FAFSA, CSS/Financial Aid PROFILE. Regular filing deadline is February 1. The Princeton Review suggests that all financial aid forms be submitted as soon as possible after January 1. *Need-based scholarships/grants offered:* Pell, SEOG, state scholarships/grants, the school's own gift aid. *Loan aid offered:* FFEL Subsidized Stafford, FFEL Unsubsidized Stafford, FFEL PLUS, Federal Perkins, Federal Nursing. Federal Work-Study Program available. Institutional employment available. Applicants will be notified of awards on or about April 1. Off-campus job opportunities are good.

FROM THE ADMISSIONS OFFICE

"Syracuse University is set on a beautiful residential campus that encompasses more than 200 acres and 170 buildings. Situated on a hill, overlooking downtown Syracuse, the school gives students the opportunity to enjoy the traditional college environment while realizing the social and recreational opportunities of a medium-size city. Syracuse University is committed to priorities that place its students first and foremost in importance. Small classes, intensive advising, emphasis on transition to college in the first year, and active learning characterize a systematic approach to assuring a productive teaching and learning environment. Improved classroom opportunities through smaller classes provide students with close attention from faculty. In virtually every aspect of students' lives at Syracuse, choices abound. The range of courses available, opportunities for study abroad and internships, the scope of residential living possibilities, the array of co-curricular and extracurricular clubs and organizations (there are nearly 300), and the opportunity to participate in the Honors Program makes SU an exciting place to attend. Students at Syracuse can choose from more than 200 undergraduate majors and nearly 70 undergraduate minors. Syracuse combines the best characteristics of a research institution with a traditional focus on the highest quality teaching, advising, and mentoring. It is a student-centered research university, and is committed to giving students the very best educational experiences available."

For even more information on this school, turn to page 365 of the "Stats" section.

TRINITY COLLEGE

300 Summit Street, Hartford, CT 06016 • Admissions: 860-297-2180 • Fax: 860-297-2287
Financial Aid: 860-297-2046 • E-mail: admissions.office@trincoll.edu • Website: www.trincoll.edu

Ratings
Quality of Life: 80   Academic: 84   Admissions: 94   Financial Aid: 82

Academics

Students at Trinity College enjoy an uncommon degree of academic intimacy and comfort. Notes one, "Trinity is a small school where it is easy to form strong relationships with professors, administration, and even the buildings and

> **SURVEY SAYS . . .**
> *Diversity lacking on campus*
> *Everyone loves the Bantams*
> *Great computer facilities, Great food on campus*
> *Class discussions encouraged*

grounds staff." Agrees another, "There is no line between faculty, administration, and students. We work hard together; we play hard together. We are a proud campus!" While students appreciate the bond they form with faculty, they also enjoy the degree of autonomy Trinity's academic approach grants them. Even the curricular requirements here provide opportunities for independence, as students are allowed to choose from a number of courses to fulfill each requirement and to design their own "integration of knowledge" sequence. One engineering major boasts, "Trinity has given me educational opportunities not normally available to undergraduates. I've been involved in graduate-level research since freshman year, have the ability to take graduate courses through the consortium, have an internship through Hartford Hospital, and have presented research at a conference." Profs here earn high marks both for teaching ability ("professors allow the make-up of the class to direct what type of class it is: discussion, group work, field trips, visual aids, lecture, etc.") and accessibility ("I have had some absolutely amazing professors who are accessible outside the classroom and go out of their way to know students"). Students save their highest praise, though, for the school president, who "is really involved. He's even called our room before regarding a question."

Life

"Trinity is a party school!" proudly exclaim students, who hasten to add that it's not all play here. "People at this school like to have fun," offers one student, "but they know when it's time to buckle down and do some work." A senior qualifies that assessment, opining that "the 'work hard, play hard' ethic still applies here, although profs are sometimes too lenient and students can get away with doing little work or getting extensions." During extracurricular hours, students enjoy theme parties such as the 1980s Dance and the Nastee Greek parties, productions by the school's "strong" theater department, lectures ("We had Cornell West and two descendents of Thomas Jefferson—one black, one white—here recently"), Greek life ("beneficial to all"), and athletic events ("Intercollegiate sports are big here. I can always count on my roommates and friends to show up [at] my games"). They also appreciate the location ("between Boston and New York") of Hartford and report that "Trinity is in a bad neighborhood, but downtown Hartford offers restaurants, theater, and a world-class museum." The lovely campus boasts "the most beautiful chapel on the East Coast."

Student Body

The students of Trinity are "so friendly, so interesting, everyone gets along." Their harshest critics say they are "rich, shallow, in a bubble. I get along with them, but I wish people cared less about how Daddy didn't put enough money in their checking account." Those looking at the bright side see that "all are passionate about something: a sport, theater, the newspaper, Saturday nights." Minority students are few and far between here. Writes one African American undergrad, "This school needs more support for minority students." Notes a white student, "Black and Hispanic kids are quite noticeably segregated."

ADMISSIONS

Very important factors considered by the admissions committee include: secondary school record. *Important factors considered include:* character/personal qualities, class rank, essays, extracurricular activities, interview, minority status, recommendations, standardized test scores, talent/ability. *Other factors considered include:* alumni/ae relation, geographical residence, volunteer work, work experience. TOEFL required of all international applicants. High school diploma or GED is required. *High school units required/recommended:* 16 total required; 4 English required, 3 math required, 2 science required, 2 science lab required, 2 foreign language required, 2 history required.

The Inside Word

Trinity's Ivy safety status and well-deserved reputation for academic quality enables it to enroll a fairly impressive student body, but many of its best applicants go elsewhere. The price tag is high, and the college's competitors include a large portion of the best schools in the country. Minority candidates with sound academic backgrounds will encounter a most accommodating admissions committee.

FINANCIAL AID

Students should submit: FAFSA, CSS/Financial Aid PROFILE, noncustodial (divorced/separated) parent's statement, federal income tax returns. Regular filing deadline is February 1. The Princeton Review suggests that all financial aid forms be submitted as soon as possible after January 1. *Need-based scholarships/grants offered:* Pell, SEOG, state scholarships/grants, private scholarships, the school's own gift aid. *Loan aid offered:* Direct Subsidized Stafford, Direct Unsubsidized Stafford, Direct PLUS, FFEL Subsidized Stafford, FFEL Unsubsidized Stafford, FFEL PLUS, Federal Perkins, college/university loans from institutional funds. Federal Work-Study Program available. Institutional employment available. Applicants will be notified of awards on or about April 1. Off-campus job opportunities are good.

FROM THE ADMISSIONS OFFICE

"An array of distinctive curricular options—including an interdisciplinary neuroscience major and a professionally accredited engineering degree program, a unique Human Rights Program, a tutorial college for selected sophomores, a Health Fellows Program, and interdisciplinary programs such as the Cities Program, Interdisciplinary Science Program, and InterArts—is one reason record numbers of students are applying to Trinity. In fact, applications are up 80 percent over the past five years. In addition, the college has been recognized for its commitment to diversity; students of color have represented approximately 20 percent of the freshman class for the past four years, setting Trinity apart from many of its peers. Trinity's capital city location offers students unparalleled 'real-world' learning experiences to complement classroom learning. Students take advantage of extensive opportunities for internships for academic credit and community service, and these opportunities extend to Trinity's global learning sites in cities around the world. Trinity's faculty is a devoted and accomplished group of exceptional teacher-scholars, our 100 acre campus is beautiful; Hartford is an educational asset that differentiates Trinity from other liberal arts colleges; our global connections and foreign study opportunities prepare students to be good citizens of the world; and our graduates go on to excel in virtually every field. We invite you to learn more about why Trinity might be the best choice for you."

For even more information on this school, turn to page 366 of the "Stats" section.

TUFTS UNIVERSITY

BENDETSON HALL, MEDFORD, MA 02155 • ADMISSIONS: 617-627-3170 • FAX: 617-627-3860
FINANCIAL AID: 617-627-3528 • E-MAIL: ADMISSIONS.INQUIRY@ASE.TUFTS.EDU • WEBSITE: WWW.TUFTS.EDU

Ratings

Quality of Life: 89   Academic: 91   Admissions: 97   Financial Aid: 84

Academics

Students at Tufts University, "a friendly school with great opportunities both at the school and in the Boston area," think it's the perfect size, "small enough to feel like a small New England liberal arts college, but big enough to offer great variety." A big plus is that "Tufts' small size gives undergrads opportunities to do individual research with excellent professors. It's fairly common for undergraduates to get published, too." Unlike many research-oriented universities, Tufts allows TAs to "only teach labs and study groups. Professors teach the actual classes, so you get a much more detailed, informed education." Professors here are "amazing, caring, intelligent individuals who take time to work with students." The school offers such a variety of courses that "the trouble is not finding enough classes to take, but rather choosing from the amazing selection." Although strong in many areas, Tufts earns especially good marks from students for its programs in engineering, international relations, pre-med studies, and the sciences. Luckily, "academics are serious without being cutthroat," which students appreciate. They also love the "awesome study abroad opportunities" the school offers. Student complaints center primarily on financial issues: "The endowment is small, so things like classroom and dorm renovation lag behind. The school tends to nickel and dime students a lot, which is also directly tied to the endowment issues," notes a typical respondent.

> **SURVEY SAYS . . .**
> *Great library*
> *Student newspaper is popular*
> *Campus easy to get around*
> *Campus feels safe*
> *Great off-campus food*
> *Campus is beautiful*
> *Great on-campus food*
> *Lots of beer drinking*

Life

Students at Tufts really do, as the old cliché goes, have the best of both worlds: a campus abuzz with activity and a world-class city just a few stops away on the T. On campus, "most kids here are pretty active in something . . . community service, writing, sports, whatever interests them." Writes one student, "I almost feel like there is too much going on at Tufts. You sometimes have to make a conscious effort to avoid the activities on campus just so you can get your work done." Adds another, "Tufts has so many performing groups, there is something to go see almost every night, and definitely every weekend. Lots of performances and exhibits are free, as are lectures. We have lots of speakers come to campus (almost every group brings people to talk), and lectures are well publicized and generally interesting." A cappella competitions are surprisingly popular; sports are less so. "The only well-attended football game is homecoming and everyone there is too drunk to even watch." As for the surrounding city, the campus is located "just down the road [from] Davis Square, home of sweet bars, nice restaurants, and a solid concert/movie/play venue. The subway is right there; Harvard Square is two stops away; Lansdowne Street is about 25 to 30 minutes away." Students here love the specialty residences (e.g., language houses, arts houses) that allow students with common interests to live together; they warn, however, that "housing for juniors and seniors is a big problem . . . because Tufts does not guarantee housing to upperclassmen."

Student Body

There are lots of stereotypes of the Tufts student body, and according to our survey, they're mostly true. "It's true what they say about Tufts; the school is filled with bitter Ivy League rejects," writes one student. Adds another, "There are a ton of well-off Jewish kids from the Northeast who wear Abercrombie and listen to Guster all the time. But there are just as many kids who don't fit that cookie-cutter view." In fact, "there is a lot of diversity for such an expensive campus. One-quarter of the student body is a racial or ethnic minority. Plus, there's an active gay community." Although diverse, the student body is not well integrated; explains one student, "The best analogy I've heard to describe Tufts students is the TV dinner. You see, we have all kinds of different flavors, but each [is] segregated into different compartments."

ADMISSIONS

Very important factors considered by the admissions committee include: secondary school record. *Important factors considered include:* character/personal qualities, class rank, essays, extracurricular activities, minority status, recommendations, standardized test scores, talent/ability, volunteer work, work experience. *Other factors considered include:* alumni/ae relation, geographical residence, interview. TOEFL required of all international applicants. High school diploma or GED is required. *High school units required/recommended:* 4 English recommended, 3 math recommended, 2 science recommended, 3 foreign language recommended, 2 history recommended.

The Inside Word

Tufts has little visibility outside the Northeast and little personality either. Still it manages to attract and keep an excellent student body, mostly from right inside its own backyard. In order to be successful, candidates must have significant academic accomplishments and submit a thoroughly well-prepared application—the review is rigorous and the standards are high.

FINANCIAL AID

Students should submit: FAFSA, CSS/Financial Aid PROFILE, noncustodial (divorced/separated) parent's statement, business/farm supplement, parent's and student's federal income tax returns. Regular filing deadline is February 15. The Princeton Review suggests that all financial aid forms be submitted as soon as possible after January 1. *Need-based scholarships/grants offered:* Pell, SEOG, state scholarships/grants, private scholarships, the school's own gift aid. *Loan aid offered:* FFEL Subsidized Stafford, FFEL Unsubsidized Stafford, FFEL PLUS, Federal Perkins, state loans, college/university loans from institutional funds. Federal Work-Study Program available. Institutional employment available. Applicants will be notified of awards on or about April 5. Off-campus job opportunities are good.

FROM THE ADMISSIONS OFFICE

"Tufts University, on the boundary between Medford and Somerville, sits on a hill overlooking Boston, five miles northwest of the city. The campus is a tranquil New England setting within easy access by subway and bus to the cultural, social, and entertainment resources of Boston and Cambridge. "Since its founding in 1852 by members of the Universalist church, Tufts has grown from a small liberal arts college into a nonsectarian university of over 7,000 students. By 1900 the college had added a medical school, a dental school, and graduate studies. The University now also includes the Fletcher School of Law and Diplomacy, the Graduate School of Arts and Sciences, the School of Veterinary Medicine, the School of Nutrition, the Sackler School of Graduate Biomedical Sciences, and the Gordon Institute of Engineering Management."

For even more information on this school, turn to page 367 of the "Stats" section.

UNION COLLEGE

GRANT HALL, SCHENECTADY, NY 12308 • ADMISSIONS: 518-388-6112 • FAX: 518-388-6986
FINANCIAL AID: 518-388-6123 • E-MAIL: ADMISSIONS@UNION.EDU • WEBSITE: WWW.UNION.EDU

Ratings
Quality of Life: 77   Academic: 87   Admissions: 91   Financial Aid: 81

Academics

Students are attracted to Union College by the great variety of courses available at a school that has fewer than 2,500 undergrads. The enrollment ensures that class sizes are small and that professors have the time to get to know their students. "Academically, Union is great," a senior political science major avers. "Classes are interest-

> **SURVEY SAYS . . .**
> *Lots of beer drinking*
> *Frats and sororities dominate social scene*
> *Popular college radio*
> *Profs teach upper-levels*
> *Hard liquor is popular*
> *Students don't like Schenectady, NY*
> *Students are cliquish*

ing," and professors are, "caring," accessible, and approachable. Professors "go out of their way to . . . get involved on campus," a junior political science major writes, and "many even give you their home numbers." TAs are nowhere to be found. There are a few professors on campus who aren't as highly regarded, and a math major grumbles, "The school puts too much emphasis on selecting professors with good reputations, [instead of] selecting profes-sors who actually can teach and speak English." Students rave about the trimester calendar, according to which they only take three classes at a time. "You never feel too bogged down," one first-year student writes. Students do, however, want to be able to register online. The "conservative" administration is, for the most part, disliked. "The bureaucracy at this school makes the IRS look like a well-oiled machine," a senior history major gripes.

Life

"Union's a blast," a sophomore beams. "We go to the same two hole-in-the-wall places where we see the same people as always," writes a less enthusiastic classmate. Campus student organizations "work hard to schedule events," but students often forsake those events for frat parties. Still, "the number of clubs we have is great," a senior Spanish major gushes. "There is a club for everything from sign language to ballroom dancing." Theme houses provide an alternative to those not interested in Greek life. Campus sports are popular, as are on-campus movies and concerts. Though students complain that there is little to do in "less-than-desir-able" Schenectady, they admit that the area offers much in the way of volunteer opportuni-ties. Many students are involved in the Big Brothers/Big Sisters program. Students are also "within a few hours of New York and Boston, and below the Adirondack Mountains, where prime skiing and hiking" opportunities abound. Students feel that campus security is too strict and that athletic facilities could stand some improvement.

Student Body

Union's students describe themselves as "apathetic" and "conservative" and "rich snobs." Most come from the East Coast. "If Daddy bought you an SUV and you're from Jersey, you'll fit right in here," a computer engineering major quips. One female student comments that most of her female peers "live by Cosmo," and a junior adds, "There's a division: the Kate Spade, Jeep Grand Cherokee, sorority and frat boy types, versus the rest of the world." Students are "cliquey," and a first-year student marvels, "I have never seen so many North

Face Jackets and Kate Spade bags in one place." A sociology major observes, "Many students, especially those involved in the Greek system, view college as one continuous party with the disadvantage of having to take finals at the end of each term to be able to come back." Many students describe their peers as "polite" and "friendly," and people "smile and say 'hi' as they pass between classes." One English major believes, however, that most of her peers view college "as a means to an end—money—[and] not an intellectual adventure."

ADMISSIONS

Very important factors considered by the admissions committee include: class rank, secondary school record. *Important factors considered include:* alumni/ae relation, character/personal qualities, essays, extracurricular activities, interview, minority status, recommendations, talent/ability, volunteer work. *Other factors considered include:* geographical residence, standardized test scores, state residency, work experience. SAT I or ACT required. TOEFL required of all international applicants. High school diploma or GED is required. *High school units required/recommended:* 16 total required; 24 total recommended; 4 English required, 3 math required, 4 math recommended, 2 science required, 4 science recommended, 2 science lab required, 4 science lab recommended, 2 foreign language required, 4 foreign language recommended, 1 social studies required, 2 social studies recommended, 1 history required, 2 history recommended.

The Inside Word

In this age of MTV-type admissions videos and ultra-glossy promotional literature, Union is decidedly more low-key than most colleges. The college is a bastion of tradition and conservatism and sticks to what it knows best when it comes to recruitment and admission. Students who are thinking about Union need to be prepared with as challenging a high school curriculum as possible and solid grades across the board.

FINANCIAL AID

Students should submit: FAFSA, CSS/Financial Aid PROFILE, state aid form, noncustodial (divorced/separated) parent's statement, business/farm supplement. Regular filing deadline is February 1. The Princeton Review suggests that all financial aid forms be submitted as soon as possible after January 1. *Need-based scholarships/grants offered:* Pell, SEOG, state scholarships/grants, private scholarships, the school's own gift aid. *Loan aid offered:* FFEL Subsidized Stafford, FFEL Unsubsidized Stafford, FFEL PLUS, Federal Perkins, college/university loans from institutional funds. Federal Work-Study Program available. Institutional employment available. Applicants will be notified of awards on or about April 1. Off-campus job opportunities are good.

FROM THE ADMISSIONS OFFICE

"'Breadth' and 'flexibility' characterize the Union academic program. Whether the subject is the poetry of ancient Greece or the possibilities of developing fields such as nanotechnology, Union students can choose among nearly 1,000 courses—a range that is unusual among America's highly selective colleges. Students can major in a single field, combine work in two or more departments, or even create their own organizing theme major. Undergraduate research is strongly encouraged, and nearly 70 percent of Union's students take advantage of the College's extensive international study program."

For even more information on this school, turn to page 367 of the "Stats" section.

UNITED STATES COAST GUARD ACADEMY

31 MOHEGAN AVENUE, NEW LONDON, CT 06320-8103 • ADMISSIONS: 800-883-8724 • FAX: 860-701-6700
E-MAIL: ADMISSIONS@CGA.USCG.MIL • WEBSITE: WWW.CGA.EDU

Ratings
Quality of Life: 85   **Academic:** 99   **Admissions:** 98   **Financial Aid:** 99

Academics

"It's free, you get paid, and you have a job promised to you when you graduate." For most at the United States Coast Guard Academy, that's a parlay too enticing to refuse. That's right; students at CGA not only get a completely free ride, but also a small stipend and a Coast Guard gig waiting at

> **SURVEY SAYS . . .**
> *Classes are small*
> *Great library*
> *Lots of classroom discussion*
> *Lab facilities are great*
> *Diverse students interact*
> *No one cheats*

the end of the line. Others choose CGA because they want an extremely challenging, extremely disciplined college experience; those cadets don't leave disappointed. "The Coast Guard Academy is one of the best overall learning opportunities that the United States has to offer. Cadets here are challenged in many aspects, including physically, mentally, and academically" by a curriculum that includes mandatory sports and drilling as well as an average of 20 credit hours per semester. "Classes are small, which allows for superb instruction." And "profs really care and will spend a lot of time out of the classroom for us." All this helps take some of the sting off the fact that "cadets get an average of 5 hours of sleep a night because the academic load is tremendous." Agrees one student, "The hardest aspect of going to school here is the lack of time to complete the assignments, or deciding which ones you are going to complete given your time." The hard work pays off, most agree: "The experience, although extremely demanding, leaves one feeling quite proud of what he has accomplished."

Life

There is "little to no downtime" for cadets at CGA, since academic and athletic requirements cram students' weekdays full. "We can basically only have fun on the weekends, when we get liberty. During the week, there is no time for anything but school" is how one cadet puts it. Many here resent the school's strict, occasionally "illogical" regulations. "Micromanaging every aspect of our lives gets old after a few days . . . let alone four years," writes one cadet. Students particularly dislike the strict drug and alcohol policy ("No drugs, ever. Caught twice drinking [underage] and you're expelled") and the rule requiring all barracks doors to remain open from 0600 to 2200. Once weekends come around, "we leave, if we can get liberty. That's the way it is in a barracks." Because "New London is a horrendously barren town," cadets try to go elsewhere; Boston, Providence, and New York are all favorite destinations. Those stuck in town "head for Connecticut College across the street," where there are "many opportunities to take part in the more artistic/scholarly activities" as well as keg parties. Life at CGA is not without its pleasures, however; the school has "an amazing sports program for a Division III school," and "the summer programs either on Coast Guard boats or spent at the Academy instructing the incoming 'Swabs'" can be "the best summers of your life. I have been able to fly Coast Guard helicopters and aircraft and participate in the exchange cadet program to the United States Military Academy at West Point during my junior year."

Student Body

"There are few other institutions on this planet that bring groups of people together the way service academies do," explains one Coast Guard cadet. "At times the closeness of the Academy can drive you crazy, but overall it enriches the institution and the experience." Puns one student, "We are all in the same boat." Coast Guard cadets "are very competitive by nature, and the corps of cadets is full of Type A personalities." They "tend to come from small communities" and be "very conservative and outgoing." Regardless of their differences, "the system requires a basic professional respect for others that one must practice most of the time." Of course, "there are a few bad apples, like anywhere." "Sometimes the Academy atmosphere, rules, etc. have a way of bringing out the worst in people," explains one cadet. "The Academy system has a way of creating conflict between people. Luckily, most of these people get weeded out eventually."

ADMISSIONS

Very important factors considered by the admissions committee include: character/personal qualities, class rank, extracurricular activities, secondary school record, standardized test scores. *Important factors considered include:* essays, recommendations, talent/ability. *Other factors considered include:* alumni/ae relation, interview, volunteer work, work experience. SAT I or ACT required. TOEFL required of all international applicants. High school diploma or GED is required. *High school units required/recommended:* 4 English required, 4 math required.

The Inside Word

The Coast Guard is the smallest service academy, regarded by many as a well-kept secret. Just like the other military service academies, admission is highly selective. Candidates must go through a rigorous admissions process that includes a medical exam and physical fitness evaluation. Those who pass muster join a very proud service. If you're a woman and thinking about a service academy, be aware that the Corps of Cadets at the Coast Guard Academy is 30 percent women!

FINANCIAL AID

The Coast Guard Academy is tuition-free.

FROM THE ADMISSIONS OFFICE

"Founded in 1876, the United State Coast Guard Academy has a proud tradition as one of the finest colleges in the country. When you've earned your four-year Bachelor of Science degree and a commission as an Ensign, you're prepared professionally, physically, and mentally as a leader and lifelong learner. You'll build friendships to last a lifetime, study with inspiring teachers in small classes, and train during the summer aboard America's Tall Ship EAGLE and the service's newest, most sophisticated ships and aircraft. Top performers spend their senior summer traveling on exciting internships. No Congressional nominations, appointments are awarded competitively on a nationwide basis. Graduates must serve for five years and have unmatched opportunities to attend flight training and graduate school, all funded by the Coast Guard. Your leadership potential and desire to serve your fellow Americans are what counts. Our student body reflects the best America has to offer—with all its potential and diversity!"

For even more information on this school, turn to page 368 of the "Stats" section.

UNITED STATES MERCHANT MARINE ACADEMY

OFFICE OF ADMISSIONS, KINGS POINT, NY 11024-1699 • ADMISSIONS: 516-773-5391 • FAX: 516-773-5390
EMAIL: ADMISSIONS@USMMA.EDU • WEBSITE: WWW.USMMA.EDU

Ratings

Quality of Life: 84   Academic: 84   Admissions: 98   Financial Aid: 99

Academics

Mention sailors and most people think of swearing, drinking, and port-of-call carousing, and while this image applies on rare occasions to students at the United States Merchant Marine Academy, the focus here is decidedly on academics. At the beginning of the second semester of freshman year, midshipmen select a major—one of six available: "deck or engine, [meaning Marine Transportation or Marine Engineering] with a few subcategories in each." From that point forward, they have their course schedule laid out by the Academy. The academic program receives high praise, specifically because classroom learning is complemented by Sea Year, "one of four years of actual working experience." Students say, "Sea Year Courses, which are done while training on various merchant ships throughout the world, are the most difficult of the academy's courses." Professors are characterized as "dedicated," some to the point of being "slave drivers." The small classes, lack of TAs, and mandatory class attendance policy ensure that students get the attention they need to manage the "very heavy course load" and regimental requirements. Even deans pitch in and "tutor students when they can." Some midshipmen perceive an "open door" attitude from administrators, but others claim that the "administration thinks we are whiny brats"; the superintendent, however, is widely respected. Most students look forward to the high-paying careers available to them after graduation and appreciate the "excellent leadership training" they receive at the Academy.

> **SURVEY SAYS . . .**
> *Instructors are good teachers*
> *No one cheats, School is well run*
> *Campus easy to get around*
> *Great computer facilities*
> *Diverse students interact*
> *Class discussions encouraged*
> *Very little drug use*

Life

"This school is a country club if you disregard the marching," one USMMA student observes. Marching and other regimental activities constitute much of life in Kings Point, prompting some students to feel at times like "inmates" on campus. Some report "sleeping two to four hours a night" to accommodate the intense academic and regimental schedule. Basically, "freshmen don't have lives," but even first-years point out, "We are here to train." Midshipmen gradually enjoy more "individual freedoms [and] privileges, which are granted based upon seniority and individual performance." To blow off steam, "most people work out nearly every day or play sports." When the weekend rolls around, "it's all about New York City," which is only 20 to 30 minutes away by train. One student writes, "I typically utilize some of our perks, such as free admission to Mets games, the U.S. Open, Yankees games, and David Letterman." "A few people have actually gone into museums," during these outings, but students mainly hit the bars, "on the prowl due to the lack of women at school." Other people choose to "sail all over Long Island on the weekends." A common sentiment goes something like, "Life at school is very busy and there are not many times to just 'chill,' as my regular college friends call it."

Student Body

The typical USMMA student is reported to be a "white male between the ages of 18 and 22"; only about 100 women attend the Academy. Also, the population includes "very few students that are of a different ethnicity," but one minority student writes frankly, "I have not found this to be a problem." This might be partly due to the pervasive notion that "having people from many different areas of the country and world makes for an increased awareness of life in general and how people act." Respondents agree that "most students have similar political views," which translates to "no hippies." "Everyone becomes 'typical' by necessity because of the regimentation of the school." Strong bonds form during an "indoctrination period" that each incoming class undergoes, the "evident esprit de corps" solidified by the "cramped quarters" and "repressive regime" in which they exist. These solid connections endure after graduates set sail: "The merchant marine community is so small that there is also the advantage of an excellent network of contacts."

ADMISSIONS

Very important factors considered by the admissions committee include: character/personal qualities, secondary school record, and standardized test scores. *Important factors considered include:* class rank, essays, extracurricular activities, recommendations, and talent/ability. *Other factors considered include:* interview, minority status, state residency, volunteer work, and work experience. SAT I or ACT required. TOEFL required of all international applicants. High school diploma is required and GED is not accepted. *High school units required/recommended:* 18 total are required; 4 English required, 4 English recommended, 3 math required, 4 math recommended, 3 science required, 4 science recommended, 1 science lab required, 2 science lab recommended, 2 foreign language recommended, 4 social studies recommended, 8 elective required.

The Inside Word

Academic criteria are only part of the admissions game here; you must also meet the Academy's physical requirements. The school catalog has three pages on requirements concerning vision, hearing, weight and body fat percent, skin condition, and respiratory health. You also need to know how to swim.

FINANCIAL AID

Students should submit: FAFSA and institution's own financial aid form. Regular filing deadline is May 1. The Princeton Review suggests that all financial aid forms be submitted as soon as possible after January 1. *Need-based scholarships/grants offered:* Pell. *Loan aid offered:* FFEL subsidized Stafford, and FFEL PLUS. Applicants will be notified of awards on a rolling basis beginning on or about January 31. Off-campus job opportunities are poor.

FROM THE ADMISSIONS OFFICE

"What makes the U.S. Merchant Marine Academy different from the other federal service academies? The difference can be summarized in two phrases that appear in our publications. The first: 'The World Is Your Campus.' You will spend a year at sea—a third of your sophomore year and two-thirds of your junior year—teamed with a classmate aboard a U.S. merchant ship. You will visit an average of 18 foreign nations while you work and learn in a mariner's true environment. You will graduate with seafaring experience and as a citizen of the world. The second phrase is 'Options and Opportunities.' Unlike students at the other federal academies, who are required to enter the service connected to their academy, you have the option of working in the seagoing merchant marine and transportation industry, or applying for active duty in the Navy, Coast Guard, Marine Corps, Air Force, or Army. Nearly 29 percent of our most recent graduating class entered various branches of the Armed Forces with an officer rank. As a graduate of the U.S. Merchant Marine Academy, you will receive a Bachelor of Science degree, a government-issued merchant marine officer's license, and a Naval Reserve commission (unless you have been accepted for active military duty). No other service academy offers so attractive a package."

For even more information on this school, turn to page 369 of the "Stats" section.

UNITED STATES MILITARY ACADEMY

600 THAYER ROAD, WEST POINT, NY 10996-1797 • ADMISSIONS: 914-938-4041 • FAX: 914-938-3021
FINANCIAL AID: 914-938-3516 • E-MAIL: 8DAD@EXMAIL.USMA.ARMY.MIL • WEBSITE: WWW.USMA.EDU

Ratings
Quality of Life: 78   Academic: 99   Admissions: 99   Financial Aid: 99

Academics

"West Point is unique in many ways: a military institution, a first-class university, and a national landmark all rolled into one," explains one cadet. "Our motto is 'duty, honor, country,' and sometimes duty looms much larger than the rest. Life is hard here, but its difficulty makes it fulfilling." The West Point approach—to cram as much activity into one day as humanly possible—is "very tough. Learn to prioritize. If

> **SURVEY SAYS . . .**
> *School is run well*
> *Campus feels safe*
> *No one cheats*
> *Registration is a breeze*
> *Different students interact*
> *Students don't like West Point, NY*
> *Very little drug use*
> *Very little hard liquor*
> *Lousy off-campus food*
> *Student publications are ignored*

you procrastinate, you die. Be ready not to sleep." Notes one student, "Academics are tough, but it's the fact that you have no time to study that makes it hard." Life is strictly regimented here, as one would expect. Writes one student, "West Point is similar to high school, at times almost too similar. We start at 7, stop for lunch at 12, and then continue until 3. Classes are small, which means every professor knows your name." For nearly all freshmen and sophomores, "There is no class choice. All classes are required." And even upperclassmen warn that "it's the military: You pick the major, they choose the classes." Fortunately for students, "the professors here, for the most part, are amazing. They understand how rigorous our life is and will tutor you personally every day for hours if you need it." Cadets are the first to admit that this school is not for everyone. "The school is focused toward military development and officership, so if you don't want to be in the Army, don't come!" warns one. Concludes another, "West Point is a machine that takes you in, chews you up, and spits you out—but somehow you are tremendously better person for it." Upon graduation, cadets are commissioned as Second Lieutenants in the U.S. Army and must serve a minimum of five years of active duty.

Life

As far as extracurricular life is concerned, a student's tenure at West Point is neatly divided in half. Simply put, for their first two years, students have no extracurricular life. Writes one student, "Because I am a sophomore, otherwise known as a 'Yuk,' I have no privileges (like going to the movies or to the mall). I am stuck in the cadet area studying." During their final two years, students are given greater freedom. Explains one upperclassman, "There is not much to do here in the first two years, but once you receive off-post privileges there is more available." The town surrounding the beautiful campus, Highland Falls, is small, so even when cadets do leave campus, they find very little to do unless they have wheels. Writes one student, "If you're not a cow (junior) or a first (senior) with a car, you are hard-pressed to have fun. If you do have a car, New York City and New Jersey aren't so far off. It also helps to be on a sports team." Intercollegiate athletic events are well attended here, even though Army's teams generally lose more often than they win. Army's popular football team, for one, competes in Conference USA, where it is usually overmatched by Tulane, Houston, Louisville, and Southern Mississippi, among others. The lacrosse team is much better, ranking 20th in the nation at the end of the 2000 season. Intramural sports are unusually popular for the simple reason that "all students not on varsity teams must play intramurals here. It's not an option." Mostly, though, life at West Point is defined by study, exercise, and plenty of drilling. "If you don't want to work hard, run, or be in the Army, do not come here," advises a senior.

Student Body

West Point's undergraduates represent a "great diversity of students and different backgrounds." However, as one cadet pointed out, "Relationships with other students are always filtered through the lens of leadership." As a result, "some get along, and some don't. But one thing about West Point is that I would trust any of [my classmates] with my life—and someday I may have to." Adds another student, "Students here all get along. They are forced to because of our mission in life: to become officers. Teamwork is essential. There are no individuals here." Minority discrimination "does not occur because it is simply not allowed here."

ADMISSIONS

Very important factors considered by the admissions committee include: essays, extracurricular activities, recommendations, secondary school record, standardized test scores. *Important factors considered include:* character/personal qualities, interview, minority status, talent/ability. *Other factors considered include:* geographical residence, volunteer work, work experience. SAT I or ACT required. High school diploma or GED is required. *High school units required/recommended:* 19 total recommended; 4 English recommended, 4 math recommended, 2 science recommended, 2 science lab recommended, 2 foreign language recommended, 3 social studies recommended, 1 history recommended, 3 elective recommended.

The Inside Word

Students considering a candidacy at West Point need to hit the ground running in the second half of their junior year. Don't delay initiating the application and nomination processes; together they constitute a long, hard road that includes not one but several highly competitive elements. Successful candidates must demonstrate strength both academically and physically, be solid citizens and contributors to society, and show true fortitude and potential for leadership. Admissions processes at other top schools can seem like a cakewalk compared to this, but those who get a nomination and pass muster through the physical part of the process have made it through the hardest part.

FINANCIAL AID

The Princeton Review suggests that all financial aid forms be submitted as soon as possible after January 1.

For even more information on this school, turn to page 369 of the "Stats" section.

UNIVERSITY OF CONNECTICUT

2131 HILLSIDE ROAD, U-3088, STORRS, CT 06268-3088 • ADMISSIONS: 860-486-3137 • FAX: 860-486-1476
FINANCIAL AID: 860-486-2819 • E-MAIL: BEAHUSKY@UCONN.EDU • WEBSITE: WWW.UCONN.EDU

Ratings
Quality of Life: 70   Academic: 71   Admissions: 79   Financial Aid: 83

Academics

Students at the University of Connecticut's flagship campus in Storrs tell us that they chose their school for "the wide variety of opportunities it provides its students to get involved and get ahead." Undergrads here also cite as big pluses "undergraduate research, study abroad, career services/internships, cooperative education programs," "more than 90 majors, including an individualized major which allows students to design their own plan of study, and over 200 clubs and activities. There is literally something for everyone." Business administration, music, theater, education, computer science, and engineering are among the disciplines garnering students' specific praise here. As at many large state schools, many warn that "introductory courses are not that great. It gets better as you progress as a student." Profs are "surprisingly helpful when students go to their office hours and tend to return emails the same day," although "with [UConn] being a research university, you sometimes get stuck with professors that are just too intelligent to be teaching." Of course, for the right student, the presence of so many researchers "provides a great experience. You can find numerous opportunities to get involved in professors' research projects." Many here appreciate the fact that "larger lectures are almost always broken into discussion sections of 20–25 students that meet once a week." Being the flagship university for the state of Connecticut doesn't hurt either. Connecticut profited, not once, but twice from state grants of $1 billion each, first in 1996 and then again in 2002. Students directly benefit from this windfall of dough in that every residence hall, academic building, sports facility, program office, etc. is being completely refurbished, torn down and rebuilt, or simply added anew to campus.

> **SURVEY SAYS . . .**
> *Everyone loves the Huskies*
> *Popular college radio*
> *Campus difficult to get around*
> *Large classes*
> *Lots of long lines and red tape*

Life

As a large university, UConn has the resources to support a wide variety of campus activities. Big-name acts "come to the university's Jorgensen Auditorium; they're amazing and with student ticket prices are a wonderfully cheap way to see great shows." On a smaller scale, "there are many students who enjoy the concerts of UConn Underground, numerous films, lectures, plays, and other activities going on in the dorms on a nightly basis." Furthermore, "there are so many clubs and organizations to be involved with that if you're bored on campus, it's because of your own laziness." Even so, a surprising number of students here claim that "there is nothing to do here except party." One reason is that many of the nonparty activities end early; explains one student, "UConn has a great campus life, which ends at 10 p.m. every day. Unfortunately because of that, alcohol is a popular late-night substitute. Activities are available . . . if you look hard enough and are open to different cultural and artistic experiences." Don't look in hometown Storrs, though, which "is not a college town. There is nothing to do off campus without driving at least 20 minutes." Do, however, look in the stadiums, arenas, and gymnasiums, as "the University of Connecticut offers strong Division I athletic programs in addition to a vast selection of club and intramural sports." Most here agree that

"Spring Weekend is the highlight of the year. Three straight days (starting on a Thursday) of parties with crowds up to and over 10,000 people: just an overall amazing experience."

Student Body

While "the large size of UConn means that there's not one typical student," we're told that most students here "have a good balance of school and social life. They work hard during the week and enjoy the weekend." Many are serious about success but not necessarily about book learning for its own sake; they "know that it's OK to skip at least one or two classes a week and to show up late because no one will say anything." Students are split regarding diversity. While some describe the typical UConn student as "white, middle/upper class, and from Connecticut," others point to "our five cultural centers, [where] it's easy for students to fit in and feel a part of a community."

ADMISSIONS

Very important factors considered by the admissions committee include: class rank, secondary school record, standardized test scores, talent/ability. *Important factors considered include:* character/personal qualities, essays, extracurricular activities, minority status, recommendations, volunteer work. *Other factors considered include:* alumni/ae relation, geographical residence, state residency, work experience. SAT I or ACT required. TOEFL required of all international applicants. High school diploma or GED is required. *High school units required/recommended:* 16 total required; 4 English required, 3 math required, 2 science required, 2 science lab required, 2 foreign language required, 3 foreign language recommended, 2 social studies required, 3 elective required.

The Inside Word

While no formulas or cutoffs may be used at UConn in the admissions process, getting in is still simply a matter of decent courses, grades, and tests. The $2 billion building program coupled with the recent high national profiles of the UConn men's and women's basketball teams has resulted in an increase in applications and in turn an increase in selectivity. With an incoming freshman class of more than 3,000, UConn is now holding enrollment steady for eager Huskies-to-be.

FINANCIAL AID

Students should submit: FAFSA. No deadline for regular filing. The Princeton Review suggests that all financial aid forms be submitted as soon as possible after January 1. *Need-based scholarships/grants offered:* Pell, SEOG, state scholarships/grants, private scholarships, the school's own gift aid. *Loan aid offered:* FFEL Subsidized Stafford, FFEL Unsubsidized Stafford, FFEL PLUS, Federal Perkins. Federal Work-Study Program available. Institutional employment available. Applicants will be notified of awards on a rolling basis beginning on or about March 1. Off-campus job opportunities are good.

FROM THE ADMISSIONS OFFICE

"The University of Connecticut provides students with high quality education, personalized attention, and a wide range of social and cultural opportunities. There are 29 students in the average undergraduate class. From award-winning actors to the federal reserve board chair, fascinating speakers and world leaders have lectured on campus within the past year, while students have taken in shows by premier dance, jazz, and rock performers. Transportation to campus events is convenient and safe, most students walk to class or ride university shuttle-buses. Through UCONN 2000 and 21st-Century UConn, landmark building programs totaling $2.3 billion, the university is erecting state-of-the-art academic and residential facilities. Among the projects: A new Center for Undergraduate Education, unifying student support services in one central location and providing speedy answers to student concerns. Because of a variety of innovations like this one, UConn is transforming the undergraduate experience and fast becoming a school of choice for a new generation of achievement-oriented students."

For even more information on this school, turn to page 370 of the "Stats" section.

THE UNIVERSITY OF MAINE

5713 Chadbourne Hall, Orono, ME 04469-5713 • Admissions: 207-581-1561 • Fax: 207-581-1213
Financial Aid: 207-581-1324 • E-mail: um-admit@maine.edu • Website: www.umaine.edu

Ratings
Quality of Life: 73   Academic: 71   Admissions: 76   Financial Aid: 81

Academics

The University of Maine is academic nirvana for any student looking to turn a love of the outdoors into a career. Top-ranked programs in wildlife ecology and forestry, as well as a major called Parks, Recreation, and Tourism, turn out the future park rangers and conservation scientists of America. "It is a nurturing and comfortable atmosphere for learning with intelligent, caring professors," writes a sophomore about

> **SURVEY SAYS . . .**
> *Everyone loves the Black Bears*
> *Students aren't religious*
> *Lots of beer drinking*
> *High cost of living*
> *Class discussions are rare*
> *Large classes*
> *Great computer facilities*
> *Campus difficult to get around*
> *Campus is beautiful*
> *Lousy food on campus*

the English department. Disagreeing, another student warns, "Don't come to U. Maine if you want one-on-one attention," referring to "huge classes" typical to freshman year students. A call for "higher academic standards" is a common sentiment; a first-year complains, "They shouldn't have graduate students teaching classes," and a senior recalls, "My advisor did nothing to help advise me." In a fair summary, one student writes that his course work has been, "challenging, tiring, inspiring, and boring all rolled into one semester." On the administrative side, there's concern that students are treated "like second-class citizens." Plus, "relations between the president and the student body are strained," a women's studies major reports. But for most attendees, the bottom line is that "you get your money's worth in terms of tuition and living costs."

Life

Smack in the middle of the "Vacation Land" state, University of Maine students hit both the hiking trails and the bottle for diversion. A native New Yorker says going to school with outdoorsy types has exposed her to a "much healthier lifestyle, socially, mentally, physically, and environmentally." But a freshman observes, "Since we live in Maine, the only thing to do is party. Every night." Cheering on Black Bear teams, especially in hockey, is a rabid obsession, to the point that many students feel the school should "focus on students, not athletics." For nonvarsity athletes, "intramural sports are the best. They give me opportunities to meet people, have fun, and stay in shape between study sessions," quips a sophomore. A typical senior tells us, "My life is made up of active involvement in campus organizations along with participation in recreational sports and outdoor activities." Other undergrads participate in "the progressive groups on campus, which are awesome and very active."

Student Body

Considering that state universities recruit mainly from their home state, a sociology major is compelled to write, "I think for our area we are pretty diverse." Since that area is Maine, that means a predominantly snow-white group, made up of "your typical Maine-iacs" and "great people with good attitudes." Describing the aesthetic of her northeastern cohorts, a senior writes, "General fashion on campus is somewhere between a Grateful Dead concert and an L.L. Bean catalog." It follows that they're concerned with things like making their campus "more green-friendly." A sophomore calls his peers "naïve about the world outside of Maine," but apparently, "you would have to try not to like them." According to another student, "There is a strong sense of community among students at this school, and that is something to be proud of." "Everyone is welcomed with open arms," concludes one of his classmates.

ADMISSIONS

Very important factors considered by the admissions committee include: secondary school record, standardized test scores. *Important factors considered include:* class rank, essays. *Other factors considered include:* alumni/ae relation, recommendations, state residency. SAT I or ACT required; SAT I preferred. TOEFL required of all international applicants. High school diploma or GED is required. *High school units required/recommended:* 17 total required; 24 total recommended; 4 English required, 3 math required, 4 math recommended, 2 science required, 3 science recommended, 2 science lab required, 3 science lab recommended, 2 foreign language required, 2 social studies required, 3 social studies recommended, 1 history recommended, 2 elective required, 4 elective recommended.

The Inside Word

The University of Maine is much smaller than most public flagship universities, and its admissions process reflects this; it is a much more personal approach than most others use. Candidates are reviewed carefully for fit with their choice of college and major, and the committee will contact students regarding a second choice if the first doesn't seem to be a good match. Prepare your application as if you are applying to a private university.

FINANCIAL AID

Students should submit: FAFSA. The Princeton Review suggests that all financial aid forms be submitted as soon as possible after January 1. *Need-based scholarships/grants offered:* Pell, SEOG, state scholarships/grants, private scholarships, the school's own gift aid. *Loan aid offered:* FFEL Subsidized Stafford, FFEL Unsubsidized Stafford, FFEL PLUS, Federal Perkins, state loans. Federal Work-Study Program available. Institutional employment available. Applicants will be notified of awards on a rolling basis beginning on or about March 15. Off-campus job opportunities are good.

FROM THE ADMISSIONS OFFICE

"The University of Maine offers students a wide array of academic and social programs, including clubs, organizations, professional societies, and religious groups. We strive to help students feel welcome and to provide opportunities for them to become an integral part of the campus community. Visit our beautiful campus and become better acquainted with this community. Take a guided campus tour and learn about campus facilities, services and technologies, and living and dining. Our student tour guides give a first-hand view of the Black Bear experience. During your visit, meet with faculty and admission staff to learn more about your program of interest and our academic climate. The University of Maine's commitment to educational excellence and community building will be reinforced when you visit our campus!"

For even more information on this school, turn to page 370 of the "Stats" section.

UNIVERSITY OF MASSACHUSETTS—AMHERST

UNIVERSITY ADMISSIONS CENTER, AMHERST, MA 01003 • ADMISSIONS: 413-545-0222
FAX: 413-545-4312 • FINANCIAL AID: 413-545-0801 • E-MAIL: MAIL@ADMISSIONS.UMASS.EDU
WEBSITE: WWW.UMASS.EDU

Ratings

Quality of Life: 74   Academic: 72   Admissions: 75   Financial Aid: 79

Academics

State-run University of Massachusetts at Amherst offers "a great education in a liberal but structured environment," according to its students. Like many large schools, it's "a wonderful university providing countless opportunities to get involved with other students. UMass is fun and active; there is always something going on at UMass every day of the week." The university also suffers from several typical large-school maladies, including a lumbering, inefficient administration and a wide range in the quality of instruction. Of profs, opinions range from the positively positive ("All the professors love their work and it shows") to the qualifiedly positive ("The professors are an amalgamation. I've had great teachers I'll never forget and ones I already have forgotten because they were so useless. Overall, this is a good experience, but that's overall"). Others complain that "the teachers are OK, but the conditions—in the auditorium-style classrooms—inhibit learning because of external irritations like stuffiness, overheating, small chairs and desks so you can't write comfortably, etc." Membership in the Five College Consortium helps to soften some of the griping, as it allows students to use the resources available at the nearby warmer-and-fuzzier campuses of Amherst, Hampshire, Smith, and Mount Holyoke.

> **SURVEY SAYS . . .**
> *Everyone loves the Minutemen*
> *Students love Amherst, MA*
> *Hard liquor is popular, Great off-campus food*
> *Class discussions are rare*
> *Large classes, Lousy food on campus*
> *Unattractive campus, Lab facilities are great*
> *Student publications are popular*

Life

Smack in the middle of the Pioneer Valley, UMass—Amherst is an idyllic setting for collegiate New England–philes. Amherst "is a great little town" with "plenty of things to do," and "good skiing and hiking are nearby." So too are the towns of Northampton, Springfield, and a little further down the line, Albany, New York. Writes one student, "We're close enough to large cities to access them but far enough away to have a small-town feel." In this environment, "there's always something to do no matter what you like." Fraternities and sororities "exist . . . but do not dominate the social scene." University-sponsored clubs are very popular; as one student notes, "There are many groups available to join—hang-gliding club, dance team, animal rights coalition, bridge club, etc." And there's always a good time to be had nearby at night: "When it comes to having fun, there's everything from parties to dancing to restaurants, movies, or a band playing anywhere at almost any given time." Are there downsides to this little slice o' heaven? The campus itself, for one. "Be prepared to eat, breathe, and live concrete," warns one student. Students also grouse loudly and frequently about the food. Says one, "They really need to improve the food. It's like a poison that kills you a little each time."

Student Body

UMass undergrads agree that theirs is a diverse population. As one student muses, "UMass is like a big bag of potpourri, made up of a thousand different scents, which, when brought together, create the strongest and sweetest of aromas." Even so, "the students, while pretty cool, are definitely segregated." Undergrads say their fellow students are "friendly, fun, and some are even concerned about real life beyond the UMass community," but they feel they're not as pointy-headed as their neighbors at Amherst College. As one student puts it, "I'd like to think this is a fairly intellectual environment and a good place to learn, but there are still quite a few dumbasses lolling about."

ADMISSIONS

Very important factors considered by the admissions committee include: essays, secondary school record. *Important factors considered include:* character/personal qualities, extracurricular activities, standardized test scores, state residency, talent/ability. *Other factors considered include:* alumni/ae relation, class rank, minority status, recommendations, volunteer work, work experience. SAT I or ACT required. TOEFL required of all international applicants. High school diploma or GED is required. *High school units required/recommended:* 16 total required; 4 English required, 3 math required, 3 science required, 2 science lab required, 2 foreign language required, 2 social studies required, 2 elective required.

The Inside Word

Gaining admission to UMass is generally not particularly difficult, but an increase in applications last year resulted in the University increasing its selectivity. Still, most applicants with solid grades in high school should be successful. UMass is a great choice for students who might have a tougher time getting in at the other Five College Consortium members.

FINANCIAL AID

Students should submit: FAFSA. The Princeton Review suggests that all financial aid forms be submitted as soon as possible after January 1. *Need-based scholarships/grants offered:* Pell, SEOG, state scholarships/grants, private scholarships, the school's own gift aid. *Loan aid offered:* Direct Subsidized Stafford, Direct Unsubsidized Stafford, Direct PLUS, Federal Perkins, state loans, William D. Ford Federal Direct (subsidized and unsubsidized) Loans. Federal Work-Study Program available. Institutional employment available. Applicants will be notified of awards on a rolling basis beginning on or about April 1. Off-campus job opportunities are good.

FROM THE ADMISSIONS OFFICE

"The University of Massachusetts—Amherst is the largest public university in New England, offering its students an almost limitless variety of academic programs and activities. Nearly 100 majors are offered, including a unique program called Bachelor's Degree with Individual Concentration (BDIC) in which students create their own program of study. The outstanding faculty of 1,100 includes novelist John Wideman, Pulitzer Prize winners Madeleine Blais and James Tate, National Medal of Science winner Lynn Margulis, and five members of the prestigious National Academy of Sciences. Students can take courses through the honors program and sample classes at nearby Amherst, Hampshire, Mount Holyoke, and Smith Colleges at no extra charge. Students can take classes in the residence halls with other dorm residents through Residential Academic Programs (RAP), and first-year students may be asked to participate in the Talent Advancement Programs (TAP) in which students with the same majors live and take classes together. And the university's extensive library system is the largest at any public institution in the Northeast. Extracurricular activities include more than 200 clubs and organizations, fraternities and sororities, multicultural and religious centers, and NCAA Division I sports for men and women. Award-winning student-operated businesses, the largest college daily newspaper in the region, and an active student government provide hands-on experiences. About 5,000 students a year participate in the intramural sports program. The picturesque New England town of Amherst offers shopping and dining, and the ski slopes of western Massachusetts and southern Vermont are close by."

For even more information on this school, turn to page 371 of the "Stats" section.

University of Massachusetts—Lowell

Office of Undergrad Admissions, 883 Broadway Street Room 110, Lowell, MA 01854-5104
Admissions: 978-934-3931 • Fax: 978-934-3086 • E-mail: admissions@uml.edu • Website: www.uml.edu

Ratings
Quality of Life: 73   Academic: 74   Admissions: 63   Financial Aid: 73

Academics

Many of the University of Massachusetts at Lowell's strengths lie in majors typically popular at state schools: the business, engineering, criminal justice, nursing programs here, to name just a few, are all fine. Lowell is distinguished from the pack, however, by a few unusual offerings, particularly in music. The music business program, for example, prepares students for the cut-throat worlds of musical performance, recording, and marketing. Better still is the sound-recording technology program, "offered in very few schools in this country. Lowell will also soon be offering a master's in sound-recording technology that won't be offered anywhere else," according to one undergrad. Students here appreciate the wide range of choices and resources available to them but still voice complaints often heard from undergraduates at state schools. Writes one student, "Up until the senior-level classes, the quality of 'teaching' was really poor. A lot of the faculty have been here forever, and it's time for them to move on. The school needs some fresh blood with innovative ideas, rather than old fogies who have taught the same class the same way for the last 40 years." Students also feel strongly that Lowell "definitely needs more faculty in order to be able to offer necessary classes," and grouse that "the administration tends to drive you around in circles."

> **SURVEY SAYS . . .**
> *Students get along with local community*
> *(Almost) everyone plays intramural sports*
> *Diverse students interact*
> *Great computer facilities*
> *School is well run*
> *Very little beer drinking*

Life

Students agree that "Lowell is a great place to be. It isn't far from Boston, and in fact, there is a commuter rail that runs from Lowell into North Station. It's about 20 minutes from Nashua and other New Hampshire cities and towns. There's a great movie theatre close by and plenty of shopping. The music organizations (concert band, wind ensemble, marching band, etc.) have been a big part of my time here." About the only drawback, students say, is that the main campus is located in a rundown neighborhood, although one undergrad notes "the safety on campus is outstanding." Lowell undergrads love to party—in bars if they're old enough, or at parties in dorms, apartments, and the school's unrecognized but active frats if they're not—but otherwise "nobody really goes to campus events, except maybe something like 'Battle of the Bands.' Most people just kind of go off campus and do their own thing." Students also tell us that "the school has great organized clubs and organizations. We have clubs for all sports and hobbies; whatever you like to do there is a club for it here." As an added bonus, "the athletic facilities over the past four years have gone through the roof with the addition of the Tsongas Arena for hockey; LeLacheur Park (home of Red Sox minor league affiliate Lowell Spinners) for baseball; an artificial turf stadium for football, field hockey, and soccer; and the newly completed student center in close proximity to the residence halls." The school's many commuter students concur that the parking situation is "horrible."

Student Body

"Located in the heart of Lowell, UML is quite a diverse school," explains one undergraduate. "Engineering is particularly strong, attracting a lot of Indian and Asian students. Some of the more active on-campus organizations are diversity oriented: ALANA is for African American, Asian, and Latino students; Spectrum, for gay and lesbian students; Bi-Gala, for bisexual, gay, and lesbian students." Students tell us that "UMass seems to have a fairly good sense of community, especially among the students that do live in the dorms. I do wish, however, that there were more events or activities planned for commuting students to get involved with each other in a nonacademic atmosphere." For the large commuter population, the sense of community is not as strong; "Basically," says one, "we are just a lot of individuals."

ADMISSIONS

Very important factors considered by the admissions committee include: secondary school record and standardized test scores. *Important factors considered include:* essays and recommendations. *Other factors considered include:* character/personal qualities, extracurricular activities, interview, talent/ability, volunteer work, and work experience. SAT I or ACT required, SAT I preferred. TOEFL required of all international applicants. High school diploma is required and GED is accepted. *High school units required/recommended:* 16 total are required; 4 English required, 3 math required, 3 science required, 2 science lab required, 2 foreign language required, 2 social studies required, 2 elective required.

The Inside Word

Solid academic disciplines attract high-caliber students to UML, many of whom strive to meet academic standards that belie moderate admissions requirements.

FINANCIAL AID

Students should submit: FAFSA. The Princeton Review suggests that all financial aid forms be submitted as soon as possible after January 1. *Need-based scholarships/grants offered:* Pell, SEOG, state scholarships/grants, private scholarships, and the school's own gift aid. *Loan aid offered:* Direct subsidized Stafford, Direct Unsubsidized Stafford, Direct PLUS, Federal Perkins, and state. Federal Work-Study Program available. Institutional employment available. Applicants will be notified of awards on a rolling basis beginning on or about March 24. Off-campus job opportunities are excellent.

For even more information on this school, turn to page 372 of the "Stats" section.

UNIVERSITY OF NEW HAMPSHIRE

4 GARRISON AVENUE, DURHAM, NH 03824 • ADMISSIONS: 603-862-1360 • FAX: 603-862-0077
FINANCIAL AID: 603-862-3600 • E-MAIL: ADMISSIONS@UNH.EDU • WEBSITE: WWW.UNH.EDU

Ratings

Quality of Life: 87   Academic: 75   Admissions: 78   Financial Aid: 86

Academics

As is the case at most large, public universities, professors at UNH don't coddle students. It's up to the latter to take the initiative to get to know the former or to locate the resources they need to develop academically. Enterprising students will find, however, that "the professors are very open" when approached. Notwithstanding a few bad-apple instructors, most students report that their "professors are excellent." Some of the

> **SURVEY SAYS . . .**
> *Lots of beer drinking*
> *Campus is beautiful*
> *Great library*
> *Athletic facilities are great*
> *Everyone loves the Wildcats*
> *Hard liquor is popular*
> *Students are happy*
> *(Almost) everyone smokes*
> *Great off-campus food*
> *(Almost) everyone plays intramural sports*

highlights of UNH academics include the Undergraduate Research Opportunities Program (UROP), which matches students interested in doing independent research with an appropriate faculty advisor and hooks them up with the necessary funds to accomplish said research. The engineering department gets rave reviews as well. Some students complain that they have trouble finding quiet space to work on their studies, though: "The library closes promptly at midnight Sunday–Thursday, and 8 p.m. on Friday and Saturday." But most of the student dissatisfaction at UNH stems from the administrative problems, such as class registration. A sophomore grumbles, "I have not been able to enroll in any of my first-choice courses. This is due to overbooking and the classes not being offered."

Life

Hockey is basically an institution at UNH, drawing a consistent stream of participants and spectators, since "UNH [intercollegiate] hockey tickets are free to students." In general, athleticism runs deep at this "beautiful" campus in the "kind of isolated" town of Durham, New Hampshire. "Skiing, biking, hiking"—all of these outdoor activities are easy to access. For the indoors-inclined, student-run activities, including "laser tag, bingo, bowling, poetry and story readings," as well as "local band performances," are popular. For chem-free students "there is an organization here called Weekend Warriors that sponsors nonalcoholic events like carnivals and movie nights." For drinkers, "Frat Row"—center of the "huge Greek life" on campus—is a popular party destination. Recreational drug use also has its place at UNH. According to an undergrad, "The University of New Hampshire is drenched with a sweet perfume—the tireless scent of a blunt and an open bottle." Still, some students say that the university's "party school" label is not entirely deserved because most people "only drink on occasion or choose not to drink at all." Students don't find much to do in tiny hometown Durham. Instead, when they need time away from school, students take advantage of the "shuttle service" to nearby "cities like Dover, Newmarket, and Portsmouth."

Student Body

About 60 percent of UNH students hail from New Hampshire, with many others coming from nearby Massachusetts, Maine, and Connecticut. "Ethnic diversity is strongly lacking" on campus, which leads some students to cry, "HOMOGENEOUS." But just in skin color. One student offers this colorful breakdown: "It works like this—there are two extremes, the Super Preps and the Hippies. The Super Preps wear Abercrombie and Fitch and drink imported beer. They are generally stodgy and stuck up, upper-class suburban kids who couldn't get into Ivy League schools. On the other side of the spectrum you have the hippies. They wear anything earthy, secondhand, or hand-made. They don't drink beer, they drink chai and smoke pot. In between these two extremes lies most of the UNH population. You have your jocks who drink Natty Ice and keg beer and generally associate with other jocks. You have your Trendoids who carry cell phones and constantly change their wardrobe. You have your Greeks who are loyal to each other despite the fact that they aren't a respectable bunch. You've got your usual conglomeration of sluts and drawer-droppers who go out on weekends in search of anything that is remotely human and willing to have sex with it. You've got your free spirits who run the Student Cable Access Network (SCAN) and will do anything anywhere as long as it's fun. You've got your druggies who smoke anything you can roll into a cigarette paper." Despite all of these cliques, "these groups will interact with each other" and "have fun together."

ADMISSIONS

Very important factors considered by the admissions committee include: secondary school record. *Important factors considered include:* class rank, essays, recommendations, standardized test scores, state residency. *Other factors considered include:* alumni/ae relation, character/personal qualities, extracurricular activities, geographical residence, minority status, talent/ability, volunteer work, work experience. SAT I or ACT required, SAT I preferred. TOEFL required of all international applicants. High school diploma or GED is required. *High school units required/recommended:* 18 total recommended; 4 English recommended, 4 math recommended, 4 science recommended, 4 science lab recommended, 3 foreign language recommended, 3 social studies recommended.

The Inside Word

New Hampshire's emphasis on academic accomplishment in the admissions process makes it clear that the admissions committee is looking for students who have taken high school seriously. Standardized tests take as much of a backseat here as is possible at a large public university.

FINANCIAL AID

Students should submit: FAFSA. The Princeton Review suggests that all financial aid forms be submitted as soon as possible after January 1. *Need-based scholarships/grants offered:* Pell, SEOG, state scholarships/grants, private scholarships, the school's own gift aid. *Loan aid offered:* FFEL Subsidized Stafford, FFEL Unsubsidized Stafford, FFEL PLUS, Federal Perkins, state loans, college/university loans from institutional funds. Federal Work-Study Program available. Institutional employment available. Applicants will be notified of awards on a rolling basis beginning on or about March 1. Off-campus job opportunities are excellent.

FROM THE ADMISSIONS OFFICE

"The University of New Hampshire is a public university founded in 1866 with an undergraduate population of 11,000 students. UNH offers an excellent education at a reasonable cost to students with a broad range of interests. Over 100 majors, 2,000 courses, and 130 student clubs and organizations are offered. Programs that provide valuable experience include the honors program, undergraduate research, internships, study abroad, and national exchange. UNH's location also caters to a wide range of interests. The campus itself is in a small town setting, surrounded by woods and farms; within 20 minutes is the Atlantic coastline, and just over an hour away are the White Mountains, Boston, and Portland."

For even more information on this school, turn to page 372 of the "Stats" section.

UNIVERSITY OF RHODE ISLAND

14 UPPER COLLEGE ROAD, KINGSTON, RI 02881-1391 • ADMISSIONS: 401-874-7000 • FAX: 401-874-5523
FINANCIAL AID: 401-874-9500 • E-MAIL: URIADMIT@ETA1.URI.EDU • WEBSITE: WWW.URI.EDU/ADMISSIONS

Ratings
Quality of Life: 81   Academic: 73   Admissions: 72   Financial Aid: 79

Academics

The mostly pre-professional students at the University of Rhode Island tell us their school has "respectable academics." Although some classes are huge, the smaller sections and seminars students deem "extremely helpful." Regarding the quality of the professors and teaching assistants who instruct these courses, student opinion is decidedly mixed. There are professors who "don't care about you at all" and whose

> **SURVEY SAYS . . .**
> *Frats and sororities dominate social scene*
> *Everyone loves the Rams*
> *(Almost) everyone smokes*
> *Great computer facilities, Lab facilities are great*
> *Hard liquor is popular, Large classes*
> *Lousy food on campus*
> *Campus difficult to get around*
> *High cost of living*
> *Musical organizations aren't popular*

"teaching skills leave much to be desired," but "there are also some good, challenging ones." Indeed, a great many profs at URI are "engaged and interested in what they're trying to teach" and "well-informed and knowledgeable in their subjects." Several electrical engineers single out the faculty in their department as "exceptional." Also, "though there are a lot of graduate assistants and new professors teaching lower-level classes, they do a great job," pledges a junior. Students give a thumbs-up to the "good computer labs" here and say the administration is "accommodating." In addition to a nationally celebrated oceanography program, popular majors at URI include education, business, engineering, psychology, communications, nursing, and pharmacy.

Life

The alcohol policies on this "quintessential New England" campus are strict—"too strict," according to some students. To drink, "we have to drive to the bars—there's not much on campus," laments a junior. Still, the parties seem to be making a comeback. Between the happening "off-campus party scene" and "strong Greek system," many students manage to "get blasted" on a regular basis. For students who do pledge, "Greek Week and Homecoming are the best times of the year." Beyond partying, students enjoy "sports, ice skating, shopping, bowling," or one of the more than 80 organizations offered by the Student Entertainment Committee and the Office of Student Life. But be aware that "this is a big school," declares a junior. "If you feel the need to be pampered, you're in the wrong place. If you are an easily adjustable person, you can find your niche and really fit in." The newly powerful men's basketball team is very popular; "I love cheering for the school," beams a freshman. URI students also focus locally, "always helping the community." On campus, "classrooms are old and buildings are run down," and security is an issue, but the "atrocious" parking situation is "the biggest problem" at the school. When they need a big-city fix, students head off to Providence, about 40 minutes away by car, or Boston, a little farther at two hours.

Student Body

Lots of students choose URI because it is "close to home" and "cheap," especially for in-state residents, who make up a majority here. Approximately 62 percent of the students at URI hail from Rhode Island; the next most represented states—New Jersey and Massachusetts—show up a distant second with about 11 percent each. While some students are "snobby," most describe themselves as "easygoing," "polite," "helpful," and "very friendly." One first-year says she gets along with other students "like friends from home." The overall population is reasonably diverse, and "for the most part, everyone gets along," although different ethnic groups "do not mesh well." Students report "quite a bit of racial tension" on campus

ADMISSIONS

Very important factors considered by the admissions committee include: secondary school record. *Important factors considered include:* character/personal qualities, class rank, geographical residence, minority status, standardized test scores, state residency, talent/ability. *Other factors considered include:* alumni/ae relation, essays, extracurricular activities, interview, recommendations, volunteer work, work experience. SAT I or ACT required. TOEFL required of all international applicants. High school diploma or GED is required. *High school units required/recommended:* 18 total required; 4 English required, 3 math required, 4 math recommended, 2 science required, 3 science recommended, 2 science lab required, 2 foreign language required, 3 foreign language recommended, 2 social studies required, 3 social studies recommended, 5 elective required.

The Inside Word

Any candidate with solid grades is likely to find the university's admissions committee to be welcoming. The yield of admits who enroll is low and the state's population small. Out-of-state students are attractive to URI because they are sorely needed to fill out the student body. Students who graduate in the top 10 percent of their class are good scholarship bets.

FINANCIAL AID

Students should submit: FAFSA. No deadline for regular filing. The Princeton Review suggests that all financial aid forms be submitted as soon as possible after January 1. *Need-based scholarships/grants offered:* Pell, SEOG, state scholarships/grants, private scholarships, the school's own gift aid. *Loan aid offered:* Direct Subsidized Stafford, Direct Unsubsidized Stafford, Direct PLUS, Federal Perkins, Federal Nursing, college/university loans from institutional funds, health professions loan. Federal Work-Study Program available. Institutional employment available. Applicants will be notified of awards on a rolling basis beginning on or about March 15. Off-campus job opportunities are excellent.

FROM THE ADMISSIONS OFFICE

"Outstanding freshman candidates with minimum SAT scores of 1150 who rank in the top third of their class are eligible for consideration for a Centennial Scholarship ranging up to full tuition. The scholarships are renewable each semester if the student maintains continuous full-time enrollment and a 3.0 average or better. Eligibility requires a completed admissions application received by our December 15 Early Action deadline. Applications and information received after December 15 cannot be considered. (High school students who present more than 23 college credits are considered transfer applicants and are not eligible for Centennial Scholarships). Like the permanent granite cornerstones that grace its stately buildings, the University of Rhode Island was founded in the lasting tradition of the land-grant colleges and later became one of the original crop of national sea-grant colleges. Observing its centennial in 1992, the state's largest university prepares its students to meet the challenges of the twenty-first century."

For even more information on this school, turn to page 373 of the "Stats" section.

UNIVERSITY OF ROCHESTER

Box 270251, ROCHESTER, NY 14627-0251 • ADMISSIONS: 716-275-3221 • FAX: 716-461-4595
FINANCIAL AID: 716-275-3226 • E-MAIL: ADMIT@ADMISSIONS.ROCHESTER.EDU • WEBSITE: WWW.ROCHESTER.EDU

Ratings

Quality of Life: 82   Academic: 88   Admissions: 88   Financial Aid: 83

Academics

The University of Rochester has traditionally been known best for its math and science departments. However, the "home of the Bausch & Lomb scholars and Xerox" has enough diversity in its academic offerings to "dispel the myth that the U of R is solely an engineering/pre-med breeding

> **SURVEY SAYS . . .**
> *Popular college radio, Great library*
> *Theater is hot, Dorms are like palaces*
> *(Almost) everyone plays intramural sports*
> *Intercollegiate sports unpopular or nonexistent*
> *Athletic facilities need improving*
> *Large classes, Musical organizations are hot*

ground." Although numerous students consider the workload "heavy and tough—they don't mess around!" most also believe their rigorous courses are "extremely rewarding." Rochester has several unique opportunities to offer its students; one is the world-renowned Eastman School of Music (the administration encourages qualified students to take courses there). Distinct to the U of R is a program called "Take Five," an attractive option for students who find themselves unable to fit enough courses of interest into a four-year schedule. One student writes, "As a chemical engineer, I have very little time to take courses outside my major. The U of R has given me the opportunity to stay here for an additional year—tuition-free—to pursue my interest in Japanese history and culture." While some students claim that certain professors "are more interested in their research than they are in undergrads," in general students here are positive and enthusiastic about their academic life; some consider the U of R "better than the Ivies but without the reputation—it's the jewel of upper New York State."

Life

Cold weather is a given in Rochester: "Siberia for eight months of the year" is a popular description among students we surveyed. It is actually possible to avoid a great deal of winter misery by using the convenient indoor tunnels beneath the campus. Nevertheless, the consensus seems to be that of one student who notes, "I just wish we could take the whole school and place it in California or somewhere where there is no snow." Despite the academic pressures at the U of R (or perhaps because of them), weekends are full of partying opportunities. Fraternities and sororities figure prominently in the social scene, and Greek activities dominate. One student observes, "Many people claim to be anti-Greek, but they tend to show up at frat parties anyway." There are varying degrees of social contentment here; some students have "too many parties to choose from," some contend that "freshman males lead lives of quiet desperation," and some prefer to socialize electronically in the generally comfy and spacious dorms.

Student Body

The typical student at the University of Rochester is politically moderate, not politically active. A small private school, despite its public-sounding name, the U of R has made an effort to increase student diversity, and minorities account for more than a fifth of the student body. However, some students still feel "the minority population is lacking . . . especially in the black and Hispanic sectors."

ADMISSIONS

Very important factors considered by the admissions committee include: secondary school record, standardized test scores. *Important factors considered include:* character/personal qualities, class rank, essays, recommendations, talent/ability. *Other factors considered include:* alumni/ae relation, extracurricular activities, minority status, volunteer work, work experience. SAT I or ACT required. TOEFL required of all international applicants. High school diploma or GED is required. *High school units required/recommended:* 4 total recommended; 4 English recommended, 4 math recommended, 3 science recommended, 4 science lab recommended, 2 foreign language recommended, 2 social studies recommended.

The Inside Word

The University of Rochester is definitely a good school, but the competition takes away three-fourths of the university's admits. Many students use Rochester as a safety; this hinders the university's ability to move up among top national institutions in selectivity. It also makes U of R a very solid choice for above-average students who aren't Ivy material.

FINANCIAL AID

Students should submit: FAFSA, CSS/Financial Aid PROFILE, state aid form, noncustodial (divorced/separated) parent's statement. Regular filing deadline is February 1. The Princeton Review suggests that all financial aid forms be submitted as soon as possible after January 1. *Need-based scholarships/grants offered:* Pell, SEOG, state scholarships/grants, private scholarships, the school's own gift aid. Federal Work-Study Program available. Institutional employment available. Applicants will be notified of awards on or about April 1. Off-campus job opportunities are excellent.

FROM THE ADMISSIONS OFFICE

"A campus visit can be one of the most important (and most enjoyable) components of a college search. Visiting Rochester can provide you with the opportunity to experience for yourself the traditions and innovations of our university. Whether you visit a class, tour the campus, or meet with a professor or coach, you'll learn a great deal about the power of a Rochester education—with advantages that begin during your undergraduate years and continue after graduation. No other school combines the wealth of academic programs on the personal scale that the University of Rochester offers. Our students achieve academic excellence in a university setting that encourages frequent, informal contact with distinguished faculty. Our faculty-designed 'Rochester Renaissance Curriculum' allows students to spend as much of their time as possible studying subjects they enjoy so much that they stop watching the clock,' says William Scott Green, dean of the undergraduate college. At the heart of the Renaissance Curriculum is the Quest Program. Quest courses are seminar-sized offerings that encourage you to solve problems through investigations and exploration . . . much the same way our faculty do. Working alongside your professor, you will test theories and explore education frontiers on a campus with some of the best resources in the world, driven by a curriculum that is truly unprecedented."

For even more information on this school, turn to page 374 of the "Stats" section.

UNIVERSITY OF SOUTHERN MAINE

37 COLLEGE AVENUE, GORHAM, ME 04038 • ADMISSIONS: 207-780-5670 • FAX: 207-780-5640
E-MAIL: USMADM@USM.MAINE.EDU • WEBSITE: WWW.USM.MAINE.EDU

Ratings
Quality of Life: 73   Academic: 72   Admissions: 65   Financial Aid: 72

Academics

Many USM students share the opinion of one transfer student who asserts that "for the price, I am still amazed at the quality of education and positive learning environment that this university

> **SURVEY SAYS . . .**
> *Diversity lacking on campus*
> *School is well run, Lousy food on campus*
> *Students get along with local community*

provides." The professors tend to be "obsessed with the subject they teach" and "focused on educating and informing their students." One student states, "I'm pleased to say that they do employ some outstanding teachers who truly care about their students and the subject matter." Instructors "are concerned not only with my scholastic achievements, but also my well-being as a maturing adult." They also represent a "variety of personalities and teaching styles" so there's something for everyone. Business classes in particular are called "very informative and helpful" in this fairly rigorous environment where "students need to work for their grades. You can't get away with as much as you'd expect" at such a large public university. The administration reportedly "works hard to support the large percentage of commuter students"; however, certain people feel that "students are treated like numbers." The advising system, called "a joke" by some, could be improved, considering that "no real advising goes on." But in the final analysis, most students are impressed by "the university's capability to be flexible," specifically "with class scheduling."

Life

Split between the rural Gorham campus and the more urban Portland location, USM enables a variety of lifestyles. One student says, "Finding things to do around either campus is pretty easy, and there are a lot of fun options, including paintball, the mall, the beaches, the bars, and tons of restaurants." A few undergraduates complain that "there aren't any activities to bring us together," but others cite the ever-popular "comedians, hypnotists, open-mic nights, karaoke, and other fun things to do on Thursday and Friday nights." If that's not enough, students can cheer on the "really good women's hockey team, men's and women's basketball teams, and baseball team." To round out the social scene, "there is always a fraternity party on the weekends," or students "spend weekend nights in downtown Portland." From the Gorham front, one undergraduate editorializes, "I don't think that the citizens of this town realize that they can't keep college life out, so they are going to have to learn to work with us, not against us."

Student Body

In a characteristic statement of the student body, one undergraduate observes, "A lot of times it feels like USM has two student bodies—the residential students and the commuter students." Of approximately 4,500 students, one undergrad estimates that "about 75 percent are commuters," largely upperclassmen who chose to live off campus in apartments and are thus less integrated in campus life. Many enjoy the fact that "most of the students going here have lives outside of college to make them a bit more real." Also, the large number of nontraditional students can "make for an eye-opening and awesome experience for those just coming out of high school." The population includes "people from all walks of life," and students note "a lot of diversity in sexuality, which is generally accepted." One out-of-state student says she "misses the diversity" of home but reminds readers that "Maine does not have much racial diversity, so it is no surprise." Some definite dividing lines crop up in the cafeteria: "The artsy students sit to the left of the salad bar, and the jocks and the frat kids sit to the right. There is an unspoken rule that you don't cross over to the other side." Despite this fatuousness, the majority of USM-ers are described as "friendly, open minded, and easygoing."

ADMISSIONS

Very important factors considered by the admissions committee include: secondary school record, GPA, class rank, and standardized test scores. *Important factors considered include:* essays and recommendations. *Other factors considered include:* alumni/ae relation, character/personal qualities, extracurricular activities, geographical residence, interview, minority status, state residency, talent/ability, volunteer work, and work experience. SAT I or ACT required. TOEFL required of all international applicants. High school diploma is required and GED is accepted. *High school units required/recommended:* 16 total are required; 4 English required, 3 math required, 4 math recommended, 2 science required, 3 science recommended, 2 science lab required, 3 science lab recommended, 2 foreign language required, 3 foreign language recommended, 1 social studies required, 3 social studies recommended, 1 history required.

The Inside Word

USM's price tag would be much higher if dollars were equated with the faculty's dedication to the students. The result: A wellspring of educational opportunity.

FINANCIAL AID

Students should submit: FAFSA. Regular Filing deadline is February 15. The Princeton Review suggests that all financial aid forms be submitted as soon as possible after January 1. *Need-based scholarships/grants offered:* Pell, SEOG, state scholarships/grants, private scholarships, and the school's own gift aid. *Loan aid offered:* FFEL Subsidized Stafford, FFEL Unsubsidized Stafford, FFEL PLUS, Federal Perkins, Federal Nursing, and state. Federal Work-Study Program available. Institutional employment available. Applicants will be notified of awards on a rolling basis beginning on or about March 15. Off-campus job opportunities are excellent.

FROM THE ADMISSIONS OFFICE

"At the University of Southern Maine you will find the personalized atmosphere and learning environment of a small, New England, residential college combined with the opportunities typically available only at large, national universities. Our student body of approximately 4,600 full-time undergraduates, 4,000 part-time and nondegree students, and 2,000 graduate students enables us to be large enough to provide a wide range of offerings, yet small enough to offer classes averaging around 22 students. USM offers more than 50 majors and 40 additional academic programs, 25 NCAA Division III athletic teams, and nearly 100 student clubs and organizations, yet our student/faculty ratio is only 13:1.

"Our students come from 35 states and 37 countries. Sixty percent of our entering freshmen choose to live on campus. Almost half of our total full-time undergraduate population resides in university housing, while many upperclassmen choose to live with their classmates in off-campus apartments in the Portland area.

"Within a two-hour drive north of Boston, the vibrant city of Portland is located along the scenic southern Maine coastline, with the Atlantic Ocean on one side and majestic mountains and lakes on the other. Our national reputation as one of the best cities for outdoor recreation; the abundant art, music, and theater scenes; and the 35,000 college students that live within an hour's drive make Portland an ideal location to be a college student."

For even more information on this school, turn to page 374 of the "Stats" section.

UNIVERSITY OF VERMONT

OFFICE OF ADMISSIONS, 194 S. PROSPECT STREET, BURLINGTON, VT 05401-3596 • ADMISSIONS: 802-656-3370
FAX: 802-656-8611 • FINANCIAL AID: 802-656-3156 • E-MAIL: ADMISSIONS@UVM.EDU
WEBSITE: WWW.UVM.EDU

Ratings

Quality of Life: 88   Academic: 76   Admissions: 77   Financial Aid: 83

Academics

There's no denying that many choose University of Vermont for its lovely ski-resort location and party-school reputation, but that doesn't mean students can't get a first-rate education here as well. Explains one student, "There may be some kids who are here for a good time and a good time only, but many of us are here for a

> **SURVEY SAYS . . .**
> *Students love Burlington, VT*
> *Diversity lacking on campus*
> *Great off-campus food*
> *Musical organizations aren't popular*
> *Students aren't religious, Large classes*
> *Student government is unpopular*
> *Dorms are like dungeons*

strong education." Others point out that "if you take an active role in your education—if you really believe that no one is going to hand it to you—it is easy to get a great education here." UVM's overall academic reputation is quite solid, and deservedly so. The university is particularly strong in animal science and health- and environment-related areas; students report that psychology, political science, and business and management are also popular majors. Undergrads note that "despite large class sizes, the professors are very dynamic and really get the class involved" and that "the larger classes are intimidating, but most offer helpful discussion groups that are small and more personal." Advises one student, "To get the most out of your tuition, use as many study aids as you can, including study groups, tutors, professors, and supplemental instruction. They will all improve your grades, and they are usually free to students." Professors receive unusually high praise for state-university instructors. Students commend them as "down-to-earth and easy to relate to" and report that they're "open [to] discussions, ideas, and suggestions. A lot of my professors encourage creativity and care about their students and their performance." The administration, on the other hand, "is a nightmare. Getting things done in the UVM bureaucracy is like pulling teeth."

Life

Just how intense the party scene is at UVM is a matter of some debate. According to many, "Our school is a shameless party school. People here think about where their next beer is coming from." Others take a more nuanced view, explaining that "it's true that UVM is a big party school, but only for those who choose it. There are many students here who study hard, have fun with their friends, participate in athletic activities, and still make the grade." For those who do choose partying, "people smoke a lot of pot, and there are some good hallucinogens floating around, but not quite as much drinking as other colleges. This is good, though—it makes the atmosphere chill instead of drunk and rowdy." That is, until "The Man" shows up. "Police are always in the dorms, and they have little respect for students and our rights," complain several undergrads. Nearly all students agree that UVM is ideally located for those who love outdoor winter activities. "What other school has ski mountains 20 minutes away, a lake 5 minutes away, and a beach 10 minutes away?" asks one student. Students love Burlington, "an amazing town for its size. There are a ton of things to do," including "concerts, shows, movies, tons of stores, the waterfront: there's always life downtown." On the weekends," notes one student, "most of us go downtown shopping or to the lake during the day. At night, we go to the dance clubs or off-campus parties," though, of course, "always pre-gamed (i.e. drunk or stoned before we arrive)."

Student Body

Many UVM undergrads feel that their student body provides "a wide variety of social groups. From hippies to jocks, UVM has it all." To these happy undergrads, "the atmosphere up here is real laid-back and relaxed. I noticed when I first came up here that if you smile at someone or say 'hi' to a stranger, they almost always say 'hi' back. People up here are cool." They also note that "the school does an excellent job of making its many out-of-state students feel comfortable, accepted, and appreciated. For us, this truly is a home away from home." Some complain that "sometimes I feel as if I'm surrounded by hippies, extreme environmentalists, and communists. [Though] they aren't that widespread on campus, they're just very vocal."

ADMISSIONS

Very important factors considered by the admissions committee include: secondary school record. *Important factors considered include:* alumni/ae relation, character/personal qualities, class rank, essays, minority status, standardized test scores, state residency. *Other factors considered include:* extracurricular activities, geographical residence, interview, recommendations, talent/ability, volunteer work, work experience. SAT I or ACT required. TOEFL required of all international applicants. High school diploma or GED is required. *High school units required/recommended:* 16 total required; 4 English required, 3 math required, 2 science required, 1 science lab required, 2 foreign language required, 3 social studies required.

The Inside Word

UVM is one of the most popular public universities in the country, and its admissions standards are significantly more competitive for out-of-state students. Nonresidents shouldn't get too anxiety-ridden about getting in; more than half of the student body comes from elsewhere. Candidates with above-average academic profiles should be in good shape.

FINANCIAL AID

Students should submit: FAFSA. Regular filing deadline is March 15. The Princeton Review suggests that all financial aid forms be submitted as soon as possible after January 1. *Need-based scholarships/grants offered:* Pell, SEOG, state scholarships/grants, private scholarships, the school's own gift aid, Federal Nursing. *Loan aid offered:* FFEL Subsidized Stafford, FFEL Unsubsidized Stafford, FFEL PLUS, Federal Perkins, Federal Nursing, college/university loans from institutional funds. Federal Work-Study Program available. Institutional employment available. Applicants will be notified of awards on a rolling basis beginning on or about March 15. Off-campus job opportunities are excellent.

FROM THE ADMISSIONS OFFICE

"The University of Vermont blends the close faculty-student relationships most commonly found in a small liberal arts college with the dynamic exchange of knowledge associated with a research university. This is not surprising because UVM is both. A comprehensive research university offering nearly 100 undergraduate majors and extensive offerings through its Graduate College and College of Medicine, UVM has chosen to keep its enrollment relatively small. UVM prides itself on the richness of its undergraduate experience. Distinguished senior faculty teach introductory courses in their fields. They also advise not only juniors and seniors, but also first- and second-year students, and work collaboratively with undergraduates on research initiatives. Students find extensive opportunities to test classroom knowledge in field through practicums, academic internships, and community service. More than 90 student organizations (involving 80 percent of the student body), 26 Division I varsity teams, 18 intercollegiate club and 24 intramural sports programs, and a packed schedule of cultural events fill in where the classroom leaves off."

For even more information on this school, turn to page 375 of the "Stats" section.

VASSAR COLLEGE

124 RAYMOND AVENUE, POUGHKEEPSIE, NY 12604 • ADMISSIONS: 845-437-7300 • FAX: 845-437-7063
FINANCIAL AID: 845-437-5320 • E-MAIL: ADMISSIONS@VASSAR.EDU • WEBSITE: WWW.VASSAR.EDU

Ratings
Quality of Life: 82   Academic: 94   Admissions: 95   Financial Aid: 86

Academics

Students say that Vassar's goal is "teaching students to think," and that the college achieves this end by affording undergraduates a high degree of academic freedom. "Vassar trusts that I can achieve my academic goals without strict guidance" is one common sentiment among students. Most here "love that we have no core curriculum," leaving them time to pursue their "genuine interests." Though the "workload is very challenging," students feel supported by their "impressive, friendly, empathetic," and "very encouraging" professors. "If you had a question for one of my professors after class, she would talk to you for half an hour and not realize how much time had gone by," writes a sophomore. Instructors "love what they do and want you to do well," and the small class sizes "force us to contribute to discussions." Students perceive "significant academic competitiveness" among undergraduates; writes one, "Sometimes Vassar students are a bit too intense about academics." A few complaints arise regarding the "limited number of classes and sections." Certain students groan that the administration "likes to maintain absurd amounts of authority." Still others call for "increased communication between administration and students." But a sophomore offer the following challenge: "Tell me any other college where the president would take the time to e-mail me personally to tell me that she's a fan of my newspaper column." In the end, a student in the American culture department avers that a Vassar education is "about self-development and intellectual glory."

> ### SURVEY SAYS . . .
> (Almost) everyone plays intramural sports
> Students get along with local community
> Diverse students interact
> Library needs improving

Life

In their fairly isolated location in the Hudson Valley, most students feel "restricted to on-campus activities." Luckily, "on any given Friday, there's usually a concert, lecture, play, and comedy performance." Other students frequent The Mug, the college's dance club and bar, or hit the live music performances at the campus café every Thursday. One student writes, "For fun, most people are drinking," and another adds that students have "no social life if you don't drink or take drugs recreationally." The administration, however, has been "cracking down lately with new party rules," putting a damper on the scene. As an alternative, students happily resort to sledding on cafeteria trays, also known as tray-ing. When this grows tiresome—or when the snow melts—students take advantage of their "great location close to New York City." Several respondents note the abundant "opportunities for leadership positions and internships" at Vassar, emphasizing that "the activist groups here are great." Surveys repeatedly praise the beautiful campus, the perfect surroundings in which to pursue Vassar students' favorite pastime of all: "finding yourself."

Student Body

The most common opinion regarding the undergraduate population of Vassar goes something like, "An atypical student here is the sort who would be a typical student elsewhere." In a place where students "conform by not conforming," the climate remains "very accepting of individuality," prompting one student to describe her peers as "tolerant, almost to the point of apathy." If forced to pin down a stereotype, one might try one or all of: "hippie, style conscious, smart, left wing, idealist, East-Village-y." Less generous characterizations call students "white rich kids with holes in their clothes" or "liberal people feeling good about it." Though some people see "no ideological diversity," others are quick to point out that the campus is "getting more conservative" and that "there are spiritual and religious people here." The student body is "very accepting in terms of sexuality," which can be a boon, considering that 60 percent of the population is female. Basically, these "pretty people with lots of talent" will continue to "pride themselves on being unique and involved" and "overthinking virtually everything."

ADMISSIONS

Very important factors considered by the admissions committee include: secondary school record. *Important factors considered include:* character/personal qualities, class rank, essays, recommendations, standardized test scores. *Other factors considered include:* alumni/ae relation, extracurricular activities, geographical residence, interview, minority status, talent/ability, volunteer work, work experience. TOEFL required of all international applicants. High school diploma or GED is required. *High school units required/recommended:* 16 total recommended; 4 English recommended, 4 math recommended, 3 science recommended, 2 science lab recommended, 4 foreign language recommended, 3 social studies recommended, 2 history recommended.

The Inside Word

Vassar is relatively frank about its standards; you won't get much more direct advice from colleges about how to get admitted. The admissions process here follows very closely the practices of most prestigious northeastern schools. Your personal side—essays, extracurriculars, interview, etc.—is not going to do a lot for you if you don't demonstrate significant academic accomplishments. Multiple applicants from the same high school will be compared against each other as well as the entire applicant pool. Males and minorities are actively courted by the admissions staff, and the college is sincere in its commitment.

FINANCIAL AID

Students should submit: FAFSA, institution's own financial aid form, CSS/Financial Aid PROFILE, state aid form, noncustodial (divorced/separated) parent's statement, business/farm supplement. Regular filing deadline is February 1. The Princeton Review suggests that all financial aid forms be submitted as soon as possible after January 1. *Need-based scholarships/grants offered:* Pell, SEOG, state scholarships/grants, private scholarships, the school's own gift aid. *Loan aid offered:* FFEL Subsidized Stafford, FFEL Unsubsidized Stafford, FFEL PLUS, Federal Perkins, college/university loans from institutional funds. Federal Work-Study Program available. Institutional employment available. Applicants will be notified of awards on or about April 3. Off-campus job opportunities are fair.

FROM THE ADMISSIONS OFFICE

"Vassar presents a rich variety of social and cultural activities, clubs, sports, living arrangements, and regional attractions. Vassar is a vital, residential college community recognized for its respect for the rights and individuality of others."

For even more information on this school, turn to page 376 of the "Stats" section.

WAGNER COLLEGE

One Campus Road, Staten Island, NY 10301 • Admissions: 718-390-3411 • Fax: 718-390-3105
Financial Aid: 718-390-3183 • E-mail: admissions@wagner.edu • Website: www.wagner.edu

Ratings

Quality of Life: 76   Academic: 76   Admissions: 78   Financial Aid: 80

Academics

Wagner has some flagship majors that earn it a national reputation, and many students apply to the college specifically for these disciplines. However, the college's recently revamped liberal arts curriculum gives it up-to-date bragging rights. Ah, and did we

> **SURVEY SAYS . . .**
> *Lots of beer drinking*
> *Students aren't very religious*
> *Hard liquor is popular*
> *Students don't like Staten Island, NY*
> *Great off-campus food*

mention that the campus overlooks La Isla MANHATTAN? Wagner students are no strangers to using the city as a classroom and for internships. As one senior puts its, "New York is our classroom." Student opinion at Wagner runs the spectrum from thrilled to disgruntled. Across the board, the small class sizes and "resourceful, witty, and inspiring" professors "create a really positive atmosphere" for study. "I feel challenged, yet professors are helpful," writes a junior, agreeing with others who note that the faculty is "always willing to give of out-of-class time to help with accelerated research projects." On the administrative side, reviews remain mixed. "The upper administration seems to distance themselves from everyone else, but if you request their attention they will give it to you." Referring to the disconnect between the administration and the student body, one student notes, "Students have a loud voice," but many wish they had more say regarding the administrative choices made for the school—both for students and the campus itself.

Life

Proximity to the unlimited opportunities of the Big Apple is one of Wagner's strongest selling points; the school provides free transportation to the Staten Island ferry, making access easy. "It's a great life here because you can go into the city, but actually get out of it and sleep when you go back to your dorm," explains a sophomore. A senior majoring in theater notes the "Location, location, location. No college is more beautiful or more beautifully located than Wagner." Oddly enough, the second most commonly mentioned aspect of Wagner life is the architectural material of choice: brick. A sociology major notes sarcastically, "I think we could use a few more bricks," and a fellow student adds, "Bricks, bricks everywhere!" Meticulous "leaf-blowing and lawn-maintenance" practices also contribute to the campus' pristine look. When they are not lured away by the city's attractions, students enjoy "on-campus activities, such as comedy nights, films, and plays." Fraternity and sorority members agree that "Greek life rocks!" though other students note that "People don't do anything unless there's alcohol." All factors considered, a sophomore declares, "[I'm] having the time of my life."

Student Body

Wagner students' general opinion of each other is pretty typical. "People here are your every-day college students: they chain smoke, bitch about the food, get drunk, go to class, [and] sleep long hours," remarks a junior majoring in technical theater. Others believe that Wagner-ites are "very open-minded" and "supportive of each other in activities," but "rumors tend to spread like wildfire." A clear division exists between students who live on campus and those who live off, with residents griping that commuters "don't realize anything outside of Staten Island exists." In spite of these opposing camps, many students laud the "sense of community" at Wagner and comment, "The people here are great. While we all have our own groups, everyone is friendly to each other." A common refrain goes, "I have made many friends here." One sophomore writes, "We are an extremely diverse social group coming from all aspects of society and different family backgrounds and different viewpoints."

ADMISSIONS

Very important factors considered by the admissions committee include: secondary school record, standardized test scores. *Important factors considered include:* class rank, essays, interview, recommendations, talent/ability. *Other factors considered include:* alumni/ae relation, character/personal qualities, extracurricular activities, geographical residence, minority status, volunteer work. SAT I or ACT required; SAT I preferred; SAT II also recommended. TOEFL required of all international applicants. High school diploma is required and GED is not accepted. *High school units required/recommended:* 18 total required; 21 total recommended; 4 English required, 3 math required, 4 math recommended, 2 science required, 3 science recommended, 2 foreign language required, 3 social studies required, 4 social studies recommended, 4 elective required.

The Inside Word

Wagner has profited in recent years from a renewed interest in urban colleges. In other words, don't take the application process too lightly. Applicants are met with a college admissions staff dedicated to finding the right students for their school. Wagner's pioneering efforts in experiential learning for all students make its recent resurgence well earned.

FINANCIAL AID

Students should submit: FAFSA. Regular filing deadline is April 15. The Princeton Review suggests that all financial aid forms be submitted as soon as possible after January 1. *Need-based scholarships/grants offered:* Pell, SEOG, state scholarships/grants, private scholarships, the school's own gift aid, Lutheran Scholarships. *Loan aid offered:* FFEL Subsidized Stafford, FFEL Unsubsidized Stafford, FFEL PLUS, Federal Perkins, Federal Nursing. Federal Work-Study Program available. Institutional employment available. Off-campus job opportunities are good.

FROM THE ADMISSIONS OFFICE

"At Wagner College, we attract and develop active learners and future leaders. Wagner College has received national acclaim (Time magazine, American Association of Colleges and Universities) for its innovative curriculum, 'The Wagner Plan for the Practical Liberal Arts.' At Wagner, we capitalize on our unique geography; we are a traditional, scenic, residential campus, which happens to sit atop a hill on an island overlooking lower Manhattan. Our location allows us to offer a program that couples required off-campus experiences (internships), with 'learning community' clusters of courses. This program begins in the first semester and continues through the senior capstone experience in the major. Fieldwork and internships, writing-intensive reflective tutorials, connected learning, 'reading, writing, and doing' . . . at Wagner College our students truly discover 'the practical liberal arts in New York City.'"

For even more information on this school, turn to page 376 of the "Stats" section.

WEBB INSTITUTE

298 Crescent Beach Road, Ocean Cove, NY 11542 • Admissions: 516-674-9838
Financial Aid: 516-671-2213 • E-mail: admissions@webb-institute.edu • Website: www.webb-institute.edu

Ratings

Quality of Life: 91   Academic: 98   Admissions: 96   Financial Aid: 99

Academics

One thing Webb students needn't worry about is a tuition bill. That's right—the Webb Institute costs "nothing except room and board." While there are only 11 full-time professors at Webb, this number is sufficient to guarantee the 73 students "a great deal of personal attention." And because Webb is such a small school, much of the red tape that crisscrosses most campuses can be avoided. "Since Webb's only major is naval architecture and marine engineering, there is no registration for courses. Everyone takes the same courses, save a few electives each year." With such a specialized educational lens, "Webb is definitely the place to get a degree . . . if you're interested in ship design." One of the unique features of the Webb curriculum is the network of "worldwide internships" that students are required to serve in during the winter, "for two months every year of the four." Students unanimously agree that these hands-on opportunities are at the core of their academic experiences. "We are taught the theory behind the engineering, but it doesn't end there," explains an undergrad. "We are also taught how to apply the theory to real-world problems." An "Honor Code" that is "adhered to by every student" does a good job at structuring the education, and an emphasis on teamwork and interaction ensures that "there is a spirit of cooperation rather than competition."

> **SURVEY SAYS . . .**
> Great computer facilities, Great on-campus food
> Lab facilities are great
> Lots of conservatives on campus
> Campus feels safe
> Diversity lacking on campus

Life

All students here have a similar schedule that includes "class from 9 A.M. to 3 P.M. and dinner at 5:30 p.m." And then there are the stacks of homework assignments. To a large extent, the massive amount of "work almost destroys any social life outside of school." When students do find some spare time, they'll go to the campus pub to grab a beer. They'll do some exercising, as well. "Over half the school plays sports, no one is cut from the teams, and everyone gets playing time." For the less competitive athletes, Webb offers "intramural sports almost year round, from basketball to floor hockey, from folf (Frisbee golf) to ultimate Frisbee, and everything in between." The institute provides rent-free boats and a private beach for its students. It also provides tuition-wavers for every student who gets accepted to the school, which allows students to spend late nights talking about things other than how they're planning to pay back college loans. "Speaking for the male population," comments a student, "we spend hours scheming as to how to lure more girls to our school." Some students, however, say to hell with trying to find mates and parties on campus. Day trips to places like nearby New York City provide outlets. "Cutting loose in the city is fantastic after having worked like a dog for five whole days."

Student Body

"Since Webb is a very small school, it is imperative that the students get along with each other and are able to work well together." And by and large they do. Many of the students at the Webb Institute will agree that they seem "more like an extended family than a student body."

Because they "all live in the same damned building" ("a mansion!") during their four years at Webb, the students "become very close," whether or not they want to be. And there's a common interest that binds these students: naval engineering. Typical "Webbies," as they're known, are "Caucasian guys from middle- to upper-class families" and self-declared "nerds." In other words, "there is no—repeat NO—diversity at this school. No gays. No minorities." And as one male student pleads, "Girls . . . we need more girls." But the females who do come are able to fit in well, and they often form tight friendships with each other. A first-year female reports that "all six of the freshman girls bonded within 15 minutes after our parents left orientation." Men and women alike have thick skin and appetites for hard work

ADMISSIONS

Very important factors considered by the admissions committee include: class rank, interview, secondary school record, standardized test scores. *Important factors considered include:* character/personal qualities, recommendations, talent/ability. *Other factors considered include:* extracurricular activities, minority status, volunteer work, work experience. SAT I or ACT required; SAT I preferred; SAT II also required. High school diploma is required and GED is not accepted. *High school units required/recommended:* 16 total required; 4 English required, 4 math required, 2 science required, 2 science lab required, 2 social studies required, 4 elective required.

The Inside Word

Let's not mince words; admission to Webb is mega-tough. Webb's admissions counselors are out to find the right kid for their curriculum—one that can survive the school's rigorous academics. The applicant pool is highly self-selected because of the focused program of study: Naval Architecture and Marine Engineering.

FINANCIAL AID

Students should submit: FAFSA. Regular filing deadline is July 1. The Princeton Review suggests that all financial aid forms be submitted as soon as possible after January 1. *Need-based scholarships/grants offered:* Pell, state scholarships/grants, private scholarships. *Loan aid offered:* FFEL Subsidized Stafford, FFEL Unsubsidized Stafford, FFEL PLUS. Applicants will be notified of awards on or about August 1. Off-campus job opportunities are good.

FROM THE ADMISSIONS OFFICE

"Webb, the only college in the country that specializes in the engineering field of Naval Architecture and Marine Engineering, seeks young men and women of all races from all over the country who are interested in receiving an excellent engineering education with a full-tuition scholarship. Students don't have to know anything about ships, they just have to be motivated to study how mechanical, civil, structural, and electrical engineering come together with the design elements that make up a ship and all its systems. Being small and private has its major advantages. Every applicant is special and the President will interview all entering students personally. The student/faculty ratio is 6:1, and since there are no teaching assistants, interaction with the faculty occurs daily in class and labs at a level not found at most other colleges. The college provides each student with a high-end laptop computer they get to keep. The entire campus operates under the Student Organization's Honor System that allows unsupervised exams and 24-hour access to the library, every classroom and laboratory, and the shop and gymnasium. Despite a total enrollment of between 70 and 80 students and a demanding workload, Webb manages to field six intercollegiate teams. Currently more than 60 percent of the members of the student body play on one or more intercollegiate teams. Work hard, play hard and the payoff is a job for every student upon graduation. The placement record of the college is 100 percent every year."

For even more information on this school, turn to page 377 of the "Stats" section.

WELLESLEY COLLEGE

BOARD OF ADMISSION, 106 CENTRAL STREET, WELLESLEY, MA 02481-8203 • ADMISSIONS: 781-283-2270
FAX: 781-283-3678 • FINANCIAL AID: 781-283-2360 • E-MAIL: ADMISSION@WELLESLEY.EDU
WEBSITE: WWW.WELLESLEY.EDU

Ratings
Quality of Life: 85   Academic: 98   Admissions: 98   Financial Aid: 80

Academics

Wellesley, an all-women's under-graduate institution near Boston, is not just a college; it is also, according to one typical enthusiast, "a community dedicated to developing women of superior intellect, life skills, and savvy. It's simply the best. Wellesley has shown me that it is okay to be a fabulous woman with so much to offer." Most stu-

> **SURVEY SAYS . . .**
> *No one cheats, Beautiful campus*
> *Dorms are like palaces*
> *Student government is popular*
> *Political activism is hot*
> *Very little beer drinking, Very little hard liquor*
> *(Almost) no one smokes*
> *No one plays intramural sports*

dents here simply can't decide what they like most about the school. It could be that classes "are small and well taught. There's good atmosphere for discussion in and out of the classroom." Or, it might be that students have "access to some of the best lecturers and facilities in the world. World-renowned experts give presentations here." Most likely, though, it's the professors. They "are Wellesley's gold. They give individual attention and that's why I'm here," writes one student. Another explains, "The professors are very knowledgeable but also very approachable. It's obvious they love teaching." Faculty and students "are very fond of each other—but not in a way that could get anyone fired." Students probably are less enthusiastic about the brutal workload the school demands, although most accept it as an essential part of the Wellesley experience. "It'll be the hardest four years of your life, but also the most rewarding," sums up one student.

Life

Despite the rigorous academic requirements of a Wellesley education, most students try to build an active extracurricular life around their studies, a situation that helps to explain the "popular bumper sticker: 'Wellesley—We'll Sleep When We're Dead.' " Writes one student, "Everyone is always busy. Over-programming for activities can be a problem." Many students become involved in some of the "many student organizations, such as Pre-Law Society and Russian Club. There are also many opportunities to volunteer in this area and the greater Boston region." While there are "student groups doing things, as far [as] parties on campus, sporting events, heavy drinking, etc., it's not here. There is no 'college life' per se. If you want fun, you have to go off campus." Explains one student, "People work hard during the week. On weekends, about one-third of the students get dressed up in tube tops and black pants, hop on the Senate Bus, and go to frat parties; one-third watch movies and do laundry or other on-campus events; and the other one-third study all weekend." Hometown Wellesley, Massachusetts, "is a little too upscale—lots of art dealers and people pushing baby strollers past Ann Taylor. But very safe." Writes one student, "Wellesley is not the best town to go out and have a good time. For fun we usually go to Boston," only 30 minutes away by car or bus. For those who simply choose to stay home, "the campus is beautiful and the dorms are fabulous."

Student Body

Wellesley's "extremely motivated, dedicated, and ambitious" students are "very intelligent. I have great conversations with everyone. I feel so privileged to be around people who have done fantastic things and will have a major impact on the future." Undergrads enjoy a "very strong sense of community" and the fact that there is "no competition here. Eveyone is competing with themselves." Students "are extremely politically conscious. There is a strong tradition of activism and social efficacy," but they are "sometimes too dogmatic. I get tired of the sidewalk telling me what to do and think." Writes one student, "They don't smile enough. People are so stressed that they (myself included) forget to relax and have fun." As for the "typical" Wellesley woman, "everyone jokes about 'Wendy Wellesley,' but in truth there are a dozen different kinds of typical Wellesley students." Concludes one student, "At an all-women's college, people learn to be themselves, whoever that might be. From Wendy Wellesley, Frat Ho, to Wendy Wellesley, Raging Dyke, we're defining who we are daily, and that is awesome!"

ADMISSIONS

Very important factors considered by the admissions committee include: essays, recommendations, secondary school record, standardized test scores. *Important factors considered include:* character/personal qualities, class rank, extracurricular activities. *Other factors considered include:* alumni/ae relation, geographical residence, interview, minority status, state residency, talent/ability, volunteer work, work experience. TOEFL required of all international applicants. *High school units required/recommended:* 4 English recommended, 4 math recommended, 3 science recommended, 2 science lab recommended, 4 foreign language recommended, 4 social studies recommended, 4 history recommended.

The Inside Word

While the majority of women's colleges have gone coed or even closed over the past two decades, Wellesley has continued with vigor. As a surviving member of the Seven Sisters, the nation's most prestigious women's colleges, Wellesley enjoys even more popularity with students who choose the single-sex option. Admissions standards are rigorous, but among institutions of such high reputation Wellesley's admissions staff is friendlier and more open than the majority. Their willingness to conduct preliminary evaluations for candidates is especially commendable and in some form or another should be the rule rather than an exception at highly selective colleges.

FINANCIAL AID

Students should submit: FAFSA, institution's own financial aid form, CSS/Financial Aid PROFILE, noncustodial (divorced/separated) parent's statement, business/farm supplement, parent's and student's tax returns and W-2s. The Princeton Review suggests that all financial aid forms be submitted as soon as possible after January 1. *Need-based scholarships/grants offered:* Pell, SEOG, state scholarships/grants, private scholarships, the school's own gift aid. *Loan aid offered:* FFEL Subsidized Stafford, FFEL Unsubsidized Stafford, FFEL PLUS, Federal Perkins, state loans, college/university loans from institutional funds. Federal Work-Study Program available. Institutional employment available. Applicants will be notified of awards on or about April 1. Off-campus job opportunities are excellent.

FROM THE ADMISSIONS OFFICE

"A student's years at Wellesley are the beginning—not the end—of an education. A Wellesley College degree signifies not that the graduate has memorized certain blocks of material, but that she has acquired the curiosity, the desire, and the ability to seek and assimilate new information. Four years at Wellesley can provide the foundation for the widest possible range of ambitions and the necessary self-confidence to fulfill them. At Wellesley, a student has every educational opportunity. Above all, it is Wellesley's purpose to teach students to apply knowledge wisely and to use the advantages of talent and education to seek new ways to serve the wider community."

For even more information on this school, turn to page 378 of the "Stats" section.

WELLS COLLEGE

ROUTE 90, AURORA, NY 13026 • ADMISSIONS: 315-364-3264 • FAX: 315-364-3327
FINANCIAL AID: 315-364-3289 • E-MAIL: ADMISSIONS@WELLS.EDU • WEBSITE: WWW.WELLS.EDU

Ratings
Quality of Life: 85   **Academic:** 86   **Admissions:** 80   **Financial Aid:** 80

Academics

One effusive sophomore calls Wells College "an Ivy League education in disguise as the best time of our lives," and most students on this all-women campus agree. Not only is "advising a very personal encounter at Wells," but the professors also make students "want to sing and dance" with their engaging lectures and personal involvement. "The greatest strength here at Wells is the time that the professors dedicate to tutoring students outside class time," notes a junior. Apparently, a rash of "bad puns" among faculty doesn't impede the "constant exchange of ideas." The cutthroat competition of many top schools is swapped for a spirit of cooperation at Wells. "Everyone wants to help each other," in the experience of one sophomore. The administration is said to have "a well-rounded view of people's abilities" and to be "very in tune with the students." A few complaints are logged regarding the library, which needs "more books from 1970–present." The issue of "low variety of classes and few teachers" is solved by an arrangement that allows Wells students to take courses at nearby Cornell. Some students also suggest putting more money into "educational funding than [campus] aesthetics." But the mentoring students receive plus the influential network of alumnae awaiting them after graduation makes Wells, overall, a "rewarding" place to hit the books.

SURVEY SAYS . . .
No one cheats
Musical organizations are hot
Students get along with local community
Very little beer drinking
Student government is popular
Dorms are like palaces
Class discussions encouraged
Theater is hot
Very small frat/sorority scene
Student publications are ignored
Lousy food on campus

Life

Travel for 25 miles in any direction from Wells, and you won't find a whole lot. Thus, students pride themselves on being "self-sufficient" and "making our own fun." On-campus life is described as "one big sleepover" or like "living at home with 400 sisters." Inevitably, this results in an "intimate" community, with more than one student commenting, "Everyone knows you, for better or worse." A senior tells us, "We always find amusement in each other doing something seemingly boring to anyone outside of the 'bubble.' " Some of these activities include, "just being silly, cooking, and playing games" as well as hitting the lone bar in the quiet "village" of Aurora. For a more extensive social life, students utilize the school-sponsored "van runs" to Ithaca and nearby college campuses. Cornell, Ithaca, Syracuse, and Hobart and William Smith are all within striking distance and ready to host the Wells women. "I haven't had any problems meeting guys," comments a junior. To round life out, students take advantage of their picturesque location on Cayuga Lake, especially during the warmer months.

Student Body

A senior woman characterizes her fellow students thusly: "Wells women tend to be independent thinkers, kind and generous, and mostly very outgoing. They tend to be unusual people, somehow slightly out of the box." These unique individuals are nonetheless still somewhat prone to "gossip" and "way too much drama." Some students observe a "lack of respect for different social classes" and describe their classmates as "prissy." But the consensus is that there is a strong sense of community, where students often "get along more like sisters"; the "very accepting" student body is diverse in nature. A freshman summarizes the warm, fuzzy, estrogen feeling in concluding, "As a community, our ability to communicate is only surpassed by our friendship."

ADMISSIONS

Very important factors considered by the admissions committee include: extracurricular activities, recommendations, secondary school record, standardized test scores. *Important factors considered include:* essays, interview. *Other factors considered include:* alumni/ae relation, character/personal qualities, class rank, talent/ability, volunteer work, work experience. SAT I or ACT required. TOEFL required of all international applicants. High school diploma or GED is required. *High school units required/recommended:* 16 total required; 23 total recommended; 4 English required, 3 math required, 4 math recommended, 2 science required, 3 science recommended, 2 science lab required, 3 science lab recommended, 3 foreign language required, 4 foreign language recommended, 2 history required, 3 history recommended, 2 elective required, 3 elective recommended.

The Inside Word

Wells is engaged in that age-old admissions game called matchmaking. There are no minimums or cutoffs in the admissions process here. But don't be fooled by the high admit rate. The admissions committee will look closely at your academic accomplishments, but also gives attention to your essay, recommendations, and extracurricular pursuits. The committee also recommends an interview; we suggest taking them up on it.

FINANCIAL AID

Students should submit: FAFSA, CSS/Financial Aid Profile for early decision Applicants only. No deadline for regular filing. The Princeton Review suggests that all financial aid forms be submitted as soon as possible after January 1. *Need-based scholarships/grants offered:* Pell, SEOG, state scholarships/grants, private scholarships, the school's own gift aid. *Loan aid offered:* FFEL Subsidized Stafford, FFEL Unsubsidized Stafford, FFEL PLUS, Federal Perkins. Federal Work-Study Program available. Institutional employment available. Applicants will be notified of awards on a rolling basis beginning on or about March 1. Off-campus job opportunities are fair.

FROM THE ADMISSIONS OFFICE

"Sixty percent of Wells women pursue advanced degrees at some point in their careers. Our recent graduates have gained admission to programs at Cornell University, Harvard University, Georgetown University, Duke University, University of California at Berkeley, Yale University, and many others."

For even more information on this school, turn to page 378 of the "Stats" section.

WESLEYAN UNIVERSITY

THE STEWART M. REID HOUSE, 70 WYLLYS AVENUE, MIDDLETOWN, CT 06459-0265
ADMISSIONS: 860-685-3000 • FAX: 860-685-3001 • FINANCIAL AID: 860-685-2800
E-MAIL: ADMISSIONS@WESLEYAN.EDU • WEBSITE: WWW.WESLEYAN.EDU

Ratings
Quality of Life: 77   Academic: 94   Admissions: 98   Financial Aid: 81

Academics

"You live with the coolest people in the world, which is interrupted periodically by instruction from the smartest people on campus," says a sophomore about a Wesleyan education. "There is a serious but noncompetitive academic environment," reports a senior art history major. A junior government major says, "When

> **SURVEY SAYS . . .**
> *Political activism is hot*
> *Great library, No one cheats*
> *Students aren't religious*
> *Athletic facilities are great*
> *Students don't like Middletown, CT*
> *(Almost) no one listens to college radio*
> *Very small frat/sorority scene*

your government professor is on a first-name basis with the White House and is an excellent teacher [to boot], you can't ask for better academics." A senior chemistry major proclaims, "Our hippie, flower-child reputation overshadows the fact that we have a great science department with opportunities you can't get anywhere else." A sophomore writes, "Professors really care about your opinions, and you're treated as an intellectual equal." Still, one junior dance major laments that "diversity university does not have a diverse faculty." Students enjoy their academic freedom. "Wesleyan's academic requirements give you tremendous freedom to design your own curriculum and to take classes you really want to be in." Learning takes place both in and out of class. Writes a sophomore, "I feel like much of my academic experience occurs outside of class because there is so much political activity and passionate discussion about campus and global issues." While the professors are universally admired, the registrar's office is the focus of displeasure. The online registration system might be revolutionary, but "online registration is hell; you're basically racing with all the people on the computers next to you," one junior writes.

Life

A senior East Asian studies major describes life at Wesleyan thusly: "What do people do for fun? Stage a rally during the president's office hours and simultaneously have a knitting bee and discussion about pro-feminist activism." Though some complain that the party policy is getting too strict, a junior English major says, "If you want frat parties, we've got them. If you want naked parties, we've got those too." Others note that while "the beer flows like water if you know where to look, there's not a lot of pressure to drink." Explains one, "Campus life doesn't revolve around drinking because there are always so many other things going on." Students call Middletown "boring" and "like a sketchy ghost town" but love the university's central New England location and its "great sledding hill." Students don't seem too happy that they are required to remain on the meal plan for four years.

Student Body

Wesleyan "is a school full of very idealistic people who really want to make a significant impact on the world before they even graduate." Though sometimes described as "self-righteous," Wesleyan is home to a "passionate, involved student body. At best, they change the world. At worst, they're entertaining." While the student body is racially mixed, a senior chemistry major notes that "we are diverse and very accepting as long as you've never worn a white hat or had any Republican sympathies." Still, most students overlook the lack of political heterogeneity because they appreciate that "there is no such thing as a typical Wesleyan student. You can meet a lacrosse jock at a fraternity party and then run into him the next day at an Amnesty International meeting or see him later in a theater performance." Another student adds, "My friends are a motley crew of musicians, artists, intellectuals . . . united by good herb." Even the senior art history major who believes that "the school is populated by a lot of whiny left-wing rich kids who have no concept of reality and how an administration must sometimes make unpopular choices," admits that she "like[s] that students are politically active."

ADMISSIONS

Very important factors considered by the admissions committee include: secondary school record. *Important factors considered include:* class rank, character/personal qualities, recommendations, essays, talent/ability, standardized test scores, minority/alumni status, volunteer work. *Other factors considered include:* geographical residence, interview, work experience. TOEFL required of all international applicants. *High school units required/recommended:* 20 total recommended; 4 English recommended, 4 math recommended, 4 science recommended, 3 science lab recommended, 4 foreign language recommended, 4 social studies recommended.

The Inside Word

Wesleyan stacks up well against its very formidable competitors academically, yet due to these same competitors the university admits at a fairly high rate for an institution of its high caliber. Candidate evaluation is nonetheless rigorous. If you aren't one of the best students in your graduating class, it isn't likely that you will be very competitive in Wesleyan's applicant pool. Strong communicators can help open the doors by submitting persuasive essays and interviews that clearly demonstrate an effective match with the university.

FINANCIAL AID

Students should submit: FAFSA, CSS/Financial Aid PROFILE, noncustodial (divorced/separated) parent's statement, business/farm supplement. Regular filing deadline is February 1. The Princeton Review suggests that all financial aid forms be submitted as soon as possible after January 1. *Need-based scholarships/grants offered:* Pell, SEOG, state scholarships/grants, private scholarships, the school's own gift aid. *Loan aid offered:* FFEL Subsidized Stafford, FFEL Unsubsidized Stafford, FFEL PLUS, Federal Perkins. Federal Work-Study Program available. Institutional employment available. Applicants will be notified of awards on or about April 1. Off-campus job opportunities are good.

FROM THE ADMISSIONS OFFICE

"Wesleyan faculty believe in an education that is flexible and affords individual freedom, and that a strong liberal arts education is the best foundation for success in any endeavor. The broad curriculum focuses on essential skills and abilities through course content and teaching methodology, allowing students to pursue their intellectual interests with passion while honing those skills and abilities. As a result, Wesleyan students achieve a very personalized but coherent education. Wesleyan's dean of admission and financial aid, Nancy Hargrave-Meislahn, describes the qualities Wesleyan seeks in its students: 'Our very holistic process seeks to identify academically accomplished and intellectually curious students who can thrive in Wesleyan's rigorous and vibrant academic environment, and to also see in a candidate the personal strengths, accomplishments, and potential for real contribution to our diverse community.'"

For even more information on this school, turn to page 379 of the "Stats" section.

WHEATON COLLEGE

Office of Admission, Norton, MA 02766 • Admissions: 508-286-8251 • Fax: 508-286-8271
Financial Aid: 508-286-8232 • E-mail: admission@wheatoncollege.edu
Website: www.wheatoncollege.edu

Ratings
Quality of Life: 79   Academic: 85   Admissions: 82   Financial Aid: 85

Academics

A comfortable, nurturing environment, Wheaton College offers students a faculty and staff that, as one typical respondant says, feels like "an extension of my family." Even underclassmen enjoy close relationships with professors: "They take special care of freshmen so we don't get forgotten. They spread the love." One senior writes that her professors are "very dedicated to their students and love what they teach," while another characterizes them as "extremely accessible and accommodating." Thanks to the small class sizes, students receive individual attention and perks like "senior seminars conducted in professors' living rooms over tea and cookies." In terms of administration, a senior comments that the Student Life Office is "run poorly and fails to help students." But others note that rather than ride a reputation, the Wheaton administration is "always looking for ways to improve." Internship opportunities and career planning services at the Filene Center are universally lauded by students. One freshman comments, "Our greatest strength is our second transcript—our resume. The school helps you build that while studying."

> **SURVEY SAYS . . .**
> *Lots of conservatives*
> *Registration is a breeze*
> *Students are happy*
> *Students are cliquish*
> *Very little drug use*

Life

Life in the "ghost town" of Norton, Massachusetts, could get boring if it weren't for the "beautiful campus" and "activities that keep students busy and connected" within the "Wheaton bubble." Luckily, both Boston and Providence are within striking distance so students can escape for "nightlife, shopping, and museums." On campus, people hang out at the Lyon's Den café or attend the concerts that frequently come through campus. Most students like the fact that there is no Greek system at Wheaton, but they grumble about school-sponsored social events, including dances that bolster one student's portrayal of Wheaton as "a big high school." A freshman comments, "I think that those who are creative and adventurous find things to do on the weekend." Athletics are popular at this Division III school, with one student stating, "Everyone plays a sport or works out." Synchronized swimming, soccer, and basketball get a lot of attention, but a high percentage of students are also involved in Wheaton's radio station, WCCS. There are complaints of dorm overcrowding, which recently led to some "forced triples," but the opening of a new 100-bed dorm in February alleviated the problem. All in all, students agree that it's "easy to make Wheaton home."

Student Body

Formerly an all-women school, Wheaton's admissions department is still trying to even out the high female-to-male ratio. "Thank God more men are being admitted!" a female sophomore writes. Generally, the student body is alternately described as "wealthy, snobby, and cliquish" or "rich, white, and preppy." Some students wonder if they've stumbled into an Abercrombie and Fitch advertisement and note a "lack of diversity in interests, ethnicity, and mentality." Though there is "some of that high school grouping" to contend with, others call the student body a "highly interactive community" with a "high level of acceptance." Apparently, "it's almost disturbing how friendly people are." "Everybody says hello," even to people they don't know. Detractors claim that Wheaton-ites are "apathetic" and "should be more political," but others say "people are very concerned with what's going on in the world." Either way, it's maintained that "you won't find a friendlier group."

ADMISSIONS

Very important factors considered by the admissions committee include: character/personal qualities, essays, extracurricular activities, secondary school record, talent/ability. *Important factors considered include:* alumni/ae relation, class rank, interview, recommendations, volunteer work, work experience. *Other factors considered include:* geographical residence, minority status, standardized test scores, state residency. TOEFL required of all international applicants. High school diploma or GED is required. *High school units required/recommended:* 16 total recommended; 4 English recommended, 3 math recommended, 3 science recommended, 2 science lab recommended, 4 foreign language recommended, 2 social studies recommended.

The Inside Word

Wheaton is to be applauded for periodically re-examining its admissions process; some colleges use virtually the same application process eternally, never acknowledging the fluid nature of societal attitudes and institutional circumstances. Approaches that emphasize individuals, or even their accomplishments, over their numbers are unfortunately rare in the world of college admission, where GPA and SAT I reign supreme. Wheaton has an easier time than some colleges in taking this step because it isn't prohibitively selective.

FINANCIAL AID

Students should submit: FAFSA, CSS/Financial Aid PROFILE, noncustodial (divorced/separated) parent's statement, business/farm supplement, parent's and student's federal tax returns and W-2s. Regular filing deadline is February 1. The Princeton Review suggests that all financial aid forms be submitted as soon as possible after January 1. *Need-based scholarships/grants offered:* Pell, SEOG, state scholarships/grants, private scholarships, the school's own gift aid. *Loan aid offered:* FFEL Subsidized Stafford, FFEL Unsubsidized Stafford, FFEL PLUS, Federal Perkins, state loans, college/university loans from institutional funds, MEFA, TERI, CitiAssist, other private educational loans. Federal Work-Study Program available. Institutional employment available. Applicants will be notified of awards on or about April 1. Off-campus job opportunities are good.

FROM THE ADMISSIONS OFFICE

"What makes for a 'best college'? Is it merely the hard-to-define notions of prestige or image? We don't think so. We think what makes college 'best' and best for you is a school that will make you a first-rate thinker and writer, a pragmatic professional in your work, and an ethical practitioner in your life. To get you to all these places, Wheaton takes advantage of its great combinations: a beautiful, secluded New England campus combined with access to Boston and Providence; a high quality, classic liberal arts and sciences curriculum combined with award-winning internship, job, and community service programs; and a campus that respects your individuality in the context of the larger community. What's the 'best' outcome of a Wheaton education? A start on life that combines meaningful work, significant relationships, and a commitment to your local and global community. Far more than for what they've studied or for what they've gone on to do for a living, we're most proud of Wheaton graduates for who they become."

For even more information on this school, turn to page 380 of the "Stats" section.

WILLIAM PATERSON UNIVERSITY

OFFICE OF ADMISSION, 300 POMPTON ROAD, WAYNE, NJ 07470 • ADMISSIONS: 973-720-2125
FAX: 973-720-2910 • E-MAIL: ADMISSIONS@WPUNJ.EDU • WEBSITE: WWW.WPUNJ.EDU

Ratings
Quality of Life: 78   Academic: 76   Admissions: 77   Financial Aid: 73

Academics

William Paterson University is one of nine institutions in New Jersey's state higher education system. And like many state universities, WPU receives its fair share of administrative complaints. However, most students are fair in their assessment that although some areas need improvements, the perks shouln't be overlooked: "diversity of students," "passionate faculty,"

SURVEY SAYS . . .
Diverse students interact
No one cheats
Classes are small
Frats and sororities dominate social scene
Lousy food on campus
No one plays intramural sports
Student publications are ignored
Students get along with local community

and "financial value." Many students note that once they hack through the red tape, they find themselves in an academic environment that wears several masks. Because WPU is a large school, professors waste little time on disinterested students. For students who show the moxie, "teachers eat up the ambition . . . and have the ability to give an educational experience that seems . . . real." Go-getters discover that their professors are "people who you can talk to after class, during the week, or even call them at home." And if students start sliding behind in class and don't feel comfortable contacting the instructor, "academic support services are excellent when tutoring is needed." The WPU programs that get the most press in this part of the world are music, teaching, nursing, history, communications, and business. But there are more than 30 undergrad programs in all, offered through five colleges: arts and communication, business, education, humanities and social sciences, and science and health.

Life

While it's fair to assume that much of the student life at William Paterson—just 20 miles west of New York City—takes place off campus, there are a number of social distractions on the campus itself. The "beautiful student center" is the hub of social activity during the weekdays, where students can shoot pool or play video games. When you need a boost, there's a Starbucks on campus. And when caffeine won't do the trick, there's a recreation center, fully equipped with tons of athletic equipment and a swimming pool. The campus also hosts lecturers, "musical performances, and theatrical productions," but "most aren't widely advertised." For the students who live on campus, alcohol is a staple part of an evening's activities. This is particularly the case on Thursday nights, a.k.a. "party night." Students also note, "We are just a half-hour bus trip from New York City." A little closer to home, the "very nice and quiet town" of Wayne offers a few shops and some small-town serenity. About 15 minutes away, towns like Clifton and Paterson provide students with "clubs" and "a lot of shopping." But even the pleasant campus itself can provide some getaways: "There is a waterfall on the wooded campus" adding to the campus's park-like feel, notes an undergraduate.

Student Body

Nearly three quarters of William Paterson's student body are commuters. Reflecting the wide variety of people in Northern Jersey, WPU's student population "is amazingly diverse—a little United Nations." With about 11,000 students on campus coming from such a wide spectrum of cultural backdrops and spending so much time away from campus, it's hard to paint a clear picture of the average student. Some see their classmates as "very interesting, friendly, intelligent people," "liberal, open-minded, and respectful." Others say you need to watch out for the "airheads" and the people who are "ill-mannered and un-intellectual," not to forget those who are just plain "rude and inconsiderate." Because there are all sorts of people at WPU, the onus is upon the student to determine who is worth hanging around with. "There are many different groups, and you can always find 'your group' or a group you feel comfortable with."

ADMISSIONS

Very important factors considered by the admissions committee include: secondary school record and standardized test scores. *Important factors considered include:* class rank. *Other factors considered include:* alumni/ae relation, character/personal qualities, essays, extracurricular activities, minority status, recommendations, talent/ability, and volunteer work. SAT I or ACT required. TOEFL required of all international applicants. High school diploma or GED is required. *High school units required/recommended:* 16 total required; 4 English required, 3 math required, 2 science required, 2 science lab required, 2 social studies required.

The Inside Word

Variety is the spice of life at WPU, where opportunities enable all types of students to satisfy their academic goals. Its location also enables students to tap into the environment that suits them socially, either on or off campus, where New York City awaits.

FINANCIAL AID

Students should submit: FAFSA. Regular filing deadline is April 1. The Princeton Review suggests that all financial aid forms be submitted as soon as possible after January 1. *Need-based scholarships/grants offered:* Pell, SEOG, state scholarships/grants, and the school's own gift aid. *Loan aid offered:* Direct Subsidized Stafford, Direct Unsubsidized Stafford, Direct PLUS, and Federal Perkins. Federal Work-Study Program available. Institutional employment available. Applicants will be notified of awards on a rolling basis beginning on or about March 1. Off-campus job opportunities are excellent.

FROM THE ADMISSIONS OFFICE

"William Paterson University's 370-acre, wooded hilltop campus in Wayne, New Jersey, encompasses more than 38 buildings, and a sleek glass-covered Atrium stands within sight of a nineteenth-century Victorian mansion, Hobart Manor. William Paterson has continued to grow with the recent addition of a new 150,000-square-foot building set on 50 acres of scenic woodland. This new building, 1600 Valley Road, is home to the E*Trade Financial Learning Center—a state-of-the-art facility featuring live real-time datafeeds of financial information—as well as the Russ Berrie Institute for Professional Sales. A quiet setting with a distinctive collegiate atmosphere, William Paterson University is dotted with sculpture, flowers, and even a waterfall, but is easily transformed into a flurry of activity by nearly 11,000 students. A comprehensive, public, liberal arts institution committed to academic excellence and student success, William Paterson University is accredited by the Middle States Association of Schools and Colleges. It offers 30 undergraduate and 19 graduate degree programs through its five colleges: Arts and Communication, Christos M. Cotsakos College of Business, Education, Humanities and Social Sciences, and Science and Health. As a state-assisted institution, the university offers students the value of a first-rate education at a fraction of the cost experienced by those at private colleges and universities. It also offers a wide variety of student activities, modern on-campus housing, and the most up-to-date educational facilities."

For even more information on this school, turn to page 380 of the "Stats" section.

WILLIAMS COLLEGE

33 STETSON COURT, WILLIAMSTOWN, MA 01267 • ADMISSIONS: 413-597-2211 • FAX: 413-597-4052
FINANCIAL AID: 413-597-4181 • E-MAIL: ADMISSIONS@WILLIAMS.EDU • WEBSITE: WWW.WILLIAMS.EDU

Ratings
Quality of Life: 94   Academic: 98   Admissions: 99   Financial Aid: 83

Academics

With only 2,000 undergraduates and no core curriculum, Williams College offers a supportive and idyllic "boot camp for your brain." Professors reportedly "love meeting with us individually" and are personable enough to "let you dog-sit and drive their cars." Many

> **SURVEY SAYS . . .**
> *Everyone loves the Ephs*
> *(Almost) everyone plays intramural sports*
> *Dorms are like palaces, Registration is a breeze*
> *Campus feels safe, (Almost) no one smokes*
> *Musical organizations are hot*

students agree that the Romance language departments fall short, and some note that class sizes are sometimes not as miniscule as advertised. The popular new president, Morty Shapiro, however, who also makes time to teach Economics 101, has "initiated a massive overhaul of the curriculum" to make it "a little less Anglo-Saxon." Distinctive academic programs include rigorous tutorials—"two students, one professor, and a fascinating topic"—and Winter Study, a January term where students study anything from book publishing to the stock market to auto mechanics. Study abroad is widely encouraged at Williams: "They provide lots of grants and fellowships for summer and winter research or travels." The generally "hands-off" administration, one student explains, "knows that I'm a real person, not a number or some drain on their time or energy." After it's all over, loyal alumni serve as "a great family for the rest of your life."

Life

Reputedly a school for smart jocks, Williams life indeed "revolves around sports," with 40 percent of students participating in varsity athletics. "At Williams people are very proud of our athletes, so we go to support them often." Many undergraduates report meeting their closest friends in their "entry," a residential group of 20 diverse freshmen and two upperclassmen JAs, whose role is to "wipe our noses and take us shopping and buy us alcohol and generally make sure that everyone is surviving and getting along." The dictum "drinking is a way of life" is backed by the administration's attitude of being "concerned with students' health and safety rather than busting people for alcohol." Williamstown shows up as a very small dot on any map; some say it "doesn't even exist." Though the not one, not two, but three local art museums draw high praise, "nothing is open past five," and a new Thai restaurant on Spring Street receives disproportionate buzz. Considering the school's small size and remote Berkshires location, students stay occupied with their "strange devotion to a cappella groups" or the "slightly dorky, albeit well-attended, on-campus events such as movies or lectures." Also, a "ridiculous percentage of the campus knows how to swing dance (well)." When the weather is survivable, the popular Outing Club sponsors excursions through the "amazing fall foliage" and "winter skiing."

Student Body

The typical Williams student is described as "preppy and athletic," as well as "incredibly driven, even when they pretend to be slackers." One student comments, "Everyone is friendly and down-to-earth, not to mention enormously talented at something." Though they may not be too "interested in the outside world," the inward focus makes for "a cozy atmosphere." In terms of diversity, some note "a polarization of the campus—at one end the minorities and at the other the mainly white jock population." Yet others report, "My group of friends is like a United Colors of Benetton ad." Concurring, another student writes that amid "such diversity of backgrounds and interests, the spirit and unity remains amazingly strong." All in all, "Everyone sees each other all the time, and so there's a real sense of community and caring for each other."

ADMISSIONS

Very important factors considered by the admissions committee include: essays, recommendations, secondary school record, standardized test scores. *Important factors considered include:* class rank, extracurricular activities, talent/ability. *Other factors considered include:* alumni/ae relation, character/personal qualities, geographical residence, minority status, volunteer work, work experience. SAT I or ACT required; SAT II also required. *High school units required/recommended:* 4 English recommended, 4 math recommended, 3 science recommended, 3 science lab recommended, 4 foreign language recommended, 3 social studies recommended.

The Inside Word

As is typical of highly selective colleges, at Williams high grades and test scores work more as qualifiers than to determine admissibility. Beyond a strong record of achievement, evidence of intellectual curiosity, noteworthy nonacademic talents, and a noncollege family background are some aspects of a candidate's application that might make for an offer of admission. But there are no guarantees—the evaluation process here is rigorous. The admissions committee (the entire admissions staff) discusses each candidate in comparison to the entire applicant pool. The pool is divided alphabetically for individual reading; after weak candidates are eliminated, those who remain undergo additional evaluations by different members of the staff. Admission decisions must be confirmed by the agreement of a plurality of the committee. Such close scrutiny demands a well-prepared candidate and application.

FINANCIAL AID

Students should submit: FAFSA, CSS/Financial Aid PROFILE. Regular filing deadline is February 1. The Princeton Review suggests that all financial aid forms be submitted as soon as possible after January 1. *Need-based scholarships/grants offered:* Pell, SEOG, state scholarships/grants, private scholarships, the school's own gift aid. *Loan aid offered:* Direct Subsidized Stafford, Direct Unsubsidized Stafford, Direct PLUS, Federal Perkins, college/university loans from institutional funds. Federal Work-Study Program available. Institutional employment available. Applicants will be notified of awards on or about April 1. Off-campus job opportunities are fair.

FROM THE ADMISSIONS OFFICE

"Special course offerings at Williams include Oxford-style tutorials, where students research and defend ideas, engaging in weekly debate with a peer and a faculty tutor. Annually 30 Williams students devote a full year to the tutorial method of study at Oxford; half of Williams students pursue their education overseas. Four weeks of Winter Study each January provide time for individualized projects, research, and novel fields of study. Students compete in 28 Division III athletic teams, perform in 25 musical groups, stage 10 theatrical productions, and volunteer in 30 service organizations. The college receives several million dollars annually for undergraduate science research and equipment. The town offers two distinguished art museums, and 2,200 forest acres—complete with a treetop canopy walkway—for environmental research and recreation."

For even more information on this school, turn to page 381 of the "Stats" section.

WORCESTER POLYTECHNIC INSTITUTE

100 INSTITUTE ROAD, WORCESTER, MA 01609 • ADMISSIONS: 508-831-5286 • FAX: 508-831-5875
FINANCIAL AID: 508-831-5469 • E-MAIL: ADMISSIONS@WPI.EDU • WEBSITE: WWW.WPI.EDU

Ratings
Quality of Life: 74   Academic: 83   Admissions: 87   Financial Aid: 86

Academics

The WPI undergraduate experience centers around the "WPI Plan," a series of required independent projects designed to build research ability and teamwork skills. Components of the plan include the "Sufficiency," a five-course sequence outside the student's major that culminates in an independent project; the "Interactive Project," which studies the interrelationship of science with social and ethical issues; and the

> **SURVEY SAYS . . .**
> *Frats and sororities dominate social scene*
> *Class discussions are rare*
> *Student publications are ignored*
> *Students aren't religious*
> *Great computer facilities*
> *Lousy food on campus*
> *Students don't like Worcester, MA*
> *Political activism is (almost) nonexistent*
> *Athletic facilities need improving*

"Major Project," a senior research/design project that allows undergraduates to work closely with graduate students, professors, and occasionally, business leaders. Students approve of WPI's unique approach. Writes one, "The projects force one to apply knowledge in real life, and they are awesome." Another agrees, "The WPI plan forces real-world experience on college students." Adds a third, "If you put the effort in, there are unparalleled opportunities for innovation in the academic experience." The workload is tough at this science, engineering, and computer science heavyweight, made even tougher by a quarterly academic calendar. Warns one engineering major, "You have to work hard here. The classes seem very fast, but it is better because you don't get bored." WPI professors "are different from class to class and really make the difference in your grade. They're like a Clint Eastwood movie: The Good, The Bad, and the Ugly." While many are "always willing to help if you have any questions," others "do not speak much English, making it hard to understand what they are trying to get across." Administrators "are very friendly. It is not uncommon to find the president or vice president walking around campus or eating in the cafeteria."

Life

A heavy workload and a lopsided male-female ratio leave little time or opportunity for a social life at WPI. Explains one student, "Life is pretty fast. Classes in the morning and afternoon, and games in the evening along with homework." Weekends offer "not much besides fraternities. If you don't belong to a fraternity or a sports team, I don't know what else people would do except visit friends at liberal arts colleges. There are no girls here!" Parties in student apartments are also popular, if not to everyone's taste. Reports one naysayer, "Fun for most is going to one of the party houses off campus. I, however, personally don't like being crammed into a small room with 50 other people huddled around a keg." Under the circumstances, it is not surprising that "school spirit is low," and students feel that they "need more support for athletics and other campus events. A lot of people get involved, but we need a lot more!" Hometown Worcester offers little help; it's a "small, homogeneous city. There are not many opportunities for fun." On the upside, "rooms are spacious and the food is not bad" on campus.

Student Body

The "international and diverse" students of WPI include "a lot of dorks and weirdoes, but there are also a lot of cool kids." Writes one, "It's a broad range of people from total dorks to total potheads. Frat parties are big with about half the campus. The other half has probably never seen a beer." Students enjoy a spirit of community fostered by a sense that they "have more in common with the students here than I could have at any other school" and because "most people are easygoing and work hard. There is a real sense of helping each other to succeed." On the downside, WPI's "terrible" male-female ratio "causes a strange social scene that most are not used to."

ADMISSIONS

Very important factors considered by the admissions committee include: class rank, secondary school record, standardized test scores. *Important factors considered include:* essays, extracurricular activities, minority status, recommendations. *Other factors considered include:* alumni/ae relation, character/personal qualities, geographical residence, interview, state residency, talent/ability, volunteer work, work experience. TOEFL required of all international applicants. High school diploma is required and GED is not accepted. *High school units required/recommended:* 10 total required; 4 English recommended, 4 math required, 2 science required, 2 science lab required.

The Inside Word

Worcester's applicant pool is small but very well qualified. Its high acceptance rate makes it a good safety choice for those aiming at more difficult tech schools and for those who are solid but aren't MIT material. As is the case at most technical institutes, women will meet with a very receptive admissions committee.

FINANCIAL AID

Students should submit: FAFSA, CSS/Financial Aid PROFILE, noncustodial (divorced/separated) parent's statement, parent's and student's prior year's federal tax return and W-2s. Regular filing deadline is March 1. The Princeton Review suggests that all financial aid forms be submitted as soon as possible after January 1. *Need-based scholarships/grants offered:* Pell, SEOG, state scholarships/grants, the school's own gift aid. *Loan aid offered:* FFEL Subsidized Stafford, FFEL Unsubsidized Stafford, FFEL PLUS, Federal Perkins, state loans, college/university loans from institutional funds. Federal Work-Study Program available. Institutional employment available. Applicants will be notified of awards on or about April 1. Off-campus job opportunities are good.

FROM THE ADMISSIONS OFFICE

"Projects and research are a distinctive element of the WPI plan. WPI believes that in these times simply passing courses and accumulating theoretical knowledge is not enough to truly educate tomorrow's leaders. Tomorrow's professionals ought to be involved in project work that prepares them today for future challenges. Projects at WPI come as close to professional experience as a college program can possibly achieve. In fact, WPI works with more than 200 companies, government agencies, and private organizations each year. These groups provide project opportunities where students get a chance to work in real, professional settings. Students gain experience in planning, coordinating team efforts, meeting deadlines, writing proposals and reports, making oral presentations, doing cost analyses, and making decisions."

For even more information on this school, turn to page 382 of the "Stats" section.

YALE UNIVERSITY

PO Box 208234, New Haven, CT 06520-8234 • Admissions: 203-432-9316 • Fax: 203-432-9392
Financial Aid: 203-432-2700 • E-mail: student.questions@yale.edu • Website: www.yale.edu/admit

Ratings

| Quality of Life: 81 | Academic: 99 | Admissions: 99 | Financial Aid: 80 |

Academics

Neither professors nor students at Yale rest on their laurels, though there are certainly many laurels to rest upon if they wanted to. Yale's professors, "in addition to being top scholars, actually seem to enjoy teaching undergrads." That's no mean feat at one of the preeminent research institutions in the country. Professors are "incredibly knowledgeable" but also "fascinated with their students, consummately available, and

> **SURVEY SAYS . . .**
> *Registration is a breeze*
> *Ethnic diversity on campus*
> *Students are happy*
> *Lots of classroom discussion*
> *No one cheats*
> *Very little hard liquor*
> *Very little drug use*
> *(Almost) no one listens to college radio*
> *Very small frat/sorority scene*

friendly and helpful to an awesome degree." Some, however, "are less talented [than others] in the department of effectively conveying the vast stores of knowledge they possess." Still, students admit that it's sort of thrilling when professors "use their own textbooks in class." Yale can afford to be extremely selective with a huge surplus of applicants beating down the doors, but "once you're in, they will pamper you and support your ambitions." And the university can afford it, too. As one student put it, "Our reputation, and thus our resources, are impressive." Another says, "Yale is so well equipped for students to explore their academic interests that being at a well-known institution almost seems to be only an added bonus." Some students do think, however, that the administration could improve a bit: "The school's administration likes to maintain an official distance from the general student population, but frequently publishes newsletters and responds to articles in the newspaper to keep us informed of its thoughts and plans." Students love the shopping system of registration, which allows them to visit classes for up to two weeks before registering, enabling them to avoid poor instructors and uninteresting classes. Lest you forget, it's worth repeating that "the schoolwork itself is hard, very hard, but rewarding, very rewarding."

Life

"Yalies take advantage of every free moment," and they have to, balancing rigorous academic requirements with exciting social lives and extracurricular activities. Something has to give, so for some students "sleep becomes a friend you only really get to hang out with on weekends." Yalies applaud the residential college system, where students live together all four years, as "awesome because you really get to know a group of people and get to live with a large portion of them for four years." Residential life also provides access to "key administrators because each college has a master and a dean." Students can depend on help from their college deans when wrangling with university bureaucracy. On campus, Yale provides all kinds of activities, from a cappella performances to parties. Hometown New Haven gets decent marks by students: "The city has its good points (the best pizza in the world among them), and they're doing a good job revitalizing it." New Haven is starkly separate from the university, though students note with pleasure that "the crime rate is down more than 60 percent since

1990." Mostly, Yale students like doing "Lacanian readings of Friends" or just "talking about anything and everything until 4 a.m." And sometimes, Yalies get excited about simply being at Yale, where, "heck, the showers in my building are all solid marble." Still, Yalies are kids like the rest of us, too: "What do we think about? Finishing our work and trying to get laid."

Student Body

"Yale does a wonderful job selecting students from a broad base," describes one student. "I now have friends in every corner of the globe." With its resources and reputation, Yale manages to bring together students from every racial, ethnic, and socioeconomic background. "The incredible student body provides an education by itself." Over and over, students repeat that what they love best about Yale are their peers. Mind you, Yalies are "intense" ("No one here is lukewarm about anything"), but "no one is trying to fit into a mold." Students are "the smartest people I've ever met." One student glows with pride, "It is easy to believe that we will be the future leaders of tomorrow."

ADMISSIONS

Very important factors considered by the admissions committee include: character/personal qualities, class rank, essays, extracurricular activities, recommendations, secondary school record, standardized test scores, talent/ability. *Other factors considered include:* alumni/ae relation, geographical residence, interview, minority status, state residency, volunteer work, work experience. SAT I or ACT required; SAT II also required. TOEFL required of all international applicants.

The Inside Word

There is no grey area here; Yale is ultra-selective with growing applicant pools each year. And there's nothing to be gained by appealing a denial here—the admissions committee considers all of its decisions final. Yale uses a regional review process that serves as a preliminary screening for all candidates, and only the best-qualified, well-matched candidates actually come before the admissions committee.

FINANCIAL AID

Students should submit: FAFSA, CSS/Financial Aid PROFILE, state aid form, noncustodial (divorced/separated) parent's statement, business/farm supplement, tax returns. Regular filing deadline is February 1. The Princeton Review suggests that all financial aid forms be submitted as soon as possible after January 1. *Need-based scholarships/grants offered:* Pell, SEOG, state scholarships/grants, private scholarships, the school's own gift aid, United Negro College Fund. *Loan aid offered:* FFEL Subsidized Stafford, FFEL Unsubsidized Stafford, FFEL PLUS, Federal Perkins, state loans, college/university loans from institutional funds. Federal Work-Study Program available. Institutional employment available. Applicants will be notified of awards on or about April 1. Off-campus job opportunities are good.

FROM THE ADMISSIONS OFFICE

"The most important questions the admissions committee must resolve are 'Who is likely to make the most of Yale's resources?' and 'Who will contribute significantly to the Yale community?' These questions suggest an approach to evaluating applicants that is more complex than whether Yale would rather admit well-rounded people or those with specialized talents. In selecting a class of 1,300 from approximately 17,700 applicants, the admissions committee looks for academic ability and achievement combined with such personal characteristics as motivation, curiosity, energy, and leadership ability. The nature of these qualities is such that there is no simple profile of grades, scores, interests, and activities that will assure admission. Diversity within the student population is important, and the admissions committee selects a class of able and contributing individuals from a variety of backgrounds and with a broad range of interests and skills."

For even more information on this school, turn to page 382 of the "Stats" section.

PART 3

THE STATS

Adelphi University

CAMPUS LIFE
Quality of Life Rating **76**
Type of school   private
Affiliation   none
Environment   urban

STUDENTS
Total undergrad enrollment   3,391
% male/female   29/71
% from out of state   11
% from public high school   75
% live on campus   26
% in (# of) fraternities   6 (3)
% in (# of) sororities   6 (6)
% African American   12
% Asian   4
% Caucasian   51
% Hispanic   7
% international   4

ACADEMICS
Academic Rating **69**
Calendar   semester
Student/faculty ratio   14:1
Profs interesting rating   83
Profs accessible rating   83
% profs teaching UG courses   100
% classes taught by TAs   0
Avg lab size   10-19 students
Avg reg class size   20-29 students

MOST POPULAR MAJORS
Social work
Social sciences
Business administration/management

SELECTIVITY
Admissions Rating **63**
# of applicants   3,703
% of applicants accepted   68
% of acceptees attending   27

FRESHMAN PROFILE
Range SAT Verbal   480-580
Average SAT Verbal   533
Range SAT Math   480-590
Average SAT Math   536
Minimum TOEFL   550
Average HS GPA   3.3
% graduated top 10% of class   17
% graduated top 25% of class   48
% graduated top 50% of class   89

DEADLINES
Nonfall registration?   yes

FINANCIAL FACTS
Financial Aid Rating **89**
Tuition $16,100
Room and board $7,050
Books and supplies $1,000
Avg frosh grant $5,853
Avg frosh loan $3,219

Alfred University

CAMPUS LIFE
Quality of Life Rating **79**
Type of school   private
Environment   rural

STUDENTS
Total undergrad enrollment   2,080
% male/female   48/52
% from out of state   35
% live on campus   65
% African American   5
% Asian   2
% Caucasian   78
% Hispanic   4
% international   2

ACADEMICS
Academic Rating **76**
Calendar   semester
Student/faculty ratio   12:1
Profs interesting rating   93
Profs accessible rating   92
% profs teaching UG courses   100
Avg lab size   10-19 students
Avg reg class size   10-19 students

MOST POPULAR MAJORS
Business administration/management
Ceramic sciences and engineering
Fine/studio arts

SELECTIVITY
Admissions Rating **77**
# of applicants   2,050
% of applicants accepted   65
% of acceptees attending   33

| # of early decision applicants | 45 |
| % accepted early decision | 93 |

FRESHMAN PROFILE
Range SAT Verbal	490-640
Range SAT Math	490-640
Range ACT Composite	26-30
Minimum TOEFL	550
% graduated top 10% of class	23
% graduated top 25% of class	51
% graduated top 50% of class	83

DEADLINES
Early decision	12/1
Early decision notification	12/15
Priority admission	2/1
Nonfall registration?	yes

FINANCIAL FACTS
Financial Aid Rating	**88**
Tuition	$18,498
Room and board	$8,500
Books and supplies	$700
Required fees	$698
% frosh receiving aid	90
% undergrads receiving aid	90

AMHERST COLLEGE

CAMPUS LIFE
Quality of Life Rating	**92**
Type of school	private
Environment	rural

STUDENTS
Total undergrad enrollment	1,618
% from out of state	85
% from public high school	60
% live on campus	98
% African American	9
% Asian	13
% Caucasian	62
% Hispanic	8
% international	5
# of countries represented	34

ACADEMICS
Academic Rating	**99**
Calendar	semester
Student/faculty ratio	9:1
Profs interesting rating	97
Profs accessible rating	96
% profs teaching UG courses	100

| Avg lab size | under 10 students |
| Avg reg class size | 10-19 students |

MOST POPULAR MAJORS
English language and literature
Economics
Political science and government

SELECTIVITY
Admissions Rating	**99**
# of applicants	5,238
% of applicants accepted	18
# accepting a place on wait list	321
% admitted from wait list	6
# of early decision applicants	368
% accepted early decision	36

FRESHMAN PROFILE
Range SAT Verbal	660-770
Average SAT Verbal	710
Range SAT Math	650-770
Average SAT Math	707
Range ACT Composite	28-33
Average ACT Composite	30
Minimum TOEFL	600
% graduated top 10% of class	82
% graduated top 25% of class	98
% graduated top 50% of class	100

DEADLINES
Early decision	11/15
Regular admission	12/31
Regular notification	4/3

FINANCIAL FACTS
Financial Aid Rating	**88**
Tuition	$27,800
Room and board	$7,380
Books and supplies	$850
Required fees	$510
% frosh receiving aid	47
% undergrads receiving aid	49
Avg frosh grant	$25,534
Avg frosh loan	$2,150

ASSUMPTION COLLEGE

CAMPUS LIFE
Quality of Life Rating	**79**
Type of school	private
Affiliation	Roman Catholic
Environment	urban

STUDENTS

Total undergrad enrollment	2,081
% male/female	39/61
% from out of state	32
% from public high school	67
% live on campus	88
% African American	1
% Asian	2
% Caucasian	85
% Hispanic	2
% international	1
# of countries represented	17

ACADEMICS

Academic Rating	**76**
Calendar	semester
Student/faculty ratio	13:1
Profs interesting rating	79
Profs accessible rating	77
% profs teaching UG courses	100
% classes taught by TAs	0
Avg lab size	18 students
Avg reg class size	20 students

MOST POPULAR MAJORS
English
Psychology
Business

SELECTIVITY

Admissions Rating	**79**
# of applicants	2,766
% of applicants accepted	76
% of acceptees attending	29
# accepting a place on wait list	145
% admitted from wait list	50
# of early decision applicants	31
% accepted early decision	85

FRESHMAN PROFILE

Range SAT Verbal	490-580
Average SAT Verbal	535
Range SAT Math	540
Average SAT Math	534
Range ACT Composite	18-23
Average ACT Composite	21
Minimum TOEFL	200
Average HS GPA	3.2
% graduated top 10% of class	13.3
% graduated top 25% of class	41.6
% graduated top 50% of class	80.5

DEADLINES

Early decision	11/15
Regular admission	3/1
Nonfall registration?	yes

FINANCIAL FACTS

Financial Aid Rating	**79**
Tuition	$19,835
Room and board	$7,820
Books and supplies	$700
Avg frosh grant	$10,731
Avg frosh loan	$3,377

BABSON COLLEGE

CAMPUS LIFE

Quality of Life Rating	**89**
Type of school	private
Environment	suburban

STUDENTS

Total undergrad enrollment	1,735
% from out of state	44
% from public high school	52
% live on campus	81
% African American	3
% Asian	11
% Caucasian	57
% Hispanic	4
% international	19
# of countries represented	64

ACADEMICS

Academic Rating	**87**
Calendar	semester
Student/faculty ratio	13:1
Profs interesting rating	73
Profs accessible rating	73
% profs teaching UG courses	100
Avg lab size	10-19 students
Avg reg class size	30-39 students

MOST POPULAR MAJORS
Business administration/management

SELECTIVITY

Admissions Rating	**90**
# of applicants	2,402
% of applicants accepted	48
% of acceptees attending	35
# accepting a place on wait list	268
% admitted from wait list	7

# of early decision applicants	122
% accepted early decision	58

FRESHMAN PROFILE
Range SAT Verbal	550-630
Average SAT Verbal	600
Range SAT Math	600-690
Average SAT Math	640
Minimum TOEFL	550
% graduated top 10% of class	44
% graduated top 25% of class	81
% graduated top 50% of class	100

DEADLINES
Early decision	12/1
Early decision notification	1/1
Priority admission	12/1
Regular admission	2/1
Regular notification	4/1

FINANCIAL FACTS
Financial Aid Rating — 80
Tuition	$24,544
Room and board	$9,226
Books and supplies	$658
% frosh receiving aid	44
% undergrads receiving aid	42
Avg frosh grant	$14,247
Avg frosh loan	$2,887

BARD COLLEGE

CAMPUS LIFE
Quality of Life Rating — 84
Type of school	private
Environment	rural

STUDENTS
Total undergrad enrollment	1,454
% male/female	45/55
% from out of state	76
% from public high school	67
% live on campus	85
% African American	3
% Asian	4
% Caucasian	77
% Hispanic	5
% international	6
# of countries represented	48

ACADEMICS
Academic Rating — 95
Calendar	4-1-4
Student/faculty ratio	9:1
% profs teaching UG courses	100
Avg reg class size	under 10 students

MOST POPULAR MAJORS
Visual and performing arts
English language and literature
Social sciences

SELECTIVITY
Admissions Rating — 95
# of applicants	3,118
% of applicants accepted	36
% of acceptees attending	31
# accepting a place on wait list	216
% admitted from wait list	17

FRESHMAN PROFILE
Range SAT Verbal	650-750
Average SAT Verbal	670
Range SAT Math	590-690
Average SAT Math	630
Minimum TOEFL	600
Average HS GPA	3.5
% graduated top 10% of class	64
% graduated top 25% of class	90
% graduated top 50% of class	99

DEADLINES
Regular admission	1/15
Regular notification	4/1
Nonfall registration?	yes

FINANCIAL FACTS
Financial Aid Rating — 87
Tuition	$26,900
Room and board	$8,134
Books and supplies	$700
Required fees	$550
% frosh receiving aid	60
% undergrads receiving aid	61
Avg frosh grant	$18,282
Avg frosh loan	$3,351

BARNARD COLLEGE

CAMPUS LIFE
Quality of Life Rating **91**
Type of school | private
Environment | urban

STUDENTS
Total undergrad enrollment | 2,297
% from out of state | 65
% from public high school | 58
% live on campus | 88
% African American | 5
% Asian | 20
% Caucasian | 65
% Hispanic | 6
% international | 3
# of countries represented | 35

ACADEMICS
Academic Rating **91**
Calendar | semester
Student/faculty ratio | 10:1
Profs interesting rating | 94
Profs accessible rating | 93
% profs teaching UG courses | 100
Avg lab size | under 10 students
Avg reg class size | 10-19 students

MOST POPULAR MAJORS
English language and literature
Psychology
Economics

SELECTIVITY
Admissions Rating **97**
# of applicants | 3,686
% of applicants accepted | 34
% of acceptees attending | 43
# accepting a place on wait list | 484
% admitted from wait list | 1
# of early decision applicants | 317
% accepted early decision | 45

FRESHMAN PROFILE
Range SAT Verbal | 630-710
Average SAT Verbal | 660
Range SAT Math | 620-700
Average SAT Math | 670
Range ACT Composite | 27-30
Average ACT Composite | 29
Minimum TOEFL | 600
Average HS GPA | 3.9

% graduated top 10% of class | 84
% graduated top 25% of class | 98
% graduated top 50% of class | 100

DEADLINES
Early decision | 11/15
Early decision notification | 12/15
Regular admission | 1/1
Regular notification | 4/2
Nonfall registration? | yes

FINANCIAL FACTS
Financial Aid Rating **84**
Tuition | $24,090
Room and board | $10,140
Books and supplies | $900
Required fees | $1,180
% frosh receiving aid | 41
% undergrads receiving aid | 41
Avg frosh grant | $21,914
Avg frosh loan | $2,625

BATES COLLEGE

CAMPUS LIFE
Quality of Life Rating **83**
Type of school | private
Environment | suburban

STUDENTS
Total undergrad enrollment | 1,738
% from out of state | 89
% from public high school | 56
% live on campus | 90
% African American | 2
% Asian | 4
% Caucasian | 89
% Hispanic | 2
% international | 6

ACADEMICS
Academic Rating **98**
Calendar | other
Student/faculty ratio | 10:1
Profs interesting rating | 95
Profs accessible rating | 98
% profs teaching UG courses | 100
Avg lab size | 10-19 students
Avg reg class size | 10-19 students

MOST POPULAR MAJORS
English language and literature
Psychology
Political science and government

SELECTIVITY

Admissions Rating	**98**
# of applicants	4,012
% of applicants accepted	28
% of acceptees attending	37
# accepting a place on wait list	300
# of early decision applicants	430
% accepted early decision	38

FRESHMAN PROFILE

Range SAT Verbal	630-710
Average SAT Verbal	671
Range SAT Math	630-720
Average SAT Math	677
Minimum TOEFL	200 (CBT)
% graduated top 10% of class	62
% graduated top 25% of class	93
% graduated top 50% of class	100

DEADLINES

Early decision	11/15
Regular admission	1/15
Regular notification	4/1
Nonfall registration?	yes

FINANCIAL FACTS

Financial Aid Rating	**82**
Tuition	$37,500
Books and supplies	$1,750
Required fees	$0
% frosh receiving aid	46
% undergrads receiving aid	39
Avg frosh grant	$21,160
Avg frosh loan	$2,500

BENNINGTON COLLEGE

CAMPUS LIFE

Quality of Life Rating	**83**
Type of school	private
Environment	rural

STUDENTS

Total undergrad enrollment	580
% male/female	33/67
% from out of state	95
% live on campus	95
% African American	1
% Asian	1
% Caucasian	82
% Hispanic	2
% international	9
# of countries represented	19

ACADEMICS

Academic Rating	**93**
Calendar	other
Student/faculty ratio	9:1
% profs teaching UG courses	100
% classes taught by TAs	2
Avg lab size	10-19 students
Avg reg class size	10-19 students

MOST POPULAR MAJORS
Multi/interdisciplinary studies
Visual and performing arts
Social sciences

SELECTIVITY

Admissions Rating	**84**
# of applicants	701
% of applicants accepted	70
% of acceptees attending	35
# of early decision applicants	49
% accepted early decision	86

FRESHMAN PROFILE

Range SAT Verbal	580-690
Average SAT Verbal	630
Range SAT Math	500-630
Average SAT Math	568
Minimum TOEFL	550
Average HS GPA	3.4
% graduated top 10% of class	40
% graduated top 25% of class	68
% graduated top 50% of class	89

DEADLINES

Early decision	11/15
Early decision notification	12/1
Regular admission	1/1
Regular notification	4/1
Nonfall registration?	yes

FINANCIAL FACTS

Financial Aid Rating	**85**
Tuition	$28,030
Room and board	$7,140
Books and supplies	$800
Required fees	$740
% frosh receiving aid	64
% undergrads receiving aid	59

| Avg frosh grant | $14,500 |
| Avg frosh loan | $2,977 |

BENTLEY COLLEGE

CAMPUS LIFE
Quality of Life Rating **79**
Type of school | private
Environment | suburban

STUDENTS
Total undergrad enrollment	4,325
% male/female	57/43
% from out of state	40
% from public high school	70
% live on campus	71
% African American	4
% Asian	8
% Caucasian	78
% Hispanic	4
% international	8
# of countries represented	61

ACADEMICS
Academic Rating **77**
Calendar	semester
Student/faculty ratio	14:1
Profs interesting rating	92
Profs accessible rating	91
% profs teaching UG courses	100
Avg reg class size	20-29 students

MOST POPULAR MAJORS
Accounting
International Studies
Marketing

SELECTIVITY
Admissions Rating **81**
# of applicants	5,082
% of applicants accepted	46
% of acceptees attending	39
# accepting a place on wait list	936
% admitted from wait list	1
# of early decision applicants	162
% accepted early decision	65

FRESHMAN PROFILE
Range SAT Verbal	520-600
Average SAT Verbal	559
Range SAT Math	560-650
Average SAT Math	603

Range ACT Composite	22-26
Minimum TOEFL	550
% graduated top 10% of class	31
% graduated top 25% of class	65
% graduated top 50% of class	95

DEADLINES
Early decision	12/1
Early decision notification	11/15
Priority admission	2/1
Regular admission	2/1
Regular notification	4/1
Nonfall registration?	yes

FINANCIAL FACTS
Financial Aid Rating **80**
Tuition	$20,880
Room and board	$9,350
Books and supplies	$900
Required fees	$195
% frosh receiving aid	57
% undergrads receiving aid	50
Avg frosh grant	$15,170
Avg frosh loan	$2,810

BOSTON COLLEGE

CAMPUS LIFE
Quality of Life Rating **80**
Type of school | private
Affiliation | Roman Catholic
Environment | suburban

STUDENTS
Total undergrad enrollment	8,916
% from out of state	73
% from public high school	60
% live on campus	73
% African American	5
% Asian	9
% Caucasian	75
% Hispanic	6
% international	2
# of countries represented	86

ACADEMICS
Academic Rating **92**
Calendar	semester
Student/faculty ratio	13:1
Profs interesting rating	91
Profs accessible rating	89

| % profs teaching UG courses | 100 |
| Avg reg class size | 10-19 students |

SELECTIVITY
Admissions Rating **96**

# of applicants	21,133
% of applicants accepted	32
% of acceptees attending	34

FRESHMAN PROFILE
Range SAT Verbal	600-690
Range SAT Math	620-710
Minimum TOEFL	600
% graduated top 10% of class	72
% graduated top 25% of class	94
% graduated top 50% of class	99

DEADLINES
Regular admission	1/2
Regular notification	4/15
Nonfall registration?	yes

FINANCIAL FACTS
Financial Aid Rating **84**

Tuition	$27,080
Room and board	$9,300
Books and supplies	$600
Required fees	$442
% frosh receiving aid	60
% undergrads receiving aid	42
Avg frosh grant	$15,880
Avg frosh loan	$3,459

BOSTON UNIVERSITY

CAMPUS LIFE
Quality of Life Rating **84**

| Type of school | private |
| Environment | urban |

STUDENTS
Total undergrad enrollment	17,860
% male/female	40/60
% from out of state	76
% from public high school	70
% live on campus	74
% in (# of) fraternities	3 (9)
% in (# of) sororities	5 (10)
% African American	2
% Asian	12
% Caucasian	62

% Hispanic	5
% international	7
# of countries represented	101

ACADEMICS
Academic Rating **92**

Calendar	semester
Student/faculty ratio	14:1
Profs interesting rating	91
Profs accessible rating	95
% profs teaching UG courses	74
% classes taught by TAs	7
Avg lab size	20-29 students
Avg reg class size	10-19 students

SELECTIVITY
Admissions Rating **91**

# of applicants	27,038
% of applicants accepted	58
% of acceptees attending	29
# accepting a place on wait list	558
% admitted from wait list	12
# of early decision applicants	399
% accepted early decision	47

FRESHMAN PROFILE
Range SAT Verbal	590-680
Average SAT Verbal	634
Range SAT Math	610-690
Average SAT Math	647
Range ACT Composite	25-29
Average ACT Composite	28
Minimum TOEFL	550
Average HS GPA	3.5
% graduated top 10% of class	56
% graduated top 25% of class	90

DEADLINES
Early decision	11/1
Early decision notification	12/15
Regular admission	1/1
Nonfall registration?	yes

FINANCIAL FACTS
Financial Aid Rating **87**

Tuition	$28,512
Room and board	$9,288
Books and supplies	$753
Required fees	$394
% frosh receiving aid	52
% undergrads receiving aid	46
Avg frosh grant	$16,825
Avg frosh loan	$4,614

BOWDOIN COLLEGE

CAMPUS LIFE
Quality of Life Rating   **91**
Type of school   private
Environment   suburban

STUDENTS
Total undergrad enrollment	1,657
% male/female	49/51
% from out of state	86
% from public high school	54
% live on campus	90
% African American	4
% Asian	8
% Caucasian	77
% Hispanic	4
% international	3
# of countries represented	27

ACADEMICS
Academic Rating   **94**
Calendar	semester
Student/faculty ratio	10:1
Profs interesting rating	94
Profs accessible rating	95
% profs teaching UG courses	100
Avg lab size	10-19 students
Avg reg class size	10-19 students

MOST POPULAR MAJORS
Government and legal studies
English
Economics

SELECTIVITY
Admissions Rating   **97**
# of applicants	4,505
% of applicants accepted	25
% of acceptees attending	41
# of early decision applicants	627
% accepted early decision	28

FRESHMAN PROFILE
Range SAT Verbal	640-730
Average SAT Verbal	680
Range SAT Math	640-720
Average SAT Math	680
Minimum TOEFL	600
% graduated top 10% of class	72
% graduated top 25% of class	94
% graduated top 50% of class	100

DEADLINES
Early decision	11/15 & 1/1
Early decision notification	12/15 & 2/7
Regular admission	1/1
Regular notification	4/1

FINANCIAL FACTS
Financial Aid Rating   **80**
Tuition	$28,070
Room and board	$7,305
Books and supplies	$850
Required fees	$615
% frosh receiving aid	45
% undergrads receiving aid	40
Avg frosh grant	$22,096
Avg frosh loan	$2,891

BRANDEIS UNIVERSITY

CAMPUS LIFE
Quality of Life Rating   **80**
Type of school   private
Environment   suburban

STUDENTS
Total undergrad enrollment	3,057
% male/female	44/56
% from out of state	75
% from public high school	70
% live on campus	84
% African American	3
% Asian	10
% Caucasian	75
% Hispanic	3
% international	6
# of countries represented	54

ACADEMICS
Academic Rating   **83**
Calendar	semester
Student/faculty ratio	8:1
Profs interesting rating	94
Profs accessible rating	97
% profs teaching UG courses	100
Avg reg class size	10-19 students

MOST POPULAR MAJORS
Biology/biological sciences
Economics
Political science and government

SELECTIVITY

Admissions Rating	**91**
# of applicants	6,080
% of applicants accepted	42
% of acceptees attending	33
# accepting a place on wait list	165
% admitted from wait list	33
# of early decision applicants	297
% accepted early decision	72

FRESHMAN PROFILE

Range SAT Verbal	627-710
Average SAT Verbal	660
Range SAT Math	630-710
Average SAT Math	670
Minimum TOEFL	600
Average HS GPA	3.8
% graduated top 10% of class	62
% graduated top 25% of class	93
% graduated top 50% of class	100

DEADLINES

Early decision	1/1
Early decision notification	2/1
Regular admission	1/15
Regular notification	4/1
Nonfall registration?	yes

FINANCIAL FACTS

Financial Aid Rating	**85**
Tuition	$27,345
Room and board	$7,849
Books and supplies	$700
Required fees	$820
% frosh receiving aid	50
% undergrads receiving aid	50
Avg frosh grant	$15,012
Avg frosh loan	$4,647

BROWN UNIVERSITY

CAMPUS LIFE

Quality of Life Rating	**87**
Type of school	private
Environment	urban

STUDENTS

Total undergrad enrollment	6,030
% male/female	45/55
% from out of state	96
% from public high school	60

% live on campus	85
% in (# of) fraternities	15 (10)
% in (# of) sororities	5 (3)
% African American	6
% Asian	15
% Caucasian	53
% Hispanic	7
% international	6
# of countries represented	72

ACADEMICS

Academic Rating	**96**
Calendar	semester
Student/faculty ratio	8:1
Profs interesting rating	94
Profs accessible rating	90
% profs teaching UG courses	100
% classes taught by TAs	13

MOST POPULAR MAJORS
Biology/biological sciences
International relations and affairs
History

SELECTIVITY

Admissions Rating	**99**
# of applicants	14,612
% of applicants accepted	17
% of acceptees attending	59
# accepting a place on wait list	400
# of early decision applicants	1,918
% accepted early decision	27

FRESHMAN PROFILE

Range SAT Verbal	640-750
Average SAT Verbal	690
Range SAT Math	650-750
Average SAT Math	700
Range ACT Composite	26-32
Average ACT Composite	29
Minimum TOEFL	600
% graduated top 10% of class	87
% graduated top 25% of class	97
% graduated top 50% of class	100

DEADLINES

Early decision	11/1
Early decision notification	12/15
Regular admission	1/1
Regular notification	4/1

FINANCIAL FACTS

Financial Aid Rating	**79**

Tuition	$27,856
Room and board	$7,876
Books and supplies	$960
Required fees	$851
% frosh receiving aid	41
% undergrads receiving aid	40
Avg frosh grant	$20,800
Avg frosh loan	$2,700

BRYANT COLLEGE

CAMPUS LIFE
Quality of Life Rating	**86**
Type of school	private
Environment	suburban

STUDENTS
Total undergrad enrollment	2,912
% male/female	60/40
% from out of state	74
% from public high school	78
% live on campus	75
% in (# of) fraternities	8 (6)
% in (# of) sororities	8 (3)
% African American	3
% Asian	2
% Caucasian	86
% Hispanic	3
% international	4
# of countries represented	37

ACADEMICS
Academic Rating	**79**
Calendar	semester
Student/faculty ratio	16:1
Profs interesting rating	82
Profs accessible rating	86
% profs teaching UG courses	100
Avg lab size	20-29 students
Avg reg class size	30-39 students

MOST POPULAR MAJORS
Business administration/management
Finance and financial management services
Marketing

SELECTIVITY
Admissions Rating	**75**
# of applicants	2,811
% of applicants accepted	74
% of acceptees attending	36
# accepting a place on wait list	283

% admitted from wait list	23
# of early decision applicants	14
% accepted early decision	93

FRESHMAN PROFILE
Range SAT Verbal	480-560
Average SAT Verbal	522
Range SAT Math	510-610
Average SAT Math	557
Range ACT Composite	19-24
Average ACT Composite	22
Minimum TOEFL	550
Average HS GPA	3.0
% graduated top 10% of class	9
% graduated top 25% of class	36
% graduated top 50% of class	80

DEADLINES
Early decision & early action	11/15
Early decision notification	12/15
Regular admission	2/15
Regular notification	3/15
Nonfall registration?	yes

FINANCIAL FACTS
Financial Aid Rating	**86**
Tuition	$21,160
Room and board	$8,546
Books and supplies	$900
% undergrads receiving aid	70
Avg frosh grant	$7,774
Avg frosh loan	$3,914

CENTRAL CONNECTICUT STATE UNIVERSITY

CAMPUS LIFE
Quality of Life Rating	**77**
Type of school	public
Affiliation	none
Environment	suburban

STUDENTS
Total undergrad enrollment	9,551
% male/female	48/52
% from out of state	2
% live on campus	28
% African American	7
% Asian	3
% Caucasian	76
% Hispanic	5
% international	1

ACADEMICS
Academic Rating   **69**

Calendar	semester
Student/faculty ratio	16;1
Profs interesting rating	82
Profs accessible rating	80
% profs teaching UG courses	100
% classes taught by TAs	0
Avg lab size	10-19 students
Avg reg class size	20-29 students

MOST POPULAR MAJORS
Teacher education, multiple levels
Education
Accounting

SELECTIVITY
Admissions Rating   **67**

# of applicants	4,660
% of applicants accepted	65
% of acceptees attending	43

FRESHMAN PROFILE

Range SAT Verbal	440-540
Average SAT Verbal	489
Range SAT Math	440-540
Average SAT Math	492
Minimum TOEFL	500
% graduated top 10% of class	5
% graduated top 25% of class	18
% graduated top 50% of class	56

DEADLINES

Regular admission	5/1
Nonfall registration?	yes

FINANCIAL FACTS
Financial Aid Rating   **80**

In-state tuition	$2,313
Out-of-state tuition	$7,485
Room and board	$6,280
Books and supplies	$750
Avg frosh grant	$3,000
Avg frosh loan	$2,625

CITY UNIVERSITY OF NEW YORK—BARUCH COLLEGE

CAMPUS LIFE
Quality of Life Rating   **80**

Type of school	public
Affiliation	none
Environment	urban

STUDENTS

Total undergrad enrollment	12,969
% male/female	43/57
% from out of state	3
% African American	19
% Asian	25
% Caucasian	29
% Hispanic	19
% international	9

ACADEMICS
Academic Rating   **65**

Calendar	semester
Student/faculty ratio	17:1
Profs interesting rating	89
Profs accessible rating	86
% profs teaching UG courses	95
% classes taught by TAs	1

MOST POPULAR MAJORS
Accounting
Computer information systems
Finance

SELECTIVITY
Admissions Rating   **63**

# of applicants	13,337
% of applicants accepted	33
% of acceptees attending	34

FRESHMAN PROFILE

Range SAT Verbal	460-560
Average SAT Verbal	511
Range SAT Math	520-620
Average SAT Math	572
Minimum TOEFL	620
Average HS GPA	3.1
% graduated top 10% of class	22
% graduated top 25% of class	54
% graduated top 50% of class	82

DEADLINES

Regular admission	3/1
Regular notification	4/1
Nonfall registration?	yes

FINANCIAL FACTS
Financial Aid Rating   **82**

In-state tuition	$3,200
Out-of-state tuition	$6,800
Avg frosh grant	$4,650
Avg frosh loan	$1,928

CITY UNIVERSITY OF NEW YORK—BROOKLYN COLLEGE

CAMPUS LIFE

Quality of Life Rating	**90**
Type of school	public
Environment	urban

STUDENTS

Total undergrad enrollment	10,767
% male/female	39/61
% from out of state	2
% from public high school	71
% in (# of) fraternities	2 (5)
% in (# of) sororities	2 (4)
% African American	30
% Asian	10
% Caucasian	48
% Hispanic	11
% international	5

ACADEMICS

Academic Rating	**83**
Calendar	semester
Student/faculty ratio	16:1
Profs interesting rating	90
Profs accessible rating	87
% classes taught by TAs	8
Avg reg class size	20-29 students

MOST POPULAR MAJORS
Business administration/management
Computer and information sciences
Education

ADMISSIONS

Admissions Rating	**75**
# of applicants	6,184
% of applicants accepted	36
% of acceptees attending	55

FRESHMAN PROFILE

Range SAT Verbal	440-550
Average SAT Verbal	497
Range SAT Math	470-570
Average SAT Math	523
Minimum TOEFL	500
Average HS GPA	3.0

DEADLINES

Priority admission	12/15
Regular admission	rolling
Nonfall registration?	yes

FINANCIAL FACTS

Financial Aid Rating	**90**
In-state tuition	$3,200
Out-of-state tuition	$6,800
Room and board	$4,200
Required fees	$353
% frosh receiving aid	59
% undergrads receiving aid	75

CITY UNIVERSITY OF NEW YORK—HUNTER COLLEGE

CAMPUS LIFE

Quality of Life Rating	**71**
Type of school	public
Environment	urban

STUDENTS

Total undergrad enrollment	15,494
% male/female	30/70
% from out of state	2
% from public high school	74
% in (# of) fraternities	1 (2)
% in (# of) sororities	1 (2)
% African American	18
% Asian	14
% Caucasian	40
% Hispanic	21
% international	6

ACADEMICS

Academic Rating	**73**
Calendar	semester
Profs interesting rating	84
Profs accessible rating	86

SELECTIVITY

Admissions Rating	**79**
# of applicants	10,550
% of applicants accepted	29
% of acceptees attending	49

FRESHMAN PROFILE

Range SAT Verbal	470-570
Average SAT Verbal	523
Range SAT Math	480-580
Average SAT Math	534
Minimum TOEFL	500

DEADLINES

Priority admission	1/2
Nonfall registration?	yes

FINANCIAL FACTS

Financial Aid Rating	**80**
In-state tuition	$3,200
Out-of-state tuition	$6,800
Books and supplies	$759
Required fees	$329
% frosh receiving aid	60
% undergrads receiving aid	60
Avg frosh grant	$4,250
Avg frosh loan	$2,600

CITY UNIVERSITY OF NEW YORK—QUEENS COLLEGE

CAMPUS LIFE

Quality of Life Rating	**67**
Type of school	public
Environment	urban

STUDENTS

Total undergrad enrollment	12,012
% male/female	37/63
% from out of state	1
% from public high school	67
% in (# of) fraternities	1 (3)
% in (# of) sororities	1 (2)
% African American	10
% Asian	20
% Caucasian	53
% Hispanic	16
% international	5

ACADEMICS

Academic Rating	**74**
Calendar	semester
Student/faculty ratio	17:1
Profs interesting rating	90
Profs accessible rating	87
% profs teaching UG courses	90
% classes taught by TAs	2
Avg reg class size	20-29 students

MOST POPULAR MAJORS
Psychology
Sociology
Accounting

SELECTIVITY

Admissions Rating	**75**
# of applicants	6,280
% of applicants accepted	41
% of acceptees attending	48

FRESHMAN PROFILE

Range SAT Verbal	440-550
Average SAT Verbal	504
Range SAT Math	480-590
Average SAT Math	537
Minimum TOEFL	500
Average HS GPA	3.1

DEADLINES

Priority admission	10/15
Nonfall registration?	yes

FINANCIAL FACTS

Financial Aid Rating	**82**
In-state tuition	$3,200
Out-of-state tuition	$6,800
Required fees	$203
% frosh receiving aid	83
% undergrads receiving aid	61
Avg frosh grant	$3,500
Avg frosh loan	$2,500

CLARK UNIVERSITY

CAMPUS LIFE

Quality of Life Rating	**71**
Type of school	private
Environment	urban

STUDENTS

Total undergrad enrollment	1,947
% male/female	39/61
% from out of state	62
% from public high school	70
% live on campus	76
% African American	3
% Asian	4
% Caucasian	66
% Hispanic	3
% international	8
# of countries represented	57

ACADEMICS

Academic Rating	**79**
Calendar	semester

Student/faculty ratio 10:1
Profs interesting rating 94
Profs accessible rating 89
% profs teaching UG courses 100
Avg lab size 10-19 students
Avg reg class size 10-19 students

MOST POPULAR MAJORS
Psychology
Government and international relations
Business management

SELECTIVITY
Admissions Rating 82
# of applicants 3,694
% of applicants accepted 68
% of acceptees attending 23
# accepting a place on wait list 28
% admitted from wait list 4
# of early decision applicants 85
% accepted early decision 85

FRESHMAN PROFILE
Range SAT Verbal 540-650
Average SAT Verbal 589
Range SAT Math 540-640
Average SAT Math 586
Range ACT Composite 22-27
Average ACT Composite 25
Minimum TOEFL 550
Average HS GPA 3.4
% graduated top 10% of class 29
% graduated top 25% of class 67
% graduated top 50% of class 93

DEADLINES
Early decision 11/15
Early decision notification 12/15
Regular admission 2/1
Regular notification 4/1
Nonfall registration? yes

FINANCIAL FACTS
Financial Aid Rating 83
Tuition $26,700
Room and board $5,150
Books and supplies $800
Required fees $265
% frosh receiving aid 84
% undergrads receiving aid 84
Avg frosh grant $13,957
Avg frosh loan $3,717

CLARKSON UNIVERSITY

CAMPUS LIFE
Quality of Life Rating 73
Type of school private
Environment rural

STUDENTS
Total undergrad enrollment 2,756
% male/female 75/25
% from out of state 23
% from public high school 87
% live on campus 75
% in (# of) fraternities 15 (10)
% in (# of) sororities 12 (2)
% African American 2
% Asian 3
% Caucasian 93
% Hispanic 2
% international 3
# of countries represented 46

ACADEMICS
Academic Rating 76
Calendar semester
Student/faculty ratio 17:1
Profs interesting rating 89
Profs accessible rating 93
% profs teaching UG courses 95
% classes taught by TAs 1
Avg lab size 20-29 students
Avg reg class size 20-29 students

MOST POPULAR MAJORS
Mechanical engineering/mechanical
technology/technician
Multi/interdisciplinary studies
Civil engineering technologies/
technicians

SELECTIVITY
Admissions Rating 82
# of applicants 2,556
% of applicants accepted 82
% of acceptees attending 35
# accepting a place on wait list 4
# of early decision applicants 221
% accepted early decision 89

FRESHMAN PROFILE
Range SAT Verbal 520-620
Average SAT Verbal 570
Range SAT Math 580-670
Average SAT Math 621

Minimum TOEFL	500
Average HS GPA	3.5
% graduated top 10% of class	36
% graduated top 25% of class	72
% graduated top 50% of class	95

DEADLINES
Early decision	12/1
Early decision notification	12/30
Priority admission	2/1
Regular admission	3/1
Nonfall registration?	yes

FINANCIAL FACTS
Financial Aid Rating	**86**
Tuition	$23,100
Room and board	$8,726
Books and supplies	$900
Required fees	$400
% frosh receiving aid	80
% undergrads receiving aid	81
Avg frosh grant	$10,662
Avg frosh loan	$5,388

COLBY COLLEGE

CAMPUS LIFE
Quality of Life Rating	**90**
Type of school	private
Environment	urban

STUDENTS
Total undergrad enrollment	1,830
% from out of state	84
% from public high school	58
% live on campus	94
% African American	3
% Asian	6
% Caucasian	89
% Hispanic	2
% international	6
# of countries represented	63

ACADEMICS
Academic Rating	**94**
Calendar	4-1-4
Student/faculty ratio	11:1
Profs interesting rating	96
Profs accessible rating	98
% profs teaching UG courses	100

Avg lab size	10-19 students
Avg reg class size	10-19 students

MOST POPULAR MAJORS
English language and literature
Biology/biological sciences
Political science and government

SELECTIVITY
Admissions Rating	**96**
# of applicants	3,873
% of applicants accepted	33
% of acceptees attending	37
# accepting a place on wait list	308
% admitted from wait list	11
# of early decision applicants	512
% accepted early decision	42

FRESHMAN PROFILE
Range SAT Verbal	620-700
Average SAT Verbal	660
Range SAT Math	640-710
Average SAT Math	670
Range ACT Composite	27-30
Average ACT Composite	28
Minimum TOEFL	600
% graduated top 10% of class	64
% graduated top 25% of class	90
% graduated top 50% of class	99

DEADLINES
Early decision	11/15
Early decision notification	12/15
Regular admission	1/1
Regular notification	4/1
Nonfall registration?	yes

FINANCIAL FACTS
Financial Aid Rating	**79**
Tuition	$35,800
Books and supplies	$650
% frosh receiving aid	43
% undergrads receiving aid	38
Avg frosh grant	$21,966
Avg frosh loan	$3,243

COLGATE UNIVERSITY

CAMPUS LIFE
Quality of Life Rating	**88**
Type of school	private
Environment	rural

STUDENTS

Total undergrad enrollment	2,827
% male/female	49/51
% from out of state	67
% from public high school	70
% live on campus	87
% in (# of) fraternities	35 (8)
% in (# of) sororities	32 (4)
% African American	4
% Asian	5
% Caucasian	85
% Hispanic	3
% international	5
# of countries represented	32

ACADEMICS

Academic Rating	**92**
Calendar	semester
Student/faculty ratio	10:1
Profs interesting rating	95
Profs accessible rating	99
% profs teaching UG courses	100
Avg lab size	10-19 students
Avg reg class size	10-19 students

MOST POPULAR MAJORS
History
English language and literature
Economics

SELECTIVITY

Admissions Rating	**95**
# of applicants	6,268
% of applicants accepted	34
% of acceptees attending	35
# accepting a place on wait list	427
% admitted from wait list	2
# of early decision applicants	613
% accepted early decision	49

FRESHMAN PROFILE

Range SAT Verbal	610-700
Average SAT Verbal	652
Range SAT Math	630-710
Average SAT Math	665
Range ACT Composite	27-31
Average ACT Composite	29
Minimum TOEFL	600
Average HS GPA	3.6
% graduated top 10% of class	68
% graduated top 25% of class	92
% graduated top 50% of class	100

DEADLINES

Early decision	11/15
Early decision notification	12/15
Regular admission	1/15
Regular notification	4/1

FINANCIAL FACTS

Financial Aid Rating	**82**
Tuition	$26,845
Room and board	$6,455
Books and supplies	$620
Required fees	$180
% frosh receiving aid	49
% undergrads receiving aid	45
Avg frosh grant	$25,261
Avg frosh loan	$2,625

COLLEGE OF MOUNT SAINT VINCENT

CAMPUS LIFE

Quality of Life Rating	**77**
Type of school	private
Affiliation	Roman Catholic
Environment	urban

STUDENTS

Total undergrad enrollment	1,202
% male/female	22/78
% from out of state	10
% live on campus	50
% African American	18
% Asian	8
% Caucasian	40
% Hispanic	26
% international	3

ACADEMICS

Academic Rating	**69**
Calendar	semester
Student/faculty ratio	12:1
Profs interesting rating	90
Profs accessible rating	90
% profs teaching UG courses	100
% classes taught by TAs	0

MOST POPULAR MAJORS
Nursing
Education
Business and psychology

SELECTIVITY

Admissions Rating	**63**
# of applicants	1,184
% of applicants accepted	70
% of acceptees attending	35

FRESHMAN PROFILE

Range SAT Verbal	450-550
Average SAT Verbal	513
Range SAT Math	420-520
Average SAT Math	499
Average ACT Composite	19
Minimum TOEFL	500
% graduated top 10% of class	16
% graduated top 25% of class	41
% graduated top 50% of class	75

DEADLINES

Early decision	11/15
Nonfall registration?	yes

FINANCIAL FACTS

Financial Aid Rating	**89**
Tuition	$17,880
Room and board	$7,550
Books and supplies	$600
Avg frosh grant	$6,550
Avg frosh loan	$2,625

THE COLLEGE OF NEW JERSEY

CAMPUS LIFE

Quality of Life Rating	**84**
Type of school	public
Environment	suburban

STUDENTS

Total undergrad enrollment	5,961
% male/female	41/59
% from out of state	5
% from public high school	66
% live on campus	61
% in (# of) fraternities	6 (13)
% in (# of) sororities	8 (11)
% African American	6
% Asian	5
% Caucasian	77
% Hispanic	6
# of countries represented	17

ACADEMICS

Academic Rating	**84**
Calendar	semester
Student/faculty ratio	13:1
% profs teaching UG courses	95
Avg lab size	20-29 students
Avg reg class size	20-29 students

MOST POPULAR MAJORS
Elementary education and teaching
English language and literature
Biology/biological sciences

SELECTIVITY

Admissions Rating	**91**
# of applicants	6,323
% of applicants accepted	48
% of acceptees attending	41
# accepting a place on wait list	300
% admitted from wait list	3
# of early decision applicants	510
% accepted early decision	39

FRESHMAN PROFILE

Range SAT Verbal	570-660
Average SAT Verbal	610
Range SAT Math	590-690
Average SAT Math	630
Minimum TOEFL	550
% graduated top 10% of class	61
% graduated top 25% of class	89
% graduated top 50% of class	98

DEADLINES

Early decision	11/15
Early decision notification	12/15
Regular admission	2/15
Nonfall registration?	yes

FINANCIAL FACTS

Financial Aid Rating	**80**
Out-of-state tuition	$9,822
Room and board	$7,416
Books and supplies	$736
Required fees	$1,891
Avg frosh grant	$3,500
Avg frosh loan	$3,000

COLLEGE OF THE ATLANTIC

CAMPUS LIFE
Quality of Life Rating   **94**
Type of school   private
Environment   rural

STUDENTS
Total undergrad enrollment   278
% male/female   36/64
% from out of state   70
% from public high school   67
% live on campus   40
% Caucasian   83
% international   14
# of countries represented   23

ACADEMICS
Academic Rating   **93**
Calendar   trimester
Student/faculty ratio   10:1
% profs teaching UG courses   100

SELECTIVITY
Admissions Rating   **85**
# of applicants   282
% of applicants accepted   71
% of acceptees attending   34
# accepting a place on wait list   3
% admitted from wait list   33
# of early decision applicants   38
% accepted early decision   87

FRESHMAN PROFILE
Range SAT Verbal   570-670
Average SAT Verbal   624
Range SAT Math   550-640
Average SAT Math   586
Range ACT Composite   25-29
Average ACT Composite   28
Minimum TOEFL   550
% graduated top 10% of class   34
% graduated top 25% of class   73
% graduated top 50% of class   93

DEADLINES
Early decision   12/1
Early decision notification   12/15
Priority admission   2/15
Regular admission   2/15
Regular notification   4/1
Nonfall registration?   yes

FINANCIAL FACTS
Financial Aid Rating   **89**
Tuition $23,601
Room and board $6,543
Books and supplies $500
Required fees $360
% frosh receiving aid   90
% undergrads receiving aid   77
Avg frosh grant $11,000
Avg frosh loan $2,625

COLLEGE OF THE HOLY CROSS

CAMPUS LIFE
Quality of Life Rating   **83**
Type of school   private
Affiliation   Roman Catholic
Environment   suburban

STUDENTS
Total undergrad enrollment   2,801
% male/female   47/53
% from out of state   66
% from public high school   42
% live on campus   79
% African American   3
% Asian   4
% Caucasian   79
% Hispanic   5
% international   1
# of countries represented   17

ACADEMICS
Academic Rating   **94**
Calendar   semester
Student/faculty ratio   11:1
Profs interesting rating   75
Profs accessible rating   72
% profs teaching UG courses   100
Avg lab size   under 10 students
Avg reg class size   10-19 students

MOST POPULAR MAJORS
English language and literature
Psychology
Political science and government

SELECTIVITY
Admissions Rating   **92**

# of applicants	4,884
% of applicants accepted	43
% of acceptees attending	34
# accepting a place on wait list	412
% admitted from wait list	9
# of early decicion applicants	357
% accepted early decision	68

FRESHMAN PROFILE

Range SAT Verbal	570-650
Average SAT Verbal	627
Range SAT Math	590-670
Average SAT Math	630
Minimum TOEFL	550
% graduated top 10% of class	59
% graduated top 50% of class	100

DEADLINES

Early decision	12/15
Early decision notification	2/15
Regular admission	1/15
Regular notification	4/1
Nonfall registration?	yes

FINANCIAL FACTS

Financial Aid Rating	**81**
Tuition	$27,560
Room and board	$8,440
Books and supplies	$400
Required fees	$451
% frosh receiving aid	53
% undergrads receiving aid	50
Avg frosh grant	$13,433
Avg frosh loan	$3,904

COLUMBIA UNIVERSITY

CAMPUS LIFE

Quality of Life Rating	**84**
Type of school	private
Environment	urban

STUDENTS

Total undergrad enrollment	4,109
% from out of state	75
% live on campus	98
% African American	9
% Asian	13
% Caucasian	55
% Hispanic	8
% international	5

ACADEMICS

Academic Rating	**98**
Calendar	semester
Avg reg class size	10-19 students

SELECTIVITY

Admissions Rating	**99**
# of applicants	14,129
% of applicants accepted	12
% of acceptees attending	63
# accepting a place on wait list	600
% admitted from wait list	1
# of early decision applicants	1,611
% accepted early decision	31

FRESHMAN PROFILE

Range SAT Verbal	660-760
Average SAT Verbal	701
Range SAT Math	660-750
Average SAT Math	693
Range ACT Composite	27-33
Minimum TOEFL	600
Average HS GPA	3.8
% graduated top 10% of class	84
% graduated top 25% of class	95
% graduated top 50% of class	100

DEADLINES

Early decision	11/1
Early decision notification	12/15
Regular admission	1/1
Regular notification	4/4

FINANCIAL FACTS

Financial Aid Rating	**85**
Tuition	$27,190
Room and board	$8,546
Required fees	$1,016
Avg frosh grant	$18,662
Avg frosh loan	$2,445

CONNECTICUT COLLEGE

CAMPUS LIFE

Quality of Life Rating	**78**
Type of school	private
Environment	suburban

STUDENTS

| Total undergrad enrollment | 1,890 |
| % male/female | 40/60 |

% from out of state	81
% from public high school	49
% live on campus	96
% African American	3
% Asian	3
% Caucasian	76
% Hispanic	4
% international	8
# of countries represented	56

ACADEMICS
Academic Rating	**82**
Calendar	semester
Student/faculty ratio	11:1
% profs teaching UG courses	100
Avg lab size	10-19 students
Avg reg class size	10-19 students

MOST POPULAR MAJORS
English language and literature
Psychology
Political science and government

SELECTIVITY
Admissions Rating	**93**
# of applicants	4,395
% of applicants accepted	35
% of acceptees attending	35
# accepting a place on wait list	275
# of early decision applicants	329
% accepted early decision	63

FRESHMAN PROFILE
Average SAT Verbal	660
Average SAT Math	650
Average ACT Composite	27
% graduated top 10% of class	47
% graduated top 50% of class	98

DEADLINES
Early decision	11/15
Early decision notification	12/15
Regular admission	1/1
Regular notification	4/1
Nonfall registration?	yes

FINANCIAL FACTS
Financial Aid Rating	**83**
Tuition	$37,900
% frosh receiving aid	41
% undergrads receiving aid	44
Avg frosh grant	$21,509
Avg frosh loan	$2,708

COOPER UNION

CAMPUS LIFE
Quality of Life Rating	**80**
Type of school	private
Environment	urban

STUDENTS
Total undergrad enrollment	896
% male/female	66/34
% from out of state	44
% from public high school	65
% live on campus	20
% in (# of) fraternities	10 (2)
% in (# of) sororities	5 (1)
% African American	4
% Asian	23
% Caucasian	56
% Hispanic	8
% international	8

ACADEMICS
Academic Rating	**97**
Calendar	semester
Student/faculty ratio	7:1
Profs interesting rating	93
Profs accessible rating	89
% profs teaching UG courses	100
Avg reg class size	10-19 students

SELECTIVITY
Admissions Rating	**99**
# of applicants	2,041
% of applicants accepted	14
% of acceptees attending	70
# accepting a place on wait list	100
# of early decision applicants	223
% accepted early decision	61

FRESHMAN PROFILE
Range SAT Verbal	600-720
Average SAT Verbal	680
Range SAT Math	670-750
Average SAT Math	710
Minimum TOEFL	600
Average HS GPA	3.2
% graduated top 10% of class	80
% graduated top 25% of class	100

DEADLINES
Early decision	12/1
Early decision notification	12/23

| Regular admission | 1/1 |
| Regular notification | 4/1 |

FINANCIAL FACTS
Financial Aid Rating **83**

Room and board	$10,000
Books and supplies	$1,350
Required fees	$500
% frosh receiving aid	100
% undergrads receiving aid	100
Avg frosh grant	$12,247
Avg frosh loan	$2,519

CORNELL UNIVERSITY

CAMPUS LIFE
Quality of Life Rating **80**

| Type of school | private |
| Environment | rural |

STUDENTS
Total undergrad enrollment	13,725
% from out of state	66
% live on campus	51
% in (# of) fraternities	25 (44)
% in (# of) sororities	24 (21)
% African American	5
% Asian	15
% Caucasian	54
% Hispanic	5
% international	8
# of countries represented	79

ACADEMICS
Academic Rating **94**

Calendar	semester
Student/faculty ratio	9:1
Profs interesting rating	91
Profs accessible rating	94
% profs teaching UG courses	100
Avg lab size	10-19 students
Avg reg class size	10-19 students

MOST POPULAR MAJORS
History
Engineering
Biology/biological sciences

SELECTIVITY
Admissions Rating **98**

| # of applicants | 21,502 |

% of applicants accepted	29
% of acceptees attending	49
# accepting a place on wait list	1,942
% admitted from wait list	6
# of early decision applicants	2,679
% accepted early decision	43

FRESHMAN PROFILE
Range SAT Verbal	620-720
Average SAT Verbal	007
Range SAT Math	660-750
Average SAT Math	700
Range ACT Composite	25-30
Average ACT Composite	27
Minimum TOEFL	550
% graduated top 10% of class	83
% graduated top 25% of class	95
% graduated top 50% of class	100

DEADLINES
Early decision	11/10
Early decision notification	12/15
Regular admission	1/1
Regular notification	4/1
Nonfall registration?	yes

FINANCIAL FACTS
Financial Aid Rating **86**

Tuition	$28,630
Room and board	$9,580
Books and supplies	$640
Required fees	$124
% frosh receiving aid	49
% undergrads receiving aid	47
Avg frosh grant	$17,021
Avg frosh loan	$5,811

DARTMOUTH COLLEGE

CAMPUS LIFE
Quality of Life Rating **95**

| Type of school | private |
| Environment | rural |

STUDENTS
Total undergrad enrollment	4,118
% male/female	51/49
% from out of state	98
% from public high school	62
% live on campus	87
% in (# of) fraternities	23 (14)

% in (# of) sororities	21 (8)
% African American	7
% Asian	12
% Caucasian	61
% Hispanic	7
% international	5

ACADEMICS
Academic Rating — 98
Calendar	quarter
Student/faculty ratio	8:1
Profs interesting rating	94
Profs accessible rating	98
% profs teaching UG courses	100
Avg reg class size	10-19 students

SELECTIVITY
Admissions Rating — 99
# of applicants	11,853
% of applicants accepted	18
% of acceptees attending	51
# accepting a place on wait list	250
% admitted from wait list	5
# of early decision applicants	1,216
% accepted early decision	33

FRESHMAN PROFILE
Range SAT Verbal	650-750
Average SAT Verbal	702
Range SAT Math	680-770
Average SAT Math	713
Range ACT Composite	28-33
Average ACT Composite	31
Minimum TOEFL	580
% graduated top 10% of class	87
% graduated top 50% of class	100

DEADLINES
Early decision	11/1
Early decision notification	12/15
Regular admission	1/1
Regular notification	4/10

FINANCIAL FACTS
Financial Aid Rating — 87
Tuition	$28,965
Room and board	$8,740
Books and supplies	$810
Required fees	$162
% frosh receiving aid	51
% undergrads receiving aid	47
Avg frosh grant	$22,900
Avg frosh loan	$2,050

DREW UNIVERSITY

CAMPUS LIFE
Quality of Life Rating — 87
Type of school	private
Affiliation	Methodist
Environment	suburban

STUDENTS
Total undergrad enrollment	1,558
% male/female	39/61
% from out of state	44
% from public high school	65
% live on campus	89
% African American	4
% Asian	6
% Caucasian	62
% Hispanic	5
% international	1

ACADEMICS
Academic Rating — 90
Calendar	semester
Student/faculty ratio	12:1
Profs interesting rating	95
Profs accessible rating	98
% profs teaching UG courses	100
Avg lab size	10-19 students
Avg reg class size	10-19 students

MOST POPULAR MAJORS
Political science and government
Psychology
English language and literature

SELECTIVITY
Admissions Rating — 89
# of applicants	2,587
% of applicants accepted	72
% of acceptees attending	21
# of early decision applicants	75
% accepted early decision	97

FRESHMAN PROFILE
Range SAT Verbal	560-670
Average SAT Verbal	620
Range SAT Math	540-640
Average SAT Math	590
Minimum TOEFL	550
% graduated top 10% of class	33
% graduated top 25% of class	71
% graduated top 50% of class	92

DEADLINES

Early decision	12/1
Early decision notification	12/24
Regular admission	2/15
Regular notification	3/20
Nonfall registration?	yes

FINANCIAL FACTS
Financial Aid Rating **84**

Tuition	$27,360
Room and board	$7,644
Books and supplies	$821
Required fees	$546
% undergrads receiving aid	48
Avg frosh grant	$13,986
Avg frosh loan	$3,490

ELMIRA COLLEGE

CAMPUS LIFE
Quality of Life Rating **78**

Type of school	private
Affiliation	none
Environment	suburban

STUDENTS

Total undergrad enrollment	1,584
% male/female	31/69
% from out of state	51
% from public high school	70
% live on campus	92
% African American	2
% Asian	1
% Caucasian	76
% Hispanic	2
% international	6
# of countries represented	23

ACADEMICS
Academic Rating **83**

Calendar	other
Student/faculty ratio	12:1
Profs interesting rating	84
Profs accessible rating	82
% profs teaching UG courses	100
% classes taught by TAs	0
Avg lab size	10-19 students
Avg reg class size	16 students

MOST POPULAR MAJORS
Business administration/management
Elementary education and teaching
Psychology

SELECTIVITY
Admissions Rating **78**

# of applicants	1,691
% of applicants accepted	80
% of acceptees attending	28
# accepting a place on wait list	28
% admitted from wait list	11
# of early decision applicants	86
% accepted early decision	67

FRESHMAN PROFILE

Range SAT Verbal	490-610
Average SAT Verbal	550
Range SAT Math	480-600
Average SAT Math	540
Range ACT Composite	20-26
Average ACT Composite	25
Minimum TOEFL	500
Average HS GPA	3.5
% graduated top 10% of class	32
% graduated top 25% of class	59
% graduated top 50% of class	87

DEADLINES

Early decision	11/15
Regular admission	rolling
Nonfall registration?	yes

FINANCIAL FACTS
Financial Aid Rating **80**

Tuition	$23,980
Room and board	$7,850
Books and supplies	$450
Avg frosh grant	$13,200
Avg frosh loan	$5,000

EMERSON COLLEGE

CAMPUS LIFE
Quality of Life Rating **79**

Type of school	private
Environment	urban

STUDENTS

Total undergrad enrollment	3,518
% male/female	38/62

% from out of state	65
% from public high school	76
% live on campus	48
% in (# of) fraternities	5 (5)
% in (# of) sororities	4 (4)
% African American	2
% Asian	3
% Caucasian	86
% Hispanic	5
% international	4
# of countries represented	62

ACADEMICS

Academic Rating	**75**
Calendar	semester
Student/faculty ratio	15:1
Profs interesting rating	82
Profs accessible rating	89
% profs teaching UG courses	97
% classes taught by TAs	3
Avg lab size	10-19 students
Avg reg class size	10-19 students

MOST POPULAR MAJORS
Visual and performing arts
Cinematography and film/video
production
Communications, journalism, and related fields

SELECTIVITY

Admissions Rating	**82**
# of applicants	3,805
% of applicants accepted	52
% of acceptees attending	33
# accepting a place on wait list	305
% admitted from wait list	4

FRESHMAN PROFILE

Range SAT Verbal	570-660
Average SAT Verbal	619
Range SAT Math	540-630
Average SAT Math	584
Range ACT Composite	24-28
Average ACT Composite	27
Minimum TOEFL	550
Average HS GPA	3.5
% graduated top 10% of class	29
% graduated top 25% of class	71
% graduated top 50% of class	98

DEADLINES

Regular admission	2/1
Regular notification	4/1
Nonfall registration?	yes

FINANCIAL FACTS

Financial Aid Rating	**84**
Tuition	$21,120
Room and board	$9,542
Books and supplies	$680
Required fees	$504
% frosh receiving aid	70
% undergrads receiving aid	61
Avg frosh grant	$13,000
Avg frosh loan	$3,000

EMMANUEL COLLEGE

CAMPUS LIFE

Quality of Life Rating	**85**
Type of school	private
Affiliation	Roman Catholic
Environment	urban

STUDENTS

Total undergrad enrollment	1,578
% male/female	21/79
% from out of state	15
% from public high school	77
% live on campus	77
% African American	10
% Asian	3
% Caucasian	60
% Hispanic	5
% international	6
# of countries represented	33

ACADEMICS

Academic Rating	**68**
Calendar	semester
Student/faculty ratio	14:1
Profs interesting rating	81
Profs accessible rating	81
% profs teaching UG courses	100
% classes taught by TAs	0
Avg lab size	10-19 students
Avg reg class size	20 students

MOST POPULAR MAJORS
Economics & management
Education
Art

SELECTIVITY

Admissions Rating	**62**
# of applicants	1,831
% of applicants accepted	66

FRESHMAN PROFILE

Range SAT Verbal	550-625
Range SAT Math	528-596
Range ACT Composite	24-28
Minimum TOEFL	500
Average HS GPA	3.2
% graduated top 10% of class	13
% graduated top 25% of class	43
% graduated top 50% of class	73

DEADLINES

Early decision	11/1
Nonfall registration?	yes

FINANCIAL FACTS
Financial Aid Rating   **80**

Tuition	$17,800
Room and board	$8,000
Books and supplies	$750
Avg frosh grant	$14,134

EUGENE LANG COLLEGE

CAMPUS LIFE
Quality of Life Rating   **87**

Type of school	private
Environment	urban

STUDENTS

Total undergrad enrollment	637
% male/female	32/68
% from out of state	57
% from public high school	64
% live on campus	39
% African American	5
% Asian	4
% Caucasian	55
% Hispanic	4
% international	3

ACADEMICS
Academic Rating   **85**

Calendar	semester
Student/faculty ratio	11:1
Profs interesting rating	95
Profs accessible rating	96
% profs teaching UG courses	100
% classes taught by TAs	25
Avg reg class size	10-19 students

MOST POPULAR MAJORS
Creative writing
Area, ethnic, cultural, and gender studies
Social sciences

SELECTIVITY
Admissions Rating   **77**

# of applicants	696
% of applicants accepted	67
% of acceptees attending	37
# accepting a place on wait list	12
% admitted from wait list	25
# of early decision applicants	34
% accepted early decision	76

FRESHMAN PROFILE

Range SAT Verbal	580-690
Average SAT Verbal	610
Range SAT Math	510-610
Average SAT Math	570
Range ACT Composite	21-27
Average ACT Composite	27
Minimum TOEFL	550
Average HS GPA	3.2
% graduated top 10% of class	18
% graduated top 25% of class	50
% graduated top 50% of class	87

DEADLINES

Early decision	11/15
Early decision notification	12/15
Regular admission	2/1
Nonfall registration?	yes

FINANCIAL FACTS
Financial Aid Rating   **83**

Tuition	$22,500
Room and board	$9,896
Books and supplies	$918
Required fees	$490
% frosh receiving aid	69
% undergrads receiving aid	64
Avg frosh grant	$10,906
Avg frosh loan	$3,125

FAIRFIELD UNIVERSITY

CAMPUS LIFE
Quality of Life Rating   **89**

Type of school	private

| Affiliation | Roman Catholic–Jesuit |
| Environment | suburban |

STUDENTS

Total undergrad enrollment	4,073
% male/female	44/56
% from out of state	76
% live on campus	80
% African American	2
% Asian	3
% Caucasian	90
% Hispanic	5
% international	1
# of countries represented	43

ACADEMICS

Academic Rating	**79**
Calendar	semester
Student/faculty ratio	13:1
Profs interesting rating	93
Profs accessible rating	94
% profs teaching UG courses	100
Avg lab size	10-19 students
Avg reg class size	20-29 students

SELECTIVITY

Admissions Rating	**80**
# of applicants	6,974
% of applicants accepted	50
% of acceptees attending	24
# accepting a place on wait list	973
% admitted from wait list	9
# of early decision applicants	172
% accepted early decision	67

FRESHMAN PROFILE

Range SAT Verbal	540-630
Average SAT Verbal	585
Range SAT Math	570-650
Average SAT Math	610
Average ACT Composite	28
Minimum TOEFL	550
Average HS GPA	3.6
% graduated top 10% of class	33
% graduated top 25% of class	70
% graduated top 50% of class	97

DEADLINES

Early decision	11/15
Early decision notification	12/15
Regular admission	1/15
Regular notification	4/1

FINANCIAL FACTS

Financial Aid Rating	**84**
Tuition	$24,100
Room and board	$8,560
Books and supplies	$800
Required fees	$455
% frosh receiving aid	52
% undergrads receiving aid	52
Avg frosh grant	$11,683
Avg frosh loan	$3,556

FORDHAM UNIVERSITY

CAMPUS LIFE

Quality of Life Rating	**81**
Type of school	private
Affiliation	Roman Catholic
Environment	urban

STUDENTS

Total undergrad enrollment	7,228
% male/female	41/59
% from out of state	39
% from public high school	40
% live on campus	58
% African American	6
% Asian	6
% Caucasian	60
% Hispanic	11
% international	1
# of countries represented	38

ACADEMICS

Academic Rating	**76**
Calendar	semester
Student/faculty ratio	11:1
Profs interesting rating	93
Profs accessible rating	88
% profs teaching UG courses	77
Avg lab size	10-19 students
Avg reg class size	10-19 students

SELECTIVITY

Admissions Rating	**83**
# of applicants	11,380
% of applicants accepted	57
% of acceptees attending	27
# accepting a place on wait list	441
% admitted from wait list	6

FRESHMAN PROFILE

Range SAT Verbal	530-630
Average SAT Verbal	606
Range SAT Math	530-630
Average SAT Math	606
Range ACT Composite	23-27
Average ACT Composite	26
Minimum TOEFL	550
Average HS GPA	3.6
% graduated top 10% of class	30
% graduated top 25% of class	68
% graduated top 50% of class	94

DEADLINES

Priority admission	2/1
Regular admission	2/1
Regular notification	4/1
Nonfall registration?	yes

FINANCIAL FACTS
Financial Aid Rating 83

Tuition	$21,210
Room and board	$8,745
Books and supplies	$660
Required fees	$460
% frosh receiving aid	73
% undergrads receiving aid	73

GODDARD COLLEGE

CAMPUS LIFE
Quality of Life Rating 94

Type of school	private
Environment	rural

STUDENTS

Total undergrad enrollment	319
% from out of state	87
% from public high school	93
% live on campus	87
% African American	3
% Asian	2
% Caucasian	87
% Hispanic	0
% international	2
# of countries represented	2

ACADEMICS
Academic Rating 88

Calendar	semester
Student/faculty ratio	11:1

Profs interesting rating	97
Profs accessible rating	97
% profs teaching UG courses	100
Avg reg class size	under 10 students

MOST POPULAR MAJORS
Liberal arts and sciences/liberal studies
Education
Psychology

SELECTIVITY
Admissions Rating 73

# of applicants	128
% of applicants accepted	93
% of acceptees attending	40

FRESHMAN PROFILE

Range SAT Verbal	550-680
Average SAT Verbal	609
Range SAT Math	480-590
Average SAT Math	541
Range ACT Composite	19-27
Minimum TOEFL	550
Average HS GPA	2.5
% graduated top 10% of class	7
% graduated top 25% of class	27
% graduated top 50% of class	63

DEADLINES

Regular notification	rolling
Nonfall registration?	yes

FINANCIAL FACTS
Financial Aid Rating 89

Tuition	$17,840
Room and board	$2,964
Books and supplies	$508
Required fees	$252
% frosh receiving aid	90
% undergrads receiving aid	88
Avg frosh grant	$2,000
Avg frosh loan	$6,189

GORDON COLLEGE

CAMPUS LIFE
Quality of Life Rating 79

Type of school	private
Affiliation	Protestant
Environment	suburban

STUDENTS

Total undergrad enrollment	1,624
% male/female	34/66
% from out of state	73
% from public high school	70
% live on campus	88
% African American	1
% Asian	1
% Caucasian	93
% Hispanic	2
% international	2
# of countries represented	21

ACADEMICS

Academic Rating	**75**
Calendar	semester
Student/faculty ratio	15:1
Profs interesting rating	81
Profs accessible rating	81
% profs teaching UG courses	100
% classes taught by TAs	0
Avg lab size	10-19 students
Avg reg class size	10-19 students

MOST POPULAR MAJORS
Bible/biblical studies
English language and literature
Communications studies/speech
communication and rhetoric

SELECTIVITY

Admissions Rating	**71**
# of applicants	1,089
% of applicants accepted	78
% of acceptees attending	52
# accepting a place on wait list	46
% admitted from wait list	4
# of early decision applicants	105
% accepted early decision	59

FRESHMAN PROFILE

Range SAT Verbal	560-650
Average SAT Verbal	608
Range SAT Math	540-640
Average SAT Math	590
Average ACT Composite	27
Minimum TOEFL	550
Average HS GPA	3.6
% graduated top 10% of class	28
% graduated top 25% of class	55
% graduated top 50% of class	74

DEADLINES

Early decision	12/1
Nonfall registration?	yes

FINANCIAL FACTS

Financial Aid Rating	**78**
Tuition	$17,378
Room and board	$5,200
Books and supplies	$600
Avg frosh grant	$12,707
Avg frosh loan	$2,794

HAMILTON COLLEGE

CAMPUS LIFE

Quality of Life Rating	**89**
Type of school	private
Environment	rural

STUDENTS

Total undergrad enrollment	1,760
% from out of state	61
% from public high school	63
% live on campus	96
% in (# of) fraternities	34 (7)
% in (# of) sororities	20 (3)
% African American	4
% Asian	5
% Caucasian	87
% Hispanic	4
% international	3
# of countries represented	31

ACADEMICS

Academic Rating	**94**
Calendar	semester
Student/faculty ratio	10:1
Profs interesting rating	76
Profs accessible rating	74
% profs teaching UG courses	100
Avg lab size	10-19 students
Avg reg class size	10-19 students

MOST POPULAR MAJORS
Psychology
Economics
Political science and government

SELECTIVITY

Admissions Rating	**92**
# of applicants	4,395

% of applicants accepted	33
% of acceptees attending	31
# accepting a place on wait list	455
% admitted from wait list	2
# of early decision applicants	434
% accepted early decision	45

FRESHMAN PROFILE
Range SAT Verbal	600-700
Range SAT Math	610-700
Minimum TOEFL	600
% graduated top 10% of class	60
% graduated top 25% of class	92
% graduated top 50% of class	99

DEADLINES
Early decision	11/15
Early decision notification	12/15
Regular admission	1/1
Regular notification	4/1
Nonfall registration?	yes

FINANCIAL FACTS
Financial Aid Rating	**85**
Tuition	$28,610
Room and board	$7,040
Required fees	$150
% frosh receiving aid	51
% undergrads receiving aid	54
Avg frosh grant	$21,520
Avg frosh loan	$2,531

HAMPSHIRE COLLEGE

CAMPUS LIFE
Quality of Life Rating	**85**
Type of school	private
Environment	rural

STUDENTS
Total undergrad enrollment	1,267
% from out of state	81
% from public high school	65
% live on campus	89
% African American	3
% Asian	4
% Caucasian	79
% Hispanic	5
% international	3

ACADEMICS
Academic Rating	**87**
Calendar	4-1-4
Student/faculty ratio	11:1
% profs teaching UG courses	100
Avg reg class size	10-19 students

SELECTIVITY
Admissions Rating	**83**
# of applicants	2,094
% of applicants accepted	51
% of acceptees attending	29
# accepting a place on wait list	100
% admitted from wait list	81
# of early decision applicants	65
% accepted early decision	72

FRESHMAN PROFILE
Range SAT Verbal	600-700
Average SAT Verbal	648
Range SAT Math	540-660
Average SAT Math	597
Range ACT Composite	25-29
Minimum TOEFL	577
Average HS GPA	3.4
% graduated top 10% of class	23
% graduated top 25% of class	58
% graduated top 50% of class	95

DEADLINES
Early decision	11/15
Early decision notification	12/15
Regular admission	2/1
Regular notification	4/1
Nonfall registration?	yes

FINANCIAL FACTS
Financial Aid Rating	**85**
Tuition	$27,354
Room and board	$7,294
Books and supplies	$400
Required fees	$516
% frosh receiving aid	53
% undergrads receiving aid	52
Avg frosh grant	$14,900
Avg frosh loan	$2,625

HARTWICK COLLEGE

CAMPUS LIFE
Quality of Life Rating   **75**
Type of school   private
Affiliation   none
Environment   rural

STUDENTS
Total undergrad enrollment   1,446
% male/female   44/56
% live on campus   86
% in (# of) fraternities   15 (5)
% in (# of) sororities   17 (4)
% African American   4
% Asian   1
% Caucasian   65
% Hispanic   2
% international   3
# of countries represented   35

ACADEMICS
Academic Rating   **70**
Calendar   4-1-4
Student/faculty ratio   11:1
Profs interesting rating   83
Profs accessible rating   81
% profs teaching UG courses   100
% classes taught by TAs   0
Avg lab size   10-19 students
Avg reg class size   10-19 students

MOST POPULAR MAJORS
Biology/biological sciences
Business administration/management
Nursing/registered nurse
training (RN, ASN, BSN, MSN)

SELECTIVITY
Admissions Rating   **65**
# of applicants   1,970
% of applicants accepted   89
% of acceptees attending   25
# accepting a place on wait list   65
% admitted from wait list   66
# of early decision applicants   80
% accepted early decision   89

FRESHMAN PROFILE
Range SAT Verbal   500-610
Average SAT Verbal   558
Range SAT Math   510-610
Average SAT Math   554

Average ACT Composite   23
Minimum TOEFL   500
% graduated top 10% of class   21
% graduated top 25% of class   36
% graduated top 50% of class   77

DEADLINES
Regular admission   2/15
Regular notification   3/7
Nonfall registration?   yes

FINANCIAL FACTS
Financial Aid Rating   **81**
Tuition $25,715
Room and board $7,050
Books and supplies $700
Avg frosh grant $20,014

HARVARD COLLEGE

CAMPUS LIFE
Quality of Life Rating   **94**
Type of school   private
Environment   urban

STUDENTS
Total undergrad enrollment   6,649
% male/female   53/47
% from out of state   84
% from public high school   65
% live on campus   96
% African American   9
% Asian   19
% Caucasian   46
% Hispanic   8
% international   7

ACADEMICS
Academic Rating   **97**
Calendar   semester
Student/faculty ratio   8:1
Profs interesting rating   93
Profs accessible rating   86
% profs teaching UG courses   100
Avg lab size   under 10 students
Avg reg class size   10-19 students

MOST POPULAR MAJORS
Psychology
Economics
Political science and government

SELECTIVITY
Admissions Rating   **99**
# of applicants   20,986
% of applicants accepted   10
% of acceptees attending   79

FRESHMAN PROFILE
Range SAT Verbal   700 800
Range SAT Math   700-790
Range ACT Composite   30-34
% graduated top 10% of class   90
% graduated top 25% of class   98
% graduated top 50% of class   100

DEADLINES
Priority admission   12/15
Regular admission   1/1
Regular notification   4/1

FINANCIAL FACTS
Financial Aid Rating   **88**
Tuition $26,066
Room and board $8,868
Books and supplies $2,522
Required fees $2,994
% frosh receiving aid   47
% undergrads receiving aid   47
Avg frosh grant $23,750
Avg frosh loan $1,100

HOBART AND WILLIAM SMITH COLLEGES

CAMPUS LIFE
Quality of Life Rating   **82**
Type of school   private
Environment   rural

STUDENTS
Total undergrad enrollment   1,893
% male/female   45/55
% from out of state   50
% from public high school   65
% live on campus   90
% in (# of) fraternities   17 (5)
% African American   4
% Asian   2
% Caucasian   86
% Hispanic   4
% international   2
# of countries represented   19

ACADEMICS
Academic Rating   **87**
Calendar   semester
Student/faculty ratio   11:1
Profs interesting rating   95
Profs accessible rating   98
% profs teaching UG courses   100
Avg reg class size   10-19 students

MOST POPULAR MAJORS
History
English language and literature
Economics

SELECTIVITY
Admissions Rating   **86**
# of applicants   3,108
% of applicants accepted   66
% of acceptees attending   26
# accepting a place on wait list   93
% admitted from wait list   19
# of early decision applicants   159
% accepted early decision   81

FRESHMAN PROFILE
Range SAT Verbal   540-630
Average SAT Verbal   550
Range SAT Math   540-630
Average SAT Math   600
Minimum TOEFL   550
Average HS GPA   3.3
% graduated top 10% of class   31
% graduated top 25% of class   60
% graduated top 50% of class   93

DEADLINES
Early decision   11/15
Early decision notification   12/15
Regular admission   2/1
Regular notification   4/1

FINANCIAL FACTS
Financial Aid Rating   **84**
Tuition $26,818
Room and board $7,230
Books and supplies $850
Required fees $690
% frosh receiving aid   70
% undergrads receiving aid   69
Avg frosh grant $17,918
Avg frosh loan $3,420

HOFSTRA UNIVERSITY

CAMPUS LIFE
Quality of Life Rating	**70**
Type of school	private
Environment	suburban

STUDENTS
Total undergrad enrollment	9,469
% male/female	46/54
% from out of state	22
% live on campus	41
% in (# of) fraternities	6 (21)
% in (# of) sororities	7 (15)
% African American	9
% Asian	4
% Caucasian	60
% Hispanic	7
% international	2
# of countries represented	67

ACADEMICS
Academic Rating	**73**
Calendar	4-1-4
Student/faculty ratio	15:1
Profs interesting rating	90
Profs accessible rating	90
% profs teaching UG courses	79
Avg reg class size	10-19 students

MOST POPULAR MAJORS
Management
Marketing
Psychology

SELECTIVITY
Admissions Rating	**76**
# of applicants	11,741
% of applicants accepted	72
% of acceptees attending	21

FRESHMAN PROFILE
Range SAT Verbal	510-600
Average SAT Verbal	559
Range SAT Math	520-610
Average SAT Math	570
Range ACT Composite	23-27
Average ACT Composite	25
Minimum TOEFL	550
Average HS GPA	2.9
% graduated top 10% of class	16
% graduated top 25% of class	41
% graduated top 50% of class	77

DEADLINES
Nonfall registration?	yes

FINANCIAL FACTS
Financial Aid Rating	**82**
Tuition	$15,740
Room and board	$8,450
Books and supplies	$760
Required fees	$802
% frosh receiving aid	58
% undergrads receiving aid	58
Avg frosh grant	$6,935
Avg frosh loan	$3,026

HOUGHTON COLLEGE

CAMPUS LIFE
Quality of Life Rating	**75**
Type of school	private
Affiliation	other
Environment	rural

STUDENTS
Total undergrad enrollment	1,380
% male/female	37/63
% from out of state	38
% from public high school	70
% live on campus	82
% African American	1
% Asian	1
% Caucasian	92
% Hispanic	1
% international	4
# of countries represented	27

ACADEMICS
Academic Rating	**78**
Calendar	semester
Student/faculty ratio	14:1
Profs interesting rating	81
Profs accessible rating	81
% profs teaching UG courses	100
% classes taught by TAs	0
Avg lab size	10-19 students
Avg regular class size	10-19 students

MOST POPULAR MAJORS
Psychology
Elementary education
Biology

SELECTIVITY

Admissions Rating   **71**
# of applicants   1,160
% of applicants accepted   88
% of acceptees attending   35

FRESHMAN PROFILE

Range SAT Verbal	540-650
Average SAT Verbal	597
Range SAT Math	520-630
Average SAT Math	579
Range ACT Composite	21-27
Average ACT Composite	25
Minimum TOEFL	550
Average HS GPA	3.16
% graduated top 10% of class	30
% graduated top 25% of class	62
% graduated top 50% of class	89

DEADLINES

Nonfall registration?   yes

FINANCIAL FACTS

Financial Aid Rating   **76**
Tuition	$15,180
Room and board	$5,400
Books and supplies	$750
Avg frosh grant	$7,164
Avg frosh loan	$6,711

ITHACA COLLEGE

CAMPUS LIFE

Quality of Life Rating   **74**
Type of school   private
Environment   suburban

STUDENTS

Total undergrad enrollment	6,190
% male/female	43/57
% from out of state	51
% from public high school	85
% live on campus	70
% in (# of) sororities	2 (1)
% African American	2
% Asian	3
% Caucasian	89
% Hispanic	3
% international	3
# of countries represented	76

ACADEMICS

Academic Rating   **76**
Calendar	semester
Student/faculty ratio	12:1
Profs interesting rating	68
Profs accessible rating	77
% profs teaching UG courses	99
% classes taught by TAs	1
Avg reg class size	10-19 students

MOST POPULAR MAJORS
Mass communications/media studies
Music/music and performing arts studies
Business administration/management

SELECTIVITY

Admissions Rating   **83**
# of applicants	11,305
% of applicants accepted	56
% of acceptees attending	24
# of early decision applicants	309
% accepted early decision	50

FRESHMAN PROFILE

Range SAT Verbal	540-630
Average SAT Verbal	587
Range SAT Math	550-640
Average SAT Math	595
Minimum TOEFL	550
% graduated top 10% of class	36
% graduated top 25% of class	76
% graduated top 50% of class	98

DEADLINES

Early decision	11/1
Early decision notification	12/15
Priority admission	3/1
Regular notification	4/15
Nonfall registration?	yes

FINANCIAL FACTS

Financial Aid Rating   **80**
Tuition	$21,102
Room and board	$8,960
Books and supplies	$876
% frosh receiving aid	71
% undergrads receiving aid	68
Avg frosh grant	$13,111
Avg frosh loan	$3,868

Keene State College

CAMPUS LIFE
Quality of Life Rating   **78**
Type of school   public
Affiliation   none
Environment   suburban

STUDENTS
Total undergrad enrollment	4,690
% male/female	42/58
% from out of state	46
% live on campus	56
% in (# of) fraternities	11 (6)
% in (# of) sororities	8 (6)
% Asian	1
% Caucasian	94
% Hispanic	1
# of countries represented	25

ACADEMICS
Academic Rating   **71**
Calendar	semester
Student/faculty ratio	17:1
Profs interesting rating	86
Profs accessible rating	80
% profs teaching UG courses	100
% classes taught by TAs	0
Avg reg class size	10-19 students

MOST POPULAR MAJORS
Psychology
Education
Management / safety studies

SELECTIVITY
Admissions Rating   **67**
# of applicants	3,925
% of applicants accepted	78
% of acceptees attending	39

FRESHMAN PROFILE
Range SAT Verbal	450-550
Average SAT Verbal	500
Range SAT Math	440-540
Average SAT Math	495
Range ACT Composite	17-22
Minimum TOEFL	500
Average HS GPA	2.9
% graduated top 10% of class	4
% graduated top 25% of class	19
% graduated top 50% of class	57

DEADLINES
Regular admission	4/1
Nonfall registration?	yes

FINANCIAL FACTS
Financial Aid Rating   **77**
In-state tuition	$4,450
Out-of-state tuition	$10,110
Room and board	$5,430
Books and supplies	$600
Avg frosh grant	$4,012
Avg frosh loan	$3,009

Lesley University

CAMPUS LIFE
Quality of Life Rating   **70**
Type of school   private
Affiliation   none
Environment   urban

STUDENTS
Total undergrad enrollment	1,071
% male/female	22/78
% from out of state	39
% from public high school	80
% live on campus	63
% African American	10
% Asian	5
% Caucasian	64
% Hispanic	7
% international	8
# of countries represented	27

ACADEMICS
Academic Rating   **71**
Calendar	semester
Student/faculty ratio	12:1
Profs interesting rating	87
Profs accessible rating	87
% profs teaching UG courses	100
% classes taught by TAs	0
Avg regular class size	10-19 students

SELECTIVITY
Admissions Rating   **68**
# of applicants	825
% of applicants accepted	70
% of acceptees attending	41

FRESHMAN PROFILE

Range SAT Verbal	450-580
Average SAT Verbal	520
Range SAT Math	430-540
Average SAT Math	500
Minimum TOEFL	500
Average HS GPA	2.89
% graduated top 10% of class	15
% graduated top 25% of class	48
% graduated top 50% of class	77

DEADLINES

Nonfall registration?	yes

FINANCIAL FACTS (LESLEY/AIB)

Financial Aid Rating	**73**
Tuition	$19,525/$16,400
Room and board	$8,800/$8,800
Books and supplies	$700/$1,575
Avg frosh grant	$12,491/$4,845
Avg frosh loan	$4,520/$3,207

MANHATTAN COLLEGE

CAMPUS LIFE

Quality of Life Rating	**75**
Type of school	private
Affiliation	Roman Catholic
Environment	urban

STUDENTS

Total undergrad enrollment	2,703
% male/female	52/48
% from out of state	17
% from public high school	60
% live on campus	73
% in (# of) fraternities	8 (5)
% in (# of) sororities	7 (3)
% African American	7
% Asian	6
% Caucasian	73
% Hispanic	17
% international	2

ACADEMICS

Academic Rating	**76**
Calendar	semester
Student/faculty ratio	14:1
Profs interesting rating	83
Profs accessible rating	80

% profs teaching UG courses	100
% classes taught by TAs	0

MOST POPULAR MAJORS
Finance
Marketing
Elementary education

SELECTIVITY

Admissions Rating	**75**
# of applicants	3,860
% of applicants accepted	66
% of acceptees attending	32
# of early decision applicants	30
% accepted early decision	60

FRESHMAN PROFILE

Range SAT Verbal	490-620
Average SAT Verbal	539
Range SAT Math	490-640
Average SAT Math	551
Minimum TOEFL	520
Average HS GPA	3.4

DEADLINES

Early decision	11/15
Regular notification	rolling
Nonfall registration?	yes

FINANCIAL FACTS

Financial Aid Rating	**70**
Tuition	$18,700
Room and board	$7,450
Books and supplies	$250
Avg frosh grant	$6,200
Avg frosh loan	$2,625

MANHATTANVILLE COLLEGE

CAMPUS LIFE

Quality of Life Rating	**77**
Type of school	private
Affiliation	none
Environment	suburban

STUDENTS

Total undergrad enrollment	1,618
% male/female	32/69
% from out of state	31
% live on campus	71
% African American	6
% Asian	3

% Caucasian	60
% Hispanic	13
% international	8

ACADEMICS
Academic Rating **75**

Calendar	semester
Student/faculty ratio	12:1
% profs teaching UG courses	100
% classes taught by TAs	0
Avg reg class size	10-19 students

SELECTIVITY
Admissions Rating **74**

# of applicants	2,330
% of applicants accepted	55
% of acceptees attending	32
# accepting a place on wait list	80
% admitted from wait list	2
# of early decision applicants	50
% accepted early decision	44

FRESHMAN PROFILE
Average SAT Verbal	530
Average SAT Math	530
Range ACT Composite	22-26
Average ACT Composite	24
Minimum TOEFL	550
Average HS GPA	3.0

DEADLINES
Early decision	12/1
Regular admission	3/1
Nonfall registration?	yes

FINANCIAL FACTS
Financial Aid Rating **83**

Tuition	$22,150
Room and board	$9,380
Books and supplies	$800
Avg frosh grant	$15,322
Avg frosh loan	$3,071

MARIST COLLEGE

CAMPUS LIFE
Quality of Life Rating **76**

Type of school	private
Affiliation	none
Environment	suburban

STUDENTS
Total undergrad enrollment	4,000
% male/female	42/58
% from out of state	50
% from public high school	77
% live on campus	68
% in (# of) fraternities	3 (5)
% in (# of) sororities	4 (4)
% African American	3
% Asian	2
% Caucasian	77
% Hispanic	6
# of countries represented	18

ACADEMICS
Academic Rating **86**

Calendar	semester
Student/faculty ratio	14:1
Profs interesting rating	81
Profs accessible rating	78
% profs teaching UG courses	96
% classes taught by TAs	0
Avg lab size	under 10 students
Avg reg class size	10-19 students

MOST POPULAR MAJORS
Psychology
Communications
Business

SELECTIVITY
Admissions Rating **83**

# of applicants	6,204
% of applicants accepted	54
% of acceptees attending	31
# accepting a place on wait list	334

FRESHMAN PROFILE
Range SAT Verbal	500-600
Average SAT Verbal	560
Range SAT Math	510-610
Average SAT Math	565
Range ACT Composite	21-25
Average ACT Composite	24
Minimum TOEFL	550
Average HS GPA	3.2
% graduated top 10% of class	18
% graduated top 25% of class	60
% graduated top 50% of class	98

DEADLINES
Regular admission	2/15

Regular notification	3/15
Nonfall registration?	yes

FINANCIAL FACTS
Financial Aid Rating **79**

Tuition	$17,444
Room and board	$8,332
Books and supplies	$850
Avg frosh grant	$6,031
Avg frosh loan	$2,966

MARLBORO COLLEGE

CAMPUS LIFE
Quality of Life Rating **94**

Type of school	private
Environment	rural

STUDENTS
Total undergrad enrollment	290
% male/female	41/59
% from out of state	82
% from public high school	65
% live on campus	78
% African American	1
% Asian	1
% Caucasian	87
% Hispanic	2
% international	2
# of countries represented	6

ACADEMICS
Academic Rating **95**

Calendar	semester
Student/faculty ratio	8:1
Profs interesting rating	98
Profs accessible rating	98
% profs teaching UG courses	100

SELECTIVITY
Admissions Rating **82**

# of applicants	308
% of applicants accepted	80
% of acceptees attending	40
# of early decision applicants	19
% accepted early decision	79

FRESHMAN PROFILE
Range SAT Verbal	580-680
Average SAT Verbal	610
Range SAT Math	500-620

Average SAT Math	580
Minimum TOEFL	550
Average HS GPA	3.2
% graduated top 10% of class	31
% graduated top 25% of class	51
% graduated top 50% of class	79

DEADLINES
Early decision	11/15
Early decision notification	12/15
Priority admission	3/1
Regular admission	3/1
Nonfall registration?	yes

FINANCIAL FACTS
Financial Aid Rating **91**

Tuition	$20,950
Room and board	$7,425
Books and supplies	$600
Required fees	$680
% frosh receiving aid	82
% undergrads receiving aid	76
Avg frosh grant	$12,007
Avg frosh loan	$2,619

MASSACHUSETTS INSTITUTE OF TECHNOLOGY

CAMPUS LIFE
Quality of Life Rating **83**

Type of school	private
Environment	urban

STUDENTS
Total undergrad enrollment	4,178
% male/female	57/43
% from out of state	91
% from public high school	68
% live on campus	97
% in (# of) fraternities	26 (27)
% in (# of) sororities	8 (5)
% African American	7
% Asian	30
% Caucasian	38
% Hispanic	13
% international	8
# of countries represented	108

ACADEMICS
Academic Rating **99**

Calendar	4-1-4
Student/faculty ratio	6:1
Profs interesting rating	91
Profs accessible rating	88
% profs teaching UG courses	100
Avg lab size	under 10 students
Avg reg class size	under 10 students

MOST POPULAR MAJORS
Business administration/management
Computer science
Electrical, electronics, and
communications engineering

SELECTIVITY
Admissions Rating	**99**
# of applicants	10,664
% of applicants accepted	16
% of acceptees attending	57
# accepting a place on wait list	296
% admitted from wait list	13

FRESHMAN PROFILE
Range SAT Verbal	680-760
Average SAT Verbal	712
Range SAT Math	740-800
Average SAT Math	757
Range ACT Composite	30-34
Average ACT Composite	31
Minimum TOEFL	577
% graduated top 10% of class	99
% graduated top 25% of class	100

DEADLINES
| Regular admission | 1/1 |
| Regular notification | 3/15 |

FINANCIAL FACTS
Financial Aid Rating	**88**
Tuition	$28,030
Room and board	$7,830
Required fees	$1,100
% frosh receiving aid	57
% undergrads receiving aid	57
Avg frosh grant	$17,267
Avg frosh loan	$4,638

MERRIMACK COLLEGE

CAMPUS LIFE
| **Quality of Life Rating** | **74** |
| Type of school | private |

| Affiliation | Roman Catholic |
| Environment | suburban |

STUDENTS
Total undergrad enrollment	2,150
% male/female	48/52
% from out of state	30
% from public high school	68
% live on campus	75
% in (# of) fraternities	3 (3)
% in (# of) sororities	3 (3)
% African American	1
% Asian	1
% Caucasian	72
% Hispanic	2
% international	1
# of countries represented	23

ACADEMICS
Academic Rating	**80**
Calendar	semester
Student/faculty ratio	14:1
Profs interesting rating	88
Profs accessible rating	87
% profs teaching UG courses	100
% classes taught by TAs	0
Avg lab size	under 10 students
Avg reg class size	20-29 students

MOST POPULAR MAJORS
Business administration
Social sciences and history
Psychology

SELECTIVITY
Admissions Rating	**75**
# of applicants	3,400
% of applicants accepted	62
% of acceptees attending	29
# accepting a place on wait list	200

FRESHMAN PROFILE
Average SAT Verbal	540
Average SAT Math	560
Average ACT Composite	23
Minimum TOEFL	600
Average HS GPA	3.2
% graduated top 10% of class	18
% graduated top 25% of class	38
% graduated top 50% of class	90

DEADLINES
| Regular admission | 2/15 |
| Nonfall registration? | yes |

FINANCIAL FACTS
Financial Aid Rating   **75**

Tuition	$18,800
Room and board	$8,400
Books and supplies	$600
Avg frosh grant	$9,000
Avg frosh loan	$3,500

MIDDLEBURY COLLEGE

CAMPUS LIFE
Quality of Life Rating   **81**

Type of school	private
Environment	rural

STUDENTS

Total undergrad enrollment	2,297
% male/female	49/51
% from out of state	94
% live on campus	96
% African American	3
% Asian	8
% Caucasian	76
% Hispanic	6
% international	8
# of countries represented	71

ACADEMICS
Academic Rating   **92**

Calendar	4-1-4
Student/faculty ratio	11:1
Profs interesting rating	96
Profs accessible rating	97
% profs teaching UG courses	100
Avg lab size	10-19 students
Avg reg class size	10-19 students

MOST POPULAR MAJORS
Economics
Psychology
English language and literature

SELECTIVITY
Admissions Rating   **98**

# of applicants	5,299
% of applicants accepted	27
% of acceptees attending	41
# accepting a place on wait list	600
# of early decision applicants	827
% accepted early decision	27

FRESHMAN PROFILE

Range SAT Verbal	680-750
Average SAT Verbal	710
Range SAT Math	670-740
Average SAT Math	700
Range ACT Composite	29-32
Average ACT Composite	30
% graduated top 10% of class	74
% graduated top 25% of class	92
% graduated top 50% of class	99

DEADLINES

Early decision	11/15
Early decision notification	12/15
Regular admission	12/15
Regular notification	4/1
Nonfall registration?	yes

FINANCIAL FACTS
Financial Aid Rating   **74**

Comprehensive tuition	$35,900
Books and supplies	$750
% undergrads receiving aid	36
Avg frosh grant	$20,161
Avg frosh loan	$5,377

MONMOUTH UNIVERSITY

CAMPUS LIFE
Quality of Life Rating   **79**

Type of school	private
Affiliation	none
Environment	suburban

STUDENTS

Total undergrad enrollment	4,179
% male/female	42/58
% from out of state	6
% live on campus	38
% in (# of) fraternities	8 (7)
% in (# of) sororities	9 (6)
% African American	6
% Asian	2
% Caucasian	77
% Hispanic	4

ACADEMICS
Academic Rating   **70**

Calendar	semester
Student/faculty ratio	18:1
Profs interesting rating	82

Profs accessible rating	78
% profs teaching UG courses	85
% classes taught by TAs	0
Avg reg class size	10-19 students

MOST POPULAR MAJORS
Business administration
Education
Communication

SELECTIVITY
Admissions Rating	**60**
# of applicants	4,964
% of applicants accepted	82
% of acceptees attending	22
# accepting a place on wait list	306
% admitted from wait list	21
# of early decision applicants	189
% accepted early decision	78

FRESHMAN PROFILE
Range SAT Verbal	470-560
Average SAT Verbal	500
Range SAT Math	470-570
Average SAT Math	524
Range ACT Composite	18-22
Minimum TOEFL	525
Average HS GPA	3.0
% graduated top 10% of class	8
% graduated top 25% of class	28
% graduated top 50% of class	61

DEADLINES
Early decision	12/1
Regular admission	3/1
Nonfall registration?	yes

FINANCIAL FACTS
Financial Aid Rating	**77**
Tuition	$16,506
Room and board	$7,076
Books and supplies	$600
Avg frosh grant	$7,986

MOUNT HOLYOKE COLLEGE

CAMPUS LIFE
Quality of Life Rating	**90**
Type of school	private
Environment	suburban

STUDENTS
Total undergrad enrollment	2,191
% male/female	0/100
% from out of state	65
% from public high school	66
% live on campus	93
% African American	5
% Asian	12
% Caucasian	67
% Hispanic	5
% international	15

ACADEMICS
Academic Rating	**93**
Calendar	semester
Student/faculty ratio	10:1
% profs teaching UG courses	100
Avg lab size	10-19 students
Avg reg class size	10-19 students

MOST POPULAR MAJORS
English language and literature
Biology/biological sciences
Psychology

SELECTIVITY
Admissions Rating	**87**
# of applicants	2,936
% of applicants accepted	52
% of acceptees attending	38
# accepting a place on wait list	278
% admitted from wait list	9
# of early decision applicants	259
% accepted early decision	65

FRESHMAN PROFILE
Range SAT Verbal	608-700
Average SAT Verbal	651
Range SAT Math	580-670
Average SAT Math	627
Range ACT Composite	26-30
Average ACT Composite	28
Minimum TOEFL	600
Average HS GPA	3.7
% graduated top 10% of class	52
% graduated top 25% of class	84
% graduated top 50% of class	98

DEADLINES
Early decision	11/15
Early decision notification	1/1
Regular admission	1/15
Regular notification	4/1
Nonfall registration?	yes

FINANCIAL FACTS

Financial Aid Rating	**93**
Tuition	$27,540
Room and board	$8,100
Required fees	$168
% undergrads receiving aid	67
Avg frosh grant	$21,087
Avg frosh loan	$2,700

NAZARETH COLLEGE OF ROCHESTER

CAMPUS LIFE

Quality of Life Rating	**75**
Type of school	private
Affiliation	none
Environment	suburban

STUDENTS

Total undergrad enrollment	1,969
% male/female	25/75
% from out of state	6
% from public high school	90
% live on campus	57
% African American	4
% Asian	2
% Caucasian	90
% Hispanic	2
# of countries represented	8

ACADEMICS

Academic Rating	**80**
Calendar	semester
Student/faculty ratio	13:1
Profs interesting rating	78
Profs accessible rating	75
% profs teaching UG courses	97
% classes taught by TAs	0
Avg lab size	10-19 students
Avg reg class size	10-19 students

MOST POPULAR MAJORS
Education
Psychology
Business administration/management

SELECTIVITY

Admissions Rating	**72**
# of applicants	1,654
% of applicants accepted	84
% of acceptees attending	28

# accepting a place on wait list	0
% admitted from wait list	0
# of early decision applicants	53
% accepted early decision	64

FRESHMAN PROFILE

Range SAT Verbal	525-625
Average SAT Verbal	569
Range SAT Math	515-615
Average SAT Math	502
Average ACT Composite	25
Minimum TOEFL	550
Average HS GPA	3.4
% graduated top 10% of class	31
% graduated top 25% of class	70
% graduated top 50% of class	90

DEADLINES

Early decision	12/1
Regular admission	2/15
Nonfall registration?	yes

FINANCIAL FACTS

Financial Aid Rating	**82**
Tuition	$15,910
Room and board	$6,930
Books and supplies	$800
Avg frosh grant	$10,802
Avg frosh loan	$2,964

NEW JERSEY INSTITUTE OF TECHNOLOGY

CAMPUS LIFE

Quality of Life Rating	**66**
Type of school	public
Environment	urban

STUDENTS

Total undergrad enrollment	5,730
% male/female	79/21
% from out of state	4
% from public high school	80
% live on campus	23
% in (# of) fraternities	7 (19)
% in (# of) sororities	5 (8)
% African American	11
% Asian	22
% Caucasian	33
% Hispanic	12
% international	6

ACADEMICS
Academic Rating   **79**

Calendar	semester
Student/faculty ratio	13:1
Profs interesting rating	87
Profs accessible rating	87
% profs teaching UG courses	70
% classes taught by TAs	7

MOST POPULAR MAJORS
Computer science
Computer engineering
Architecture

SELECTIVITY
Admissions Rating   **80**

# of applicants	2,591
% of applicants accepted	58
% of acceptees attending	44

FRESHMAN PROFILE

Range SAT Verbal	490-590
Average SAT Verbal	546
Range SAT Math	550-650
Average SAT Math	606
Minimum TOEFL	550
% graduated top 10% of class	24
% graduated top 25% of class	59
% graduated top 50% of class	90

DEADLINES

Priority admission	4/1
Nonfall registration?	yes

FINANCIAL FACTS
Financial Aid Rating   **85**

In-state tuition	$6,758
Out-of-state tuition	$11,710
Room and board	$7,864
Books and supplies	$1,000
Required fees	$1,148
% frosh receiving aid	65
% undergrads receiving aid	57
Avg frosh grant	$4,400
Avg frosh loan	$2,500

NEW YORK UNIVERSITY

CAMPUS LIFE
Quality of Life Rating   **88**

Type of school	private
Environment	urban

STUDENTS

Total undergrad enrollment	19,490
% male/female	40/60
% from out of state	51
% from public high school	72
% live on campus	56
% in (# of) fraternities	4 (13)
% in (# of) sororities	2 (13)
% African American	6
% Asian	15
% Caucasian	45
% Hispanic	7
% international	4
# of countries represented	137

ACADEMICS
Academic Rating   **89**

Calendar	semester
Student/faculty ratio	12:1
Avg lab size	20-29 students
Avg reg class size	10-19 students

SELECTIVITY
Admissions Rating   **90**

# of applicants	29,581
% of applicants accepted	28
% of acceptees attending	40
# accepting a place on wait list	1,430
% admitted from wait list	13
# of early decision applicants	2,935
% accepted early decision	39

FRESHMAN PROFILE

Range SAT Verbal	620-710
Average SAT Verbal	672
Range SAT Math	630-720
Average SAT Math	666
Range ACT Composite	28-32
Average ACT Composite	29
Minimum TOEFL	600
Average HS GPA	3.7
% graduated top 10% of class	70
% graduated top 25% of class	93
% graduated top 50% of class	100

DEADLINES

Early decision	11/15
Early decision notification	12/15
Priority admission	11/15
Regular admission	1/15
Regular notification	4/1
Nonfall registration?	yes

FINANCIAL FACTS

Financial Aid Rating	**83**
Tuition	$26,646
Room and board	$10,430
Books and supplies	$450
% frosh receiving aid	61
% undergrads receiving aid	55
Avg frosh grant	$18,444
Avg frosh loan	$4,384

NORTHEASTERN UNIVERSITY

CAMPUS LIFE

Quality of Life Rating	**76**
Type of school	private
Environment	urban

STUDENTS

Total undergrad enrollment	14,144
% from out of state	63
% in (# of) fraternities	4 (11)
% in (# of) sororities	3 (8)
# of countries represented	110

ACADEMICS

Academic Rating	**76**
Calendar	semester
Student/faculty ratio	16:1
Profs interesting rating	91
Profs accessible rating	92
% profs teaching UG courses	100
Avg reg class size	10-19 students

MOST POPULAR MAJORS
Business/commerce
Engineering
Health services/allied health

SELECTIVITY

Admissions Rating	**77**
# of applicants	17,037
% of applicants accepted	61
% of acceptees attending	28
# accepting a place on wait list	472

FRESHMAN PROFILE

Range SAT Verbal	520-620
Average SAT Verbal	565
Range SAT Math	540-640
Average SAT Math	588
Range ACT Composite	22-27

Average ACT Composite	24
Minimum TOEFL	550
Average HS GPA	3.2
% graduated top 10% of class	21
% graduated top 25% of class	57
% graduated top 50% of class	88

DEADLINES

Priority admission	2/15
Nonfall registration?	yes

FINANCIAL FACTS

Financial Aid Rating	**88**
Tuition	$24,266
Room and board	$5,160
Books and supplies	$900
Required fees	$201
% frosh receiving aid	67
% undergrads receiving aid	63
Avg frosh grant	$12,321
Avg frosh loan	$3,028

PLYMOUTH STATE COLLEGE

CAMPUS LIFE

Quality of Life Rating	**75**
Type of school	public
Affiliation	none
Environment	rural

STUDENTS

Total undergrad enrollment	3,790
% male/female	49/51
% from out of state	45
% from public high school	98
% live on campus	57
% in (# of) fraternities	4 (2)
% in (# of) sororities	7 (5)
% African American	1
% Asian	1
% Caucasian	90
% Hispanic	1

ACADEMICS

Academic Rating	**68**
Calendar	semester
Student/faculty ratio	17:1
Profs interesting rating	82
Profs accessible rating	78
% profs teaching UG courses	100
% classes taught by TAs	0

Avg lab size	10-19 students
Avg reg class size	10-19 students

MOST POPULAR MAJORS
Physical education teaching and coaching
Business administration/management
Elementary education and teaching

SELECTIVITY
Admissions Rating	**60**
# of applicants	3,573
% of applicants accepted	77
% of acceptees attending	34

FRESHMAN PROFILE
Range SAT Verbal	430-530
Average SAT Verbal	483
Range SAT Math	540
Average SAT Math	483
Range ACT Composite	17-21
Average ACT Composite	19
Minimum TOEFL	520
Average HS GPA	2.8
% graduated top 10% of class	3
% graduated top 25% of class	15
% graduated top 50% of class	48

DEADLINES
Regular admission	4/1
Nonfall registration?	yes

FINANCIAL FACTS
Financial Aid Rating	**80**
In-state tuition	$4,450
Out-of-state tuition	$10,110
Room and board	$5,768
Books and supplies	$700
Avg frosh grant	$4,016
Avg frosh loan	$2,806

POLYTECHNIC UNIVERSITY

CAMPUS LIFE
Quality of Life Rating	**75**
Type of school	private
Affiliation	none
Environment	urban

STUDENTS
Total undergrad enrollment	1,709
% male/female	80/20
% from out of state	3

% from public high school	82
% live on campus	11
% in (# of) fraternities	3 (3)
% in (# of) sororities	4 (1)
% African American	9
% Asian	38
% Caucasian	40
% Hispanic	6
% international	6
# of countries represented	6

ACADEMICS
Academic Rating	**82**
Calendar	semester
Student/faculty ratio	12:1
Profs interesting rating	86
Profs accessible rating	82
% profs teaching UG courses	100
% classes taught by TAs	0
Avg lab size	20-29 students
Avg regular class size	10-19 students

MOST POPULAR MAJORS
electrical, electronics, and communications engineering
computer engineering
computer science

SELECTIVITY
Admissions Rating	**80**
# of applicants	1,573
% of applicants accepted	69
% of acceptees attending	42

FRESHMAN PROFILE
Range SAT Verbal	530-610
Average SAT Verbal	590
Range SAT Math	620-690
Average SAT Math	660
Minimum TOEFL	500
Average HS GPA	3.45

DEADLINES
Regular notification	rolling
Nonfall registration?	yes

FINANCIAL FACTS
Financial Aid Rating	**80**
Tuition	$22,280
Room and board	$5,250
Books and supplies	$700

PRINCETON UNIVERSITY

CAMPUS LIFE
Quality of Life Rating	**86**
Type of school	private
Environment	suburban

STUDENTS
Total undergrad enrollment	4,779
% male/female	52/48
% from out of state	86
% from public high school	55
% live on campus	97
% African American	9
% Asian	13
% Caucasian	70
% Hispanic	7
% international	7

ACADEMICS
Academic Rating	**99**
Calendar	semester
Student/faculty ratio	6:1
Profs interesting rating	94
Profs accessible rating	91

MOST POPULAR MAJORS
History
English language and literature
Political science and government

SELECTIVITY
Admissions Rating	**99**
# of applicants	14,521
% of applicants accepted	11
% of acceptees attending	73

FRESHMAN PROFILE
Minimum TOEFL	630
% graduated top 10% of class	95
% graduated top 25% of class	99
% graduated top 50% of class	100

DEADLINES
Early decision	11/1
Early decision notification	12/15
Regular admission	1/1
Regular notification	4/3

FINANCIAL FACTS
Financial Aid Rating	**83**
Tuition	$28,540
Room and board	$8,109
Books and supplies	$790
% frosh receiving aid	46
% undergrads receiving aid	43
Avg frosh grant	$23,000

PROVIDENCE COLLEGE

CAMPUS LIFE
Quality of Life Rating	**79**
Type of school	private
Affiliation	Roman Catholic
Environment	suburban

STUDENTS
Total undergrad enrollment	4,371
% male/female	42/58
% from out of state	87
% from public high school	63
% live on campus	76
% African American	2
% Asian	2
% Caucasian	85
% Hispanic	2
% international	1

ACADEMICS
Academic Rating	**78**
Calendar	semester
Student/faculty ratio	14:1
Profs interesting rating	92
Profs accessible rating	89
% profs teaching UG courses	100
Avg lab size	10-19 students
Avg reg class size	10-19 students

MOST POPULAR MAJORS
Marketing/marketing management
Special education
Biology/biological sciences

SELECTIVITY
Admissions Rating	**83**
# of applicants	7,347
% of applicants accepted	49
% of acceptees attending	24
# accepting a place on wait list	399
% admitted from wait list	88

FRESHMAN PROFILE
Range SAT Verbal	540-630
Average SAT Verbal	587
Range SAT Math	550-640
Average SAT Math	596

Range ACT Composite	23-28
Average ACT Composite	25
Minimum TOEFL	550
Average HS GPA	3.4
% graduated top 10% of class	42
% graduated top 25% of class	81
% graduated top 50% of class	99

DEADLINES

Regular admission	1/15
Regular notification	4/1
Nonfall registration?	yes

FINANCIAL FACTS
Financial Aid Rating — 81

Tuition	$21,665
Room and board	$8,500
Books and supplies	$650
Required fees	$320
% frosh receiving aid	67
% undergrads receiving aid	64
Avg frosh grant	$9,570
Avg frosh loan	$4,125

QUINNIPIAC UNIVERSITY

CAMPUS LIFE
Quality of Life Rating — 74

Type of school	private
Affiliation	none
Environment	suburban

STUDENTS

Total undergrad enrollment	4,843
% male/female	39/61
% from out of state	70
% from public high school	80
% live on campus	70
% in (# of) fraternities	10 (4)
% in (# of) sororities	8 (3)
% African American	2
% Asian	2
% Caucasian	90
% Hispanic	3
# of countries represented	18

ACADEMICS
Academic Rating — 79

Calendar	semester
Student/faculty ratio	16:1
Profs interesting rating	82

Profs accessible rating	78
% profs teaching UG courses	83
% classes taught by TAs	0
Avg lab size	10-19 students
Avg reg class size	10-19 students

MOST POPULAR MAJORS
physical therapy
psychology
mass communications/media studies

SELECTIVITY
Admissions Rating — 75

# of applicants	7,281
% of applicants accepted	74
% of acceptees attending	24
# accepting a place on wait list	250
% admitted from wait list	80

FRESHMAN PROFILE

Range SAT Verbal	500-610
Average SAT Verbal	535
Range SAT Math	500-600
Average SAT Math	545
Range ACT Composite	22-27
Average ACT Composite	24
Minimum TOEFL	550
Average HS GPA	3.2
% graduated top 10% of class	14
% graduated top 25% of class	45
% graduated top 50% of class	90

DEADLINES

Nonfall registration?	yes

FINANCIAL FACTS
Financial Aid Rating — 78

Tuition	$18,000
Room and board	$8,530
Books and supplies	$600
Avg frosh grant	$10,702
Avg frosh loan	$2,625

RAMAPO COLLEGE OF NEW JERSEY

CAMPUS LIFE
Quality of Life Rating — 80

Type of school	public
Affiliation	none
Environment	suburban

STUDENTS

Total undergrad enrollment	5,143
% male/female	40/60
% from out of state	15
% live on campus	56
% in (# of) fraternities	7 (9)
% in (# of) sororities	5 (8)
% African American	7
% Asian	4
% Caucasian	81
% Hispanic	8
% international	5
# of countries represented	66

ACADEMICS

Academic Rating	**84**
Calendar	semester
Student/faculty ratio	16:1
Profs interesting rating	78
Profs accessible rating	76
% profs teaching UG courses	100
% classes taught by TAs	0
Avg lab size	10-19 students
Avg reg class size	10-19 students

MOST POPULAR MAJORS
Psychology
Communications studies/speech
communication and rhetoric
Business administration/management

SELECTIVITY

Admissions Rating	**79**
# of applicants	3,785
% of applicants accepted	43
% of acceptees attending	42

FRESHMAN PROFILE

Range SAT Verbal	520-600
Average SAT Verbal	570
Range SAT Math	530-610
Average SAT Math	570
Minimum TOEFL	550
Average HS GPA	3.2
% graduated top 10% of class	21
% graduated top 25% of class	54
% graduated top 50% of class	95

DEADLINES

Regular admission	2/15
Nonfall registration?	yes

FINANCIAL FACTS

Financial Aid Rating	**76**
In-state tuition	$4,836
Out-of-state tuition	$8,738
Room and board	$7,372
Books and supplies	$750
Avg frosh grant	$9,231
Avg frosh loan	$2,578

RENSSELAER POLYTECHNIC INSTITUTE

CAMPUS LIFE

Quality of Life Rating	**82**
Type of school	private
Environment	suburban

STUDENTS

Total undergrad enrollment	5,139
% male/female	75/25
% from out of state	47
% from public high school	79
% live on campus	55
% in (# of) fraternities	35 (29)
% in (# of) sororities	20 (6)
% African American	4
% Asian	13
% Caucasian	71
% Hispanic	5
% international	4

ACADEMICS

Academic Rating	**87**
Calendar	semester
Student/faculty ratio	16:1
Avg lab size	10-19 students
Avg reg class size	20-29 students

SELECTIVITY

Admissions Rating	**83**
# of applicants	5,480
% of applicants accepted	70
% of acceptees attending	27
# of early decision applicants	200
% accepted early decision	83

FRESHMAN PROFILE

Range SAT Verbal	580-680
Average SAT Verbal	611
Range SAT Math	640-720

Average SAT Math	671
Range ACT Composite	24-28
Average ACT Composite	27
Minimum TOEFL	550
% graduated top 10% of class	65
% graduated top 25% of class	91
% graduated top 50% of class	99

DEADLINES

Early decision	11/15
Early decision notification	12/31
Regular admission	1/1
Regular notification	3/31
Nonfall registration?	yes

FINANCIAL FACTS
Financial Aid Rating   **85**

Tuition	$26,400
Room and board	$8,902
Books and supplies	$1,528
Required fees	$770
% frosh receiving aid	70
% undergrads receiving aid	70
Avg frosh grant	$16,992
Avg frosh loan	$4,800

RICHARD STOCKTON
COLLEGE OF NEW JERSEY

CAMPUS LIFE
Quality of Life Rating   **75**

Type of school	public
Affiliation	none
Environment	suburban

STUDENTS

Total undergrad enrollment	6,138
% male/female	42/58
% from out of state	2
% from public high school	74
% live on campus	41
% in (# of) fraternities	5 (9)
% in (# of) sororities	5 (9)
% African American	8
% Asian	5
% Caucasian	82
% Hispanic	5
% international	1
# of countries represented	21

ACADEMICS
Academic Rating   **82**

Calendar	semester
Student/faculty ratio	19:1
Profs interesting rating	83
Profs accessible rating	79
% profs teaching UG courses	97
% classes taught by TAs	0
Avg lab size	under 10 students
Avg reg class size	20-29 students

MOST POPULAR MAJORS
Business
Psychology
Biology/biological sciences

SELECTIVITY
Admissions Rating   **84**

# of applicants	3,384
% of applicants accepted	45
% of acceptees attending	51
# accepting a place on wait list	324
% admitted from wait list	16

FRESHMAN PROFILE

Range SAT Verbal	490-570
Average SAT Verbal	551
Range SAT Math	490-590
Average SAT Math	559
Range ACT Composite	23-26
Average ACT Composite	25
Minimum TOEFL	550
Average HS GPA	3.2
% graduated top 10% of class	18
% graduated top 25% of class	60
% graduated top 50% of class	92

DEADLINES

| Regular admission | 5/1 |
| Nonfall registration? | yes |

FINANCIAL FACTS
Financial Aid Rating   **74**

In-state tuition	$3,952
Out-of-state tuition	$6,400
Room and board	$5,845
Books and supplies	$825
Avg frosh grant	$5,251
Avg frosh loan	$2,432

Rider University

CAMPUS LIFE
Quality of Life Rating   78
Type of school   private
Environment   suburban

STUDENTS
Total undergrad enrollment	4,284
% male/female	41/59
% from out of state	21
% from public high school	80
% live on campus	64
% in (# of) fraternities	15 (8)
% in (# of) sororities	16 (7)
% African American	8
% Asian	4
% Caucasian	78
% Hispanic	5
% international	2

ACADEMICS
Academic Rating   77
Calendar	semester
Student/faculty ratio	13:1
Profs interesting rating	74
Profs accessible rating	81
% profs teaching UG courses	95
Avg lab size	10-19 students
Avg reg class size	10-19 students

MOST POPULAR MAJORS
Business
Communications studies/speech
communication and rhetoric
Elementary education and teaching

SELECTIVITY
Admissions Rating   75
# of applicants	4,091
% of applicants accepted	82
% of acceptees attending	20

FRESHMAN PROFILE
Range SAT Verbal	470-560
Average SAT Verbal	510
Range SAT Math	470-580
Average SAT Math	520
Minimum TOEFL	550
Average HS GPA	3.1
% graduated top 10% of class	11
% graduated top 25% of class	37
% graduated top 50% of class	71

DEADLINES
Nonfall registration?   yes

FINANCIAL FACTS
Financial Aid Rating   84
Tuition	$20,590
Room and board	$8,060
Books and supplies	$1,000
Required fees	$460
% frosh receiving aid	69
% undergrads receiving aid	65
Avg frosh grant	$17,171
Avg frosh loan	$3,613

Rochester Institute of Technology

CAMPUS LIFE
Quality of Life Rating   74
Type of school   private
Environment   suburban

STUDENTS
Total undergrad enrollment	12,279
% male/female	69/31
% from out of state	40
% from public high school	85
% live on campus	60
% in (# of) fraternities	7 (19)
% in (# of) sororities	5 (10)
% African American	5
% Asian	7
% Caucasian	75
% Hispanic	3
% international	5
# of countries represented	90

ACADEMICS
Academic Rating   80
Calendar	quarter
Student/faculty ratio	13:1
Profs interesting rating	91
Profs accessible rating	94
% profs teaching UG courses	95
Avg lab size	10-19 students
Avg reg class size	10-19 students

MOST POPULAR MAJORS
Information technology
Mechanical engineering
Photography

SELECTIVITY

Admissions Rating   **85**

# of applicants	8,697
% of applicants accepted	69
% of acceptees attending	39
# accepting a place on wait list	125
% admitted from wait list	20
# of early decision applicants	830
% accepted early decision	81

FRESHMAN PROFILE

Range SAT Verbal	540-640
Range SAT Math	570-670
Range ACT Composite	25-28
Minimum TOEFL	525
Average HS GPA	3.7
% graduated top 10% of class	31
% graduated top 25% of class	65
% graduated top 50% of class	92

DEADLINES

Early decision	12/15
Early decision notification	1/15
Priority admission	2/15
Regular admission	3/15
Nonfall registration?	yes

FINANCIAL FACTS

Financial Aid Rating   **81**

Tuition	$19,470
Room and board	$7,527
Books and supplies	$600
Required fees	$510
% frosh receiving aid	70
% undergrads receiving aid	67
Avg frosh grant	$9,800
Avg frosh loan	$3,900

ROGER WILLIAMS UNIVERSITY

CAMPUS LIFE

Quality of Life Rating   **75**

Type of school	private
Affiliation	none
Environment	suburban

STUDENTS

Total undergrad enrollment	3,300
% male/female	49/51

% from out of state	80
% from public high school	78
% live on campus	79
% African American	2
% Asian	1
% Caucasian	82
% Hispanic	2
% international	3

ACADEMICS

Academic Rating   **71**

Calendar	4-1-4
Student/faculty ratio	17:1
Profs interesting rating	81
Profs accessible rating	80
% profs teaching UG courses	100
% classes taught by TAs	0
Avg lab size	20-29 students
Avg reg class size	20-29 students

MOST POPULAR MAJORS
Architecture (BArch, BA/BS, MArch, MA/MS, PhD)
Psychology
Criminal justice

SELECTIVITY

Admissions Rating   **64**

# of applicants	4,793
% of applicants accepted	84
% of acceptees attending	24
# of early decision applicants	171
% accepted early decision	150

FRESHMAN PROFILE

Range SAT Verbal	480-570
Average SAT Verbal	531
Range SAT Math	480-585
Average SAT Math	536
Average HS GPA	3.0
% graduated top 10% of class	12
% graduated top 25% of class	36
% graduated top 50% of class	69

DEADLINES

Early decision	12/1
Regular notification	rolling
Nonfall registration?	yes

FINANCIAL FACTS

Financial Aid Rating   **78**

Tuition	$20,280
Room and board	$9,375
Books and supplies	$600

| Avg frosh grant | $7,200 |
| Avg frosh loan | $4,125 |

ROWAN UNIVERSITY

CAMPUS LIFE
Quality of Life Rating	**77**
Type of school	public
Affiliation	none
Environment	suburban

STUDENTS
Total undergrad enrollment	6,514
% male/female	44/56
% from out of state	3
% from public high school	90
% live on campus	25
% in (# of) fraternities	12 (12)
% in (# of) sororities	7 (13)
% African American	9
% Asian	4
% Caucasian	79
% Hispanic	6
# of countries represented	31

ACADEMICS
Academic Rating	**74**
Calendar	semester
Student/faculty ratio	14:1
Profs interesting rating	81
Profs accessible rating	78
% profs teaching UG courses	100
% classes taught by TAs	0
Avg reg class size	20-23 students

MOST POPULAR MAJORS
Business administration
Elementary/early childhood education
Communications

SELECTIVITY
Admissions Rating	**66**
# of applicants	6,891
% of applicants accepted	46
% of acceptees attending	42
# accepting a place on wait list	150

FRESHMAN PROFILE
Range SAT Verbal	515-615
Average SAT Verbal	565
Range SAT Math	533-633
Average SAT Math	583

Minimum TOEFL	550
Average HS GPA	3.4
% graduated top 10% of class	15
% graduated top 25% of class	45
% graduated top 50% of class	79

DEADLINES
Regular admission	3/15
Regular notification	4/15
Nonfall registration?	yes

FINANCIAL FACTS
Financial Aid Rating	**77**
In-state tuition	$4,950
Out-of-state tuition	$9,900
Room and board	$6,846
Avg frosh grant	$5,050
Avg frosh loan	$2,625

RUTGERS UNIVERSITY— NEW BRUNSWICK

CAMPUS LIFE
Quality of Life Rating	**72**
Type of school	public
Environment	suburban

STUDENTS
Total undergrad enrollment	28,070
% male/female	47/53
% from out of state	11
% African American	8
% Asian	22
% Caucasian	56
% Hispanic	8
% international	3
# of countries represented	99

ACADEMICS
Academic Rating	**82**
Calendar	semester
Student/faculty ratio	14:1
Profs interesting rating	89
Profs accessible rating	90
% profs teaching UG courses	80
% classes taught by TAs	20

SELECTIVITY
| **Admissions Rating** | **88** |
| # of applicants | 26,678 |

% of applicants accepted	44
% of acceptees attending	24

FRESHMAN PROFILE
Range SAT Verbal	530-630
Average SAT Verbal	582
Range SAT Math	560-670
Average SAT Math	613
Minimum TOEFL	550
% graduated top 10% of class	36
% graduated top 25% of class	75
% graduated top 50% of class	98

DEADLINES
Priority admission	12/01
Regular notification	2/28

FINANCIAL FACTS
Financial Aid Rating 82
In-state tuition	$5,770
Out-of-state tuition	$11,746
Room and board	$7,200
Books and supplies	$750
Required fees	$1,538
% frosh receiving aid	49
% undergrads receiving aid	47
Avg frosh grant	$6,598
Avg frosh loan	$3,816

St. Anselm College

CAMPUS LIFE
Quality of Life Rating 80
Type of school	private
Affiliation	Roman Catholic
Environment	suburban

STUDENTS
Total undergrad enrollment	1,956
% male/female	43/57
% from out of state	77
% from public high school	65
% live on campus	85
% Asian	1
% Caucasian	96
% Hispanic	1
% international	1
# of countries represented	15

ACADEMICS
Academic Rating 79
Calendar	semester
Student/faculty ratio	14:1
Profs interesting rating	81
Profs accessible rating	82
% profs teaching UG courses	100
Avg lab size	10-19 students
Avg reg class size	10-19 students

MOST POPULAR MAJORS
Nursing
Business administration/management
Psychology

ADMISSIONS
Admissions Rating 86
# of applicants	3,018
% of applicants accepted	73
% of acceptees attending	29
# accepting a place on wait list	213
# of early decision applicants	81
% accepted early decision	83

FRESHMAN PROFILE
Range SAT Verbal	510-600
Average SAT Verbal	551
Range SAT Math	510-600
Average SAT Math	556
Range ACT Composite	21-25
Average ACT Composite	23
Minimum TOEFL	550
Average HS GPA	3.1
% graduated top 10% of class	14
% graduated top 25% of class	47
% graduated top 50% of class	87

DEADLINES
Early decision	12/1
Early decision notification	12/15
Nonfall registration?	yes

FINANCIAL FACTS
Financial Aid Rating 82
Tuition	$21,410
Room and board	$8,090
Books and supplies	$750
Required fees	$520
% frosh receiving aid	91
% undergrads receiving aid	82
Avg frosh grant	$7,696
Avg frosh loan	$2,427

SAINT BONAVENTURE UNIVERSITY

CAMPUS LIFE
Quality of Life Rating   **85**

Type of school	private
Affiliation	Roman Catholic
Environment	rural

STUDENTS

Total undergrad enrollment	2,229
% male/female	46/54
% from out of state	21
% from public high school	71
% live on campus	76

ACADEMICS
Academic Rating   **77**

Calendar	semester
Student/faculty ratio	15:1
Profs interesting rating	78
Profs accessible rating	94
% profs teaching UG courses	98
Avg lab size	10-19 students
Avg reg class size	10-19 students

MOST POPULAR MAJORS
Journalism
Elementary education and teaching
Psychology

SELECTIVITY
Admissions Rating   **77**

# of applicants	1,704
% of applicants accepted	88
% of acceptees attending	39

FRESHMAN PROFILE

Range SAT Verbal	480-570
Average SAT Verbal	523
Range SAT Math	480-580
Average SAT Math	531
Range ACT Composite	20-25
Average ACT Composite	22
Minimum TOEFL	550
Average HS GPA	3.1
% graduated top 10% of class	12
% graduated top 25% of class	35
% graduated top 50% of class	70

DEADLINES

Priority admission	2/1
Regular admission	4/15
Nonfall registration?	yes

FINANCIAL FACTS
Financial Aid Rating   **88**

Tuition	$17,190
Room and board	$6,594
Books and supplies	$735
Required food	$635
% frosh receiving aid	74
% undergrads receiving aid	71
Avg frosh grant	$8,641
Avg frosh loan	$3,050

ST. JOHN'S UNIVERSITY— QUEENS

CAMPUS LIFE
Quality of Life Rating   **80**

Type of school	private
Affiliation	Roman Catholic
Environment	urban

STUDENTS

Total undergrad enrollment	14,485
% male/female	43/57
% from out of state	7
% from public high school	59
% live on campus	12
% in (# of) fraternities	7 (34)
% in (# of) sororities	7 (19)
% African American	14
% Asian	14
% Caucasian	43
% Hispanic	16
% international	3

ACADEMICS
Academic Rating   **73**

Calendar	semester
Student/faculty ratio	18:1
Profs interesting rating	82
Profs accessible rating	80
% profs teaching UG courses	91
% classes taught by TAs	0
Avg lab size	20-29 students
Avg regular class size	20-29 students

MOST POPULAR MAJORS
Computer science
Finance
Pharmacy (PharmD, BS/BPharm)

SELECTIVITY
Admissions Rating	**66**
# of applicants	12,274
% of applicants accepted	59
% of acceptees attending	30

FRESHMAN PROFILE
Range SAT Verbal	460-560
Average SAT Verbal	516
Range SAT Math	480-580
Average SAT Math	535
Minimum TOEFL	500
Average HS GPA	3.2
% graduated top 10% of class	24
% graduated top 25% of class	54
% graduated top 50% of class	86

DEADLINES
Nonfall registration?	yes

FINANCIAL FACTS
Financial Aid Rating	**79**
Tuition	$16,900
Room and board	$9,330
Books and supplies	$1,000
Avg frosh grant	$4,527
Avg frosh loan	$3,749

SAINT JOSEPH COLLEGE

CAMPUS LIFE
Quality of Life Rating	**79**
Type of school	private
Affiliation	Roman Catholic
Environment	suburban

STUDENTS
Total undergrad enrollment	1,287
% from out of state	10
% from public high school	79
% live on campus	47
% African American	9
% Asian	1
% Caucasian	61
% Hispanic	4

ACADEMICS
Academic Rating	**73**
Calendar	semester
Student/faculty ratio	11:1
Profs interesting rating	81
Profs accessible rating	78
% profs teaching UG courses	75
% classes taught by TAs	0
Avg lab size	under 10 students
Avg reg class size	10-19 students

MOST POPULAR MAJORS
Social work
Nursing
Psychology

SELECTIVITY
Admissions Rating	**64**
# of applicants	478
% of applicants accepted	80
% of acceptees attending	50
# of early decision applicants	3
% accepted early decision	100

FRESHMAN PROFILE
Range SAT Verbal	390-590
Average SAT Verbal	500
Range SAT Math	390-590
Average SAT Math	486
% graduated top 10% of class	17
% graduated top 25% of class	49
% graduated top 50% of class	77

DEADLINES
Regular notification	rolling
Nonfall registration?	yes

FINANCIAL FACTS
Financial Aid Rating	**80**
Tuition	$17,860
Room and board	$7,600
Books and supplies	$750
Avg frosh grant	$13,246
Avg frosh loan	$3,200

ST. LAWRENCE UNIVERSITY

CAMPUS LIFE
Quality of Life Rating	**83**
Type of school	private
Environment	rural

STUDENTS

Total undergrad enrollment	2,150
% male/female	47/53
% from out of state	46
% from public high school	72
% live on campus	95
% in (# of) fraternities	15 (4)
% in (# of) sororities	23 (4)
% African American	2
% Asian	1
% Caucasian	74
% Hispanic	2
% international	4

ACADEMICS

Academic Rating	**91**
Calendar	semester
Student/faculty ratio	12:1
Profs interesting rating	75
Profs accessible rating	75
% profs teaching UG courses	99
Avg lab size	10-19 students
Avg reg class size	10-19 students

MOST POPULAR MAJORS
Psychology
Economics
English language and literature

SELECTIVITY

Admissions Rating	**86**
# of applicants	2,867
% of applicants accepted	65
% of acceptees attending	33
# accepting a place on wait list	123
% admitted from wait list	2
# of early decision applicants	166
% accepted early decision	80

FRESHMAN PROFILE

Range SAT Verbal	520-620
Average SAT Verbal	570
Range SAT Math	520-620
Average SAT Math	570
Range ACT Composite	21-27
Average ACT Composite	24
Minimum TOEFL	600
Average HS GPA	3.3
% graduated top 10% of class	31
% graduated top 25% of class	62
% graduated top 50% of class	92

DEADLINES

Early decision	11/15
Early decision notification	12/15
Regular admission	2/15
Nonfall registration?	yes

FINANCIAL FACTS

Financial Aid Rating	**83**
Tuition	$27,985
Room and board	$7,755
Required fees	$205
Books and supplies	$650
% frosh receiving aid	85
% undergrads receiving aid	85
Avg frosh grant	$18,341
Avg frosh loan	$5,009

SAINT MICHAEL'S COLLEGE

CAMPUS LIFE

Quality of Life Rating	**75**
Type of school	private
Affiliation	Roman Catholic
Environment	suburban

STUDENTS

Total undergrad enrollment	1,981
% male/female	46/54
% from out of state	78
% from public high school	70
% live on campus	87
% African American	1
% Asian	2
% Caucasian	93
% Hispanic	1
% international	3

ACADEMICS

Academic Rating	**80**
Calendar	semester
Student/faculty ratio	13:1
Profs interesting rating	77
Profs accessible rating	75
% profs teaching UG courses	100
% classes taught by TAs	0
Avg lab size	10-19 students
Avg reg class size	20-29 students

MOST POPULAR MAJORS
Psychology
Biology/biological sciences
Business administration/management

SELECTIVITY

Admissions Rating	**87**
# of applicants	2,552
% of applicants accepted	68
# accepting a place on wait list	126

FRESHMAN PROFILE

Range SAT Verbal	510-600
Average SAT Verbal	560
Range SAT Math	500-610
Average SAT Math	560
Minimum TOEFL	550
% graduated top 10% of class	20
% graduated top 25% of class	50
% graduated top 50% of class	86

DEADLINES

Regular admission	2/1
Regular notification	4/1

FINANCIAL FACTS

Financial Aid Rating	**77**
Tuition	$21,010
Room and board	$7,255
Books and supplies	$600
Avg frosh grant	$10,288
Avg frosh loan	$4,656

SALVE REGINA UNIVERSITY

CAMPUS LIFE

Quality of Life Rating	**77**
Type of school	private
Affiliation	Roman Catholic
Environment	suburban

STUDENTS

Total undergrad enrollment	1,894
% male/female	34/66
% from out of state	80
% from public high school	68
% live on campus	65
% African American	1
% Asian	1
% Caucasian	89
% Hispanic	2
% international	1

ACADEMICS

Academic Rating	**71**
Calendar	semester

Student/faculty ratio	12:1
Profs interesting rating	79
Profs accessible rating	76
% profs teaching UG courses	100
% classes taught by TAs	0
Avg lab size	20-29 students
Avg reg class size	10-19 students

MOST POPULAR MAJORS
Special education
Criminal justice/law enforcement administration
Business administration/management

SELECTIVITY

Admissions Rating	**63**
# of applicants	3,563
% of applicants accepted	60
% of acceptees attending	26
# accepting a place on wait list	109
% admitted from wait list	24

FRESHMAN PROFILE

Range SAT Verbal	490-570
Average SAT Verbal	525
Range SAT Math	480-560
Average SAT Math	518
Minimum TOEFL	500
Average HS GPA	3.2
% graduated top 10% of class	12
% graduated top 25% of class	35
% graduated top 50% of class	75

DEADLINES

Nonfall registration?	yes

FINANCIAL FACTS

Financial Aid Rating	**75**
Tuition	$19,000
Room and board	$8,400
Books and supplies	$700
Avg frosh grant	$10,200
Avg frosh loan	$3,609

SARAH LAWRENCE COLLEGE

CAMPUS LIFE

Quality of Life Rating	**76**
Type of school	private
Environment	suburban

STUDENTS

Total undergrad enrollment	1,226

% male/female	26/74
% from out of state	79
% from public high school	65
% live on campus	87
% African American	6
% Asian	5
% Caucasian	77
% Hispanic	4
% international	4

ACADEMICS
Academic Rating **93**

Calendar	semester
Student/faculty ratio	6:1
Profs interesting rating	95
Profs accessible rating	98
% profs teaching UG courses	100
Avg reg class size	10-19 students

SELECTIVITY
Admissions Rating **90**

# of applicants	2,667
% of applicants accepted	40
% of acceptees attending	30
# accepting a place on wait list	264
# of early decision applicants	192
% accepted early decision	46

FRESHMAN PROFILE

Range SAT Verbal	610-710
Average SAT Verbal	660
Range SAT Math	530-650
Average SAT Math	590
Range ACT Composite	24-29
Average ACT Composite	27
Minimum TOEFL	600
Average HS GPA	3.6
% graduated top 10% of class	34
% graduated top 25% of class	77
% graduated top 50% of class	97

DEADLINES

Early decision	11/15
Early decision notification	12/15
Regular admission	1/1
Regular notification	4/1

FINANCIAL FACTS
Financial Aid Rating **80**

Tuition	$28,680
Room and board	$10,494
Books and supplies	$600
Required fees	$680

% frosh receiving aid	46
% undergrads receiving aid	51
Avg frosh grant	$18,268
Avg frosh loan	$2,370

SETON HALL UNIVERSITY

CAMPUS LIFE
Quality of Life Rating **80**

Type of school	private
Affiliation	Roman Catholic
Environment	suburban

STUDENTS

Total undergrad enrollment	5,080
% male/female	48/52
% from out of state	21
% from public high school	70
% live on campus	42
% in (# of) fraternities	6 (11)
% in (# of) sororities	5 (12)
% African American	11
% Asian	9
% Caucasian	54
% Hispanic	9
% international	2

ACADEMICS
Academic Rating **83**

Calendar	semester
Student/faculty ratio	14:1
% profs teaching UG courses	65
% classes taught by TAs	1
Avg lab size	10-19 students
Avg reg class size	10-19 students

MOST POPULAR MAJORS
Finance
Communications studies/speech
communication and rhetoric
Nursing/registered nurse training (RN,
ASN, BSN, MSN)

SELECTIVITY
Admissions Rating **77**

# of applicants	5,575
% of applicants accepted	85
% of acceptees attending	25
# accepting a place on wait list	1,239
% admitted from wait list	87

FRESHMAN PROFILE

Range SAT Verbal	480-590
Average SAT Verbal	539
Range SAT Math	490-600
Average SAT Math	548
Range ACT Composite	22-27
Average ACT Composite	25
Minimum TOEFL	550
Average HS GPA	3.2
% graduated top 10% of class	24
% graduated top 25% of class	50
% graduated top 50% of class	80

DEADLINES

Priority admission	3/1
Nonfall registration?	yes

FINANCIAL FACTS

Financial Aid Rating	**81**
Tuition	$18,780
Room and board	$8,302
Books and supplies	$1,100
Required fees	$2,050

SIENA COLLEGE

CAMPUS LIFE

Quality of Life Rating	**75**
Type of school	private
Affiliation	Roman Catholic
Environment	suburban

STUDENTS

Total undergrad enrollment	3,405
% male/female	43/57
% from out of state	20
% live on campus	70
% African American	2
% Asian	2
% Caucasian	90
% Hispanic	3
# of countries represented	6

ACADEMICS

Academic Rating	**74**
Calendar	semester
Student/faculty ratio	14:1
Profs interesting rating	91
Profs accessible rating	92
% profs teaching UG courses	100

Avg lab size	10-19 students
Avg reg class size	20-29 students

MOST POPULAR MAJORS
Biology
Accounting
Psychology

SELECTIVITY

Admissions Rating	**74**
# of applicants	3,945
% of applicants accepted	58
% of acceptees attending	30
# of early decision applicants	117
% accepted early decision	9

FRESHMAN PROFILE

Range SAT Verbal	510-590
Average SAT Verbal	550
Range SAT Math	520-610
Average SAT Math	567
Range ACT Composite	24-27
Average ACT Composite	26
Minimum TOEFL	550
% graduated top 10% of class	24
% graduated top 25% of class	63
% graduated top 50% of class	94

DEADLINES

Early decision	12/1
Early decision notification	12/15
Priority admission	3/1
Regular admission	3/1
Regular notification	3/15
Nonfall registration?	yes

FINANCIAL FACTS

Financial Aid Rating	**80**
Tuition	$17,555
Room and board	$7,215
Books and supplies	$745
Required fees	$540
% frosh receiving aid	92
% undergrads receiving aid	89

SIMMONS COLLEGE

CAMPUS LIFE

Quality of Life Rating	**86**
Type of school	private
Environment	urban

STUDENTS

Total undergrad enrollment	1,373
% from out of state	43
% from public high school	81
% live on campus	75
% African American	7
% Asian	7
% Caucasian	76
% Hispanic	4
% international	4
# of countries represented	26

ACADEMICS

Academic Rating	**88**
Calendar	semester
Student/faculty ratio	12:1
Profs interesting rating	94
Profs accessible rating	94
% profs teaching UG courses	100
Avg reg class size	10-19 students

MOST POPULAR MAJORS
Nursing/registered nurse training (RN, ASN, BSN, MSN)
Biology
Communications

SELECTIVITY

Admissions Rating	**77**
# of applicants	1,753
% of applicants accepted	68
% of acceptees attending	27
# accepting a place on wait list	18
% admitted from wait list	0

FRESHMAN PROFILE

Range SAT Verbal	500-600
Average SAT Verbal	554
Range SAT Math	490-590
Average SAT Math	542
Range ACT Composite	19-25
Average ACT Composite	23
Minimum TOEFL	560
% graduated top 10% of class	24
% graduated top 25% of class	47
% graduated top 50% of class	80
Average HS GPA	3.1

DEADLINES

Regular admission	2/1
Regular notification	4/15
Nonfall registration?	yes

FINANCIAL FACTS

Financial Aid Rating	**80**
Tuition	$22,860
Room and board	$9,458
Books and supplies	$640
Required fees	$690
% frosh receiving aid	88
% undergrads receiving aid	65

SIMON'S ROCK COLLEGE OF BARD

CAMPUS LIFE

Quality of Life Rating	**84**
Type of school	private
Environment	rural

STUDENTS

Total undergrad enrollment	409
% male/female	41/59
% from out of state	80
% from public high school	70
% live on campus	86
% African American	3
% Asian	5
% Caucasian	74
% Hispanic	3
% international	1

ACADEMICS

Academic Rating	**93**
Calendar	semester
Student/faculty ratio	8:1
Profs interesting rating	80
Profs accessible rating	76
% profs teaching UG courses	100
Avg lab size	10-19 students
Avg reg class size	10-19 students

MOST POPULAR MAJORS
Dramatic/theatre arts and stagecraft
Mathematics
Ethnic, cultural minority, and gender studies

SELECTIVITY

Admissions Rating	**91**
# of applicants	480
% of applicants accepted	50
% of acceptees attending	64

FRESHMAN PROFILE

Range SAT Verbal	580-660
Average SAT Verbal	640
Range SAT Math	490-640
Average SAT Math	600
Range ACT Composite	22-28
Average ACT Composite	26
Minimum TOEFL	550

DEADLINES

Regular admission	7/1
Regular notification	rolling

FINANCIAL FACTS
Financial Aid Rating 88

Tuition	$27,180
Room and board	$7,160
Books and supplies	$1,000
Required fees	$235
% frosh receiving aid	68
% undergrads receiving aid	63

SKIDMORE COLLEGE

CAMPUS LIFE
Quality of Life Rating 94

Type of school	private
Environment	suburban

STUDENTS

Total undergrad enrollment	2,506
% male/female	40/60
% from out of state	71
% from public high school	60
% live on campus	77
% African American	3
% Asian	5
% Caucasian	75
% Hispanic	4
% international	1

ACADEMICS
Academic Rating 84

Calendar	semester
Student/faculty ratio	11:1
Profs interesting rating	94
Profs accessible rating	94
% profs teaching UG courses	100
Avg lab size	10-19 students
Avg reg class size	10-19 students

SELECTIVITY
Admissions Rating 83

# of applicants	5,606
% of applicants accepted	46
% of acceptees attending	25
# accepting a place on wait list	347
% admitted from wait list	1
# of early decision applicants	406
% accepted early decision	57

FRESHMAN PROFILE

Range SAT Verbal	580-670
Average SAT Verbal	630
Range SAT Math	580-660
Average SAT Math	620
Range ACT Composite	25-28
Average ACT Composite	27
Minimum TOEFL	580
Average HS GPA	3.4
% graduated top 10% of class	41
% graduated top 25% of class	74
% graduated top 50% of class	97

DEADLINES

Early decision	12/1
Early decision notification	1/1
Regular admission	1/15
Regular notification	4/1
Nonfall registration?	yes

FINANCIAL FACTS
Financial Aid Rating 81

Tuition	$27,700
Room and board	$7,835
Books and supplies	$650
Required fees	$280
% frosh receiving aid	40
% undergrads receiving aid	42
Avg frosh grant	$17,342
Avg frosh loan	$2,336

SMITH COLLEGE

CAMPUS LIFE
Quality of Life Rating 92

Type of school	private
Environment	suburban

STUDENTS

Total undergrad enrollment	2,647
% from out of state	76

% from public high school	74
% live on campus	87
% African American	5
% Asian	10
% Caucasian	62
% Hispanic	6
% international	6
# of countries represented	55

ACADEMICS
Academic Rating **94**

Calendar	semester
Student/faculty ratio	9:1
Profs interesting rating	97
Profs accessible rating	98
% profs teaching UG courses	100
Avg lab size	10-19 students
Avg reg class size	10-19 students

MOST POPULAR MAJORS
Psychology
Economics
Political science and government

SELECTIVITY
Admissions Rating **97**

# of applicants	3,047
% of applicants accepted	53
% of acceptees attending	42
# accepting a place on wait list	174
# of early decision applicants	224
% accepted early decision	70

FRESHMAN PROFILE
Range SAT Verbal	590-700
Average SAT Verbal	660
Range SAT Math	580-670
Average SAT Math	640
Range ACT Composite	24-30
Average ACT Composite	27
Minimum TOEFL	600
Average HS GPA	3.8
% graduated top 10% of class	58
% graduated top 25% of class	90
% graduated top 50% of class	99

DEADLINES
Early decision	11/15
Early decision notification	12/15
Regular admission	1/15
Regular notification	4/1

FINANCIAL FACTS
Financial Aid Rating **79**

Tuition	$27,330
Room and board	$9,490
Books and supplies	$1,500
Required fees	$214
% frosh receiving aid	61
% undergrads receiving aid	64
Avg frosh grant	$21,874
Avg frosh loan	$2,674

STEVENS INSTITUTE OF TECHNOLOGY

CAMPUS LIFE
Quality of Life Rating **74**

Type of school	private
Environment	suburban

STUDENTS
Total undergrad enrollment	1,729
% male/female	75/25
% from out of state	35
% live on campus	75
% in (# of) fraternities	30 (9)
% in (# of) sororities	33 (3)
% African American	5
% Asian	25
% Caucasian	51
% Hispanic	10
% international	7
# of countries represented	68

ACADEMICS
Academic Rating **82**

Calendar	semester
Student/faculty ratio	9:1
Profs interesting rating	86
Profs accessible rating	91
% profs teaching UG courses	100
Avg lab size	10-19 students
Avg reg class size	20-29 students

MOST POPULAR MAJORS
Computer science
Computer engineering
Mechanical engineering

SELECTIVITY

Admissions Rating **85**

# of applicants	2,049
% of applicants accepted	50
% of acceptees attending	38
# accepting a place on wait list	166
% admitted from wait list	17
# of early decision applicants	76
% accepted early decision	47

FRESHMAN PROFILE

Range SAT Verbal	540-660
Range SAT Math	610-730
Minimum TOEFL	550
Average HS GPA	3.8

DEADLINES

Early decision	11/1
Early decision notification	12/15
Priority admission	11/15
Regular admission	2/15

FINANCIAL FACTS

Financial Aid Rating **89**

Tuition	$24,500
Room and board	$8,100
Books and supplies	$900
Required fees	$250
% frosh receiving aid	74
% undergrads receiving aid	70
Avg frosh grant	$19,140
Avg frosh loan	$2,500

STONEHILL COLLEGE

CAMPUS LIFE

Quality of Life Rating **74**

Type of school	private
Affiliation	Roman Catholic
Environment	suburban

STUDENTS

Total undergrad enrollment	2,602
% male/female	40/60
% from out of state	39
% from public high school	74
% live on campus	85
% African American	2
% Asian	2
% Caucasian	91

% Hispanic	3
% international	1
# of countries represented	5

ACADEMICS

Academic Rating **78**

Calendar	semester
Student/faculty ratio	15:1
Profs interesting rating	79
Profs accessible rating	75
% profs teaching UG courses	100
% classes taught by TAs	0
Avg lab size	10-19 students
Avg reg class size	20-29 students

MOST POPULAR MAJORS
Education studies
Psychology
Biology

SELECTIVITY

Admissions Rating **76**

# of applicants	5,331
% of applicants accepted	42
% of acceptees attending	25
# accepting a place on wait list	432
% admitted from wait list	2
# of early decision applicants	98
% accepted early decision	55

FRESHMAN PROFILE

Range SAT Verbal	540-630
Average SAT Verbal	590
Range SAT Math	560-640
Average SAT Math	600
Average ACT Composite	25
Minimum TOEFL	550
Average HS GPA	3.53
% graduated top 10% of class	51
% graduated top 25% of class	92
% graduated top 50% of class	100

DEADLINES

Early decision	11/1
Regular admission	1/15
Regular notification	4/1
Nonfall registration?	yes

FINANCIAL FACTS

Financial Aid Rating **73**

Tuition	$19,094
Room and board	$9,172
Books and supplies	$740

| Avg frosh grant | $7,724 |
| Avg frosh loan | $3,141 |

SUFFOLK UNIVERSITY

CAMPUS LIFE
Quality of Life Rating	**73**
Type of school	private
Affiliation	none
Environment	urban

STUDENTS
Total undergrad enrollment	3,437
% male/female	43/57
% from out of state	15
% from public high school	63
% live on campus	15
% in (# of) fraternities	1 (2)
% African American	4
% Asian	6
% Caucasian	59
% Hispanic	6
% international	13

ACADEMICS
Academic Rating	**70**
Calendar	semester
Student/faculty ratio	12:1
% profs teaching UG courses	90
% classes taught by TAs	0
Avg lab size	Under 10 students
Avg regular class size	10-19 students

SELECTIVITY
Admissions Rating	**69**
# of applicants	3,283
% of applicants accepted	83
% of acceptees attending	26

FRESHMAN PROFILE
Range SAT Verbal	450-560
Average SAT Verbal	502
Range SAT Math	440-540
Average SAT Math	493
Minimum TOEFL	525
Average HS GPA	2.9
% graduated top 10% of class	7
% graduated top 25% of class	24
% graduated top 50% of class	60

DEADLINES
| Nonfall registration? | yes |

FINANCIAL FACTS
Financial Aid Rating	**75**
Tuition	$15,538
Room and board	$9,660
Books and supplies	$500
Avg frosh grant	$6,800
Avg frosh loan	$7,300

SUNY AT ALBANY

CAMPUS LIFE
Quality of Life Rating	**68**
Type of school	public
Environment	suburban

STUDENTS
Total undergrad enrollment	11,953
% male/female	50/50
% from out of state	5
% live on campus	58
% in (# of) fraternities	4 (19)
% in (# of) sororities	5 (15)
% African American	9
% Asian	6
% Caucasian	65
% Hispanic	7
% international	2
# of countries represented	87

ACADEMICS
Academic Rating	**70**
Calendar	semester
Student/faculty ratio	21:1
Profs interesting rating	89
Profs accessible rating	88
% profs teaching UG courses	91
% classes taught by TAs	13
Avg lab size	10-19 students
Avg reg class size	20-29 students

MOST POPULAR MAJORS
Business administration/management
English language and literature
Psychology

SELECTIVITY
| Admissions Rating | **79** |
| # of applicants | 17,667 |

% of applicants accepted	56
% of acceptees attending	23

FRESHMAN PROFILE
Range SAT Verbal	500-600
Average SAT Verbal	567
Range SAT Math	520-610
Average SAT Math	583
Minimum TOEFL	550
Average HS GPA	3.6
% graduated top 10% of class	16
% graduated top 25% of class	54
% graduated top 50% of class	92

DEADLINES
Priority admission	12/1
Regular admission	3/1
Nonfall registration?	yes

FINANCIAL FACTS
Financial Aid Rating	**74**
In-state tuition	$3,400
Out-of-state tuition	$8,300
Room and board	$7,052
Books and supplies	$800
Required fees	$1,420
% frosh receiving aid	54
% undergrads receiving aid	53
Avg frosh grant	$4,310
Avg frosh loan	$4,113

SUNY AT BINGHAMTON

CAMPUS LIFE
Quality of Life Rating	**75**
Type of school	public
Affiliation	none
Environment	suburban

STUDENTS
Total undergrad enrollment	10,328
% male/female	48/52
% from out of state	4
% from public high school	87
% live on campus	57
% in (# of) fraternities	10 (10)
% in (# of) sororities	10 (10)
% African American	5
% Asian	17
% Caucasian	52
% Hispanic	6

% international	3
# of countries represented	85

ACADEMICS
Academic Rating	**84**
Calendar	semester
Student/faculty ratio	21:1
Profs interesting rating	91
Profs accessible rating	88
% profs teaching UG courses	90
% classes taught by TAs	10
Avg lab size	20-29 students
Avg reg class size	10-19 students

MOST POPULAR MAJORS
Business administration/management
English language and literature
Psychology

SELECTIVITY
Admissions Rating	**92**
# of applicants	18,315
% of applicants accepted	42
% of acceptees attending	27
# accepting a place on wait list	219
% admitted from wait list	100

FRESHMAN PROFILE
Range SAT Verbal	550-640
Average SAT Verbal	599
Range SAT Math	590-690
Average SAT Math	637
Range ACT Composite	24-29
Average ACT Composite	26
Minimum TOEFL	550
Average HS GPA	3.6
% graduated top 25% of class	86
% graduated top 50% of class	99

DEADLINES
Priority admission	1/15
Nonfall registration?	yes

FINANCIAL FACTS
Financial Aid Rating	**75**
In-state tuition	$3,400
Out-of-state tuition	$8,300
Room and board	$6,412
Books and supplies	$800
Required fees	$1,317
% frosh receiving aid	43
% undergrads receiving aid	49
Avg frosh grant	$3,806
Avg frosh loan	$3,116

SUNY AT BUFFALO

CAMPUS LIFE
Quality of Life Rating	**69**
Type of school	public
Environment	suburban

STUDENTS
Total undergrad enrollment	16,636
% male/female	55/45
% from out of state	2
% live on campus	21
% in (# of) fraternities	1 (10)
% in (# of) sororities	1 (12)
% African American	8
% Asian	10
% Caucasian	71
% Hispanic	4
% international	5
# of countries represented	106

ACADEMICS
Academic Rating	**76**
Calendar	semester
Student/faculty ratio	14:1
% profs teaching UG courses	64
% classes taught by TAs	20
Avg lab size	20-29 students
Avg reg class size	20-29 students

MOST POPULAR MAJORS
Business administration/management
Communications studies/speech
communication and rhetoric
Psychology

SELECTIVITY
Admissions Rating	**82**
# of applicants	16,057
% of applicants accepted	61
% of acceptees attending	31
# of early decision applicants	417
% accepted early decision	63

FRESHMAN PROFILE
Range SAT Verbal	500-600
Average SAT Verbal	566
Range SAT Math	520-630
Average SAT Math	589
Average ACT Composite	29
Minimum TOEFL	550
Average HS GPA	3.1
% graduated top 10% of class	21
% graduated top 25% of class	57
% graduated top 50% of class	92

DEADLINES
Early decision	11/1
Early decision notification	12/1
Priority admission	11/1
Nonfall registration?	yes

FINANCIAL FACTS
Financial Aid Rating	**80**
In-state tuition	$3,400
Out-of-state tuition	$8,300
Room and board	$6,512
Books and supplies	$750
Required fees	$1,450
% frosh receiving aid	65
% undergrads receiving aid	52
Avg frosh grant	$5,225
Avg frosh loan	$4,050

SUNY AT NEW PALTZ

CAMPUS LIFE
Quality of Life Rating	**75**
Type of school	public
Affiliation	none
Environment	rural

STUDENTS
Total undergrad enrollment	6,082
% male/female	37/63
% from out of state	5
% from public high school	92
% live on campus	49
% in (# of) fraternities	3 (10)
% in (# of) sororities	2 (14)
% African American	8
% Asian	4
% Caucasian	68
% Hispanic	9
% international	3
# of countries represented	30

ACADEMICS
Academic Rating	**83**
Calendar	semester
Student/faculty ratio	17:1
Profs interesting rating	82
Profs accessible rating	82
% profs teaching UG courses	98

| % classes taught by TAs | 0 |
| Avg reg class size | 10-19 students |

MOST POPULAR MAJORS
Sociology
Business administration/management
Special education

SELECTIVITY
Admissions Rating	**82**
# of applicants	9,617
% of applicants accepted	35
% of acceptees attending	27
# accepting a place on wait list	42
% admitted from wait list	5
# of early decision applicants	56
% accepted early decision	29

FRESHMAN PROFILE
Range SAT Verbal	500-620
Average SAT Verbal	564
Range SAT Math	510-620
Average SAT Math	566
Minimum TOEFL	550
Average HS GPA	3.2
% graduated top 10% of class	13
% graduated top 25% of class	47
% graduated top 50% of class	91

DEADLINES
Early decision	11/15
Regular admission	5/1
Nonfall registration?	yes

FINANCIAL FACTS
Financial Aid Rating	**70**
In-state tuition	$3,400
Out-of-state tuition	$8,300
Room and board	$5,246
Books and supplies	$750
Avg frosh grant	$2,625
Avg frosh loan	$2,200

SUNY AT STONY BROOK

CAMPUS LIFE
Quality of Life Rating	**68**
Type of school	public
Environment	suburban

STUDENTS
Total undergrad enrollment	14,224

% male/female	52/48
% from out of state	3
% from public high school	90
% live on campus	50
% African American	10
% Asian	25
% Caucasian	37
% Hispanic	8
% international	4

ACADEMICS
Academic Rating	**75**
Calendar	semester
Student/faculty ratio	18:1
Profs interesting rating	87
Profs accessible rating	88
Avg lab size	20-29 students
Avg reg class size	10-19 students

MOST POPULAR MAJORS
Psychology
Business management
Biology

SELECTIVITY
Admissions Rating	**80**
# of applicants	16,849
% of applicants accepted	54
% of acceptees attending	27

FRESHMAN PROFILE
Range SAT Verbal	500-590
Average SAT Verbal	545
Range SAT Math	550-650
Average SAT Math	599
Minimum TOEFL	550
Average HS GPA	3.5
% graduated top 10% of class	26
% graduated top 25% of class	63
% graduated top 50% of class	93

DEADLINES
Priority admission	12/1
Regular admission	rolling
Regular notification	rolling
Nonfall registration?	yes

FINANCIAL FACTS
Financial Aid Rating	**73**
In-state tuition	$3,400
Out-of-state tuition	$8,300
Room and board	$7,174
Books and supplies	$900

Required fees	$958
% frosh receiving aid	50
% undergrads receiving aid	60
Avg frosh grant	$4,043
Avg frosh loan	$2,153

SUNY COLLEGE AT BROCKPORT

CAMPUS LIFE

Quality of Life Rating	**80**
Type of school	public
Affiliation	none
Environment	suburban

STUDENTS

Total undergrad enrollment	6,764
% male/female	42/58
% from out of state	2
% live on campus	37
% in (# of) fraternities	2 (5)
% in (# of) sororities	2 (4)
% African American	6
% Asian	1
% Caucasian	88
% Hispanic	2
% international	1
# of countries represented	28

ACADEMICS

Academic Rating	**72**
Calendar	semester
Student/faculty ratio	19:1
Profs interesting rating	87
Profs accessible rating	82
% profs teaching UG courses	95
% classes taught by TAs	0
Avg lab size	20-29 students
Avg reg class size	20-29 students

MOST POPULAR MAJORS
Criminal justice/safety studies
Business administration/management
Physical education teaching and coaching

SELECTIVITY

Admissions Rating	**67**
# of applicants	6,947
% of applicants accepted	54
% of acceptees attending	29

FRESHMAN PROFILE

Range SAT Verbal	475-565
Average SAT Verbal	519
Range SAT Math	480-575
Average SAT Math	528
Range ACT Composite	19-25
Average ACT Composite	22
Minimum TOEFL	530
Average HS GPA	87%
% graduated top 10% of class	10
% graduated top 25% of class	35
% graduated top 50% of class	78

DEADLINES

Nonfall registration?	yes

FINANCIAL FACTS

Financial Aid Rating	**72**
In-state tuition	$3,400
Out-of-state tuition	$8,300
Room and board	$6,140
Books and supplies	$800
Avg frosh grant	$2,695
Avg frosh loan	$2,715

SUNY COLLEGE AT CORTLAND

CAMPUS LIFE

Quality of Life Rating	**75**
Type of school	public
Affiliation	none
Environment	suburban

STUDENTS

Total undergrad enrollment	5,850
% male/female	41/59
% from out of state	2
% from public high school	91
% live on campus	55
% in (# of) fraternities	4 (4)
% in (# of) sororities	9 (1)
% African American	2
% Asian	1
% Caucasian	90
% Hispanic	3
# of countries represented	14

ACADEMICS

Academic Rating	**73**

Calendar	semester
Student/faculty ratio	16:1
Profs interesting rating	82
Profs accessible rating	79
% profs teaching UG courses	97
% classes taught by TAs	0
Avg lab size	20-29 students
Avg reg class size	20-29 students

MOST POPULAR MAJORS
Elementary education
Physical education
Psychology

SELECTIVITY
Admissions Rating	72
# of applicants	8,341
% of applicants accepted	55
% of acceptees attending	28
# of early decision applicants	90
% accepted early decision	71

FRESHMAN PROFILE
Range SAT Verbal	485-580
Average SAT Verbal	520
Range SAT Math	470-555
Average SAT Math	520
Range ACT Composite	22-25
Average ACT Composite	23
Minimum TOEFL	550
Average HS GPA	3.2

DEADLINES
Early decision	11/15
Nonfall registration?	yes

FINANCIAL FACTS
Financial Aid Rating	68
Out-of-state tuition	$8,300
Room and board	$6,390
Books and supplies	$700

SUNY COLLEGE AT FREDONIA

CAMPUS LIFE
Quality of Life Rating	77
Type of school	public
Affiliation	none
Environment	rural

STUDENTS
Total undergrad enrollment	4,900
% male/female	42/58
% from out of state	2
% from public high school	75
% live on campus	51
% in (# of) fraternities	5 (4)
% in (# of) sororities	3 (3)
% African American	1
% Asian	1
% Caucasian	94
% Hispanic	2

ACADEMICS
Academic Rating	79
Calendar	semester
Student/faculty ratio	19:1
Profs interesting rating	85
Profs accessible rating	83
% profs teaching UG courses	100
% classes taught by TAs	0
Avg lab size	20-29 students
Avg reg class size	under 10 students

MOST POPULAR MAJORS
Elementary education
Business
Communications

SELECTIVITY
Admissions Rating	74
# of applicants	6,150
% of applicants accepted	52
% of acceptees attending	33
# of early decision applicants	68
% accepted early decision	60

FRESHMAN PROFILE
Range SAT Verbal	510-590
Average SAT Verbal	557
Range SAT Math	520-590
Average SAT Math	561
Range ACT Composite	21-26
Average ACT Composite	24
Minimum TOEFL	277
Average HS GPA	3.4
% graduated top 10% of class	14
% graduated top 25% of class	46
% graduated top 50% of class	91

DEADLINES
Early decision	11/1
Nonfall registration?	yes

FINANCIAL FACTS

Financial Aid Rating	**75**
In-state tuition	$3,400
Out-of-state tuition	$8,300
Room and board	$5,650
Books and supplies	$620
Avg frosh grant	$2,581
Avg frosh loan	$2,944

SUNY COLLEGE AT GENESEO

CAMPUS LIFE

Quality of Life Rating	**71**
Type of school	public
Environment	rural

STUDENTS

Total undergrad enrollment	5,387
% male/female	36/64
% from out of state	1
% from public high school	94
% live on campus	58
% in (# of) fraternities	10 (10)
% in (# of) sororities	12 (10)
% African American	2
% Asian	5
% Caucasian	90
% Hispanic	3
% international	1

ACADEMICS

Academic Rating	**77**
Calendar	semester
Student/faculty ratio	19:1
Profs interesting rating	71
Profs accessible rating	76
% profs teaching UG courses	100
Avg reg class size	20-29 students

MOST POPULAR MAJORS
Special education
Psychology
Business administration/management

SELECTIVITY

Admissions Rating	**92**
# accepting a place on wait list	2,735
% admitted from wait list	7
# of early decision applicants	265
% accepted early decision	50

FRESHMAN PROFILE

Range SAT Verbal	580-650
Average SAT Verbal	619
Range SAT Math	590-660
Average SAT Math	626
Range ACT Composite	25-28
Average ACT Composite	27
Minimum TOEFL	525
Average HS GPA	3.6
% graduated top 10% of class	49
% graduated top 25% of class	81
% graduated top 50% of class	99

DEADLINES

Early decision	11/15
Early decision notification	12/15
Regular admission	1/15
Nonfall registration?	yes

FINANCIAL FACTS

Financial Aid Rating	**79**
In-state tuition	$3,400
Out-of-state tuition	$8,300
Room and board	$5,660
Books and supplies	$700
Required fees	$910
% frosh receiving aid	45
% undergrads receiving aid	47
Avg frosh grant	$1,585
Avg frosh loan	$2,975

SUNY COLLEGE AT ONEONTA

CAMPUS LIFE

Quality of Life Rating	**80**
Type of school	public
Affiliation	none
Environment	suburban

STUDENTS

Total undergrad enrollment	5,458
% male/female	40/60
% from out of state	2
% from public high school	92
% live on campus	59
% in (# of) sororities	7 (3)
% African American	3
% Asian	2
% Caucasian	81

% Hispanic	4
% international	1
# of countries represented	30

ACADEMICS
Academic Rating — 69

Calendar	semester
Student/faculty ratio	18:1
Profs interesting rating	81
Profs accessible rating	79
% profs teaching UG courses	98
% classes taught by TAs	0
Avg reg class size	10-19 students

MOST POPULAR MAJORS
Psychology
Business/managerial economics
Elementary education and teaching

SELECTIVITY
Admissions Rating — 64

# of applicants	9,286
% of applicants accepted	52
% of acceptees attending	24
# accepting a place on wait list	452
% admitted from wait list	27
# of early decision applicants	166
% accepted early decision	43

FRESHMAN PROFILE

Range SAT Verbal	490-560
Average SAT Verbal	527
Range SAT Math	490-570
Average SAT Math	532
Range ACT Composite	21-24
Average ACT Composite	22
Minimum TOEFL	500
Average HS GPA	3.1
% graduated top 10% of class	8
% graduated top 25% of class	32
% graduated top 50% of class	83

DEADLINES

Early decision	11/1
Nonfall registration?	yes

FINANCIAL FACTS
Financial Aid Rating — 74

In-state tuition	$3,400
Out-of-state tuition	$8,300
Room and board	$5,750
Books and supplies	$800
Avg frosh grant	$6,312
Avg frosh loan	$3,033

SUNY COLLEGE AT OSWEGO

CAMPUS LIFE
Quality of Life Rating — 81

Type of school	public
Affiliation	none
Environment	suburban

STUDENTS

Total undergrad enrollment	7,337
% male/female	46/54
% from out of state	2
% from public high school	94
% live on campus	50
% in (# of) fraternities	12 (15)
% in (# of) sororities	12 (14)
% African American	4
% Asian	2
% Caucasian	90
% Hispanic	3
# of countries represented	21

ACADEMICS
Academic Rating — 68

Calendar	semester
Student/faculty ratio	19:1
Profs interesting rating	86
Profs accessible rating	82
% profs teaching UG courses	93
% classes taught by TAs	0
Avg lab size	10-19 students
Avg reg class size	20-29 students

MOST POPULAR MAJORS
Cusiness administration
Communication studies
Elementary education

SELECTIVITY
Admissions Rating — 65

# of applicants	7,697
% of applicants accepted	56
% of acceptees attending	32
# of early decision applicants	84
% accepted early decision	83

FRESHMAN PROFILE

Range SAT Verbal	510-600
Average SAT Verbal	541
Range SAT Math	530-590
Average SAT Math	544
Range ACT Composite	21-25

Average ACT Composite	24
Minimum TOEFL	550
Average HS GPA	3.2
% graduated top 10% of class	10
% graduated top 25% of class	43
% graduated top 50% of class	86

DEADLINES

Early decision	11/15
Nonfall registration?	yes

FINANCIAL FACTS

Financial Aid Rating	**78**
In-state tuition	$3,400
Out-of-state tuition	$8,300
Room and board	$6,696
Books and supplies	$650
Avg frosh grant	$2,300
Avg frosh loan	$2,625

SUNY COLLEGE AT POTSDAM

CAMPUS LIFE

Quality of Life Rating	**76**
Type of school	public
Affiliation	none
Environment	rural

STUDENTS

Total undergrad enrollment	3,475
% male/female	41/59
% from out of state	3
% live on campus	49
% African American	2
% Asian	1
% Caucasian	82
% Hispanic	2
% international	2
# of countries represented	10

ACADEMICS

Academic Rating	**70**
Calendar	semester
Student/faculty ratio	18:1
Profs interesting rating	89
Profs accessible rating	82
% profs teaching UG courses	95
Avg lab size	10-19 students
Avg reg class size	10-19 students

MOST POPULAR MAJORS
Music teacher education
Psychology
Elementary education and teaching

SELECTIVITY

Admissions Rating	**66**
# of applicants	3,397
% of applicants accepted	67
% of acceptees attending	28
# accepting a place on wait list	47
% admitted from wait list	19

FRESHMAN PROFILE

Range SAT Verbal	470-590
Average SAT Verbal	534
Range SAT Math	480-580
Average SAT Math	533
Range ACT Composite	20-26
Average ACT Composite	23
Minimum TOEFL	520
Average HS GPA	85%
% graduated top 10% of class	11
% graduated top 25% of class	37
% graduated top 50% of class	78

DEADLINES

Nonfall registration?	yes

FINANCIAL FACTS

Financial Aid Rating	**76**
In-state tuition	$3,400
Out-of-state tuition	$8,300
Room and board	$6,390
Books and supplies	$800
Avg frosh grant	$4,042
Avg frosh loan	$6,290

SYRACUSE UNIVERSITY

CAMPUS LIFE

Quality of Life Rating	**84**
Type of school	private
Environment	urban

STUDENTS

Total undergrad enrollment	10,936
% male/female	44/56
% from out of state	56
% from public high school	78
% live on campus	73

% in (# of) fraternities	8 (22)
% in (# of) sororities	13 (20)
% African American	6
% Asian	5
% Caucasian	73
% Hispanic	4
% international	3
# of countries represented	61

ACADEMICS
Academic Rating — 87
Calendar	semester
Student/faculty ratio	12:1
Profs interesting rating	73
Profs accessible rating	73
% profs teaching UG courses	98
% classes taught by TAs	6
Avg lab size	10-19 students
Avg reg class size	20-29 students

MOST POPULAR MAJORS
Information science/studies
Psychology
Political science and government

SELECTIVITY
Admissions Rating — 88
# of applicants	13,644
% of applicants accepted	69
% of acceptees attending	31
# of early decision applicants	715
% accepted early decision	65

FRESHMAN PROFILE
Range SAT Verbal	550-640
Range SAT Math	570-660
Minimum TOEFL	550
Average HS GPA	3.5
% graduated top 10% of class	41
% graduated top 25% of class	79
% graduated top 50% of class	98

DEADLINES
Early decision	11/15
Early decision notification	12/31
Regular admission	1/1
Nonfall registration?	yes

FINANCIAL FACTS
Financial Aid Rating — 83
Tuition	$24,170
Room and board	$9,590
Books and supplies	$1,162
Required fees	$960

% frosh receiving aid	55
% undergrads receiving aid	56
Avg frosh grant	$13,400
Avg frosh loan	$3,300

TRINITY COLLEGE

CAMPUS LIFE
Quality of Life Rating — 80
| Type of school | private |
| Environment | urban |

STUDENTS
Total undergrad enrollment	2,098
% male/female	48/52
% from out of state	78
% from public high school	54
% live on campus	95
% in (# of) fraternities	27 (7)
% in (# of) sororities	22 (7)
% African American	6
% Asian	6
% Caucasian	69
% Hispanic	5
% international	2
# of countries represented	35

ACADEMICS
Academic Rating — 84
Calendar	semester
Student/faculty ratio	9:1
Profs interesting rating	95
Profs accessible rating	98
% profs teaching UG courses	100
Avg lab size	20-29 students
Avg reg class size	10-19 students

MOST POPULAR MAJORS
History
Economics
Political science and government

SELECTIVITY
Admissions Rating — 94
# of applicants	5,417
% of applicants accepted	36
% of acceptees attending	28
# accepting a place on wait list	433
# of early decision applicants	522
% accepted early decision	50

FRESHMAN PROFILE

Range SAT Verbal	590-690
Average SAT Verbal	630
Range SAT Math	600-690
Average SAT Math	642
Range ACT Composite	24-29
Average ACT Composite	27
Minimum TOEFL	550
% graduated top 10% of class	50
% graduated top 25% of class	83
% graduated top 50% of class	98

DEADLINES

Early decision	11/15
Early decision notification	12/15
Regular admission	1/15
Regular notification	4/1

FINANCIAL FACTS

Financial Aid Rating	**82**
Tuition	$27,170
Room and board	$7,380
Books and supplies	$850
Required fees	$1,432
% frosh receiving aid	44
% undergrads receiving aid	47
Avg frosh grant	$25,000
Avg frosh loan	$3,521

TUFTS UNIVERSITY

CAMPUS LIFE

Quality of Life Rating	**89**
Type of school	private
Environment	suburban

STUDENTS

Total undergrad enrollment	4,910
% male/female	45/55
% from out of state	76
% from public high school	61
% live on campus	75
% in (# of) fraternities	15 (10)
% in (# of) sororities	4 (3)
% African American	8
% Asian	14
% Caucasian	58
% Hispanic	9
% international	7

ACADEMICS

Academic Rating	**91**
Calendar	semester
Student/faculty ratio	9:1
% profs teaching UG courses	100
% classes taught by TAs	1
Avg lab size	10-19 students
Avg reg class size	10-19 students

SELECTIVITY

Admissions Rating	**97**
# of applicants	14,308
% of applicants accepted	27
% of acceptees attending	34
# of early decision applicants	1,230
% accepted early decision	43

FRESHMAN PROFILE

Range SAT Verbal	610-710
Range SAT Math	640-720
Range ACT Composite	26-31
Minimum TOEFL	100 (CBT)
% graduated top 10% of class	72
% graduated top 25% of class	94
% graduated top 50% of class	100

DEADLINES

Early decision	11/15
Early decision notification	12/15
Regular admission	1/1
Regular notification	4/1

FINANCIAL FACTS

Financial Aid Rating	**84**
Tuition	$26,213
Room and board	$7,987
Books and supplies	$700
Required fees	$679
% frosh receiving aid	36
% undergrads receiving aid	41
Avg frosh grant	$19,183
Avg frosh loan	$3,356

UNION COLLEGE

CAMPUS LIFE

Quality of Life Rating	**77**
Type of school	private
Environment	suburban

STUDENTS

Total undergrad enrollment	2,147
% male/female	53/47
% from out of state	54
% from public high school	70
% live on campus	80
% in (# of) fraternities	21 (14)
% in (# of) sororities	25 (4)
% African American	3
% Asian	5
% Caucasian	84
% Hispanic	4
% international	3
# of countries represented	21

ACADEMICS

Academic Rating	**87**
Calendar	trimester
Student/faculty ratio	11:1
Profs interesting rating	95
Profs accessible rating	98
% profs teaching UG courses	100
Avg lab size	10-19 students
Avg reg class size	10-19 students

MOST POPULAR MAJORS
Psychology
Political science and government
Economics

ADMISSIONS

Admissions Rating	**91**
# of applicants	3,828
% of applicants accepted	45
% of acceptees attending	33
# accepting a place on wait list	405
% admitted from wait list	18
# of early decision applicants	249
% accepted early decision	74

FRESHMAN PROFILE

Range SAT Verbal	550-650
Average SAT Verbal	610
Range SAT Math	590-680
Average SAT Math	630
Minimum TOEFL	600
Average HS GPA	3.5
% graduated top 10% of class	58
% graduated top 25% of class	81
% graduated top 50% of class	96

DEADLINES

Early decision	11/15
Early decision notification	12/15
Regular admission	1/15
Regular notification	4/1

FINANCIAL FACTS

Financial Aid Rating	**81**
Tuition	$27,246
Room and board	$6,738
Books and supplies	$450
Required fees	$268
% frosh receiving aid	48
% undergrads receiving aid	51
Avg frosh grant	$19,846
Avg frosh loan	$2,745

UNITED STATES COAST GUARD ACADEMY

CAMPUS LIFE

Quality of Life Rating	**85**
Type of school	public
Environment	suburban

STUDENTS

Total undergrad enrollment	985
% from out of state	93
% live on campus	100
% African American	5
% Asian	5
% Caucasian	82
% Hispanic	6
% international	2

ACADEMICS

Academic Rating	**99**
Calendar	semester
Student/faculty ratio	10:1
% profs teaching UG courses	100
Avg lab size	10-19 students
Avg reg class size	20-29 students

MOST POPULAR MAJORS
Civil engineering
Electrical, electronics, and
communications engineering
Environmental/environmental health engineering

SELECTIVITY

Admissions Rating	**98**
# accepting a place on wait list	161

FRESHMAN PROFILE

Range SAT Verbal	580-670

Average SAT Verbal	620
Range SAT Math	610-680
Average SAT Math	640
Range ACT Composite	25-30
Average ACT Composite	27
Minimum TOEFL	500
% graduated top 10% of class	48
% graduated top 25% of class	88
% graduated top 50% of class	100

DEADLINES

Regular admission	12/15

FINANCIAL FACTS

Financial Aid Rating	**99**
Required fees	$3,000

UNITED STATES MERCHANT MARINE ACADEMY

CAMPUS LIFE

Quality of Life Rating	**84**
Type of school	public
Affiliation	none
Environment	suburban

STUDENTS

Total undergrad enrollment	943
% from out of state	86
% from public high school	50
% live on campus	100
% international	2
# of countries represented	4

ACADEMICS

Academic Rating	**84**
Calendar	trimester
Student/faculty ratio	11:1
Profs interesting Rating	84
Profs accessible Rating	83

SELECTIVITY

Admissions Rating	**98**
# of applicants	1,586
% of applicants accepted	24
% of acceptees attending	74
# accepting a place on wait list	113
% admitted from wait list	15

FRESHMAN PROFILE

Range SAT Verbal	620-670
Average SAT Verbal	600
Range SAT Math	600-650
Average SAT Math	610
Average ACT Composite	27
Minimum TOEFL	550
% graduated top 10% of class	16
% graduated top 25% of class	75
% graduated top 50% of class	100

DEADLINES

Early decision	11/1
Regular admission	3/1

FINANCIAL FACTS

Financial Aid Rating	**80**
Avg frosh loan	$2,625

UNITED STATES MILITARY ACADEMY

CAMPUS LIFE

Quality of Life Rating	**78**
Type of school	public
Environment	suburban

STUDENTS

Total undergrad enrollment	4,154
% from out of state	92
% from public high school	86
% live on campus	100
% African American	8
% Asian	5
% Caucasian	79
% Hispanic	6
% international	1

ACADEMICS

Academic Rating	**99**
Calendar	semester
Student/faculty ratio	7:1
Profs interesting rating	96
Profs accessible rating	99
% profs teaching UG courses	100

SELECTIVITY

Admissions Rating	**99**
# of applicants	11,473
% of applicants accepted	13
% of acceptees attending	74

FRESHMAN PROFILE

Range SAT Verbal	570-670
Average SAT Verbal	627
Range SAT Math	590-680
Average SAT Math	641
Range ACT Composite	26-30
Average ACT Composite	28
Average HS GPA	3.7
% graduated top 10% of class	50
% graduated top 25% of class	81
% graduated top 50% of class	97

DEADLINES

Priority admission	12/1
Regular admission	3/21

FINANCIAL FACTS

Financial Aid Rating	**99**
Books and supplies	$664

UNIVERSITY OF CONNECTICUT

CAMPUS LIFE

Quality of Life Rating	**70**
Type of school	public
Environment	rural

STUDENTS

Total undergrad enrollment	14,716
% male/female	48/52
% from out of state	23
% live on campus	72
% in (# of) fraternities	7 (18)
% in (# of) sororities	7 (9)
% African American	5
% Asian	6
% Caucasian	75
% Hispanic	5
% international	1
# of countries represented	107

ACADEMICS

Academic Rating	**71**
Calendar	semester
Student/faculty ratio	17:1
Profs interesting rating	89
Profs accessible rating	89
Avg lab size	10-19 students
Avg reg class size	10-19 students

MOST POPULAR MAJORS

Business
Political science
Engineering

SELECTIVITY

Admissions Rating	**79**
# of applicants	13,760
% of applicants accepted	62
% of acceptees attending	37
# accepting a place on wait list	628
% admitted from wait list	9

FRESHMAN PROFILE

Range SAT Verbal	520-610
Average SAT Verbal	565
Range SAT Math	530-630
Average SAT Math	584
Minimum TOEFL	550
% graduated top 10% of class	26
% graduated top 25% of class	65
% graduated top 50% of class	96

DEADLINES

Regular admission	3/1
Nonfall registration?	yes

FINANCIAL FACTS

Financial Aid Rating	**83**
In-state tuition	$5,260
Out-of-state tuition	$16,044
Room and board	$6,888
Books and supplies	$725
Required fees	$1,540
% frosh receiving aid	48
% undergrads receiving aid	47
Avg frosh grant	$5,124
Avg frosh loan	$3,108

THE UNIVERSITY OF MAINE

CAMPUS LIFE

Quality of Life Rating	**73**
Type of school	public
Environment	rural

STUDENTS

Total undergrad enrollment	8,817
% male/female	48/52
% from out of state	14
% live on campus	43
% African American	1
	%

Asian	1
% Caucasian	95
% Hispanic	1
% international	2
# of countries represented	73

ACADEMICS

Academic Rating	**71**
Calendar	semester
Student/faculty ratio	15:1
Profs interesting rating	91
Profs accessible rating	94
% profs teaching UG courses	76
% classes taught by TAs	6
Avg lab size	10-19 students
Avg reg class size	20-29 students

MOST POPULAR MAJORS
Business administration/management
Education
Engineering

SELECTIVITY

Admissions Rating	**76**
# of applicants	5,249
% of applicants accepted	79
% of acceptees attending	43

FRESHMAN PROFILE

Range SAT Verbal	480-590
Average SAT Verbal	539
Range SAT Math	490-610
Average SAT Math	547
Range ACT Composite	20-26
Average ACT Composite	23
Minimum TOEFL	530
Average HS GPA	3.2
% graduated top 10% of class	23
% graduated top 25% of class	50
% graduated top 50% of class	89

DEADLINES

Nonfall registration?	yes

FINANCIAL FACTS

Financial Aid Rating	**81**
In-state tuition	$4,380
Out-of-state tuition	$12,450
Room and board	$5,922
Books and supplies	$700
Required fees	$1,170
% frosh receiving aid	73
% undergrads receiving aid	57

Avg frosh grant	$5,329
Avg frosh loan	$2,974

UNIVERSITY OF MASSACHUSETTS— AMHERST

CAMPUS LIFE

Quality of Life Rating	**74**
Type of school	public
Environment	suburban

STUDENTS

Total undergrad enrollment	18,606
% male/female	49/51
% from out of state	18
% from public high school	90
% live on campus	60
% in (# of) fraternities	3 (21)
% in (# of) sororities	7 (12)
% African American	5
% Asian	7
% Caucasian	76
% Hispanic	4
% international	2
# of countries represented	114

ACADEMICS

Academic Rating	**72**
Calendar	semester
Student/faculty ratio	19:1
Profs interesting rating	92
Profs accessible rating	95
% profs teaching UG courses	88
% classes taught by TAs	12
Avg lab size	20-29 students
Avg reg class size	20-29 students

MOST POPULAR MAJORS
Communications studies/speech
communication and rhetoric
English language and literature
Biology/biological sciences

SELECTIVITY

Admissions Rating	**75**
# of applicants	20,449
% of applicants accepted	58
% of acceptees attending	28

FRESHMAN PROFILE

Range SAT Verbal	500-620
Average SAT Verbal	554
Range SAT Math	510-630
Average SAT Math	571
Minimum TOEFL	550
Average HS GPA	3.4
% graduated top 10% of class	21
% graduated top 25% of class	56
% graduated top 50% of class	92

DEADLINES

Regular admission	1/15
Nonfall registration?	yes

FINANCIAL FACTS

Financial Aid Rating	**79**
In-state tuition	$1,714
Out-of-state tuition	$9,937
Room and board	$5,472
Books and supplies	$500
% frosh receiving aid	46
% undergrads receiving aid	44

UNIVERSITY OF MASSACHUSETTS—LOWELL

CAMPUS LIFE

Quality of Life Rating	**73**
Type of school	public
Affiliation	none
Environment	urban

STUDENTS

Total undergrad enrollment	9,650
% male/female	59/41
% from out of state	13
% live on campus	33
% African American	2
% Asian	8
% Caucasian	52
% Hispanic	3
% international	2
# of countries represented	73

ACADEMICS

Academic Rating	**74**
Calendar	semester
Student/faculty ratio	15:1
Profs interesting rating	87
Profs accessible rating	84

MOST POPULAR MAJORS

Business administration
Criminal justice
Electrical engineering

SELECTIVITY

Admissions Rating	**63**
# of applicants	3,286
% of applicants accepted	70
% of acceptees attending	43

FRESHMAN PROFILE

Range SAT Verbal	470-570
Average SAT Verbal	519
Range SAT Math	490-580
Average SAT Math	537
Minimum TOEFL	500
Average HS GPA	2.98

DEADLINES

Nonfall registration?	yes

FINANCIAL FACTS

Financial Aid Rating	**73**
In-state tuition	$1,454
Out-of-state tuition	$8,567
Room and board	$5,095
Books and supplies	$500
Avg frosh grant	$3,755
Avg frosh loan	$2,040

UNIVERSITY OF NEW HAMPSHIRE

CAMPUS LIFE

Quality of Life Rating	**87**
Type of school	public
Environment	rural

STUDENTS

Total undergrad enrollment	11,496
% male/female	43/57
% from out of state	43
% from public high school	78
% live on campus	51
% in (# of) fraternities	5 (10)
% in (# of) sororities	5 (5)
% African American	1
% Asian	2
% Caucasian	90
% Hispanic	1

% international	1
# of countries represented	28

ACADEMICS
Academic Rating **75**

Calendar	semester
Student/faculty ratio	14:1
% profs teaching UG courses	77
% classes taught by TAs	1
Avg lab size	10-19 students
Avg reg class size	10-19 students

MOST POPULAR MAJORS
Business administration/management
English language and literature
Psychology

SELECTIVITY
Admissions Rating **78**

# of applicants	10,376
% of applicants accepted	77
% of acceptees attending	34

FRESHMAN PROFILE
Range SAT Verbal	500-590
Average SAT Verbal	546
Range SAT Math	510-610
Average SAT Math	558
Minimum TOEFL	550
% graduated top 10% of class	18
% graduated top 25% of class	53
% graduated top 50% of class	94

DEADLINES
Regular admission	2/1
Regular notification	4/15
Nonfall registration?	yes

FINANCIAL FACTS
Financial Aid Rating **86**

Books and supplies	$1,300
% frosh receiving aid	54
% undergrads receiving aid	53
Avg frosh grant	$6,630
Avg frosh loan	$3,538

UNIVERSITY OF RHODE ISLAND

CAMPUS LIFE
Quality of Life Rating **81**

Type of school	public
Environment	rural

STUDENTS
Total undergrad enrollment	10,784
% male/female	44/56
% from out of state	38
% from public high school	92
% live on campus	33
% in (# of) fraternities	7 (9)
% in (# of) sororities	11 (11)
% African American	4
% Asian	3
% Caucasian	77
% Hispanic	4

ACADEMICS
Academic Rating **73**

Calendar	semester
Student/faculty ratio	18:1
Profs interesting rating	91
Profs accessible rating	93
% profs teaching UG courses	83
% classes taught by TAs	8
Avg lab size	10-19 students
Avg reg class size	20-29 students

MOST POPULAR MAJORS
Pharmacy (PharmD, BS/BPharm)
Communications studies/speech
communication and rhetoric
Psychology

SELECTIVITY
Admissions Rating **72**

# of applicants	11,072
% of applicants accepted	69
% of acceptees attending	31

FRESHMAN PROFILE
Range SAT Verbal	490-590
Average SAT Verbal	549
Range SAT Math	500-610
Average SAT Math	562
Minimum TOEFL	550
Average HS GPA	3.4
% graduated top 10% of class	16
% graduated top 25% of class	59
% graduated top 50% of class	89

DEADLINES
Priority admission	12/15
Regular admission	2/1
Nonfall registration?	yes

FINANCIAL FACTS
Financial Aid Rating   **79**

In-state tuition	$3,864
Out-of-state tuition	$13,334
Room and board	$7,402
Books and supplies	$800
Required fees	$1,990
% frosh receiving aid	74
% undergrads receiving aid	72

UNIVERSITY OF ROCHESTER

CAMPUS LIFE
Quality of Life Rating   **82**

Type of school	private
Environment	suburban

STUDENTS

Total undergrad enrollment	4,665
% male/female	54/46
% from out of state	50
% live on campus	80
% in (# of) fraternities	26 (17)
% in (# of) sororities	19 (11)
% African American	5
% Asian	13
% Caucasian	66
% Hispanic	4
% international	4

ACADEMICS
Academic Rating   **88**

Calendar	semester
Student/faculty ratio	8:1
Profs interesting rating	94
Profs accessible rating	90
Avg reg class size	10-19 students

SELECTIVITY
Admissions Rating   **88**

# of applicants	10,930
% of applicants accepted	49
% of acceptees attending	21
# accepting a place on wait list	336
# of early decision applicants	375
% accepted early decision	52

FRESHMAN PROFILE

Range SAT Verbal	600-700
Average SAT Verbal	665
Range SAT Math	620-710
Average SAT Math	687
Range ACT Composite	27-32
Average ACT Composite	30
Minimum TOEFL	550
% graduated top 10% of class	60
% graduated top 25% of class	88
% graduated top 50% of class	99

DEADLINES

Early decision	11/15
Early decision notification	12/15
Regular admission	1/20
Regular notification	4/1
Nonfall registration?	yes

FINANCIAL FACTS
Financial Aid Rating   **83**

Tuition	$24,150
Room and board	$8,185
Books and supplies	$575
Required fees	$644
% frosh receiving aid	55
% undergrads receiving aid	59

UNIVERSITY OF SOUTHERN MAINE

CAMPUS LIFE
Quality of Life Rating   **73**

Type of school	public
Affiliation	none
Environment	multicampus: urban & rural

STUDENTS

Total undergrad enrollment	4,596
% male/female	39/61
% from out of state	14
% live on campus	38
% in (# of) fraternities	4 (4)
% in (# of) sororities	4 (4)
% African American	1
% Asian	1
% Caucasian	96
% Hispanic	1
# of countries represented	38

ACADEMICS
Academic Rating   **72**

Calendar	semester

Student/faculty ratio	13:1
Profs interesting rating	86
Profs accessible rating	86
% profs teaching UG courses	90
% classes taught by TAs	0

MOST POPULAR MAJORS
Surgical nurse/nursing
Psychology
Business/commerce

SELECTIVITY
Admissions Rating	**65**
# of applicants	3,664
% of applicants accepted	69
% of acceptees attending	38

FRESHMAN PROFILE
Range SAT Verbal	470-560
Average SAT Verbal	516
Range SAT Math	470-560
Average SAT Math	512
Minimum TOEFL	550
Average HS GPA	2.99
% graduated top 10% of class	8
% graduated top 25% of class	30
% graduated top 50% of class	70

DEADLINES
Priority admission	2/15
Regular admission	rolling
Nonfall registration?	yes

FINANCIAL FACTS
Financial Aid Rating	**72**
In-state tuition	$4,020
Out-of-state tuition	$11,190
Room and board	$5,328
Books and supplies	$800
Avg frosh grant	$3,762
Avg frosh loan	$4,373

UNIVERSITY OF VERMONT

CAMPUS LIFE
Quality of Life Rating	**88**
Type of school	public
Environment	suburban

STUDENTS
Total undergrad enrollment	8,792
% male/female	44/56

% from out of state	61
% from public high school	70
% live on campus	52
% in (# of) fraternities	9 (10)
% in (# of) sororities	6 (5)
% African American	1
% Asian	2
% Caucasian	94
% Hispanic	2
% international	1
# of countries represented	40

ACADEMICS
Academic Rating	**76**
Calendar	semester
Student/faculty ratio	13:1
Profs interesting rating	92
Profs accessible rating	94
% profs teaching UG courses	85
% classes taught by TAs	2
Avg lab size	10-19 students
Avg reg class size	10-19 students

MOST POPULAR MAJORS
Business administration/management
English language and literature
Psychology

SELECTIVITY
Admissions Rating	**77**
# of applicants	9,776
% of applicants accepted	71
% of acceptees attending	26
# accepting a place on wait list	380
% admitted from wait list	24
# of early decision applicants	245
% accepted early decision	70

FRESHMAN PROFILE
Range SAT Verbal	520-620
Average SAT Verbal	568
Range SAT Math	520-620
Average SAT Math	574
Range ACT Composite	22-27
Average ACT Composite	24
Minimum TOEFL	550
% graduated top 10% of class	19
% graduated top 25% of class	55
% graduated top 50% of class	91

DEADLINES
Early decision	11/1
Early decision notification	12/15

Regular admission 1/15
Regular notification 3/31
Nonfall registration? yes

FINANCIAL FACTS
Financial Aid Rating **83**
In-state tuition $8,696
Out-of-state tuition $21,748
Room and board $6,680
Books and supplies $800
Required fees $940
% frosh receiving aid 54
% undergrads receiving aid 50
Avg frosh grant $8,208
Avg frosh loan $4,239

VASSAR COLLEGE

CAMPUS LIFE
Quality of Life Rating **82**
Type of school private
Environment suburban

STUDENTS
Total undergrad enrollment 2,472
% male/female 40/60
% from out of state 72
% from public high school 60
% live on campus 95
% African American 5
% Asian 10
% Caucasian 78
% Hispanic 6
% international 5
# of countries represented 41

ACADEMICS
Academic Rating **94**
Calendar semester
Student/faculty ratio 9:1
Profs interesting rating 70
Profs accessible rating 70
% profs teaching UG courses 100
Avg lab size 10-19 students
Avg reg class size 10-19 students

MOST POPULAR MAJORS
English language and literature
Psychology
Political science and government

SELECTIVITY
Admissions Rating **95**
# of applicants 5,733
% of applicants accepted 26
% of acceptees attending 43
# accepting a place on wait list 400
# of early decision applicants 508
% accepted early decision 50

FRESHMAN PROFILE
Range SAT Verbal 640-730
Average SAT Verbal 686
Range SAT Math 630-700
Average SAT Math 664
Range ACT Composite 28-32
Minimum TOEFL 600
% graduated top 10% of class 65
% graduated top 25% of class 95
% graduated top 50% of class 99

DEADLINES
Early decision 11/15
Early decision notification 12/15
Regular admission 1/1
Regular notification 4/1

FINANCIAL FACTS
Financial Aid Rating **86**
Tuition $27,550
Room and board $7,340
Books and supplies $800
Required fees $410
% frosh receiving aid 54
% undergrads receiving aid 53
Avg frosh grant $19,917
Avg frosh loan $2,797

WAGNER COLLEGE

CAMPUS LIFE
Quality of Life Rating **76**
Type of school private
Affiliation Lutheran
Environment urban

STUDENTS
Total undergrad enrollment 1,739
% male/female 41/59
% from out of state 55
% from public high school 57
% live on campus 77

% African American	6
% Asian	4
% Caucasian	77
% Hispanic	6
% international	2
# of countries represented	16

ACADEMICS
Academic Rating	**70**
Calendar	semester
Student/faculty ratio	15:1
Profs interesting rating	73
Profs accessible rating	80
% profs teaching UG courses	100

ADMISSIONS
Admissions Rating	**78**
# of applicants	2,413
% of applicants accepted	66
% of acceptees attending	33
# of early decision applicants	74
% accepted early decision	29

FRESHMAN PROFILE
Range SAT Verbal	510-620
Average SAT Verbal	560
Range SAT Math	520-610
Average SAT Math	560
Average ACT Composite	25
Minimum TOEFL	550
Average HS GPA	3.5
% graduated top 10% of class	17
% graduated top 25% of class	50
% graduated top 50% of class	91

DEADLINES
Early decision	11/15
Early decision notification	1/1
Priority admission	2/15
Regular admission	3/15
Nonfall registration?	yes

FINANCIAL FACTS
Financial Aid Rating	**80**
Tuition	$18,000
Room and board	$6,500
Books and supplies	$625
% frosh receiving aid	75
% undergrads receiving aid	68
Avg frosh grant	$6,965
Avg frosh loan	$5,660

WEBB INSTITUTE

CAMPUS LIFE
Quality of Life Rating	**91**
Type of school	private
Environment	suburban

STUDENTS
Total undergrad enrollment	67
% from out of state	78
% from public high school	88
% live on campus	100
% African American	1
% Asian	3
% Caucasian	96

ACADEMICS
Academic Rating	**98**
Calendar	semester
Student/faculty ratio	6:1
Profs interesting rating	92
Profs accessible rating	94
% profs teaching UG courses	100
Avg reg class size	10-19 students

ADMISSIONS
Admissions Rating	**96**
# of applicants	85
% of applicants accepted	41
% of acceptees attending	50
# of early decision applicants	10
% accepted early decision	70

FRESHMAN PROFILE
Range SAT Verbal	620-710
Average SAT Verbal	670
Range SAT Math	700-740
Average SAT Math	720
Average HS GPA	3.9
% graduated top 10% of class	83
% graduated top 25% of class	100

DEADLINES
Early decision	10/15
Early decision notification	12/15
Priority admission	10/15
Regular admission	2/15

FINANCIAL FACTS
Financial Aid Rating	**99**
Room and board	$6,950
Books and supplies	$600
% frosh receiving aid	53

% undergrads receiving aid	28
Avg frosh grant	$2,750
Avg frosh loan	$2,625

WELLESLEY COLLEGE

CAMPUS LIFE
Quality of Life Rating **85**
Type of school	private
Environment	suburban

STUDENTS
Total undergrad enrollment	2,300
% from out of state	84
% from public high school	65
% live on campus	94
% African American	6
% Asian	26
% Caucasian	48
% Hispanic	5
% international	7

ACADEMICS
Academic Rating **98**
Calendar	semester
Student/faculty ratio	9:1
Profs interesting rating	96
Profs accessible rating	99
% profs teaching UG courses	100
Avg lab size	10-19 students
Avg reg class size	10-19 students

MOST POPULAR MAJORS
English language and literature
Psychology
Economics

SELECTIVITY
Admissions Rating **98**
# of applicants	2,877
% of applicants accepted	47
% of acceptees attending	44
# accepting a place on wait list	287
% admitted from wait list	18
# of early decision applicants	154
% accepted early decision	62

FRESHMAN PROFILE
Range SAT Verbal	620-720
Average SAT Verbal	671
Range SAT Math	630-720
Average SAT Math	671

Range ACT Composite	27-31
Average ACT Composite	29
Minimum TOEFL	600
% graduated top 10% of class	59
% graduated top 25% of class	92
% graduated top 50% of class	100

DEADLINES
Early decision	11/1
Early decision notification	12/15
Regular admission	1/15
Regular notification	4/1

FINANCIAL FACTS
Financial Aid Rating **80**
Tuition	$26,138
Room and board	$8,242
Books and supplies	$800
Required fees	$564
% frosh receiving aid	56
% undergrads receiving aid	56
Avg frosh grant	$21,701
Avg frosh loan	$2,360

WELLS COLLEGE

CAMPUS LIFE
Quality of Life Rating **85**
Type of school	private
Environment	rural

STUDENTS
Total undergrad enrollment	437
% from out of state	27
% from public high school	90
% live on campus	75
% African American	5
% Asian	4
% Caucasian	76
% Hispanic	5
% international	2
# of countries represented	8

ACADEMICS
Academic Rating **86**
Calendar	semester
Student/faculty ratio	7:1
Profs interesting rating	80
Profs accessible rating	84
% profs teaching UG courses	100

| Avg lab size | 10-19 students |
| Avg reg class size | 10-19 students |

MOST POPULAR MAJORS
Psychology
English language and literature
Biology/biological sciences

SELECTIVITY
Admissions Rating	**80**
# of applicants	404
% of applicants accepted	86
% of acceptees attending	31
# of early decision applicants	23
% accepted early decision	96

FRESHMAN PROFILE
Range SAT Verbal	530-650
Average SAT Verbal	580
Range SAT Math	500-590
Average SAT Math	550
Range ACT Composite	22-26
Average ACT Composite	25
Minimum TOEFL	550
Average HS GPA	3.5
% graduated top 10% of class	30
% graduated top 25% of class	67
% graduated top 50% of class	94

DEADLINES
Early decision	12/15
Early decision notification	1/15
Priority admission	12/15
Regular admission	3/1
Regular notification	4/1

FINANCIAL FACTS
Financial Aid Rating	**80**
Tuition	$13,070
Room and board	$6,450
Books and supplies	$600
Required fees	$680
% frosh receiving aid	80
% undergrads receiving aid	78
Avg frosh grant	$9,978
Avg frosh loan	$3,066

WESLEYAN UNIVERSITY

CAMPUS LIFE
Quality of Life Rating	**78**
Type of school	private
Environment	suburban

STUDENTS
Total undergrad enrollment	2,733
% male/female	48/52
% from out of state	90
% from public high school	56
% live on campus	94
% in (# of) fraternities	5 (9)
% in (# of) sororities	1 (4)
% African American	9
% Asian	8
% Caucasian	67
% Hispanic	7
% international	6

ACADEMICS
Academic Rating	**94**
Calendar	semester
Student/faculty ratio	9:1
Profs interesting rating	95
Profs accessible rating	96
% profs teaching UG courses	100
% classes taught by TAs	1
Avg lab size	10-19 students
Avg reg class size	10-19 students

SELECTIVITY
Admissions Rating	**98**
# of applicants	6,474
% of applicants accepted	28
% of acceptees attending	40
# of early decision applicants	676
% accepted early decision	46

FRESHMAN PROFILE
Range SAT Verbal	640-740
Average SAT Verbal	700
Range SAT Math	650-730
Average SAT Math	690
Average ACT Composite	29
Minimum TOEFL	250 (CBT)
% graduated top 10% of class	73
% graduated top 25% of class	94
% graduated top 50% of class	99

DEADLINES
Early decision	11/15

Early decision notification	12/15
Regular admission	1/1
Regular notification	4/1

FINANCIAL FACTS
Financial Aid Rating	**81**
Tuition	$29,784
Room and board	$8,226
% undergrads receiving aid	47
Avg frosh grant	$23,992
Avg frosh loan	$2,770

WHEATON COLLEGE

CAMPUS LIFE
Quality of Life Rating	**79**
Type of school	private
Environment	suburban

STUDENTS
Total undergrad enrollment	1,521
% male/female	36/64
% from out of state	67
% from public high school	65
% live on campus	97
% African American	3
% Asian	3
% Caucasian	83
% Hispanic	4
% international	6
# of countries represented	29

ACADEMICS
Academic Rating	**85**
Calendar	semester
Student/faculty ratio	11:1
Profs interesting rating	96
Profs accessible rating	97
% profs teaching UG courses	100
Avg lab size	10-19 students
Avg reg class size	10-19 students

MOST POPULAR MAJORS
Psychology
English language and literature
Fine/studio arts

SELECTIVITY
Admissions Rating	**82**
# of applicants	3,534
% of applicants accepted	44
% of acceptees attending	27

# accepting a place on wait list	248
% admitted from wait list	6
# of early decision applicants	243
% accepted early decision	66

FRESHMAN PROFILE
Range SAT Verbal	590-670
Average SAT Verbal	630
Range SAT Math	550-650
Average SAT Math	610
Range ACT Composite	26-29
Average ACT Composite	27
Minimum TOEFL	550
Average HS GPA	3.4
% graduated top 10% of class	43
% graduated top 25% of class	76
% graduated top 50% of class	93

DEADLINES
Early decision	11/15
Early decision notification	12/15
Regular admission	1/15
Regular notification	4/1
Nonfall registration?	yes

FINANCIAL FACTS
Financial Aid Rating	**85**
Tuition	$27,105
Room and board	$7,260
Books and supplies	$1,060
Required fees	$225
% frosh receiving aid	51
% undergrads receiving aid	58
Avg frosh grant	$14,416
Avg frosh loan	$3,602

WILLIAM PATERSON UNIVERSITY

CAMPUS LIFE
Quality of Life Rating	**78**
Type of school	public
Affiliation	none
Environment	suburban

STUDENTS
Total undergrad enrollment	8,862
% male/female	41/59
% from out of state	2
% from public high school	88
% live on campus	26
% in (# of) fraternities	3 (13)

% in (# of) sororities	2 (11)
% African American	12
% Asian	4
% Caucasian	66
% Hispanic	14
% international	1
# of countries represented	57

ACADEMICS
Academic Rating	**76**
Calendar	semester
Student/faculty ratio	12:1
Profs interesting rating	85
Profs accessible rating	85
% profs teaching UG courses	100
% classes taught by TAs	0
Avg reg class size	20-29 students

MOST POPULAR MAJORS
Business administration/management
Communications studies/speech
communication and rhetoric
Sociology

SELECTIVITY
Admissions Rating	**77**
# of applicants	3,543
% of applicants accepted	137
% of acceptees attending	29
# accepting a place on wait list	50
% admitted from wait list	40

FRESHMAN PROFILE
Range SAT Verbal	450-540
Average SAT Verbal	522
Range SAT Math	450-550
Average SAT Math	530
Minimum TOEFL	550
% graduated top 10% of class	8
% graduated top 25% of class	26
% graduated top 50% of class	65

DEADLINES
Regular admission	5/1
Nonfall registration?	yes

FINANCIAL FACTS
Financial Aid Rating	**73**
In-state tuition	$6,400
Out-of-state tuition	$10,200
Room and board	$7,030
Books and supplies	$800
Avg frosh grant	$5,814
Avg frosh loan	$3,437

WILLIAMS COLLEGE

CAMPUS LIFE
Quality of Life Rating	**94**
Type of school	private
Environment	rural

STUDENTS
Total undergrad enrollment	1,983
% male/female	51/49
% from out of state	80
% from public high school	54
% live on campus	93
% African American	8
% Asian	9
% Caucasian	74
% Hispanic	8
% international	6
# of countries represented	52

ACADEMICS
Academic Rating	**98**
Calendar	4-1-4
Student/faculty ratio	8:1
Profs interesting rating	96
Profs accessible rating	98
% profs teaching UG courses	100
Avg lab size	10-19 students
Avg reg class size	10-19 students

SELECTIVITY
Admissions Rating	**99**
# of applicants	4,931
% of applicants accepted	23
# of early decision applicants	496
% accepted early decision	39

FRESHMAN PROFILE
Range SAT Verbal	660-760
Average SAT Verbal	701
Range SAT Math	660-750
Average SAT Math	694
Average ACT Composite	30

DEADLINES
Early decision	11/15
Early decision notification	12/15
Regular admission	1/1
Regular notification	4/8

FINANCIAL FACTS
Financial Aid Rating	**83**
Tuition	$26,326

Room and board	$7,230
Books and supplies	$800
Required fees	$194
% frosh receiving aid	45
% undergrads receiving aid	41
Avg frosh grant	$18,187
Avg frosh loan	$2,533

WORCESTER POLYTECHNIC INSTITUTE

CAMPUS LIFE

Quality of Life Rating	**74**
Type of school	private
Environment	suburban

STUDENTS

Total undergrad enrollment	2,767
% male/female	77/23
% from out of state	48
% from public high school	79
% live on campus	83
% in (# of) fraternities	35 (12)
% in (# of) sororities	25 (2)
% African American	1
% Asian	7
% Caucasian	85
% Hispanic	3
% international	5
# of countries represented	68

ACADEMICS

Academic Rating	**83**
Calendar	quarter
Student/faculty ratio	12:1
Profs interesting rating	91
Profs accessible rating	96
% profs teaching UG courses	100
Avg lab size	20-29 students
Avg reg class size	under 10 students

MOST POPULAR MAJORS
Mechanical engineering
Electrical, electronics, and communications engineering
Computer science

SELECTIVITY

Admissions Rating	**87**
# of applicants	3,560

% of applicants accepted	70
% of acceptees attending	29
# of early decision applicants	200
% accepted early decision	77

FRESHMAN PROFILE

Range SAT Verbal	540-660
Average SAT Verbal	620
Range SAT Math	630-730
Average SAT Math	680
Average ACT Composite	29
Minimum TOEFL	550
Average HS GPA	3.7
% graduated top 10% of class	47
% graduated top 25% of class	82
% graduated top 50% of class	98

DEADLINES

Early decision	11/15
Early decision notification	12/15
Early action	11/15
Early action notification	12/15
Regular admission	2/1
Regular notification	4/1
Nonfall registration?	yes

FINANCIAL FACTS

Financial Aid Rating	**86**
Tuition	$28,420
Room and board	$8,984
Books and supplies	$692
Required fees	$170
% frosh receiving aid	77
% undergrads receiving aid	51
Avg frosh grant	$12,121
Avg frosh loan	$4,620

YALE UNIVERSITY

CAMPUS LIFE

Quality of Life Rating	**81**
Type of school	private
Environment	urban

STUDENTS

Total undergrad enrollment	5,339
% male/female	50/50
% from out of state	92
% from public high school	53
% live on campus	87
% African American	9

% Asian	17
% Caucasian	55
% Hispanic	9
% international	10

ACADEMICS
Academic Rating **99**

Calendar	semester
Student/faculty ratio	/:1
Profs interesting rating	92
Profs accessible rating	90
Avg reg class size	10-19 students

SELECTIVITY
Admissions Rating **99**

# of applicants	15,466
% of applicants accepted	13
% of acceptees attending	67
# accepting a place on wait list	633
% admitted from wait list	0
# of early action applicants	1,795
% accepted early action	29

FRESHMAN PROFILE

Range SAT Verbal	680-770
Range SAT Math	680-770
Range ACT Composite	28-33
Minimum TOEFL	600
% graduated top 10% of class	95
% graduated top 25% of class	99
% graduated top 50% of class	100

DEADLINES

Early action	11/1
Early action notification	12/15
Regular admission	12/31
Regular notification	4/1

FINANCIAL FACTS
Financial Aid Rating **80**

Tuition	$28,400
Room and board	$8,600
Books and supplies	$2,520
% frosh receiving aid	42
% undergrads receiving aid	39

PART 4

INDEX

INDEX BY STATE

NEW HAMPSHIRE

NEW JERSEY

NEW YORK

ABOUT THE AUTHORS

Robert Franek is a graduate of Drew University and has been a member of The Princeton Review Staff for four years. Robert comes to The Princeton Review with an extensive admissions background, most recently at Wagner College in Staten Island, New York. In addition, he owns a walking tour business and leads historically driven, yet not boring, tours of his home town!

Tom Meltzer is a graduate of Columbia University. He has taught for The Princeton Review since 1986 and is the author or co-author of seven TPR titles, the most recent of which is *Illustrated Word Smart*, which Tom co-wrote with his wife, Lisa. He is also a professional musician and songwriter. A native of Baltimore, Tom now lives in Hillsborough, North Carolina.

Roy Opochinski is a graduate of Drew University and has been a member of The Princeton Review staff since 1990. He has taught courses for TPR for 11 years and has edited several other books for TPR, including *Word Smart II* and *Math Smart*. In addition, Roy is the executive editor at Groovevolt.com, a music website. He now lives in Toms River, New Jersey.

Tara Bray is a resident of New York City by way of Hawaii, New Hampshire, Oregon, and Chicago, and is a graduate of Dartmouth College as well as Columbia University's School of the Arts. When she's not writing, Tara likes to spend her time figuring out how to pay the rent. She is also the author of The Princeton Review's guide to life after college, *Why Won't the Landlord Take Visa?*

Christopher Maier is a graduate of Dickinson College. During the past five years, he's lived variously in New York City, coastal Maine, western Oregon, central Pennsylvania, and eastern England. Now he's at an oasis somewhere in the midwestern cornfields—the University of Illinois—where he's earning his MFA in fiction. Aside from writing for magazines, newspapers, and The Princeton Review, he's worked as a radio disc jockey, a helping hand in a bakery, and a laborer on a highway construction crew. He's trying to avoid highway construction these days.

Carson Brown graduated from Stanford University in 1998, and after getting paid too much for working for various Internet companies for several years, sold her BMW and moved to Mexico. She has now overstayed her welcome south of the border and is returning to San Francisco to be responsible and further her career working as a writer and editor.

Julie Doherty is a freelance writer, Web designer, and preschool teacher. She lives in Mexico City.

K. Nadine Kavanaugh is pursuing her Master of Fine Arts at Columbia University. Her fiction has appeared on NYCBigCityLit.com and SlackFaith.com.

Catherine Monaco—ACADEMICS: Graduated from Dickinson College and earned a master's degree from Fordham University. STUDENT BODY: Bigger hair, bushier eyebrows (but learned to pluck after junior year). LIFE: Works as NYC public school teacher, lives in Tribeca, and "always has fun quoting other people for The Princeton Review."

Dinaw Mengestu is a graduate of Georgetown University and is currently completing his MFA in fiction at Columbia University. He lives in Brooklyn, New York.

Countdown to the SAT: The Week Before the Test

Studying Tips

- Make sure that you get enough sleep every night. Try going to bed earlier and waking up earlier.
- Get up early on the weekend and take a practice test. You need to train your mind to be alert in the morning and able to think for three hours. Treat the practice test as the "real thing."
- Get into a pattern of doing 30-45 minutes' worth of SAT problems each day from now until the test day. You're probably really busy, but think of it this way: you can make this tiny sacrifice now, or go through the entire process all over again.
- When you practice at home, do so under timed conditions. You need to get the feeling of what it will be like on the day of the test. As always, don't do your homework in front of the television or with the radio playing.
- Review all of the formulas and strategies that you've learned so far.

Got What You Need?

- Make sure you have your admission ticket. If you lose it or if it hasn't arrived at least one week before the test, call ETS at (609) 771-7600.
- Put new batteries in your calculator.
- Buy some No. 2 pencils, an eraser, and a sharpener.
- Confirm the location of the test center and make sure you know exactly where it is. If you haven't been there before, take a test run. How long does it take to get there? What's traffic like on Saturdays? Where should you park?
- Make sure you have a picture ID (e.g., driver's license, school ID with photo, passport). If you don't have one, see your counselor. Have him or her write a brief physical description of you on school stationery, and then both you and your counselor should sign it.

Extra Study Tip

Get a 3" x 7" index card; write math strategies on one side and verbal strategies on the other. Keep this card with you all week. Study it whenever you have free time: in study hall, in between classes, or on the ride home.

Countdown to the SAT:
The Day Before the Test

Studying Tips

- DON'T STUDY!!! Cramming just won't help. Put your books away on a high shelf where you can't see them.
- Take it easy and let your brain relax. Catch an early movie or have dinner with friends.

At Night

- Go to bed at a reasonable hour. However, don't try to go to sleep at 7:00 p.m. It won't work.
- Set your alarm clock.

"Don't Forget" Checklist

Prepare everything that you'll need for the morning of the test:

- Admission ticket
- Photo ID
- No. 2 pencils
- Eraser
- Sharpener
- Calculator
- Watch or clock (one that doesn't beep)
- Morning warm-up problems

Countdown to the SAT: The Morning of the Test

At Home

- Eat a healthy breakfast. It will give you the energy you need to make it through three hours of testing. However, don't give your body what it's not used to. For example, don't eat steak and eggs if you normally have toast and a glass of juice.
- Wear comfortable clothes. Also, dress in layers. You never know whether the test center will be unusually hot or cold.
- Take everything from the "Don't Forget" Checklist with you.
- Leave yourself 20 minutes more than you think you'll need to get to the test center. Be sure to arrive at least 20 minutes before the scheduled test time.

At the Test Center

- Use the bathroom before the test starts. You'll also have a chance to go to the bathroom during the first break (after Section 2). However, you will not have a chance to go during the second break (after Section 4).
- Do your warm-up problems. A great time to work on these questions is before you're seated.
- Try to maintain your focus. Do not listen to what other people say about the test, including which section they think is the experimental one.

Classroom Courses From The Princeton Review

The Classic Way to Prep

Classrooms may remind you of school, but in Princeton Review classes, the feeling is different. You're in a friendly, supportive place where everyone has the same goal: to beat the test.

Teachers that really know their stuff.

Not only do our teachers know how to keep you interested and involved, they also know our methods inside out. And by the end of your course, so will you.

Small, focused classes.

We never put more than 12 students in any class. So you'll get the personal attention you need and work at a pace that's right for you.

Extra help when you need it.

Admit it: occasionally you might need a little bit of extra help. Your Princeton Review teacher is available to meet with you outside of class at no extra charge. (And no one else has to know.)

Online resources 24/7.

Our Online Student Center is just a click away. You can go there whenever you want to check on your class times and locations, email your teacher, review lessons, practice tough concepts, or make up a missed class.

Materials that work for you.

Ask anyone who's taken our course: our manuals are the best. They have it all. Plus, you'll take a series of full-length practice tests, so you can monitor your progress and get comfortable with the exam.

Guaranteed results.

We know our courses work. In fact, we guarantee it: your SAT score will improve by at least 100 points, or your ACT score by 4 points, or we'll work with you again for up to a year, FREE.

Classroom Courses Available: *

SAT
ACT
SAT II – Writing, Math IC and IIC,
   Biology, Chemistry, Physics
PSAT
Word Smart, Math Smart

* Availability of specific courses varies by month
  and by location.

1-2-1 Private Tutoring From The Princeton Review

The Ultimate in Personalized Attention

If you're too busy for a classroom course, prefer learning at your own kitchen table, or simply like being the center of the universe, *1-2-1* Private Tutoring may be for you.

The focus is on you.

Forget about what some other kid doesn't understand. With *1-2-1* Private Tutoring, it really is all about you. Just you. So you'll get the best instruction in less time than you'd spend in a class.

Your tutor is your coach.

1-2-1 tutors are our best, most experienced teachers. Your tutor will work side-by-side with you, doing whatever it takes to help you get your best score. No push-ups are required.

Pick a time, any time.

We know you're very, very (very) busy. So you and your tutor will meet when it's convenient for you.

Guaranteed results.

As with our classroom and online courses, your results with a full *1-2-1* Private Tutoring program are guaranteed: your SAT score will improve by at least 100 points, or your ACT score by at least 4 points, or we'll work with you again for free.

Tutoring programs available: *

SAT
ACT
SAT II (all subject tests)
PSAT
AP tests
Academic subjects

*Availability varies by location.

Online Courses
From The Princeton Review

The Best of Both Worlds

Take the newest and best in software design, combine it with our time-tested strategies, and voilà: dynamic test prep where, when, and how you want it!

Lively, engaging lessons.

Our online courses are totally different from others you may have seen. You'll never passively scroll through pages of text or watch boring, choppy video clips. These courses feature animation, audio, interactive lessons, and self-directed navigation. We put you in the driver's seat.

Customized, focused practice.

The course software will discover your personal strengths and weaknesses and will help you to prioritize. You'll get extra practice only in the areas where you need it. Of course, you'll have access to dozens of hours' worth of lessons and drills covering all areas of the test. So you can practice as much or as little as you choose. (Just don't give yourself carpal tunnel syndrome, okay?)

Real-time interaction.

Our *LiveOnline* course includes eight additional sessions that take place in a virtual classroom over the Internet. You'll interact with your specially certified teacher and your fellow students in real time, using live audio, a virtual whiteboard, and a chat interface.

Help at your fingertips.

Any time of the day or night, help is there for you: chat online with a live Coach, check our Frequently Asked Questions (FAQ) database, or talk to other students in our discussion groups.

Guaranteed results.

We stand behind our *Online* and *LiveOnline* courses with complete confidence. Your SAT score will improve by at least 100 points, or your ACT score by at least 4 points. Guaranteed.

Online Courses Available:*

SAT *Online*
SAT *LiveOnline*
SAT *ExpressOnline*
ACT *Online*
ACT *LiveOnline*
ACT *ExpressOnline*

*Available EVERYWHERE!

Hit Parade

abstract general; not concrete

aesthetic having to do with the appreciation of beauty

alleviate to ease a pain or a burden

ambivalent simultaneously feeling opposing feelings

apathetic feeling or showing little emotion

auspicious favorable; promising

benevolent well-meaning; generous

candor sincerity; openness

cogent convincing; reasonable

comprehensive large in scope or content

contemporary current, modern; from the same time

conviction a fixed or strong belief

diligent marked by painstaking effort; hard-working

dubious doubtful; of unlikely authenticity

eclectic made up of a variety of sources or styles

egregious conspicuously bad or offensive

exculpate to free from guilt or blame

florid describing flowery or elaborate speech

gratuitous given freely; unearned; unwarranted

hackneyed worn-out through overuse; trite

idealize to consider perfect

impartial not in favor of one side or the other; unbiased

imperious arrogantly domineering or overbearing

inherent inborn; built-in

innovative introducing something new

inveterate long established; deep-rooted; habitual

laudatory giving praise

maverick one who resists adherence to a group

mollify to calm or soothe

novel strikingly new or unusual

obdurate stubborn; inflexible

objectivity treating facts uninfluenced by emotion

obstinate stubbornly adhering to an opinion

ornate elaborately decorated

ostentatious describing a pretentious display

paramount of chief concern or importance

penitent expressing remorse for one's misdeeds

pervasive dispersed throughout

plausible seemingly valid or acceptable; credible

profound having great depth or seriousness

prosaic unimaginative; dull

quandary a state of uncertainty or perplexity

rancorous hateful; marked by deep-seated ill will

spurious not genuine; false; counterfeit

stoic indifferent to pleasure or pain; impassive

superfluous extra; unnecessary

tenuous having little substance or strength; unsure; weak

timorous timid; fearful about the future

transitory short-lived; temporary

vindicated freed from blame

SAT vs. ACT

	SAT	ACT
Preferred by?	Private schools, and schools on the east and west coasts.	Public schools, and schools in the middle of the country. ACT is preferred by more U.S. colleges than the SAT.
Accepted by?	Nearly all U.S. colleges and universities.	Nearly all U.S. colleges and universities.
When is it administered?	Seven times per year.	Six times per year.
Test structure	Seven-section exam: Three Verbal, three Math, and one Experimental. The Experimental section is masked to look like a regular section.	Four-section exam: English, Math, Reading, and Science Reasoning. An Experimental section is added to tests on certain dates only, and is clearly experimental.
Test content	Math: up to 9th grade basic geometry. No science section. Reading: one passage with roughly one minute to answer each question. Stresses vocabulary. A test of strategy and testmanship.	Math: up to trigonometry. Science section included. Reading: four passages with less than one minute to answer each question. Stresses grammar. A test of time management and studiousness.
Is there a penalty for wrong answers?	Yes	No
How the test is scored/highest possible score	200-800 for each subject, added together for a combined score. A 1600 is the highest possible combined score.	1-36 for each subject, averaged together for a composite score. A 36 is the highest possible composite score.
Are all scores sent to schools?	Yes. If a student requests a score report be sent to specific colleges, the report will include the scores the student received on every SAT taken.	No. There is a "score choice" option. Students can choose which schools will receive their scores AND which scores the schools will see.
Other uses for the exams	Scholarship purposes.	Scholarship purposes. Certain statewide testing programs.
When to register	At least six weeks before the test date.	At least four weeks before the test date.
For more information	Educational Testing Service (ETS) (609) 771-7600 www.ets.org The College Board www.collegeboard.com	ACT, Inc. (319) 337-1270 www.act.org

To help you decide which test is right for you, take a side-by-side glance at these important exams.

www.PrincetonReview.com

The Princeton Review
Admissions Services

At The Princeton Review, we care about your ability to get accepted to the best school for you. But, we all know getting accepting involves much more than just doing well on standardized tests. That's why, in addition to our test preparation services, we also offer free admissions services to students looking to enter college or graduate school. You can find these services on our website, *www.PrincetonReview.com*, the best online resource for researching, applying to, and learning how to pay for the right school for you.

No matter what type of program you're applying to—undergraduate, graduate, law, business, or medical—**PrincetonReview.com has the free tools, services, and advice you need to navigate the admissions process.** Read on to learn more about the services we offer.

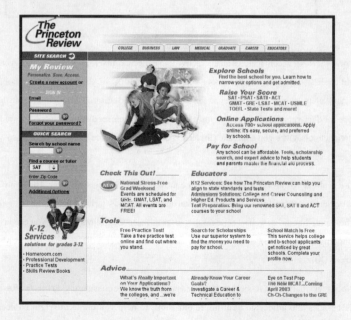

Research Schools
www.PrincetonReview.com/Research

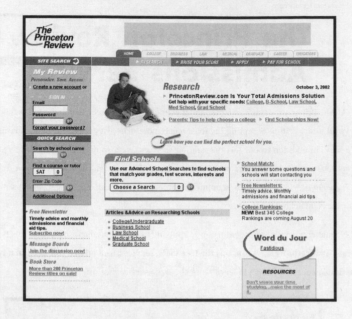

PrincetonReview.com features an interactive tool called **Counselor-O-Matic.** When you use this tool, you enter stats and information about yourself to find a list of your best match schools, reach schools, and safety schools. From there you can read statistical and editorial information about thousands of colleges and universities. In addition, you can find out what currently enrolled college students say about their schools. Once you complete Counselor-O-Matic make sure you opt in to School Match so that colleges can come to you.

Our **College Majors Search** is one of the most popular features we offer. Here you can read profiles on hundreds of majors to find information on curriculum, salaries, careers, and the appropriate high school preparation, as well as colleges that offer it. From the Majors Search, you can investigate corresponding Careers, read **Career Profiles**, and learn what career is the best match for you by taking our **Career Quiz**.

No matter what type of school or specialized program you are considering, **PrincetonReview.com has free articles and advice, in addition to our tools, to help you make the right choice.**

Apply to School
www.PrincetonReview.com/Apply

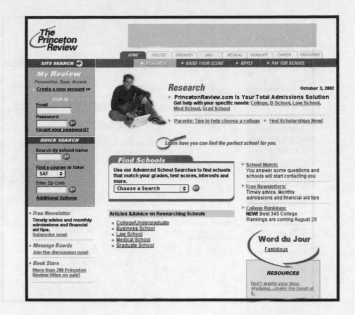

For most students, completing the school application is the most stressful part of the admissions process. PrincetonReview.com's powerful **Online School Application Engine** makes it easy to apply.

Paper applications are mostly a thing of the past. And, our hundreds of partner schools tell us they prefer to receive your applications online.

Using our online application service is simple:

- Enter information once and the common data automatically transfers onto each application.
- Save your applications and access them at any time to edit and perfect.
- Submit electronically or print and mail in.
- Pay your application fee online, using an e-check, or mail the school a check.

Our powerful application engine is built to accommodate all your needs.

Pay for School
www.PrincetonReview.com/Finance

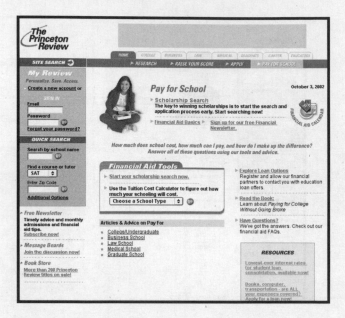

The financial aid process is confusing for everyone. But don't worry. Our free online tools, services, and advice can help you plan for the future and get the money you need to pay for school.

Our **Scholarship Search** engine will help you find free money, although often scholarships alone won't cover the cost of high tuitions. So, we offer other tools and resources to help you navigate the entire process.

Filling out the FAFSA and CSS Profile can be a daunting process, use our **Strategies for both forms** to make sure you answer the questions correctly the first time.

If scholarships and government aid aren't enough to swing the cost of tuition, we'll help you secure student loans. The Princeton Review has partnered with a select group of reputable financial institutions who will help **explore all your loans options**.

If you know how to work the financial aid process, you'll learn you don't have to **eliminate a school based on tuition.**

Be a Part of the
PrincetonReview.com Community

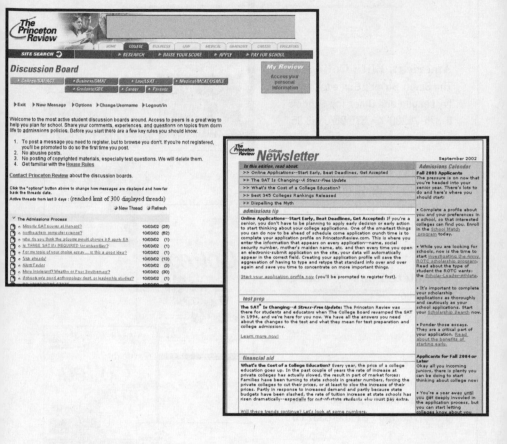

PrincetonReview.com's **Discussion Boards** and **Free Newsletters** are additional services to help you to get information about the admissions process from your peers and from The Princeton Review experts.

MORE BOOKS FOR YOUR
COLLEGE SEARCH

America's Elite Colleges
The Smart Buyer's Guide to the
Ivy League and Other Top Schools
0-375-76206-X • $15.95/C$23.95

Best 351 Colleges
The Smart Student's Guide to Colleges
2004 Edition
0-375-76337-6 • $21.95/C$32.95

Complete Book of Colleges
2004 Edition
0-375-76339-2 • $24.95/C$37.95

Guide to College Majors
Everything You Need to Know
to Choose the Right Major
0-375-76276-0 • $21.00/C$32.00

The Internship Bible
2003 Edition
0-375-76307-4 • $25.00/C$38.00

The Princeton Review

The K&W Guide to Colleges for Students with Learning Disabilities or Attention Deficit Disorder
7th Edition
0-375-76357-0 • $27.00/C$41.00

Paying for College Without Going Broke
2004 Edition
0-375-76350-3 • $20.00/C$30.00

The Scholarship Advisor
5th Edition
0-375-76210-8 • $26.00/C$40.00

Taking Time Off
2nd Edition
0-375-76303-1 • $13.00/C$20.00

Visiting College Campuses
6th Edition
0-375-76208-6 • $20.00/C$30.00

Book Store
www.PrincetonReview.com/college/ Bookstore.asp

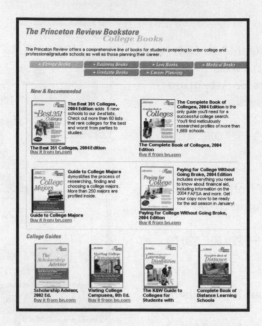

In addition to this book, we publish hundreds of other titles, including guidebooks that highlight life on campus, student opinion, and all the statistical data that you need to know about any school you are considering. Just a few of the titles that we offer are:

- Complete Book of Business Schools
- Complete Book of Law Schools
- Complete Book of Medical Schools
- The Best 351 Colleges
- The K&W Guide to Colleges for Students with Learning Disabilities or Attention Deficit Disorder
- Guide to College Majors
- Paying for College Without Going Broke

For a complete listing of all of our titles, visit our **online book store**:

www.princetonreview.com/college/bookstore.asp